Economic, Political, and Demographic Drivers of Social Isolation

Volkan Kaymaz
Istanbul Yeni Yuzyil University, Turkey

IGI Global
Scientific Publishing
Publishing Tomorrow's Research Today

Vice President of Editorial	Melissa Wagner
Director of Acquisitions	Mikaela Felty
Director of Book Development	Jocelynn Hessler
Production Manager	Mike Brehm
Cover Design	Jose Rosado

Published in the United States of America by
IGI Global Scientific Publishing
701 East Chocolate Avenue
Hershey, PA, 17033, USA
Tel: 717-533-8845 | Fax: 717-533-7115
Website: https://www.igi-global.com E-mail: cust@igi-global.com

Library of Congress Cataloging-in-Publication Data

LCCN: 2025044748 (CIP Data Pending)
ISBN13: 979-8-3373-5811-6
Isbn13Softcover: 979-8-3373-5812-3
EISBN13: 979-8-3373-5813-0

British Cataloguing in Publication Data
A Cataloguing in Publication record for this book is available from the British Library.

To everyone who has ever felt unseen in a crowded world, to those who quietly carry the weight of loneliness, and to the people who choose kindness, connection, and understanding—even on the days it feels hardest. This book is for you.

Table of Contents

Detailed Table of Contents

This chapter argues that loneliness has become a structural condition under neoliberal capitalism, produced and monetized by systems privileging individualism, marketization, and precarious labor. Neoliberal reforms—through deregulation, austerity, privatization, and welfare erosion—dismantle community ties, embedding loneliness into urban design, digital culture, and work practices. Advancing the notion of "loneliness as infrastructure," it shows how isolation sustains the loneliness economy, normalizes exploitative gig and remote work, and fuels consumer dependence on commodified intimacy via apps, pet industries, and wellness markets. Drawing on political economy, sociology, and media studies, and comparing India, Japan, and the West, the chapter demonstrates that loneliness is not incidental but foundational to post-crisis capitalism. It concludes by critiquing policies that individualize loneliness as self-help, calling instead for collective interventions rooted in solidarity and public investment.

This chapter examines the emergence of the "loneliness economy" through a mixed-methods approach, combining a review of recent literature with analysis of small-scale empirical studies and case reports from urban and semi-urban regions. Drawing on demographic data, sociological surveys, and prior research in mental health and technology adoption, the study explores how urbanization, migration, and shifting family structures have eroded traditional support systems. It critically evaluates digital mental health platforms, AI companionship tools, and community-based applications in terms of accessibility, efficacy, and ethical implications. The findings reveal a persistent gap between market-driven interventions and the authentic interpersonal connections essential for emotional well-being. The chapter concludes with policy recommendations and culturally attuned design principles aimed at fostering inclusive, community-rooted responses to loneliness in India's rapidly evolving social environment.

This chapter examines how nationality laws function as instruments of structural discrimination that institutionalize social isolation and inequality. Drawing on theories from Arendt, Carens, Shachar, Soysal, and Brubaker, it shows how legal definitions of citizenship create exclusionary hierarchies within national communities. The discussion integrates emerging issues—digital identification systems, biometric governance, and global migration regimes—to demonstrate that exclusion is not merely historical but technologically reproduced. Comparative case studies reveal how discriminatory nationality laws entrench poverty, restrict mobility, and fracture identity across generations. The chapter concludes by outlining pathways toward inclusive citizenship through gender-equal reforms, post-national rights, and recognition of digital personhood.

This study investigates how microeconomic conditions, trust, and neighborhood safety satisfaction, jointly shape dimensions of social isolation in Adana. A combination of binary and ordinal logistic regressions are applied to estimate direct and moderation effects based on survey data (N=972). Results show that higher levels of trust reduce emotional isolation and increase perceived connectedness. Consistent with latent deprivation theory, employment status moderates the effect of trust on social isolation. Microeconomic constraints such as low income, housing cost dissatisfaction, and unemployment increase vulnerabilities to perceived and objective isolation. These findings expand theoretical explanations of social isolation by integrating trust, perceived safety, and material circumstances into a single framework. Policy implications highlight the importance of neighborhood safety, inclusive labor markets, and social infrastructure in reducing the risks of social isolation across the lifespan.

The focus of this chapter is on loneliness. Specifically, this chapter provides an overview of loneliness in academia and offers guidance to university stakeholders on how to manage loneliness. Using secondary literature sources identified through a scoping review, this chapter explains what loneliness is and how it manifests itself in academia. It explains the causes and consequences of loneliness and identifies the key vulnerable cohorts most at risk of loneliness. It also offers recommendations on strategies that can be deployed by university stakeholders to combat loneliness. Additionally, this chapter proposes recommendations to universities on the strategies to help their stakeholders combat loneliness. Understanding what loneliness is and how to manage it is essential, as it can have detrimental effects that range from poor academic performance to health-related problems.

This chapter reframes loneliness among globally mobile healthcare professionals as a structural outcome of political economy rather than an individual shortcoming. Using an interdisciplinary review and a U.S–China comparison (with selective UK references), it traces how migration regimes, credentialing bottlenecks, institutional hierarchies, and market logics jointly produce isolation among migrant clinicians. Four interlocking dynamics emerge—bureaucratic precarity, emotional dislocation, professional invisibility, and commodification of care—each linked to burnout, attrition, and underused cultural–linguistic assets. We translate this synthesis into multi-level remedies: institution-level onboarding, mentorship, mental-health supports, and anti-bias systems; national reforms to visas, fair-contract enforcement, and credential recognition; and cross-border adherence to the WHO Code, bilateral supports, and better migration data.

A paradox exists in contemporary society, characterized by the rise of advanced digital technologies, increasing wealth that supports consumer independence, an increasingly personalized consumer culture, and rising life expectancy, which has given rise to an economy of loneliness, which diminishes the need for human interaction and reduces social dependency. Loneliness has become a product of capitalism and contributed to the creation of an industry that deepens social isolation. Islamic social finance, with its empathy for the socially and economically marginalized, helps build a framework for shifting individualism to community to enhance social cohesion, strengthen social solidarity, and social resilience. This chapter employs an integrative review and netnography techniques through a qualitative research design with thematic analysis to address the economy of loneliness by illustrating the transformative potential of Islamic social finance instruments as antidotes in addressing both material deprivation and social disconnection.

This chapter analyses the global phenomenon of loneliness and the rise of the "loneliness economy" through Islamic social ethics and an integrative analytical framework. It examines microeconomic, macroeconomic, and political-economic aspects over a decade. At the micro level, Islamic teachings such as Ukhuwwah, Silat al-Rahm, Zakat, Waqf, and Sadaqah are highlighted as means of meeting material needs and strengthening relational capital, countering commodified social bonds. At the macro level, it considers social isolation as a cost to productivity and healthcare, showing how mosques, families, and communal responsibilities reduce alienation. Politically, it critiques neoliberalism and consumerist individualism, proposing Islamic values, Shura, Maslaha, and Adl, to foster inclusive, just, and interdependent communities.

Preface

INTRODUCTION

In an age characterized by unprecedented technological advancement and instantaneous global communication, one of the most profound paradoxes of contemporary life has been the steady rise of social isolation. Across societies—whether highly industrialized or rapidly developing—individuals are reporting diminished social bonds, weakened community structures, and a growing sense of emotional detachment. Loneliness, once considered a private emotional state, has increasingly become recognized as a structural and systemic outcome of economic pressures, political shifts, demographic transformations, and cultural change. It is not merely that individuals feel alone; rather, our social landscapes, economic policies, digital environments, and demographic patterns are collectively producing conditions that normalize isolation.

This edited volume, *Economic, Political, and Demographic Drivers of Social Isolation*, is among the first comprehensive scholarly efforts to examine loneliness through an integrated, multidimensional lens. Whereas traditional research has predominantly approached loneliness as a psychological or interpersonal issue, the chapters compiled here extend far beyond individual-level explanations. Together, they illuminate how economic instability, widening inequality, labor market precarity, educational disparities, demographic aging, migration flows, urbanization, and shifting family structures all converge to reshape the experience of connection and disconnection. Loneliness is no longer a matter of personal disposition; it is increasingly the byproduct of broader structural arrangements.

The accelerating dominance of digital technologies plays a central role in this emerging reality. While digital platforms have expanded communication networks, they have simultaneously fostered new forms of superficial engagement and algorithmically curated echo chambers. The result is a complex interplay between perceived connectivity and experienced isolation. Moreover, the commercialization of loneliness—often referred to as the "loneliness economy"—has introduced new market responses that frame companionship, emotional support, and social belonging as services to be purchased. These developments raise important ethical questions about authenticity, vulnerability, commodification, and the blurred boundaries between emotional care and economic exchange.

Demographic transitions further intensify this dynamic. Population aging, declining fertility rates, increased mobility, and the fragmentation of extended family structures are altering the rhythms of daily life and the patterns of social support. Urbanization has amplified anonymity; rural-to-urban migration has disrupted traditional kinship networks; and individualistic cultural norms have encouraged self-reliance over community interdependence. Taken together, these forces reveal how loneliness has become embedded within the very fabric of economic development, political priorities, and demographic change.

This book emerges from a recognition that addressing loneliness requires a holistic understanding of these forces. As editor, my own motivation in developing this volume stems from observing how profoundly loneliness shapes perceptions, behaviors, cultural practices, and economic decisions. Loneliness influences how individuals consume, live, work, trust, and connect. It affects mental and physical health, productivity, civic participation, and even patterns of political engagement. Yet despite its wide-ranging effects, loneliness has rarely been studied through a framework that integrates the economic, political, and demographic underpinnings of the phenomenon.

By assembling contributions from multiple countries and disciplinary perspectives, this volume seeks to fill that gap. The chapters collectively illustrate that loneliness is not a uniform experience; rather, it manifests differently across contexts, cultures, and demographic groups. These variations reveal important insights into how states, markets, communities, and individuals negotiate the meaning and impact of social isolation. The authors draw from microeconomic modeling, qualitative research, sociological theory, digital literacy studies, healthcare experiences, Islamic social finance perspectives, and analyses of structural discrimination—to uncover the diverse ways in which isolation is produced, sustained, and potentially overcome.

THE GLOBAL RELEVANCE OF SOCIAL ISOLATION IN CONTEMPORARY SOCIETIES

Loneliness today has evolved into one of the most pressing public concerns of the 21st century. Governments, international organizations, and public health institutions increasingly recognize social isolation as both a symptom and a driver of wider societal distress. The World Health Organization has recently identified loneliness as a global health threat with consequences comparable to smoking, obesity, and physical inactivity. Several countries—including the United Kingdom, Japan, and Australia—have appointed ministers or task forces to address loneliness on a national scale. This institutional response illustrates a powerful reality: loneliness is no longer a peripheral phenomenon but a central feature of modern socio-economic life.

Globalization and digitalization have simultaneously connected and fragmented communities. Individuals interact across continents in real time, yet local institutions of belonging—from neighborhood associations to extended families—have weakened considerably. Economic transformations have intensified this shift. Labor market volatility, the rise of precarious work, and increasing income inequality have eroded the stability that once grounded social relationships. As people move more frequently in search of employment or educational opportunities, traditional community anchors dissolve, making it increasingly difficult to form durable networks.

Political developments compound these trends. Polarization, declining trust in public institutions, and the erosion of collective civic engagement have created environments where individuals feel disconnected not only from each other but from the broader social system. Social media, once celebrated as a democratizing force, often amplifies political hostility and performative interaction rather than fostering meaningful dialogue. These changes reveal how political structures—both formal and informal—shape the emotional contours of everyday life.

Demographic shifts further complicate the landscape. Many countries face rapidly aging populations, altering household structures and increasing the prevalence of single-person living arrangements. Fertility declines, intergenerational distance, and migration patterns create conditions where social support systems weaken, and individuals increasingly rely on formal institutions or market substitutes for companionship and care. At the same time, in younger populations, the pressures of academic competition, economic insecurity, and digital overwhelm contribute to new forms of emotional isolation.

Against this backdrop, the study of social isolation requires a framework that captures its interconnected causes and consequences. Traditional approaches—which locate loneliness primarily in psychological predispositions or interpersonal challenges—cannot fully account for its accelerating prevalence across varied sociocultural contexts. Understanding social isolation as an outcome of economic structures, political configurations, and demographic transitions offers a far more accurate and comprehensive analytic lens.

This book positions itself precisely at this intersection, emphasizing the importance of recognizing loneliness as a structural condition, not simply a personal experience. Each chapter in this volume contributes to this broader argument, demonstrating that loneliness emerges from shifts in economic incentives, market behaviors, educational systems, healthcare practices, migration flows, religious and cultural transformations, and policy discourses. By centering these structural dimensions, the book challenges the notion that loneliness can be addressed solely through individualized interventions or technological quick fixes.

Moreover, this volume responds to an urgent need to diversify the geography of loneliness research. Much of the existing literature is heavily Western-centric, with limited attention to the experiences of the Global South. Yet countries such as India, Indonesia, Pakistan, and Türkiye offer distinct socio-cultural and economic landscapes that reshape how isolation is felt, expressed, and addressed. By bringing together scholars from a wide range of regions, this book provides one of the few interdisciplinary, multinational examinations of loneliness and its systemic drivers.

In doing so, it expands not only the empirical base of loneliness studies but also the conceptual and theoretical frameworks available to researchers, policymakers, psychologists, economists, and sociologists. The chapters collectively highlight that loneliness cannot be reduced to a single cause or remedy; instead, it represents a complex interplay of structural pressures and cultural narratives. Addressing it requires a commitment to understanding its roots within broader social transformations—and ultimately, reimagining the economic, political, and demographic systems that shape human connection.

This book is designed for a wide and interdisciplinary audience, reflecting the complex and multifaceted nature of social isolation. While loneliness is often viewed through the lens of psychology or public health, the economic, political, and demographic dimensions explored in this volume broaden the readership far beyond any single discipline.

The primary audience includes academicians, researchers, and graduate students in fields such as sociology, economics, political science, psychology, public policy, and demography. For scholars seeking to understand how structural forces shape emotional and social experiences, this book provides an integrated analytical framework supported by empirical evidence and global case studies. It is particularly valuable for those who study social capital, inequality, migration, digitalization, and changing family structures.

Policy makers, government agencies, and international organizations also constitute a critical part of the readership. As loneliness becomes increasingly recognized as a public policy challenge—affecting healthcare expenditures, productivity, political engagement, and community resilience—there is a growing need for research that explains the structural roots of isolation. The insights presented here can inform social welfare programs, digital governance strategies, urban planning, and demographic policy interventions. Decision makers will find in this volume a nuanced understanding that goes beyond diagnostic statistics to illuminate the systemic dynamics that produce isolation.

Healthcare professionals, psychologists, social workers, and counselors can similarly benefit from the broader perspective offered in this book. While therapeutic approaches address the individual experience of loneliness, the structural explanations presented here allow practitioners to contextualize emotional distress within larger societal forces. Understanding how labor precarity, migration, urban anonymity, and digital consumption patterns drive isolation can enrich practice-based interventions and improve community-level outcomes.

The book also speaks to those in the nonprofit and civil society sectors, particularly organizations working on mental health, community development, digital literacy, refugee integration, and youth empowerment. These groups often witness firsthand how economic and political systems affect social belonging. By providing conceptual tools and region-specific analyses, this volume enables a more informed, evidence-based engagement with vulnerable populations.

Lastly, the book invites engagement from the general educated reader, especially those interested in how modern life reshapes relationships, identity, and well-being. Loneliness touches nearly every aspect of human existence—from how people consume information to how they work, live, and form meaning. Readers seeking to understand these rapid transformations will find in this volume a rich and accessible exploration of the forces shaping social connection in the 21st century.

By bridging academic disciplines, global contexts, and methodological approaches, this book positions itself as a comprehensive resource for anyone seeking to understand the systemic foundations of social isolation. Its interdisciplinary orientation and international authorship make it a uniquely relevant contribution at a time when societies across the world are grappling with the social consequences of economic instability, demographic change, and cultural fragmentation.

CHAPTER OVERVIEW

Chapter 1 – Neoliberalism, Social Disconnection, and Economic Reinvention: Loneliness as Infrastructure

This chapter provides a critical theoretical framework for understanding how neoliberal systems reshape emotional and social life. By examining how market-driven policies, privatization, and individualistic value structures alter the foundations of community and solidarity, the authors argue that loneliness is not an accidental outcome but a predictable structural byproduct of neoliberal economic logics. The chapter anchors the entire volume by demonstrating how macro-level economic reforms—intended to promote efficiency and growth—unintentionally generate environments of competition, insecurity, and isolation. In doing so, it establishes loneliness as a form of modern infrastructure embedded within contemporary socio-economic systems.

Chapter 2 – The Loneliness Economy in India: Market Responses to Social Disconnection in the Digital Age

This chapter investigates the rise of the "loneliness economy" in India, where digitalization, rapid urbanization, and shifting family structures have created both widespread social isolation and new commercial responses. Drawing on a systematic literature review and empirical insights, the authors show how the market has stepped in to fill the void left by weakening traditional support networks. Mental health apps, curated social events, virtual companionship services, and youth-oriented digital communities illustrate how loneliness is commodified in emerging economies. The chapter deepens the book's perspective by revealing how demographic pressures and digital divides intersect with emotional well-being in the Global South.

Chapter 3 – Social Isolation by Design: Structural Discrimination and Belonging in Contemporary Nationality Laws

Bridging political science and social psychology, this chapter highlights how modern nationality laws and bureaucratic regimes can institutionalize social exclusion. By examining citizenship policies, residency requirements, and legal frameworks that determine belonging, the author demonstrates that loneliness is often embedded within state structures. The chapter offers a powerful argument: when access to identity, rights, and community is mediated by restrictive legal systems, individuals experience a profound form of structural loneliness. This contribution broadens the book's scope by underscoring the political drivers of isolation and the emotional consequences of legal marginalization.

Chapter 4 – Microeconomic and Psychosocial Determinants of Social Isolation: An Econometric Analysis

Employing econometric tools and empirical modeling, this chapter identifies key micro-level factors that influence loneliness. Income variability, employment conditions, educational attainment, and social capital emerge as strong predictors of isolation. The findings reveal how economic stress, limited social resources, and demographic constraints directly shape emotional well-being. By integrating microeconomic behavior with psychosocial theory, the chapter strengthens the book's multidisciplinary orientation and offers evidence-based insights relevant to policy makers and researchers seeking to address loneliness through targeted economic interventions.

Chapter 5 – Invisible Struggles: Loneliness in Higher Education

This chapter focuses on loneliness among university students—a population often assumed to be socially connected yet deeply vulnerable. Through qualitative accounts and institutional analysis, the authors illustrate how academic pressure, migration for education, digital dependency, and cultural expectations create environments of silent suffering. The chapter contributes to the volume by demonstrating how loneliness manifests within competitive educational systems and how institutions can unintentionally exacerbate isolation. It highlights an urgent need for student-centered, mental-health-oriented interventions that acknowledge the complex lived realities of young adults.

Chapter 6 – Isolation in White Coats: The Political Economy of Loneliness Among Global Healthcare Migrants

By exploring loneliness among healthcare workers who migrate across borders, this chapter adds a global labor and migration dimension to the book. The authors show how long hours, cultural dislocation, precarious employment, and emotional labor intensify isolation, even within professions dedicated to caring for others. Their analysis reveals how global health systems depend on migrant labor while failing to provide adequate social or emotional support. This chapter powerfully underscores the human cost of global mobility and introduces a nuanced understanding of how professional identities intersect with loneliness.

Chapter 7 – Drivers of Social Isolation: The Role of Digital Literacy and Migration – A Qualitative Study

This chapter investigates how digital literacy, technology adoption, and migration patterns shape social isolation in contemporary societies. It highlights the paradox that while digital tools offer opportunities for connection, individuals with limited digital literacy or who face linguistic and cultural barriers are pushed toward isolation. Through qualitative insights, the chapter shows how digital exclusion becomes a new form of social exclusion, especially among migrants and marginalized groups. This contribution enriches the volume's exploration of digital inequalities and their emotional consequences.

Chapter 8 – Objectified Bodies: Roots of Disconnection and Isolation

Focusing on embodiment, gender, and identity, this chapter argues that objectification—whether mediated by media, culture, or social norms—plays a central role in shaping experiences of loneliness. When individuals internalize objectified identities or face judgment based on appearance, gender, or social expectations, they experience emotional alienation and loss of agency. This chapter deepens the book's theoretical scope by linking isolation to the politics of the body, social representation, and cultural narratives surrounding worth and belonging.

Chapter 9 – From Individualism to Community: Islamic Social Finance as Antidotes to the Loneliness Economy

This chapter introduces a religious and ethical perspective by examining how Islamic social finance mechanisms—such as zakat, waqf, and community solidarity practices—can counteract the loneliness produced by individualistic economic systems. The author argues that community-oriented financial structures promote social cohesion, shared responsibility, and interpersonal connection. This chapter expands the book's geographic and conceptual reach, showing how non-Western economic traditions offer meaningful alternatives to isolation-producing market logics.

Chapter 10 – Islamic Approaches to Social Inclusion: Addressing the Economic, Political, and Demographic Drivers of Social Isolation

Building on Chapter 9, this chapter explores how Islamic principles of social justice, community, and mutual care address structural forms of exclusion. It demonstrates the relevance of faith-based frameworks in creating inclusive environments for women, marginalized groups, and communities experiencing political or economic instability. This chapter broadens the analytical lens by connecting social isolation with cultural values, institutional structures, and religious understandings of solidarity.

Chapter 11 – An Assessment of the Commodification of Loneliness

The concluding chapter offers a sharp critique of the growing commercialization of loneliness. By examining how markets convert emotional needs into monetizable services—ranging from digital companionship to commercial therapy—the author questions whether profit-driven models can ever provide genuine human connection. This chapter synthesizes many of the themes present in the volume and poses an essential ethical question: when care becomes a commodity, what happens to authenticity, trust, and emotional well-being? It provides a compelling and thought-provoking end to the book's interdisciplinary narrative.

This volume makes a significant contribution to the growing body of research that seeks to understand loneliness not as an isolated emotional state but as a deeply structural and multidimensional phenomenon. By bringing together perspectives from economics, political science, sociology, psychology, religious studies, healthcare, digital literacy, migration studies, and cultural analysis, the book challenges conventional approaches that confine loneliness to the realm of individual pathology. Instead, it positions social isolation at the intersection of broader systemic forces—economic pressures, demographic transitions, political structures, technological environments, labor markets, and cultural expectations.

One of the most distinctive contributions of this book is its explicit attention to global diversity. Much of the existing literature on loneliness is rooted in Western contexts, yet the experience of social isolation varies dramatically across countries with different economic models, cultural traditions, and demographic structures. By including chapters from India, Türkiye, Pakistan, Indonesia, China, the United Kingdom, and the United States, the volume expands the geographic scope of loneliness research and highlights how local conditions shape the nature and consequences of isolation. These cross-national perspectives not only enrich the academic discourse but also demonstrate the need for policy solutions that are culturally informed and contextually grounded.

The book also offers valuable methodological diversity. Quantitative analyses, qualitative studies, conceptual frameworks, and interdisciplinary syntheses interact across the chapters, creating a holistic picture of how loneliness is produced and experienced. This combination of empirical evidence and theoretical reflection contributes to the development of new research pathways that extend beyond traditional disciplinary boundaries. Scholars and practitioners can draw on these insights to better understand how loneliness manifests in educational institutions, healthcare systems, labor markets, digital spaces, and legal frameworks.

A central message that emerges from this volume is that loneliness cannot be addressed through individual-level interventions alone. While therapy, counseling, and digital tools offer support, they do not fundamentally alter the structural conditions that give rise to isolation. Effective solutions require systemic change—policies that strengthen community bonds, reduce economic precarity, expand digital literacy, support migrant integration, protect workers, and promote inclusive citizenship. The chapters collectively underscore the importance of building environments where individuals can cultivate meaningful connections, experience belonging, and participate fully in social and economic life.

Looking ahead, this book opens the door to several promising directions for future research. Scholars may explore longitudinal analyses of social isolation in rapidly changing societies, comparative studies across demographic groups, or evaluations of policy interventions aimed at reducing loneliness. The ethical dimensions of the loneliness economy, including the commodification of emotional labor and digital companionship, warrant ongoing attention. Additionally, as global crises—such as pandemics, displacement, economic instability, and climate-related disruptions—reshape the fabric of social life, understanding the evolving dynamics of isolation will remain an urgent priority.

In compiling this volume, my intention has been not only to highlight the complexity of loneliness but also to emphasize its profound relevance to human well-being and societal resilience. Social isolation is a defining challenge of our time, yet it is also a lens through which we can rethink social policy, economic systems, cultural norms, and the fundamental meaning of connection. By situating loneliness within broader structural and global contexts, this book seeks to inspire new scholarly inquiry and inform evidence-based approaches that foster healthier, more connected societies.

Acknowledgement

I would like to extend my sincere appreciation to all contributors whose scholarly efforts have shaped the development of this volume. Their commitment to advancing interdisciplinary research on social isolation made this book possible.

I am also grateful to the reviewers for their constructive feedback throughout the editorial process, as well as to the editorial team at IGI Global for their guidance and professional support.

This work has also benefited greatly from the support of colleagues and institutions who helped cultivate an environment conducive to collaboration and scholarly exchange. Their encouragement and cooperation played a meaningful role in bringing this volume to completion.

I would also like to offer a respectful acknowledgment to those whose experiences often remain unseen—individuals who struggle with loneliness, who feel detached from the social rhythms around them, or who navigate the world with a sense of distance from belonging. Likewise, this book recognizes communities whose lives unfold at the margins of dominant social and economic structures. Their realities remind us that social isolation is not only a personal condition but also a reflection of broader systems that shape inclusion and exclusion. This work is, in part, dedicated to making those experiences more visible.

Introduction

Social isolation has emerged as a structural outcome of contemporary economic and political transformations rather than a mere personal experience. Rising inequality, labor market precarity, demographic shifts, and the erosion of collective institutions have fundamentally altered the ways individuals connect to society. Understanding loneliness today requires situating it within these broader macro-level dynamics.

Economic, Political, and Demographic Drivers of Social Isolation offers a timely and analytically rigorous contribution to this debate. The chapters collectively demonstrate how market structures, state policies, migration patterns, and demographic transitions interact to reshape social relations and civic life. By linking micro-level experiences of disconnection to macro-level political economy processes, this volume challenges individualistic explanations of loneliness and reframes it as a systemic, policy-relevant issue.

The volume adopts an interdisciplinary perspective, examining economic mechanisms, governance structures, global health mobility, digital participation, and shifting social norms as interconnected factors shaping experiences of isolation

In a period marked by democratic backsliding, rising populism, and weakening social cohesion, examining social isolation through the lens of political economy offers a useful framework for understanding these dynamics. Positioning isolation within broader structural processes may support researchers and policymakers in evaluating how social capital and collective resilience are shaped across contemporary societies.

Chapter 1

Neoliberalism, Social Disconnection, and Economic Reinvention: Loneliness as Infrastructure

Ratan Sarkar
https://orcid.org/0009-0008-5480-0165
Tezpur University, India

J. Santhosh
https://orcid.org/0009-0008-2825-1035
Assam Don Bosco University, India

ABSTRACT

This chapter argues that loneliness has become a structural condition under neoliberal capitalism, produced and monetized by systems privileging individualism, marketization, and precarious labor. Neoliberal reforms—through deregulation, austerity, privatization, and welfare erosion—dismantle community ties, embedding loneliness into urban design, digital culture, and work practices. Advancing the notion of "loneliness as infrastructure," it shows how isolation sustains the loneliness economy, normalizes exploitative gig and remote work, and fuels consumer dependence on commodified intimacy via apps, pet industries, and wellness markets. Drawing on political economy, sociology, and media studies, and comparing India, Japan, and the West, the chapter demonstrates that loneliness is not incidental but foundational to post-crisis capitalism. It concludes by critiquing policies that individualize loneliness as self-help, calling instead for collective interventions rooted in solidarity and public investment.

DOI: 10.4018/979-8-3373-5811-6.ch001

1. INTRODUCTION

Loneliness, long perceived as a private emotion or psychological affliction, has gradually transformed into a defining structural feature of late modern life. In its psychological conception, loneliness was primarily understood through the lens of individual pathology—an emotional void to be cured through therapy, mindfulness, or self-help regimes (Perlman & Peplau, 1981; Weiss, 1973). This framing situated loneliness within the realm of personal responsibility, resonating with neoliberal ideals of self-regulation and emotional resilience (Illouz, 2008). Over time, however, scholars began to advance a social-structural view, revealing how loneliness arises not merely from personal deficits but from systemic transformations in social and economic life: urban fragmentation, the erosion of communal institutions, precarious employment, and the commodification of everyday interactions (Bauman, 2001; Putnam, 2000). Within this view, loneliness becomes symptomatic of the atomization and competitive individualism inherent in neoliberal societies. In the contemporary infrastructural perspective, loneliness is recognized as embedded within the architectures of global capitalism—manifest in algorithmic mediation, the gig economy, digital labor platforms, and affective economies that monetize connection and isolation alike (Crary, 2013; Han, 2017). The shift from emotion to infrastructure signals a deepening analysis of how loneliness functions not only as a subjective experience but also as a designed and reproducible condition sustaining economic, technological, and spatial systems. As recent public health data and policy discourses attest (Holt-Lunstad, 2017; Murthy, 2020), the scale and persistence of loneliness are inseparable from the infrastructures that produce and profit from disconnection. In this sense, loneliness is no longer an accidental by-product of modernity but a central logic of its operation—an affective infrastructure of neoliberal capitalism.

Figure 1. Conceptual evolution of loneliness from individual emotion to systemic infrastructure.

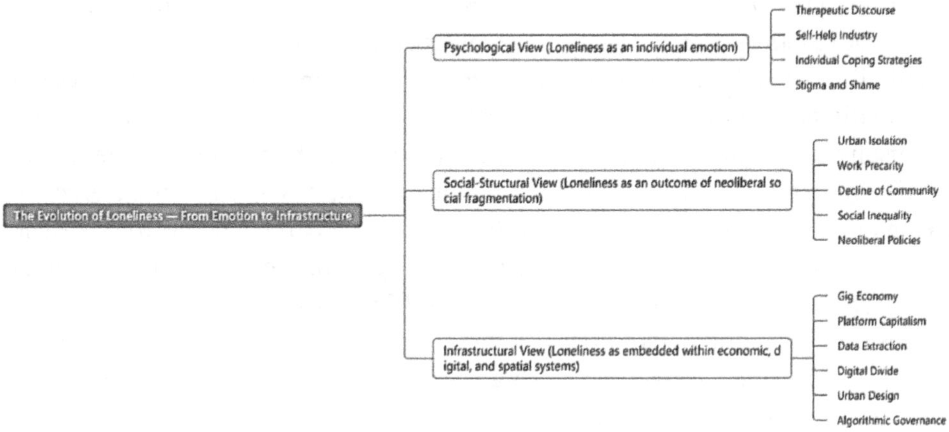

1.1 From Private Malaise to Public Condition

In conventional discourse, loneliness has been treated as a psychological state, an emotional consequence of lacking satisfying social relationships (Perlman & Peplau, 1981). While this individualised framing remains dominant in clinical psychology and public health, it obscures the socio-economic determinants that produce and normalise isolation. The global COVID-19 pandemic starkly exposed this fallacy. Social distancing mandates amplified pre-existing trends of withdrawal, revealing that "normal" social life in many urban, market-oriented societies was already underpinned by fragmented networks and transactional interactions (Klinenberg, 2018). When public life contracted, the fragility of connection was laid bare, especially for those in precarious work or unstable housing.

Neoliberalism, broadly understood as a set of political-economic practices promoting market primacy, deregulation, and the rollback of state welfare (Harvey, 2005; Peck, 2010), has intensified the structural drivers of loneliness. The emphasis on individual responsibility, entrepreneurial selfhood, and competitive self-optimisation has eroded collective institutions and social safety nets. Public spaces are increasingly privatised or commodified, while housing and labour markets deepen segregation along class and income lines. This reorganisation of economic and spatial life not only undermines traditional community structures but also cultivates conditions in which loneliness can flourish as both a lived experience and a profitable opportunity.

1.2 Loneliness as Infrastructure

The notion of *loneliness as infrastructure* shifts analytical focus from loneliness as an episodic emotion to loneliness as a systemic condition embedded in the organisation of daily life. By infrastructure, we mean both the tangible and intangible systems — from digital platforms to urban design to labour arrangements — that facilitate and sustain particular social patterns (Larkin, 2013). In this framing, loneliness is not merely an unintended side effect of neoliberalism; it is a stabilising element of its economic logic. Disconnected individuals become ideal consumers for industries that commodify intimacy, from dating apps and pet economies to wellness retreats and subscription friendship services (Illouz, 2007; Banet-Weiser, 2018).

This infrastructural perspective also foregrounds the role of technological mediation. Digital platforms are often celebrated as tools for connection, yet their profit models depend on extracting attention, data, and affective labour from users (Zuboff, 2019). These logics can paradoxically deepen isolation by substituting algorithmically curated interaction for sustained, embodied social life. As urban sociologist Eric Klinenberg (2018) observes, "We have built an architecture of disconnection, both physical and virtual, that makes aloneness the path of least resistance."

Figure 2. The architecture of disconnection: Interacting infrastructures producing systemic loneliness.

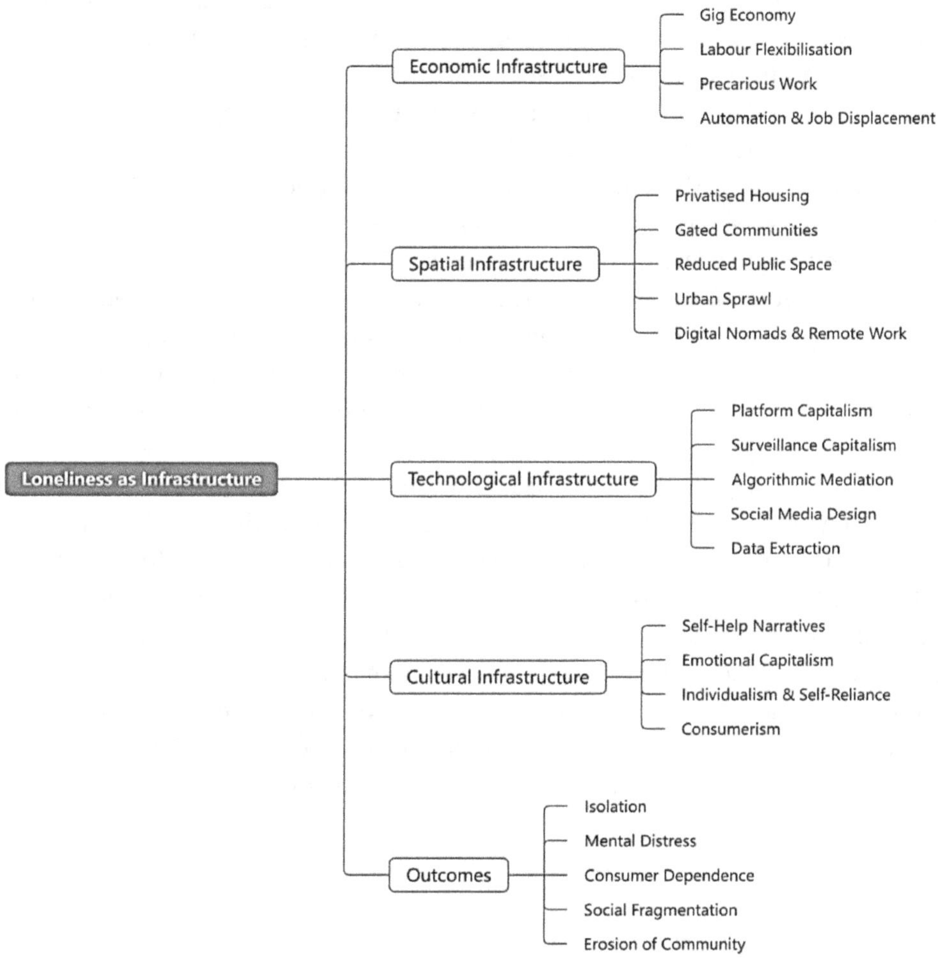

1.3 Neoliberal Restructuring and the Political Economy of Disconnection

Three interlinked processes define the neoliberal restructuring that has institutionalised loneliness as a systemic condition rather than a personal state. *First*, the *flexibilisation of labour markets* has dismantled stable, long-term employment in favour of short-term contracts, gig work, and remote freelancing (Standing, 2011). Marketed as "freedom" and "autonomy," this flexibility has instead fragmented work schedules, dispersed workers geographically, and eroded the workplace as a traditional site of solidarity and collective identity. The resulting precarity generates not only economic insecurity but also profound relational instability, as individuals struggle to sustain consistent social ties. *Second*, the *privatisation and withdrawal of public goods* have hollowed out the social commons. As public libraries, parks, and community centres face defunding, social life increasingly migrates to commercial spaces—cafés, malls, gyms—where access is regulated by pricing, surveillance, and design (Harvey, 2012). The shared public sphere has been replaced by transactional environments mediated by consumption, where participation depends on purchasing power. *Third*, the *technologisation of intimacy* has recast human connection as a commodified service. Digital platforms such as Tinder, Bumble, and RentAFriend.com transform relationships into algorithmically curated portfolios, subject to ranking, matching, and monetisation (Davies, 2015; Turkle, 2011). These infrastructures promise connectivity yet often deepen alienation, embedding affective life within corporate systems driven by data extraction and profit maximisation rather than collective wellbeing.

Across time, key neoliberal milestones have accelerated this trajectory: the 1980s deregulation under Thatcher and Reagan institutionalised market supremacy; India's 1991 economic liberalisation extended global neoliberal logics into the Global South; the 2008 global financial crisis normalised precarity as a permanent feature of post-industrial economies; and the 2020 COVID-19 pandemic intensified digital mediation and social isolation, rendering loneliness both infrastructural and endemic. Together, these developments illustrate how the neoliberal project has not merely restructured economies but also re-engineered the emotional architecture of everyday life—producing loneliness as both symptom and system.

Figure 3. Global neoliberal restructuring and the parallel intensification of loneliness.

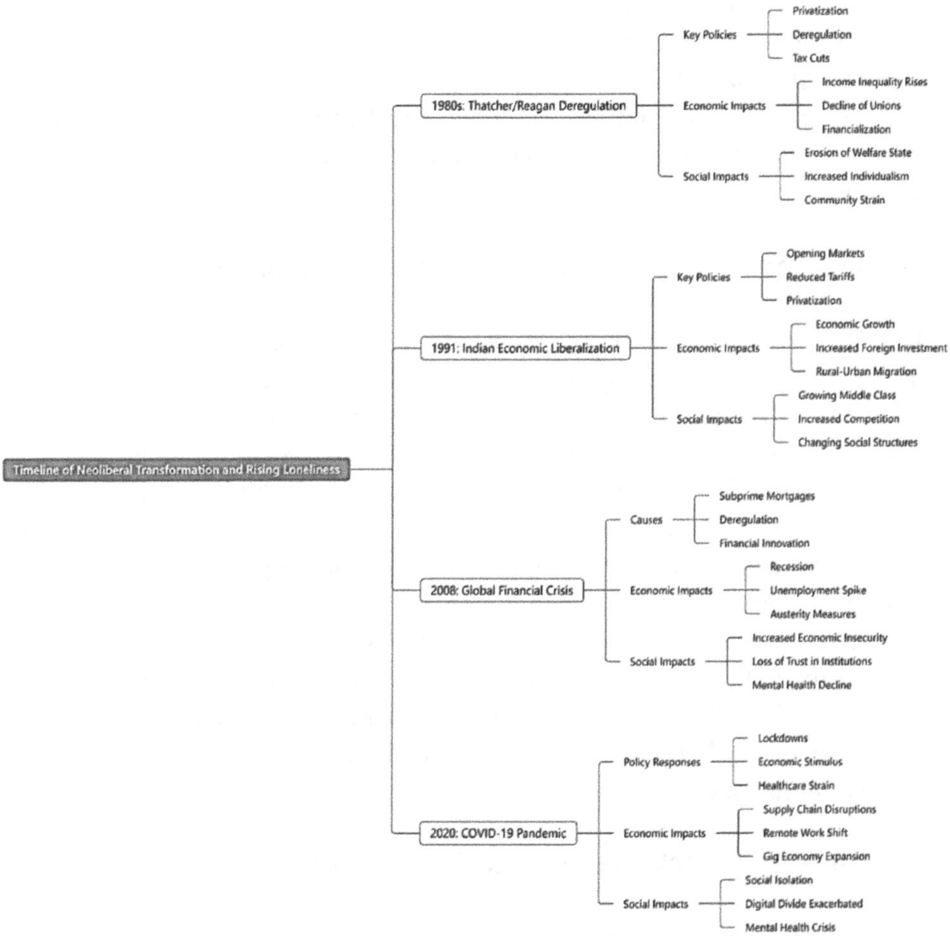

1.4 Globalising Loneliness: Beyond Cultural Exceptionalism

Although loneliness manifests differently across cultural contexts, the structural conditions enabling it are increasingly globalised. In India, rural-to-urban migration and rapid urbanisation disrupt traditional kinship networks, while digital platforms emerge as both substitutes and intensifiers of isolation (Jeffrey & Young, 2012). In Japan, the hikikomori phenomenon - extreme social withdrawal - is linked to rigid educational and employment structures, yet is also commodified through rent-a-family services and robotic companions (Tateno et al., 2012). In Western contexts, rising rates of solo living intersect with neoliberal individualism, producing markets for therapeutic self-care and curated experiences that promise connection without requiring structural change (Klinenberg, 2012; Banet-Weiser, 2018).

These diverse expressions of loneliness reveal the adaptability of the loneliness economy to different cultural and regulatory settings. While cultural norms shape the form of commodified solutions, the underlying drivers - precarity, commodification of public life, and technological mediation - are widely shared under neoliberal globalisation.

1.5 The Contradiction of the Loneliness Economy

The rise of the *loneliness economy* poses a fundamental contradiction. On one hand, loneliness is increasingly framed as a public health crisis, with measurable costs in morbidity, mortality, and healthcare expenditure (Holt-Lunstad, 2017). On the other hand, it is a lucrative growth sector, attracting investment in products and services that monetise disconnection. This dual status - as both a social harm and a profitable market - creates tensions for policy, as interventions may be co-opted by commercial actors whose profitability depends on the persistence of the very problem they claim to solve.

For example, corporate wellness programmes may address symptoms of workplace isolation without altering exploitative labour practices; dating apps may facilitate connections while structuring interaction in ways that encourage churn and continuous engagement. In both cases, the resolution of loneliness is subordinated to the imperatives of market growth.

1.6 Reframing Policy and Public Discourse

Public discourse often reproduces the individualised framing of loneliness, promoting self-help strategies, resilience training, and lifestyle adjustments while neglecting systemic causes. This mirrors broader neoliberal tendencies to depoliticise structural problems by reframing them as personal challenges (Brown, 2015). As a result, interventions tend to focus on individual behaviour change rather than collective provision or structural reform.

Yet, as scholars of social infrastructure argue, sustainable solutions to loneliness require investments in the public realm: well-designed communal spaces, equitable housing policies, inclusive urban planning, and labour protections that facilitate stable, meaningful work (Klinenberg, 2018; Harvey, 2012). Addressing loneliness thus demands a re-politicisation of connection - treating it as a public good rather than a private luxury.

2. STRUCTURE OF THE CHAPTER

This introduction has outlined the central claim that loneliness in the neoliberal era functions as an infrastructural condition, reproduced through economic, spatial, and technological systems. The remainder of the chapter is organised as follows:

- Conceptual foundations elaborate the theoretical underpinnings of "loneliness as infrastructure," drawing on political economy, sociology, and infrastructure studies.
- The loneliness economy examines how markets identify, commodify, and profit from disconnection.
- Empirical case studies compare manifestations in India, Japan, and the west, highlighting both common structural drivers and culturally specific adaptations.
- Macroeconomic consequences explore the public health and productivity impacts of systemic loneliness.
- Policy critique interrogates the individualisation of loneliness in official responses.
- Structural interventions propose collective, systemic remedies.

The chapter concludes by reframing loneliness as a political-economic crisis, calling for solidarity-driven alternatives to its commodification.

3. CONCEPTUAL FOUNDATIONS: FROM EMOTION TO INFRASTRUCTURE

3.1 Reframing Loneliness

Loneliness has traditionally been approached through the lenses of psychology, gerontology, and public health, where it is defined as the perceived gap between desired and actual social relationships (Perlman & Peplau, 1981; Hawkley & Cacioppo, 2010). This framing often assumes that loneliness is primarily an individual emotional state, to be resolved through behavioural adjustment or therapeutic intervention. While valuable for clinical treatment, such perspectives underplay the socio-economic and political structures that shape how and why disconnection emerges, persists, and becomes normalised.

The challenge, then, is to shift from viewing loneliness merely as an episodic affective condition toward understanding it as a systemic phenomenon - produced, managed, and sometimes exploited by the organisation of economic life under neoliberalism (Brown, 2015; Harvey, 2005). This conceptual expansion allows us to link subjective feelings to macro-structural transformations: from welfare retrenchment to digital platform capitalism.

3.2 The Emotional Turn in Capitalism

Eva Illouz's concept of *emotional capitalism* provides a critical starting point. She argues that late capitalism has not only commodified goods and services but also emotions themselves, reshaping intimacy, self-expression, and desire according to market logics (Illouz, 2007). In this view, loneliness is not simply an unintended by-product of economic change; it is actively structured by a system that commodifies connection and instrumentalises affective bonds.

Emotions like loneliness acquire market value because they can be targeted by products and services - dating apps, mental health platforms, self-care industries - designed to promise resolution. But the resolution is often partial and temporary, ensuring continued demand. This "engineered incompletion" mirrors the strategies of other consumer industries, from fashion to gaming, where satisfaction is intentionally deferred.

3.3 From Infrastructure as Objects to Infrastructure as Relations

Anthropologist Brian Larkin (2013) reminds us that infrastructure is more than material artefacts such as roads, pipes, or networks. It is a socio-technical system that "mediates and structures the possibility of social life." In this sense, the infrastructure of connection is not simply the smartphone that enables a video call, but the entire assemblage of digital platforms, labour regimes, urban designs, and cultural narratives that organise how people interact.

Under neoliberalism, these infrastructures have been reconfigured to privilege individualised and commodified encounters over collective, public, and freely accessible forms of sociality. Urban infrastructures increasingly take the form of gated communities, surveillance-heavy public spaces, and commercialised leisure zones that restrict spontaneous association (Low, 2003). Digital infrastructures, driven by platform capitalism, are designed to maximise engagement and extract data rather than to nurture meaningful connection (Zuboff, 2019). Economic infrastructures, shaped by flexible labour markets, disperse workers, undermine unions, and weaken workplace solidarities (Standing, 2011).

To frame loneliness infrastructurally, then, is to recognise that disconnection is not a random psychological accident but something "built in" to the very systems that organise everyday life.

3.4 Political Economy and the Production of Disconnection

The political economy of loneliness is inseparable from the broader transformations of neoliberal globalisation. Central among these are four interlinked dynamics.

First, deregulation and market primacy have reshaped welfare states, as governments retreat from public provision and market actors step in to fill gaps in care — always at a price (Harvey, 2005). Second, the privatisation of social goods has hollowed out libraries, parks, and community centres, replacing them with commercialised "third places" like cafés or co-working spaces where entry depends on consumption (Oldenburg, 1999). Third, labour precarity has intensified through the gig economy, fragmenting working life and replacing stable, community-oriented employment with atomised, contingent forms of work (Standing, 2011). Finally, technological mediation increasingly channels social interaction through digital platforms whose profit models depend on maximising screen time and extracting behavioural data (Srnicek, 2017).

Taken together, these dynamics generate disconnection at scale. They do not merely reduce the number of opportunities for in-person contact; they fundamentally reshape how individuals imagine, pursue, and sustain relationships. Loneliness, in this sense, is produced not at the margins of neoliberal capitalism but at its very core.

3.5 Social Infrastructure and Its Erosion

Eric Klinenberg's (2018) notion of *social infrastructure* — the physical places and organisational frameworks that shape our capacity to interact — is essential for understanding how systemic loneliness emerges. Social infrastructure includes parks, libraries, public transit, and community organisations. Its presence encourages sustained, diverse social contact; its absence fosters isolation.

Neoliberal austerity measures often target these infrastructures for cuts, citing efficiency and cost-saving. The result is a gradual erosion of the everyday spaces where trust and reciprocity are built. This is compounded by the digital displacement of social life, where interactions migrate to online platforms that lack the density, diversity, and serendipity of in-person public life.

3.6 Cultural Narratives and the Individualisation of Loneliness

The cultural narratives surrounding loneliness under neoliberalism emphasise self-responsibility, self-improvement, and entrepreneurial solutions. Popular media portray isolation as a personal failing - to be remedied through mindfulness training, networking events, or "finding your tribe" via curated experiences. This framing aligns with what Wendy Brown (2015) calls the *homo oeconomicus* paradigm: individuals are reimagined as competitive market actors responsible for maximising their own "human capital," including social and emotional capacities. The depoliticisation of loneliness serves a strategic function: it deflects attention from structural determinants, thereby preserving the status quo. As Berlant (2011) notes in her work on cruel optimism, the very things we turn to for relief - self-care industries, personalised digital connection - can sustain the conditions that produce the problem.

3.7 Comparative Perspectives

The infrastructural lens on loneliness acquires sharper clarity when examined across different cultural and socio-economic contexts. In Japan, the hikikomori phenomenon demonstrates how rigid educational and corporate structures, coupled with technological mediation, can channel individuals into prolonged withdrawal from society (Tateno et al., 2012). In India, rapid urban migration has disrupted extended kinship networks, leaving vacuums of support that are increasingly filled by app-based social and romantic services seeking to monetise the absence of traditional forms of connection (Jeffrey & Young, 2012). In the West, the rise of solo-living intersects with the neoliberal valorisation of independence, fuelling industries of therapeutic self-care and commodified experience designed to manage, rather than resolve, disconnection (Klinenberg, 2012).

Though culturally distinct, these cases converge on a common pattern: infrastructures — whether educational, urban, economic, or digital — both sustain disconnection and simultaneously generate commodified palliatives to manage it.

3.8 Conceptual Synthesis

The conceptual shift from viewing loneliness as an emotion to analysing it as infrastructure signals a deeper recognition of its structural, economic, and political embeddedness. Rather than a transient feeling or private affliction, loneliness becomes a systemic condition, produced and maintained by the socio-material configurations of modernity.

Critically, this approach disrupts the moral psychology of individual blame. By locating loneliness within urban design, labour organization, and technological mediation, it reframes isolation as an outcome of capitalist and neoliberal rationalities that prioritise productivity, surveillance, and consumption over relational wellbeing. For instance, algorithmic architectures of social media, designed to maximise engagement, engineer a sense of perpetual connection while deepening affective fragmentation — a "connected loneliness" that mirrors Berlant's notion of *cruel optimism*.

The economic functionality of loneliness further exposes its commodification. In late capitalism, affective deficits become market opportunities: from wellness apps to "emotional AI" companions, industries profit from sustaining the very alienation they promise to heal. Thus, loneliness becomes both symptom and resource — a circulatory mechanism of emotional capitalism. This recalls Marx's critique of commodity fetishism, where the social relations of people are replaced by relations between things.

Finally, the political obfuscation of loneliness as an individual failing depoliticizes structural harm. As Fraser (2017) and Illouz (2007) argue, neoliberal affective regimes transform collective suffering into matters of personal responsibility and self-care. "Seeking help" or "staying positive" replaces demands for equitable housing, humane work conditions, or public spaces that nurture community. In this sense, loneliness functions ideologically — as a tool to maintain compliance within a disintegrating social fabric.

Hence, to treat loneliness as infrastructure is to expose its reproductive logic: how built environments, digital ecologies, and labour relations co-produce the affective economies of disconnection. It demands a politics of repair, not resilience — a collective re-imagining of how we design cities, workplaces, and technologies to sustain interdependence rather than isolation. Loneliness, then, is not a private wound to be soothed but a public failure to be redressed.

3.9 Implications for Research and Policy

Reconceptualising loneliness as an infrastructural condition rather than a personal deficit generates profound implications for both research and policy. It calls for a fundamental shift—from understanding loneliness as a psychological symptom to analysing it as a systemic configuration of disconnection embedded in economic, spatial, and technological structures.

For research, this perspective demands an explicitly interdisciplinary and critical framework that bridges political economy, urban sociology, digital media studies, and public health. Isolated disciplinary approaches that treat loneliness as a variable of individual well-being cannot capture the structural logics that reproduce it. Instead, research must map the material infrastructures and institutional arrangements—labour flexibilisation, urban privatisation, and algorithmic governance—that generate and sustain social isolation. This requires methodologies capable of tracing how neoliberal reforms reconfigure time, space, and affective life: ethnographies of gig work, spatial analyses of fragmented urban design, or political-economic assessments of welfare retrenchment. The goal is not merely to describe loneliness but to expose the systems that manufacture it as a reproducible condition of modern capitalism.

For policy, the infrastructural lens reveals the inadequacy of counselling, awareness drives, or social-prescribing programmes that locate responsibility within the individual. Such interventions, while well-intentioned, remain palliative rather than transformative. Genuine structural responses must involve the rebuilding of social infrastructure—accessible libraries, parks, community centres, and inclusive housing—that foster sustained, non-commercial interaction. Policies must also regulate the digital infrastructures that commodify connection: ensuring algorithmic transparency, curbing exploitative data practices, and holding platforms accountable for engineering dependence. Equally crucial is addressing labour precarity, which depletes the time, energy, and emotional capacity necessary for relational life.

At the same time, this reframing complicates the seductive appeal of market-based "solutions." Wellness industries, dating apps, and therapeutic platforms promise comfort yet often entrench dependence on commodified interaction, perpetuating the very isolation they claim to heal. They convert vulnerability into profit, transforming disconnection into a renewable economic resource.

Thus, the imperative is not merely to alleviate loneliness but to transform the structural conditions that reproduce it. Policies must move from managing individual symptoms to reconstructing collective systems of belonging—reclaiming connection as a public good rather than a purchasable service. Only through such a structural and ethical reorientation can societies shift from coping with loneliness to confronting its political-economic roots. The following section operationalises these theoretical insights by examining how disconnection is monetised through specific market forms—the "loneliness economy."

4. THE LONELINESS ECONOMY: COMMODIFYING DISCONNECTION

The "loneliness economy" refers to the set of markets, industries, and business models that monetise the absence or erosion of social connection. It operates by identifying loneliness as a problem, framing it in ways amenable to commodification, and delivering partial solutions that create recurring demand. While loneliness has long been addressed through informal networks - family, community, religious institutions - its transformation into a lucrative market sector is a recent phenomenon linked to neoliberal restructuring, digital platformisation, and the erosion of public social infrastructure (Illouz, 2007; Banet-Weiser, 2018). The loneliness economy thrives on a paradox: it promises to alleviate disconnection while often reinforcing the conditions that produce it. The commodification of intimacy, friendship, and care reframes these relationships as transactional encounters mediated by market logics.

The result is not only a shift in how people connect but also a deep entanglement of emotional life with corporate profit imperatives.

4.1 Market Typologies

The loneliness economy comprises diverse sub-sectors, each targeting different dimensions of disconnection.

Figure 4. Typologies of the loneliness economy: Market sectors profiting from disconnection.

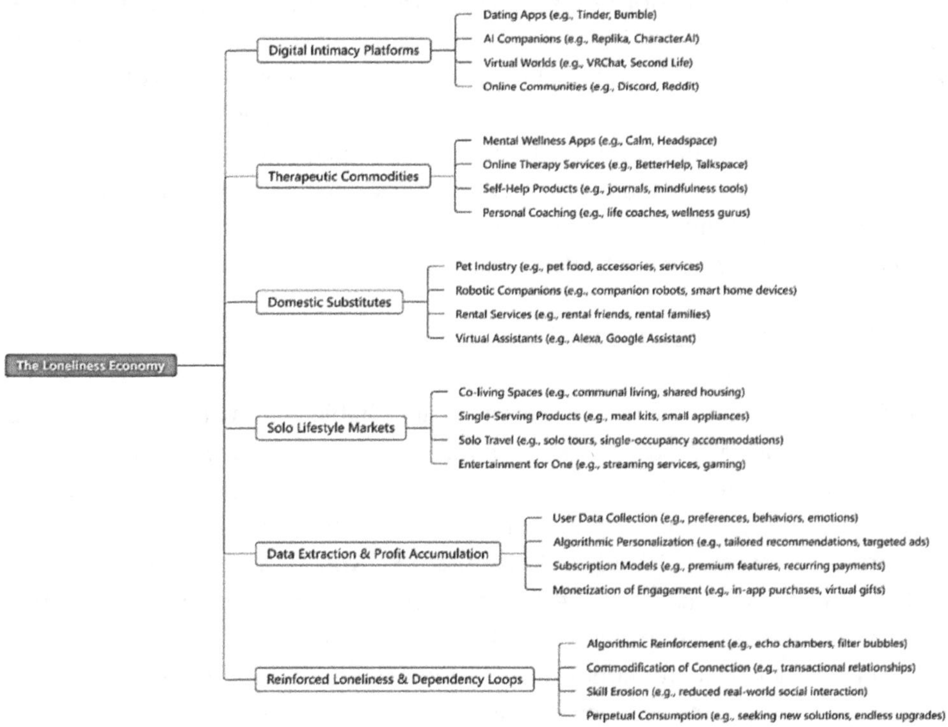

4.1.1 Digital Intimacy Platforms

Dating apps, matchmaking websites, and virtual companion services are perhaps the most visible faces of the loneliness economy. Platforms such as Tinder, Bumble, and OkCupid offer algorithmically mediated access to potential romantic or sexual partners (Chan, 2018). Meanwhile, AI-driven chatbot companions like Replika and virtual reality friendship environments provide simulated intimacy that is available on-demand, subscription-based, and infinitely customisable (Turkle, 2011). While these services expand the scope of possible connections, they also commodify the search for intimacy. Interaction becomes subject to metrics, gamified interfaces, and monetisable "premium" features, embedding personal relationships in a profit-driven ecosystem (Heino, Ellison, & Gibbs, 2010).

4.1.2 Therapeutic Commodities

A parallel industry targets the emotional distress associated with loneliness through wellness and self-care products. Subscription meditation apps (Headspace, Calm), online therapy platforms (BetterHelp, Talkspace), and mental health start-ups frame isolation as an individual wellness challenge solvable through purchase (Davies, 2015). Here, the discourse shifts from the social determinants of loneliness to personal resilience and self-optimisation, aligning with neoliberal ideals of individual responsibility (Illouz, 2007). These platforms also illustrate the datafication of emotional life. Users' mood logs, therapy transcripts, and meditation habits are mined to refine algorithmic targeting, turning emotional vulnerability into a resource for behavioural prediction (Zuboff, 2019).

4.1.3 Domestic Substitutes

When human relationships are absent or unreliable, the market steps in with substitutes. Pet care industries promote animals as companionship solutions, with associated markets in food, grooming, and veterinary services (Kaufman, 2021). In Japan, rental family services allow clients to hire actors to play relatives or friends, fulfilling emotional roles for a fee (Allison, 2013). Robotic caregivers and socially assistive devices, such as Sony's Aibo or SoftBank's Pepper, blend technological novelty with companionship marketing (Tateno et al., 2012). These substitutes reveal the extent to which the care economy has become intertwined with marketised loneliness — and how the line between functional utility and emotional labour is blurred.

4.1.4 Solo Lifestyle Markets

Rising rates of solo living in cities like Tokyo, New York, and Stockholm have spurred a range of products and services tailored to single-person households (Klinenberg, 2012). These include micro-apartments, subscription communal kitchens, minimalist homeware, and solo travel packages. The marketing narrative reframes living alone as a lifestyle choice rather than a social risk, while selling goods that support this mode of life.

4.2 Cultural Engineering of Consumption

The profitability of the loneliness economy rests on its capacity to reframe vulnerability as opportunity. Loneliness is not positioned as a collective failure of social systems but as an individual challenge to be overcome through consumption. Advertising narratives translate disconnection into empowerment: self-care products become pathways to self-actualisation, dating apps function as arenas of self-branding, and even pet adoption is marketed as an expression of individual authenticity (Banet-Weiser, 2018).

This "cultural engineering" performs two key functions. First, *normalisation*: it makes the purchase of social and emotional experiences appear not only ordinary but aspirational, embedding commodified connection into the rhythms of everyday life. Second, *depoliticisation*: by framing loneliness as a lifestyle challenge, it diverts attention from structural drivers such as unaffordable housing, precarious labour markets, and the decline of public infrastructure (Brown, 2015). The result is a culture in which vulnerability is rebranded as "self-investment," where upgrading one's emotional life is synonymous with consuming new goods and services.

4.3 Invisible Labour and Data Economies

Beneath the polished veneer of digital intimacy platforms and wellness technologies lies an extensive architecture of invisible labour and data extraction. What appears to users as effortless connection or emotional support is, in reality, sustained by precarious workers and algorithmic infrastructures designed to convert human vulnerability into profit.

4.3.1 Invisible Labour

The loneliness economy is underpinned by a workforce that remains largely unseen, undervalued, and dispossessed. Behind every swipe, chat, or delivery lies the labour of content moderators, customer service agents, digital therapists, and gig couriers—workers who enable the illusion of seamless interaction. Many operate under insecure contracts, fragmented schedules, and algorithmic surveillance, conditions that not only erode job stability but also reproduce the very isolation the system claims to address (Graham, Hjorth, & Lehdonvirta, 2017).

Moreover, the emotional labour embedded in this economy—performed by counsellors, moderators, or even "rental family" actors—is systematically devalued. These workers perform affective maintenance for others while being denied recognition, adequate pay, or psychological support. The irony is striking: those who sustain the infrastructures of connection are themselves structurally disconnected, alienated from the emotional and material rewards of their work. The loneliness economy thus externalises both emotional and economic costs onto a hidden class of labourers who constitute its moral and material backbone.

4.3.2 Data Capitalism

Parallel to this invisible workforce is a deeper process of data appropriation, where intimacy itself becomes a site of extraction. Every digital interaction—each swipe, message, or mood log—is harvested as data to refine behavioural prediction models and targeted advertising (Zuboff, 2019). Users' affective expressions, from therapy transcripts to dating preferences, are algorithmically mined to create new forms of emotional capital.

This process generates what might be called dependency loops: platforms that promise relief from loneliness optimise for perpetual engagement rather than resolution. The longer users interact, the more data is produced, and the more precisely algorithms can manipulate emotional triggers to keep them returning. What begins as a search for connection becomes an engineered cycle of affective dependence, ensuring that the business of curing loneliness never runs out of customers.

4.4 The Commodification Cycle

The loneliness economy operates through a self-reinforcing circuit of commodification, transforming disconnection into a renewable resource for capital accumulation:

a) **Identification of Need:** Loneliness is reframed as a personal deficit or lifestyle flaw, detached from its structural origins in precarious labour, urban alienation, and digital fragmentation.
b) **Product Design:** Industries package partial "solutions"—apps, wellness retreats, virtual companions—that promise connection but deliver temporary relief, ensuring continuous use and subscription.
c) **Labour and Data Capture:** The infrastructure of connection is sustained by invisible workers and fuelled by users' behavioural and emotional data, both of which serve as sources of surplus value.
d) **Reinforcement of Conditions:** By normalising market-mediated intimacy and displacing public alternatives, these platforms entrench systemic disconnection, ensuring that loneliness remains profitable.

Through this cycle, loneliness is not merely commodified—it is engineered as an enduring condition. Its persistence is essential to the reproduction of digital capitalism, transforming human isolation into a stable asset class. In this way, the loneliness economy reveals capitalism's ultimate paradox: it monetises the erosion of community while claiming to restore it.

4.6 Comparative Examples

The comparative case studies presented in this chapter adopt a qualitative and interpretive methodology, combining secondary data analysis, policy review, and cultural discourse analysis. Rather than relying on quantitative surveys, the cases of India, Japan, and selected Western contexts were chosen for their illustrative power in demonstrating how neoliberal restructuring manifests across distinct socio-economic and cultural settings. The study synthesises findings from existing sociological and policy research, public reports, and media analyses to trace the infrastructures of disconnection and their commercial adaptations. This method follows the comparative political-economy approach, which examines parallel logics rather than identical variables, allowing the analysis to highlight how shared neoliberal reforms—labour flexibilisation, welfare retrenchment, and digital platformisation—generate context-specific expressions of engineered loneliness. By situating each case within its policy, cultural, and economic milieu, the chapter provides an empirically grounded yet conceptually coherent understanding of loneliness as infrastructure.

Japan

In Japan, the *hikikomori* phenomenon—characterised by prolonged social withdrawal—illustrates the intersection between cultural pressures and the commodification of isolation. A combination of rigid educational hierarchies, precarious employment structures, and social stigma surrounding vulnerability has given rise to a unique segment of the loneliness economy. Services such as *rent-a-family* agencies, host and hostess clubs, and robotic pets function as both coping mechanisms and market opportunities (Tateno et al., 2012). These high-tech yet emotionally performative industries blur the line between care and commerce, offering simulated intimacy within a society where expressing loneliness often remains taboo. What emerges is a hybrid marketplace of affect, where human connection is technologically mediated, emotionally scripted, and economically transactional.

India

In India, rapid urbanisation and large-scale migration from rural to metropolitan areas have disrupted traditional kinship networks and collective forms of care. The resulting social vacuum has been swiftly occupied by digital intermediaries that market connection as a lifestyle asset. Dating platforms such as TrulyMadly and matrimony sites like Shaadi.com localise global models of digital intimacy to align with cultural expectations of caste, class, and familial consent. Simultaneously, app-based friendship and event platforms like Meetup and NoStranger target urban professionals seeking community in highly individualised environments. However, participation in these digital ecosystems presupposes access to smartphones, internet connectivity, and cultural capital—privileges concentrated among the urban middle class (Jeffrey & Young, 2012). The result is a digitally stratified landscape of belonging, where connection itself becomes a marker of social and economic privilege.

Western Contexts

Across the United States and Europe, the rise of solo living and the decline of civic participation have catalysed new markets for curated sociability. Co-living spaces, wellness retreats, and social dining platforms like *EatWith* promise community and "authentic connection," yet at a cost that often excludes those most affected by isolation (Klinenberg, 2012). These enterprises commodify the very social life they displace, transforming everyday acts of togetherness into subscription-based experiences. What was once spontaneous community becomes a premium commodity, accessible primarily to those who can afford to purchase participation. The Western iteration of the loneliness economy thus reveals a paradox: in attempting to sell belonging, it reinforces the structural inequalities that make genuine community increasingly unattainable.

Across these contexts—Japan's technologised intimacy, India's digitally mediated kinship, and the West's commercialised community—the underlying pattern remains consistent: loneliness is not simply experienced but engineered, shaped by infrastructures that convert disconnection into a sustainable market resource.

4.7 Critical Perspectives

Critical engagement with the loneliness economy exposes it as more than a benign market response to social need—it is a mechanism of capitalist extraction and affective governance. Scholars argue that this phenomenon exemplifies what David Harvey (2005) terms *accumulation by dispossession*: the systematic dismantling of public goods and communal infrastructures, followed by their reconstitution as private, monetisable commodities. Public parks give way to fee-based wellness spaces; neighbourhood associations are displaced by subscription-based "community platforms." What were once spontaneous, reciprocal social exchanges are now mediated through corporate infrastructures that monetise access to belonging. In this sense, loneliness is not merely exploited but actively manufactured to sustain cycles of consumption and dependency.

Beyond economic appropriation, critics highlight the subtler forms of affective capture operating within digital and cultural economies. Platforms do not simply commodify loneliness; they discipline emotional expression through algorithmic visibility and reward structures. As Berlant (2011) suggests, users are nudged toward affective styles that align with platform logics—optimism, irony, and "relatable" vulnerability—while deeper forms of grief, anger, or political critique are rendered less visible. Dating apps, social media feeds, and wellness platforms thus cultivate a curated emotional public sphere where loneliness is aestheticised, performable, and monetisable but rarely politicised.

This affective governance serves a dual purpose: it maintains engagement by ensuring that users continually seek emotional resolution within the platform, and it neutralises dissent by transforming collective suffering into individualised self-expression. The result is a feedback loop of commodified emotion, in which loneliness becomes both the raw material and the product of digital capitalism.

Critically, such dynamics reflect the broader neoliberal restructuring of emotional life: the conversion of relational capacities into market assets and the replacement of solidarity with self-optimisation. The loneliness economy, therefore, is not a marginal aberration but a central feature of contemporary capitalism's moral economy, in which the management of feeling becomes a new frontier of accumulation and control.

4.8 Policy Implications

Interpreting loneliness through the lens of political economy highlights urgent regulatory and policy interventions. Left unchecked, the loneliness economy risks transforming meaningful connection into a stratified privilege - accessible primarily to those who can afford commodified solutions - while deepening inequality in emotional and social life.

Consumer protection must be central. Emotional and intimate data represent some of the most sensitive forms of personal information, yet they are routinely harvested, analysed, and sold. Transparent standards on how such data are collected, stored, and monetised are essential to prevent exploitation and to ensure informed consent in contexts where vulnerability is easily leveraged.

Labour rights also demand attention. The invisible workers who sustain the loneliness economy - from content moderators to on-demand couriers to "emotional service" providers - often labour under precarious contracts with little recognition of the affective dimensions of their work. Policy must extend protections, fair wages, and benefits to these workers, acknowledging emotional labour as real labour deserving of compensation and security.

Public alternatives are equally critical. Investment in libraries, parks, community hubs, and affordable housing provides non-market spaces for connection, reducing dependence on commercial substitutes. By treating social infrastructure as a public good, governments can counterbalance the encroachment of commodified solutions and restore conditions for organic, collective forms of belonging.

Finally, regulation of platform power is necessary to address monopolistic control over digital intimacy. Antitrust measures, algorithmic accountability, and requirements for interoperability could limit the concentration of power in a few corporations that currently dictate how billions of people experience connection (Zuboff, 2019).

Taken together, these interventions shift the frame from loneliness as a private problem to loneliness as a public concern. They foreground the principle that connection should not be treated as a luxury commodity but protected as a social right and democratic necessity. While these markets demonstrate the economic logic of loneliness, their real-world expression varies across societies. Section 5 explores these patterns through comparative case studies.

5. EMPIRICAL CASE STUDIES: GLOBAL PATTERNS OF ENGINEERED LONELINESS

The concept of "engineered loneliness" moves beyond the idea that disconnection is an unfortunate by-product of modernity. Instead, it views loneliness as a condition actively shaped - and sometimes intentionally sustained - by social, economic, and technological infrastructures. These infrastructures vary across geographies, but share underlying logics: commodification of connection, erosion of public and communal spaces, and digital mediation of intimacy.

This section presents three empirical case studies - Japan, India, and selected Western contexts (United States and parts of Europe) - to illustrate how different socio-economic, cultural, and political configurations produce distinctive patterns of engineered loneliness. The analysis focuses on (1) structural drivers, (2) cultural narratives, (3) commercial interventions, and (4) policy landscapes, while also considering the transnational circulation of loneliness-related markets.

Table 1. Comparative patterns of engineered loneliness across global contexts.

Region	*Structural Drivers*	*Cultural Narratives*	*Market Interventions*	*Policy Response*
Japan	Aging, rigid work	Emotional restraint	Rental family, robots	Counselling focus
India	Urban migration, precarity	Modern individualism	Dating apps, co-living	Limited state role
West	Welfare retrenchment	Self-help culture	Wellness retreats	Symbolic policy

5.1 Japan: High-Tech Isolation and the Commodification of Care

5.1.1 Structural Drivers

Japan presents one of the most studied cases of socially embedded loneliness. According to the Cabinet Office (2021), more than 1.5 million individuals are estimated to live in prolonged social withdrawal (hikikomori), while nearly 40 per cent of households now consist of single occupants—a demographic trend that amplifies isolation in dense urban settings (Statistics Japan, 2022).

Japan presents one of the most studied cases of socially embedded loneliness. Demographic changes - an ageing population, declining birth rates, and increasing solo living - intersect with rigid corporate structures and educational systems that place high demands on individuals while limiting opportunities for unstructured social interaction (Allison, 2013). Urban housing design, favouring small apartments, further constrains communal living arrangements.

The *hikikomori* phenomenon, where individuals (often young men) withdraw from school or work and remain isolated for months or years, exemplifies the intersection of structural and cultural pressures (Tateno et al., 2012). While initially understood as a psychological condition, research now points to structural underpinnings, including employment precarity, bullying in competitive educational environments, and the stigma associated with “failure” to meet normative life milestones.

5.1.2 Cultural Narratives

Cultural scripts emphasising self-reliance and emotional restraint can inhibit help-seeking behaviours. Expressions of loneliness may be interpreted as weakness or social incompetence, making individuals more vulnerable to prolonged isolation (Furlong, 2008). At the same time, a cultural premium on technological innovation has normalised the use of machines as emotional supports, reinforcing the marketability of non-human companionship.

5.1.3 Commercial Interventions

The Japanese loneliness economy includes:

- Rental family and friend services: Agencies provide actors to play roles in personal events - from weddings to routine family visits (Yamamoto, 2016).
- Host and hostess clubs: Patrons pay for simulated romantic or platonic attention, often in highly stylised environments.
- Robotic caregivers and pets: Products such as Aibo (robot dog) and Paro (therapeutic seal) are marketed for companionship, particularly among the elderly (Broadbent et al., 2009).

These services commodify both the performance of intimacy and the objects that substitute for it, embedding emotional life in market transactions.

5.1.4 Policy Landscape

In 2021, Japan appointed a *Minister for Loneliness and Isolation*, launching a national strategy that linked loneliness to suicide prevention and ageing policy (Cabinet Office of Japan, 2021).

While the Japanese government has acknowledged loneliness as a public health issue - particularly among older adults - interventions often focus on individual counselling or volunteer networks rather than structural reforms in labour or housing policy (Cabinet Office of Japan, 2021). This limited scope reflects the broader neoliberal trend of framing loneliness as a matter for individual or community management, rather than systemic restructuring.

5.2 India: Urban Migration, Digital Mediation, and Market Capture

5.2.1 Structural Drivers

Rapid urbanisation continues to reshape India's social fabric: between 2001 and 2021, the urban population increased from 27.8 per cent to 36 per cent, while migration surveys show that over 45 per cent of internal migrants live apart from extended families (Census of India, 2021; NSSO, 2020). These trends, combined with gig-based employment models, have intensified spatial and relational fragmentation in metropolitan centres.

India's rapid urbanisation and economic liberalisation have disrupted traditional kinship networks and community-based support systems. Migration from rural to urban areas for education and employment often results in nuclear or solo living arrangements, particularly among young professionals (Jeffrey & Young, 2012). Urban design in metropolitan centres like Bengaluru and Mumbai tends toward privatised, gated communities, reducing public spaces for interaction.

Labour market transformations, especially the expansion of IT services and gig work, have introduced flexible but isolating work arrangements. The precarity of employment and long working hours also reduce opportunities for sustained offline social engagement.

5.2.2 Cultural Narratives

While collectivist ideals remain strong in many parts of India, middle-class urban culture increasingly incorporates globalised narratives of individual achievement and self-branding (Nisbett, 2009). Loneliness is often unspoken due to stigma, but it is indirectly addressed through consumption - for example, "anti-loneliness" dining experiences or premium dating services positioned as lifestyle enhancers.

5.2.3 Commercial Interventions

The Indian loneliness economy includes:

- Dating and matrimony platforms: Apps like TrulyMadly and global players like Tinder adapt to local norms, often offering parental involvement features or horoscope compatibility checks.
- Friendship and networking apps: Platforms such as Meetup and NoStranger facilitate interest-based connections, but require digital literacy and disposable income.
- Coworking spaces: Marketed as professional networking hubs, these also serve as curated social environments for remote workers.

These services monetise connection by offering structured, often membership-based, alternatives to informal community life.

5.2.4 Policy Landscape

India's *National Mental Health Policy (2014)* acknowledges social isolation as a determinant of mental well-being, yet programmatic attention remains limited to counselling initiatives rather than urban or labour reforms (Ministry of Health and Family Welfare, 2014).

Loneliness has not been a central policy concern in India, but mental health initiatives (e.g., the National Mental Health Programme) occasionally address it indirectly. Social sector interventions by NGOs - such as senior citizen helplines - often fill gaps left by the state. However, such efforts rarely address urban design or labour market structures that produce disconnection.

5.3 Western Contexts: Platformised Sociality and the Retreat of Public Space

5.3.1 Structural Drivers

In the United Kingdom, nearly 25 per cent of adults report feeling lonely often or always (ONS, 2023), prompting the creation of the *Loneliness Strategy (2018)* and a dedicated *Minister for Loneliness*. In the United States, the U.S. Surgeon General's *2023 Advisory on the Healing Effects of Social Connection* estimated that disconnection carries health risks comparable to smoking 15 cigarettes per day (Murthy, 2023).

In the United States and much of Western Europe, several structural dynamics have created fertile ground for the commodification of connection. Rising rates of solo living, declining participation in civic associations, and cuts to public services have reduced opportunities for collective interaction (Klinenberg, 2012). Suburbanisation and car-dependent urban design limit spontaneous encounters, while the digitalisation of both work and leisure channels interaction through commercial platforms. The neoliberal restructuring of welfare states has further redefined social goods — from recreation to mental health — as matters of private responsibility. Public libraries, parks, and community centres face chronic underfunding, pushing citizens toward fee-based alternatives that transform once-shared spaces into commodities.

5.3.2 Cultural Narratives

Western cultural imaginaries valorise independence, mobility, and self-actualisation. Within this framework, loneliness is often pathologised as a personal deficiency rather than recognised as a systemic outcome. Such framing encourages therapeutic or consumer-oriented solutions (Illouz, 2007). The booming self-help industry and the proliferation of wellness products and services exemplify how disconnection is rebranded as an individual challenge to be solved through lifestyle consumption rather than collective reform.

5.3.3 Commercial Interventions

The Western loneliness economy manifests in a range of commodified interventions. Co-living spaces, marketed primarily to millennials and remote workers, promise curated communities but at premium rents that often exclude lower-income groups. Wellness retreats blend tourism with mental health branding, offering reconnection and "digital detox" in ways that reproduce exclusivity through cost barriers. Social dining platforms, such as EatWith, commodify the simple act of eating together by turning hospitality into a market transaction. Across these interventions, platform capitalism provides the dominant mediation, with companies harvesting and analysing user data to refine targeting strategies and maximise engagement (Srnicek, 2017).

5.3.4 Policy Landscape

Governments in Western contexts have begun to acknowledge loneliness as a public health concern. The most visible example is the United Kingdom's appointment of a "Minister for Loneliness" in 2018 (UK Government, 2018). Yet, most initiatives focus on soft interventions - awareness campaigns, volunteer programmes, or community partnerships — while leaving intact the structural conditions that fuel disconnection. Few policies confront the deeper issues of labour precarity, housing unaffordability, declining public space, or the monopolistic dominance of digital platforms. As a result, policy responses risk legitimising individualised and market-based remedies rather than pursuing systemic reform.

5.4 Cross-Case Comparative Insights

Comparing cases across regions reveals several recurring themes.

a. **Structural Commonalities:** Despite cultural and economic differences, a consistent pattern emerges: neoliberal restructuring has diminished public and collective spaces while promoting individualised, market-mediated forms of connection. Whether through Japan's cramped urban housing, India's proliferation of gated communities, or the United States' underfunded public libraries, the retreat of the commons emerges as a key driver of engineered loneliness.
b. **Cultural Mediation:** While the stigma and expression of loneliness differ — from Japan's valorisation of emotional restraint to Western self-help narratives — each context exhibits some degree of individualisation in framing the problem. These cultural framings provide legitimacy for market-based "solutions," presenting loneliness less as a structural condition than as a personal deficit to be addressed through consumption.

c. **Market Innovation:** The commodification of connection is highly adaptive, embedding itself within local cultural scripts. Host clubs in Japan, matrimony apps in India, and co-living spaces in Western cities each package sociality for sale in ways that resonate with local norms while maintaining underlying market logics.
d. **Policy Limitations:** Government interventions tend to remain soft and symbolic, emphasising awareness campaigns, volunteerism, or individual coping strategies. Few policies confront the structural political economy of disconnection — whether through labour deregulation, housing unaffordability, or platform monopolisation — leaving the underlying conditions intact.

5.5 Transnational Circulation of the Loneliness Economy

The loneliness economy is not confined within national borders but circulates transnationally through digital platforms and lifestyle marketing. A dating app developed in Silicon Valley can be localised for Indian markets; robotic pets designed in Japan are marketed to European eldercare facilities.

This circulation produces two dynamics. *Standardisation* occurs as core business models — subscription fees, data monetisation, and engagement-driven design — remain consistent across borders. At the same time, *diversification* emerges through adaptation to local cultural scripts and regulatory environments: what is marketed as "companionship" in one setting may be sold as "wellness" or "productivity" in another.

Taken together, these dynamics highlight loneliness not as an accidental by-product of modernity but as a core feature of globalised emotional capitalism (Illouz, 2007). The infrastructures of disconnection are increasingly shared, even as their manifestations are locally inflected.

5.6 Implications for Future Research and Policy

The comparative cases make clear that engineered loneliness cannot be mitigated through individual-level interventions alone. What is required is a systemic approach that recognises disconnection as an outcome of political economy rather than personal psychology.

Future research should:

- Investigate how urban design, labour markets, and digital platforms intersect to structurally produce disconnection.

- Examine the often-invisible labour - from content moderators to care workers - that sustains markets for connection while simultaneously generating isolation among those workers themselves.
- Critically assess the unintended consequences of commercial "solutions," including the ways they create dependency on commodified intimacy and foreclose non-market alternatives.

Policy frameworks must:

- Reinvest in social infrastructure such as parks, libraries, and community centres, ensuring spaces for connection remain accessible outside the market.
- Regulate platform monopolies and data exploitation, particularly in the domain of emotional and intimate life.
- Address housing affordability and labour precarity as upstream determinants of relational well-being, recognising that stable living and working conditions are preconditions for social connection.

Without such systemic measures, the loneliness economy will not diminish loneliness but will continue to thrive by managing it as a renewable resource for profit.

6. MACROECONOMIC CONSEQUENCES OF LONELINESS AND POLICY CRITIQUE

Loneliness is often understood as an individual or public health problem, but its macroeconomic consequences are substantial, far-reaching, and systemic. Beyond its personal toll, loneliness contributes to measurable declines in productivity, increased healthcare expenditures, reduced workforce participation, and long-term fiscal burdens. In a neoliberal political economy - where market logics permeate social life - loneliness is paradoxically both an economic liability (through lost output and public health costs) and an asset (as a driver of consumer demand in the "loneliness economy").

This section examines these macroeconomic impacts through four lenses: (1) productivity and labour market effects, (2) healthcare and welfare costs, (3) economic externalities and intergenerational effects, and (4) the contradictions in policy approaches. It concludes with a critical review of existing policy responses and a framework for systemic intervention.

6.1 Productivity and Labour Market Effects

Loneliness undermines productivity in ways that are both immediate and structural. Research shows that socially isolated workers experience higher rates of absenteeism, presenteeism, and burnout, with significant reductions in engagement, morale, and cognitive performance (Holt-Lunstad, 2017; Cigna, 2020). For employers, this translates into lost efficiency; for economies, it compounds into slowed growth and weaker competitiveness.

National contexts reveal the scale of underutilised human capital. In Japan, an estimated one million hikikomori remain outside the labour market altogether, representing not just individual withdrawal but systemic loss of productive capacity (Cabinet Office of Japan, 2021). In India, urban migration and hyper-competitive labour environments disrupt kinship networks and intensify isolation, leading to higher job turnover and underinvestment in skill development — costs ultimately borne by employers through repeated recruitment and training.

Labour market withdrawal magnifies these effects. Chronic loneliness can drive early retirement, long-term unemployment, or permanent exclusion from economic participation. Older adults who lose workplace-based networks face accelerated disengagement, adding to pension and healthcare burdens. Younger workers, particularly those with untreated mental health conditions, may exit competitive markets entirely, deepening long-term dependency.

Paradoxically, the very labour models that exacerbate loneliness also exploit it. Remote gig work and other atomised forms of employment, often celebrated for flexibility, leave workers socially isolated and structurally disempowered. Cut off from peers and organisational support, many accept unfavourable terms, trading stability and skill development for short-term solitary income streams (Graham, Hjorth, & Lehdonvirta, 2017). In this way, loneliness is not merely a by-product of precarious labour but also a condition that sustains it.

6.2 Healthcare and Welfare Costs

The health implications of loneliness are severe and well-documented. Chronic disconnection increases the risk of premature mortality by up to 26%, a risk comparable to smoking and obesity (Holt-Lunstad et al., 2015). It is strongly correlated with cardiovascular disease, depression, anxiety, and cognitive decline - all conditions that impose heavy demands on public healthcare systems. In the UK, loneliness-related illnesses are estimated to cost billions annually in additional healthcare and social care spending (UK Government, 2018). While national cost estimates in Japan and

India are less developed, the rising prevalence of mental health challenges linked to social isolation suggests comparable fiscal pressures.

Loneliness also drives welfare dependence, further entrenching its economic consequences. Individuals facing prolonged isolation and mental health difficulties are more likely to rely on disability allowances, subsidised housing, or other welfare supports. This produces a damaging feedback loop: disconnection reduces the likelihood of re-entering the workforce, which in turn deepens dependency and expands state expenditures. In this sense, loneliness is not only a public health burden but also a structural drain on welfare systems, reinforcing cycles of exclusion and fiscal strain.

6.3 Economic Externalities and Intergenerational Effects

From a macroeconomic standpoint, loneliness erodes what Putnam (2000) termed *social capital* - the networks, trust, and norms that sustain cooperation and collective action. Social capital is not a soft cultural add-on but a productive resource: it underpins economic dynamism, strengthens democratic institutions, and enhances resilience in times of crisis. Its depletion through widespread disconnection undermines trust, weakens civic engagement, and narrows the capacity of societies to innovate or respond collectively to shocks.

The effects of loneliness are also intergenerational. Children raised in socially isolated households often face reduced opportunities to develop social skills and civic habits, limiting future employability and participation in democratic life. This "social inheritance" of isolation creates a compounding effect, embedding diminished productivity and weakened civic ties across generations.

At the local level, communities marked by high loneliness rates often experience economic stagnation. Declines in volunteerism, civic associations, and informal care provision undermine the social infrastructure that sustains small businesses and public services. In this sense, loneliness is not only an individual burden but a corrosive force at multiple scales - household, community, and macroeconomy.

6.4 The Contradictions of the Loneliness Economy

Yet loneliness is not simply a social cost; it is also a source of market opportunity. A growing set of industries - from dating apps to wellness retreats - thrive precisely because disconnection is widespread. This generates a structural contradiction: from a public policy perspective, loneliness is a problem to be solved in order to reduce healthcare expenditure and boost productivity; from a market perspective, it is a renewable resource, to be managed rather than eliminated, in order to sustain consumer demand.

As Zuboff (2019) observes in the context of surveillance capitalism, the commodification of deficits relies on their ongoing reproduction. The loneliness economy functions in a similar way. It offers partial solutions that provide temporary relief - a weekend retreat, a curated co-living space, a new platform promising companionship - but leaves untouched the deeper structural causes of disconnection. In doing so, it ensures that loneliness remains both an economic liability for society and a lucrative market for capital.

6.5 Policy Critique

Most existing policy approaches to loneliness remain trapped within an individualised framework, treating disconnection as a matter of personal resilience or lifestyle adjustment rather than as the outcome of systemic arrangements. Governments often promote mindfulness classes, volunteering schemes, or social clubs as solutions, but such measures obscure the deeper forces of housing unaffordability, precarious labour markets, and exclusionary urban design. This mirrors broader neoliberal health strategies, which shift responsibility from the state to the citizen while leaving structural determinants untouched.

Even where more ambitious policies have emerged - such as the UK's appointment of a Minister for Loneliness - interventions remain fragmented and underfunded, siloed across departments with little capacity for structural reform. Symbolism without resources risks reducing loneliness policy to gesture politics, legitimising the idea that something is being done while core drivers remain unchallenged.

A particularly glaring blind spot is the economic and digital dimension of loneliness. Policies rarely confront the fact that insecure work, flexible contracts, and inadequate housing erode the stability necessary for sustained social bonds. Nor do they regulate the platform monopolies that increasingly mediate social life, extracting data and engineering engagement loops that mimic, but cannot replace, genuine connection. By neglecting these domains, policy inadvertently reinforces the very infrastructures of disconnection it seeks to address.

In short, current strategies risk managing loneliness at the margins rather than transforming its conditions of production. Without a structural shift - linking housing, labour, urban planning, and digital governance to the politics of connection - policy will remain palliative at best and complicit at worst.

6.6 Toward a Structural Policy Approach

Reducing the macroeconomic burden of loneliness requires moving beyond symbolic gestures and individualised fixes toward structural reform. Loneliness must be treated not as a lifestyle ailment but as a predictable outcome of policy choices and economic arrangements. The erosion of public space, the casualisation of labour, exclusionary urban design, and the unregulated power of digital platforms are not accidental backdrops to disconnection; they are its structural foundations.

A structural policy approach would prioritise rebuilding social infrastructure - libraries, parks, community hubs, and affordable co-housing - as non-market spaces for sustained connection. It would involve labour reforms that guarantee security, fair wages, and flexibility without isolation, recognising that stable work is inseparable from social participation. It would demand urban planning oriented toward connection, embedding walkability, mixed-use neighbourhoods, and inclusive shared spaces into the design of everyday life. Just as crucially, it would extend to platform regulation, imposing transparency on algorithms, restricting exploitative data practices, and supporting public-interest digital environments that privilege human well-being over engagement metrics.

Yet structural reform is not only about discrete sectors. An integrated policy framework linking health, housing, labour, and technology would be required to address disconnection at its roots. This means treating loneliness as a cross-sectoral priority, on par with climate or inequality, rather than a siloed public health concern.

The stakes are clear: loneliness is not only a personal tragedy but a macroeconomic liability, visible in lost productivity, increased healthcare costs, and the corrosion of social capital. Under neoliberal capitalism, however, the very conditions that generate disconnection have been repurposed into profitable markets - from dating apps to wellness retreats - that thrive on scarcity of connection. Current responses, fragmented and underfunded, are at best palliative and at worst complicit, allowing loneliness to be managed as a renewable resource for capital.

A critical political economy perspective makes the conclusion inescapable: tackling loneliness requires systemic interventions that rebuild commons, regulate extractive industries, reform labour, and reimagine cities as sites of encounter. Without such changes, loneliness will persist not only as an individual affliction but as an entrenched economic logic - a symptom and strategy of contemporary capitalism.

7. THE INDIVIDUALIZATION OF LONELINESS IN POLICY AND PUBLIC DISCOURSE

In recent years, loneliness has shifted from a private emotional experience to a recognised social issue, appearing in public health strategies, governmental reports, and popular media. However, this recognition has often come with a subtle reframing: loneliness is presented less as a systemic or structural outcome of economic, spatial, and technological arrangements, and more as an individual challenge to be managed through personal action. This "individualization" process mirrors wider neoliberal policy trends in which collective problems are reframed as matters of personal responsibility (Brown, 2015).

This section examines how policy frameworks, media narratives, and corporate messaging converge to produce an individualised understanding of loneliness. It explores (A) the discursive construction of loneliness as a lifestyle problem, (B) the therapeutic and self-help framing in public policy, (C) the role of commercial actors in sustaining the individualised lens, and (D) the consequences of this framing for systemic reform.

Figure 5. The discursive individualisation of loneliness: From structural causes to personal responsibility.

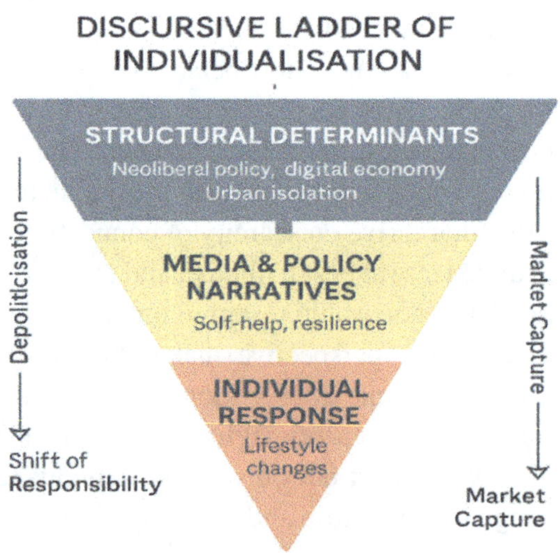

7.1 Loneliness as a Lifestyle Problem

7.1.1 Media Narratives

Mainstream media representations of loneliness often personalise what is, in essence, a structural and collective problem. News outlets and lifestyle journalism frame loneliness through individual testimonies—stories of "isolated individuals" seeking reconnection—while neglecting the social, economic, and technological systems that produce disconnection. Headlines such as *"How to Beat Loneliness"* or *"Tips for Staying Connected"* (The Guardian, 2019) reproduce the logic of individual responsibilisation, encouraging readers to view loneliness as a failure of personal agency or social competence.

This framing aligns with Eva Illouz's (2007) theory of *emotional capitalism*, wherein emotional life becomes both commodified and privatised. The "solutions" offered—self-help routines, mindfulness apps, and lifestyle adjustments—convert emotional distress into an economic opportunity. As Illouz argues, capitalism reorganises affect by translating psychological suffering into consumer demand, encouraging individuals to "fix" structural alienation through consumption. In this sense, media discourse naturalises neoliberal values of self-regulation and self-improvement, obscuring the political economy of loneliness. Rather than interrogating the erosion of community infrastructures or the precarity of work, it redefines connection as a personal project—a matter of resilience and self-management (Brown, 2015; Davies, 2015).

7.1.2 Social Media and the Performance of Connection

The rise of digital culture intensifies this individualisation by conflating visibility with belonging. Social media platforms—Twitter/X, Instagram, Facebook, TikTok—create what Sherry Turkle (2011) calls *"performance intimacy"*, a mode of relational life mediated through constant display and surveillance. Within this logic, loneliness becomes evidence of personal failure to "stay connected," while hyperactivity online is misread as social health.

Algorithms reinforce this illusion by rewarding engagement metrics—likes, shares, comments—as proxies for social worth. Users internalise these metrics, curating their digital identities to perform connection while experiencing deeper affective isolation (Kross et al., 2013). The result is a paradox of "connected loneliness" (Nowland, Necka, & Cacioppo, 2018): users remain perpetually networked but emotionally detached, trapped within infrastructures that monetise their interactions. The media's silence on this paradox reflects a deeper ideological function—by equating connectivity with sociality, it sustains a market for digital "solutions" while depoliticising the architectures of disconnection.

7.2 Therapeutic and Self-Help Framing in Public Policy

7.2.1 Health Policy Integration

Governments have increasingly incorporated loneliness into public health frameworks, as seen in the UK's *A Connected Society* report (UK Government, 2018). While such initiatives mark institutional recognition of loneliness, their operational logic remains therapeutic rather than structural. Strategies emphasise early intervention through *GP referrals, social prescribing,* and *volunteer-led programmes*—interventions that target individual behaviour rather than the socio-economic infrastructures that generate isolation.

As Wendy Brown (2015) and Nikolas Rose (2006) note, such policies epitomise neoliberal governance: they translate systemic failures into psychological deficits to be managed through behaviour modification. By framing loneliness as a personal health risk, states avoid confronting upstream determinants—housing unaffordability, labour precarity, and digital monopolisation—that sustain chronic disconnection (Klinenberg, 2018). The medicalisation of loneliness therefore serves a double purpose: it legitimises the problem's visibility while simultaneously narrowing its political horizon.

7.2.2 Social Prescribing as Behavioural Nudging

Social prescribing—where patients are referred to non-clinical activities like walking clubs or art classes—is often heralded as a low-cost, community-based intervention. Yet, in practice, it operates as a behavioural "nudge" within the neo-liberal paradigm of *self-governance* (Thaler & Sunstein, 2008). Patients are urged to "get out more" or "join a group" without addressing the material conditions that make participation difficult: long working hours, unsafe neighbourhoods, or unaffordable transit.

As William Davies (2015) argues, this shift replaces political intervention with psychological adaptation, positioning individuals as entrepreneurs of their own wellbeing. The structural roots of disconnection—welfare retrenchment, spatial segregation, and privatisation of public life—remain untouched. Social prescribing thus exemplifies a post-welfare logic, where states outsource social repair to individual initiative under the guise of empowerment.

7.2.3 The Responsibility Shift

The therapeutic framing of loneliness extends a broader responsibility shift from collective institutions to individuals. The citizen is reimagined as a self-regulating emotional subject, responsible for managing the social fallout of market-driven disconnection. This echoes Foucault's (2008) notion of *governmentality*, where the neoliberal state governs not by direct coercion but through cultivating self-disciplining subjects.

Policies that ignore the structural causes—deregulated housing markets, cuts to public infrastructure, and exploitative labour regimes—effectively privatise the social costs of neoliberalism. Loneliness becomes a moral failure rather than a policy failure. As a result, state and corporate actors absolve themselves of accountability, while individuals are urged to consume, adapt, and self-optimize in the face of structural alienation.

7.3 Corporate Narratives and the Market for Self-Connection

7.3.1 Commodifying the Cure

Corporate marketing has seamlessly absorbed loneliness into the language of lifestyle management. From dating apps and friendship platforms to mindfulness subscriptions and ergonomic home-office setups, corporations position themselves as architects of emotional fulfilment. The message is consistent: the individual can—and must—purchase connection through consumption.

Wellness industries promote "digital detox" retreats and subscription therapy apps; tech companies advertise AI companions and virtual meetups; retailers link products such as books, pets, and kitchenware to narratives of comfort and self-sufficiency. These commodified "cures" echo Illouz's (2007) critique of emotional capitalism, where feelings are rebranded as market opportunities. Under the guise of empowerment, corporations cultivate dependency: consumers must continually buy to sustain emotional equilibrium.

This commodification of affect displaces collective solutions—such as investment in social infrastructure or labour protections—by offering temporary comfort through goods and services. In doing so, it redefines social connection as a private luxury rather than a public right, deepening class-based inequalities in access to belonging (Banet-Weiser, 2018).

7.3.2 The Self-Optimisation Imperative

In the corporate discourse, loneliness is reframed not as a symptom of structural alienation but as evidence of personal underinvestment in social capital. The language of "networking," "relationship building," and "emotional intelligence" transforms relational life into a productivity metric. This mirrors what Byung-Chul Han (2017) calls the *"achievement society"*, where individuals internalise the logic of competition and constant self-improvement even in intimate domains.

Under these conditions, connection becomes instrumental—something to be cultivated for advantage, not solidarity. Workers are told to "expand their networks" or "leverage social ties" within conditions of overwork, algorithmic management, and economic insecurity. The contradiction is acute: systems that erode the foundations of collective life simultaneously demand that individuals perform relational competence to remain employable. Thus, loneliness is not a failure of individual initiative but the outcome of structural contradictions—a condition engineered by capitalism yet pathologised as a personal flaw.

7.4 Consequences of the Individualised Framing

7.4.1 Depoliticisation of Loneliness

The individualisation of loneliness functions as a form of depoliticisation, obscuring the structural and systemic forces that produce social disconnection. When loneliness is narrated as a personal affliction or psychological deficit, its political and economic determinants—the erosion of public infrastructure, the privatisation of leisure, the spatial segregation of cities, and the precarisation of labour—fade into the background (Peck & Tickell, 2002; Brown, 2015). This rhetorical shift transforms collective experiences of alienation into matters of private responsibility, foreclosing the possibility of structural critique or political mobilisation.

By casting loneliness as an individual management problem, the state and market evade accountability for policies that dismantle the social commons—public spaces, affordable housing, community services, and labour protections. In the process, loneliness is recoded from a symptom of neoliberal restructuring into a moralised failure of self-care. As Wendy Brown (2015) argues, neoliberal rationality reframes social suffering as a failure of entrepreneurial subjectivity, leaving individuals to navigate systemic disconnection with the limited tools of self-discipline and optimism. The result is an affective depoliticisation: loneliness becomes something to be treated, not contested.

7.4.2 Victim-Blaming Dynamics

The discourse of personal responsibility embedded in this framing also generates victim-blaming dynamics, subtly implying that individuals are at fault for their isolation. Public narratives urging citizens to "reach out," "stay connected," or "try harder" presuppose equal access to time, mobility, and emotional energy—resources unequally distributed across class, gender, and ability lines. As Lauren Berlant (2011) observes, neoliberal culture celebrates "cruel optimism," in which people are encouraged to pursue unattainable ideals of happiness and connection despite structural impediments.

This moralisation of loneliness fosters stigma and silence, discouraging open discussion and collective solidarity among those most affected. Individuals internalise structural alienation as personal inadequacy, reinforcing cycles of shame and withdrawal. The paradox is that interventions designed to alleviate loneliness often reproduce the very psychological burden of failure that intensifies it.

7.4.3 Reinforcing Inequality

Self-help and lifestyle solutions to loneliness are invariably classed, gendered, and spatially uneven. They presume access to time, disposable income, and safe, accessible environments—all privileges unavailable to many. Wellness retreats, paid social platforms, and subscription-based therapy services remain accessible largely to the urban middle classes, while low-income or marginalised populations face structural barriers to participation (Klinenberg, 2018).

This uneven access creates a "stratified sociality"—a hierarchy of connection in which belonging becomes a commodity. The more loneliness is defined as a problem of individual initiative, the more interventions reward those already equipped with cultural and economic capital to "invest" in relationships. As Bourdieu (1986) noted, social capital itself is unequally distributed and structurally reproduced; policies that ignore this dynamic risk amplifying the very inequalities they claim to address. Thus, the individualised framing not only marginalises the structurally disconnected but actively institutionalises inequality within the discourse of emotional well-being.

7.4.4 Market Dependence

Finally, the individualised framing entrenches market dependence, transforming the quest for connection into a perpetual cycle of consumption. By making individuals responsible for their own emotional and social maintenance, neoliberal culture sustains the profitability of the loneliness economy—a constellation of industries offering commodified "solutions" to disconnection (Illouz, 2007; Zuboff, 2019).

Apps, wellness platforms, and digital communities promise empowerment while ensuring users' continued reliance on paid services. This logic mirrors what Shoshana Zuboff (2019) calls *surveillance capitalism*: a system that monetises human vulnerability by transforming emotional expression into data and profit. The more individuals turn to market solutions for companionship or comfort, the more their social lives become entangled within circuits of commodification.

In effect, the neoliberal solution to loneliness becomes its own perpetuation: by offering temporary relief, it reproduces the very conditions of isolation it purports to cure. The outcome is a self-reinforcing loop of dependency, where disconnection is continuously regenerated as both a social reality and a profitable asset.

8. TOWARD A COLLECTIVE REFRAMING

Countering the individualisation of loneliness requires shifting both discourse and policy:

1) *Repoliticise the Narrative:* Public messaging should explicitly acknowledge how housing policy, labour practices, and urban design contribute to disconnection.
2) *Expand Social Infrastructure:* Investment in shared spaces and public amenities is as crucial as healthcare or education in reducing loneliness at scale.
3) *Regulate Corporate Practices:* Platforms and companies profiting from engineered disconnection should face transparency and reinvestment obligations.
4) *Integrate Structural Indicators into Policy:* Loneliness strategies should track indicators such as public space availability, housing affordability, and work-life balance alongside health metrics.

The individualisation of loneliness in policy and public discourse reflects a broader neoliberal logic in which citizens are framed as autonomous managers of their own well-being. This framing obscures the structural determinants of disconnection and sustains a cycle where loneliness serves as both a personal burden and a profitable market opportunity. Breaking this cycle requires reimagining loneliness not as a private affliction to be "fixed" through self-help, but as a public, structural challenge intertwined with the political economy of contemporary life. Only by restoring collective responsibility- through policy, infrastructure, and cultural reframing- can societies address the root causes of disconnection and move beyond the commodified management of loneliness.

9. TOWARD AN ETHICS OF CONNECTION: ALTERNATIVES AND STRUCTURAL INTERVENTIONS

As established in previous sections, loneliness is not simply a personal emotion but a structural outcome of neoliberal political economy, produced by the erosion of public goods, precarisation of work, and commodification of human connection (Brown, 2015; Illouz, 2007). An ethics of connection begins with the recognition that relationships are shaped - and often constrained - by collective arrangements, not merely by private choice. Drawing on Iris Marion Young's (2011) "social connection model of responsibility" and Martha Nussbaum's (2006) capabilities approach, this ethics positions social connection as a public good and a basic capability that must be cultivated through political and institutional design. This section sets out systemic interventions in five domains- social infrastructure, labour and economic policy, urban design, digital governance, and cultural-political reframing - to move from critique toward transformation.

9.1 Social Infrastructure as a Public Good

Social infrastructure, defined as "the physical places and organizations that shape the way people interact" (Klinenberg, 2018, p. 5), constitutes the invisible scaffolding of collective life. Just as transportation systems sustain mobility, these civic institutions and spaces sustain human connection. Yet, under neoliberal austerity, libraries, parks, and community centres have suffered systematic underfunding, leading to a slow erosion of everyday opportunities for interaction (Harvey, 2005). The consequences are not merely cultural but profoundly political, as diminished social infrastructure weakens democratic life and the capacity for solidarity.

Rebuilding these infrastructures requires deliberate public investment. Community hubs and cultural venues, if funded to provide free access, can create sustained contexts for association and exchange. Cooperative and co-housing models that integrate shared kitchens, gardens, and meeting spaces resist the isolating tendencies of privatised housing and commodified urban design (Jarvis, 2015). Likewise, intergenerational facilities that combine childcare and eldercare break down age segregation while cultivating reciprocal forms of care. Critically, such interventions should not depend on market philanthropy or temporary programmes but on institutional guarantees. Allocating a fixed share of municipal budgets to social infrastructure, administered through participatory budgeting, not only safeguards funding stability but also embeds democratic responsiveness into its governance (Fung, 2006).

9.2 Labour and Economic Policy

Work and economic structures are not neutral backdrops to social life; they are central determinants of relational capacity. Precarious contracts, long commutes, and solitary gig work systematically undermine the time and energy individuals can devote to meaningful connection (Standing, 2011). A society oriented toward social well-being must therefore secure rights to social breaks and common spaces within workplaces, regulate hybrid work to preserve both flexibility and in-person collaboration (Messenger, 2019), and establish living wages with predictable scheduling to ease temporal and financial precarity.

Equally critical is the recognition of unpaid care. Despite being central to the fabric of connection, caregiving continues to be excluded from GDP metrics and remains invisible in mainstream economics (Folbre, 2001). By providing pension credits and tax benefits to unpaid caregivers, and by funding local care cooperatives, governments can begin to integrate care into economic recognition while affirming its social value. This shift redefines care not as a private sacrifice but as a collective good.

9.3 Urban Design for Connection

The built environment is one of the most decisive yet overlooked factors in shaping social life. Urban design can either foster spontaneous encounters or entrench isolation. Mixed-use zoning, for example, integrates residential, commercial, and public spaces, enabling incidental interaction across daily routines (Gehl, 2010). Walkable neighbourhoods, as emphasised in Jacobs' (1961) critique of car-centric planning, allow street-level connections that cannot be replicated in fragmented urban sprawls. Even micro-public spaces—pocket parks, benches, shared courtyards—create low-threshold meeting points that restore conviviality to everyday life.

Yet, spatial design alone is insufficient if it excludes vulnerable groups. Perceived and actual safety are preconditions for participation in public life. Investment in lighting, barrier-free access, and inclusive design ensures that elders, disabled persons, and marginalised groups can claim these spaces as their own (Whyte, 1980). Urban design, then, is not simply about aesthetics but about equity and accessibility.

9.4 Digital Governance and Platform Accountability

In the digital age, social connection is increasingly mediated by corporate platforms whose architectures reflect commercial rather than public values. Zuboff (2019) shows how surveillance capitalism thrives on extracting behavioural data and monetising attention, often at the expense of user well-being. This raises a critical need for publicly funded, non-commercial platforms designed around well-being rather than engagement metrics, and for interoperability standards that prevent monopolistic lock-in.

Equally important is algorithmic transparency. The opaque systems that determine what users see and with whom they interact can amplify divisive or addictive behaviours. Independent auditing and mandatory disclosure of algorithms are necessary steps to align digital infrastructures with democratic accountability (Pasquale, 2015). Moreover, strict data protection regimes, such as those outlined in the European Commission's (2018) GDPR, should limit behavioural extraction and establish opt-in consent as a baseline, resisting the normalisation of dependency loops.

9.5 Cultural-Political Reframing

Addressing loneliness requires more than technical fixes; it requires a cultural reframing. Public messaging that locates loneliness primarily in individual shortcomings obscures the structural drivers of disconnection, such as housing policy, labour precarity, and disinvestment in public goods (Holt-Lunstad, 2017). Narratives must instead highlight these systemic contributors, thereby shifting responsibility from isolated individuals to collective arrangements.

This reframing also requires cultural resistance to what Rosa (2013) terms "acceleration culture." By promoting unstructured, offline time as a public health goal, akin to anti-sedentary campaigns, societies can counter the commodification of speed and presence. Similarly, reviving civic associations—unions, neighbourhood councils, voluntary organisations—creates durable contexts for participation and solidarity, reversing the civic decline documented by Putnam (2000).

9.6 Integrative Policy Framework

The crisis of disconnection cannot be addressed through siloed interventions; it demands systemic integration. Health ministries must embed loneliness prevention into non-communicable disease strategies, recognising its impact on morbidity and mortality. Urban planning should collaborate with public health to design environments that encourage interaction. Labour ministries need to integrate indicators of social connection into workplace regulation, while digital regulators align platform governance with cultural and educational policies.

Metrics for success must move beyond GDP. Indicators such as per-capita public space, average commuting time, and frequency of in-person contact provide a more accurate account of social well-being. Tracking these alongside conventional economic and health statistics would make visible the value of connection, repositioning it as a matter of political economy rather than private coping.

9.7 Ethical Grounding

The capability approach frames social connection as essential to human flourishing, requiring both individual agency and enabling conditions (Sen, 1999; Nussbaum, 2006). Young's (2011) social connection model asserts that all members of society share responsibility for structural injustices, including systemic disconnection. This ethical stance rejects the neoliberal tendency to privatise social risks, insisting instead on collective responsibility and structural investment. An ethics of connection demands a shift from reactive, individualised fixes toward proactive, systemic design. Recognising loneliness as a structural crisis - rather than a personal failing - means restoring the commons in physical, digital, and relational domains. This reorientation challenges the neoliberal settlement in which individuals absorb the costs of disconnection while markets profit from commodified cures (Brown, 2015; Zuboff, 2019). By asserting connection as a public good and political right, societies can move from a loneliness economy toward an infrastructure of belonging.

Figure 6. The ethics of connection: Integrated domains for systemic intervention.

10. REFRAMING LONELINESS AS A POLITICAL-ECONOMIC CRISIS

Loneliness is too often misrepresented as a private emotional shortcoming, when in fact it is structurally produced and politically sustained. This chapter has argued that loneliness must be reframed as a political-economic crisis, generated by the arrangements of contemporary capitalism. Neoliberal restructuring, commodification, and the erosion of collective goods have not merely coincided with the rise of loneliness — they have actively engineered and profited from it (Brown, 2015; Illouz, 2007; Zuboff, 2019). To treat loneliness only as a "social determinant of health" is insufficient. It is more accurately understood as an outcome of deliberate policy decisions and institutional designs. Insecure work, housing precarity, and digital platforms optimised for surveillance and monetisation reorganise the social fabric in ways that privilege efficiency, competition, and self-reliance over reciprocity, solidarity, and shared presence (Harvey, 2005; Standing, 2011).

Dominant public narratives, however, continue to individualise the problem. Government loneliness strategies and self-help literature commonly frame disconnection as a deficit of skills, resilience, or effort. This aligns with neoliberal responsibilisation, where structural harms are reframed as personal challenges to be overcome through consumption, therapy, or "positive thinking" (Beck, 1992; Fraser, 2013). Such framings misdiagnose the problem and thereby restrict the solutions to market-friendly, self-reinforcing interventions. The structural determinants of loneliness are both visible and measurable: zoning laws that limit public meeting places, corporate ownership models that turn digital interaction into data-mining operations, and fiscal austerity that hollows out libraries, parks, and community centres (Klinenberg, 2018). When these systemic drivers are ignored, interventions reduce to private coping mechanisms or commodified fixes — an outcome profitable for markets but corrosive for collective life.

The health consequences of loneliness are stark. Empirical research demonstrates that loneliness carries a mortality risk comparable to smoking and obesity (Holt-Lunstad et al., 2015). Economically, it generates indirect costs through reduced productivity, higher healthcare expenditure, and the expansion of parasitic industries that monetise social deficits - what might be termed the "loneliness economy" (ONS, 2020). The democratic stakes are equally significant. Loneliness erodes trust, civic engagement, and solidarity, conditions that leave individuals more susceptible to authoritarian populist appeals promising illusory forms of belonging (Mounk, 2018; Putnam, 2000). Thus, structural disconnection imperils not only public health but also the resilience of democratic institutions. Market-driven solutions exacerbate the problem. Dating apps, wellness retreats, and commercialised social platforms commodify human needs for connection, profiting from scarcity while undermining public alternatives (Zuboff, 2019). As publicly funded infrastructures wither, these privatised substitutes appear not as choices but as inevitabilities. The system thus reproduces the very disconnection it claims to cure.

Confronting this requires a political-economic reorientation. Just as climate change has been reframed as a systemic crisis of fossil-fuel capitalism, loneliness must be recognised as a systemic crisis of neoliberal capitalism. It can only be addressed through collective, structural interventions rather than individualised fixes. An "ethics of connection" provides the normative foundation for such a shift. Grounded in the capability approach (Sen, 1999; Nussbaum, 2006) and Young's (2011) social connection model, this framework recognises that relational well-being is not a luxury but a basic human capability - one that depends on enabling economic, infrastructural, and cultural conditions. Rejecting neoliberal privatisation of social risks, it insists on collective responsibility for fostering conditions of belonging. This ethics translates into concrete policy prescriptions: sustained investment in libraries, parks, and community hubs; regulation of labour markets to ensure secure and humane work; recognition and economic valuation of unpaid care; urban design that enables incidental interaction; digital governance that prioritises well-being over profit; and public narratives that shift responsibility from self-help to collective structures.

Such reframing is not a purely academic exercise but a mobilising narrative. By shifting the focus from the individual psyche to the collective polis, it opens political space for alliances between health advocates, labour organisers, urban planners, digital rights activists, and community movements. In doing so, it reframes loneliness as a structural crisis requiring systemic remedies. This shift also demands new metrics of success. Instead of measuring prosperity solely through GDP growth, societies should track indicators of social connection: per-capita access to public space, frequency of in-person contact, and levels of civic participation. Elevating such measures would reposition relational well-being as a political priority, rendering widespread disconnection as unacceptable as unemployment or inflation.

In sum, loneliness is not simply a psychological state but a structural outcome of neoliberal capitalism. Reframing it as a political-economic crisis compels us to treat connection as a public good and a political right, moving societies away from a loneliness economy and toward an infrastructure of belonging.

11. CONCLUSION

Loneliness is too significant to be treated as a private misfortune or left to fragmented health campaigns. Like clean air or safe water, social connection is a collective good whose value is political, economic, and democratic. To reduce it to an individual failing obscures the structural arrangements — precarious work, housing insecurity, digital surveillance platforms, and austerity-driven disinvestment — that generate disconnection while fuelling demand for commodified "cures." Connection must therefore be recognised as infrastructure: the everyday fabric of libraries, community hubs, shared spaces, and civic associations through which trust and solidarity are cultivated. Without such connective tissues, democracies weaken, leaving societies vulnerable to authoritarian appeals that exploit isolation and fear. If the twenty-first century is to resist engineered isolation, connection must be affirmed as a political right, a human capability, and a collective achievement. This requires institutional commitments: investment in social infrastructure, secure and humane labour markets, inclusive urban design, transparent digital governance, and cultural narratives that reject neoliberal responsibilisation in favour of collective responsibility. Success must be measured not by GDP alone but by indicators of relational well-being - access to public space, frequency of contact, and levels of civic participation. Reframing loneliness as a political-economic crisis is not only an academic task but a mobilising narrative. It creates the basis for coalitions among health advocates, labour organisers, urban planners, digital rights activists, and community movements, united by the recognition that connection is the foundation of resilience, democracy, and human flourishing. The choice is stark: invest in connection to build more humane societies, or accept commodified isolation and civic decline. The pathway forward is clear - connection must be reclaimed as a right, protected as a public good, and nurtured as the foundation of belonging in the twenty-first century.

Figure 7. Pathway from the loneliness economy to an infrastructure of belonging

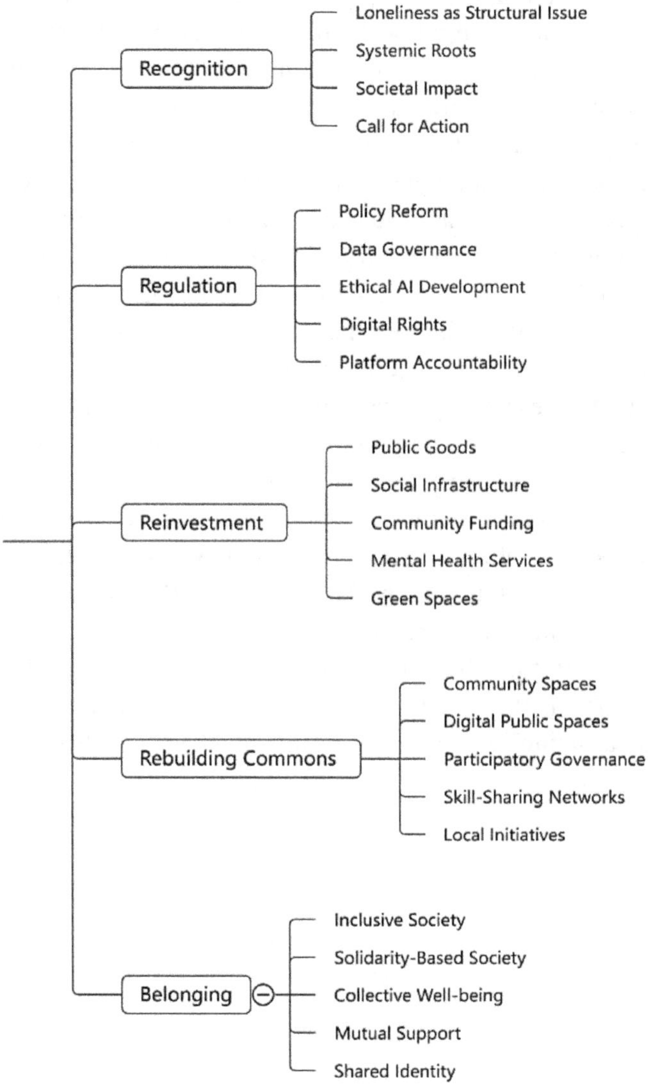

AUTHOR CONTRIBUTIONS

All contributing authors participated equally in the conceptualization, critical framing, drafting, and final revision of this chapter. Each author takes full responsibility for the integrity, originality, and intellectual content of the work presented herein.

DECLARATIONS

- **Ethical Considerations:** This chapter adheres to all established academic, ethical, and publication standards in research and writing.
- **Consent to Participate:** Not applicable (conceptual and theoretical book chapter).
- **Consent for Publication:** All authors have reviewed and approved the final manuscript for publication.
- **Declaration of Conflicting Interest:** The authors declare no potential conflicts of interest with respect to the authorship or publication of this chapter.
- **Funding Statement:** This chapter received no external funding or financial support.
- **Data Availability:** Not applicable (conceptual and theoretical book chapter).

ACKNOWLEDGEMENT

The author(s) express sincere gratitude to the editors of this volume for their scholarly vision and guidance. Appreciation is also extended to all scholars and researchers whose works have been cited and referenced in this chapter; their insights and contributions provided the intellectual foundation for the present analysis. The author(s) gratefully acknowledge the academic community whose continued engagement with issues of inclusion, technology, and human connection has informed and inspired this work.

REFERENCES

Allison, A. (2013). *Precarious Japan*. Duke University Press. DOI: 10.1215/9780822377245

Banet-Weiser, S. (2018). *Empowered: Popular feminism and popular misogyny*. Duke University Press.

Bauman, Z. (2001). *The individualized society*. Polity Press.

Beck, U. (1992). Risk society: Towards a new modernity. *Sage (Atlanta, Ga.)*.

Berlant, L. (2011). *Cruel optimism*. Duke University Press.

Bourdieu, P. (1986). The forms of capital. In J. Richardson (Ed.), *Handbook of theory and research for the sociology of education* (pp. 241–258). Greenwood.

Broadbent, E., Stafford, R., & MacDonald, B. (2009). Acceptance of healthcare robots for the older population: Review and future directions. *International Journal of Social Robotics*, *1*(4), 319–330. DOI: 10.1007/s12369-009-0030-6

Brown, W. (2015). *Undoing the demos: Neoliberalism's stealth revolution*. MIT Press. DOI: 10.2307/j.ctt17kk9p8

Cabinet Office of Japan. (2021). *Annual report on the ageing society*. Government of Japan.

Cacioppo, J. T., & Cacioppo, S. (2018). The growing problem of loneliness. *Lancet*, *391*(10119), 426. DOI: 10.1016/S0140-6736(18)30142-9 PMID: 29407030

Chan, L. S. (2018). Online dating apps as a marketing platform. *Journal of Marketing Management*, *34*(15-16), 1373–1392.

. Cigna. (2020). *Loneliness and the workplace: 2020 U.S. report*. Cigna.

Crary, J. (2013). *24/7: Late capitalism and the ends of sleep*. Verso.

Davies, W. (2015). *The happiness industry: How the government and big business sold us well-being*. Verso.

. European Commission. (2018). *General Data Protection Regulation.*

Folbre, N. (2001). *The invisible heart: Economics and family values*. The New Press.

Foucault, M. (2008). *The birth of biopolitics: Lectures at the Collège de France, 1978–1979*. Palgrave Macmillan.

Fraser, N. (2013). *Fortunes of feminism*. Verso.

Fraser, N. (2017). Crisis of care? On the social-reproductive contradictions of contemporary capitalism. *Socialist Register, 113*, 21–45. DOI: 10.2307/j.ctt1vz494j.6

Fung, A. (2006). Varieties of participation in complex governance. *Public Administration Review, 66*(s1), 66–75. DOI: 10.1111/j.1540-6210.2006.00667.x

Furlong, A. (2008). The Japanese hikikomori phenomenon: Acute social withdrawal among young people. *The Sociological Review, 56*(2), 309–325. DOI: 10.1111/j.1467-954X.2008.00790.x

Gehl, J. (2010). *Cities for people*. Island Press.

Graham, M., Hjorth, I., & Lehdonvirta, V. (2017). Digital labour and development. *Development Studies Research, 4*(1), 13–29. PMID: 28781494

Han, B.-C. (2017). *Psychopolitics: Neoliberalism and new technologies of power*. Verso.

Harvey, D. (2005). *A brief history of neoliberalism*. Oxford University Press. DOI: 10.1093/oso/9780199283262.001.0001

Harvey, D. (2012). *Rebel cities: From the right to the city to the urban revolution*. Verso.

Hawkley, L. C., & Cacioppo, J. T. (2010). Loneliness matters: A theoretical and empirical review. *Annals of Behavioral Medicine, 40*(2), 218–227. DOI: 10.1007/s12160-010-9210-8 PMID: 20652462

Heino, R. D., Ellison, N. B., & Gibbs, J. L. (2010). Relationships on the line: Dating and intimacy in the digital age. *New Media & Society, 12*(3), 477–494.

Holt-Lunstad, J. (2017). The potential public health relevance of social isolation and loneliness: Prevalence, epidemiology, and risk factors. *The Public Policy and Aging Report, 27*(4), 127–130. DOI: 10.1093/ppar/prx030

Holt-Lunstad, J., Smith, T. B., & Layton, J. B. (2015). Social relationships and mortality risk: A meta-analytic review. *Perspectives on Psychological Science, 10*(2), 227–237. DOI: 10.1177/1745691614568352 PMID: 25910392

Illouz, E. (2007). Cold intimacies: The making of emotional capitalism. *Polity.*

Illouz, E. (2008). *Saving the modern soul: Therapy, emotions, and the culture of self-help.* University of California Press. DOI: 10.1525/9780520941311

Jacobs, J. (1961). *The death and life of great American cities.* Random House.

Jarvis, H. (2015). Towards a deeper understanding of the social architecture of co-housing. *Urban Research & Practice, 8*(1), 93–105. DOI: 10.1080/17535069.2015.1011429

Jeffrey, C., & Young, S. (2012). Waiting for change: Youth, caste and politics in India. *Economy and Society, 41*(4), 507–536. DOI: 10.1080/03085147.2011.635435

Kaufman, A. B. (2021). Pet companionship in the age of urban isolation. *Journal of Urban Studies, 58*(4), 811–828.

Klinenberg, E. (2012). *Going solo: The extraordinary rise and surprising appeal of living alone.* Penguin.

Klinenberg, E. (2018). *Palaces for the people: How social infrastructure can help fight inequality, polarization, and the decline of civic life.* Crown.

Kross, E., Verduyn, P., Demiralp, E., Park, J., Lee, D. S., Lin, N., Shablack, H., Jonides, J., & Ybarra, O. (2013). Facebook use predicts declines in subjective well-being in young adults. *PLoS One, 8*(8), e69841. DOI: 10.1371/journal.pone.0069841 PMID: 23967061

Larkin, B. (2013). The politics and poetics of infrastructure. *Annual Review of Anthropology, 42*(1), 327–343. DOI: 10.1146/annurev-anthro-092412-155522

Low, S. (2003). *Behind the gates: Life, security, and the pursuit of happiness in fortress America.* Routledge.

Messenger, J. (2019). *Telework in the 21st century.* Edward Elgar. DOI: 10.4337/9781789903751

Mounk, Y. (2018). *The people vs. democracy.* Harvard University Press. DOI: 10.4159/9780674984776

Murthy, V. (2020). *Together: The healing power of human connection in a sometimes lonely world.* Harper Wave.

Nisbett, N. (2009). *Growing up in the knowledge society: Living the IT dream in Bangalore*. Routledge.

Nowland, R., Necka, E. A., & Cacioppo, J. T. (2018). Loneliness and social internet use: Pathways to reconnection in a digital world? *Perspectives on Psychological Science, 13*(1), 70–87. DOI: 10.1177/1745691617713052 PMID: 28937910

Nussbaum, M. (2006). *Frontiers of justice*. Harvard University Press.

Oldenburg, R. (1999). *The great good place*. Marlowe.

ONS. (2020). *The cost of loneliness to the UK economy*. Office for National Statistics.

Pasquale, F. (2015). *The black box society*. Harvard University Press. DOI: 10.4159/harvard.9780674736061

Peck, J. (2010). *Constructions of neoliberal reason*. Oxford University Press. DOI: 10.1093/acprof:oso/9780199580576.001.0001

Peck, J., & Tickell, A. (2002). Neoliberalizing space. *Antipode, 34*(3), 380–404. DOI: 10.1111/1467-8330.00247

Perlman, D., & Peplau, L. A. (1981). Toward a social psychology of loneliness. In Gilmour, R., & Duck, S. (Eds.), *Personal relationships in disorder* (pp. 31–56). Academic Press.

Putnam, R. D. (2000). *Bowling alone: The collapse and revival of American community*. Simon & Schuster.

Rosa, H. (2013). *Social acceleration*. Columbia University Press. DOI: 10.7312/rosa14834

Rose, N. (2006). *The politics of life itself: Biomedicine, power, and subjectivity in the twenty-first century*. Princeton University Press.

Sen, A. (1999). *Development as freedom*. Oxford University Press.

Srnicek, N. (2017). Platform capitalism. *Polity*.

Standing, G. (2011). *The Precariat: The New Dangerous Class*. Bloomsbury Academic.

Tateno, M., Park, T. W., Kato, T. A., Umene-Nakano, W., & Saito, T. (2012). Hikikomori as a possible clinical term in psychiatry: A questionnaire survey. *BMC Psychiatry, 12*(1), 169. DOI: 10.1186/1471-244X-12-169 PMID: 23061675

Thaler, R. H., & Sunstein, C. R. (2008). *Nudge: Improving decisions about health, wealth, and happiness*. Yale University Press.

Turkle, S. (2011). *Alone together: Why we expect more from technology and less from each other*. Basic Books.

UK Government. (2018). *A connected society: A strategy for tackling loneliness*. HM Government.

Weiss, R. S. (1973). *Loneliness: The experience of emotional and social isolation*. MIT Press.

Whyte, W. H. (1980). *The social life of small urban spaces*. Project for Public Spaces.

Yamamoto, M. (2016). Performing family in Japan's rental services industry. *Asian Anthropology, 15*(3), 193–210.

Young, I. M. (2011). *Responsibility for justice*. Oxford University Press. DOI: 10.1093/acprof:oso/9780195392388.001.0001

Zuboff, S. (2019). *The age of surveillance capitalism: The fight for a human future at the new frontier of power*. Profile Books.

KEY TERMS AND DEFINITIONS

Neoliberalism: An ideology promoting free markets, deregulation, and individual responsibility while reducing welfare provisions; it reshapes social life around competition and self-optimisation.

Loneliness Economy: A market system that commodifies isolation through products and services—such as dating apps or wellness retreats—that promise connection while sustaining dependence.

Social Infrastructure: Institutions and public spaces—like parks, libraries, and community centres—that enable social interaction, trust, and collective belonging.

Commodification of Connection: The conversion of emotional and social relationships into marketable goods and services within capitalist economies.

Gig Economy: A flexible yet insecure labour system based on short-term, platform-mediated work that fragments stability and increases social isolation.

Political Economy of Disconnection: A framework analysing how neoliberal structures in labour, housing, and technology produce and maintain systemic social isolation.

Emotional Capitalism: A condition in which emotions and relationships become entangled with market logic, turning feelings into sources of economic value.

Engineered Loneliness: The systemic creation of isolation through economic, technological, and spatial mechanisms that also monetise disconnection.

Digital Mediation: The technological structuring of social interactions through digital platforms and algorithms that shape how people connect and relate.

Urban Design and Isolation: The influence of privatised architecture and fragmented urban planning in restricting public encounters and deepening disconnection.

Affective Labour: Emotionally driven work—such as caregiving or counselling—often undervalued despite its essential role in sustaining social life.

Surveillance Capitalism: An economic model where human behaviour and emotions are extracted as data for profit, fostering dependency and emotional commodification.

Individualisation of Loneliness: The neoliberal framing of loneliness as a personal problem rather than a structural condition, shifting responsibility to individuals.

Ethics of Connection: A moral framework that recognises social connection as a public good and promotes collective responsibility and inclusion.

Collective Reframing: A structural perspective that treats loneliness as a systemic issue requiring policy reform and public investment to rebuild solidarity.

Chapter 2

The Loneliness Economy in India:

Market Responses to Social Disconnection in the Digital Age

Megha Bakshi
https://orcid.org/0000-0002-2651-3184
Sri Balaji University, India

Monica C. Singh
Sri Balaji University, India

ABSTRACT

This chapter examines the emergence of the "loneliness economy" through a mixed-methods approach, combining a review of recent literature with analysis of small-scale empirical studies and case reports from urban and semi-urban regions. Drawing on demographic data, sociological surveys, and prior research in mental health and technology adoption, the study explores how urbanization, migration, and shifting family structures have eroded traditional support systems. It critically evaluates digital mental health platforms, AI companionship tools, and community-based applications in terms of accessibility, efficacy, and ethical implications. The findings reveal a persistent gap between market-driven interventions and the authentic interpersonal connections essential for emotional well-being. The chapter concludes with policy recommendations and culturally attuned design principles aimed at fostering inclusive, community-rooted responses to loneliness in India's rapidly evolving social environment.

DOI: 10.4018/979-8-3373-5811-6.ch002

1. INTRODUCTION: THE PARADOX OF CONNECTED-LONELINESS IN CONTEMPORARY INDIA

India stands at a critical 21st-century juncture, where rapid technological advancement and profound socio-cultural shifts are simultaneously deepening connectivity and fuelling a paradox of emotional and social disconnection (Banerjee et al., 2023). India's digital transformation is unmistakable the number of internet users, which stood at around 700 million in 2020, is expected to exceed 974 million by 2025, with smartphones accounting for nearly 73 percent of total web traffic (Gloria, 2022).This mobile-centric engagement is massive, with 294 million Indians active on social media in 2019, averaging 17 hours per week surpassing usage in China and the United States (McKinsey Global Institute, 2019). Yet, the very tools designed for connection often foster superficial relationships and algorithm-driven echo chambers, culminating in a noted "loneliness epidemic" (Gloria, 2022). This crisis is starkly visible in urban India, where individuals feel emotionally detached amidst densely populated cities. In response, a "loneliness economy" has emerged, treating the experience of isolation as a commercial opportunity (Kiliç and Daldal, 2024). The market now offers a wave of services, from mental health apps like *InnerHour* and *YourDOST* to curated social clubs, targeting millennials and Gen Z (Bakshi and Bhattacharyya, 2021). These commercial solutions arise against a backdrop of large-scale social change. Accelerated urbanisation, migration, and the shift from joint to nuclear and single-person households have eroded traditional, informal support systems (Yadav et al., 2022).

Concurrently, the weakening of community ties and a growing emphasis on individualism have intensified feelings of disconnection (Chandra, 2024). The public health implications are severe, with chronic loneliness linked to cardiovascular disease, cognitive decline, depression, and premature mortality risks comparable to smoking or obesity (Mihalopoulos et al., 2020). India's commercial response, while innovative, raises critical questions. Can services like "rent-a-friend" or virtual companionship act as genuine substitutes for authentic relationships, or do they merely offer temporary relief? There are profound doubts about whether commodified empathy can ever fulfill the human need for authenticity, trust, and physical closeness (Jain et al., 2025). Despite the scale of the crisis with millions in isolation and 8% of Indian youth reporting frequent loneliness (Gloria, 2022) the phenomenon remains critically underexplored within India's unique context of urbanization, evolving family structures, and a digital divide (Hossain et al., 2020). This analysis seeks to address that gap, moving beyond Western frameworks to examine the drivers, market responses, and potential solutions to loneliness within India's distinct socio-cultural landscape. This chapter approaches the loneliness economy in India through a comprehensive, multi-dimensional lens, tracing its origins within shifting demographic, economic, and cultural contexts. It examines the interplay between the breakdown of traditional community structures and the emergence of market-driven interventions. Drawing upon recent empirical studies, sociological surveys, and interdisciplinary literature, it offers a critical evaluation of both the accessibility and the ethical dimensions of these responses. In doing so, it seeks to illuminate the persistent tension between digital forms of connectivity and the deeper human need for meaningful, in-person connection, as well as the role of market forces in shaping the lived experience of loneliness in contemporary India.

1.1 Research Methodology

A systematic literature review was conducted following the PRISMA framework (Figure 1) to analyze recent research on loneliness and the "loneliness economy" in India. The review focused on studies published between 2020 and 2024. Initial searches across academic databases and institutional repositories, using keywords like "loneliness," "digital mental health," and "India," yielded 1,247 records. After removing duplicates, 1,036 unique records were screened by title and abstract. The 302-remaining full-text articles were assessed for eligibility based on predefined criteria. Studies were included if they were empirical or conceptual works examining loneliness in the Indian context and related interventions. Exclusion criteria removed studies outside the date range, those lacking methodological rigor, or those not focused on loneliness. This process, involving two independent assessors, resulted in 63 studies for final synthesis. Data from these studies were extracted and thematically analyzed, categorizing findings into areas like digital mental health apps, AI companionship, and community initiatives. This rigorous, PRISMA-guided approach ensured a comprehensive and replicable review of the contemporary Indian landscape of loneliness and its associated market responses.

Figure 1. PRISMA 2020 Flow Diagram for the Systematic Review on Loneliness and the Loneliness Economy in India (2020–2024)

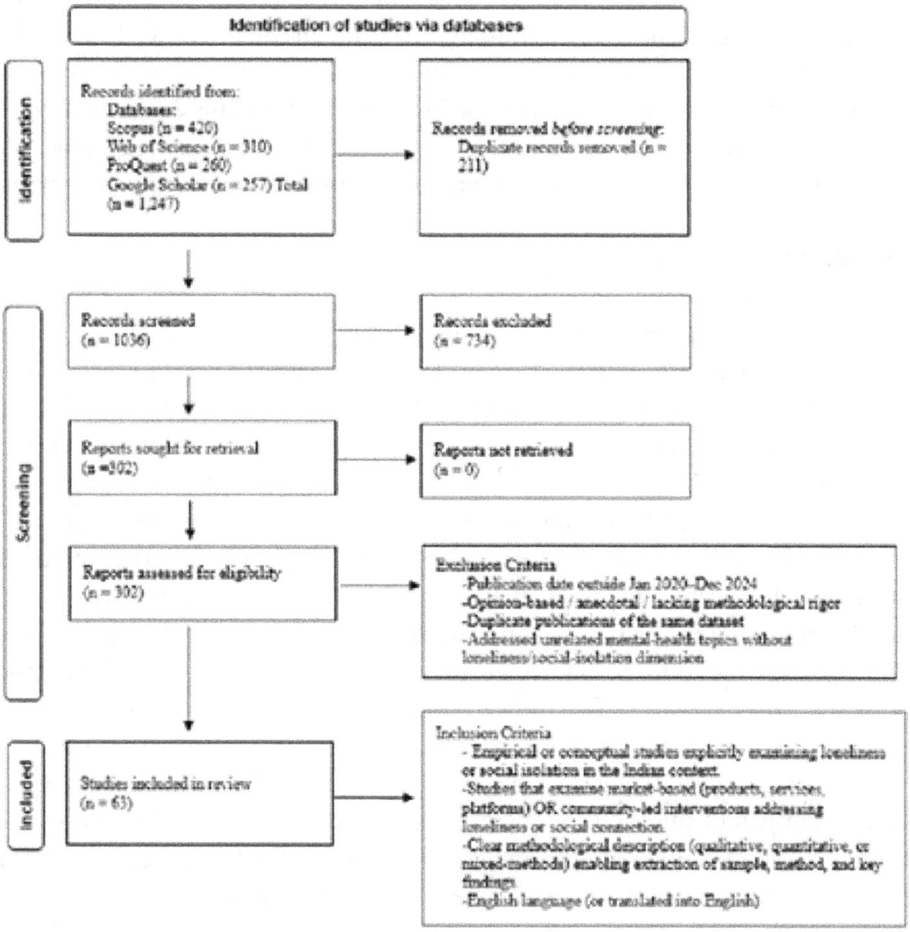

2. THEORETICAL FOUNDATIONS: UNDERSTANDING LONELINESS IN SOCIAL AND CULTURAL CONTEXT

2.1 Defining Loneliness: Psychological and Sociological Perspectives

Loneliness is a multifaceted subjective experience, defined as a perceived discrepancy between one's desired and actual social relationships. As outlined in Table 1, contemporary research classifies it into several distinct types. These include the foundational distinction between emotional loneliness (a lack of intimate bonds) and social loneliness (a lack of a broader community), as well as the more profound existential loneliness, which stems from a sense of fundamental separation from the world. Furthermore, the causes extend beyond the individual to encompass societal factors, such as the structural loneliness identified in contexts like India, which results from modernization and eroding traditional networks. Underpinning all these types is a significant biological component, with neuroimaging studies showing that social pain and physical pain share common neural pathways. Therefore, Table 1 illustrates that a comprehensive understanding of loneliness requires an integrated perspective, considering its psychological, sociological, and biological dimensions.

Table 1. Loneliness Types

Type of Loneliness	Primary Cause / Origin	Key Characteristics and Manifestations	Contextual Notes
Emotional Loneliness	Absence of a close, intimate, attachment figure.	Lack of deep emotional bonds and authentic connection.	Identified by Weiss (1975). Can be experienced even within a crowd.
Social Loneliness	Absence of a broader social network, community, or group belonging.	Feeling disconnected from a community; lacking a social web.	Identified by Weiss (1975). Relevant in both individualist and collectivist societies.
Existential Loneliness	Major life transitions (aging, migration, bereavement); a sense of fundamental separation from the world.	A profound isolation not resolved by social contact; requires psychological or philosophical engagement.	Differs from social/ emotional types in its cause and remedy (e.g., Moustakas, 1961).
Structural Loneliness (e.g., in the Indian context)	Macro-social forces: modernization, urban migration, digital mediation of relationships.	Decline of extended family/ kinship networks, erosion of communal rituals, substitution of face-to-face interaction.	Leads to what scholars term *"Invisible Loneliness"* (Ansari et al., 2023).
Biological Substrate (Underpinning all types)	Neural mechanisms related to social pain and exclusion.	Brain regions for physical pain (dACC, anterior insula) are activated.	Suggests an evolutionary basis for social bonding (Brilliant et al., 2022).

2.2 Cultural Dimensions of Loneliness in India

Traditionally grounded in collectivist values, Indian society has placed strong emphasis on interdependence, filial duty, and integration within dense social networks such as joint families, caste-based communities, and religious institutions

(Verma and Singh, 2024). These systems historically acted as protective buffers against emotional isolation, offering individuals multiple layers of belonging, identity reinforcement, and social support. Over the past two decades, however, forces of modernization, urban migration, and neoliberal consumer culture have introduced more individualistic orientations, contributing to the weakening of extended family structures and community-based living (Vinod, 2023). In this shifting landscape, Bauman's notion of liquid modernity marked by transient, flexible, and individualized forms of association finds growing relevance. In contemporary urban India, many interpersonal relationships are initiated through digital platforms and sustained with minimal emotional intimacy, reflecting a transformation in the very nature of social connectedness (Dervin, 2024).This shift creates a cultural tension: while individual autonomy is increasingly celebrated, emotional support systems that were previously taken for granted are weakened or absent, particularly for young professionals, elderly populations living alone, and migrants disconnected from their native social fabrics. For many, especially in megacities like Mumbai and Delhi, loneliness manifests in silent and invisible ways masked by digital connectivity yet devoid of deep interpersonal engagement.

Another critical factor is the cultural stigma around emotional expression and mental health, which discourages individuals from acknowledging loneliness. In Indian patriarchal norms, masculine ideals of stoicism and self-sufficiency often prevent men from articulating emotional distress, leading to the internalization of loneliness and delayed or absent help-seeking behavior. The cultural value placed on izzat a concept encompassing honor, dignity, and social reputation adds another layer of complexity to the experience of loneliness in India. Concerns about potential social judgment or the risk of bringing perceived shame to one's family can discourage individuals from openly discussing emotional distress. This reluctance not only reinforces feelings of isolation but also limits access to both formal mental health resources and informal networks of support (Veale et al., 2023). Consequently, while traditional cultural norms once operated as a robust emotional safety net, the ongoing transformation driven by modernization, urban migration, and socio-economic mobility has introduced new forms of vulnerability. These are particularly evident among urban, educated, and digitally connected populations, who must navigate the tension between long-standing cultural expectations and the evolving demands of increasingly globalized social identities.

3. THE INDIAN CONTEXT: DRIVERS OF THE LONELINESS EPIDEMIC

3.1 Demographic Shifts

- **The Rise of Nuclear Families and Single-Person Households:** A key demographic shift is the rapid nuclearization of Indian families. Data shows 50% of India's 318 million households were nuclear in 2022, a significant increase from 37% in 2008 (Singh and Srivastva, 2024). This trend is most pronounced in metropolitan areas, where high cost of living and smaller housing units physically necessitate nuclear family setups.
- **An Ageing Population and the "Empty Nest":** India's elderly population is projected to more than double to 347 million by 2050, constituting 20.8% of the total population (Yadav and Prakash, 2024). This rapid ageing occurs alongside a declining fertility rate, shifting the dependency ratio and placing immense pressure on both families and state support systems. The out-migration of younger generations for work or education leaves many older adults in rural or semi-urban areas with limited social contact and inadequate institutional care, exacerbating issues like "empty-nest syndrome" (Mishra et al., 2024). This "left behind" cohort often experiences financial dependency and a loss of decision-making authority within the household, intensifying feelings of uselessness and isolation.
- **The Cross-Generational Burden:** This demographic transition fuels "demographic loneliness" across age groups:
    - For **young adults**, factors include delayed marriage, competitive careers, and the pressure to succeed in a globalized economy, often at the cost of deep, offline friendships.
    - **Middle-aged individuals** become the "sandwich generation," squeezed between caring for ageing parents and supporting their own children, with their own social needs becoming a low priority.
    - The **elderly**, particularly widows and those with chronic illness, face loneliness compounded by physical constraints, sensory disabilities, and social marginalization. The decline of multigenerational co-residence means fewer daily interactions and a loss of their traditional role as knowledge repositories.

3.2 Urban Migration and the Erosion of Social Capital

- **Scale of Urbanization:** India is undergoing one of the largest internal demographic shifts, with its urban population projected to reach 600 million by 2030 (Mishra, et al., 2022). This is not limited to megacities but includes rapid growth in Tier-2 and Tier-3 cities, which are also beginning to exhibit classic urban anomie.

- **The Migrant Experience:** This movement to cities severs traditional social capital kinship, village networks, and cultural familiarity making migrants highly susceptible to urban loneliness (Ali, and Ali, 2021). New migrants often face "cultural lag," where urban, individualistic values clash with their more collectivist rural upbringing, creating internal conflict and identity-based isolation.
- **Urban Living Conditions:** Life in rented accommodations or gated communities fosters transient relationships that lack emotional depth, replacing long-standing social ties (Hepat, et al., 2024). Urban architecture high-rise apartments with closed doors reduces spontaneous community interaction. Relationships become more contractual and less communal.
- **The Urban Work Culture:** In cities like Bengaluru and Gurugram, demanding work cultures in sectors like IT and finance lead to long, irregular hours and "time poverty," where individuals lack the time and energy to invest in building and maintaining robust social networks outside of work.
- **Gendered Vulnerability:** Female migrants face a heavier burden, as safety concerns, patriarchal restrictions, and cultural stigma often prevent them from forming new social networks in urban spaces. Working women may be confined to the home-work commute loop, while non-working female migrants can experience extreme isolation within the confines of a new, unfamiliar apartment.

3.3 Cultural and Intersectional Vulnerabilities

- **Women and Patriarchal Structures:**
  - Loneliness for women is often linked to patriarchal expectations, economic dependence, and social invisibility (Guha, and Kadam, 2024). Their social worth is frequently tied to their roles as caregivers, leaving little room for identity-based peer connections.
  - Housewives in nuclear families report high emotional isolation due to limited mobility and unpaid care work that is monotonous and lacks social recognition.
  - Working women experience a "double burden" that leaves little time for social relationships, a reality often concealed by productivity narratives (Samanta, 2021). They may also face a "guilt complex" when engaging in leisure activities, further limiting their social outlets.

- Widows frequently encounter a severe form of structural loneliness, marked by ritualistic marginalization, loss of financial security, and reduced social participation.

- **The LGBTQ+ Community:**
    - This group faces systematic ostracization from traditional support networks like family and community due to cultural stigma and familial rejection (Gaur et al., 2023). This often forces them to create "chosen families," which, while supportive, may not fully compensate for the loss of biological kin.
    - This profound isolation, explained by Minority Stress Theory (encompassing distal stressors like discrimination and proximal stressors like internalized homophobia), directly increases their reliance on market-based solutions such as digital mental health platforms (Gaur et al., 2023).
    - However, discriminatory attitudes within systems, including healthcare, can render even market-driven solutions ineffective if not designed to be LGBTQ+-affirmative (Gaur et al., 2023). This creates a paradox where the community most in need of connection is funneled toward transactional alternatives that may not meet their core need for authentic acceptance.
- **Class-Based Divergence:**
    - The **middle and upper classes** may experience loneliness linked to competitive lifestyles, hyper-individualism, and social comparison fueled by social media. Their connections can be broad but shallow, focused on networking rather than emotional intimacy.
    - The **working class and urban poor** face more existential isolation from unstable employment, physical exhaustion, precarious living conditions, and limited access to leisure spaces. Their social marginalization is reinforced by caste and ethnic identities in urban settings.
    - The **digital divide** intensifies this inequality: while wealthier groups use digital tools (dating apps, online therapy, virtual communities) to cope with loneliness, lower-income groups are excluded due to cost, language barriers, and low digital literacy (Hossain et al., 2024). This exclusion denies them access to emerging forms of social support, deepening their isolation.

4. THE DIGITAL TRANSFORMATION OF SOCIAL CONNECTION

4.1 Technology Adoption and Social Media in India

Over the last ten years, India's digital landscape has changed dramatically. On average, Indians now spend about 2.5 to 3 hours each day on social media, making digital platforms a central part of social connection, self-expression, and emotional engagement (Rahman et al., 2024). Everyday communication is strongly tied to apps like WhatsApp, Facebook, Instagram, and Telegram, which help people maintain long-distance bonds, connect with relatives abroad, join online communities, and share content instantly. For many migrants, young people, and older adults these platforms function as vital lifelines, sustaining emotional continuity across fragmented or geographically dispersed social networks. Yet, this constant connectivity does not necessarily translate into deeper emotional intimacy. The phenomenon of *"social media loneliness"* describes the paradox where individuals feel socially isolated despite constant digital interaction. Excessive screen time, passive scrolling, and exposure to idealized portrayals of others' lives may foster feelings of inadequacy, envy, and social disconnection. Research suggests that passive use of social media, such as consuming content without meaningful interaction, correlates with increased loneliness and reduced well-being. Moreover, digital interactions often lack emotional cues such as tone, facial expression, and body language, making it difficult to convey empathy and build deep relationships (Audrin, and Audrin, 2024). The curated nature of social media posts can distort perceptions of reality, create a constant sense of social comparison and fueling feelings of exclusion or being left behind. As such, social media can be both a connector and a contributor to loneliness, depending on how it is used and experienced (Kouros, and Papa, 2024).

4.2 The Rise of Digital Mental Health Platforms

In response to rising mental health concerns, including loneliness, India has witnessed the growth of digital mental health ecosystems. Platforms like Wysa, YourDOST, MindPeers, InnerHour, and Talkspace India offer therapy services, AI-assisted self-help tools, emotional tracking, peer support, and crisis intervention. These platforms have transformed access to mental health care, particularly for urban youth and working professionals, offering 24/7 availability, cost-effectiveness, and reduced stigma through anonymity. The COVID-19 pandemic further accelerated digital mental health adoption, normalizing app-based counseling and teletherapy sessions for emotional support. However, there are significant concerns regarding quality control, standardization, and data privacy (Sinha, et al., 2023). Unlike traditional therapy models governed by ethical frameworks, many digital platforms operate in regulatory grey zones, lacking oversight in therapist accreditation, intervention efficacy, or user confidentiality. Additionally, algorithm-driven content or in-app nudges designed for user engagement may prioritize platform retention over psychological outcomes. Evidence on the efficacy of digital interventions for loneliness remains mixed. While cognitive behavioral therapy (CBT)-based apps show promise for short-term relief, sustained impact on chronic or existential loneliness is limited, especially when human interaction is absent. For emotionally complex individuals such as those with trauma or social anxiety platforms may fall short in delivering the empathetic nuance required for recovery (Harsh, et al., 2024).

4.3 AI Companionship and Chatbot Technology

One of the most technologically novel and ethically contested responses to loneliness is the rise of artificial companions. Applications such as *Replika, Woebot,* and *Wysa AI Coach* employ natural language processing and related computational techniques to simulate conversation, provide emotional support, and offer a sense of companionship (Tewari et al., 2021). These technologies are designed to provide steady, non-judgmental, and responsive interactions, making them particularly valuable for individuals who lack reliable social networks. Their appeal often lies in key psychological benefits: freedom from the fear of rejection, the ability to express emotions openly without restraint, and the convenience of constant availability. For people coping with social anxiety, depression, or past trauma, such companions can sometimes serve as temporary supports on the path back to meaningful human relationships. At the same time, digitally mediated companionship raises complex ethical and psychological questions (Nazareth et al., 2024). Although these systems can convincingly mirror empathy, they lack genuine emotional understanding, creating the danger of false intimacy and misrepresentation of connection. Heavy reliance on them may limit opportunities for real-world social interaction, foster dependency, and gradually weaken interpersonal skills. The tendency to *anthropomorphize* AI treating non-human agents as if they were human can blur the line between simulated interaction and authentic relationships, with some users even forming romantic or familial bonds with digital personas. These concerns have led to increasing calls for ethical regulation, awareness-building, and the integration of safeguards to protect vulnerable or socially isolated users. As such technologies advance and become more widespread, the priority must be to ensure that they complement, rather than replace, the irreplaceable depth of genuine human relationships.

5. MARKET RESPONSES: LONELINESS ECONOMY

5.1 Mapping the Loneliness Economy in India

India's loneliness economy has matured into a multifaceted ecosystem where commercial solutions target different aspects of social isolation through technological and service innovations. This emerging sector illustrates a significant societal shift, showing how entrepreneurial ventures are attempting to compensate for weakening traditional support systems (Yadav et al., 2022; Chandra, 2024).

- **Digital Mental Health Platforms: Structured Psychological Support**

The most established segment includes digital mental health platforms that provide professional, accessible psychological care. Leading services like *YourDost* and *InnerHour* offer online counselling and therapy programs, particularly serving urban youth and professionals. *TrustCircle* and *MindPeers* have pioneered anonymous peer support and gamified mental fitness tools for younger demographics. These private initiatives are complemented by public-sector responses like the government-backed NIMHANS (National Institute of Mental Health and Neuro-Sciences) developed MANAS app (Mental Health and Normalcy Augmentation System), which extend affordable, multilingual support to underserved communities.

- **AI Companionship Applications: Simulated Social Connection**

A rapidly growing category features AI-powered companionship tools that provide constant, simulated social interaction. Platforms like *NeoSaathi* and *Deep Talk* use advanced emotional intelligence algorithms to offer personalized conversational partners. Specialized applications such as *myBuddy* cater to corporate employees, while *Evolve* and *Inaya* focus on vulnerable groups including LGBTQ+ youth and those in acute distress, representing targeted approaches to specific demographic needs (Wadhwa, 2021).

- **Community and Social Connection Platforms: Rebuilding Social Infrastructure**

This sector focuses on restoring community bonds through organized engagement. While international platforms like *Meetup* maintain strong Indian presence, domestic solutions like *Nyburs* and *Kutumb* enable hyperlocal neighbourhood and cultural connections. Innovative platforms such as *Leher* facilitate spontaneous conversations through audio rooms, and *Jamm* organizes carefully curated intimate gatherings. Notably, *Bultoo Radio* serves remote communities through innovative offline technology, addressing isolation in regions with limited digital access.

- **Lifestyle and Wellness Services: Integrated Social Solutions**

This category embeds social connectivity into daily living arrangements. Co-living providers like *Stanza Living* and *Zolostays* create built-in communities for urban migrants. Senior living solutions such as *Antara Senior Living* offer socially structured environments for the elderly. The pet wellness sector has unexpectedly emerged as a powerful antidote to loneliness, with platforms like *Sploot* and *Pets of Paradise* creating extensive pet-owner networks, while *Pet Fed India* organizes large-scale social events that foster community bonding.

- **Elder Care and Support Services: Specialized Senior Support**

A critically important segment addresses the profound isolation affecting India's aging population. Comprehensive services like *Emoha* and *ElderAid* combine healthcare with social activities, while companion services like *Sakhi4Life* provide regular social interaction for seniors. Digital solutions including *We Care App* and *GenWise Saathi* enable virtual companionship, while community platforms such as *60Plus India* and *MAITYS ElderTech* combine digital tools with physical events specifically designed for elders living alone.

Key Takeaways:

1. **Precise Market Segmentation**: The ecosystem has evolved beyond generic solutions to address specific demographic needs through tailored approaches for different age groups, professions, and geographic locations.
2. **Hybrid Service Models**: Successful platforms increasingly blend digital accessibility with real-world interactions, recognizing that sustainable connection requires both technological convenience and genuine human contact.
3. **Public-Private Integration**: While private ventures dominate the landscape, increasing government involvement demonstrates institutional recognition of loneliness as a significant public health concern.
4. **Cultural Contextualization**: India-specific platforms addressing regional languages, family dynamics, and social structures show the necessity of culturally appropriate solutions rather than imported Western models (Hossain et al., 2020).
5. **Ethical Considerations**: The expansion of AI companions and commercialized emotional support raises important questions about the authenticity of

manufactured relationships and the long-term impact of outsourcing human connection (Jain et al., 2025; Babu and Prasad, 2024).

The sophisticated development of this ecosystem underscores how deeply market-based approaches have penetrated the realm of emotional well-being, presenting both innovative solutions and fundamental questions about whether commercial interventions can adequately address what remains essentially a social and relational deficit (Kiliç and Daldal, 2024; Alabed et al., 2024).

5.2 Business Models and Market Dynamics

Digital platforms in India that address loneliness are experimenting with diverse business models to balance financial sustainability with the need for scale (Nandamuri et al., 2020; Noushad Yashan et al., 2024). While these models (Table 6) help ensure revenue stability, they also shape accessibility, affordability, and user experience in ways that raise important ethical questions.

Table 2. Dominant Business Models in India's Loneliness Economy Platforms

Business Model	Key Features	Implications
Subscription-Based	Users pay monthly/annual fees for access to services. Often includes tiered plans with added features.	Ensures recurring revenue but may exclude low-income and rural users needing affordable care.
Freemium Model	Basic features are free; users must pay to access premium services like live counselling or deeper insights.	Offers initial access but creates a two-tier system where full support is only available to paying users.
Corporate Partnership (B2B)	Services offered via employer HR departments as part of employee wellness programs.	Enables scalability and affordability for employees but raises concerns about confidentiality and surveillance.
Commission-Based	Platform earns a commission for matching users with counsellors or therapists, often per session.	Can incentivize quality service delivery but may also encourage upselling or over-servicing.
Advertising-Based	Revenue generated from behavioural data used for targeted ads within community features or forums.	Rare in therapy-focused platforms; raises ethical concerns about emotional data exploitation and manipulation.

Note. While these monetization strategies enable scalability and innovation in addressing loneliness, they also risk commodifying emotional vulnerability. Ensuring ethical safeguards—such as transparency, informed consent, and equitable access—is essential to prevent exploitation in the name of emotional support.

6. CRITICAL ANALYSIS: LIMITATIONS AND ETHICAL CONCERNS

The digital response to loneliness, while promising, is fraught with significant limitations and ethical challenges that threaten its efficacy and equity.

6.1 Digital Access and Equity Issues

The potential of digital platforms is undermined by pervasive access barriers, creating a "therapeutic inequality" (Munikrishnappa et al., 2024). Key concerns include:

- **Infrastructural Divide:** A stark rural-urban gap persists, with only approximately 30% of rural households having internet access compared to 70% in urban areas (Asrani, 2022). This excludes vulnerable groups like the elderly and rural poor.
- **Economic Barriers:** Premium features essential for comprehensive care (e.g., video therapy) are often locked behind paywalls, making support a function of affordability.
- **Cultural and Linguistic Exclusion:** Most platforms operate primarily in English and Hindi, failing to accommodate India's diverse languages and culturally specific expressions of distress.
- **Geographic Limitations:** Poor connectivity in remote, hilly, and tribal areas negates the promise of location-agnostic support.

6.2 Privacy and Data Security Concerns

Digital mental health involves collecting highly sensitive data, yet protections remain inadequate.

- **Regulatory Gaps:** Critics argue that the Digital Personal Data Protection Act (2023) does not provide the heightened safeguards mental health data deserves.
- **Informed Consent Issues:** Opaque terms and conditions mean users often unknowingly consent to extensive data collection and third-party sharing (Dey, 2024).
- **Emotional Surveillance:** AI chatbots that train on user input raise ethical questions about manipulation and data use for advertising or profiling.

- **Cybersecurity Risks:** Centralized data storage, often on international servers, creates vulnerabilities to breaches and complicates jurisdictional oversight (Herzog and Sulaiman, 2024).

6.3 Therapeutic Effectiveness and Professional Standards

The rapid growth of digital services has outpaced the establishment of clinical and safety standards.

- **Unregulated Practitioners:** Platforms exhibit wide variation in provider qualifications, from licensed clinicians to unregulated "wellness coaches," raising concerns about competence and accountability (Wang and Yu, 2020).
- **Lack of Localized Evidence:** The evidence base for digital loneliness interventions in India is emergent, with many platforms relying on internal feedback rather than peer-reviewed, longitudinal studies.
- **Inadequate Crisis Response:** Few platforms have robust protocols for emergencies, creating a dangerous gap for users in acute distress or expressing suicidal ideation (Sanghvi and Mehrotra, 2022).
- **Blurred Ethical Boundaries:** Gamification and engagement-driven designs can conflict with therapeutic goals, prioritizing revenue over user well-being.

6.4 Commodification and Authenticity Concerns

The market-based approach to loneliness presents a fundamental paradox by attempting to solve a human problem with transactional tools.

- **Artificial Intimacy:** AI companions provide empathy simulations that are incapable of genuine reciprocity, which may foster emotional dependency and a condition termed "algorithmic attachment disorder" (Babu and Prasad, 2024).
- **Misaligned Incentives:** Business models that profit from user engagement are inherently at odds with the therapeutic aim of fostering self-sufficiency and reducing reliance on intervention (Alabed et al., 2024).
- **Mechanization of Empathy:** The core of this issue is the commodification of emotional labor, where empathy becomes a purchasable product, raising profound questions about the authenticity of connection in the digital age.

7. COMMUNITY-BASED AND CULTURAL ALTERNATIVES

7.1 Traditional Support Systems and Their Evolution

India's community-oriented structures provide emotional resilience through relational depth absent in digital interventions. Key elements include:

- **Familial Networks**: Extended familial ties and the *kutumb* (joint family) concept remain strong, ensuring intergenerational caregiving and emotional support, particularly in semi-urban and rural India.
- **Religious Institutions**: Gurudwaras, temples, mosques, and churches function as community anchors through rituals, volunteerism, and community meals (e.g., *langar*) that promote social bonding, especially for the elderly and isolated individuals.
- **Community Organizations**: Neighbourhood associations including Resident Welfare Associations facilitate local social networks, organizing events and establishing informal safety nets (Bose, 2021).
- **Occupational Communities**: Professional groups among teachers, defense families, and trade clusters provide identity, belonging, and emotional reinforcement through shared experiences.

7.2 Contemporary Community Initiatives

Grassroots innovations are adapting traditional collectivist values to modern loneliness challenges:

- **Organizational Models**: Groups like Dignity Foundation and The Banyan provide community-based mental health and eldercare with home visits, group counseling, and telephonic support, particularly effective in resource-limited settings (Namrata Rao et al., 2024).
- **Self-Help Groups**: Women-led SHGs in rural areas have evolved from microfinance platforms into robust social networks offering emotional support and empowerment.
- **Integrated Mental Health**: Community-based programs by organizations like SCARF *(Schizophrenia Research Foundation)* demonstrate the benefits of embedding mental health services within local institutions (Anganwadis, panchayats, schools), enhancing outcomes while reducing stigma (Murthy, 2021).
- **Faith-Based Initiatives**: Organizations including ISKCON *(International Society for Krishna Consciousness)* and Jamaat-e-Islami Hind provide cul-

turally resonant spaces through community kitchens and spiritual discussions (Banerjee, 2021).

7.3 Cultural Practices and Healing Traditions

India's cultural heritage offers non-commercial avenues for emotional well-being:

- **Spiritual Practices**: *Satsangs* and *bhajan* gatherings serve as structured forums for collective reflection and connection, positively impacting mental health, particularly among older adults (Vliegenthart, 2023).
- **Festival Culture**: Diwali, Eid, Pongal, and Bihu facilitate community participation and intergenerational connection through cyclical social traditions.
- **Wellness Frameworks**: Ayurvedic traditions emphasize social balance through concepts like *satsanga* (positive company) and *dinacharya* (daily routines) that implicitly address loneliness (Soni and Sharma, 2023).
- **Oral Traditions**: Storytelling and folktales in tribal and rural communities provide emotional resonance and narrative therapy, with cultural NGOs reviving these practices to bridge intergenerational divides.

7.4 Innovative Hybrid Approaches

Hybrid models combine digital scalability with traditional community depth:

- **Technology-Facilitated Engagement**: Platforms like Humans of Safe Spaces use digital tools to enable safe, in-person interactions while overcoming geographic barriers.
- **Intergenerational Programs**: Initiatives such as Adopt a Grandparent connect youth and elders for mutual dialogue and companionship, reducing isolation across generations (Venters and Jones, 2021).
- **Collaborative Learning**: Skill-sharing platforms like Stirring Minds offer online and offline opportunities for creative collaboration and community building.
- **Cultural Preservation**: Projects like Project Katha engage youth in documenting and performing stories from elders, fostering empathy and collective identity while addressing loneliness (Katha, 2019).

8. CURRENT POLICY LANDSCAPE

India has made notable strides in the field of mental health, yet loneliness continues to receive minimal direct attention within national policy frameworks. This is especially concerning, as recent research underscores the link between chronic loneliness and elevated risks of depression, cardiovascular disease, and even mortality. The National Mental Health Programme (NMHP), which dates back to 1982 and has been updated periodically, remains central to India's mental health infrastructure. Still, loneliness has not been explicitly prioritized within its mandates, resulting in limited targeted resource allocation or intervention development (Ministry of Health and Family Welfare [MoHFW], 2023). While the Mental Healthcare Act (2017) enshrines the right to mental health services and champions community-based care, its implementation varies considerably across states, and loneliness-specific supports or assessments are not yet routine components of care pathways. Although telemedicine platforms such as Digital India and eSanjeevani have expanded access to services, their primary focus remains on general mental health or physical health, with loneliness occupying a marginal position in these initiatives. Policies aimed at the elderly—like the National Programme for Healthcare of the Elderly (NPHCE)—do acknowledge social isolation, but the emphasis typically remains on physical ailments and geriatric care rather than emotional well-being (United Nations Population Fund [UNFPA], 2023). Likewise, programs for youth, migrants, or individuals in single-person households rarely include loneliness as a targeted outcome.

9. FUTURE DIRECTIONS AND EMERGING TRENDS

India's experience with loneliness is unfolding amid sweeping technological, demographic, and cultural transformations. Recent advances virtual and augmented reality, conversational AI companions, biometric wearables, and IoT-based behavioral monitoring are reshaping the landscape for detecting and alleviating loneliness, particularly for older adults and digitally engaged youth. These technologies may foster a sense of social presence, provide emotional support, and enable timely interventions. At the same time, they bring ethical dilemmas data privacy, emotional dependency on technology, and persistent digital divides that shape equitable access remain significant concerns. Social structures in India are simultaneously shifting. Trends such as remote work, expansion of gig economies, delayed marriage, and the proliferation of high-rise urban housing have reduced opportunities for face-to-face interaction, especially in cities. Among younger generations Gen Z and millennials mental health discourse is increasingly visible, but deep-rooted stigma and silence persist in rural and traditional communities.

Even as India invests in physical infrastructure and "smart cities," there is an urgent need to prioritize the social fabric supporting emotional well-being and human connection. Despite these changes, research on loneliness in India remains limited. There is scant large-scale data on its prevalence, regional or caste-based patterns, or the cultural nuances of social disconnection. Existing assessment tools, such as the UCLA Loneliness Scale, often lack contextual sensitivity. India requires culturally relevant frameworks and rigorous evaluations of both digital and community-based interventions. While NGOs and grassroots initiatives have shown promise, most evidence remains anecdotal and lacks systematic evaluation. Looking ahead, the most sustainable solutions will likely be hybrid—integrating the scalability of digital tools with the trust and familiarity of community-based practices. Approaches that blend traditional gatherings (such as satsangs, self-help groups, or neighbourhood festivals) with mobile apps and tele-counseling platforms can broaden reach and deepen impact. Government initiatives such as Ayushman Bharat and NEP 2020 provide opportunities to embed loneliness screening and intervention at scale, while training frontline workers including teachers, ASHA workers, nurses, and software developers could decentralize detection and support. Addressing loneliness in India will demand more than piecemeal interventions. It requires a multi-sectoral, culturally grounded, and future-oriented approach one where innovation, tradition, and empathy are interwoven to create a society that fosters meaningful social connection and psychological well-being for all.

10. CONCLUSION: TOWARD A COMPREHENSIVE APPROACH TO LONELINESS IN INDIA

Tackling loneliness in India requires a coordinated, context-aware strategy that acknowledges the country's social and cultural complexity as well as disparities in digital access (Table 7). At the policy level, it is essential for stakeholders to formally recognize loneliness as a significant public health issue and to integrate solutions across domains healthcare, education, urban development, and technology. Technology platforms must be designed with India's linguistic and cultural diversity in mind, ensuring that digital solutions are accessible and relevant to users from a wide array of backgrounds and levels of digital literacy. In healthcare settings, particularly within public health initiatives such as Ayushman Bharat and Primary Health Centres, routine screening and intervention for loneliness should become standard practice. At the community level, organizations grounded in collectivist traditions, self-help groups, and local leaders are well-placed to develop and implement solutions that are both culturally resonant and locally adaptable. Finally, researchers in India must produce evidence that captures the nuances of regional and cultural variation, combining traditional perspectives with contemporary approaches to ensure that interventions remain contextually appropriate and effective. By aligning efforts across sectors and remaining attentive to India's unique social fabric, stakeholders can advance strategies that address loneliness in ways that are sustainable, culturally informed, and impactful.

Table 3. Stakeholder-Specific Recommendations to Address Loneliness in India

Stakeholder	Recommendations (Specific to India)
Policymakers	• Recognize loneliness as a public health issue in India's National Health Policy and SDG frameworks • Establish regulatory guidelines for digital mental health startups under frameworks like the Digital Personal Data Protection Act • Increase funding for community health and wellness centres to serve as hubs for connection • Embed loneliness reduction goals in policies across urban housing (e.g., PMAY), education (e.g., NEP 2020), and workplace reforms • Support localized research through institutions like ICMR, NIMHANS, and ICSSR
Technology Companies	• Design platforms in Indian languages, considering low bandwidth and accessibility constraints in rural and semi-urban areas • Prioritize ethical design principles aligned with India's digital public infrastructure goals (e.g., India Stack) • Collaborate with Indian NGOs, mental health experts, and government schemes (e.g., Tele-MANAS) for culturally tailored content • Ensure compliance with India-specific data privacy and mental health standards • Invest in impact studies involving Tier 2 and Tier 3 cities and rural India
Healthcare Providers	• Train ASHAs, ANMs, and PHC staff to recognize and respond to signs of social isolation, especially among the elderly and adolescents • Promote integration of mental and social well-being in public programs like Ayushman Bharat and Mental Health Helplines • Encourage partnerships between traditional Indian healing systems (Ayurveda, Yoga) and modern psychiatry • Embed loneliness indicators into health MIS systems • Conduct outreach in regional languages to improve inclusivity and reach

continued on following page

Table 3. Continued

Stakeholder	Recommendations (Specific to India)
Community Organizations	• Leverage India's social capital—religious groups, youth clubs (e.g., NSS, NYKS), SHGs, and local panchayats—to run anti-loneliness campaigns • Use festivals, storytelling, and spiritual gatherings as platforms to build belonging • Seek CSR partnerships for scalable, locally-run social inclusion programs • Train local volunteers and peer leaders in identifying and supporting lonely individuals • Share best practices through national-level coalitions and summits
Researchers	• Conduct large-scale, regionally representative studies on loneliness patterns among youth, elderly, migrants, and homemakers in India • Develop culturally valid loneliness scales adapted for Indian languages and socio-economic realities • Evaluate effectiveness of both tech-based and non-tech interventions in rural and urban Indian settings • Examine intersections between caste, gender, income, and loneliness • Study how India's traditional practices (e.g., joint family systems) can be integrated into contemporary interventions

REFERENCES

Alabed, A., Javornik, A., Gregory-Smith, D., & Casey, R. (2024). More than just a chat: A taxonomy of consumers' relationships with conversational AI agents and their well-being implications. *European Journal of Marketing, 58*(2), 373–409. DOI: 10.1108/EJM-01-2023-0037

Ali, S., George, A., & Ali, S. A. A. (2021, December). Urban isolation-A state of the art report on addressing complexities in urban communities. In. AIP Conference Proceedings: Vol. 2409. *No. 1* (p. 020006). AIP Publishing LLC. DOI: 10.1063/5.0067612

Ansari, S., Muhammad, T., & Dhar, M. (2023). How does multi-morbidity relate to feeling of loneliness among older adults? Evidence from a population-based survey in India. *Journal of Population Ageing, 16*(1), 45–66. DOI: 10.1007/s12062-021-09343-5

Asrani, C. (2022). Spanning the digital divide in India: Barriers to ICT adoption and usage. *Journal of Public Affairs, 22*(4), e2598. DOI: 10.1002/pa.2598

Audrin, C., & Audrin, B. (2024). Emotional intelligence in digital interactions–A call for renewed assessments. *Personality and Individual Differences, 223*, 112613. DOI: 10.1016/j.paid.2024.112613

Babu, K. V., and Prasad, V. N. (2024). Can Replika's Emotional AI Replace Human Companionship?. *IUP Journal of Knowledge Management, 22*(2).

Bakshi, T., & Bhattacharyya, A. (2021). Socially distanced or socially connected? Well-being through ICT usage among the Indian elderly during COVID-19. *Millennial Asia, 12*(2), 190–208. DOI: 10.1177/0976399621989910

Banerjee, A., Duflo, E., Grela, E., McKelway, M., Schilbach, F., Sharma, G., & Vaidyanathan, G. (2023). Depression and loneliness among the elderly in low-and middle-income countries. *The Journal of Economic Perspectives, 37*(2), 179–202. DOI: 10.1257/jep.37.2.179

Banerjee, D. (2021). Loneliness in older people: Spiritual practices as an alternative pathway to action, a treatise from India. *Journal of Geriatric Mental Health, 8*(2), 63–69. DOI: 10.4103/jgmh.jgmh_37_21

Bose, N. (2021). Citizens' participation in local governance: A study of Residents Welfare Associations in Delhi. In *Decentralisation in Contemporary India* (pp. 240-254). Routledge India.

Brilliant, T. (2022). Loneliness inside of the brain: Evidence from a large dataset of resting-state fMRI in young adult. *Scientific Reports*, *12*(1), 7856. DOI: 10.1038/s41598-022-11724-5 PMID: 35550564

Chandra, V. (2024). Changing Landscape of Indian Family. In *Indian Families: Contemporary Family. Structures and Dynamics*, *26*, 65–76. Emerald Publishing Limited.

Dervin, F. (2024). From Language to Listening. *Interculturologies: Moving Forward with Interculturality in Research and Education*, 197-210.

Dey, D. N. C. (2024). Mental health of adolescents and youth in India: A critical analysis in the era of AI. *Available at SSRN* 5056368. DOI: 10.2139/ssrn.5056368

Gaur, P. S., Saha, S., Goel, A., Ovseiko, P., Aggarwal, S., Agarwal, V., Haq, A. U., Danda, D., Hartle, A., Sandhu, N. K., & Gupta, L. (2023). Mental healthcare for young and adolescent LGBTQ+ individuals in the Indian subcontinent. *Frontiers in Psychology*, *14*, 1060543. DOI: 10.3389/fpsyg.2023.1060543 PMID: 36743255

Gloria, K. (2022). Loneliness in India: Recognizing the role of history, technology, & culture. Aspen Digital, Aspen Institute.

Guha, S., and Rajesh Kadam, S. (2024). Review of recent studies on Women in Management. *An Inquiry into Women Representation in Management: A Case Study of Indian Industries*, 23-95.

Harsh, S., Ritik, B., Rushikesh, K., Purvanshu, M., & Suman, S. (2024). AI Being used to Tackle Mental Health Issues Conversify: A Robot Therapist. *International Journal of Trend in Scientific Research and Development*, *8*(5), 584–592.

Hepat, A., Khode, D., Chakole, S., & Chitransha, S. (2024). A narrative review of urbanization and mental health: An Indian perspective. *Cureus*, *16*(3). Advance online publication. DOI: 10.7759/cureus.55381 PMID: 38562368

Herzog, N. J., Celik, D., & Sulaiman, R. B. (2024). Artificial intelligence in health-care and medical records security. In *Cybersecurity and Artificial Intelligence: Transformational Strategies and Disruptive Innovation* (pp. 35–57). Springer Nature Switzerland. DOI: 10.1007/978-3-031-52272-7_2

Hossain, M. M., Purohit, N., Khan, N., McKyer, E. L. J., Ma, P., Bhattacharya, S., & Pawar, P. (2020). Prevalence and correlates of loneliness in India: A systematic review. *Advance.*_https://www.mckinsey.com/~/media/McKinsey/Featured%20Insights/Innovation/Ten%20highlights%20from%20our%202019%20research/MGI-in-2019-A-compendium-of-our-research-this-year-vF.pdf

Hossain, M. M., Purohit, N., Khan, N., McKyer, E. L. J., Ma, P., Bhattacharya, S., & Pawar, P. (2024). Loneliness in India: A systematic review of empirical studies. *Authorea Preprints.*

Jain, S., Singh, R., Agarwal, B., & Singh, A. K. (2025). Understanding the Role of Emerging Technology in Human Resilience in the Digital Age and Artificial Intelligence. In *Exploring Psychology, Social Innovation and Advanced Applications of Machine Learning* (pp. 131-152). IGI Global Scientific Publishing. DOI: 10.4018/979-8-3693-6910-4.ch007

Katha. (2019, June 19). *Current projects.* https://www.katha.org/current-projects/

Kiliç, S., and Daldal, K. M. (2024). Economy of loneliness and consumer behavior. *Journal of Financial Politic and Economic Reviews/Finans Politik and Ekonomik Yorumlar, 61*(667).

Kouros, T., & Papa, V. (2024). Digital mirrors: AI companions and the self. *Societies (Basel, Switzerland), 14*(10), 200. DOI: 10.3390/soc14100200

McKinsey Global Institute. (2019). *MGI in 2019: A compendium of our research this year.* McKinsey and Company.

Mihalopoulos, C., Le, L. K. D., Chatterton, M. L., Bucholc, J., Holt-Lunstad, J., Lim, M. H., & Engel, L. (2020). The economic costs of loneliness: A review of cost-of-illness and economic evaluation studies. *Social Psychiatry and Psychiatric Epidemiology, 55*(7), 823–836. DOI: 10.1007/s00127-019-01733-7 PMID: 31119308

Mishra, P. S., Singh, R., Srivastava, S., & Aditya, A. (2024). Predicting the risk of depression by migration status: A cross-sectional study on older adults in India. *Journal of Population Ageing, 17*(4), 693–720. DOI: 10.1007/s12062-024-09453-w

Mishra, R. K., Kumari, C. L., Janaki Krishna, P. S., and Dubey, A. (2022). Smart cities for sustainable development: An overview. *Smart cities for sustainable development*, 1-12.

Munikrishnappa, D., Majumder, J., Kalita, M., Shivarudraiah, M., Saha, I., & Chakrabarti, A. (2024). Bridging the Mental Health Treatment Gap in India: Opportunities and Challenges: A Narrative Review. *Journal of Mental Health and Human Behaviour, 29*(2), 55–61. DOI: 10.4103/jmhhb.jmhhb_167_24

Murthy, R. S. (2021). Schizophrenia Research Foundation-Caring for the Mind: A Journey of 35 Years.... and Counting. *Indian Journal of Social Psychiatry, 37*(4), 378–379. DOI: 10.4103/ijsp.ijsp_320_21

Namrata Rao, M., Lakshmi Ravikanth, A., Sankaran, L., Bansal, P., & Chowdhury, R. (2024). The Banyan Journey: A Continuum in Community Mental Health Care. In *Mental Health Care Resource Book: Concepts and Praxis for Social Workers and Mental Health Professionals* (pp. 229–250). Springer Nature Singapore. DOI: 10.1007/978-981-97-1203-8_14

Nandamuri, P. P., Rao, K. V. G., & Mishra, M. K. (2020). Sustainable competitive advantage through business model innovation: The Indian perspective. In *Disruptive technology: Concepts, methodologies, tools, and applications* (pp. 191–213). IGI Global Scientific Publishing. DOI: 10.4018/978-1-5225-9273-0.ch010

Nazareth, P., Nikhil, G. B., Chirag, G., Prathik, N. R., & Pratham, P. (2024, June). Exploring the Efficacy of Mental Health Care Chatbots: A Comprehensive Review. In *2024 15th International Conference on Computing Communication and Networking Technologies (ICCCNT)* (pp. 1-6). IEEE. DOI: 10.1109/ICCCNT61001.2024.10725176

Noushad Yashan, D. S. R. S., Kohli, N. K., Kalakumari, T., & Mistry, V. (2024). Innovative business models in the digital age: a comparative analysis. *Cahiers Magellanes-NS*, *6*(2), 5170–5181.

Rahman, E., Webb, W. R., Rao, P., Yu, N., Garcia, P. E., Ioannidis, S., Sayed, K., Philipp-Dormston, W. G., Carruthers, J. D. A., & Mosahebi, A. (2024). A systematic review on the reinforcement loop in aesthetic medicine and surgery: The interplay of social media, self-perception, and repeat procedures. *Aesthetic Plastic Surgery*, *48*(17), 3475–3487. DOI: 10.1007/s00266-024-04016-y PMID: 38724639

Samanta, T. (2021). Living solo at midlife: Can the pandemic de-stigmatize living alone in India? *Journal of Aging Studies*, *56*, 100907. DOI: 10.1016/j.jaging.2020.100907 PMID: 33712092

Sanghvi, P. B., & Mehrotra, S. (2022). Help-seeking for mental health concerns: Review of Indian research and emergent insights. *Warasan Wichai Witthayasat Kanphaet*, *36*(3), 428–441. DOI: 10.1108/JHR-02-2020-0040

Singh, S., & Sirvastva, N. (2024). Loneliness and satisfaction with life among young adults belonging to nuclear and joint families. *International Journal of Indian Psychology*, *12*(2).

Sinha, C., Meheli, S., & Kadaba, M. (2023). Understanding digital mental health needs and usage with an artificial intelligence–led mental health app (Wysa) during the COVID-19 pandemic: Retrospective analysis. *JMIR Formative Research*, *7*(1), e41913. DOI: 10.2196/41913 PMID: 36540052

Soni, S. K. & Sharma, S. (2023). *Ayurveda and Social Health: Need for healthy society.*

Tewari, A., Chhabria, A., Khalsa, A. S., Chaudhary, S., & Kanal, H. (2021, April). A survey of mental health chatbots using NLP. In *Proceedings of the International Conference on Innovative Computing and Communication (ICICC)*. DOI: 10.2139/ssrn.3833914

Veale, D., Robins, E., Thomson, A. B., & Gilbert, P. (2023). No safety without emotional safety. *The Lancet. Psychiatry*, *10*(1), 65–70. DOI: 10.1016/S2215-0366(22)00373-X PMID: 36442491

Venters, S., & Jones, C. J. (2021). The experiences of grandchildren who provide care for a grandparent with dementia: A systematic review. *Dementia (London)*, *20*(6), 2205–2230. DOI: 10.1177/1471301220980243 PMID: 33372548

Verma, S. K., Bhattacharya, S., & Singh, T. (2024). Family Dynamics and Inter-generational Relation in Interdependent Society: An Indian Perspective. In *Indian Families: Contemporary Family. Structures and Dynamics*, *26*, 97–125. Emerald Publishing Limited.

Vinod, R. (2023). *Modernity in India: Issues, Perspectives and Challenges*. Routledge India. DOI: 10.4324/9781032622880

Vliegenthart, D. (2023). Meaningless spirituality?: The Satsang Network as a Grassroots Response to the Modern Western Crisis of Meaning. In *Combating Crises from Below*

Wadhwa, M. (2021). *Digital Mental Health Initiatives in India* (No. 60). ICT India Working Paper.

Wang, L., Fagan, C., & Yu, C. L. (2020). Popular mental health apps (MH apps) as a complement to telepsychotherapy: Guidelines for consideration. *Journal of Psychotherapy Integration*, *30*(2), 265–273. DOI: 10.1037/int0000204

Weiss, R. (1975). *Loneliness: The experience of emotional and social isolation.* MIT press.

Yadav, U., & Prakash, B. (2024). A Socio-Legal Analysis of the Health and Well-Being of the Ageing Population. In *Intersections of Law and Computational Intelligence in Health Governance* (pp. 142–160). IGI Global. DOI: 10.4018/979-8-3693-5976-1.ch007

Yadav, V., Chauhan, S., & Patel, R. (2022). What causes loneliness among household heads: A study based in primary setting in Mumbai, India. *BMC Public Health*, *22*(1), 730. DOI: 10.1186/s12889-022-13108-w PMID: 35413809

ABBREVIATIONS

ANMs: Auxiliary Nurse Midwives
ASHAs: Accredited Social Health Activists
CSR: Corporate Social Responsibility
ICMR: Indian Council of Medical Research
ICSSR: Indian Council of Social Science Research
NEP 2020: National Education Policy 2020
NGO: Non-Governmental Organization
NIMHANS: National Institute of Mental Health and Neurosciences
NSS: National Service Scheme
NYKS: Nehru Yuva Kendra Sangathan
PHC: Primary Health Centre
PMAY: Pradhan Mantri Awas Yojana
SDG: Sustainable Development Goals
SHGs: Self-Help Groups; MIS – Management Information System
Tele-MANAS: Tele Mental Health Assistance and Networking Across States

Chapter 3
Social Isolation by Design:
Structural Discrimination and Belonging in Contemporary Nationality Laws

Cassadee Orinthia Yan
https://orcid.org/0009-0005-2737-3434
Maslow Quest Foundation, Cook Islands

ABSTRACT

This chapter examines how nationality laws function as instruments of structural discrimination that institutionalize social isolation and inequality. Drawing on theories from Arendt, Carens, Shachar, Soysal, and Brubaker, it shows how legal definitions of citizenship create exclusionary hierarchies within national communities. The discussion integrates emerging issues—digital identification systems, biometric governance, and global migration regimes—to demonstrate that exclusion is not merely historical but technologically reproduced. Comparative case studies reveal how discriminatory nationality laws entrench poverty, restrict mobility, and fracture identity across generations. The chapter concludes by outlining pathways toward inclusive citizenship through gender-equal reforms, post-national rights, and recognition of digital personhood.

INTRODUCTION AND CONCEPTUAL FRAMEWORK

Citizenship has long been the legal and moral framework of modern political life, delineating who is entitled to rights and who is excluded. Hannah Arendt's

DOI: 10.4018/979-8-3373-5811-6.ch003

renowned assertion that citizenship is "the right to have rights" encapsulates both its potential and its danger: inclusion within a polity allows for the realization of human dignity, while exclusion leaves individuals beyond the reach of justice (Arendt, 2004). Yet, the institution that affirms belonging can also facilitate exclusion. Nationality laws— rules that determine how citizenship is acquired, transmitted, or lost—often execute this exclusionary function by translating social hierarchies of ethnicity, gender, class, and religion into formal legal categories. In doing so, they create not just legal outsiders, but also social isolation as a structural condition of life.

This chapter contends that social isolation is not merely a byproduct of discriminatory nationality regimes but an intended outcome of their design. Law serves as a tool through which states institutionalize differences, allocate privileges, and perpetuate inequality across generations. Joseph Carens (1987) famously described citizenship as a modern feudal status, a hereditary condition largely determined at birth and profoundly influencing one's life chances. Shachar (2009) expanded this analysis to the concept of the birthright lottery, highlighting that birthright citizenship, like inherited wealth, perpetuates inequality over time. Rogers Brubaker (1992) conceptualized citizenship as a form of social closure, where the state delineates insiders and outsiders to maintain the scarcity that gives membership its value. Yasemin Soysal (1994) and Linda Bosniak (2006) further examined how global human-rights norms and migration have complicated these boundaries, suggesting an emerging form of post-national membership that anchors rights in personhood rather than nationality. Despite these normative developments, the empirical reality remains that states continue to use citizenship laws as a tool of exclusion.

In this context, nationality law embodies what Charles Mills (1997) termed the racial contract, a political order that formally advocates equality while structurally embedding hierarchy. The deprivation or denial of nationality has historically targeted minorities deemed ethnically or politically undesirable, whether the Rohingya in Myanmar, Dominicans of Haitian descent, or Black South Africans, during apartheid. Legal exclusion ensures social subordination by denying access to the means of participation—work, education, property, and representation—thereby normalizing inequality. Studies of statelessness and denationalization reveal that once people are excluded from their legal identity, they are more easily deprived of physical security and social respect (Blitz & Lynch, 2011; van Waas, 2008; UNHCR, 2023).

Contemporary landscapes amplify these dynamics through emerging identification and surveillance technologies. Today, citizenship is increasingly mediated by data. Governments worldwide have implemented biometric identity systems, such as India's Aadhaar, Kenya's Huduma Namba, Pakistan's NADRA, and the European Union's Entry/Exit System, which promise efficiency and security, but often perpetuate existing exclusions. Errors in biometric capture, documentary gaps, or discretionary enrollment rules can render entire communities digitally invisible

(Gelb and Clark, 2013; Khera, 2019; Eubanks, 2018). Scholars refer to this as "digital statelessness," in which individuals are denied access to welfare, employment, or movement because a database fails to recognize them (Hosein & Nyst, 2013; Privacy International, 2021). Far from being neutral, these infrastructures encode political hierarchies into algorithmic forms, extending Arendt's mid-twentieth-century insight into the digital age: when belonging is mediated by code, exclusion becomes automated.

At the same time, nationalist and populist movements have re-ethnicized the concept of citizenship. Across Europe, South Asia, and the Americas, appeals to sovereignty and cultural authenticity have justified restrictive naturalization policies and denationalization powers. The rhetoric has shifted from overt racial superiority to the language of "security," "integration," or "national identity," but the outcomes remain similar: the legal contraction of the political community. Recent comparative research shows that tightening citizenship laws correlates with rising xenophobia and social polarization (Joppke, 2019; Howard, 2020). These developments highlight that citizenship, far from a stable legal status, is a dynamic battleground where inclusion and exclusion are continually renegotiated.

Understanding how these processes generate social isolation requires attention to two interrelated mechanisms, structural discrimination and othering. Structural discrimination refers to the systematic production of inequality through ostensibly neutral legal and institutional practices (Fredman 2011). It is not the bias of individuals but the bias of systems—procedures that, by design or inertia, perpetuates disadvantage. Nationality laws exemplify this when they set conditions that certain groups cannot meet: ancestry cut-off dates excluding minorities, documentation requirements impossible for the poor, or paternal-line transmission rules that subordinate women's citizenship to men's citizenship. In addition, is the discursive process through which differences are constructed and devalued (Said 1978). When institutionalized in law, it transforms prejudice into governance. The "other" is rendered administratively manageable: counted, classified, and excluded.

These two forces reinforce each other. Legal frameworks of citizenship formalize othering by identifying who belongs, while social narratives of otherness legitimize the law's exclusions. The result is what Nira Yuval-Davis (2011) calls the *politics of belonging*—the constant negotiation of boundaries that decides who may share in collective life. Once encoded in the law, these boundaries are remarkably durable. For example, gender-discriminatory nationality statutes still present in more than twenty-five countries, deny women the equal right to transmit nationality to their children or spouses. The United Nations High Commissioner for Refugees (2023) identifies these provisions as leading drivers of intergenerational statelessness. Discrimination is doubly structural: women's legal status is subordinated, and their children's belonging is contingent on a male relative.

The consequences of these exclusions are multidimensional. Empirical studies have consistently linked statelessness and precarious nationality to poverty, health disparities, and restricted mobility (Blitz & Lynch 2011; Manby 2016). Without recognized citizenship, individuals are often barred from formal employment, property ownership, or education. They are also vulnerable to detention, trafficking, and exploitation. The World Bank (2018) notes that foundational identity documentation is now essential for economic participation; its absence directly translates into material deprivation. The sociological literature adds that the absence of legal identity also corrodes social cohesion: individuals denied recognition experience what Liisa Malkki (1995) termed *categorical homelessness*, a form of existential displacement even within one's homeland.

The psychological dimension of exclusion was equally severe. Research on stateless communities documents feelings of invisibility, fear, and shame, which compound material deprivation (Kingston, 2017). Arendt (2004) warned that a stateless person is deprived of not only rights but also the public space in which those rights can appear. This loss produces civic loneliness that mirrors the isolation described by contemporary mental health studies of marginalized groups. Thus, the isolation produced by nationality law is both structural and affective; it reorganizes society while disfiguring the self.

Using an analytical approach, this chapter examines nationality laws as a framework for exclusion. It uses a comparative documentary method, integrating legal texts, human rights reports, and scholarly research to trace how states convert social differences into legal hierarchies. Instead of relying on fieldwork, it draws from verified sources to identify recurring patterns in various cases. The chosen examples—Myanmar, the Dominican Republic, South Africa, Kuwait, and the Baltic states—represent different legal systems and historical contexts, but reveal similar techniques of isolation. Each case illustrates how denial or restriction of citizenship functions as a political tool that perpetuates inequality under the guise of legality.

This discussion unfolds through four analytical steps. The first examines ethnic and racial exclusion, demonstrating how citizenship laws in Myanmar, the Dominican Republic, and apartheid South Africa have transformed notions of purity and ancestry into tools of segregation. The second explores gender and structural exclusions, from patriarchal nationality laws to documentary and linguistic barriers in Kuwait and Baltics, linking these to the emerging issue of algorithmic exclusion in digital ID regimes. The third analyzes the consequences of these legal frameworks—economic marginalization, political disempowerment, and psychosocial harm—while highlighting resistance through activism, litigation, and international advocacy. The final section proposed a framework for inclusive citizenship based on human rights, gender equality, and digital ethics.

Ultimately, this chapter argues that the persistence of social isolation through nationality law reveals the incomplete project of political modernity. The Enlightenment's promise of universal equality was built on an exclusionary foundation of national membership. As global mobility, technological governance, and transnational inequality reshape the landscape of belonging, reimagining citizenship has become essential. The task is not merely to extend membership to more people but to redefine the meaning of membership itself. A truly inclusive polity would recognize that the right to belong precedes the state's authority to define it. Citizenship must evolve from an inherited privilege into a relational practice of mutual recognition—an affirmation that no one should be rendered invisible by design.

ETHNIC AND RACIAL EXCLUSION IN NATIONALITY LAWS

Nationality law has never merely been an administrative device for managing citizenship; it has always been a political technology for shaping the boundaries of belonging. Scholars of nationalism and legal sociology argue that law constructs demos through exclusion as much as inclusion (Brubaker, 1992; Anderson, 2013). In this sense, citizenship is not simply a status of membership, but a system of differentiation—a form of *social closure* that integrates and isolates. Modern states have used nationality laws to define an ethnically homogenous "people," while relegating minorities and racialized groups to categories of partial or non-belonging. These exclusions do not occur at the margins of sovereignty, but rather constitute its essence: sovereignty is exercised through the power to decide who belongs (Mamdani, 1996; Shachar, 2009).

The exclusion of Myanmar's Rohingya, the denationalization of Dominicans of Haitian descent, and the citizenship segregation of apartheid South Africa exemplify how states translate social hierarchies into legal regimes of exclusion. Each case represents a distinct modality of what Mahmood Mamdani (2001) termed the *bifurcated state*: a political order that simultaneously produces citizens endowed with rights and deprived subjects. These instances demonstrate how the codification of ancestry, race, or ethnicity into citizenship law generates a structural inequality that endures long after the law itself is enacted.

Myanmar's 1982 *Citizenship Law* remains one of the most explicit racialized nationality regimes in the modern era. The law established a tripartite hierarchy—full, associate, and naturalized citizenship—based on membership in 135 officially recognized "national races." The Rohingya, a Muslim minority with a century-long settlement in Rakhine State, was deliberately omitted. As Cheesman (2017) observes, this act was not an administrative oversight, but a deliberate attempt to define Myanmar's political community as exclusively Buddhist and Burman. By legal design, the

Rohingya were rendered *stateless in situ* and trapped within the borders of a state that denied their existence. The law's exclusionary logic produced the conditions for subsequent persecution. The United Nations Independent International Fact-Finding Mission on Myanmar (2018) documented systematic violations—murder, rape, and forced displacement—that it deemed possible precisely because the Rohingya lacked a legal personality. The loss of citizenship has become an enabling condition for atrocity. Hannah Arendt's (2004) insight that the deprivation of nationality is the deprivation of rights finds its fullest expression here: once outside the circle of citizenship, one is stripped of political existence itself.

Rohingya's plight demonstrates that statelessness functions as a form of governance. By defining the Rohingya as "illegal immigrants," Myanmar's state apparatus institutionalized its exclusion from civil registration, education, and healthcare (Leider, 2018). Kingston (2017) describes this as "bureaucratic violence"—harm inflicted not by overt coercion but by the slow, systemic denial of recognition. As of 2023, more than one million Rohingya will remain in exile in Bangladesh, while those remaining in Rakhine will live under segregation orders and movement restrictions (UNHCR, 2023). Citizenship law here performs what Didier Fassin (2011) calls *biolegitimacy*: it decides whose lives matter and whose can be left unprotected.

A comparable though distinct process unfolded in the Dominican Republic, where the Constitutional Tribunal's 2013 Judgment TC 168-13 reinterpreted nationality to exclude those born to parents considered "in transit." Applied retroactively to 1929, the ruling revoked citizenship from tens of thousands of Dominicans of Haitian descent. Scholars trace this judicial maneuver to the racialized ideology of *antihaitianismo*, which constructs a Dominican identity through opposition to Blackness and Haitian ancestry (García Peña, 2016; Nkrumah, 2017). By reframing the legal meaning of birth rights, the Tribunal effectively converted a racially defined minority into foreigners overnight. The Inter-American Commission on Human Rights (2015) concluded that the decision constituted an arbitrary deprivation of nationality and violated both the Dominican Constitution and international law.

Empirical research has revealed the consequences of this exclusion. Stateless Dominicans have lost access to formal education, healthcare, and employment and face deportation threats despite generational residence in the country (Manby, 2016; Fernández, 2020). Many live in limbo, neither Dominican nor Haitian, illustrating van Waas and Blitz's (2014) notion of *quasi-citizenship*, a status of partial inclusion without substantive rights. The government's "regularization plan," designed to remedy the ruling's effects, remains bureaucratically inaccessible to those lacking birth certificates or funds. Racialized exclusion thus persists through administrative inertia as much as overt racism.

Civil-society responses, such as the *Reconoci.do* movement, reveal the counter-politics of belonging. By organizing demonstrations and pursuing litigation before regional human rights bodies, these activists enact what Isin (2009) calls *acts of citizenship*: performances through which excluded subjects assert political agency despite their legal erasure. Their activism underscores that citizenship is not a static status but a contested practice that is continually redefined through struggle.

Apartheid South Africa represents a paradigmatic historical instance of racialized citizenship codified into law. The 1970 *Bantu Homelands Citizenship Act* forcibly assigned all Black South Africans to one of ten ethnically defined "homelands," simultaneously stripping them of South African citizenship. As Posel (1991) explains, the law transformed racial segregation into a regime of differentiated nationality: whites retained full citizenship; "coloureds" and Indians were semi-citizens; and Black Africans were rendered foreign in their own country. Mamdani (1996) characterizes this system as *decentralized despotism*, in which the fiction of separate homelands justifies the exclusion of black people from political participation while preserving their economic subordination. The Bantustans were never viable sovereign entities—they were mechanisms for controlling labor and fragmenting resistance. Even after the abolition of apartheids, the spatial and economic legacies of this stratified citizenship persist, visible in South Africa's persistent racialized inequality and land dispossession (Seekings & Nattrass, 2005; Southall, 2019).

These cases share a structural logic. Whether through statutory classification (Myanmar), judicial reinterpretation (Dominican Republic), or legislative partition (South Africa), the state redefined membership around racialized criteria to consolidate power. In each instance, the formal rationality of law—citizenship tests, ancestry lists, or territorial assignments —masked a deeper project of exclusion. As Mamdani (2001) and Brubaker (1992) observe, the liberal conception of citizenship as equal membership coexists uneasily with the political imperative to preserve a homogeneous nation. Law reconciles this tension by creating a hierarchy of belonging: citizens, second-class citizens, and rightless subjects.

The socioeconomic and psychological consequences of exclusion are severe and enduring. Empirical studies confirm that stateless and denationalized populations experience higher rates of poverty, lower educational attainment, and greater exposure to violence (Blitz and Lynch 2011; Manby 2016). Citizenship operates as a form of social capital; its absence systematically constrains opportunity. For the Rohingya, exclusion confines communities to camps, where economic life is virtually extinguished. For the Dominicans of Haitian descent, lack of identification precludes formal work and political participation. For Black South Africans under apartheid, fabricated "homeland" citizenship legitimized dispossession. In each case, legal nonrecognition produces material impoverishment and symbolic degradation.

Psychologically, the effects of exclusion manifest as a loss of identity, shame, and social withdrawal. Research on stateless populations describes a pervasive sense of invisibility and humiliation (Kingston 2017; van Waas 2008). Malkki's (1995) ethnography of refugees introduced the concept of *categorical homelessness*: the dislocation of people stripped not only of home but also of classification. Such civic homelessness persisted in the denationalized. The destruction of legal identity fractures personal and collective narratives, leaving individuals, as Arendt (2004) wrote, 'superfluous' in political life.

The adaptability of racialized citizenship to new political forms underscores its resilience. In contemporary democracies, exclusionary practices reappear under the guise of security and bureaucratic modernization. States deploy citizenship deprivation, stringent naturalization tests, and digital identity systems to replicate historical inequities. Gibney (2013) documents how the United Kingdom, Australia, and Canada have expanded citizenship-revocation powers, disproportionately targeting racialized dual nationals. Digital identity programs, often lauded as inclusive, can reproduce exclusion when documentation gaps intersect with social disadvantages (Eubanks, 2018; Khera, 2019). These new mechanisms translate the same old hierarchies into algorithmic forms: citizenship by data rather than by blood but exclusion nonetheless.

At the structural level, these regimes persist because statelessness serves the state's interests. Denial of membership allows governments to manage population demographics, suppress dissent, and externalize social responsibility. Bloom (2017) terms this the *politics of responsibility denial*: by erasing individuals from the citizenry, states absolve their obligations toward them. International law remains constrained by its capacity to counteract this dynamic. Although the *1961 Convention on the Reduction of Statelessness* prohibits arbitrary deprivation of nationality, compliance is inconsistent and enforcement mechanisms are weak (van Waas, 2008; UNHCR, 2023). Thus, sovereignty continues to function as a shield from discrimination.

Nevertheless, resistance to exclusion persisted across the scales. The global campaign against statelessness—epitomized by UNHCR's *#IBelong* initiative launched in 2014—has catalyzed reforms in states such as Kenya, Morocco, and Thailand (Blitz & Sawyer, 2011; UNHCR, 2014). Grassroots mobilizations, from the Rohingya diaspora's advocacy to Dominican and South African rights movements, reassert belonging through alternative narratives of community and solidarity. These struggles demonstrate that citizenship, though juridically defined by the state, can also be reimagined from below as a moral and political claim to equality:

Thus, ethnic and racial exclusion through nationality law reveals a foundational paradox in the modern state system. The state derives its legitimacy from the promise of equal citizenship, yet reproduces inequality by tethering to lineage, race, or faith. As long as the legal definition of a citizen remains a proxy for cultural or racial purity, social isolation remains an institutional outcome rather than an aberration. The challenge is not simply to include the excluded, but to transform the logic of membership itself—from a mechanism of closure to a practice of universal recognition. Reimagining citizenship in this way requires confronting what Arendt (2004) called "the calamity of the rightless": that the power to exclude, once legalized, corrodes the idea of human equality.

GENDER AND STRUCTURAL EXCLUSIONS IN NATIONALITY LAWS

Gendered hierarchies in nationality law reveal that citizenship is not a neutral legal category but a political institution embedded in systems of patriarchy, class, and colonial inheritance. While liberal theory celebrates citizenship as the equalizing bond between state and individual, the actual legal frameworks that determine belonging often treat women as conduits of lineage and national continuity, as opposed to autonomous bearers of rights. Feminist and postcolonial scholars have long noted that the gendered division of citizenship—who can confer, inherit, or lose it—reflects the state's control over reproduction and kinship (Yuval-Davis 2011; Lister 1997; Shachar 2009). In most societies, the boundaries of the nation are drawn through men's bodies and names, while women's membership remains derivative, contingent, or revocable. These gendered logics of descent do not simply mirror social inequality; they institutionalize it, producing what Kimberlé Crenshaw (1989) called *structural intersectionality*, in which gendered subordination amplifies other forms of exclusion, such as ethnicity, class, and statelessness.

Legal discrimination regarding nationality transmission remains one of the most enduring forms of gender inequality worldwide. Even after decades of international reform, the United Nations High Commissioner for Refugees (UNHCR, 2023) identifies twenty-three countries that still deny women the right to pass citizenship to their children on the same terms as men and over 50 that restrict their ability to confer nationality on foreign spouses. These limitations violate Article 9 of the *Convention on the Elimination of All Forms of Discrimination against Women* (1979), yet persist through the legal fiction that the family's political identity is patrilineal. Ayelet Shachar (2009) describes this as the "birthright lottery": citizenship operates as an inherited property transmitted through the father's line, locking inequality into the genetic metaphor of the nation. Laura van Waas (2008) demonstrates that this patriarchal transmission system is a leading global cause of child statelessness, depriving millions of legal recognition from birth.

The consequences of these laws are not confined to formal inequality, but they produce tangible and intergenerational isolation. In Lebanon, where women cannot confer nationality on children or foreign husbands, entire families exist as "legal ghosts," denied access to public education and healthcare. In Kuwait, patriarchal logic intersects with tribal and racial hierarchies. The *Bidun*—literally "without"—remain excluded from citizenship because nationality passes only through fathers. Human Rights Watch (2011) and Amnesty International (2023) estimate that more than 100,000 Bidun live in Kuwait without legal status and are deprived of education, employment, and health services. Women married to Bidun men cannot protect their children from statelessness, reproducing both gender and ethnic inequalities. Shachar's (2009) concept of *citizenship inheritance inequality* captures this circularity: the law transforms biological descent into a mechanism for reproducing political hierarchy. Despite sporadic proposals for reform, patriarchal and nationalist anxieties about "diluting" citizenship continue to block change (Manby 2016).

Nepal, Iran, and numerous other states in North Africa show similar patterns. Nepal's pre-2015 nationality law required mothers to prove the citizenship of their child's father to transmit nationality, effectively excluding single mothers and children with unknown paternity (Dhakal, 2018). Although the 2015 Constitution nominally guaranteed equality, provincial bureaucracies continued to apply older standards (Manby, 2016). In Iran, the 2019 amendment to the Nationality Law allowed Iranian mothers to confer nationality on their children; however, its implementation remains uneven. Applicants undergo security screening that disproportionately affects families of Afghan origin (Shahrzad and Kian 2020). These examples demonstrate that legal reform alone cannot undo deep social hierarchies; patriarchal bureaucracies reproduce inequality through discretionary enforcement. As Ruth Lister (1997) argued, citizenship equality requires not only formal inclusion, but also transformation of the institutions that define who counts as a rights-bearing subject.

Gender discrimination often operates in tandem with other structural exclusions, particularly those based on language, ancestry, or class. In the Baltic states, post-Soviet nationality regimes created large populations of Russian-speaking "non-citizens." Latvia's 1994 Citizenship Law granted automatic citizenship only to descendants of pre-1940 citizens, while others were required to pass demanding language and civic tests (Järve, 2000). Although the number of non-citizens has declined, tens of thousands have remained without full rights. Dzenovska (2018) and Galbreath (2013) show that this exclusion produces not only legal inequality but a hierarchy of linguistic belonging, where cultural conformity determines access to political membership. The resulting marginalization—limited voting rights, restricted mobility, and stigmatization—illustrates how structural discrimination can persist in democratic states under the guise of linguistic integration.

Technological changes in governance have added new layers to these exclusions. Biometric identification and digital databases now determine who is recognized by the state, often replicating historical bias. Eubanks (2018) and Benjamin (2019) describe this phenomenon as "automating inequality," in which algorithmic systems reproduce racial and gendered hierarchies under the veneer of neutrality. In India, Kenya, and Pakistan, biometric programs such as *Aadhaar*, *Huduma Namba*, and

NADRA have been criticized for excluding women, minorities, and the poor from essential services because of data mismatches or lack of documentation (Khera, 2019; Masiero & Das, 2022). Technologies designed to ensure inclusion can thus recreate statelessness in a digital form. When citizenship rights depend on algorithmic legibility, those misrecognized by the database become invisible to the state. Shoshana Zuboff (2019) calls this a new "instrumentarian power," whereby control is exerted through data surveillance rather than overt law. The continuity between paper- and data-based exclusion underscores that technology does not erase hierarchy; it merely translates it into code.

Gendered and structural exclusions incur material, psychological, and developmental costs. Empirical studies consistently link statelessness and gender discrimination to heightened poverty, child mortality, and vulnerability to violence (Blitz & Lynch, 2011; UNHCR, 2023). Without a legal identity, women cannot own property, access credit, or work formally, perpetuating economic dependence. Equality Now (2025) documents that discriminatory nationality laws increase exposure to human trafficking and early marriage as women seek security through dependent relationships. Loss of nationality also inflicts psychosocial harm. Kingston (2017) describes this as "civic invisibility," a condition of existential uncertainty and shame. In contexts where citizenship is the key to recognition, legal absence translates into social erasure. Liisa Malkki's (1995) concept of *categorical homelessness* captures this experience: to be outside the classificatory order of the state is to be rendered socially weightless.

The economic cost of exclusion was substantial. The World Bank (2018) and UNDP (2021) research shows that countries with gender-equal nationality laws experience higher female labor-force participation, better child health outcomes, and greater overall productivity. Conversely, exclusionary citizenship laws suppress growth by restricting human capital and perpetuating dependency. Citizenship inequality thus functions as both a human-rights violation and an economic inefficiency. Charlesworth and Chinkin (2000) contended that feminist engagement with international law reveals how formal equality remains hollow without dismantling the gendered assumptions underpinning legal categories. Therefore, gender-equal nationality reform is not only a moral imperative, but also a pragmatic necessity for sustainable development.

Reform movements demonstrate that legal change is possible when equality is framed as a question of human dignity, rather than national identity. The *Global Campaign for Equal Nationality Rights*, coordinated by the UNHCR, UN Women, and Equality Now, has driven reforms in more than a dozen countries since 2003, including Morocco, Egypt, Algeria, and Jordan, enabling women to transmit their nationality to their children (Equality Now, 2025). However, these victories coexist with persistent structural barriers. Administrative discretion, documentary requirements, and conservative jurisprudence often neutralize the spirit of reform. As Shachar (2009) notes, citizenship's power lies in its function as a boundary technology; even progressive amendments can entrench hierarchy when they fail to challenge the assumption that belonging must be inherited rather than lived.

Recent feminist theories of citizenship attemptedtempt to reconceptualize belonging beyond the nation-state's patriarchal frame. Engin Isin (2009) proposes viewing citizenship as an *act*—a practice through which individuals constitute themselves as political agents regardless of legal status. Kim Rubenstein (2017) extends this idea, arguing for "gendered citizenship" that recognizes care, social reproduction, and community participation as civic contributions equal to formal political acts. Yuval-Davis (2011) advances the concept of *transversal politics*, emphasizing solidarity across difference rather than assimilation into homogeneity. Together, these frameworks point toward reimagined citizenship grounded in residence, participation, and mutual recognition, instead of descent and conformity. They also suggest that digital infrastructure could, if ethically designed, facilitate inclusion by recording residence and contribution rather than lineage. This requires embedding equality and transparency into algorithmic governance, a task that remains largely aspirational.

The persistence of gender and structural exclusion underscores the limits of the current international law. Despite normative frameworks such as CEDAW and the *1961 Convention on the Reduction of Statelessness*, enforcement mechanisms remain weak and compliance depends on political will (van Waas, 2008; Manby, 2016). States often invoke sovereignty to resist reform, asserting that control over citizenship is the last domain of absolute authority. Yet, as Bloom (2017) argues, sovereignty cannot justify the systematic production of rightlessness. When citizenship law institutionalizes inequality, it undermines the legitimacy of the state. The future of inclusive citizenship, therefore, depends on shifting the epistemology of sovereignty—from possession to responsibility–from exclusion to care.

CONSEQUENCES AND RESISTANCE

The consequences of exclusionary nationality laws are neither incidental nor contained in the juridical domain. They operate across ontological, political, and epistemic registers, eroding not only the material foundations of existence but also the very conditions under which persons can appear as subjects of rights. Citizenship's absence marks the threshold between recognition and invisibility. Hannah Arendt's (2004) diagnosis of the stateless as "the calamity of the rightless" remains the conceptual axis through which contemporary exclusion must be read: once deprived of nationality, individuals lose the political space in which action and speech become meaningful. To be without citizenship is not simply to lack legal documentation, but to be stripped of the grammar through which human worth is publicly acknowledged.

Modern states deploy nationality law as a disciplinary regime that naturalizes rightlessness. It is an architecture of silence that converts social hierarchies into legal facts and transforms membership into an instrument of control. The effects of exclusion radiate outward through what Bourdieu would call the "symbolic economy" of the state—where recognition, status, and access to resources are allocated according to legally defined belonging. Statelessness and denationalization thus enact profound redistribution of vulnerability. Individuals without citizenship exist in a perpetual state of contingency; they may work, move, or survive only through the temporary tolerance of the state or international agencies. This condition epitomizes Agamben 's(1998) terms of *bare life*: life exposed to power without protection. However, unlike Agamben's camp, which he imagined as an exception to law, exclusionary citizenship regimes demonstrate that the exception has become the rule.

The deprivation of nationality therefore constitutes not merely an administrative failure, but a reconfiguration of political subjectivity itself. Citizenship functions as the interface between personhood and sovereignty; its withdrawal renders the individual an object of governance rather than a participant in it. The consequence is civic paralysis that Arendt associated with totalitarianism: the reduction of human plurality to isolation, a social condition in which speech no longer registers as action. Statelessness generates a peculiar ontology—existence without audibility—where even suffering must be mediated by institutions that recognize it as legitimate. Humanitarian interventions, when necessary, often reinforce this dynamic. As Didier Fassin (2011) observes, humanitarianism replaces the political logic of rights with the moral logic of compassion, transforming the stateless into recipients of care, rather than agents of justice. In this sense, compassion becomes the affective corollary of exclusion.

At the structural level, exclusionary nationality regimes materialize as economies of dispossession. Citizenship determines access to labor markets, property, and social welfare; its absence transforms rights into privileges contingent on benevolence. Joseph Carens (1987) described citizenship as a modern form of feudal status—an inherited position that predetermines life chances. Denationalization and statelessness reproduce this feudal logic on a global scale. The Rohingya's enforced immobility, the Bidun's denial of public employment, and the continued marginalization of "non-citizens" in the Baltic states exemplify how the law's silence perpetuates economic subordination. However, beyond its material consequences, exclusion also structures the epistemology of development: those without citizenship are uncounted in national statistics, invisible in policy frameworks, and, therefore, absent from the epistemic universe of governance. Thus, exclusion is both ontological and cognitive: it erases subjects from being and knowing.

The psychological dimension of exclusion has been well documented, yet insufficiently theorized. Studies of stateless populations have revealed pervasive feelings of humiliation, fear, and self-doubt (Kingston, 2017; Blitz & Lynch, 2011). These are not simply emotional reactions to deprivation, but indicators of how law penetrates the subject. The stateless internalize the verdict of nonexistence imposed upon them; they come to experience their invisibility as ontological rather than political. In this sense, exclusion operates as a biopolitical technique that reshapes subjectivity from within. Michel Foucault's (1978) notion of *governmentality* helps elucidate this process: citizenship laws do not merely regulate populations externally; they produce the governed subject who consents to her own marginality. To be stateless is to be disciplined with gratitude for mere survival. This internalization of precarity ensures that exclusion reproduces itself even in the absence of overt coercion.

The entanglement of exclusion and humanitarianism further complicates this resistance. As Arendt (2004) observed in her critique of interwar refugee policies, the international community tends to treat statelessness as a humanitarian crisis rather than political injustice. This framing obscures the structural nature of exclusion by reducing it to the management of the bodies in need. Humanitarian protection sustains life but suspends politics; it preserves statelessness, while preventing the reconstitution of citizenship. The camp, shelter, and NGO—each becomes a site where survival replaces participation. The result is what Ruha Benjamin (2019) calls "the benevolent algorithm of inequality": systems that appear to save lives while reproducing the hierarchies that endangered them.

Resistance to exclusion therefore begins with the reclamation of politics. Engin Isin (2009) conceptualizes such acts as *performative citizenship*: moments when individuals enact the rights they are denied, thereby constituting themselves as political agents. These acts disrupt the state's monopoly on recognition by asserting that belonging can be claimed, rather than granted. The Dominican Movement *Reconoci. do*, the Rohingya diaspora's documentation of atrocities, and women's nationality-rights campaigns across the Middle East exemplify this performativity. However, Isin's insight extends beyond activism; it identifies a new ontology of citizenship in which agency precedes legality. Resistance, in this framework, is not a reaction but an invention—it produces the very subject that exclusion seeks to erase.

Theoretically, this performative politics aligns with what Nira Yuval-Davis (2011) describes as *transversal belonging*: solidarity across differences that refuses assimilation while seeking shared responsibility. Transversal belonging disrupts the binary of citizens and foreigners by positioning the political community as relational rather than bounded. It reframes inclusion as interdependence, emphasizing that no polity is autonomous, because all are constituted through the recognition of others. This perspective transforms the problem of statelessness from membership to one of ethics: who is responsible for ensuring that the human condition does not collapse into a national condition? Tendayi Bloom (2017) advances a parallel argument in her theory of *responsible sovereignty*, contending that the right to nationality entails a duty not to produce statelessness. Sovereignty, reimagined as stewardship rather than dominion, reorients power toward care rather than control.

Resistance also requires confronting the epistemic foundations of exclusion. As Ayelet Shachar (2009) warns, even well-intentioned reforms risk-entrenching inequality when they leave the principle that belonging must be inherited. The modern state's obsession with descent, whether biological, cultural, or digital, ensures that inclusion is always conditional. Algorithmic governance represents the latest iteration of this descent logic: belonging is now verified by data lineage rather than the bloodline. The biometric registry, such as the birth certificate, encodes the same assumption that legitimacy must be authenticated. Feminist theorists, such as Kim Rubenstein (2017) and Nira Yuval-Davis (2011), have criticized this logic as patriarchal and exclusionary, arguing instead for citizenship as participation—a relational practice grounded in care, residence, and contribution. Such redefinitions move beyond the legalistic expansion of rights toward the transformation of political subjectivity.

At the normative level, these theories converge on the reimagining of human rights as politics of mutual recognition. Arendt's (2004) insight that rights depend on belonging to a community is not an argument against universality, but a call to construct communities that embody it. The stateless and denationalized expose the inadequacy of both nation-state and cosmopolitan utopianism: the former confines humanity to territory, and the latter abstracts it from responsibility. Resistance must navigate between these poles by cultivating what Iris Marion Young (2011) calls *relational responsibility*, the ethical awareness that freedom and belonging are sustained only through shared vulnerability. Such ethos underpins global movements that challenge statelessness today. The UNHCR's *#IBelong* campaign, while institutional in form, gestures toward this ethical horizon by framing nationality not as a privilege of sovereignty, but as a universal human need. Its success in catalyzing legislative reform in states such as Kenya, Thailand, and Morocco demonstrates that moral arguments can occasionally reconfigure political possibilities.

However, structural resistance requires more than reformist accommodation. It demands a new grammar for the political community—one that displaces the citizen as the sole bearer of rights. Étienne Balibar (2014) envisions such a post-national democracy grounded in *equaliberty*: the simultaneous affirmation of equality and freedom across borders. Citizenship, in this view, must cease to function as the threshold of humanity. Similarly, Benhabib (2004) argued for the *democratic iteration* of rights, a process through which excluded groups reinterpret universal principles to include themselves. This iterative politics, evident in the self-advocacy of stateless communities, expands the meaning of universality by forcing institutions to confront their exclusion. Resistance, thus conceived, is a form of translation that transforms the language of the law from possession to participation.

The enduring challenge lies in translating these theoretical reimaginings into institutional forms. International law continues to privilege state consent; global governance mechanisms remain structurally dependent on the sovereignties they seek to constrain. The paradox is that stateless persons must appeal to states for recognition while contesting the legitimacy of the system that renders them invisible. Arendt (2004) called this the "perplexity of rights": the right to have rights depends on a polity willing to recognize it. Resistance must, therefore, operate simultaneously inside and against law, using legal claims to expose the insufficiency of legality. Strategic litigation before regional human rights courts, such as the Inter-American Court's jurisprudence on denationalization, exemplifies this dual strategy; it affirms the law's authority while demanding its transformation.

Finally, the consequences of exclusionary nationality laws are inseparable from the forms of resistance that they provoke. Each of them produces the other. Exclusion generates the silence that resistance seeks to break; resistance, in turn, reveals the fragility of the categories through which exclusion operates. A stateless person who speaks—who insists on being seen—disrupts the state's fiction of homogeneity. This disruption is the essence of political action in Arendt's sense–the appearance of the new in a world that had rendered it impossible. The task of theory is not to domesticate this appearance but to sustain it—to recognize that in the moment of resistance, a new conception of citizenship is born, one grounded not in inheritance but in responsibility, not in identity, but in relation. The political community that could emerge from this recognition would not eliminate differences, but refuse to weaponize it. Its foundation would be the mutual acknowledgment that, as Arendt wrote, "we are all the same in that we are all unique." To imagine such a community is to resist isolation by the design that nationality law continues to impose on the world.

TOWARD INCLUSIVE CITIZENSHIP

The political, moral, and epistemic crises of exclusionary nationality laws converge on a single paradox: the very institution that promises universal equality, citizenship, operates as the central mechanism through which inequality is reproduced. The modern state's legitimacy rests on the notion that its authority is derived from the collective will of equal members. However, the legal frameworks that define membership remain founded on the asymmetries of descent, privilege, and documentation. The challenge, therefore, is not simply reforming these laws, but reimagining the ontological and ethical foundations of citizenship itself. To move toward inclusion requires dismantling the inherited assumptions that ties belong to ancestry, territory, or algorithmic recognition and replacing them with an understanding of citizenship as a practice of reciprocal responsibility and shared visibility.

The philosophical genealogy of exclusion reveals that the modern state's capacity to define belonging is both its constitutive power and moral limitations. Hannah Arendt's (2004) insight that the loss of citizenship amounts to the loss of the world remains the most concise diagnosis of this paradox. Arendt understood citizenship not as a possession of the individual but as a collective condition that enables the appearance of humanity in public. To be a citizen is to be seen and heard; to be stateless is to inhabit silence in which action cannot resonate. However, the nation-state, by monopolizing the power to bestow or withdraw citizenship, transformed this relational condition into an instrument of control. Thus, the entity most capable of denying it mediates the right to have rights. Any theory of inclusive citizenship should begin by acknowledging this contradiction.

Ayelet Shachar (2009) exposed another dimension of this paradox in her critique of *birthright citizenship*. She describes nationality as a "birthright lottery," a global mechanism for the intergenerational transmission of inequality. Citizenship, she argues, functions like inherited property: it distributes opportunities and protections along arbitrary lines of descent. Reforming nationality laws without challenging this genealogical principle merely redistributes privileges while preserving their hereditary form. The persistence of patrilineal descent in nationality transmission, the naturalization hurdles faced by migrant communities, and the digital codification of belonging through identification systems all reflect the same underlying logicthat legitimacy must be inherited rather than lived. Transcending this logic requires redefining membership as *participation*, not lineage and rights arising from presence, not pedigree.

Tendayi Bloom (2017) extends this critique through her notion of *responsible sovereignty*, which reinterprets the right to nationality as a correlative duty of states. Sovereignty, she argues, must be understood not as the power to exclude, but as an obligation to prevent rightlessness. Sovereign that produces statelessness betrays its moral foundation. In this conception, the legitimacy of state authority depends on its capacity to sustain inclusion rather than manage exclusion. The shift from control to responsibility redefines the political community as a structure of care rather than domination. It also reframes international law: The universal right to nationality becomes enforceable only when sovereignty is conceived as accountable. Bloom's argument suggests that global governance mechanisms should not merely respond to statelessness but should prevent it through collective stewardship, a paradigm that could transform the politics of belonging from possession to co-responsibility.

Theorists of post-national and feminist citizenship similarly call for dismantling the nation-state's monopolization of belonging. Yasemin Soysal's (1994) concept of *post-national membership* identified early manifestations of this shift in Europe, where residence and human rights rather than descent increasingly anchored entitlement. However, as Linda Bosniak (2006) and Nira Yuval-Davis (2011) note, post-national tendencies coexist with resurgent nationalism; the inclusive potential of human rights often falters when confronted with the state's gatekeeping power. Yuval-Davis proposes *transversal belonging* as an ethical and political alternative: a mode of solidarity that acknowledges difference while building community through mutual recognition. Transversality is not assimilation; it is coexistence that is premised on empathy and accountability. Applied to citizenship, it suggests a pluralist model of membership in which individuals belong to multiple overlapping communities—local, national, and global—without a hierarchy among them. This model undermines the exclusionary fiction of a homogenous nation while preserving the social bonds that make rights meaningful.

The possibility of such inclusive citizenship also depends on reconfiguring the epistemology of the law. Law's traditional ontology is classificatory: it defines categories, delineates insiders from outsiders, and stabilizes differences. But as feminist legal scholars such as Kim Rubenstein (2017) and Hilary Charlesworth and Christine Chinkin (2000) have argued, this classificatory impulse embeds the hierarchies it seeks to regulate. A truly inclusive legal order must be dialogical, rather than taxonomic. Rubenstein's notion of *gendered citizenship* and Isin's (2009) concept of *acts of citizenship* converge on this point: citizenship should be seen as an ongoing conversation between the governed and the governing–an iterative process of mutual recognition. In this view, belonging cannot be conferred once and, for all, it must be continually enacted through participation. Therefore, the inclusionary project requires institutionalizing mechanisms for voicespaces where marginalized groups can articulate grievances and reshape the law that defines them.

At the normative level, the transformation of citizenship from inheritance to participation entails a shift in the moral imagination. Étienne Balibar's (2014) idea of *equaliberty*—the inseparability of equality and liberty—captures the essence of this reorientation. Citizenship as equaliberty posits that freedom is meaningful only when universally shared; exclusion, by conferring freedom on some at the expense of others, negates its own premise. Similarly, Young's (2011) theory of *relational responsibility* argues that justice requires acknowledging interdependence: individuals and states are bound in networks of obligation that transcend territorial boundaries. These theories converge on a single principlethat inclusion is not an act of generosity but a condition of justice. Citizenship, redefined through this lens, becomes an ethical relation of reciprocity rather than a juridical contract of rights and duties.

The transformation of this moral horizon demands shifts in institutional practices. Universal birth registration, gender-equal nationality laws, and accessible pathways to naturalization are necessary, but insufficient. As Shachar (2009) warns, reforms that retain the hereditary logic of belonging risk reproduce inequality in new forms. The deeper task is to restructure the social imaginaries that sustain exclusion—the idea that nations must protect purity, citizenship must be scarce, and belonging must be proven. Changing laws without altering imaginations yields only procedural inclusion within unchanged hierarchies. Education, public discourse, and transnational cooperation must therefore become sites of democratic pedagogy, cultivating what Balibar (2014) calls "civic universalism"the recognition that our differences are the condition, not the obstacle, of shared life.

Resistance movements across the world prefigure inclusive citizenship. When stateless women demand the right to confer nationality, when migrants document their presence through art or protest, and when digital rights advocate contest algorithmic exclusion, they enact what Isin (2009) terms *ruptural citizenship*: the creation of political subjects through acts that defy the law's boundaries. These practices illustrate that belonging emerges not from recognition, but from assertion. The political community of the future may thus be imagined as an assemblage of such acts, a living network of mutual acknowledgment. Arendt's notion of *natality*–the capacity to begin anew–captures this generative potential: every act of claiming rights produces a new space of appearance, expanding the world itself. The politics of inclusion, therefore, is the politics of the beginning.

At its most profound level, inclusive citizenship demands a redefinition of the humanity's relationship with the state. The state's historical claim to represent the nation presupposes a unity that has never existed; its promise of equality is limited by its power to exclude. If the twentieth century was defined by the consolidation of national citizenship, the twenty-first century must be defined by its transcendence. The emerging global order, characterized by mobility, digital interconnection, and ecological interdependence, renders isolation impossible and destructive. The crises of displacement, climate migration, and statelessness are not anomalies, but a mirror in which contradictions of sovereignty are revealed. To respond to inclusion is not utopian idealism but pragmatic necessity. As Bloom (2017) notes, states that produce rightlessness undermine the stability of international order itself: exclusion destabilizes belonging everywhere.

In this light, citizenship must be reconceived as an *infrastructure of solidarity*, a framework for sustaining mutual care in a shared world. It must shift from the logic of entitlement to the ethics of relation and from sovereignty to cohabitation. This does not abolish the state, but transforms its purpose: the state becomes the guarantor of inclusion rather than its gatekeeper. Such a transformation requires rethinking global governance beyond humanitarian responses toward a politics of co-responsibility, where inclusion is institutionalized as a collective good. The movement toward universal citizenship is not a negation of diversity, but its affirmation; it acknowledges that equality does not imply sameness and that belonging can be plural without being exclusionary.

Ultimately, the project of inclusive citizenship is a reassertion of the human capacity for renewal. Contrary to the bureaucratic fatalism of exclusionary law, it insists that political life can be remade through imagination and responsibility. The right to have rights, reinterpreted for the twenty-first century, is the right to participate in shaping the conditions of common life. Citizenship so conceived would no longer be a privilege bestowed at birth or verified by database; it would be a shared practice of recognition sustained by equality and care. To move toward such a horizon is to transform the architecture of isolation into a politics of belonging—one in which, to echo Arendt, freedom and plurality become not privileges of the few, but the reality of all.

REFERENCES

Agamben, G. (1998). *Homo sacer: Sovereign power and bare life*. Stanford University Press.

Amnesty International. (2023). *"I don't have a future": Stateless Kuwaitis and the right to education* (Report No. MDE 17/6990/2023). Amnesty International.

Anderson, B. (2013). *Us and them? The dangerous politics of immigration control*. Oxford University Press. DOI: 10.1093/acprof:oso/9780199691593.001.0001

Arendt, H. (2004). *The origins of totalitarianism*. Schocken Books.

Balibar, É. (2014). *Equaliberty: Political Essays* (J.) Ingram, Ed.). Duke University Press.

Benhabib, S. (2004). *The rights of others: aliens, residents, and citizens*. Cambridge University Press. DOI: 10.1017/CBO9780511790799

Benjamin, R. (2019). *Race after Technology: Abolitionist Tools for the New Jim Code*. Polity Press.

Blitz, B. K., & Lynch, M. (Eds.). (2011). *Statelessness and the benefits of citizenship: A comparative study*. Oxford Brookes University/Kingston University. DOI: 10.4337/9781849808996

Blitz, B. K., & Sawyer, C. (Eds.). (2011). *Statelessness in the European Union: Displaced, undocumented, unwanted*. Cambridge University Press. DOI: 10.1017/CBO9780511921438.001

Bloom, T. (2017). *Noncitizenism: recognizing non-citizen capabilities in the world of citizens*. Routledge. DOI: 10.4324/9781315169736

Bosniak, L. (2006). *The citizen and the alien: Dilemmas of contemporary membership*. Princeton University Press. DOI: 10.1515/9781400827510

Bourdieu, P. (1998). *Practical reason: On the theory of action*. Stanford University Press.

Brubaker, R. (1992). *Citizenship and nationhood in France and Germany*. Harvard University Press. DOI: 10.4159/9780674028944

Carens, J. H. (1987). Aliens and citizens: The case for open borders. *The Review of Politics*, *49*(2), 251–273. DOI: 10.1017/S0034670500033817

Charlesworth, H., & Chinkin, C. (2000). *The boundaries of international law: A feminist analysis*. Manchester University Press.

Cheesman, N. (2017). How in Myanmar "national races" came to surpass citizenship and exclude Rohingya. *Journal of Contemporary Asia, 47*(3), 461–483. DOI: 10.1080/00472336.2017.1297476

Crenshaw, K. (1989). Demarginalizing the intersection of race and sex: A Black feminist critique of antidiscrimination doctrine, feminist theory and antiracist politics. *University of Chicago Legal Forum, 1989*(1), 139–167.

Dhakal, S. (2018). Citizenship and belonging: Gendered nationality law in Nepal. *Asian Journal of Women's Studies, 24*(2), 137–158.

Dzenovska, D. (2018). *School of Europeanness: Tolerance and other lessons in political liberalism in Latvia*. Cornell University Press.

Eubanks, V. (2018). *Automating inequality: How high-tech tools profile, police, and punish the poor*. St. Martin's Press.

Fassin, D. (2011). *Humanitarian reason: A moral history of the present*. University of California Press.

Fernández, M. (2020). The politics of denationalization in the Dominican Republic. *Latin American and Caribbean Ethnic Studies, 15*(1), 44–68.

Fredman, S. (2011). *Discrimination law* (2nd ed.). Oxford University Press.

Galbreath, D. J. (2013). Latvia's non-citizens: Between ethnic discrimination and democratic inclusion. *Ethnopolitics, 12*(4), 372–391.

García Peña, L. (2016). *The borders of Dominicanidad: Race, nation, and archives of contradiction*. Duke University Press.

Gelb, A., & Clark, J. (2013). Identification for development: The biometrics revolution. *Center for Global Development Working Paper*, (315).

Gibney, M. J. (2013). A very transcendental power: Denationalization and the liberalization of citizenship in the United Kingdom. *Political Studies, 61*(3), 637–655. DOI: 10.1111/j.1467-9248.2012.00980.x

Hosein, G., & Nyst, C. (2013). Aiding surveillance: an exploration of how development and humanitarian aid initiatives are enabling surveillance in developing countries.

Howard, M. M. (2020). *The politics of citizenship in Europe* (2nd ed.). Cambridge University Press.

Human Rights Watch. (2011). *Prisoners of the past: Kuwaiti Bidun and the burden of statelessness*. Human Rights Watch.

Inter-American Commission on Human Rights. (2015). *Report on the situation of human rights in the Dominican Republic*. Organization of American States.

Isin, E. F. (2009). Citizenship in flux: The figure of the activist citizen. *Subjectivity*, *29*(1), 367–388. DOI: 10.1057/sub.2009.25

Järve, P. (2000). *Ethnic and language policy in Estonia*. European Centre for Minority Issues Working Paper No. 6.

Joppke, C. (2019). *Neoliberal nationalism: Immigration and the rise of the populist right*. Cambridge University Press.

Khera, R. (2019). Aadhaar and the invisible exclusion of India's poor. *Economic and Political Weekly*, *54*(5), 35–40.

Kingston, L. N. (2017). *Fully human: Personhood, citizenship, and rights*. Oxford University Press.

Leider, J. (2018). *Rohingya*. Oxford Research Encyclopedia of Asian History.

Lister, R. (1997). *Citizenship: Feminist perspectives*. Macmillan. DOI: 10.1007/978-1-349-26209-0

Mamdani, M. (1996). *Citizen and subject: Contemporary Africa and the legacy of late colonialism*. Princeton University Press.

Mamdani, M. (2001). *When victims become killers: Colonialism, nativism, and the genocide in Rwanda*. Princeton University Press.

Manby, B. (2016). *Citizenship law in Africa: A comparative study* (3rd ed.). African Minds. DOI: 10.47622/9781928331087

Masiero, S., & Das, S. (2022). The datafied welfare state: Citizenship and social assistance in India. *Information Communication and Society*, *25*(3), 329–346.

Mills, C. W. (1997). *The racial contract*. Cornell University Press.

Nkrumah, J. (2017). Statelessness and racial exclusion in the Dominican Republic. *Georgetown Journal of International Affairs*, *18*(1), 93–103.

Equality Now, & Global Campaign for Equal Nationality Rights. (2025). *Gender-discriminatory nationality laws are fueling poverty and violence against women*. Equality Now.

Posel, D. (1991). *The making of apartheid, 1948–1961: Conflict and compromise*. Clarendon Press. DOI: 10.1093/acprof:oso/9780198273349.001.0001

Privacy International. (2021). *Digital identity and human rights: Building inclusive systems*. Privacy International.

Rubenstein, K. (2017). *Gender, citizenship, and the politics of belonging*. Cambridge University Press.

Said, E. W. (1978). *Orientalism*. Pantheon Books.

Seekings, J., & Nattrass, N. (2005). *Class, race, and inequality in South Africa*. Yale University Press. DOI: 10.12987/yale/9780300108927.001.0001

Shachar, A. (2009). *The birthright lottery: Citizenship and global inequality*. Harvard University Press.

Shahrzad, A., & Kian, A. (2020). Women, nationality, and the politics of belonging in Iran. *International Feminist Journal of Politics*, *22*(3), 369–388.

Southall, R. (2019). *Inequality in South Africa: Nature, causes and responses*. Palgrave Macmillan.

Soysal, Y. N. (1994). *Limits of citizenship: Migrants and postnational membership in Europe*. University of Chicago Press.

UNDP. (2021). *Human development report 2021/2022: Uncertain times, unsettled lives*. United Nations Development Programme.

United Nations. (1948). *Universal declaration of human rights*. United Nations.

United Nations. (1961). *Convention on the reduction of statelessness*. United Nations.

United Nations. (1979). *Convention on the elimination of all forms of discrimination against women*. United Nations.

United Nations. (1989). *Convention on the rights of the child*. United Nations.

United Nations High Commissioner for Refugees. (2014). *IBelong campaign to end statelessness within 10 years*. UNHCR.

United Nations High Commissioner for Refugees. (2023). *Global trends: Forced displacement in 2023*. UNHCR.

van Waas, L. (2008). *Nationality matters: Statelessness under international law*. Intersentia.

Warria, A., & Chikadzi, V. (2022). Statelessness, trauma, and mental well-being: Implications for practice, research, and advocacy. *African Human Mobility Review*, *8*(3), 41–55. DOI: 10.14426/ahmr.v8i3.1135

World Bank. (2018). *Identification for development (ID4D): The state of identification systems in the world.* World Bank.

Young, I. M. (2011). *Responsibility for justice.* Oxford University Press. DOI: 10.1093/acprof:oso/9780195392388.001.0001

Yuval-Davis, N. (2011). *The politics of belonging: Intersectional contestations.* Sage Publications. DOI: 10.4135/9781446251041

Chapter 4

Microeconomic and Psychosocial Determinants of Social Isolation: An Econometric Analysis

Can Mavruk
https://orcid.org/0000-0002-4084-7447
Nigde Omer Halisdemir University, Turkey

ABSTRACT

This study investigates how microeconomic conditions, trust, and neighborhood safety satisfaction, jointly shape dimensions of social isolation in Adana. A combination of binary and ordinal logistic regressions are applied to estimate direct and moderation effects based on survey data (N=972). Results show that higher levels of trust reduce emotional isolation and increase perceived connectedness. Consistent with latent deprivation theory, employment status moderates the effect of trust on social isolation. Microeconomic constraints such as low income, housing cost dissatisfaction, and unemployment increase vulnerabilities to perceived and objective isolation. These findings expand theoretical explanations of social isolation by integrating trust, perceived safety, and material circumstances into a single framework. Policy implications highlight the importance of neighborhood safety, inclusive labor markets, and social infrastructure in reducing the risks of social isolation across the lifespan.

DOI: 10.4018/979-8-3373-5811-6.ch004

INTRODUCTION

Social isolation has emerged as a defining challenge in contemporary societies, particularly as demographic shifts, economic volatility, and urban transformations reshape social life conditions. Defined as a lack of meaningful social contacts or reduced participation in community life, social isolation encompasses multiple dimensions, including objective indicators of network size, subjective experiences of loneliness, and perceptions of belonging or exclusion (Hawkley & Cacioppo, 2010). The consequences of social isolation extend beyond individual distress, with evidence linking it to adverse health outcomes such as depression, cardiovascular disease, and premature mortality (Holt-Lunstad et al., 2015). At a societal level, widespread isolation erodes social capital, undermines civic participation, and increases demands on welfare and healthcare systems (Putnam, 2000).

While research has extensively documented the detrimental effects of isolation, less attention has been given to the interplay of microeconomic and psychosocial determinants. Existing studies emphasize the protective role of social trust and neighborhood safety in fostering social connectedness (Lancee & Dronkers, 2011; Sampson, 2012). Some exceptions note that trust mediates the effects of neighborhood disadvantage on social participation (Kawachi et al., 1999), while others show that financial stress amplifies the consequences of low trust on health and well-being (Layte & Whelan, 2002). At the same time, economic precarity manifested in unemployment, low income, and insecure housing remains a persistent risk factor for social withdrawal (Gallie et al., 2003). However, most analyses treat these domains in isolation rather than examining their interactions. Systematic examinations of how trust, safety, and microeconomic constraints jointly shape multiple dimensions of isolation remain scarce.

This study addresses that gap through a comprehensive analytical strategy that combines regression and moderation models, integrating microeconomic and psychosocial perspectives in analyzing the determinants of social isolation. Specifically, the study investigates the direct effects of microeconomic constraints, trust, and neighborhood safety satisfaction on isolation outcomes; and the moderating role of microeconomic factors (employment) in shaping how trust influences social isolation. The approach draws on Putnam's (2000) theory of social capital, which emphasizes trust and reciprocity as foundations of collective life, and Jahoda's (1982) latent deprivation model, which identifies employment as central to maintaining social integration and identity.

By adopting a multidimensional framework, the study aims to advance a more nuanced understanding of how both material and psychosocial conditions contribute to social isolation forms. In doing so, this study contributes to ongoing debates in sociology, public health, and social policy about the structural and relational roots of social exclusion.

LITERATURE REVIEW

Research on social isolation has evolved from individual-level explanations toward multidimensional frameworks that integrate structural, economic, and psychosocial factors. This section reviews the literature on key determinants—trust, economic conditions, and health—before synthesizing the theoretical advancements and identifying the specific research gap this study aims to fill.

Psychosocial and Neighborhood Determinants

A robust line of inquiry establishes trust and neighborhood context as critical determinants of social connectedness. Seminal work by Hawkley & Cacioppo (2010) elucidated the cognitive, behavioral, and physiological mechanisms linking loneliness to diminished physical and mental well-being, establishing a critical distinction between objective and subjective isolation. The profound health impact is further underscored by meta-analytic evidence; Holt-Lunstad et al. (2015) demonstrated that social isolation, loneliness, and living alone significantly increase mortality risk, with effects consistent across genders and world regions. Recent global data confirms the urgency of this issue, showing a 13.4% increase in social isolation prevalence between 2009 and 2024, a trend exacerbated by socioeconomic disparities (Fuller-Rowell et al., 2025).

The neighborhood environment serves as a crucial arena where trust is built or eroded. Analyzing Dutch data, Lancee & Dronkers (2011) revealed that the impact of diversity is multidimensional; while ethnic and religious diversity had divergent effects on native and immigrant groups, economic diversity uniformly fostered trust. Similarly, Sampson (2012), in his landmark study of Chicago, demonstrated that collective efficacy and perceived safety are foundational for local engagement and resilience against isolation. Recent studies continue to affirm these associations. Kim et al. (2020), using Korean community health data, found that neighborhood cohesion reduces isolation by strengthening mutual trust, while Taylor et al. (2023), analyzing a U.S. national sample of Black older adults, confirmed that neighborhood conditions and sociodemographic factors are significant predictors of social isolation. The COVID-19 pandemic highlighted these psychosocial mechanisms, with Chung et al. (2023) finding that loneliness, interpersonal mistrust, and poor numeracy skills were key predictors of fear, with effects varying by age and gender.

Economic and Employment-Related Factors

Economic precarity is a well-established driver of isolation risk. Early longitudinal research by Gallie et al. (2003) using the European Community Household Panel provided strong evidence for a "vicious cycle" in which unemployment leads to poverty, which in turn hinders re-employment. However, their findings complicated the social exclusion model, showing that social isolation's role was contingent on national cultural patterns rather than a direct consequence of joblessness.

More recent analyses have quantified the staggering economic burden of isolation. Casal et al. (2025) estimated the tangible costs of loneliness in Spain at €14.1 billion (1.2% of GDP), primarily from productivity losses and healthcare consumption. Similarly, Lyu et al. (2024) established longitudinal associations between economic precarity, isolation, and mortality across OECD countries. The link between socio-economic strain and isolation is also mediated by psychosocial factors; a 2025 study found social isolation partially mediated the relationship between stigma and reduced work ability in stroke survivors, accounting for 22% of the effect (Kotozaki, 2025).

Theoretical Advancements and Health Consequences

The field's theoretical development is increasingly capturing the complexity of isolation. Cornwell & Waite (2009), using U.S. national data, operationalized a crucial distinction between *social disconnectedness* (objective network characteristics) and *perceived isolation* (subjective loneliness), finding that while both predict poor physical health, perceived isolation is the primary pathway to poor mental health. This multidimensional understanding is advanced by the proposed "Resilience and Social Isolation Model of Aging (RSIMA)" (Wister et al., 2025), which frames isolation as a dynamic process on a continuum.

In aging populations, isolation is a critical public health concern. Studies have linked chronic loneliness to cognitive decline and dementia risk (Guarnera et al., 2023), while also highlighting the protective role of digital tools (Latikka et al., 2021). Recent research further disentangles these pathways; a 2025 UK Biobank study found loneliness and social isolation to be independent risk factors for depression, a finding complemented by qualitative insights that their combination creates a particularly harmful feedback loop (Wan et al., 2025).

Identified Research Gaps and This Study's Contribution

Despite this progress, critical gaps remain. First, studies often examine economic or psychosocial factors in isolation, rarely investigating their interactive effects—for instance, integrating the trust mechanism identified by Kawachi et al. (1999) with labor market variables. Second, the evidence base is heavily skewed toward Western European and North American contexts, leaving emerging economies profoundly underrepresented.

This Western-centric focus is mirrored within Turkey's research landscape. Although the country faces high exposure to isolation due to urbanization and economic volatility, empirical analyses are limited and fragmented. Existing studies primarily focus on scale validations (Çevik Özdemir & Ayran, 2025; Keskin & Lajunen, 2024), specific clinical populations (Eren et al., 2025; Kaşak et al., 2022), or rural-urban comparisons (Gümüş Demir & Yılmaz, 2024). While research exists in cities like Mersin and Bursa, major industrial and agricultural hubs central to Turkey's economy, such as Adana, remain critically understudied.

Consequently, this study addresses a triple gap by:

1. Shifting the focus to the understudied urban context of Adana, Turkey.
2. Moving beyond siloed approaches to integrate microeconomic indicators (income, employment, housing) with psychosocial variables (trust, safety) in a unified econometric model.
3. Employing a multidimensional analytical framework that simultaneously assesses perceived (PSI), emotional (ESI), and objective social isolation (OSI).

This research advances the literature by (a) analyzing these multiple dimensions of isolation, (b) jointly modeling their microeconomic and psychosocial determinants, and (c) explicitly testing the moderating effects of employment status and neighborhood safety. In doing so, it provides novel theoretical and empirical insights into the trust-isolation dynamic within a non-Western, urban-regional setting.

Why Adana?

This study focuses on Adana for three interrelated reasons (demographic, structural, and cultural) that make it uniquely suited to analyze the effects of trust on isolation through the interaction of perceptions of neighborhood safety and employment.

With a population exceeding 2.2 million, Adana is one of Türkiye's largest metropolitan regions and is characterized by sharp internal disparities among industrial, agricultural, and service sector districts. Simultaneously embodying both urban density and rural proximity, Adana offers a microcosm of Türkiye's broader socioeconomic heterogeneity. This diversity allows for a comparative analysis of trust and social isolation across different neighborhood types within the same metropolitan framework.

As one of Türkiye's oldest industrial and agricultural centers, Adana has long relied on informal trust networks (kinship, neighborhood ties, and community associations), particularly during periods of economic recession. While these forms of "bonding" social capital (Putnam, 2000) have historically compensated for the lack of weak formal institutions, they can also lead to exclusionary effects that deepen emotional or social isolation for certain groups (Poortinga, 2012; Yang and Victor, 2011).

In recent years, Adana has experienced industrial restructuring, urban migration, and fluctuating employment opportunities. These factors increase the importance of institutional trust in municipal government, welfare provision, and access to healthcare as a moderating factor in the trust-isolation relationship. The city's mixed governance performance and socio-spatial fragmentation provide theoretically fertile ground for examining how different forms of trust (personal, social, institutional) interact with indicators of perceived isolation (emotional, social, general).

Therefore, Adana is not only a useful research area but also a strategic analytical context within which Türkiye's broader trust-isolation dynamics can be distilled and observed within a single metropolitan setting.

Conceptual Framework

This study is guided by an integrated framework that combines social capital theory, human capital theory, and insights from behavioral economics to explain the multifaceted nature of social isolation.

Social capital theory posits that the structure and quality of social relationships provide tangible and intangible resources that enhance well-being and facilitate collective action (Bourdieu, 1986; Putnam, 2000). Central to this work is the concept of social trust, a psychological state that involves the willingness to accept vulnerability based on positive expectations about another's intentions or behavior (Rousseau et al., 1998). This encompasses generalized trust, the belief that most people in one's community or society are fundamentally trustworthy, honest, and benevolent (Uslaner, 2002). This is distinct from specialized trust (trust in familiar individuals) and is a cornerstone of social cohesion. It also encompasses the cognitive mechanism by which trust reduces the perceived risk and cognitive load of social interaction, making it safer and more rewarding (Helliwell & Putnam, 2004), and its behavioral consequences; for example, higher trust leads to stronger, more supportive social ties by promoting reciprocity (the mutual exchange of favors and support) and cooperation. Conversely, insecurity acts as a psychological barrier, triggering social withdrawal and hypervigilance, which directly increases perceived isolation (Paxton, 2007).

In the Turkish context, traditional, kin-based trust has historically been a powerful buffer against isolation (Kağıtçıbaşı, 2007). However, urban migration and the atomization of family structures have eroded these informal networks, making generalized trust a more critical, yet increasingly fragile resource for social connection (Aytaç & Rankin, 2009).

Human capital theory emphasizes how individuals' resources, specifically education, health, and economic assets, enable effective social and economic participation (Becker, 1965).

From a psychological standpoint, education enhances cognitive and social skills, thereby increasing self-efficacy and the capacity to navigate complex social environments. Similarly, stable employment and income provide not merely the financial means for social engagement but also furnish a key source of identity, regular social contact, and a structured daily routine. Conversely, resource deprivation manifested through unemployment and income insecurity erodes an individual's material and psychological capacity to invest in social participation. This erosion can lead to the atrophy of social skills and a diminished sense of self-worth, creating a self-reinforcing cycle of withdrawal. Furthermore, housing instability and overcrowding act as critical constraints, limiting the physical privacy and mental space necessary for initiating and sustaining meaningful relationships.

Behavioral economics provides a micro-level lens on how cognitive constraints shape social decision-making (Kahneman & Tversky, 1979; Mullainathan & Shafir, 2013). Bounded rationality leads individuals to rely on mental shortcuts, which can result in suboptimal social choices like misinterpreting cues or avoiding unfamiliar interactions. Furthermore, a scarcity mindset—triggered by financial or time poverty—captures cognitive resources, creating a "tunneling" effect that prioritizes immediate pressures over long-term social investments, causing social participation to be neglected (Shah et al., 2012). Finally, unsafe neighborhoods function by heightening the perceived risk and cost of engagement, further discouraging social interaction.

This exacerbates avoidance behaviors and reinforces a psychological state of threat vigilance, making social outreach feel too risky (Ross & Jang, 2000; Sampson, 2012). This can create a behavioral feedback loop, where loneliness itself drains the motivation and cognitive energy required to initiate contact, thereby deepening isolation (Kang et al., 2025).

Figure 1. General Conceptual Framework Integrating Social Capital, Human Capital, and Behavioral Economics Perspectives on Social Isolation

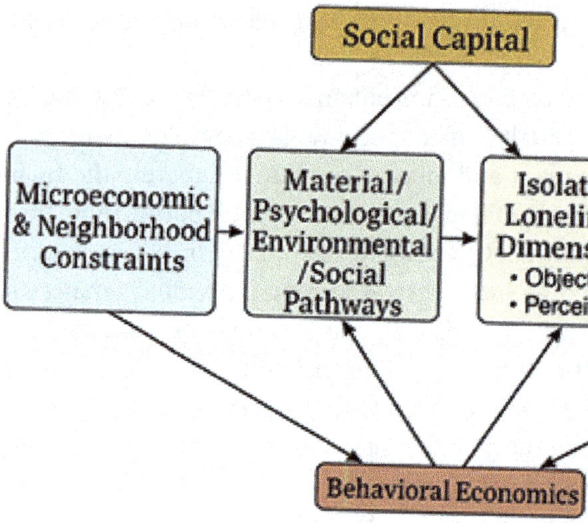

Note: This framework is drawn using Python

As illustrated in Figure 1, the framework adopted here integrates the theoretical perspectives of social capital, human capital, and behavioral economics. Social capital is operationalized through generalized trust, which is hypothesized to directly reduce perceived (PSI) and emotional (ESI) isolation, while also buffering the adverse effects of economic and neighborhood constraints (Bjørnskov, 2007; Putnam, 2000). Concurrently, human capital factors (education, income, employment) determine the structural opportunities for social participation, and behavioral responses to scarcity and risk explain psychological withdrawal. Together, these mechanisms shape the three primary outcomes of this study: objective isolation - the tangible lack of social contacts and integration (Cornwell & Waite, 2009), perceived loneliness - the cognitive awareness and dissatisfaction with one's social network size, often synonymous with loneliness (Peplau & Perlman, 1982), and emotional isolation - the affective distress arising from a lack of intimate, confiding relationships (Weiss, 1973). The critical need for this multidimensional approach is validated by evidence showing these dimensions have independent pathways to negative health outcomes, including depression and mortality (Cacioppo & Cacioppo, 2018; Holt-Lunstad et al., 2015; Wan et al., 2025).

Empirical Operationalization: The Adana Model and Hypotheses

Guided by the general conceptual framework in Figure 1, this study develops a specific empirical model to examine how trust, neighborhood safety, and economic constraints shape the three dimensions of isolation: perceived (PSI), emotional (ESI), and objective (OSI). Figure 2 operationalizes this by modeling trust as a multilayered construct, illustrating how personal, social, and institutional trust theoretically influences isolation through distinct pathways.

However, for the purpose of this empirical analysis, the focus is narrowed to general interpersonal trust (measured as "trust in people in general"). This specific construct is positioned within the broader model to test its direct and moderating effects on isolation.

The empirical design implements this focused approach using survey data from Adana residents. The dataset includes validated indicators of general interpersonal trust, perceived safety, employment status, and the three isolation outcomes (PSI, ESI, OSI). This allows for multivariate regression models that test both the direct effects of trust and its interaction with the contextual moderators—neighborhood safety and employment status—thereby assessing how local conditions and economic security alter the relationship between trust and different types of isolation.

Figure 2. Empirical Model Linking Trust, Moderators, and Social Isolation Outcomes in Adana

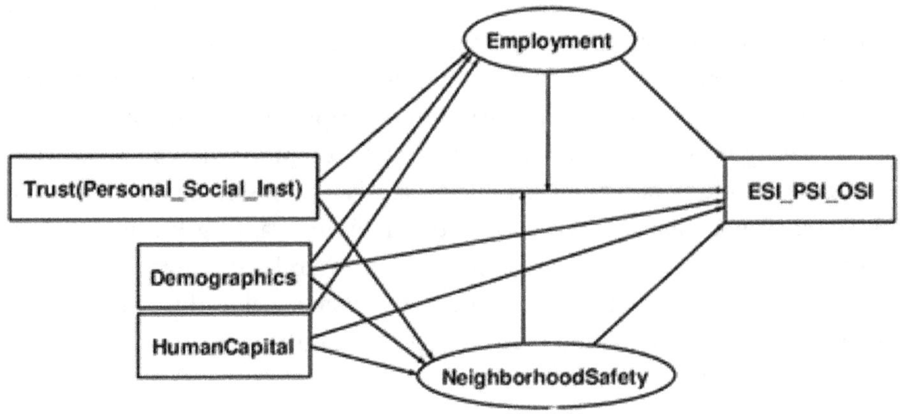

Note: This model is constructed using Stata's Structural Equation Modelling. The empirical analysis focuses only on general interpersonal trust, measured as "trust in people in general." Inst: Institutional

As summarized in Figure 2, this study narrows its focus to general interpersonal trust. The empirical design implements this focused approach using survey data from

Adana residents. This allows for multivariate regression models that test both the direct effects of trust and its interaction with the contextual moderators.

The conceptual model depicts hypothesized pathways from trust to isolation, moderated by neighborhood safety and employment status. The model integrates relational and structural dimensions specific to Adana's socioeconomic and institutional context (adapted from Weiss, 1973; Putnam, 2000; Cornwell & Waite, 2009; Holt-Lunstad et al., 2015).

Based on the models, the hypotheses are stated as follows.

> **H1:** Higher levels of general interpersonal trust will be directly associated with lower levels of (a) PSI, (b) ESI, and (c) OSI.
> **H2:** The negative association between trust and social isolation will be stronger for employed individuals than for unemployed individuals.
> **H3:** The negative association between trust and social isolation will be stronger for individuals reporting higher neighborhood safety satisfaction.

MATERIALS AND METHODS

Data and Sample

The empirical analysis is based on original survey data collected in 2018 from 972 adult respondents aged 19 to 67 living in the metropolitan province of Adana, Turkey. Adana was deliberately selected as the research site because it exemplifies a transitional urban environment where industrial and agricultural sectors, informal employment, and neighborhood-level inequalities coexist. As Turkey's fifth-largest city, Adana combines dense urban districts and peripheral settlements, offering a distinctive setting in which to examine how microeconomic constraints, neighborhood safety, and interpersonal trust jointly shape experiences of social isolation. The city's heterogeneous social composition including varying levels of income, education, and migration backgrounds provides a natural laboratory for exploring the interaction of structural and psychosocial factors central to this study.

The data were obtained using a cross-sectional convenience sampling design, capturing a broad range of demographic and economic profiles. The survey instrument included validated measures of perceived (PSI), emotional (ESI), and objective (OSI) isolation, alongside items on generalized trust ("To what extent do you trust people in general?"), housing satisfaction, employment status, income adequacy, and neighborhood safety. These variables were selected to operationalize the study's conceptual model (Figure 1), linking microeconomic and psychosocial determinants of social isolation.

At the time of survey, formal ethical review procedures were not yet standardized in local institutions; however, participation was voluntary, anonymous, and conducted with informed consent. Respondents were briefed on confidentiality and the academic purpose of the study. The resulting dataset offers a representative urban case that integrates economic and psychosocial indicators, providing a robust empirical foundation for the multivariate analyses presented in the following sections.

Response Variables

Social isolation was measured using objective and subjective dimensions. Objective indicator is frequency of social contacts (family, friends), using a survey question "How often do you see friends or relatives who don't live with you?" Individuals were categorized as socially isolated if they reported no social contact frequency in the last two weeks. This is measured with ordinal response categories are 1 = no contact, 2 = less than once a month, 3 = 1-3 times a month, 4 = 1-2 times a week and 5 =every day.

Subjective dimension includes feeling alone, disconnected, or lacking companionship assessed using Ryff's (1989) negative relation loneliness (PSI) and Bradburn's (1969) negative affect loneliness (ESI).

ESI was assessed using a single-item measure. Participants were asked, "Did you feel very lonely or remote from other people over the past few weeks?" Responses were dichotomized (1 = Yes, 0= No).

PSI was measured using a single survey item "I often feel lonely because I have few close friends to share my problems with" with five ordinal response categories from 1=strongly disagree to 5=strongly agree, where higher values indicate greater PSI.

Explanatory Variables

The set of explanatory variables reflects both microeconomic and contextual determinants. Microeconomic factors include personal income (log-transformed or categorical) and employment status (dummy variables for employed and retired, with unemployed as the reference). Housing and neighborhood quality are measured by perceived neighborhood safety satisfaction, categorized into low, moderate, and high safety perceptions. Demographic controls include age (categorized into life-course groups) and gender. These variables align with prior research demonstrating that economic resources, labor market participation, and neighborhood conditions jointly structure opportunities for social connection (Cornwell & Waite, 2009; Kawachi & Berkman, 2001).

Income is measured using individual monthly income in TL ("Your individual monthly income?"). This data was updated from 2018 to 2025 based on (Reported

Income)/(2018 minimum wage)*(2025 minimum wage) and converted into binary using minimum wage (0=less than or equal to 22020 and 1=above 22020 TL) and into three categories using minimum wage and poverty levels (1=less than or equal to 22K, 2=greater than 22K and less than or equal to 55K, 3=greater than 55K).

Employment data originally was categorized as paid-income earner (employed formal/informal), currently unemployed, unemployed for less than 12 months, out of work due to illness or disability and economically inactive (retired, homemaker, unpaid family worker, student). Economically inactive categories except retired are combined into unemployed category, dropping categories to three (0 = unemployed, 1 = employed, 2 = retired; unemployed as base).

Financial problems were categorized from 1=strongly disagree to 5=strongly agree based on single item "I am having financial problems"

Housing stability was measured using tenure status (owned, rented, public housing, informal occupancy), and residential moves within the past one year.

Perceived neighborhood safety is measured by respondents' satisfaction with neighborhood safety and perceptions of local crime/disorder (To what extent are you satisfied with the safety of your neighborhood?), 5-point scaled (1=very dissatisfied, 2=dissatisfied, 3=neither nor, 4= satisfied, 5=very satisfied).

Neighborhood disturbance level is measured by respondents' experience ("How much do the problems you encounter bother you?" (1 = bothers a lot, 2 = bothers, 3 = neither nor, 4 = does not bother, 5 = does not bother at all, 6 = does not bother because it is not a problem).

Demographics include age (18-27, 28-37, 38-47, 48-57, 58-67) and gender (male or female).

Human capital includes self-rated health based on "how is your health in general" (1=very poor, 2=poor, 3=moderate, 4=good, 5=very good) and education based on "what is your educational background" (1=primary-middle school, 2=high school, 3=associates, 4=bachelors, 5=graduate degree).

Social capital variable is human trust measured using a standard item on generalized trust ("To what extent do you trust people in general?"), scaled (1=I do not trust at all, 2=I do not trust, 3=neither nor, 4=I trust, 5=I trust very much).

Econometric Model Specification

Logit models were estimated for each isolation dimension, testing direct effects of trust and interaction terms with neighborhood safety and employment status. In moderation (interaction) models, human trust and employment status are potential moderators with microeconomic constraints. Effect sizes were reported as unstandardized coefficients with confidence intervals.

Interaction terms tested whether trust's effects vary across categories of employment status and neighborhood safety satisfaction. Independent variable of interest is human trust (social capital), entered as a categorical predictor. Control variables are microeconomic constraints (income, employment), neighborhood safety (ordered categories), housing status (rent, owner, public, other). Binary and ordered logistic regressions are used to estimate associations between microeconomic conditions and isolation, and interactions testing whether microeconomic and neighborhood constraints condition the effect of trust on isolation.

To examine the association between these predictors and emotional isolation, binary logistic regression analysis was conducted. The probability that individual i reports "very lonely and isolated from other people" (Y_i=1) was modeled as$P(Y_i = 1|X_i) = \frac{1}{1+e^{-X\beta}}$ where Y_i is binary ESI outcome, X_i is vector of predictors for individual i and β is vector of parameters to be estimated. In log-odds form, with interacting variable X_j added, the model is represented as

$$ln\left(\frac{P(Y_i = 1|X_i)}{1 - P(Y_i = 1|X_i)}\right) = \beta_0 + \beta_1 X_{i1} + \beta_2 X_{i2} + \ldots + \beta_p X_{ip} + \beta_j X_j + \beta_{jk} X_{ij} X_{ik} \quad (1)$$

Where:

- $X_i = \left(X_{i1}, X_{i2}, \ldots, X_{ip}\right)$ is the vector of all predictors for individual i.
- $X_{ij}X_{ik}$ are the two specific predictors involved in the interaction (e.g., "human trust" and "employment status")
- β_0 is the intercept.
- $\beta_0, \beta_1, \beta_2, \ldots, \beta_p$ are the coefficients for the main effects.
- β_{jk} is the coefficient for the interaction term $X_{ij}X_{ik}$.

Given the ordered nature of the dependent variable, an ordinal logistic regression model was employed to estimate the association between each predictor and the odds of reporting greater social isolation. The ordinal logistic model assumes proportional odds across outcome thresholds.

Formally, the probability that individual i reports a level of social isolation less than or equal to category j is modeled as $P(Y_i \leq j|X_i) = \frac{1}{1+e^{-\kappa_j + X\beta}}$ for j=1,…, J-1, where Y_i is social isolation response for individual i, κ_j cut point (threshold) parameter for category j, X_i vector of predictors for individual i, and β vector of coefficients for the predictors. The model estimates a single coefficient vector β that applies across all cumulative splits of the ordinal outcome, reflecting the proportional odds assumption.

In log-odds form, the model is

$$ln\left(\frac{P(Y \leq j|X_i)}{1 - P(Y \leq j|X_i)}\right) = ln\left(\frac{P(Y \leq j|X_i)}{P(Y > j|X_i)}\right) = \kappa_j - \left(\beta_1 X_1 + \ldots + \beta_p X_p + \beta_k X_k + \beta_{pk} X_p X_k\right) \quad (2)$$

The interaction coefficient β_{pk} tells that the effect of X_p on social contact frequency depends on the level of X_k. The proportional odds assumption implies that the coefficients are constant across all thresholds j, indicating that the effect of predictors is consistent across different cut points of the outcome.

The study runs ordinal logistic models for OSI and PSI.

To enhance interpretability for policy and practice, Average Marginal Effects (AMEs) were computed following the logistic regression estimation. For each predictor, AME for the probability of reporting j^{th} category of social isolation can be estimated as

$$AME_j = \frac{1}{N}\sum_{i=1}^{N}\frac{\partial P(Y_i = j|X_i)}{\partial X_{ij}} \quad (3)$$

Where N is sample size (972). The estimated coefficients represent log-odds of being in outcome *j* relative to the baseline. AMEs quantify the average change in predicted probabilities of each isolation outcome with respect to a one-unit change in the predictor (continuous variable or a discrete change from the reference category for categorical variables), while holding other variables constant (Train, 2009). This approach allows the results to be interpreted as percentage point changes in loneliness probability associated with each predictor, facilitating clearer policy and practical implications. AME provides a direct and policy-relevant measure of effect size, especially in contexts where raw log-odds are difficult to interpret.

Robust standard errors for the marginal effects were calculated using the delta method, and statistical significance was evaluated at the 0.05 level. Variance inflation factors (VIF) were monitored to assess multicollinearity among microeconomic predictors. Sensitivity analyses were conducted using alternative social isolation definitions and stratification by age and gender. All models were estimated using maximum likelihood method. Statistical significance was evaluated at the 0.05 level, with robustness checks for multicollinearity and alternative model specifications.

No multicollinearity issues were detected (all VIF<5, mean VIF=1.29) in the logit model. The Hosmer-Lemeshow test ($p > 0.05$) indicated good model fit, while link tests did not suggest specification errors. Link test indicated _hat ($p<0.0001$, model predicts well) and _hatsq ($p=0.35>0.05$, no specification error). No outliers were detected. Residual analyses and leverage diagnostics were conducted to identify potential outliers or influential observations. All diagnostics supported the robustness of the logistic regression model. For ordinal logit models, the proportional odds (parallel lines) assumption was assessed using the Brant test. Prob(chi^2) was greater than 0.05, indicating the assumption was not violated. Joint Wald test confirmed significance of interaction effects with Prob(chi^2) less than 0.001.

RESULTS

Descriptive Statistics

Table 1 represents frequency distribution of the variables. Substantial variation across dimensions of social isolation is observed. Approximately one-fifth of respondents (20%) experience objective isolation, over half (51.7%) report emotional isolation, and 57.4% perceive themselves as socially isolated. The sample is predominantly women (56%), and the majority are between 18–27 years old (74%), with 13% aged 28–37. Most respondents hold a bachelor's degree (75.6%) and report good health status (81%). In terms of employment, 68% are unemployed, 29% employed, and 3.4% retired. The socioeconomic profile indicates that 76.6% have incomes below the minimum wage (22K), and an additional 22.6% report income between the minimum wage (22K) and poverty line (55K). Financial difficulties are salient, as 42% agree or strongly agree that they face affordability problems. Housing constraints are also evident: half of respondents (50%) are dissatisfied or very dissatisfied with housing costs, 64% rent their homes, 29% own, and 25% have changed residence in recent years. Regarding social trust and safety, 44.4% report no trust in other people, while 36% are dissatisfied or very dissatisfied with neighborhood safety.

Table 1. Frequencies and Percentages of Variables (N = 972)

Variable	n	%	Variable	n	%	Variable	n	%	Variable	n	%
PSI			**ESI**			**OSI**			**Age**		
Strongly Disagree	78	8.0	No	470	48.3	Never	21	2.2	18-27	721	74.2
Disagree	168	17.3	Yes	502	51.7	<1 a month	173	17.8	28-37	128	13.2
Neither Nor	168	17.3				1-3 times/month	353	36.3	38-47	64	6.6
Agree	280	28.8				1-2 times/week	332	34.2	48-57	52	5.3
Strongly Agree	278	28.6				Everyday	93	9.6	58-67	7	0.7
Gender			**Education**			**Employment**			**Income Category**		
Women	543	55.9	Primary-Middle	73	7.5	Unemployed	660	67.9	< Min. wage	744	76.6
Men	429	44.1	High School	96	9.9	Employed	279	28.7	Min. wage<< poverty	220	22.6

continued on following page

Table 1. Continued

Variable	n	%	Variable	n	%	Variable	n	%	Variable	n	%
			Associate	40	4.0	Retired	33	3.4	> Poverty line	8	0.8
			Bachelor	735	76.0						
			MSc-PhD	28	2.9						
Human Trust			**Nbhd Safety**			**Housing Status**			**Housing Cost**		
No trust	432	44.4	Very dissatisfied	141	14.5	Owner	284	29.2	Very dissatisfied	230	23.7
Neutral	382	39.3	Dissatisfied	210	21.6	Rent	619	63.7	Dissatisfied	253	26.0
Trust	158	16.3	Neither Nor	267	27.5	Public	13	1.3	Neither Nor	239	24.6
			Satisfied	274	28.2	Other	56	5.8	Satisfied	195	20.0
			Very satisfied	80	8.2				Very satisfied	55	5.7
Financial Prob.			**Residence Change**			**Health Status**					
Strongly Disagree	148	15.2	Strongly Disagree	450	46.3	Poor	19	2.0			
Disagree	157	16.2	Disagree	191	19.7	Neutral	165	17.0			
Neither Nor	260	26.8	Neither Nor	90	9.3	Good	788	81.0			
Agree	218	22.4	Agree	130	13.4						
Strongly Agree	189	19.4	Strongly Agree	111	11.4						

Correlations

The correlation analysis provides preliminary insights into the bivariate associations among social isolation measures and the individual- and household-level covariates. Table 2 shows Spearman correlations between the variables which confirm theoretically expected relationships. Economic stress (low income, financial problems) and residential instability predict greater loneliness and weaker connectedness. Human trust (social capital), neighborhood safety, and good health (human capital) show protective associations. Different isolation dimensions are only weakly correlated, supporting the importance of analyzing them separately.

Table 2. Spearman Correlations

	Variable	1	2	3	4	5	6	7	8	9	10	11	12	13	14
1	PSI	—													
2	ESI	-0.19***	—												
3	OSI	0.04	-0.08**	—											

continued on following page

Table 2. Continued

	Variable	1	2	3	4	5	6	7	8	9	10	11	12	13	14
4	Age	-0.02	-0.12***	-0.06	—										
5	Gender	−0.00	−0.09**	0.03	-0.03	—									
6	Edu	0.01	0.08*	0.01	-0.49***	-0.01	—								
7	Employment	0.03	-0.12***	-0.00	0.39***	0.20***	-0.26***	—							
8	Income	0.07*	-0.15***	-0.04	0.31***	0.16***	-0.11*	0.59***	—						
9	Health	0.14***	−0.11***	0.11***	-0.17***	-0.00	0.17***	-0.03	0.01	—					
10	Nbhd Safety	0.02	−0.12***	0.12***	0.04	0.01	0.05	0.02	0.04	0.11***	—				
11	Housing Cost	0.08*	-0.11***	0.07*	0.08*	-0.06	-0.00	0.05	0.05	0.10**	0.50***	—			
12	Human Trust	0.13***	-0.09**	0.11***	-0.04	0.05	0.05	0.04	0.01	0.21***	0.20***	0.15***	—		
13	Housing Status	0.01	-0.07*	0.05	-0.07*	-0.08*	0.04	-0.11***	-0.08**	0.06	0.03	0.13***	0.05	—	
14	Money Prob.	-0.23***	0.15***	-0.00	-0.02	-0.02	0.03	-0.08*	-0.15***	-0.09**	0.06	-0.08*	-0.01	-0.04	—
15	Residence Change	-0.17***	0.08*	-0.04	-0.04	0.09**	0.03	-0.03	0.06	0.02	0.01	-0.06	-0.03	-0.05	0.05

Note: $^*p<0.05$, $^{**}p<0.01$, $^{***}p<0.001$

Model Results

OSI Results

Table 3 shows that trust is significantly associated with OSI outcomes. OSI displays both convergences and divergences with PSI and ESI. Higher trust and neighborhood safety are associated with more frequent contact, particularly for those who are satisfied with their local environment. Higher trust reduces the probability of reporting the lowest isolation categories (−0.3 pp for OSI 1; −2.1 pp for OSI 2; −1.2 pp for OSI 3), while increasing the likelihood of higher isolation responses (+2.3 pp for OSI 4; +1.3 pp for OSI 5). This pattern contrasts with the protective role of trust observed in PSI and ESI, suggesting that in the case of objective isolation, trust may align more with selective social engagement (fewer but stronger ties) than with sheer contact frequency. Neighborhood safety satisfaction is also strongly predictive. Being moderately satisfied (vs. not satisfied) decreases the probability of low-isolation responses (−4.7 pp for OSI 2; −3.1 pp for OSI 3) while increasing higher-isolation outcomes (+5.4 pp for OSI 4; +3.1 pp for OSI 5). Similarly, full satisfaction amplifies this pattern, producing a −5.4 pp and −2.9 pp decrease in OSI 2 and OSI 3, and a +6.1 pp and +3.0 pp increase in OSI 4 and OSI 5.

Table 3. Objective Social Isolation AME

	Ologit	**OSI 1**	**OSI 2**	**OSI 3**	**OSI 4**	**OSI 5**
	Coef	dy/dx (se)	dy/dx (se)	dy/dx (se)	dy/dx (se)	dy/dx (se)
Nbhd Safety Satisfaction x trust_c		—	—	—	—	—
(x moderately satisfied)	0.111 (0.163)					
(x satisfied)	-0.117 (0.139)					
Emplotment x trust_c		—	—	—	—	—
(x employed)	-0.166 (0.126)					
(x retired)	0.527 (0.586)					
trust_c	0.187 (0.077)*	-0.003 (0.016)*	-0.021 (0.009)*	-0.012 (0.005)*	0.023 (0.010)*	0.013 (0.005)*
Log(income)	0.030 (0.058)	-0.001 (0.001)	-0.004 (0.009)	-0.002 (0.006)	0.004 (0.010)	0.002 (0.006)
Employment (retired vs unemployed)		-0.009 (0.007)	-0.064 (0.051)	-0.059 (0.063)	0.074 (0.057)	0.057 (0.064)
Health status (moderate vs poor)		0.008 (0.011)	0.048 (0.072)	0.020 (0.043)	-0.052 (0.082)	-0.024 (0.044)
Nbhd Safety Satisfaction						
(moderate vs not)	0.357 (0.171)*		-0.047 (0.021)*	-0.031 (0.014)*	0.054 (0.024)*	0.031 (0.014)*
(satisfied vs not)	0.337 (0.171)*	-0.008 (0.003)*	-0.054 (0.020)**	-0.029 (0.012)*	0.061 (0.023)**	0.030 (0.012)*
Pseudo R2= 0.0126						

Note: *p<0.05, **p<0.01, ***p<0.001. dy/dx is the percentage point (pp) change in the predicted probability of objective (frequency of contact) loneliness when the variable changes from the base category (no loneliness) to the indicated category. Results are from ordinal logistic regression using the dataset (N = 972).

Employment status also matters. Compared to unemployed respondents, retirees are somewhat less integrated into daily contact networks. Income effects are positive but weaker than in PSI or ESI. Interaction effects suggest that trust's protective role is conditional: it reduces OSI risk more strongly in safe neighborhoods but is less effective where safety satisfaction is low.

Figures 2 and 3 present predictive margins of neighborhood safety satisfaction by levels of interpersonal trust, for the lowest (OSI = 1, no contact) and highest

(OSI = 5, daily contact) categories of OSI. The probability of reporting no contact decreases as neighborhood safety satisfaction improves, though this decline is steeper among low-trust respondents (–1 SD). Conversely, the second plot indicates that the probability of reporting daily contact rises with neighborhood safety satisfaction, particularly among high-trust respondents, who show the sharpest increase at moderate safety levels. Taken together, these patterns suggest that trust amplifies the positive role of neighborhood safety in fostering social contact, reducing the risk of structural isolation at the extreme low end. The plots can also be interpreted in terms of trust. Among all satisfaction levels, the probability of reporting no contact decreases as trust increases and the probability of daily contact increases as trust increases. However, the margin is the highest at moderate satisfaction level.

Figure 3. Predictive Margins of Lowest OSI Across Neighborhood Safety Satisfaction By Trust

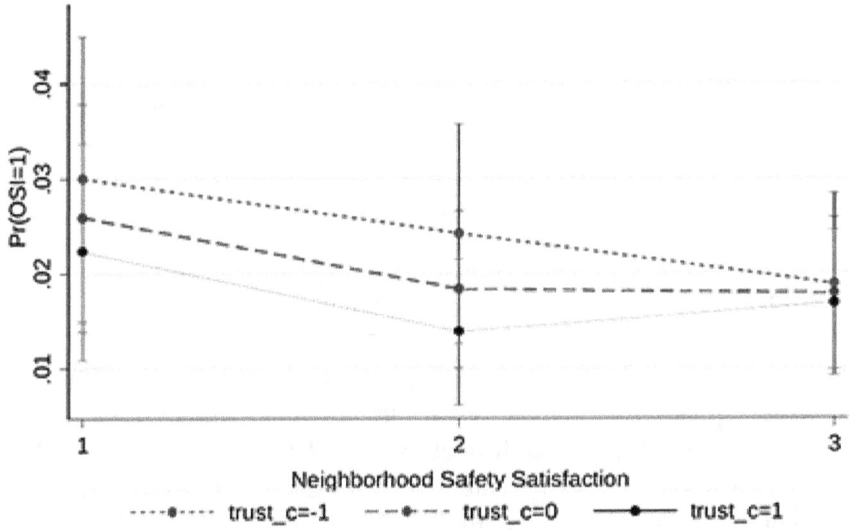

Figure 4. Predictive Margins of Highest OSI Across Neighborhood Safety Satisfaction By Trust

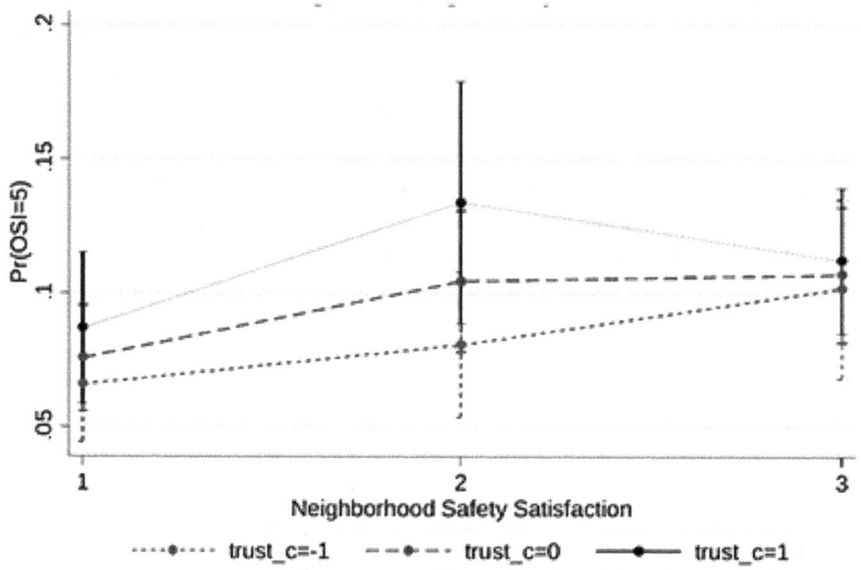

ESI Results

Table 4 presents the AMEs from the logistic regression examining predictors of ESI among respondents. The results show that trust has a modest but significant protective effect when interpreted through AMEs. While the raw logit coefficient is nonsignificant (0.047, $p > 0.10$), the marginal effects indicate that higher trust reduces the probability of reporting emotional isolation by about 3.7–3.8 percentage points (pp). Demographic effects are notable. Men are significantly less likely than women to report emotional loneliness (−8.0 to −8.4 pp), and older age is consistently protective, both as a continuous measure (−0.6 pp per year, $p \approx 0.06$) and in categorical comparisons (e.g., those aged 58–67 are 36 pp less likely to be emotionally isolated than those aged 19–27). Employment status and retirement show no strong effects relative to unemployment. Socioeconomic conditions matter strongly. Higher income reduces emotional loneliness, particularly for respondents above the poverty line (−35.8 pp), and neighborhood safety satisfaction has one of the most substantial associations, with those in the safest environments reporting a 24–25 pp lower probability of ESI compared to those in unsafe neighborhoods. Housing cost satisfaction also trends protective (≈ -8 pp, marginal).

Table 4. AME Results for Neighborhood Safety x Trust on ESI

Logit	Coef	AME (1) dy/dx (se)		AME (2) dy/dx (se)
Trust	0.047 (0.198)	-0.037(0.016)*		-0.038(0.016)*
Neigh.Safety x Trust	ns	—		—
Men vs women	-0.364 (0.142)**	-0.084(0.032)**		-0.080 (0.033)*
Age	-0.024 p=0.061 (0.012)	-0.006 p=0.059 (0.029)		-0.006(0.041)*
Age Cat. 58-67 vs 19-27		-0.375(0.169)*		-0.360(0.179)*
Employment status (employed vs unemployed	-0.223 (0.181)	-0.051(0.042)		-0.019(0.042)
(retired vs unemployed)	0.264 (0.510)	0.059(0.113)		0.065(0.110)
log(income)	-0.036 (0.075)	-0.008(0.017)	Income (between min. wage and poverty line vs below min. wage)	-0.089 p=0.057 (0.047)
			Income (above poverty line vs below min. wage)	-0.358(0.145)**
Education (Associate vs Primary)	0.828 p=0.069 (0.455)	0.189 p=0.063 (0.102)	Education (Associates vs Primary)	0.151 p=0.055 (0.078)
			(Bachelors vs Primary)	0.214(0.102)*
			(MS-PhD vs Primary)	0.207 p=0.065 (0.112)
Nbhd Safety Satisfact. (Highest vs Lowest)	-1.070 (0.346)	-0.246(0.076)**		-0.240(0.076)**
Housing Cost Satisfact.				
(satisfied vs not)	-0.373 p=0.053 (0.192)	-0.086 p=0.054 (0.045)		-0.080 p=0.069 (0.044)
Financial Prob.				
(moderately have vs not)	0.360 (0.177)*	0.084(0.041)*		0.075 p=0.065 (0.041)

continued on following page

Table 4. Continued

Logit	Coef	AME (1) dy/dx (se)		AME (2) dy/dx (se)
(have vs not)	0.650 (0.165)***	0.150(0.038)***		0.140(0.037)***
	R2=0.080	Pseudo R2=0.039		Pseudo R2=0.689

Notes: *p<0.05, **p<0.01, ***p<0.001. dy/dx is the is the percentage point (pp) change in the predicted probability of Bradburn loneliness when the variable changes from the base category (no loneliness) to the indicated category (very lonely and isolated). se: robust standard errors in parenthesis.

By contrast, consistent with PSI findings, financial difficulties are consistently associated with higher loneliness and increase ESI risk. Respondents with moderate financial problems are about 7–8 pp more likely to be emotionally isolated, while those with severe problems face a 14–15 pp increase. Educational attainment shows a complex pattern: while higher degrees (BA or MS/PhD) are associated with elevated odds in the logit, the AMEs suggest these effects are smaller and only marginally significant, potentially reflecting compositional or cohort effects.

Overall, the ESI model underscores the salience of trust, income security, neighborhood safety, and financial stability in mitigating feelings of loneliness, while pointing to age and gender as key social patterning dimensions. The AMEs reveal clearer substantive impacts than the logit coefficients alone, highlighting how protective resources buffer against subjective experiences of emotional isolation.

In Figure 5, the predictive margins plot for ESI reveals that differences by trust are most pronounced at intermediate levels of neighborhood safety satisfaction. At the lowest satisfaction category (very unsafe) and at the highest (very safe), the probabilities of reporting emotional isolation converge across all trust levels, suggesting little or no moderating effect. However, in the middle categories, individuals with lower trust report consistently higher probabilities of ESI than those with higher trust, indicating that trust exerts its buffering effect most strongly when neighborhood conditions are neither highly adverse nor highly favorable.

Figure 5. Predictive Margins of ESI Across Neighborhood Safety Satisfaction by Trust

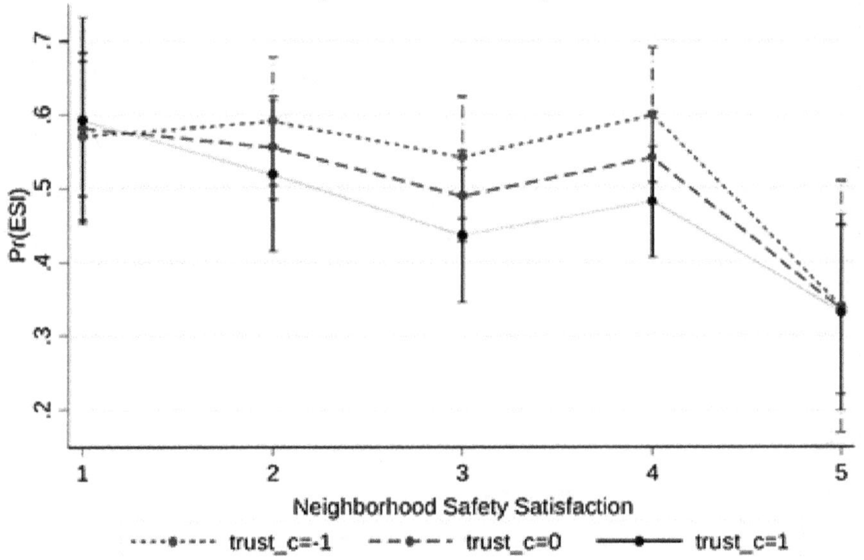

In Figure 6, AME results for employment and trust interaction on ESI show that interaction is not significant and therefore trust is not a moderator of the link between employment status and ESI. This model differs from safety-trust interaction model with safety losing significance and housing cost gaining significance at 5%, while the other variables keep their significance at the same levels. Interaction effects suggest that trust's protective role is conditional: it reduces ESI risk more strongly among retirees but is less effective among employed compared to unemployed participants.

Figure 6. Linear Prediction of ESI Across Employment Status by Trust

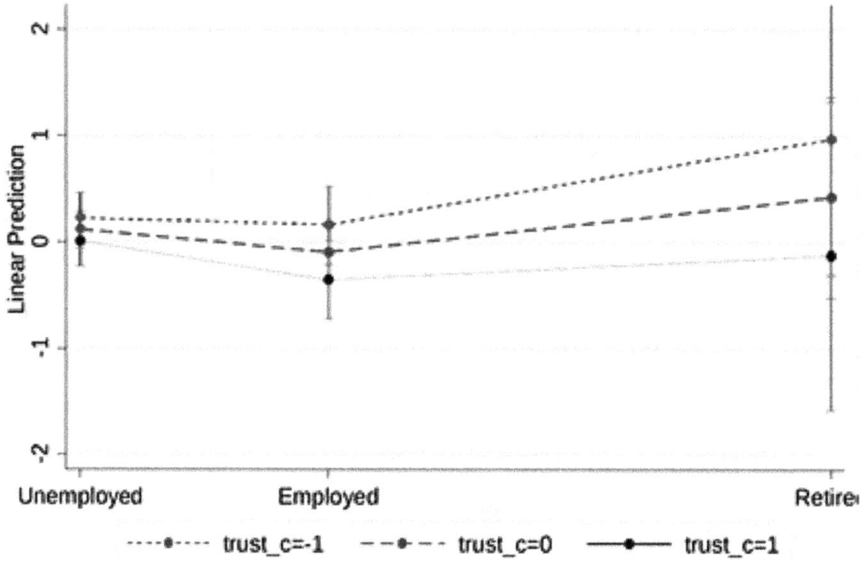

Figure 7 shows AMEs of the variables in employment and trust interaction model. Confidence intervals over and under the Y=0 reference line indicates significance of the variable. Confidence intervals slightly crossing the line or on the line may have significance close to 5% or at 5%.

Figure 7. Effects on Pr(ESI) Across Variables of the Model

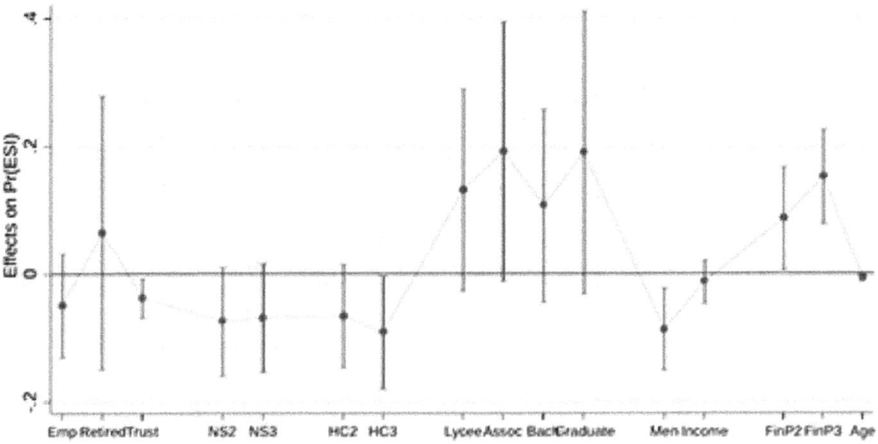

Note: NS2 and NS3=Moderately satisfied and satisfied with neighborhood safety, HC2 and HC3= Moderately satisfied and satisfied with housing cost, FinP2 and FinP3=Moderately have and have financial problems.

PSI Results

Table 5 presents the AMEs from ordered logistic regression model examining predictors of PSI among respondents. The model highlights several robust predictors of perceived social isolation. Generalized trust significantly reduces the probability of reporting higher levels of loneliness. A one-unit increase in trust decreases the probability of being in PSI categories 2 and 3 (–2.2 and –0.8 percentage points, respectively) while increasing the probability of reporting no isolation (PSI 1) by 1.7 points and strong isolation (PSI 5) by 3.8 points. Contextual and microeconomic conditions also matter. Similarly, higher income reduces PSI, with each log-point increase in income lowering the probability of moderate isolation while increasing the likelihood of reporting severe PSI (4.3 points). By contrast, financial strain strongly increases PSI. Compared to those with no financial problems, respondents with moderate financial difficulties were 16.4 percentage points more likely to report perceived loneliness, and those with severe problems were 21.3 points more likely. Education decreases PSI: those with tertiary qualifications (MSc-PhD) were less likely than primary-secondary to be in the highest PSI group. Finally, housing cost satisfaction reduced the likelihood of moderate to high isolation, raising the probability of daily contact by 10.1 points. Employment interacts with trust. Retirees with higher trust report less isolation relative to the unemployed, the interaction is significant ($p<0.05$). A similar moderation effect appears for neighborhood safety, where satisfaction combined with trust predicts lower PSI, suggesting that trust amplifies the protective role of safe, stable environments.

Table 5. Neighborhood Safety-Trust Interaction and AME Results for PSI

	Ologit	PSI 1	PSI 2	PSI 3	PSI 4	PSI 5
	Coef	dy/dx (se)	dy/dx (se)	dy/dx (se)	dy/dx (se)	dy/dx (se)
Trust_c	0.364(0.105)**	-0.017 (0.005)***	-0.022 (0.007)***	-0.008 (0.003)**	0.010 (0.003)**	0.038 (0.012)***
Nbhd Safety x Trust						
(Moderately satisfied vs not)	0.209(0.160)					
(Satisfied vs not)	-0.462 (0.149)**					
Log Income	0.147(0.067)*	-0.016 (0.005)**	-0.024 (0.007)**	-0.011 (0.003)**	0.008 (0.003)**	0.043 (0.0125)**
Education (MSc-PhD) vs (Primary-Secondary)	-0.904(0.412)*	0.077 P=0.077 (0.042)	0.096(0.042)*	0.030(0.012)*	—	- 0.153(0.064)*
Financial Prob. (Moderately have vs not)	- 0.748(0.150)***	0.043 (0.009)***	0.078 (0.015)***	0.050 (0.011)***	-0.008 (0.007)	-0.164 (0.031)***
(Have vs not)	- 1.017(0.173)***	0.067 (0.011)***	0.112 (0.017)***	0.061 (0.010)***	-0.028 (0.009)**	-0.213 (0.030)***
Housing Cost (Satisfied vs not)	0.362(0.173)*	-0.034 (0.011)**	-0.054 (0.018)**	-0.028 (0.010)**	0.015 (0.006)**	0.101 (0.034)**
Pseudo R2=0.04						

Note: *p<0.05, **p<0.01, ***p<0.001. dy/dx is the percentage point (pp) change in the predicted probability of perceived loneliness when the variable changes from the base category (1=no loneliness) to the indicated category.

Overall, the PSI results underscore the salience of both individual-level resources (trust, income, education) and structural conditions (housing costs, neighborhood safety) in shaping perceptions of social isolation. Importantly, the moderating interactions suggest that trust strengthens the benefits of secure environments and buffers the risks associated with structural vulnerabilities, particularly for retirees.

Figures 8 and 9 plot predicted probability of being in *no PSI* and *strong PSI* across neighborhood safety levels at three trust levels (−1 SD, mean, +1 SD). The predictive margins plots in Figure 7 show that PSI varies systematically across neighborhood safety satisfaction, and that these effects are moderated by trust.

For neighborhood safety satisfaction, the probability of reporting *no PSI* is highest among individuals with low trust when safety satisfaction is moderate, but this probability falls as satisfaction improves. In contrast, high-trust individuals report lower probabilities of no PSI at low and moderate satisfaction, but their probability rises slightly at high satisfaction levels.

Figure 8. Predictive Margins of Lowest PSI Across Neighborhood Safety Satisfaction by Trust

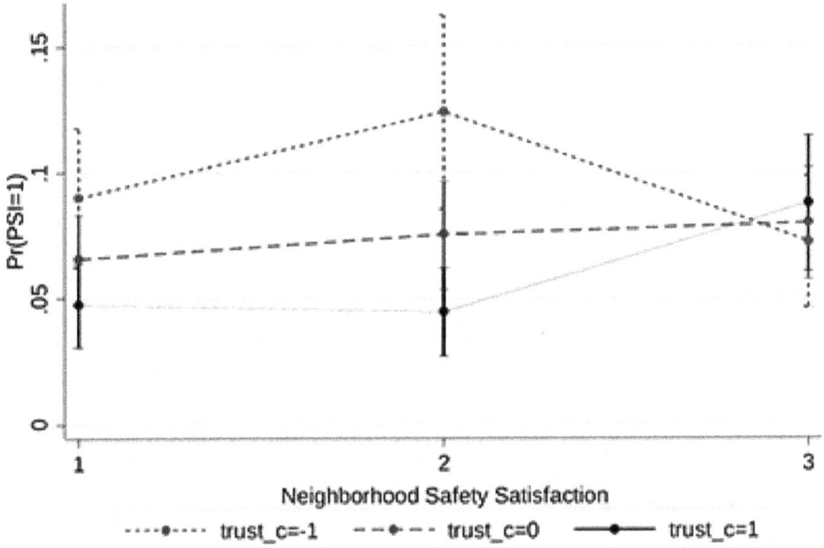

Notes: The y-axis is the predicted probability of being in the lowest category (PSI = 1). The x-axis is neighborhood safety (1 = unsatisfied 3 = satisfied). Each line corresponds to a different level of trust (centered at −1, 0, and +1). Error bars represent 95% CIs.

At the other end of the scale, Figure 9 shows that the probability of *strong PSI* is lowest among low-trust respondents, but rises among high-trust individuals as safety satisfaction improves. Together, these patterns indicate that trust not only moderates but inverts the relationship between neighborhood safety perceptions and PSI risk.

Figure 9. Predictive Margins of Highest PSI Across Neighborhood Safety Satisfaction by Trust

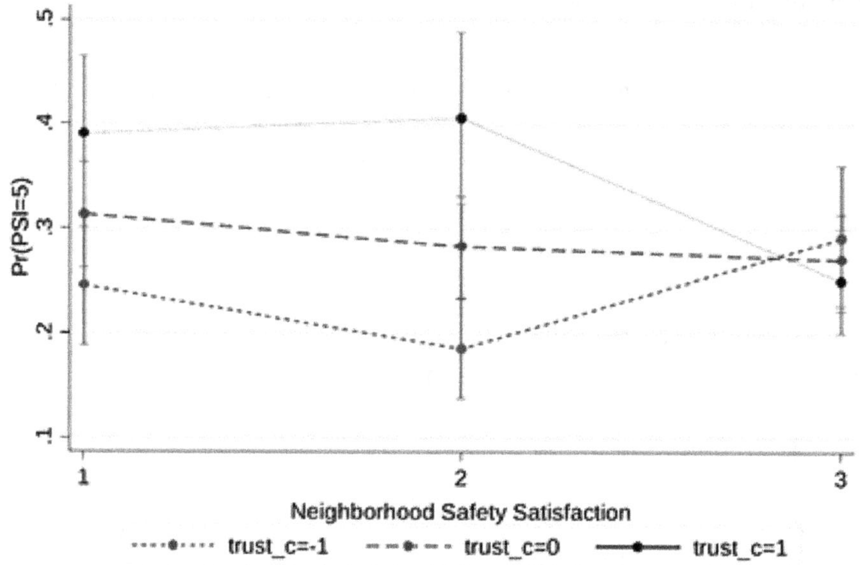

Notes: The y-axis is the predicted probability of being in the highest category (PSI=5). The x-axis is neighborhood safety (1 = unsatisfied 3 = satisfied). Each line corresponds to a different level of trust (centered at −1, 0, and +1). Error bars represent 95% CIs.

Table 6 shows the AMEs of the variables and interaction effect of employment status and trust on PSI. A one-unit increase in trust is associated with a 0.194 increase in the relative log odds of being in PSI. The positive main effect of trust ($\beta = 0.194$, $p < 0.01$) indicates that, on average, higher trust is actually associated with higher PSI, which is counterintuitive and suggests the relationship may be conditional on other factors. Indeed, the significant Trust × Employment interaction shows this is the case. For retirees, the interaction is negative and significant ($\beta = -0.539$, $p < 0.05$), meaning that the otherwise positive association between trust and isolation is dampened or even reversed among this group. By contrast, no interaction is observed for category 1, suggesting that employed individuals still show the positive slope. Neighborhood safety is marginally protective. Respondents satisfied with safety report lower PSI ($\beta = -0.281$, $p<0.10$), but significance is not at conventional level. Housing cost burdens increase PSI, with respondents in high category reporting higher odds of PSI ($\beta = 0.527$, $p = 0.007$). Other controls (age, gender, employment main effects, health status) are not statistically significant, meaning their independent contributions are limited in this specification.

Table 6. Employment Status -Trust Interaction and AME Results for PSI

	Ologit	**PSI 1**	**PSI 2**	**PSI 3**	**PSI 4**	**PSI 5**
	Coef	dy/dx (se)	dy/dx (se)	dy/dx (se)	dy/dx (se)	dy/dx (se)
Trust_c	0.194 (0.077)**	-0.015 (0.005)**	-0.023 (0.007)**	-0.011 (0.003)**	0.008 (0.003)*	0.042 (0.012)**
Employment x Trust						
(x Employed vs unemployed)	0.126 (0.140)					
(x Retired vs unemployed)	-0.539 (0.274)*					
Housing Cost (Satisfied vs not)	0.527 (0.170)**	-0.035 (0.012)**	-0.057 (0.018)**	-0.030 (0.010)**	0.016 (0.006)*	0.108 (0.035)**
Education (6 vs 1)	-0.870 (0.416)*	0.091 (0.054)	0.099 (0.044)*	0.017 (0.012)	-0.070 (0.039)	-0.138 (0.058)*
Neighborhood Safety Satisfaction	-0.281[a] (0.169)		0.031[a] (0.018)	0.015[a] (0.09)		-0.056[a] (0.033)
Pseudo R^2=0.013						

Notes: *p<0.05, **p<0.01, ***p<0.001. dy/dx is the percentage point (pp) change in the predicted probability of perceived loneliness when the variable changes from the base category (1=no loneliness) to the indicated category. [a]p<0.10

For employment status, the shape of the interaction is qualitatively similar, but overall predicted probabilities of both low and high PSI are lower compared to the neighborhood safety models. This suggests that employment-related contexts are less strongly associated with PSI than safety perceptions, though trust continues to differentiate respondents in meaningful ways.

Predictive margins of lowest-level PSI in Figure 10 show that high-trust unemployed individuals are more likely to report no isolation than low-trust unemployed. For those employed, differences by trust narrow and among retirees, the lines converge further — retirees with high trust are no more likely to report no isolation than their low-trust counterparts. Overall, trust is protective against isolation mainly for the unemployed; employment and retirement status both weaken its marginal benefit.

Figure 10. Predictive Margins of Lowest-Level PSI Across Employment Status by Trust

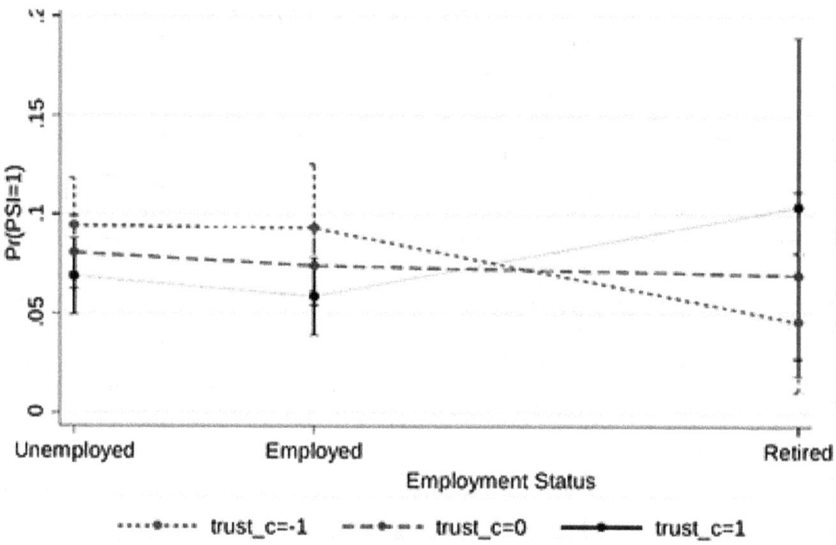

Predictive margins of highest-level PSI in Figure 11 show that among the unemployed, low trust is linked with a lower risk of severe isolation, whereas high trust protects against it. For the employed, the gap narrows and among retirees, high-trust individuals actually show a lower probability of severe isolation compared to low-trust retirees, though confidence intervals overlap. Consequently, trust strongly buffers unemployed individuals from severe isolation. But for retirees, trust does not confer the same protective effect and may even lose its role as a buffer.

Figure 11. Predictive Margins of Highest-Level PSI Across Employment Status by Trust

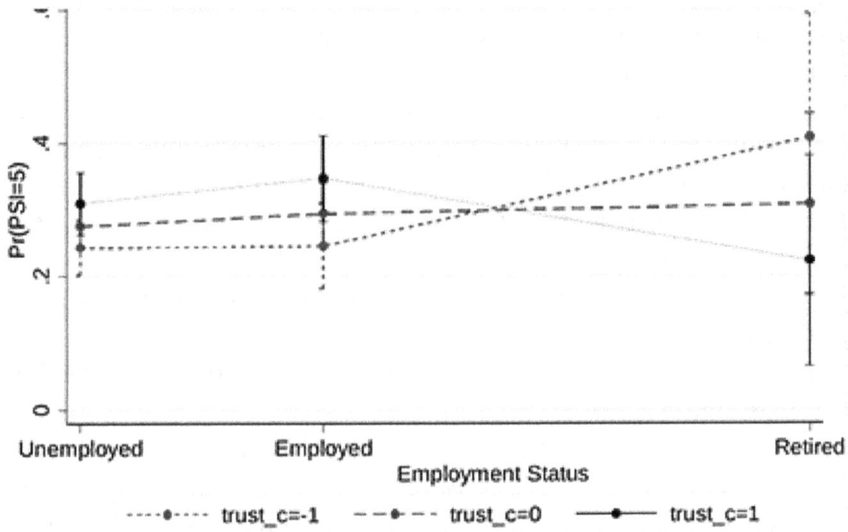

Overall, these results suggest that trust acts as a social buffer against isolation particularly for the unemployed, but its protective role diminishes once individuals are employed and may reverse in retirement, where other factors (e.g., health or income security) likely dominate the isolation experience.

Across all three models of social isolation trust emerged as a consistent differentiating factor, but its effects varied sharply by outcome and context.

For PSI, generalized trust was strongly and positively associated with higher isolation. Individuals with greater trust were less likely to report no PSI and more likely to report the highest PSI. Interaction analyses underscored this pattern. In the neighborhood safety models, high-trust individuals showed increased probabilities of strong PSI as safety satisfaction increased, whereas low-trust individuals had higher probabilities of reporting no PSI under moderate safety satisfaction. Employment status produced a similar but weaker moderation: trust differentiated isolation risks across unemployed, employed, and retired groups, though margins were flatter and at lower levels. These findings indicate that PSI is shaped by psychosocial pathways in which trust interacts with contextual resources.

For ESI, trust effects were minimal and inconsistent. Instead, structural and demographic factors dominated. Men were significantly less likely than women to report emotional loneliness, and younger adults reported higher risks than older groups. Neighborhood safety satisfaction strongly reduced ESI, with individuals most satisfied with safety showing substantially lower probabilities of loneliness, aligning with evidence that neighborhood disorder undermines emotional well-being (Schnittker & Bacak, 2014; Yang & Victor, 2011). This suggests that emotional isolation is more directly tied to structural resources and environmental security, rather than relational trust.

For OSI, results pointed in the opposite direction of PSI. Higher trust was associated with lower probabilities of reporting no contact (OSI=1) and higher probabilities of daily contact (OSI=5), suggesting a protective role of trust against objective isolation. Neighborhood safety also mattered: greater satisfaction was linked to reduced odds of low contact and increased likelihood of daily contact. Yet, interaction effects between trust and safety were weak and only marginally significant, and overall explanatory power remained low, indicating that OSI reflects broader structural constraints such as mobility, kin availability, and technology use, rather than psychosocial trust.

Taken together, these comparative findings highlight divergent pathways across isolation types. PSI is conditioned by the interplay of relational trust and contextual safety, ESI is primarily shaped by structural neighborhood conditions, and OSI is weakly predicted by either trust or safety but shows trust's protective role in sustaining daily contact. These contrasts reinforce the multidimensional nature of social isolation and the need to distinguish subjective from objective measures. They also set the stage for the Discussion, where we interpret how relational and structural pathways jointly shape the varied experiences of isolation.

DISCUSSION

This study shows that the role of trust in shaping social isolation is complex and domain-specific. Trust protects against perceived social isolation (PSI) but simultaneously predicts more frequent social contact (OSI), without necessarily reducing loneliness. This divergence reflects the distinction between relational expectations and behavioral networks (Weiss, 1973): trust facilitates civic participation and daily contact (Kawachi & Berkman, 2001; Putnam, 2000) but also raises expectations of reciprocity that, when unmet, can intensify subjective loneliness (Huxhold et al., 2022a; Luhmann & Hawkley, 2016).

For PSI, effects are conditioned by employment status. Trust reduced loneliness among the employed but not among the unemployed, while retirees displayed mixed patterns. These findings support Jahoda's (1982) latent deprivation model, where unemployment constrains the translation of trust into connectedness, and align with evidence that aging cohorts often sustain networks that may not fulfill emotional needs (Cornwell & Waite, 2009; De Jong Gierveld & Van Tilburg, 2010). By contrast, emotional isolation (ESI) was less tied to trust and more responsive to structural and demographic factors, including gender, age, and financial strain (Lyu et al., 2024).

Neighborhood safety also moderated trust's effects. Trust heightened vulnerability under unsafe conditions for PSI but reinforced protective safety effects for OSI, consistent with studies of neighborhood capital and isolation (Nyqvist et al., 2019; Poortinga, 2012). OSI models further revealed that retirees face lower risks than unemployed peers, challenging the assumption of uniformly rising isolation in older age (Malani et al., 2025; Pollak et al., 2025).

Overall, trust emerges as a two-way social resource: it can foster outward participation and embeddedness while also increasing awareness of unmet relational standards. These findings support recent studies showing that trust can both strengthen participation and exacerbate loneliness (Niedzwiedz et al., 2021; Victor and Pikhartova, 2020; Yang, 2023). From a policy perspective, this means that promoting trust and neighborhood safety is necessary but not sufficient; strategies must also address structural vulnerabilities and the psychosocial dimensions of loneliness, particularly among unemployed and retired groups.

Limitations and Future Research

This study has several limitations that offer valuable pathways for future research. First, the reliance on self-reported, cross-sectional data limits causal inference and may introduce common method bias (Podsakoff et al., 2003). While the multidimensional framework is a strength, the use of single-item indicators for some constructs may reduce validity compared to established multi-item scales (e.g., De Jong Gierveld & Van Tilburg, 2010).

Second, the geographical focus on Adana, while chosen for its representativeness of broader Turkish urban dynamics, means the findings may not generalize to rural areas or other regional contexts. Future studies could employ longitudinal or mixed-method designs and extend the analysis to different Turkish regions to capture temporal and spatial variations.

Third, the analytical scope could be expanded. Subsequent research would benefit from incorporating additional variables such as institutional trust, digital connectedness, and the emotional quality of social interactions to more fully test theoretical mechanisms.

Despite these limitations, the study possesses notable strengths. It makes a significant methodological contribution by integrating PSI, ESI, and OSI within a single analytical framework, an approach advocated for in recent literature (Courtin & Knapp, 2017; Huxhold et al., 2022b). Furthermore, the analysis of interaction effects elucidates the contextual conditions that shape isolation, and the use of a large, representative dataset with robust statistical techniques provides a solid foundation for the results.

CONCLUSION

This chapter examined the interrelations between microeconomic, psychosocial, and trust-based mechanisms that shape patterns of social isolation in Adana. Drawing on original survey data, the study revealed that both economic precarity and diminished interpersonal trust significantly heighten isolation risks, while neighborhood cohesion and perceived stability operate as protective factors. The analysis thus underscores that social isolation is not merely an individual outcome but a socially and spatially embedded process, mediated by local economic and relational contexts.

The comparative findings also demonstrated how trust functions as a pivotal connector across personal, social, and occupational isolation models. Consistent with prior evidence on the role of generalized trust in fostering social integration (Weiss, 1973; Putnam, 2000; Holt-Lunstad et al., 2015), the results from Adana highlight the continued relevance of trust as both a resource and a reflection of broader social structures.

Overall, the chapter addresses how microeconomic and psychosocial factors jointly shape patterns of social isolation within an urban Turkish context. Beyond its empirical results, the study's unique contribution lies in its focus on *trust as a moderating mechanism* within a city-specific framework—an approach rarely applied to middle-income, rapidly urbanizing settings such as Adana. By linking individual-level socioeconomic indicators with social trust and neighborhood conditions, the study provides a localized yet conceptually generalizable model of isolation dynamics.

Policy Implications

These findings extend Putnam's (2000) account of social capital by demonstrating that the benefits of trust depend on structural conditions such as employment, financial stability, housing affordability, and neighborhood safety. They also support Jahoda's (1982) model of latent deprivation, in which employment not only provides material resources but also strengthens the protective role of trust. Therefore, social isolation should be understood as the result of intertwined relational and structural dynamics.

Policy interventions should go beyond promoting interpersonal trust to address underlying vulnerabilities. Economic support, employment programs, and affordable housing can reduce material insecurity; neighborhood safety initiatives and community-based design can reduce the risks of isolation associated with environmental insecurity. Targeted measures for retirees (such as intergenerational programs and community centers) can maintain emotional connectedness, while gender- and age-sensitive initiatives can support groups more prone to loneliness.

Taken together, these results suggest that multi-sectoral approaches that integrate economic support, housing stability, security, and community participation are essential for reducing isolation and its associated health burdens.

Ultimately, social isolation emerges from the intersection of psychosocial trust, neighborhood safety, and microeconomic constraints. Therefore, effective interventions should combine investments in social capital with structural interventions to promote inclusion and resilience. Future research should extend these insights with longitudinal designs, digital-age analyses, and international comparisons to test generalizability.

Comparative Insights

The comparative findings of this study reveal that trust, neighborhood safety, and employment collectively shape distinct dimensions of social isolation—perceived (PSI), emotional (ESI), and objective (OSI). While PSI is most responsive to relational trust and its contextual moderators, ESI reflects the stronger influence of structural and environmental conditions such as safety and economic stability. OSI, in contrast, appears more dependent on tangible network and contact opportunities. These results align with international evidence (e.g., Lancee & Dronkers, 2011; Kim et al., 2020; Chung et al., 2023) and extend it by illustrating how psychosocial and economic mechanisms intersect within an urban Turkish setting.

Suggestions for Future Research

However, like many survey-based studies, this analysis has certain limitations that future research can address. The survey was conducted in Adana, a city characterized by socioeconomic heterogeneity, rapid urbanization, and pronounced income disparities making it a meaningful case for examining isolation under conditions of structural and psychosocial diversity. Nevertheless, results may not fully generalize to other Turkish regions. Future studies could replicate this framework in different cities or rural settings to identify spatial variations in trust and isolation pathways.

The literature review, while conceptually grounded, could be broadened to integrate comparative regional evidence and national surveys to strengthen contextualization. Methodologically, future research could employ probability-based sampling, longitudinal designs, or mixed-method approaches to capture change over time and deepen causal insights. Expanding the survey instrument to include institutional trust, digital connectedness, and civic participation would also enrich understanding of the multidimensional mechanisms underlying isolation. Addressing these gaps will enhance the study's external validity and theoretical reach, providing a more comprehensive account of how microeconomic and psychosocial determinants shape social connection in contemporary Turkey.

REFERENCES

Aytaç, I. A., & Rankin, B. H. (2009). Economic crisis and marital problems in Turkey: Testing the family stress model. *Journal of Marriage and Family*, *71*(3), 756–767. DOI: 10.1111/j.1741-3737.2009.00631.x

Becker, G. S. (1965). A theory of the allocation of time. *Economic Journal (London)*, *75*(299), 493–517. DOI: 10.2307/2228949

Bjørnskov, C. (2007). Determinants of generalized trust: A cross-country comparison. *Public Choice*, *130*(1–2), 1–21. DOI: 10.1007/s11127-006-9069-1

Bourdieu, P. (1986). The forms of capital. In Richardson, J. G. (Ed.), *Handbook of theory and research for the sociology of education* (pp. 241–258).

Bradburn, N. M. (1969). *The structure of psychological well-being*. Aldine.

Cacioppo, J. T., & Cacioppo, S. (2018). The growing problem of loneliness. *Lancet*, *391*(10119), 426. DOI: 10.1016/S0140-6736(18)30142-9

Casal, B., Rodríguez-Miguez, E., & Rivera, B. (2025). The societal cost of 'unwanted'loneliness in Spain. *The European Journal of Health Economics*, *26*(4), 605–617. DOI: 10.1007/s10198-024-01724-9

Çevik Özdemir, H. N., & Ayran, G. (2025). Social isolation in Turkish adolescents: Translation, cross-cultural adaptation, and validation of the social isolation questionnaire. *Children (Basel, Switzerland)*, *12*(9), 1122. DOI: 10.3390/children12091122

Chung, A. F., Teasell, M. J., Pergher, V., Thornton, A. E., & Thornton, W. L. (2023). Fear of COVID-19 is associated with trust, subjective numeracy, and differentially with loneliness in older versus younger adults. *Frontiers in Psychology*, *14*, 1080631. Advance online publication. DOI: 10.3389/fpsyg.2023.1080631

Cornwell, E. Y., & Waite, L. J. (2009). Social disconnectedness, perceived isolation, and health among older adults. *Journal of Health and Social Behavior*, *50*(1), 31–48. DOI: 10.1177/002214650905000103

Courtin, E., & Knapp, M. (2017). Social isolation, loneliness and health in old age: A scoping review. *Health & Social Care in the Community*, *25*(3), 799–812. DOI: 10.1111/hsc.12311

De Jong Gierveld, J., & Van Tilburg, T. (2010). The De Jong Gierveld short scales for emotional and social loneliness: Tested on data from 7 countries in the UN Generations and Gender Surveys. *European Journal of Ageing*, *7*(2), 121–130. DOI: 10.1007/s10433-010-0144-6

Eren, F. A., Boz, C., & Sargin, M. (2025). Exploring the relationship between obesity and social isolation: A crosssectional analysis. *Eurasian Journal of Family Medicine = Avrasya Aile Hekimligi Dergisi*, *14*(2), 57–67. DOI: 10.33880/ejfm.2025140203

Fuller-Rowell, T. E., Sultana, S., & Kawachi, I. (2025). Global trends and disparities in social isolation. *JAMA Network Open*, *8*(9), e2532008. DOI: 10.1001/jamanetworkopen.2025.32008

Gallie, D., Paugam, S., & Jacobs, S. (2003). Unemployment, poverty and social isolation: Is there a vicious circle of social exclusion? *European Societies*, *5*(1), 1–32. DOI: 10.1080/1461669032000057668

Guarnera, J., Yuen, E., & Macpherson, H. (2023). The impact of loneliness and social isolation on cognitive aging: A narrative review. *Journal of Alzheimer's Disease Reports*, *7*(1), 699–714. DOI: 10.3233/ADR-230011

Gümüş-Demir, Z., & Yılmaz, M. (2024). Loneliness, psychological well-being, depression, and social participation in the older persons: Rural and urban differences. *Current Aging Science*, *17*(3), 247–261. DOI: 10.2174/011874609829706 3240409070531

Hawkley, L. C., & Cacioppo, J. T. (2010). Loneliness matters: A theoretical and empirical review of consequences and mechanisms. *Annals of Behavioral Medicine*, *40*(2), 218–227. DOI: 10.1007/s12160-010-9210-8

Helliwell, J. F., & Putnam, R. D. (2004). The social context of well-being. *Philosophical Transactions of the Royal Society of London. Series B, Biological Sciences*, *359*(1449), 1435–1446. DOI: 10.1098/rstb.2004.1522

Holt-Lunstad, J., Smith, T. B., Baker, M., Harris, T., & Stephenson, D. (2015). Loneliness and social isolation as risk factors for mortality: A meta-analytic review. *Perspectives on Psychological Science*, *10*(2), 227–237. DOI: 10.1177/1745691614568352

Huxhold, O., Miche, M., Schüz, B., & Tesch-Römer, C. (2022a). The role of trust in shaping loneliness trajectories in later life. *The Journals of Gerontology: Series B*, *77*(3), 502–512. DOI: 10.1093/geronb/gbab004

Huxhold, O., Olaru, G., & Windsor, T. D. (2022b). Social expectations and loneliness: Testing the social expectation model of loneliness. *Journal of Personality and Social Psychology*, *123*(5), 1121–1138. DOI: 10.1037/pspp0000414

Jahoda, M. (1982). *Employment and unemployment: A social-psychological analysis*. Cambridge University Press.

Kahneman, D., & Tversky, A. (1979). Prospect theory: An analysis of decision under risk. *Econometrica, 47*(2), 263–291. DOI: 10.2307/1914185

Kang, J. W., Oga-Omenka, C., Tyas, S. L., Dubin, J. A., & Oremus, M. (2025). How social isolation and loneliness leave distinct imprints on memory: A thematic analysis informed by descriptive phenomenology. *Archives of Gerontology and Geriatrics, 139*, 106003. DOI: 10.1016/j.archger.2025.106003

Kaşak, M., Hacıosmanoğlu, C. D., Tural Hesapcioglu, S., & Ceylan, M. F. (2022). Loneliness in modern world: A case study of Hikikomori from Turkey (eng). *Klinik Psikiyatri Dergisi, 25*(1), 117–122. DOI: 10.5505/kpd.2022.59265

Kawachi, I., & Berkman, L. F. (2001). Social ties and mental health. *Journal of Urban Health, 78*(3), 458–467. DOI: 10.1093/jurban/78.3.458

Kawachi, I., Kennedy, B. P., & Glass, R. (1999). Social capital and self-rated health: A contextual analysis. *American Journal of Public Health, 89*(8), 1187–1193. DOI: 10.2105/AJPH.89.8.1187

Keskin, D., & Lajunen, T. (2024). Adaptation of the social and emotional loneliness scale for adults to Turkish culture. *Social Sciences (Basel, Switzerland), 13*(3), 174. DOI: 10.3390/socsci13030174

Kim, E. S., Chen, Y., Kawachi, I., & Van der Weele, T. J. (2020). Perceived neighborhood social cohesion and subsequent health and well-being in older adults: An outcome-wide longitudinal approach. *Health & Place, 66*, 102420. DOI: 10.1016/j.healthplace.2020.102420

Kotozaki, Y. (2025). Editorial: New insights into social isolation and loneliness, volume II. *Frontiers in Psychiatry, 16*, 1675314. DOI: 10.3389/fpsyt.2025.1675314

Lancee, B., & Dronkers, J. (2011). Ethnic, religious and economic diversity in Dutch neighborhoods: Explaining quality of contact with neighbors, trust in the neighborhood and inter-ethnic trust. *Journal of Ethnic and Migration Studies, 37*(4), 597–618. DOI: 10.1080/1369183X.2011.545277

Latikka, R., Rubio-Hernández, R., Lohan, E. S., Rantala, J., Nieto Fernández, F., Laitinen, A., & Oksanen, A. (2021). Older adults' loneliness, social isolation, and physical ICT in the era of ambient assisted living: A systematic review. *Journal of Medical Internet Research, 23*(12), e28022. DOI: 10.2196/28022

Layte, R., & Whelan, C. T. (2002). Cumulative disadvantage or individualisation? A comparative analysis of poverty risk and incidence. *European Societies, 4*(2), 209–233. DOI: 10.1080/14616690220142790

Luhmann, M., & Hawkley, L. C. (2016). Age differences in loneliness from late adolescence to oldest old age. *Developmental Psychology, 52*(6), 943–959. DOI: 10.1037/dev0000117

Lyu, C., Siu, K., Xu, I., Osman, I., & Zhong, J. (2024). Social isolation changes and long-term outcomes among older adults. *JAMA Network Open, 7*(7), e2424519. DOI: 10.1001/jamanetworkopen.2024.24519

Malani, P. N., Solway, E., Kirch, M., Singer, D. C., Roberts, J. S., & Kullgren, J. T. (2025). Loneliness and social isolation among US older adults. *Journal of the American Medical Association, 333*(3), 254–257. DOI: 10.1001/jama.2024.23213

Mullainathan, S., & Shafir, E. (2013). *Scarcity: Why having too little means so much.* Times Books.

Niedzwiedz, C. L., Richardson, E. A., Tunstall, H., Shortt, N. K., Mitchell, R. J., & Pearce, J. R. (2021). The relationship between community trust and loneliness across the adult life course: Evidence from a national survey. *Social Science & Medicine, 278*, 113933. DOI: 10.1016/j.socscimed.2021.113933

Nyqvist, F., Victor, C. R., Forsman, A. K., & Cattan, M. (2019). The association between social capital and loneliness in different age groups: A population-based study in Western Finland. *BMC Public Health, 19*, 1337. DOI: 10.1186/s12889-019-7760-y

Paxton, P. (2007). Association memberships and generalized trust: A multilevel model across 31 countries. *Social Forces, 86*(1), 47–76. DOI: 10.1353/sof.2007.0107

Peplau, L. A., & Perlman, D. (1982). Perspectives on loneliness. In Peplau, L. A., & Perlman, D. (Eds.), *Loneliness: A sourcebook of current theory, research and therapy* (pp. 1–18).

Podsakoff, P. M., MacKenzie, S. B., Lee, J. Y., & Podsakoff, N. P. (2003). Common method biases in behavioral research: A critical review of the literature and recommended remedies. *The Journal of Applied Psychology, 88*(5), 879–903. DOI: 10.1037/0021-9010.88.5.879

Pollak, C., Pham, Y., Ehrlich, A., Verghese, J., & Blumen, H. M. (2025). Loneliness and social isolation risk factors in community-dwelling older adults receiving home health services. *BMC Geriatrics, 25*(1), 290. DOI: 10.1186/s12877-025-05947-0

Poortinga, W. (2012). Community resilience and health: The role of bonding, bridging, and linking aspects of social capital. *Health & Place, 18*(2), 286–295. DOI: 10.1016/j.healthplace.2011.09.017

Putnam, R. D. (2000). *Bowling alone: The collapse and revival of American community*. Simon & Schuster.

Ross, C. E., & Jang, S. J. (2000). Neighborhood disorder, fear, and mistrust: The buffering role of social ties with neighbors. *American Journal of Community Psychology, 28*(4), 401–420. DOI: 10.1023/A:1005137713332

Ryff, C. D. (1989). Happiness is everything, or is it? Explorations on the meaning of psychological well-being. *Journal of Personality and Social Psychology, 57*(6), 1069–1081. DOI: 10.1037/0022-3514.57.6.1069

Sampson, R. J. (2012). *Great American city: Chicago and the enduring neighborhood effect*. University of Chicago Press. DOI: 10.7208/chicago/9780226733883.001.0001

Schnittker, J., & Bacak, V. (2014). The increasing predictive validity of self-rated health. *PLoS One*, *9*(1), e84933. DOI: 10.1371/journal.pone.0084933

Shah, A. K., Mullainathan, S., & Shafir, E. (2012). Some consequences of having too little. *Science, 338*(6107), 682–685. DOI: 10.1126/science.1222426

Taylor, H. O., Tsuchiya, K., Nguyen, A. W., & Mueller, C. (2023). Sociodemographic factors and neighborhood/environmental conditions associated with social isolation among black older adults. *Journal of Aging and Health, 35*(3-4), 294–306. DOI: 10.1177/08982643221118427

Train, K. E. (2009). *Discrete choice methods with simulation* (2nd ed.). Cambridge University Press., DOI: 10.1017/CBO9780511805271

Uslaner, E. M. (2002). *The moral foundations of trust*. Cambridge University Press.

Victor, C. R., & Pikhartova, J. (2020). Lonely places or lonely people? Investigating the relationship between loneliness and place of residence. *BMC Public Health, 20*(1), 778. DOI: 10.1186/s12889-020-08703-8

Wan, L. P., Zhao, Z. Y., Liu, B. P., Zhu, J. H., Jia, C. X., & Wang, X. T. (2025). Association between loneliness, social isolation and incident depression: A prospective study based on UK Biobank. *General Hospital Psychiatry, 96*, 171–177. DOI: 10.1016/j.genhosppsych.2025.07.007

Weiss, R. S. (1973). *Loneliness: The experience of emotional and social isolation*. MIT Press World Health Organization (WHO). (2021). *Social isolation and loneliness among older people: Advocacy brief*. https://www.who.int/publications/i/item/9789240030749

Wister, A., Kim, B., Levasseur, M., Poulin, V., Qiu, S., Yuwono, E., Meynet, S., Beadle, J., Kadowaki, L., Klasa, K., & Linkov, I. (2025). Resilience applications to social isolation and loneliness in older adults: A scoping review to develop a model and research agenda. *Frontiers in Public Health, 13*, 1589781. DOI: 10.3389/fpubh.2025.1589781

Yang, K. (2023). Trust, social engagement, and loneliness among older adults: Evidence from a nationally representative survey. *Aging & Mental Health, 27*(6), 1047–1056. DOI: 10.1080/13607863.2021.2009603

Yang, K., & Victor, C. R. (2011). Age and loneliness in 25 European nations. *Ageing and Society, 31*(8), 1368–1388. DOI: 10.1017/S0144686X1000139X

Yetim, N., & Yetim, Ü. (2014). Sense of community and individual well-being: A research on fulfillment of needs and social capital in the Turkish Community. *Social Indicators Research, 115*(1), 93–115. DOI: 10.1007/s11205-012-0210-x

ADDITIONAL READINGS

Cacioppo, J. T., Hawkley, L. C., & Thisted, R. A. (2010). Perceived social isolation makes me sad: 5-year cross-lagged analyses of loneliness and depressive symptomatology in the Chicago Health, Aging, and Social Relations Study. *Psychology and Aging, 25*(2), 453–463. DOI: 10.1037/a0017216

Cacioppo, J. T., Hughes, M. E., Waite, L. J., Hawkley, L. C., & Thisted, R. A. (2006). Loneliness as a specific risk factor for depressive symptoms: Cross-sectional and longitudinal analyses. *Psychology and Aging, 21*(1), 140–151. DOI: 10.1037/0882-7974.21.1.140

Heinrich, L. M., & Gullone, E. (2006). The clinical significance of loneliness: A literature review. *Clinical Psychology Review, 26*(6), 695–718. DOI: 10.1016/j.cpr.2006.04.002

Hughes, M. E., Waite, L. J., Hawkley, L. C., & Cacioppo, J. T. (2004). A short scale for measuring loneliness in large surveys: Results from two population-based studies. *Research on Aging, 26*(6), 655–672. DOI: 10.1177/0164027504268574

Masi, C. M., Chen, H.-Y., Hawkley, L. C., & Cacioppo, J. T. (2011). A meta-analysis of interventions to reduce loneliness. *Personality and Social Psychology Review, 15*(3), 219–266. DOI: 10.1177/1088868310377394

Parker, J. G., & Asher, S. R. (1993). Friendship and friendship quality in middle childhood: Links with peer group acceptance and feelings of loneliness and social dissatisfaction. *Developmental Psychology*, *29*(4), 611–621. DOI: 10.1037/0012-1649.29.4.611

Russell, D. W. (1996). UCLA Loneliness Scale (Version 3): Reliability, validity, and factor structure. *Journal of Personality Assessment*, *66*(1), 20–40. DOI: 10.1207/s15327752jpa6601_2

Steptoe, A., Shankar, A., Demakakos, P., & Wardle, J. (2013). Social isolation, loneliness, and all-cause mortality in older men and women. *Proceedings of the National Academy of Sciences of the United States of America*, *110*(15), 5797–5801. DOI: 10.1073/pnas.1219686110

KEY TERMS AND DEFINITIONS

Emotional Social Isolation: Feelings of loneliness due to the absence of close, emotionally supportive relationships, even when social contact may be frequent

Employment Status: A structural condition that shapes social integration and well-being. Employment provides material resources and hidden psychosocial benefits, while unemployment or retirement can increase the risks of isolation.

Human Trust: An individual's general trust in others. It reflects trust in the good will of others, and involves honesty and risk.

Latent Deprivation Model: A framework that assumes that employment not only provides income but also psychosocial resources such as social contact, identity and structure that reduce the risk of isolation.

Neighborhood Safety Satisfaction: An individual's perceived level of safety within local environment. Safety perceptions influence both social participation and emotional well-being.

Objective Social Isolation: Low or no frequency of social contacts and participation in activities.

Perceived Social Isolation: A feeling of being disconnected or excluded from social participation, regardless of actual frequency of contact. Often linked to psychosocial and relational factors such as trust.

Social Capital: Resources embedded in social networks, trust, and norms that facilitate cooperation and collective action.

Chapter 5
Invisible Struggles–Loneliness in Higher Education

Alan Swiercz
https://orcid.org/0009-0009-9894-6075
Glasgow Caledonian University, UK

Symela Charalampidou
https://orcid.org/0009-0005-1455-0382
Glasgow Caledonian University, UK

Umm E. Habiba Tariq
https://orcid.org/0009-0004-6857-0277
Glasgow Caledonian University, UK

ABSTRACT

The focus of this chapter is on loneliness. Specifically, this chapter provides an overview of loneliness in academia and offers guidance to university stakeholders on how to manage loneliness. Using secondary literature sources identified through a scoping review, this chapter explains what loneliness is and how it manifests itself in academia. It explains the causes and consequences of loneliness and identifies the key vulnerable cohorts most at risk of loneliness. It also offers recommendations on strategies that can be deployed by university stakeholders to combat loneliness. Additionally, this chapter proposes recommendations to universities on the strategies to help their stakeholders combat loneliness. Understanding what loneliness is and how to manage it is essential, as it can have detrimental effects that range from poor academic performance to health-related problems.

DOI: 10.4018/979-8-3373-5811-6.ch005

1. INTRODUCTION

Norman Cousins once observed, *"The eternal quest of the human spirit is to shatter its loneliness."* Loneliness is increasingly being recognized as a significant emerging global health concern (Holt-Lunstad et al., 2015). Yet, even in the 21st century, our understanding of how to overcome loneliness remains limited (Bevens et al., 2024). The authors of this book chapter believe that this may be because loneliness is a sensitive topic, making people hesitant to discuss it openly out of fear of being judged. This chapter aims to help break the stigma surrounding loneliness by exploring what loneliness is, its causes and consequences, the groups most at risk, and strategies to reduce loneliness in academia.

Loneliness refers to the distressing feeling that arises from a lack of sufficient quality or quantity in one's social relationships (Kaufmann & Vallade, 2022). A range of factors can contribute to loneliness; for instance, low educational attainment, limited income, and inadequate support from family and friends (Egaña-Marcos et al., 2025). Additionally, evidence suggests that structural inequalities and institutional cultures favoring certain groups over others contribute to loneliness by excluding individuals who share specific characteristics (Yan, 2024). Although there is no single best way to measure loneliness (Allen et al., 2021), three scales are commonly used. These scales are the Center for Epidemiologic Studies Depression Scale (CES-D) (Dahlberg et al., 2015), the UCLA Loneliness Scale (Zebhauser et al., 2014), and the de Jong Gierveld Loneliness Scale (dJGLS) (Newall et al., 2013). However, all three are susceptible to social desirability bias where respondents give false answers to be viewed favorably by others (Bugallo-Carrera et al., 2023). The authors of this chapter also argue that loneliness is complex and varies across individuals, which simple Likert scales may fail to capture.

There are three categories of loneliness: cognitive, affective, and behavioral (McCarthy et al., 2025). Cognitive loneliness involves negative thoughts and beliefs about one's social relationships, such as perceiving oneself as unwanted by others. Affective loneliness refers to the emotional distress that arises from perceived social disconnection, often manifesting as feelings of sadness or emptiness. Lastly, behavioral loneliness is characterized by actions that either result from or reinforce loneliness, such as withdrawing from social interactions or engaging in maladaptive coping strategies. Additionally, loneliness can either be chronic or situational (McCarthy et al., 2025). Chronic loneliness refers to long-term or prolonged feelings of loneliness, whereas situational loneliness refers to short-term or temporary feelings of loneliness.

Loneliness, although related, is not the same as being alone; loneliness is typically involuntary and marked by emotional distress, whereas being alone can be a voluntary and even fulfilling choice (Jandric, 2022; Zheng et al., 2023). Additionally, an individual may feel lonely despite having an active social life, while another may have limited social interaction yet not experience loneliness (Richardson et al., 2017). While everyone experiences loneliness at some stage in their lives (Holt-Lunstad et al., 2015), prolonged periods of loneliness can negatively impact wellbeing. In fact, long-term loneliness has been linked to sleep deprivation (Zhang et al., 2018), impaired cognitive function (Lim et al., 2020), stress and anxiety (Taylor et al., 2024), depression (Cacioppo et al., 2010), suicidal thoughts (Stickley & Koyanagi, 2016), and coronary heart disease (Hodgson et al., 2020). The health risks linked to loneliness can be understood through an evolutionary lens, in which social connections are essential for human survival and reproduction (Cacioppo et al., 2014; Slavich, 2020). The authors of this chapter also suggest that the link between loneliness and health problems may arise from reduced self-care, as individuals experiencing loneliness may feel they have no one to take care of themselves for.

According to academic research, university students represent a population especially vulnerable to loneliness (Diehl et al., 2018; Bu et al., 2020), with increasing numbers of students seeking support from university services (Auerbach et al., 2018). It is estimated that the prevalence of loneliness among university students rose from 61% in 2008 to 67.4% in 2019 (Shin et al., 2023). The COVID-19 pandemic exacerbated feelings of loneliness among university students (Luo et al., 2021). The global pandemic led to the closure of university campuses, forcing students into virtual learning environments and confining many to their dormitories (Ellard et al., 2023). Researchers argue that this prolonged isolation contributed to the development of alexithymia- commonly referred to as emotional blindness- where individuals struggle to identify and express their emotions (Osimo et al., 2021). This difficulty in emotional processing intensified students' feelings of loneliness, making it harder for them to recognize their loneliness and discouraging them from seeking support.

In addition, starting university represents a significant life transition, often marked by leaving the family home, adjusting to a new academic environment, and managing finances independently (Granieri et al., 2021). Overcommitted and introverted students are argued to be at a higher risk of loneliness due to their limited social life (Buecker et al., 2020; Bayraktar & Jiménez, 2022). The authors of this chapter also suggest that LGBTQ+ university stakeholders may face a heightened risk, particularly in countries where their rights are restricted. The authors also suggest that male students may be at increased risk due to the prevailing culture of toxic masculinity which expects males not to share their feelings with others. Furthermore, mature students may experience elevated loneliness due to potential exclusion from younger peers, while part-time students may feel amplified loneliness due to being disconnected from the broader academic culture. The academic literature, however, identifies certain university stakeholders as being at the greatest risk of loneliness. These are first-year students, international students, neurodivergent students, and lecturers. These four stakeholder groups constitute the primary focus of this book chapter.

The exploration of loneliness in academia is therefore necessarily, especially since university interventions are often ill-equipped to address the complex nature of loneliness (Fakoya et al., 2020; Ousman & Nazir, 2023). This can in turn impair students' academic performance, lower graduation rates, and restrict future contributions to the labor market (Von Soest et al., 2020). Additionally, drawing on the authors' own academic experience, loneliness may also damage the university's reputation and prompt valuable staff members to leave. To address this issue, this chapter identifies the most effective anti-loneliness interventions, drawing on recent cross-disciplinary studies vetted by strict inclusion and exclusion criteria.

This chapter is also helpful for introverted students or those reluctant to seek formal support, as it outlines personal strategies they can use to manage loneliness independently. Additionally, since individuals experiencing loneliness often do not recognize or acknowledge it (Kerr & Stanley, 2021), this chapter raises awareness and encourages early support-seeking before loneliness worsen. Importantly, this chapter does not treat students as a homogenous group. Instead, it explores the experiences of loneliness among diverse student populations such as first-year students, neurodivergent students, and international students ensuring the guidance is inclusive and relevant. Beyond the student body, this chapter also extends its focus to lecturers who are likewise vulnerable to loneliness (Rawat & Meena, 2014). The parents or guardians of students, as well as the university's HR and management teams, may also benefit from reading this chapter, as it broadens their understanding of how to better support the students in their care and the staff under their supervision.

Finally, the content of this book chapter is also relevant to policymakers, particularly considering initiatives such as the appointment of Ministers for Loneliness in some countries (Rippe, 2024). By presenting evidence-based best practices, this chapter offers valuable guidance for developing targeted policies to reduce loneliness in higher education. The chapter may also be useful for prospective students and academics, helping them anticipate the emotional challenges of entering university life. In sum, this chapter aims to serve as a practical guide for university stakeholders by increasing awareness of loneliness in academia and offering actionable strategies to help reduce- or potentially eliminate- these feelings.

This chapter is structured around three key sections. *Section 2.0 Research Method,* outlines how the scoping review was conducted. It also informs the reader on the aim, objectives, and research questions for this book chapter. Then, *Section 3.0 Results,* presents key literature on loneliness within the academic context. In this section, the reader is informed on the causes and consequences of loneliness. Additionally, this section outlines the university stakeholder groups who are most at risk of loneliness. This section also offers personal and university-led strategies to help combat loneliness. Furthermore, this section provides university stakeholders with final tips and words of encouragement to support them in their academic journey. Finally, *Section 4.0 Conclusion*, highlights the key points made in this book chapter. Having introduced loneliness in academia, the next section outlines the approaches used to conduct the scoping review.

2. RESEARCH METHOD

The following section discusses how the Scoping Review was developed to select the most credible literary sources.

2.1 Scoping Review

A scoping review is a form of knowledge synthesis characterized by searching, identifying, and synthesizing existing knowledge (Colquhoun et al., 2014). The value of the scoping review lies in its ability to chart intellectual territory, translate sprawling evidence into coherent summaries, and act as a platform for deeper empirical or theoretical work (Tricco et al., 2016). This project adopts a scoping review design as the aim is to chart, rather than judge, the landscape of loneliness research in higher education. To achieve this, the authors utilize the Population–Concept–Context (PCC) framework. Mapping these elements will reveal concentrations, gaps and methodological variety, information a narrowly focused systematic review would omit. The PCC framework is shown in Table 1 below.

Table 1. The PCC Framework.

PCC Framework	Relevant Components
Population	Students, faculty in HE
Concept	Loneliness
Context	Higher Education

Note: This table was created by the authors to demonstrate the Population, Concept, Context framework adopted for this book chapter.

The first step of a scoping review is to identify the gaps in literature (Tricco, 2016). The current literature on loneliness is marked by several gaps. Firstly, student loneliness within higher education has received little attention (Dagnew & Dagne, 2019). Secondly, the existing literature on student loneliness tends to adopt a one-size-fits-all approach by examining students as a homogeneous group, often overlooking their diverse circumstances (Fakoya et al., 2020). This book chapter addresses this gap by focusing on student populations that have received limited attention in the existing literature, including neurodivergent and international students (Zheng et al., 2023). Thirdly, the literature on loneliness in academia tends to overlook other key stakeholder groups, such as lecturers, who are also recognized as being vulnerable to loneliness (Rawat & Meena, 2014). This book chapter addresses this gap by exploring the experiences of these underrepresented groups.

The second step is to identify relevant studies (Tricco, 2016). To achieve this, the Boolean terms 'OR' and 'AND' was used to combine search results. 'OR' was used to combine results within the same category, while 'AND' was used to combine results between different categories. The following key terms were included: loneliness OR lonely OR "perceived isolation" AND "higher education" OR university OR college OR undergraduate* OR postgraduate* OR "graduate student*" OR lecturer* OR faculty OR supervisor* intervention* OR program* OR policy OR "student support" OR "peer support" OR "self-help" OR belonging OR wellbeing. We also focused our search on Google Scholar, PubMed, ProQuest, Wiley Online Library, SAGE, Springer, ScienceDirect, Nature, Taylor & Francis, Psychiatriki, Cambridge University Press, BMC, Oxford Academic.

The third step entails selecting relevant studies (Tricco, 2016). Once the search was complete, all citations were exported to RefWorks, where de-duplication was undertaken to create a single, unique dataset. The titles and abstracts were screened followed by full-text screening, guided by the inclusion and exclusion criteria. Every citation judged as 'include' was processed to the next phase. Discrepancies were discussed, and the coding form amended until consensus was reached. The inclusion and exclusion criteria is shown in Table 2 below.

Table 2. Inclusion and exclusion criteria.

Criteria Type	Description
INCLUSION	Empirical studies
	Reviews (systematic/scoping/narrative)
	Peer reviewed
	2010–2025
	Written or able to translate to English
	National and international studies
	Explicit focus on loneliness within HE stakeholders or HE-based interventions targeting loneliness.
EXLUSION	General-population studies not situated in HE

continued on following page

Table 2. Continued

Criteria Type	Description
	Work without a loneliness component
	Sources published before 2010
	Grey literature from non-reputable sources
	Sources that could not be translated to English

Note: The table was created by the authors to show the inclusion and exclusion criteria of studies.

Throughout the inclusion and exclusion process, the authors were able to identify a total of n=1268 sources which after screening and eligibility checks went down to a total of n=226 sources. Out of 226 sources, 126 results were deemed most suitable and therefore worthy to be included in this book chapter. From the scoping review, key themes emerged in relation to loneliness in higher education which informed the structure of the results section. The process of the scoping review enabled the authors to shape the research aim, objectives and research questions which are outlined in the section below.

2.2 Aim, Objectives and Research Questions

The aim of this book chapter is to examine loneliness in higher education- its causes, consequences, and the individuals at greatest risk- and offers evidence-based recommendations to reduce loneliness across diverse university stakeholder groups.

To achieve this aim, the following research objectives have been outlined.

1. To explore the causes and consequences of loneliness in diverse student groups within the context of higher education.
2. To identify higher education stakeholder groups most at risk of experiencing loneliness and examine the factors contributing to their vulnerability.
3. To investigate personal strategies that at-risk individuals in higher education can use to alleviate feelings of loneliness.
4. To recommend best-practice interventions for academic institutions to reduce loneliness among its stakeholders.

The specific research questions needed to achieve these objectives are outlined below.

RQ1: What are the primary causes and consequences of loneliness among individuals in higher education settings?

RQ2: Which demographic groups within higher education are most vulnerable to loneliness, and what factors contribute to their increased risk?

RQ3: What personal coping strategies do at-risk individuals in higher education employ to manage or reduce feelings of loneliness?

RQ4: How university interventions are most effective in addressing loneliness, and what improvements can be made to enhance their impact?

Having outlined the scoping review and the aim, objectives, and research questions, the next section examines the literature on loneliness in academia.

3. RESULTS

This section summarizes the academic sources identified through the scoping review on the causes and consequences of loneliness, vulnerable groups, and personal and university-led strategies to address loneliness.

3.1 Causes of Loneliness

Loneliness is pervasive across global higher education (Belkhir et al., 2019). The literature identifies several key stressors that can lead to loneliness. The first stressor that students face is homesickness caused by leaving the family home and moving to a new accommodation (Munir et al., 2015). To alleviate this stressor, the authors of this chapter recommend maintaining regular contact with family and friends and arranging periodic visits with them. Using video call apps such as *Microsoft Teams, WhatsApp,* and *FaceTime* can also be helpful in maintaining connections. Additionally, moving into new accommodation requires students to manage domestic responsibilities independently (Ellard et al., 2023). This can contribute to feelings of loneliness, especially for those living in shared housing where household tasks are not distributed equally. To address this issue, the authors recommend that students create a weekly cleaning schedule, agreed upon by all residents, assigning different household tasks to different housemates on specific days.

The second stressor refers to financial problems and concerns about dept (Dabrowski et al., 2025). Such pressures can heighten loneliness when social activities require expenditure, and when students compare themselves with non-university peers who may not face similar constraints. To alleviate this stressor, the authors recommend that universities implement clear training policies on budgeting and money management for staff members- particularly those in student support services- so they can effectively advise and guide students on financial planning. AI technology can also be useful, as students can develop their weekly and monthly budget with the help of platforms like *Copilot* and *ChatGPT*. Additionally, the authors of this chapter recommend using free budgeting apps such as *Snoop, PocketGuard*, and *Moneyhub*, which can help students monitor and plan their expenses. Furthermore, there are apps, such as *VoucherCodes, Coupert*, and *Shopmium* which can help in finding discounted products and coupons. The authors also advise universities to regularly invite guest speakers- particularly those with financial or entrepreneurial expertise- to share practical tips on effective money management.

The third stressor refers to students facing tougher coursework and assessments at university; leading to busy schedules and heightened vulnerability to isolation and withdrawal (Munir et al., 2015). To help students manage more challenging assignments, the authors recommend that universities maintain up-to-date policies on available writing support services and actively promote these resources through their websites and social media channels. Additionally, universities should implement policies requiring tutors to collect regular updates from students on their academic progress through regular meetings, ensuring they stay informed about students' performance and wellbeing. Furthermore, based on the authors' academic experience, a common issue arises when multiple assignment deadlines fall on the same day, which can be overwhelming for students. Therefore, universities should implement policies that prevent module leaders from scheduling overlapping deadlines.

The fourth stressor refers to the performance driven culture in academia. For staff, intense competition for funding and stable positions can erode collegial trust. For students, high achieving environments amplify pressure and discourage help seeking, which makes it harder to build supportive relationships when peers feel like rivals (Ueno et al., 2024; Jandric, 2022). Although this issue may be difficult, if not impossible, to eliminate entirely, universities can ensure the presence of an open-door policy that allows students to discuss their concerns with tutors. Additionally, universities should maintain an up-to-date workload policy requiring management to monitor staff workloads and address instances where staff are working excessive hours. This can be achieved by monitoring the duration of staff members' online activity to help identify excessive working hours and re-distribute the workload where necessary. Furthermore, academic work is often solitary, making it challenging for both staff and students to form and maintain friendships (Jandric, 2022; Ousman & Nazir, 2023). Therefore, the authors of this chapter recommend that universities consider establishing shared offices for departmental staff and open workspaces for students to encourage interaction and foster relationship building.

The fifth and final stressor refers to excessive use of social media which is linked to poorer wellbeing (Hu et al., 2023). Although social media can help reduce loneliness by making it easier to connect with others, it can also be a double-edged sword, as excessive use (cyberloafing) may lead to replacing genuine in-person interactions with artificial online ones (Ousman & Nazir, 2023). Therefore, the authors of this chapter recommend monitoring social media usage, which can be achieved through apps such as *Freedom* and *RescueTime*. Additionally, university stakeholders are encouraged to schedule specific times for social media and set time limits for its usage. Stakeholders should also consider removing social media triggers by, for example, moving social media apps off the home screen into a 'Later' folder. Together, these factors map the main causes of loneliness in academia and set up a discussion of its consequences. These are discussed in the next section.

3.2 Consequences of Loneliness

Loneliness within the academic context can lead to a range of negative consequences. To avoid feelings of loneliness, university stakeholders may be at risk of engaging in maladaptive coping behaviors, such as excessive alcohol consumption and drug misuse (Ahuja et al., 2024). These behaviors are detrimental to health, resulting in increased risk of addiction, high blood pressure, heart and liver problems, and increased risk of cancer (Lo et al., 2020). An additional maladaptive behavior associated with loneliness is excessive TV watching (Liu et al., 2025). Excessive TV watching has been linked to intensified feelings of stress and anxiety, sleep deprivation, risk of obesity, and poor academic performance (Nakshine et al., 2022). Evidence also indicates that loneliness can lead to cyberloafing, or excessive use of the internet and social media for non-academic purposes during study or work time (Yang et al., 2023). This may also negatively impact academic performance and further intensify feelings of loneliness. Another maladaptive coping strategy may involve denying feelings of loneliness or convincing oneself that loneliness is not present (Akbulut & Pamuk, 2025), which can hinder university stakeholders from seeking the support they need.

Loneliness is also associated with reduced cognitive functioning and concentration (Yin et al., 2019). Consequently, students who experience loneliness are at risk of being unable to complete learning activities, and recall or memorise learning materials (Le, 2021) which can lead to poor grades. The sufferers of loneliness also report diminished motivation to interact with others (Cacioppo & Cacioppo, 2018). As a result, students who experience loneliness are more likely to engage in absenteeism which explains why they are at a heightened risk of dropping out of university, as the backlog of missed work can quickly become overwhelming (Adenuga et al., 2025). Dropping out of university can be deleterious in itself, as it can lead to reduced labor market opportunities (Payne, 2023), reduced self-esteem (Andersson et al., 2024), and reduced health and life satisfaction (Klein et al., 2021). Students' dropout rates can also impact external stakeholders, such as their parents or guardians who may feel disappointed in their child for dropping out (Fathi-Ashtiani et al., 2021). Having outlined the consequences of loneliness, the following section examines the university stakeholders who are most at risk of experiencing it.

3.3 Key Vulnerable Groups

The key vulnerable groups identified through the process of the scoping review are first-year students, international students, neurodivergent students, and lecturers. These stakeholders are discussed below.

3.3.1 First-Year Students

The first year of university can be particularly challenging (Hassel & Ridout, 2018). Evidence shows that 49.5% of students report feeling lonely with first-year students being at 2.47 odds of loneliness in comparison to students in year two and above (Dagnew & Dagne, 2019). The prominence of loneliness among first-years may be caused by new undergraduates arriving at university with expectations shaped by schools that are often unrealistic in higher education (Hassel & Ridout, 2018). A common expectation is that information will be spoon-fed; the shift to self-directed learning can therefore be unsettling (Murtagh, 2012; Thompson et al., 2021), leaving some students feeling they must "figure things out" alone. Expectations about small class sizes can be similarly misplaced (Hassel & Ridout, 2018): large lecture theatres and seminars can foster anonymity and a sense of being a small cog in a large machine.

Additionally, the limits on staff availability for individual student support (Macaskill, 2013; Worsley et al., 2021) may compound these feelings. As a solution to this issue, the authors of this chapter recommend that universities revise their outreach policies to ensure that representatives visiting schools and colleges provide a realistic portrayal of university life, including both its opportunities and challenges. In addition, first-year students frequently report course dissatisfaction (van Rooij et al., 2018), which can undermine belonging to the chosen field and intensify loneliness. Therefore, the authors of this chapter suggest that universities implement questionnaires on their websites to gather information about prospective students' interests and passions, helping them choose the most suitable course of study. The next section discusses the second key vulnerable group- international students.

3.3.2 International Students

International students are those who attend university outside their home country. International students enrich host communities and contribute to local economies (Zheng et al., 2023). Yet, evidence shows that as many as 75% of international students experience loneliness (Wawera & McCamley, 2019). Loneliness may be particularly daunting for students from collectivist cultures (e.g., East Asian or Latin American countries), as they place greater emphasis on interdependence and close relationships (Barreto et al., 2021). However, this does not mean that students from individualistic cultures (e.g., Western countries) face less struggles, as evidence demonstrates that they may be less likely to seek support (Das, 2024).

International students experience loneliness in unique ways, often influenced by factors beyond their or the university's control- such as culture shock and the daunting feeling of starting life from scratch (Hasnain & Hajek, 2022; Götz et al., 2019), differences in social and cultural norms, food, and climate (Shan et al., 2020; Morris et al., 2022), as well as policy-related uncertainties surrounding visa regulations and fluctuating tuition fees, particularly in countries like the UK, the US, and Australia (Boddy, 2020; Park & Shimada, 2022). These challenges can contribute to loneliness, often leaving international students feeling as though they are facing more obstacles than their home-based peers. To ease this pressure, the authors of this chapter recommend that universities promote the services of international student support officers, who can provide tailored advice and guidance to help students navigate academic and personal challenges. Additionally, where possible, the authors recommend that universities pair international students with academic tutors who share a similar cultural or linguistic background, as this may encourage more open and honest communication about their challenges.

From the authors' own academic experience, many international students also struggle with language barriers. Being unable to communicate may make international students feel excluded and lead to loneliness. Therefore, it is advised that university policies permit the recording of lectures, allowing students to replay and translate the content as needed. International students can also benefit from apps, such as *Google Translate, Translate Me* and *Wordly Translation*, which provide real-time translation into their native languages. Evidence also shows that international students are likely to face discrimination in the form of exclusion, particularly those with foreign and difficult to pronounce names (Das, 2024; Girmay & Singh, 2019). The authors of this chapter recommend that universities develop comprehensive EDI policies. This includes establishing clear and accessible processes for reporting incidents of racial discrimination. Additionally, universities should implement anonymous assessment methods, ensuring that markers cannot view students' names or images, to promote fairness in grading. The next section examines loneliness among neurodivergent students.

3.3.3 Neurodivergent Students

Young adults who are neurodivergent are at up to four times greater risk of experiencing loneliness compared to their non-neurodivergent peers (Quadt et al., 2024). Neurodiversity is the natural variation in how people perceive and process the world, including autism, ADHD, dyslexia, and Tourette's (Stenning & Bertilsdotter-Rosqvist,

2021). Neurodivergent students face higher loneliness risk because conventional curricula favor long passive lectures and rigid norms, leading to misperceptions of disengagement (Sulaimani & Gut, 2019). To reduce disengagement, the authors of this chapter recommend that universities adopt flexible teaching policies allowing staff to use multiple instructional formats- such as visual, auditory, and written methods. This flexibility should also extend to assessment, offering alternative formats, such as written assignments in place of presentations. The provision of extended deadlines can also be beneficial for neurodivergent students, as they may require more time for reading and writing, and experience slower task completion (Cheetham, 2024).

Evidence also shows that neurodivergent students often experience sensory overload, particularly in noisy, brightly lit and crowded rooms (Sulaimani & Gut, 2019). This can lead to loneliness, making neurodivergent students feel like they do not belong. Therefore, the authors suggest that lecturers familiarize themselves with their students through available records before teaching and, where possible, reserve quiet, sensory-friendly classrooms. Teaching staff are also recommended to encourage assistive technology, such as speech-to-text, to support neurodivergent students in completing their projects. Flexibility should also extend to attendance policies, and lecturers are advised not to confront neurodivergent students who arrive late to class, as this may increase their stress and discomfort. Additionally, differences in communication and cue-reading can invite exclusion (Kusurkar et al., 2021). This difficulty in communicating can impact finding employment after university. Therefore, universities are advised to provide neurodiversity training, particularly to career advisors, who can support neurodivergent students and prepare them for work interviews. The next section examines loneliness among lecturers.

3.3.4 Lecturers

Lecturers are also at a heightened risk of loneliness. Studies reveal that 46% of academics experience the feelings of loneliness at some point in their career (Sibai et al., 2019). It is no secret that lecturing is demanding- balancing teaching, administrative duties, and continual research (Rajamanikam, 2024). The 'publish or perish' culture prevalent in academia places immense pressure on academics, often compelling them to work long and demanding hours (Rawat & Meena, 2014). This workload can disrupt a healthy work-life balance, leading to social withdrawal and weakened connections with family and social networks (Gawande, 2024). Additionally, excessive work demands are closely associated with burnout (Kusurkar et al., 2021), a condition that has been strongly linked to experiences of loneliness (McCarthy et al., 2025). Although some solutions to this issue have already been proposed, such as monitoring and redistributing staff workload, the university's management team could further address the problem by implementing new technologies to help staff streamline certain tasks. Furthermore, the management team must comply with the university's policy on staff breaks, ensuring that staff do not work during their break times.

Another challenge that lecturers face is the prevalent toxic culture in academia; characterized by bullying, mobbing, and toxic management styles (Thomas, 2023). Those who whistle-blow and expose these practices often face adverse consequences (Thomas, 2023). The inability to openly discuss the toxic culture in academia may enhance the feelings of loneliness among lecturers. As a solution, the authors of this chapter recommend that lecturers who experience hostile behavior from colleagues seek support from trade unions or regulatory bodies, which can provide advice and guidance. For the management team, it is important to conduct regular anonymous surveys that allow lecturers to openly share their experiences and challenges at work. It is also important for the management team to set clear policies on what constitutes bullying and how to report it, as well as offer regular anti-bullying training to all staff.

Interestingly, lecturers in leadership roles are argued to be most at risk of loneliness (Ong, 2022). This may stem from shifts in relationships with former colleagues- from informal to formal- where senior lecturers are viewed less as friends and more as bosses. The increase in workload for senior lecturers can also impose limitations on their social life. Furthermore, evidence shows that female lecturers in senior roles are at more risk of loneliness compared to their male counterparts (Ong, 2022). This may be attributed to gender-bias where female seniors are perceived as less competent by male seniors. To combat gender bias in academia, the authors of this chapter suggest keeping a record of all gender-biased incidents. HR team are also advised to regularly update their grievance policy to make the process as simple as possible whilst complying with industry standards. Female leaders are also advised to join associations, such as Advance HE's *Women in Higher Education Network* where they can offer each other support and guidance.

Another group of lecturers who are at a heightened risk of loneliness are those that teach online (Mosleh et al., 2022). This is because remote work is associated with reduced team cohesion (Ferreira et al., 2021) where online lecturers feel as they are not part of a team. To overcome this issue, team leaders are advised to schedule regular team meetings online and plan regular social events where all remote staff members can interact face-to-face. The following section explores personal strategies for combatting loneliness.

3.4 Personal Strategies for Combatting Loneliness.

The scoping review identified four key personal strategies that can be utilized by university stakeholders on their own. These strategies are detailed below.

3.4.1 Healthy Lifestyle

Loneliness can be eased through everyday lifestyle choices. Regular physical activity is consistently linked to lower loneliness as it boosts dopamine, serotonin and endorphins. Engaging in physical activity also gives a sense of achievement and can therefore build self-esteem which is a necessary component in building relationships with others (Harris & Orth, 2020). Regular exercise also helps in structuring one's daily routine which can reduce engagement in maladaptive behaviors like excessive internet use and cyberloafing (Davies et al., 2016). Additionally, participating in team-based sports facilitates regular contact with others and is effective at fostering a sense of belonging (Kim et al., 2019). The authors of this chapter also suggest that regular exercise can provide individuals with something to look forward to, helping to replace negative thoughts with positive ones.

To maximise the benefits of physical activity, adults should aim for 150-300 minutes of moderate or 75-100 minutes of vigorous exercise each week (Bull et al., 2020). Furthermore, it is necessary to pair exercise with a healthy diet that is rich in fruit and vegetables, whole grains, nuts and seeds, and limited in saturated fat and added sugar (Aydin, 2025). The authors of this chapter recommend joining a local gym, which often offers discounted rates for university students. For those on a limited budget, the authors suggest finding exercise groups- such as walking or running clubs- through social media platforms like *Facebook*. To assist in creating a healthy lifestyle routine, university stakeholders can benefit from AI platforms such as *ChatGPT*, which can help design personalized workout and diet plans without the cost of a personal trainer. The next section examines the effectiveness of meditation.

3.4.2 Meditation

Meditation refers to the mental ability to connect the mind with the body. Meditation is associated with multiple health benefits, such as reduced stress and anxiety (Elder et al., 2014), reduced physical and psychological pain (Grant et al., 2010), and increased cognitive functioning (Khalsa, 2015). The practice of meditation can also alleviate the feelings of loneliness through increasing the grey matter in the brain (Chételat et al., 2018). While meditation can feel challenging at the beginning, it is actually quite simple. Start by choosing a quiet, distraction-free space and adopting a comfortable position- whether standing, sitting, or lying down. Focus your attention on your breath, noticing how your body responds to each inhale and exhale. It's natural for your mind to wander; when you notice this, gently acknowledge it and bring your focus back to your breathing. For beginners, daily meditation sessions of 5-10 minutes are recommended, gradually increasing the duration as you gain experience (Saini et al., 2021). There are free apps available that can support you through your meditation journey, such as *Insight Timer*, *Smiling Mind* and *Medito*. The authors of this chapter also recommend using platforms such as *YouTube*, where university stakeholders can follow guided meditation sessions led by trainers, helping them feel less alone in their practice. The next section discusses the effectiveness of mindfulness.

3.4.3 Mindfulness

Mindfulness refers to the ability to be aware of and pay attention to one's thoughts, feelings, and surroundings as they occur in the present moment (Salvi et al., 2025). Mindfulness is also a useful tool to reduce the feelings of loneliness (Pandya, 2021). This is because it encourages the individual to acknowledge sensations- including unpleasant ones- that are often suppressed, gradually desensitizing them to these experiences (Salvi et al., 2025). Mindfulness can be practiced in many everyday situations. For instance, while eating, focus on the flavor, aroma, texture, and temperature of your food. When walking, notice your surroundings, along with the sounds and scents you encounter. Although this might seem tricky at first, there are many free apps that can support you in becoming more mindful, such as *Plum Village App, UCLA Mindful* and *Healthy Minds Program*. The authors of this chapter also suggest practicing mindfulness through journaling. Writing down one's thoughts and feelings can make them easier to process. Additionally, keeping a gratitude journal- listing things one is thankful for- can help put situations into perspective and foster a more positive outlook. The gratitude list doesn't have to include major achievements; it can also feature simple things, such as appreciating good weather, finishing an assignment on time, or enjoying a nutritious breakfast. There are many free apps that can be used for journaling, including *Penzu*, *My Diary*, and *Journey*. Engaging in skill development programs can also alleviate loneliness which is discussed in the next section.

3.4.4 Developing New Skills

Evidence shows that learning new skills is an additional strategy to manage the feeling of loneliness. This is because attending skills courses, whether in person or online, provides opportunities to meet and interact with other learners as well as the instructors (De Felice et al., 2023). Free courses can be found on websites such as *Coursera, FutureLearn*, and *Khan Academy*. Another way of learning new skills is through volunteering. Volunteering refers to engaging in unpaid work that benefits the society (Husk et al., 2016). Volunteering in itself is associated with reduced loneliness (Warner et al., 2024). In fact, it is considered so effective in reducing loneliness that scholars have advocated for its inclusion in public health initiatives, educational programs, and national policy (Yeung et al., 2017). There are many available volunteering opportunities that can be found in local newspapers and local community boards. These opportunities can also be found online through websites, such as *VolunteerMatch.org*, *All for Good*, and *Idealist.org*. These sources provide opportunities to work in food banks and soup kitchens, homeless shelters, senior centers, animal shelters, and wildlife rescue centers. However, the authors of this chapter believe that it is important to choose volunteering opportunities that align with one's passions and interests to ensure sustained engagement. Additionally, since academic workload can be demanding, individuals should also consider their current commitments and select opportunities accordingly. To help stakeholders manage their time, the authors recommend utilising the Eisenhower Matrix to help prioritise urgent and important tasks over non-urgent and non-important tasks. The next section discusses university-led interventions.

3.5 University-Led Interventions for Combatting Loneliness

The scoping review identified five key university-led strategies for combatting loneliness. These strategies are detailed below.

3.5.1 Cognitive Behavioral Therapy

Cognitive Behavioral Therapy (CBT) is an effective strategy for combatting loneliness (Ellard et al., 2023). CBT aims to help patients identify current patterns of thinking and behavior and develop skills to evaluate and change irrational maladaptive thoughts and actions into positive rational ones (Hassan Kariri & Almubaddel, 2024). During CBT, patients articulate maladaptive thoughts and behaviors while the therapist uses Socratic questioning to help them examine evidence, reframe interpretations, and develop more adaptive alternatives. Typical prompts include: 'What do you think is causing this?', 'What other ways could you look at this?', and 'What else might we assume?' (Fenn & Byrne, 2013). To ensure the most effective delivery of CBT programs, the authors of this chapter recommend that CBT be established as a key component of the university's mental health policy. This includes partnering with CBT accredited organisations and therapists to ensure service quality. The CBT section of the university's mental health policy should be updated regularly and align with the latest evidence and best practices.

The authors also recommend offering short optional modules for students on managing loneliness using CBT principles. The university's policy should also include the provision of individual and group CBT. This is important because neurodivergent students may feel uncomfortable discussing their emotions in group settings, while lecturers may be hesitant to share their feelings with students. The policy should also provide both face-to-face and online CBT options to ensure accessibility for those who cannot attend on campus (Thase et al., 2020). However, CBT does have its limitations. For example, evidence shows that patients can still relapse back to maladaptive thoughts and behaviors after completing the course (Cuijpers et al., 2013). CBT also requires the completion of regular homework (Kazantzis et al., 2016). This can be challenging to manage, particularly for university stakeholders with busy schedules. Therefore, CBT should be used in combination with other strategies, such as social skills training which is discussed below.

3.5.2 Social Skills Training

Social skills training is argued to be a useful tool for reducing loneliness (Cacioppo et al., 2015). Evidence indicates it is particularly beneficial for neurodivergent individuals (Anchieta et al., 2025). The purpose of social skills training is to teach trainees about developing and maintaining social connections, holding a conversation, and using humor appropriately (Płatos et al., 2023). Training is typically conducted in small group settings where participants first identify the skills they need to develop. They then engage in role-play activities where they utilize these skills in practice, before obtaining feedback from the instructor and other participants on their performance (Anchieta et al., 2025). Therefore, social skills training not only equips trainees with the skills to form friendships, but it also provides opportunities to meet others with similar difficulties- potentially fostering new friendships.

The authors of this chapter recommend that social skills training be incorporated into the university's student support policy. This should include providing quiet spaces where students can develop their social skills, as well as running university-wide awareness campaigns and promoting the service through the university's website, social media channels, posters, and leaflets. Self-paced digital modules should also be promoted. These courses are freely available on platforms such as *Udemy* and can be especially beneficial for introverted students and international students with language barriers. However, social skills training does have its limitations. For instance, evidence shows that the lessons learnt in training do not always generalize to real-world contexts, perhaps owing to the artificial nature of the training environment (Carruthers et al., 2020). To overcome this obstacle, the university's management team should consider introducing optional work experience modules within students' courses, allowing them to develop and apply their social skills in real-life settings. Social skills training should be used in conjunction with other strategies, such as group discussions, which is discussed below.

3.5.3 Group Discussions

Group discussions have been proven to reduce loneliness among students (Ellard et al., 2023). Discussion groups enable students to share their struggles and give each other advice and support (Gold et al., 2019). Such groups enable students to feel 'listened to' and being part of a community which are important components in combatting loneliness (Haslam et al., 2022). Group discussions can also be delivered face-to face or online (Marshall et al., 2024) to include stakeholders who are unable to attend in-person. The authors of this chapter argue that group discussions should be included in the university's policy on student and staff support.

Specifically, the policy should encourage organizing these discussion groups by cohort or affinity to enhance participation and engagement. For example, discussion groups for neurodivergent students only, can foster stronger social bonds and encourage greater openness (Pellicano et al., 2022). A likely reason is homophily based on shared neurodivergent experiences, which fosters connection more readily than with non-neurodivergent peers. The same framework could be extended to first-year and international students, but also to lecturers by running staff-only discussion groups, as lecturers may find it easier to express their feelings to colleagues than to their students. The policy should also involve parents and friends, not only to promote openness but also to help them manage potential feelings of loneliness that may result from a student leaving home for university. However, not all participants involved in group discussions may feel comfortable sharing their personal struggles with loneliness. To overcome this obstacle, the authors suggest universities introducing anonymous mental health hotlines as part of their wider wellbeing policy to provide confidential and stigma-free support. Therefore, universities should also consider providing 1-2-1 peer support which is discussed below.

3.5.4 1-2-1 Peer Support

One-to-one (1-2-1) peer mentoring is effective for reducing student loneliness (Fortuna et al., 2022). Typically, a more experienced student shares lived experience, builds rapport, and maps the mentee's current social connections before co-creating a graded action plan of societies, events, and study or interest groups for the mentee to try (Lorenzetti et al., 2019; Webber et al., 2015). The mentor then supports first steps, monitors progress and iteratively adjusts goals to fit the mentee's needs and confidence. Its core strength is the non-hierarchical peer dynamic, which can feel safer and more relatable than staff-led support (Mikolajczak-Degrauwe et al., 2023).

The authors of this chapter therefore suggest that universities introduce 1-2-1 peer support as part of their wider wellbeing policy. However, universities must be aware of the potential risks associated with peer mentoring. These risks include under-involvement (insufficient support) and over-involvement (a controlling, "parent–child" relationship). Universities can mitigate these risks by providing mentors with mentalization training, so mentors calibrate help to a professional standard (Hall et al., 2015). The authors also recommend the strategic pairing of mentors and mentees, for example, by using tools such as the Myers–Briggs Type Indicator (MBTI) to help ensure compatibility and foster positive mentoring relationships. The next section examines university-led social events.

3.5.5 Social Events

Participating in university-led social events is also associated with lower levels of loneliness (Hansen & Budtz Pedersen, 2018). Such events encourage social interaction and create shared positive experiences. Therefore, universities are recommended to include campus-based social events as part of their student support policy. To effectively deliver social events, scholars argue that they should be tailored around the specific characteristics of its target audience to foster a sense of belonging (Rodriguez & Blaney, 2021; Morrish et al., 2023). This could include, for example, faith-based events, LGBTQ+ events or neurodivergence awareness events. The authors of this chapter also suggest allowing students' family and friends to attend these events to encourage engagement. The authors also recommend allowing students to participate in the design and development of these events which can enhance their team-building skills.

For lecturers, event ideas could include academic conferences or cross-department events. Hosting such events can enable relationship building and potential collaborations on research projects with other academics (Kuzhabekova & Temerbayeva, 2018). Furthermore, given that alcohol-centered socializing can exclude non-drinkers, universities should also deliver alcohol-free events (Ross-Houle & Quigg, 2019). Moreover, as noted in Section 3.5.1 (Healthy Lifestyle), exercise is an effective strategy for reducing loneliness. Academic institutions should therefore provide sport-oriented events- preferably team-based (e.g., football, tennis or field hockey). to foster a sense of identity among students (Costello et al., 2022). The next section provides final tips and words of encouragement.

3.6 Final Tips and Words of Encouragement

Neil Strauss once said, *"Great things never come from comfort zones."* In other words, if something were easy, everyone would do it. Higher education is no exception- your academic journey will be challenging and may at times be marked by loneliness. Yet, earning a degree is an extraordinary achievement. It not only equips you with lifelong knowledge and skills to enrich both your personal and professional life but also shapes your resilience. Learning to manage loneliness along the way is an achievement in itself, preparing you to handle similar feelings in the future. By engaging with this book chapter, you have already taken your first steps towards building that skill.

Whether you are a student or an academic, remember that you are not alone in experiencing loneliness. Many others within the university community share these feelings. The key is to take steady, small steps- speak to someone, join a group, or seek support- because a problem shared is a problem halved. Focus on the present; the past cannot be changed, and the future is still to be shaped. Celebrate every small success you achieve in addressing loneliness, as these moments are milestones in your journey. Most people who have been through higher education eventually look back on their experience with joy and pride. That is exactly what the authors of this chapter hope you will one day feel too.

4. CONCLUSION

In summary, this book chapter serves as a valuable resource for university stakeholders seeking to reduce loneliness in academia. Addressing this issue is crucial, as loneliness remains a prevalent yet seldom discussed challenge in higher education, often leaving universities ill-equipped to support those affected. The chapter achieves its purpose by outlining the primary causes of loneliness in academic settings, including financial difficulties, homesickness, maladaptive behaviors such as excessive social media use, demanding academic workloads, and the solitary nature of scholarly work. It also clearly highlights the consequences of loneliness, such as diminished academic performance and motivation, absenteeism, increased dropout risk, reduced career prospects, and physical and mental health problems.

The chapter identifies four key groups most at risk of loneliness: first-year students, international students, neurodivergent students, and lecturers. First-year students often enter university with unrealistic expectations of academic life, which can lead to disappointment and isolation. To address this, universities are encouraged to implement policies that promote writing support services, prevent overlapping assignment deadlines, maintain open-door policies, provide collaborative workspaces, and ensure that outreach activities portray university life realistically. International students face additional barriers as they must adjust not only to academic demands but also to unfamiliar cultural norms and values. To support them, universities should actively promote international student support services, permit lecture recordings, adopt anonymized grading practices, and regularly update EDI policies. Neurodivergent students are also at heightened risk of loneliness, often finding everyday academic tasks more challenging. Universities should therefore ensure flexible teaching formats, offer alternative assessment methods, allow extended deadlines, provide flexibility in attendance requirements, and deliver neurodiversity awareness training for all staff. Beyond the student body, lecturers are also vulnerable to loneliness, often due to excessive workloads and the competitive, isolating culture of academia. To mitigate this, universities must ensure compliance with workload and break policies and maintain up-to-date grievance policies aligned with HR best practices.

Finally, this book chapter outlines strategies to support university stakeholders most at risk of loneliness. For self-managed approaches, it recommends maintaining a healthy lifestyle through balanced nutrition and regular exercise, practicing meditation and mindfulness- such as journaling- and developing new skills through courses or volunteering. For university-led interventions, the authors highlight the importance of making cognitive behavioural therapy (CBT) widely accessible to help individuals reframe negative thoughts. They also advocate one-to-one peer mentoring, social skills training, and discussion groups where stakeholders can openly share experiences. Additionally, organizing regular social events is encouraged to foster connection, promote inclusion, and facilitate friendship formation across the academic community, ultimately creating a more supportive and connected university environment.

REFERENCES

Adenuga, I., Tuncer, B., MacDonald, K. B., & Schermer, J. A. (2025). The relationship between loneliness and school dropout. *Current Research in Behavioral Sciences*, *9*, 100183. DOI: 10.1016/j.crbeha.2025.100183

Ahuja, M., Miller-Slough, R., Adebayo-Abikoye, E., Williams, C., Haubner, A., Dooley, M. G., Bansal, M., Sathiyaseelan, T., Pons, A., Karki, A., Al Ksir, K., Samuel, B., Tchoua, P., Schuver, T., & Fernandopulle, P. (2024). Loneliness and Alcohol use among College Students During the COVID-19 Pandemic in Rural Appalachia. *Chronic Stress (Thousand Oaks, Calif.)*, *8*, 24705470241264909. DOI: 10.1177/24705470241264909

Akbulut, Ö. F., & Pamuk, K. (2025). Rumination, Loneliness, Task-Oriented Coping and Mental Well-Being Among University Students: A Serial Mediation Model. *Psychological Reports*, *00332941251329788*, 00332941251329788. Advance online publication. DOI: 10.1177/00332941251329788

Allen, K.-A., Kern, M. L., Rozek, C. S., McInerney, D. M., & Slavich, G. M. (2021). Belonging: A review of conceptual issues, an integrative framework, and directions for future research. *Australian Journal of Psychology*, *73*(1), 87–102. DOI: 10.1080/00049530.2021.1883409

Anchieta, M. V., Torro-Alves, N., da Fonsêca, É. K. G., & de Lima Osório, F. (2025). Effects of social skills training on social responsiveness of people with Autism spectrum disorder: A systematic review with meta-analysis. *European Child & Adolescent Psychiatry*, *34*(7), 2007–2022. DOI: 10.1007/s00787-025-02697-7

Andersson, M. A., Wilkinson, R., & Maralani, V. (2024). Revisiting Health Disparities Linked to "Some College": Incorporating Gender and High School Experiences. *Social Currents*, *11*(2), 159–180. DOI: 10.1177/23294965231175822

Auerbach, R. P., Mortier, P., Bruffaerts, R., Alonso, J., Benjet, C., Cuijpers, P., Demyttenaere, K., Ebert, D. D., Green, J. G., Hasking, P., Murray, E., Nock, M. K., Pinder-Amaker, S., Sampson, N. A., Stein, D. J., Vilagut, G., Zaslavsky, A. M., & Kessler, R. C.WHO WMH-ICS Collaborators. (2018). WHO World Mental Health Surveys International College Student Project: Prevalence and distribution of mental disorders. *Journal of Abnormal Psychology*, *127*(7), 623–638. DOI: 10.1037/abn0000362

Aydin, N. (2025). Understanding of a healthy diet in relation to current guidelines: A case study of UK university students. *Health Education Journal*, *84*(2), 125–134. DOI: 10.1177/00178969251316813

Barreto, M., Victor, C., Hammond, C., Eccles, A., Richins, M. T., & Qualter, P. (2021). Loneliness around the world: Age, gender, and cultural differences in loneliness. *Personality and Individual Differences*, *169*, 110066. DOI: 10.1016/j.paid.2020.110066

Bayraktar, S., & Jiménez, A. (2022). Friend or foe? The effects of harmonious and obsessive passion on entrepreneurs' well-being, strain and social loneliness. *Cross Cultural & Strategic Management*, *29*(2), 320–348. DOI: 10.1108/CCSM-03-2021-0056

Belkhir, M., Brouard, M., Brunk, K. H., Dalmoro, M., Ferreira, M. C., Figueiredo, B., Huff, A. D., Scaraboto, D., Sibai, O., & Smith, A. N. (2019). Isolation in Globalizing Academic Fields: A Collaborative Autoethnography of Early Career Researchers. *Academy of Management Learning & Education*, *18*(2), 261–285. DOI: 10.5465/amle.2017.0329

Bevens, W., Stoeckl, S. E., Schueller, S. M., Kim, J., Cha, B. S., Chwa, C., Stadnick, N. A., Best, N. C., & Sorkin, D. H. (2024). Loneliness, online learning and student outcomes in college students living with disabilities: Results from the National College Health Assessment Spring 2022. *Frontiers in Psychology*, *15*, 1408837. DOI: 10.3389/fpsyg.2024.1408837

Boddy, C. (2020). Lonely, homesick and struggling: Undergraduate students and intention to quit university. (2020). *Quality Assurance in Education*, *28*(4), 239–253. DOI: 10.1108/QAE-05-2020-0056

Bu, F., Steptoe, A., & Fancourt, D. (2020). Who is lonely in lockdown? Cross-cohort analyses of predictors of loneliness before and during the COVID-19 pandemic. *Public Health*, *186*, 31–34. DOI: 10.1016/j.puhe.2020.06.036

Buecker, S., Maes, M., Denissen, J. J. A., & Luhmann, M. (2020). Loneliness and the Big Five Personality Traits: A Meta–Analysis. *European Journal of Personality*, *34*(1), 8–28. DOI: 10.1002/per.2229

Bugallo-Carrera, C., Dosil-Díaz, C., Anido-Rifón, L., Pacheco-Lorenzo, M., Fernández-Iglesias, M. J., & Gandoy-Crego, M. (2023). A systematic review evaluating loneliness assessment instruments in older adults. *Frontiers in Psychology*, *14*, 1101462. DOI: 10.3389/fpsyg.2023.1101462

Bull, F. C., Al-Ansari, S. S., Biddle, S., Borodulin, K., Buman, M. P., Cardon, G., Carty, C., Chaput, J.-P., Chastin, S., Chou, R., Dempsey, P. C., DiPietro, L., Ekelund, U., Firth, J., Friedenreich, C. M., Garcia, L., Gichu, M., Jago, R., Katzmarzyk, P. T., & Willumsen, J. F. (2020). World Health Organization 2020 guidelines on physical activity and sedentary behaviour. *British Journal of Sports Medicine*, *54*(24), 1451–1462. DOI: 10.1136/bjsports-2020-102955

Cacioppo, J. T., & Cacioppo, S. (2018). Chapter Three - Loneliness in the Modern Age: An Evolutionary Theory of Loneliness (ETL). In Olson, J. M. (Ed.), Vol. 58, pp. 127–197). Advances in Experimental Social Psychology. Academic Press., DOI: 10.1016/bs.aesp.2018.03.003

Cacioppo, J. T., Cacioppo, S., & Boomsma, D. I. (2014). Evolutionary mechanisms for loneliness. *Cognition and Emotion*, *28*(1), 3–21. DOI: 10.1080/02699931.2013.837379

Cacioppo, J. T., Hawkley, L. C., & Thisted, R. A. (2010). Perceived social isolation makes me sad: 5-year cross-lagged analyses of loneliness and depressive symptomatology in the Chicago Health, Aging, and Social Relations Study. *Psychology and Aging*, *25*(2), 453–463. DOI: 10.1037/a0017216

Cacioppo, S., Grippo, A. J., London, S., Goossens, L., & Cacioppo, J. T. (2015). Loneliness: clinical import and interventions. *Perspectives on psychological science: a journal of the Association for Psychological Science, 10*(2), 238–249. DOI: 10.1177/1745691615570616

Carruthers, S., Pickles, A., Slonims, V., Howlin, P., & Charman, T. (2020). Beyond intervention into daily life: A systematic review of generalisation following social communication interventions for young children with autism. *Autism Research*, *13*(4), 506–522. DOI: 10.1002/aur.2264

Cheetham, L. J. (2024). "Because people don't know what it is, they don't really know it exists": A qualitative study of postgraduate medical educators' perceptions of dyscalculia. *BMC Medical Education*, *24*(1), 896. DOI: 10.1186/s12909-024-05912-2

Chételat, G., Lutz, A., Arenaza-Urquijo, E., Collette, F., Klimecki, O., & Marchant, N. (2018). Why could meditation practice help promote mental health and well-being in aging? *Alzheimer's Research & Therapy*, *10*(1), 57. DOI: 10.1186/s13195-018-0388-5

Colquhoun, H. L., Levac, D., O'Brien, K. K., Straus, S., Tricco, A. C., Perrier, L., Kastner, M., & Moher, D. (2014). Scoping reviews: Time for clarity in definition, methods, and reporting. *Journal of Clinical Epidemiology*, *67*(12), 1291–1294. DOI: 10.1016/j.jclinepi.2014.03.013

Costello, M. A., Nagel, A. G., Hunt, G. L., Rivens, A. J., Hazelwood, O. A., Pettit, C., & Allen, J. P. (2022). Facilitating connection to enhance college student well-being: Evaluation of an experiential group program. *American Journal of Community Psychology*, *70*(3–4), 314–326. DOI: 10.1002/ajcp.12601

Cuijpers, P., Hollon, S. D., van Straten, A., Bockting, C., Berking, M., & Andersson, G. (2013). Does cognitive behaviour therapy have an enduring effect that is superior to keeping patients on continuation pharmacotherapy? A meta-analysis. *BMJ Open*, *3*(4), e002542. DOI: 10.1136/bmjopen-2012-002542

Dabrowski, V., Atas, N., Ramsey, T., & Howarth, N. (2025). 'Money anxiety': Understanding HE students' experiences of the cost-of-living crisis. *Social Policy and Administration*, *59*(2), 280–292. DOI: 10.1111/spol.13048

Dagnew, B., & Dagne, H. (2019). Year of study as predictor of loneliness among students of University of Gondar. *BMC Research Notes*, *12*(1), 240. DOI: 10.1186/s13104-019-4274-4

Das, B. (2024). Loneliness of PhD-ing: Migrant bodies of colour and Irish neo-liberal academia. *Irish Journal of Sociology*, *32*(1–2), 47–65. DOI: 10.1177/07916035241259254

Davies, N., Crowe, M., & Whitehead, L. (2016). Establishing routines to cope with the loneliness associated with widowhood: A narrative analysis. *Journal of Psychiatric and Mental Health Nursing*, *23*(8), 532–539. DOI: 10.1111/jpm.12339

De Felice, S., Hamilton, A. F. de C., Ponari, M., & Vigliocco, G. (2023). Learning from others is good, with others is better: The role of social interaction in human acquisition of new knowledge. *Philosophical Transactions of the Royal Society of London. Series B, Biological Sciences, 378*(1870), 20210357. DOI: 10.1098/rstb.2021.0357

Diehl, K., Jansen, C., Ishchanova, K., & Hilger-Kolb, J. (2018). Loneliness at Universities: Determinants of Emotional and Social Loneliness among Students. *International Journal of Environmental Research and Public Health, 15*(9), 1865. DOI: 10.3390/ijerph15091865

Egaña-Marcos, E., Collantes, E., Diez-Solinska, A., & Azkona, G. (2025). The Influence of Loneliness, Social Support and Income on Mental Well-Being. *European Journal of Investigation in Health, Psychology and Education, 15*(5), 70. DOI: 10.3390/ejihpe15050070

Elder, C., Nidich, S., Moriarty, F., & Nidich, R. (2014). Effect of transcendental meditation on employee stress, depression, and burnout: A randomized controlled study. *The Permanente Journal, 18*(1), 19–23. DOI: 10.7812/TPP/13-102

Ellard, O. B., Dennison, C., & Tuomainen, H. (2023). Review: Interventions addressing loneliness amongst university students: a systematic review. *Child and Adolescent Mental Health, 28*(4), 512–523. DOI: 10.1111/camh.12614

Fakoya, O. A., McCorry, N. K., & Donnelly, M. (2020). Loneliness and social isolation interventions for older adults: A scoping review of reviews. *BMC Public Health, 20*(1), 129. DOI: 10.1186/s12889-020-8251-6

Fathi-Ashtiani, M., Hosseinchari, M., Ahmadi, F., & Jowkar, B. (2021). Lived Experiences of Dropout University Students: A Qualitative Content Analysis. *International Journal of Behavioral Sciences, 15*(1), 41–47. DOI: 10.30491/ijbs.2021.258913.1440

Fenn, K., & Byrne, M. (2013). The key principles of cognitive behavioural therapy. *InnovAiT, 6*(9), 579–585. DOI: 10.1177/1755738012471029

Ferreira, R., Pereira, R., Bianchi, I. S., & da Silva, M. M. (2021). Decision Factors for Remote Work Adoption: Advantages, Disadvantages, Driving Forces and Challenges. *Journal of Open Innovation, 7*(1), 70. DOI: 10.3390/joitmc7010070

Fortuna, K. L., Solomon, P., & Rivera, J. (2022). An Update of Peer Support/Peer Provided Services Underlying Processes, Benefits, and Critical Ingredients. *The Psychiatric Quarterly, 93*(2), 571–586. DOI: 10.1007/s11126-022-09971-w

Gawande, R. P. (2024). Work-life balance and its impact on employees: Navigating strategies for better work-life balance at workplace. *International Journal of Cultural Studies and Social Science, 20*(1), 130–136.

Girmay, M., & Singh, G. K. (2019). Social Isolation, Loneliness, and Mental and Emotional Well-being among International Students in the United States. *International Journal of Translational Medical Research and Public Health, 3*(2), 1–8. DOI: 10.21106/ijtmrph.82

Gold, J. A., Bentzley, J. P., Franciscus, A. M., Forte, C., & De Golia, S. G. (2019). An Intervention in Social Connection: Medical Student Reflection Groups. *Academic Psychiatry, 43*(4), 375–380. DOI: 10.1007/s40596-019-01058-2

Götz, F. M., Stieger, S., & Reips, U.-D. (2019). The Emergence and Volatility of Homesickness in Exchange Students Abroad: A Smartphone-Based Longitudinal Study. *Environment and Behavior, 51*(6), 689–716. DOI: 10.1177/0013916518754610

Granieri, A., Franzoi, I. G., & Chung, M. C. (2021). Editorial: Psychological Distress Among University Students. *Frontiers in Psychology, 12*, 647940. DOI: 10.3389/fpsyg.2021.647940

Grant, J. A., Courtemanche, J., Duerden, E. G., Duncan, G. H., & Rainville, P. (2010). Cortical thickness and pain sensitivity in zen meditators. *Emotion (Washington, D.C.), 10*(1), 43–53. DOI: 10.1037/a0018334

Hall, S. L., Ryan, D. J., Beatty, J., & Grubbs, L. (2015). Recommendations for peer-to-peer support for NICU parents. *Journal of Perinatology: Official Journal of the California Perinatal Association, 35 Suppl 1*(Suppl 1), S9-13. DOI: 10.1038/jp.2015.143

Hansen, T. T., & Budtz Pedersen, D. (2018). The impact of academic events—A literature review. *Research Evaluation, 27*(4), 358–366. DOI: 10.1093/reseval/rvy025

Harris, M. A., & Orth, U. (2020). The link between self-esteem and social relationships: A meta-analysis of longitudinal studies. *Journal of Personality and Social Psychology, 119*(6), 1459–1477. DOI: 10.1037/pspp0000265

Haslam, S. A., Haslam, C., Cruwys, T., Jetten, J., Bentley, S. V., Fong, P., & Steffens, N. K. (2022). Social identity makes group-based social connection possible: Implications for loneliness and mental health. *Current Opinion in Psychology, 43*, 161–165. DOI: 10.1016/j.copsyc.2021.07.013

Hasnain, A., & Hajek, J. (2022). Understanding international student connectedness. *International Journal of Intercultural Relations, 86*, 26–35. DOI: 10.1016/j.ijintrel.2021.10.008

Hassan Kariri, H. D., & Almubaddel, A. (2024). From theory to practice: Revealing the real-world impact of cognitive behavioral therapy in psychological disorders through a dynamic bibliometric and survey study. *Heliyon, 10*(18), e37763. DOI: 10.1016/j.heliyon.2024.e37763

Hassel, S., & Ridout, N. (2018). An Investigation of First-Year Students' and Lecturers' Expectations of University Education. *Frontiers in Psychology, 8*, 2218. Advance online publication. DOI: 10.3389/fpsyg.2017.02218

Hodgson, S., Watts, I., Fraser, S., Roderick, P., & Dambha-Miller, H. (2020). Loneliness, social isolation, cardiovascular disease and mortality: A synthesis of the literature and conceptual framework. *Journal of the Royal Society of Medicine, 113*(5), 185–192. DOI: 10.1177/0141076820918236

Holt-Lunstad, J., Smith, T. B., Baker, M., Harris, T., & Stephenson, D. (2015). Loneliness and social isolation as risk factors for mortality: A meta-analytic review. *Perspectives on Psychological Science: A Journal of the Association for Psychological Science, 10*(2), 227–237. DOI: 10.1177/1745691614568352

Hu, Z., Zhu, Y., Li, J., Liu, J., & Fu, M. (2023). The COVID-19 related stress and social network addiction among Chinese college students: A moderated mediation model. *PLoS One, 18*(8), e0290577. DOI: 10.1371/journal.pone.0290577

Husk, K., Lovell, R., Cooper, C., Stahl-Timmins, W., & Garside, R. (2016). Participation in environmental enhancement and conservation activities for health and well-being in adults: A review of quantitative and qualitative evidence. *The Cochrane Library, 2016*(5), CD010351. Advance online publication. DOI: 10.1002/14651858.CD010351.pub2

Jandric, P. (2022). Alone-Time and Loneliness in the Academia. *Postdigital Science and Education, 4*(3), 633–642. DOI: 10.1007/s42438-022-00294-4

Kaufmann, R., & Vallade, J. I. (2022). Exploring connections in the online learning environment: Student perceptions of rapport, climate, and loneliness. *Interactive Learning Environments, 30*(10), 1794–1808. DOI: 10.1080/10494820.2020.1749670

Kazantzis, N., Whittington, C., Zelencich, L., Kyrios, M., Norton, P. J., & Hofmann, S. G. (2016). Quantity and Quality of Homework Compliance: A Meta-Analysis of Relations With Outcome in Cognitive Behavior Therapy. *Behavior Therapy, 47*(5), 755–772. DOI: 10.1016/j.beth.2016.05.002

Kerr, N. A., & Stanley, T. B. (2021). Revisiting the social stigma of loneliness. *Personality and Individual Differences, 171*, 110482. DOI: 10.1016/j.paid.2020.110482

Khalsa, D. S. (2015). Stress, Meditation, and Alzheimer's Disease Prevention: Where The Evidence Stands. *Journal of Alzheimer's Disease, 48*(1), 1–12. DOI: 10.3233/JAD-142766

Kim, Y.-S., O'Sullivan, D. M., & Shin, S.-K. (2019). Can 24 weeks strength training reduce feelings of depression and increase neurotransmitter in elderly females? *Experimental Gerontology, 115*, 62–68. DOI: 10.1016/j.exger.2018.11.009

Klein, D., Mishra, S., & Müller, L. (2021). Die langfristigen individuellen Konsequenzen des Studienabbruchs. In Neugebauer, M., Daniel, H.-D., & Wolter, A. (Eds.), *Studienerfolg und Studienabbruch* (pp. 279–300). Springer Fachmedien., DOI: 10.1007/978-3-658-32892-4_12

Kusurkar, R. A., van der Burgt, S. M. E., Isik, U., Mak-van der Vossen, M., Wilschut, J., Wouters, A., & Koster, A. S. (2021). Burnout and engagement among PhD students in medicine: The BEeP study. *Perspectives on Medical Education, 10*(2), 110–117. DOI: 10.1007/S40037-020-00637-6

Kuzhabekova, A., & Temerbayeva, A. (2018). The role of conferences in doctoral student socialization. *Studies in Graduate and Postdoctoral Education, 9*(2), 181–196. DOI: 10.1108/SGPE-D-18-00012

Le, H. V. (2021). An Investigation into Factors Affecting Concentration of University Students. *Journal of English Language Teaching and Applied Linguistics, 3*(6), 07–12. DOI: 10.32996/jeltal.2021.3.6.2

Lim, M. H., Eres, R., & Vasan, S. (2020). Understanding loneliness in the twenty-first century: An update on correlates, risk factors, and potential solutions. *Social Psychiatry and Psychiatric Epidemiology, 55*(7), 793–810. DOI: 10.1007/s00127-020-01889-7

Liu, Z., Werneck, A. O., Herold, F., Lowe, C. J., Hallgren, M., Cheval, B., Tari, B., Stubbs, B., Gerber, M., Falck, R. S., Kramer, A. F., Owen, N., & Zou, L. (2025). Bidirectional relationships between television viewing and loneliness in middle-aged and older men and women. *Journal of Affective Disorders, 388*, 119737. DOI: 10.1016/j.jad.2025.119737

Lo, T. W., Yeung, J. W. K., & Tam, C. H. L. (2020). Substance Abuse and Public Health: A Multilevel Perspective and Multiple Responses. *International Journal of Environmental Research and Public Health, 17*(7), 2610. DOI: 10.3390/ijerph17072610

Lorenzetti, D. L., Shipton, L., Nowell, L., Jacobsen, M., Lorenzetti, L., Clancy, T., & Paolucci, E. O. (2019). A systematic review of graduate student peer mentorship in academia. *Mentoring & Tutoring, 27*(5), 549–576. DOI: 10.1080/13611267.2019.1686694

Luo, W., Zhong, B.-L., & Chiu, H. F.-K. (2021). Prevalence of depressive symptoms among Chinese university students amid the COVID-19 pandemic: A systematic review and meta-analysis. *Epidemiology and Psychiatric Sciences, 30*, e31. DOI: 10.1017/S2045796021000202

Macaskill, A. (2013). The mental health of university students in the United Kingdom. *British Journal of Guidance & Counselling, 41*(4), 426–441. DOI: 10.1080/03069885.2012.743110

Marshall, P., Booth, M., Coole, M., Fothergill, L., Glossop, Z., Haines, J., Harding, A., Johnston, R., Jones, S., Lodge, C., Machin, K., Meacock, R., Nielson, K., Puddephatt, J.-A., Rakic, T., Rayson, P., Robinson, H., Rycroft-Malone, J., Shryane, N., & Lobban, F. (2024). Understanding the Impacts of Online Mental Health Peer Support Forums: Realist Synthesis. *JMIR Mental Health, 11*, e55750. DOI: 10.2196/55750

McCarthy, J. M., Erdogan, B., Bauer, T. N., Kudret, S., & Campion, E. (2025). All the Lonely People: An Integrated Review and Research Agenda on Work and Loneliness. *Journal of Management, 01492063241313320*, 01492063241313320. Advance online publication. DOI: 10.1177/01492063241313320

Mikolajczak-Degrauwe, K., Slimmen, S. R., Gillissen, D., de Bil, P., Bosmans, V., Keemink, C., Meyvis, I., & Kuipers, Y. J. (2023). Strengths, weaknesses, opportunities and threats of peer support among disadvantaged groups: A rapid scoping review. *International Journal of Nursing Sciences, 10*(4), 587–601. DOI: 10.1016/j.ijnss.2023.09.002

Morris, A., Mitchell, E., Wilson, S., Ramia, G., & Hastings, C. (2022). Loneliness within the Home among International Students in the Private Rental Sector in Sydney and Melbourne. *Urban Policy and Research, 40*(1), 67–81. DOI: 10.1080/08111146.2021.2005017

Morrish, N., Choudhury, S., & Medina-Lara, A. (2023). What works in interventions targeting loneliness: A systematic review of intervention characteristics. *BMC Public Health, 23*(1), 2214. DOI: 10.1186/s12889-023-17097-2

Mosleh, S. M., Kasasbeha, M. A., Aljawarneh, Y. M., Alrimawi, I., & Saifan, A. R. (2022). The impact of online teaching on stress and burnout of academics during the transition to remote teaching from home. *BMC Medical Education, 22*(1), 475. DOI: 10.1186/s12909-022-03496-3

Munir, T., Shafiq, S., Ahmad, Z., & Khan, S. (2015). Impact of loneliness and academic stress on psychological well being among college students. *Academic Research International, 6*(2), 343.

Murtagh, L. (2012). Enhancing preparation for higher education. *Practitioner Research in Higher Education, 6*(1), 31–39.

Nakshine, V. S., Thute, P., Khatib, M. N., & Sarkar, B. (2022). Increased Screen Time as a Cause of Declining Physical, Psychological Health, and Sleep Patterns: A Literary Review. *Cureus, 14*(10), e30051. DOI: 10.7759/cureus.30051

Newall, N. E. G., Chipperfield, J. G., Bailis, D. S., & Stewart, T. L. (2013). Consequences of loneliness on physical activity and mortality in older adults and the power of positive emotions. *Health Psychology: Official Journal of the Division of Health Psychology, American Psychological Association, 32*(8), 921–924. DOI: 10.1037/a0029413

Ong, W. J. (2022). Gender-contingent effects of leadership on loneliness. *The Journal of Applied Psychology, 107*(7), 1180–1202. DOI: 10.1037/apl0000907

Osimo, S. A., Aiello, M., Gentili, C., Ionta, S., & Cecchetto, C. (2021). The Influence of Personality, Resilience, and Alexithymia on Mental Health During COVID-19 Pandemic. *Frontiers in Psychology, 12*, 630751. DOI: 10.3389/fpsyg.2021.630751

Ousman, Y. I., & Nazir, T. (2023). Loneliness among University students as a growing concerne. *Journal of Family Counseling and Education, 8*(2), 85–99. DOI: 10.32568/jfce.1312556

Pandya, S. P. (2021). Meditation program mitigates loneliness and promotes well-being, life satisfaction and contentment among retired older adults: A two-year follow-up study in four South Asian cities. *Aging & Mental Health, 25*(2), 286–298. DOI: 10.1080/13607863.2019.1691143

Park, C., & Shimada, S. (2022). The impact of changing nonimmigrant visa policies on international students' psychological adjustment and well-being in the United States during the COVID-19 pandemic: A qualitative study. *BMC Public Health, 22*(1), 2227. DOI: 10.1186/s12889-022-14698-1

Payne, S. S. C. (2023). Equalization or Reproduction? "Some College" and the Social Function of Higher Education. *Sociology of Education, 96*(2), 104–128. DOI: 10.1177/00380407221134809

Pellicano, E., Lawson, W., Hall, G., Mahony, J., Lilley, R., Heyworth, M., Clapham, H., & Yudell, M. (2022). "I Knew She'd Get It, and Get Me": Participants' Perspectives of a Participatory Autism Research Project. *Autism in Adulthood: Challenges and Management, 4*(2), 120–129. DOI: 10.1089/aut.2021.0039

Płatos, M., Wojaczek, K., & Laugeson, E. A. (2023). Effects of Social Skills Training for Adolescents on the Autism Spectrum: A Randomized Controlled Trial of the Polish Adaptation of the PEERS® Intervention via Hybrid and In-Person Delivery. *Journal of Autism and Developmental Disorders, 53*(11), 4132–4146. DOI: 10.1007/s10803-022-05714-9

Quadt, L., Williams, G., Mulcahy, J., Larsson, D. E. O., Silva, M., Arnold, A. J., Critchley, H. D., & Garfinkel, S. N. (2024). "I'm Trying to Reach Out, I'm Trying to Find My People": A Mixed-Methods Investigation of the Link Between Sensory Differences, Loneliness, and Mental Health in Autistic and Nonautistic Adults. *Autism in Adulthood: Challenges and Management*, *6*(3), 284–299. DOI: 10.1089/aut.2022.0062

Rajamanikam, S. R. (2024). The Challenges of a Lecturer in a Higher Learning Institution (HLI) in Malaysia. *International Journal of Academic Research in Progressive Education and Development*, *13*(4), 368–382. DOI: 10.6007/IJARPED/v13-i4/23041

Rawat, S., & Meena, S. (2014). Publish or perish: Where are we heading? *Journal of Research in Medical Sciences : the Official Journal of Isfahan University of Medical Sciences*, *19*(2), 87–89.

Richardson, T., Elliott, P., & Roberts, R. (2017). Relationship between loneliness and mental health in students. *Journal of Public Mental Health*, *16*(2), 48–54. DOI: 10.1108/JPMH-03-2016-0013

Rippe, J. (2024). Loneliness and Lifestyle Medicine. *American Journal of Lifestyle Medicine*, *18*(4), 456–458. DOI: 10.1177/15598276231207279

Rodriguez, S. L., & Blaney, J. M. (2021). "We're the unicorns in STEM": Understanding how academic and social experiences influence sense of belonging for Latina undergraduate students. *Journal of Diversity in Higher Education*, *14*(3), 441–455. DOI: 10.1037/dhe0000176

Ross-Houle, K., & Quigg, Z. (2019). Content, perceptions and impact of alcoholic drink promotions in nightlife venues that are targeted towards students. *Addictive Behaviors Reports*, *9*, 100163. DOI: 10.1016/j.abrep.2019.100163

Saini, G. K., Haseeb, S. B., Taghi-Zada, Z., & Ng, J. Y. (2021). The effects of meditation on individuals facing loneliness: A scoping review. *BMC Psychology*, *9*(1), 88. DOI: 10.1186/s40359-021-00585-8

Salvi, D., Shah, R., & Tripathi, R. (2025). The Essence of Mindfulness: A Detailed Primer. In Dutta, G., Misra, G., & Gupta, S. (Eds.), *Handbook of Positive Psychology and Indian Thought Systems: Transforming Education for Well-being and Happiness* (pp. 261–280). Springer Nature., DOI: 10.1007/978-981-96-4210-6_17

Shan, C., Hussain, M., & Sargani, G. R. (2020). A mix-method investigation on acculturative stress among Pakistani students in China. *PLoS One*, *15*(10), e0240103. DOI: 10.1371/journal.pone.0240103

Shin, E., Bui, K., & Park, J. (2023). Loneliness Rates among Undergraduates from 2008 to 2022, according to Data from the National College Health Assessment. *Seaver College Research And Scholarly Achievement Symposium*. https://digitalcommons.pepperdine.edu/scursas/2023/posters/29

Sibai, O., Figueiredo, B. & Ferreira, M.C. (2019, January 30). The Loneliness of the Long-Suffering Researcher. *Social Sciences Space*. The Loneliness of the Long-Suffering Researcher - Social Science Space

Slavich, G. M. (2020). Social safety theory: A biologically based evolutionary perspective on life stress, health, and behavior. *Annual Review of Clinical Psychology*, *16*(1), 265–295. DOI: 10.1146/annurev-clinpsy-032816-045159

Stenning, A., & Bertilsdotter-Rosqvist, H. (2021). Neurodiversity studies: Mapping out possibilities of a new critical paradigm. *Disability & Society*, *36*(9), 1532–1537. DOI: 10.1080/09687599.2021.1919503

Stickley, A., & Koyanagi, A. (2016). Loneliness, common mental disorders and suicidal behavior: Findings from a general population survey. *Journal of Affective Disorders*, *197*, 81–87. DOI: 10.1016/j.jad.2016.02.054

Sulaimani, M. F., & Gut, D. M. (2019). Hidden Curriculum in a Special Education Context: The Case of Individuals with Autism. *Journal of Educational Research and Practice*, *9*(1), 30–39. DOI: 10.5590/JERAP.2019.09.1.03

Taylor, Z., Yankouskaya, A., & Panourgia, C. (2024). Social media use, loneliness and psychological distress in emerging adults. *Behaviour & Information Technology*, *43*(7), 1312–1325. DOI: 10.1080/0144929X.2023.2209797

Thase, M. E., McCrone, P., Barrett, M. S., Eells, T. D., Wisniewski, S. R., Balasubramani, G. K., Brown, G. K., & Wright, J. H. (2020). Improving Cost-effectiveness and Access to Cognitive Behavior Therapy for Depression: Providing Remote-Ready, Computer-Assisted Psychotherapy in Times of Crisis and Beyond. *Psychotherapy and Psychosomatics*, *89*(5), 307–313. DOI: 10.1159/000508143

Thomas, D. N. (2023). The burden of calling out toxic academic practices. *Nature*, *624*(7991), 252–252. DOI: 10.1038/d41586-023-03951-1

Thompson, M., Pawson, C., & Evans, B. (2021). Navigating entry into higher education: The transition to independent learning and living. *Journal of Further and Higher Education*, *45*(10), 1398–1410. DOI: 10.1080/0309877X.2021.1933400

Tricco, A. C., Lillie, E., Zarin, W., O'Brien, K., Colquhoun, H., Kastner, M., Levac, D., Ng, C., Sharpe, J. P., Wilson, K., Kenny, M., Warren, R., Wilson, C., Stelfox, H. T., & Straus, S. E. (2016). A scoping review on the conduct and reporting of scoping reviews. *BMC Medical Research Methodology*, *16*(1), 15. DOI: 10.1186/s12874-016-0116-4

Ueno, A., Yu, C., Curtis, L., & Dennis, C. (2024). Job demands-resources theory extended: Stress, loneliness, and care responsibilities impacting UK doctoral students' and academics' mental health. *Studies in Higher Education*, *50*(4), 808–823. DOI: 10.1080/03075079.2024.2357148

van Rooij, E. C. M., Jansen, E. P. W. A., & van de Grift, W. J. C. M. (2018). First-year university students' academic success: The importance of academic adjustment. *European Journal of Psychology of Education*, *33*(4), 749–767. DOI: 10.1007/s10212-017-0347-8

von Soest, T., Luhmann, M., & Gerstorf, D. (2020). The development of loneliness through adolescence and young adulthood: Its nature, correlates, and midlife outcomes. *Developmental Psychology*, *56*(10), 1919–1934. DOI: 10.1037/dev0001102

Warner, L. M., Yeung, D. Y.-L., Jiang, D., Choi, N. G., Ho, R. T. H., Kwok, J. Y. Y., & Chou, K.-L. (2024). Effects of volunteering over six months on loneliness, social and mental health outcomes among older adults: The HEAL-HOA Dual Randomized Controlled Trial. *The American Journal of Geriatric Psychiatry*, *32*(5), 598–610. DOI: 10.1016/j.jagp.2023.12.022

Wawera, A. S., & McCamley, A. (2019). Loneliness among international students in the UK. *Journal of Further and Higher Education*.

Webber, M., Reidy, H., Ansari, D., Stevens, M., & Morris, D. (2015). Enhancing social networks: A qualitative study of health and social care practice in UK mental health services. *Health & Social Care in the Community*, *23*(2), 180–189. DOI: 10.1111/hsc.12135

Worsley, J. D., Harrison, P., & Corcoran, R. (2021). Bridging the Gap: Exploring the Unique Transition From Home, School or College Into University. *Frontiers in Public Health*, *9*, 634285. DOI: 10.3389/fpubh.2021.634285

Yan, C. O. (2024). Non-citizens' Continuity of Citizenship in the Baltic States. *The International Journal of Interdisciplinary Social and Community Studies*, *20*(1), 1–24. DOI: 10.18848/2324-7576/CGP/v20i01/1-24

Yang, H., Lin, Z., Chen, X., & Peng, J. (2023). Workplace loneliness, ego depletion and cyberloafing: Can leader problem-focused interpersonal emotion management help? *Internet Research, 33*(4), 1473–1494. DOI: 10.1108/INTR-01-2021-0007

Yeung, J. W. K., Zhang, Z., & Kim, T. Y. (2017). Volunteering and health benefits in general adults: Cumulative effects and forms. *BMC Public Health, 18*(1), 8. DOI: 10.1186/s12889-017-4561-8

Yin, J., Lassale, C., Steptoe, A., & Cadar, D. (2019). Exploring the bidirectional associations between loneliness and cognitive functioning over 10 years: The English longitudinal study of ageing. *International Journal of Epidemiology, 48*(6), 1937–1948. DOI: 10.1093/ije/dyz085

Zebhauser, A., Hofmann-Xu, L., Baumert, J., Häfner, S., Lacruz, M. E., Emeny, R. T., Döring, A., Grill, E., Huber, D., Peters, A., & Ladwig, K. H. (2014). How much does it hurt to be lonely? Mental and physical differences between older men and women in the KORA-Age Study. *International Journal of Geriatric Psychiatry, 29*(3), 245–252. DOI: 10.1002/gps.3998

Zhang, N., Fan, F.-M., Huang, S.-Y., & Rodriguez, M. A. (2018). Mindfulness training for loneliness among Chinese college students: A pilot randomized controlled trial. *International Journal of Psychology, 53*(5), 373–378. DOI: 10.1002/ijop.12394

Zheng, K., Johnson, S., Jarvis, R., Victor, C., Barreto, M., Qualter, P., & Pitman, A. (2023). The experience of loneliness among international students participating in the BBC Loneliness Experiment: Thematic analysis of qualitative survey data. *Current Research in Behavioral Sciences, 4*, 100113. DOI: 10.1016/j.crbeha.2023.100113

ADDITIONAL READINGS

Bernardon, S., Babb, K. A., Hakim-Larson, J., & Gragg, M. (2011). Loneliness, attachment, and the perception and use of social support in university students. *Canadian Journal of Behavioural Science / Revue Canadienne. Science et Comportement, 43*(1), 40–51. DOI: 10.1037/a0021199

Blodgett, J. M., Tiley, K., Harkness, F., & Musella, M. (2025). What works to reduce loneliness: A rapid systematic review of 101 interventions. *Journal of Public Health Policy, 46*(2), 245–268. DOI: 10.1057/s41271-025-00561-1

Campbell, F., Blank, L., Cantrell, A., Baxter, S., Blackmore, C., Dixon, J., & Goyder, E. (2022). Factors that influence mental health of university and college students in the UK: A systematic review. *BMC Public Health*, *22*(1), 1778. DOI: 10.1186/s12889-022-13943-x

McIntyre, J. C., Worsley, J., Corcoran, R., Harrison Woods, P., & Bentall, R. P. (2018). Academic and non-academic predictors of student psychological distress: The role of social identity and loneliness. *Journal of Mental Health (Abingdon, England)*, *27*(3), 230–239. DOI: 10.1080/09638237.2018.1437608

Riboldi, I., Crocamo, C., Piacenti, S., Capogrosso, C. A., Calabrese, A., Lucini Paioni, S., Bartoli, F., Armes, J., Taylor, C., & Carrà, G. (2025). Mental health and loneliness in university students: A structural equation modelling comparing Italy and the UK. *The International Journal of Social Psychiatry*, *00207640251346273*(8), 1574–1586. Advance online publication. DOI: 10.1177/00207640251346273

Chapter 6
Isolation in White Coats: The Political Economy of Loneliness Among Global Healthcare Migrants

Tina Lee
https://orcid.org/0009-0000-4705-3028
Aurora High School, USA

Luna Lee
Northeast Ohio Neighborhood Health Services, Inc., USA

Chenxiao Hu
The First Hospital of Lanzhou University, China

Nicolas Melin
Adel's SAS, France

Laure C. Bouchez
Adel's SAS, France

Dylan Lee
https://orcid.org/0009-0004-3059-2841
CuraStrategix Health, USA

ABSTRACT

This chapter reframes loneliness among globally mobile healthcare professionals as a structural outcome of political economy rather than an individual shortcoming. Using an interdisciplinary review and a U.S–China comparison (with selective UK references), it traces how migration regimes, credentialing bottlenecks, institutional hierarchies, and market logics jointly produce isolation among migrant clinicians. Four interlocking dynamics emerge—bureaucratic precarity, emotional dislocation, professional invisibility, and commodification of care—each linked to burnout, attrition, and underused cultural–linguistic assets. We translate this synthesis into multi-level remedies: institution-level onboarding, mentorship, mental-health supports, and anti-bias systems; national reforms to visas, fair-contract enforcement, and credential recognition; and cross-border adherence to the WHO Code, bilateral supports, and better migration data.

DOI: 10.4018/979-8-3373-5811-6.ch006

INTRODUCTION

Loneliness is no longer a merely individual or psychological condition; it has become an institutional, economic, and political symptom of the modern world (Boniol et al., 2022; Giroud, 2024; Ramji & Etowa, 2018). The contemporary global order, characterized by rapid mobility, neoliberal labor regimes, and fragmented social ties, has produced novel forms of social isolation even among the most professionally successful and socially mobile individuals (Ahmed et al., 2018; Yeates & Pillinger, 2020). One such group, which paradoxically embodies both privilege and precarity, comprises global healthcare migrants (Ramji & Etowa, 2018). These are the doctors, nurses, researchers, and medical executives who cross borders to meet the demands of an increasingly globalized and strained healthcare workforce (General, 2023). While their mobility is often framed as opportunity and advancement, the lived experience of these professionals frequently includes a persistent sense of dislocation, bureaucratic limbo, and emotional estrangement, conditions not immediately visible but structurally embedded within contemporary political economy (Austin & Gregory, 2024; Omiyi et al., 2025).

This chapter explores loneliness as a systemic and under-theorized outcome of skilled healthcare migration, focusing on two major national systems: the United States and China. While the U.S. continues to serve as a magnet for foreign-trained healthcare professionals due to its high wages and global prestige, it also imposes rigid credentialing regimes and fragmented institutional cultures that limit integration. In China, rapid health sector modernization and internationalization have led to increasing recruitment of returnee doctors and foreign medical executives; however, these individuals often encounter localized professional silos, hierarchical rigidity, and limited institutional support (Hou et al., 2014; Hu et al., 2021; Illouz, 2007; Jakovljevic et al., 2023; Li et al., 2019). In both settings, the promise of professional success coexists with the reality of social and relational rupture. This paradox forms the foundation for analyzing how neoliberal globalization transforms not only healthcare systems, but also the emotional and existential terrain of those who serve within them (Ahmed et al., 2018; Hertz, 2021).

Framing healthcare migrants not merely as economic actors but also as subjects of political and emotional economies, this chapter contributes to a more nuanced understanding of the "loneliness economy", a term that encompasses how capitalism commodifies disconnection and reframes social isolation as a condition to be treated through consumption. Healthcare professionals are selected because their work is uniquely positioned at the intersection of state regulation, professional credentialing, and human care. Their dependence on licensure and team-based practice makes them especially sensitive indicators of how institutional and policy frameworks translate into lived social isolation. While existing studies have investigated loneliness in the context of the elderly, digital natives, or those impacted by automation, comparatively less research has been devoted to the global class of mobile professionals who, despite their outward achievements, navigate persistent relational instability (Austin & Gregory, 2024; Giroud, 2024). The chapter argues that the loneliness of healthcare migrants is not incidental or idiosyncratic but the product of a structured mismatch between labor mobility and institutional belonging.

This framework allows the chapter to serve three core objectives. First, it maps the structural production of loneliness among healthcare migrants through credentialing bottlenecks, professional segmentation, and policy intransigence. Second, it identifies how this loneliness generates demand for ancillary markets and consumption practices, contributing to the expansion of the loneliness economy. Third, it evaluates the macroeconomic implications of professional disconnection, including burnout, attrition, and reduced innovation within health systems. These threads are woven through comparative analysis of the United States and China, with selective reference to the United Kingdom, to offer a globally relevant but contextually grounded interpretation.

Methods and Approach

This chapter adopts a comparative qualitative design grounded in political economy and health labor studies. Peer-reviewed and gray literature from 2010–2024 were analyzed through directed content analysis, mapping four structural mechanisms, bureaucratic precarity, emotional dislocation, professional invisibility, and commodification of care, across the United States and China. The comparison highlights how differing policy, cultural, and market structures produce parallel outcomes of loneliness. This approach synthesizes cross-disciplinary insights to generate a theoretical framework linking macro-level policies with micro-level experiences of isolation among healthcare migrants.

To complement this qualitative design, we outline a quantitative extension: outcomes,short-form UCLA Loneliness, burnout (Maslach subscales), intent-to-leave; exposures, visa/authorization class, credentialing stage and time-to-licensure, rural/underserved assignment and shift pattern, presence of mentorship/onboarding; data sources—hospital HR and wellness surveys, licensure rosters and exam pass lists, specialty-society surveys, and program participation files (e.g., waiver/Conrad placements); designs, cross-sectional/panel models with facility and time fixed effects; difference-in-differences/event-study around policy shocks (e.g., waiver expansions, contract-penalty enforcement); and synthetic-control comparisons for hospitals adopting structured onboarding. Heterogeneity by discipline, country of training, and geography will be pre-specified, with repeated short-form instruments to minimize burden and improve response rates..

Background and Context

Neoliberalism here denotes market-centric governance of health labor, outsourcing, throughput metrics, and shifting risk onto workers, while globalization denotes cross-border integration of training pipelines, credential flows, and recruitment chains. Clinician loneliness is treated as an outcome that emerges where these forces produce prolonged status liminality, skill underuse, and thin workplace social infrastructure. The international migration of healthcare professionals is not a new phenomenon, but its scale, complexity, and internal contradictions have dramatically intensified over the past three decades (Connell, 2010; Siyam et al., 2013). Historically, physicians and nurses moved from lower-income countries to higher-income ones in response to better working conditions, wages, and professional recognition (Brush et al., 2004). However, as health systems globalized and deregulated under neoliberal reforms, these labor flows began to take on new systemic significance (Gauthier, 2009). Today, high-income countries depend structurally on the steady import of medical talent, while exporting nations simultaneously suffer from brain drain and asymmetric workforce depletion (Clemens & Pettersson, 2008; Siyam et al., 2013). The World Health Organization (2020) reported that more than one in eight doctors working in OECD countries were trained abroad, and in some contexts, such as the United Kingdom and Australia, that number exceeds one-third of the workforce .

Such migration is shaped by both push and pull factors. On the push side, inadequate infrastructure, limited research opportunities, and a lack of institutional transparency in origin countries incentivize emigration (Lopez-Abuin, 2010). On the pull side, high-income destinations offer better resources but impose rigorous credentialing regimes that delay or obstruct full professional integration (Walton-Roberts et al., 2017). The U.S., for example, requires international medical graduates to pass multi-step exams and secure limited residency slots, resulting in years-long lags between arrival and licensure (Mullan, 1995; Travis, 2023). China, while actively recruiting returnee scholars and medical professionals to enhance its domestic innovation base, has failed to provide cohesive reintegration pathways, leading to symbolic recognition but also functional marginalization (Wang & Liu, 2022).

Amid this structural entanglement, the concept of loneliness has emerged as a crucial, though often neglected, dimension of transnational medical labor. Loneliness, once narrowly defined as a lack of intimate relationships, is now reconceptualized as the erosion of embeddedness within collective institutions, civic life, and professional networks (Cacioppo & Cacioppo, 2018). Recent interdisciplinary research has highlighted how labor flexibility, privatization, and technological substitution exacerbate feelings of social isolation, even among the most formally integrated workers (Beaunoyer et al., 2020; Cunha, 2013; Guay & Drago, 2021; Singh & Steeves, 2020). The case of healthcare professionals is particularly revealing: these individuals work in collaborative and service-oriented environments, yet often report deep emotional alienation due to high workloads, regulatory uncertainty, and cultural dissonance (Walton-Roberts et al., 2017).

For migrant professionals, this isolation is not just psychological, it is structural. Credentialing regimes fragment entry and delay recognition (Mullan, 1995); visa regimes tether mobility to institutional sponsorship (Angel & Fire, 2023); hospital cultures valorize efficiency over collegiality (Sanner-Stiehr et al., 2021); and transnationalism itself weakens durable social ties (*The State and the Grassroots*, 2015). Many foreign-trained physicians in the United States, for example, live without their immediate families due to immigration constraints (Mullan, 1995). Returnee doctors in China face skepticism from domestic peers and barriers to accessing leadership roles (Ma, 2020; Wang & Liu, 2022). Even when these individuals speak the local language fluently or hold prestigious degrees, they may remain symbolically peripheral, granted professional space but denied relational inclusion (Walton-Roberts et al., 2017). The ensuing comparative analysis operationalizes these political-economy concepts within a policy-oriented framework, consistent with contemporary political-science approaches to labor and migration governance.

COMPARATIVE ANALYSIS

In comparing the United States and China, clear differences emerge in how structural conditions, credentialing regimes, institutional hierarchies, market forces, and cultural norms, shape the loneliness and isolation of migrant healthcare workers (Al-Btoush & El-Bcheraoui, 2024). Both countries' healthcare systems are embedded in distinct policy frameworks and labor market logics, which produce unique challenges for internationally mobile healthcare professionals. This section synthesizes key similarities and differences, highlighting how systemic factors in each context contribute to professional isolation among migrant doctors and nurses. Differences in immigration policies, migration pathways, labor market needs, and institutional responses in the U.S. versus China create divergent experiences of loneliness for migrant clinicians (Cho et al., 2023; Dotsey, 2023; Leitão et al., 2024). Yet, common threads, such as credentialing hurdles, precarious employment, and cultural dislocation, transcend the two settings, underscoring the global political economy of loneliness in healthcare migration (Toyin-Thomas et al., 2023).

Table 1. U.S. and China compared: Structural conditions shaping migrant clinicians' loneliness

Dimension	United States	China	Implications for Loneliness
Migration pathways & visas	High inflows via H-1B/J-1; waiver routes (e.g., Conrad 30) tie practice to underserved areas; family reunification can be slow.	Limited long-term entry for foreign clinicians; temporary practice permits; returnee diaspora prioritized; family accompaniment constrained.	Visa/permit dependence sustains liminality; separation from family and uncertainty dampen social investment.
Credentialing regimes	USMLE/NCLEX; state-by-state variability; repetition of training common; bridge programs uneven.	National exams; recognition of foreign credentials limited; institutional discretion high; re-entry norms for returnees opaque.	Delayed role congruence undermines identity and peer integration; skill underuse fuels invisibility.
Institutional hierarchy & culture	Emphasis on compliance, documentation, and productivity; formal DEI efforts exist but uneven; team hierarchies vary by specialty.	Strong seniority/departmental hierarchies; guanxi networks; deference norms; limited structured support for foreigners.	Power distance and informal networks gatekeep belonging; newcomers lack sponsors and safe voice.
Market forces & employment models	Corporate consolidation; staffing agencies; stay-or-pay contracts in some settings; throughput metrics (RVUs).	Public–private hybridity; revenue targets; rapid corporatization in top cities; niche private/expat hospitals.	Commodification thins collegial ties; precarious contracts inhibit help-seeking and candid dissent.
Typical isolation mechanisms	Rural/remote placements; accent bias; exclusion from informal networks; family separation.	Language barriers; outsider status in tight teams; symbolic inclusion without authority; festival/family-centric rhythms.	Daily micro-exclusions cumulate into chronic loneliness; holidays and off-duty time intensify it.
Protective factors	Large diasporas; professional associations; mentorship where present; EAP/mental health access.	Cohesive teams once trust established; returnee prestige in select units; emerging international clinics.	Deliberate onboarding, peers, and trusted mentors convert presence into belonging.
Policy levers	Visa portability; fair-contract enforcement; harmonized credentialing; funded bridging; anti-bias enforcement.	Longer-term licenses for experts; structured re-entry for returnees; language support; inclusion guidance for hospitals.	Reducing precarity and creating voice pathways are primary antidotes to isolation.
Data gaps	Sparse loneliness metrics in clinicians; limited disaggregation by visa/ specialty/setting.	Very limited empirical data on foreign clinicians; few validated measures in Chinese contexts.	Investment in measurement and comparative designs is prerequisite to targeted reforms.

Migration Policy Frameworks and Pathways

United States: The U.S. is a major destination for migrant healthcare workers, with longstanding reliance on foreign-trained professionals to fill workforce gaps (Bludau, 2021). As of 2021, approximately 2.8 million immigrants were employed in health occupations in the U.S., accounting for over 18% of the healthcare workforce . More than a quarter of all physicians practicing in the U.S. were educated abroad, alongside significant numbers of internationally educated nurses (IENs) and other health workers (Bludau, 2021; Hasan et al., 2021; Oliva-Arocas et al., 2022). Migration pathways into U.S. healthcare are shaped by complex immigration and visa policies (Bludau, 2021). High-skilled visa programs such as the H-1B (for specialty occupations) and J-1 (exchange visitor program for physicians) are common routes by which foreign medical graduates and nurses enter U.S. hospitals (Poon et al., 2022). These visa regimes, however, often tie workers to specific employers or impose conditions like home-country return requirements (in the case of J-1 physicians), creating a state of "bureaucratic precarity" for migrants who must constantly maintain legal status (Bludau, 2021). Research on international medical graduates in U.S. residency programs illustrates how visa restrictions and uncertainty become chronic stressors, as physicians live "in a state of bureaucratic precarity, just trying uphill constantly to ensure I can continue to live here" (Oliva-Arocas et al., 2022). This perpetual immigration insecurity can heighten feelings of isolation and anxiety, as migrant clinicians worry that any change in employment could jeopardize their legal status.

Furthermore, U.S. licensing boards and credentialing processes require most foreign-trained professionals to undergo cumbersome re-certification or additional training (Toyin-Thomas et al., 2023). For example, IMGs must pass the USMLE exams and often repeat residency training; foreign-trained nurses typically must pass the NCLEX exam and meet state nursing board requirements (Al-Btoush & El-Bcheraoui, 2024). These lengthy credentialing regimes delay full workforce integration, leaving many immigrants in under-employed positions despite their qualifications . An estimated 263,000 immigrants and refugees with health-related degrees in the U.S. were unemployed or underemployed as of the early 2020s, largely due to non-recognition of foreign credentials (Bludau, 2021; Hasan et al., 2021; Oliva-Arocas et al., 2022; Poon et al., 2022; Toyin-Thomas et al., 2023). This skills underutilization not only wastes human capital but can engender loneliness and professional disenfranchisement: physicians and nurses who held respected roles in their home countries may spend years in limbo or working in unrelated jobs, disconnected from peers and professional identity (Dotsey, 2023). One report notes that licensing barriers force many immigrant health professionals to "repeat their education and training," a time-consuming and costly process that, compounded by limited English proficiency and lack of networks, leaves them socially and professionally isolated in the interim (Toyin-Thomas et al., 2023).

Despite these challenges, U.S. policy frameworks do offer migrants the possibility of permanent career establishment. Pathways such as employment-sponsored green cards eventually allow many foreign clinicians to settle and advance. The U.S. healthcare labor market actively recruits from abroad to address shortages, especially in underserved areas. Programs like the Conrad 30 waiver encourage J-1 visa doctors to work in rural or inner-city health shortage areas in exchange for visa waivers (Poon et al., 2022). As a result, foreign-born physicians are disproportionately represented in rural communities and primary care roles (American Immigration Council, 2021). While this helps alleviate provider gaps, it can aggravate isolation: an immigrant doctor posted in a remote town may experience geographic and cultural loneliness, separated from both urban professional networks and their own ethnic community (Bludau, 2021). Indeed, the American Immigration Council (2021) observes that foreign-born physicians often relocate more willingly than natives to isolated areas, becoming "a valuable resource for medically underserved areas" (p. 3). However, these lone providers may lack collegial support and encounter cultural gaps with the local population, heightening their sense of otherness (Bludau, 2021).

China: In contrast to the U.S., China has historically been a net exporter of health professionals rather than a major destination for migrant healthcare labor (Organization, 2022). China's domestic healthcare workforce is overwhelmingly trained and employed within the country, and immigration pathways for foreign healthcare workers are relatively limited. Strict licensing rules and regulatory barriers make it challenging for foreign-educated doctors or nurses to practice in China on a long-term basis (Collins, 2021; Kuhlmann et al., 2023; Organization, 2022). According to official policy, foreign physicians are generally only permitted to practice in China on a short-term temporary basis (up to one year), and must obtain a temporary practice license under an invitation by a Chinese medical institution. These Interim Measures for Foreign Physicians signify that China tightly controls foreign medical practice, primarily allowing exchange or visiting specialists rather than permanent immigrants (Poon et al., 2022). The temporary licensure requires detailed agreements and is not easily renewed beyond one year, indicating that foreign doctors are viewed as transient contributors rather than integrated members of the health system.

Similarly, foreign nurses have very limited opportunities in China's public hospitals(Debesay et al., 2022). Anecdotal evidence suggests that outside of a few international clinics or joint-venture hospitals in major cities such as Beijing and Shanghai, it is rare for Chinese healthcare institutions to hire foreign nurses, especially given language requirements and an expectation that Chinese professionals should fill available roles (Toyin-Thomas et al., 2023). This stands in stark contrast to the U.S. model of actively recruiting overseas nurses and doctors to meet staffing needs. Indeed, one insider account notes that Chinese authorities "won't hire foreign people for what their own citizens can do" ("New China (Xinhua) News Agency," 2009), reflecting a policy preference to prioritize domestic training and self-reliance in healthcare human resources. This self-reliance likely stems from Maoist policies of the mid-1900s aiming for complete self-reliance (Aktas et al., 2022).

Impact on Loneliness: The differing policy frameworks significantly color the experience of loneliness for healthcare migrants in each country (Olofsson et al., 2021). In the U.S., the prolonged uncertainty of visa status and credentialing can leave migrants in a protracted liminal state, physically present in the workplace but socially not fully integrated or secure. One outcome is a sense of "temporary exile" (Meisters et al., 2021). By contrast, in China, the small number of foreign health workers (and the short-term nature of their stints) means those who do enter a Chinese hospital may be extremely isolated as token outsiders. Cultural and language barriers in China can therefore be even more acute given the rarity of migrant coworkers (Zhao et al., 2023). Meanwhile, Chinese doctors and nurses who migrate abroad may experience loneliness as newcomers in foreign systems, like other migrants, yet often with an additional burden of expectation to return, which can complicate their sense of belonging.

Credentialing Regimes and Institutional Hierarchies

United States: Credentialing and licensure systems in the U.S. serve as a major structural gatekeeper for migrant health workers, often with isolating effects. Foreign-trained physicians must surmount the U.S. medical licensing exams and secure a limited number of residency training slots to practice medicine. Those who succeed often find themselves steered into lower-prestige specialties or locations due to competition, which can instill a sense of being second-class in the professional hierarchy. Even after licensure, immigrant may confront subtle institutional hierarchies that favor domestic graduates (Jenkins, 2023; Kirkpatrick et al., 2023).

Research indicates that internationally educated nurses frequently perceive an "unwelcoming environment" in U.S. healthcare settings, including forms of othering by colleagues (Kirkpatrick et al., 2023). They may be left out of team communications or passed over for promotions, reinforcing a feeling of professional invisibility. An integrative review of African immigrant nurses in the U.S. found "collegial isolation and loneliness" alongside experiences of racism, discrimination, and having their voices silenced in clinical settings(Adler & Kwon, 2013). Despite the high immigration rates and cultural diversity of the U.S., such nurses reported feeling like perpetual outsiders in their workplaces, their contributions undervalued and their cultural differences treated as impediments rather than assets. This dynamic is often exacerbated by the rigid hierarchies in healthcare institutions. For example, immigrant nurses might be assigned less desirable tasks or shifts, or excluded from decision-making, reinforcing a hierarchy where they occupy a lower rung despite equal qualifications (Scott, 2000). Likewise, foreign doctors in U.S. hospitals can face skepticism from patients or colleagues. Over time, these micro-inequities erode migrants' sense of professional identity and belonging. Not feeling respected as an equal professional, "not feeling valued or valuable professionally," as one migrant nurse described is a profound contributor to loneliness at work (Currie et al., 2008).

Additionally, U.S. healthcare organizations historically provided minimal structured support for cultural integration (Currie et al., 2008). Orientation for new international staff is often perfunctory, focusing on technical onboarding rather than social incorporation. Many migrant clinicians are left to "learn the ropes" on their own, which can be an isolating trial-and-error process (Kirkpatrick et al., 2023). Differences in terminology and workplace policy further accentuate the cultural divide; little support is given to acclimate international hires to these conditions. A scoping review of migrant healthcare workers' experiences noted that insufficient workplace support and unfamiliarity with the U.S. healthcare system were common challenges that impeded integration (Scott, 2000). In addition, cultural differences play a large role in the lack of social integration. New international hires might struggle to understand unwritten norms of teamwork or patient interaction, potentially leading to misunderstandings with colleagues. Without formal mentorship or inclusion efforts by the institution, migrant workers can remain at the margins of the professional community (Currie et al., 2008; Jenkins, 2023; Olofsson et al., 2021). Work culture can be different across the world. Notably, asynchronous work can be difficult with "right to disconnect" laws in certain countries when paired with those containing the expectation to continue working outside of designated hours (Zhao et al., 2023).

China: In China's healthcare institutions, strict hierarchies and cultural norms present a different set of challenges for migrant professionals (whether foreign nationals or returning Chinese expatriates). Chinese hospitals are often characterized by a strong top-down hierarchy: senior physicians wield considerable authority, and nurses are expected to defer to doctors (Ma, 2020; Xu et al., 2008). This traditional hierarchy can be jarring for those from healthcare cultures that emphasize more egalitarian team dynamics. A foreign-trained nurse or doctor working in China may find that practices they consider routine, such as openly questioning a senior physician's decision or introducing a new idea, are frowned upon, potentially leading to conflict or isolation (Qiu et al., 2021; Wang & Liu, 2022).

The aforementioned account of a foreign nurse in China is illustrative: their more assertive style led to constant arguments with Chinese doctors "who were above him/ her," and her refusal to conform to local norms resulted in social ostracism until she resigned (Xie et al., 2021; Yang et al., 2022). In that scenario, the institutional hierarchy directly contributed to her social isolation: colleagues viewed her as insubordinate rather than collegial, and without supportive superiors, he/ she had no recourse or allies. This instance reveals the struggles of a migrant worker thrown into an environment which emphasizes filial piety and professional courtesy, highlighting how migrant workers in China can be caught between professional standards learned elsewhere and the expectation to assimilate into China's authoritative institutional culture, a tension that can leave them feeling deeply alone and misunderstood (Xu et al., 2008).

Language and communication barriers further compound hierarchical divides (Zhao et al., 2023). Even highly skilled foreign physicians in China must navigate communication in Chinese (often without fluency), which can place them at a disadvantage in meetings, documentation, and informal interactions. This dynamic can relegate a foreign clinician to the periphery of the institutional discourse, effectively muting their voice. They might, for instance, be excluded from critical discussions or find that their ideas gain little traction if not perfectly expressed in Chinese. Lack of expression can lead to feeling unheard and insignificance, which can be physically isolating and mentally exhausting.

It is worth noting that because foreign healthcare workers are few in China, institutional responses are ad hoc (Li et al., 2017). There are no large-scale programs in Chinese hospitals to support foreign staff comparable to what some Western hospitals have for international recruits. The responsibility to adapt lies largely with the individual. For example, foreign doctors usually work in private or expatriate-focused clinics where operations are in English; mainstream public hospitals seldom have the capacity (or incentive) to accommodate non-Chinese speakers beyond short-term collaborative roles (Ling et al., 2011). Therefore, those foreigners who do enter Chinese public healthcare can feel extremely isolated as "one-of-a-kind" in their setting.

Impact on Loneliness: Credentialing and hierarchy-related factors in both countries feed into migrant healthcare workers' loneliness in distinctive ways. In the U.S., credentialing delays and institutional bias contribute to a feeling of "standing apart": migrants feel they must prove themselves constantly and yet remain unseen or under-recognized (Chen & Liu, 2023). The combination of being structurally marginalized (through licensing hurdles keeping them out of practice or in junior roles longer) and socially marginalized (through subtle exclusion or prejudice at work) creates a perfect storm for professional loneliness (D. Li et al., 2021). Immigrant nurses have described walking into break rooms where conversations halt due to language differences or cliques, leaving them feeling invisible and alienated among colleagues (J. Li et al., 2021). Similarly, immigrant physicians on the bottom of a hierarchy may not have the collegial support networks that domestic-trained peers enjoy, leading to fewer consultations or informal case discussions, activities that normally bond teams (Yang et al., 2022). A qualitative study of international medical residents in the U.S. noted that many felt "excluded from the social fabric" of their training programs outside of formal duties, contributing to a sense of emotional isolation despite working among people (Zhao et al., 2023).

Political-culture inflection: In China's hospital field, pronounced power distance and networked gatekeeping (seniority, *guanxi*) intersect with language expectations to shape everyday access to influence. For rare foreign clinicians, these features magnify outsider status; for returnees, they can translate symbolic prestige into limited voice unless sponsorship is explicit. The mechanism is not simply "culture," but its institutionalization in evaluation, meetings, and role allocation—factors that mediate whether newcomers secure mentors, peer reciprocity, and the routine invitations that ground belonging (Ma, 2020; Xu et al., 2008; Wang et al., 2021).

Market Forces and Labor Market Dynamics

Both the U.S. and Chinese healthcare systems operate within neoliberal contexts, but market forces shape migrant workers' experiences differently in each. Efficiency-, competition-, and cost-focused dynamics commodify labor, with clear effects on well-being and connectedness (Caliendo et al., 2015). In the U.S., a largely market-driven sector links migrant recruitment to shortages and cost control; hospitals and agencies import nurses and other professionals as an expedient, alternative to improving wages or conditions (Caliendo et al., 2019). This transactional approach can render migrants a "captive workforce," especially where visa dependence or debt is leveraged. Investigations document exploitative "stay-or-pay" contracts that impose steep penalties for early exit (Carillon et al., 2020; Jossen, 2018); a 2023 probe described a "hidden system of exploitation," including $20,000+ breach fees, and a New York case in which such clauses were deemed illegal labor trafficking with restitution ordered (Feng & Guo, 2021).

In China, marketization has advanced within a public-dominant system: revenue pressures, high volumes, and corporatization produce intense workloads and burnout (Cai et al., 2008). For the limited number of foreign clinicians, the shock of rapid-fire appointments and quantity-over-quality routines can be disorienting (Lee & Mather, 2008). Emerging private hospitals—often expat-oriented—may buffer workload but create a separate bubble, reinforcing professional peripherality. Across both countries, global "care chains" commodify labor from lower-income regions, externalizing family care and generating transnational guilt and loneliness (Dao et al., 2017) (Qi et al., 2020). Brain-drain dynamics amplify moral strain: HICs benefit from LMIC-financed human capital, while some programs in China emphasize return, positioning workers as national resources and complicating identity and purpose (Feng et al., 2015; Zhong & Su, 2021).

Impact on Loneliness. Market logics deepen a "loneliness of commodification": when workers become mere inputs, needs for community, recognition, and rest are sidelined. In the U.S., economic tethering via visas or debt inhibits authentic collegial ties and voice (Zhong & Su, 2021); trust and openness wither in climates where migrants are viewed as contract fulfillers, not peers (Zhou, 2003). In China, revenue chasing and competitive evaluations can crowd out camaraderie; outsiders—foreigners or internal migrants—struggle to form bonds in fast-paced, target-driven environments (Gu, 2001; Zhou, 2003; Cai et al., 2008). Finally, the "loneliness economy" thesis (Hertz) is visible here: global markets optimize labor flows but at the cost of human connection, creating win–lose equilibria in which systems gain throughput while migrant clinicians lose belonging.

Cultural Norms and Emotional Dislocation

Cultural norms deeply influence migrant healthcare workers' social integration and feelings of loneliness. Both the U.S. and China present migrants with cultural environments that can diverge sharply from those of their home countries, affecting communication, socializing, and the implicit rules of workplace behavior. Adapting to these cultural differences is often an emotionally dislocating process, in which individuals feel "neither here nor there," belonging fully to neither the home nor host culture.

United States: The U.S. healthcare workplace is shaped by both American cultural traits such as a degree of informality, individualism, and direct communication and the multicultural makeup of its workforce. Migrants arriving in the U.S. may initially experience a kind of culture shock in how colleagues interact and how they are expected to relate to patients. For instance, many international nurses note that U.S. patients expect more autonomy and a say in their care, and nurses are expected to advocate for patients and collaborate with physicians in a relatively flat hierarchy compared to some other countries. A nurse coming from a culture where deference to doctors is the norm might feel anxious, disrespectful and out-of-place being asked to speak up or call a physician by their first name (Allen et al., 2014).

Simple social rituals can pose pitfalls. Immigrant health workers often mention struggling with colloquial language, humor, or small talk. In one U.S. study, 7% of migrant clinicians cited ongoing language and communication difficulties as a key concern, noting it hampered both patient care and collegial relations (Bhugra, 2004). Missing cultural references or idioms can make a migrant feel like an outsider during lunchroom conversations – jokes might elicit confusion instead of laughter. Over time, feeling excluded from these everyday social exchanges feeds loneliness. Even when migrants achieve linguistic fluency, accent discrimination can persist; an international medical graduate in the U.S. might find patients or colleagues occasionally asking for someone "who speaks English," undermining their confidence and willingness to engage socially (Kim & Silverstein, 2021; Nishio & Bilmes, 1987; Sun, 2012).

Studies have documented that migrant doctors and nurses frequently face subtle or overt discrimination based on language or ethnicity, which not only affects career opportunities but also erodes the sense of belonging, for example, nurses in Ireland reported that strong accents led to patient complaints or mocking, contributing to feelings of isolation. This can be especially prominent in areas which are known to be ethnically homogenous, as people tend to be more sensitized to cultures different than their own (Sue, 1994).

As a result, immigrant workers can feel rebuffed or lonely even when no exclusion was intended – it may simply be that their coworkers assume everyone is handling their own personal life. For example, an immigrant nurse might be hurt that U.S. colleagues do not invite her to weekend gatherings, while the colleagues assume she prefers her own time. This mismatch of expectations contributes to what researchers call a lack of "sense of cultural belongingness" for many migrant professionals (Kim, 2017). They are present in the host culture but not truly part of it, which is a recipe for loneliness. A migrant interviewee in one study poignantly described feeling estranged and misunderstood, lacking "appropriate social partners for desired activities" and emotional intimacy. This captures how one can feel lonely despite many coworkers around – if those relationships lack depth or mutual understanding, the emotional needs remain unfulfilled.

China: For migrant healthcare workers in China, cultural challenges are if anything even more formidable given the relatively insular nature of Chinese society regarding foreigners. Language is the most obvious barrier: fluency in Mandarin (and perhaps local dialects) is essentially a prerequisite to function in a Chinese clinical setting, but attaining fluency with medical terminology is a years-long endeavor that few foreign clinicians achieve. Those lacking language skills are confined to practicing in expatriate-focused facilities where translation is provided, which by design limits their social integration with Chinese colleagues. For those who do speak Mandarin, understanding the nuanced social etiquette of Chinese workplaces is crucial (Lee, 1998; Ng, 2009).

Chinese communication tends to be high-context, indirect, and rooted in concepts of face (mianzi) and harmony. In a culture that is much different from one's own, it can be difficult to read A foreigner unaccustomed to reading between the lines may inadvertently violate norms, perhaps by openly pointing out a mistake (causing someone to lose face) or by failing to partake in group activities in the expected way. Such missteps can lead to social sanction or exclusion. For example, not joining an after-work dinner when invited could be seen as aloof or disrespectful, closing off future invitations. Over time, a foreign worker might find themselves simply not included in social gatherings, deepening their isolation (Lee, 1998)

For Chinese healthcare workers who have migrated overseas and possibly returned, the cultural re-adjustment can also be lonely. They may have adopted some Western professional norms while abroad, which on returning can set them apart from local colleagues (as noted earlier). Psychologically, they might have changed in ways family and friends back home do not entirely grasp, causing a feeling of distance (Cai et al., 2008; Kim & Silverstein, 2021). This is a common phenomenon among return migrants (the so-called "re-entry shock"), where one no longer fits neatly into the old cultural patterns. Initial feelings of excitment can be replaced by nostalgia for what was in the past, and a sense of loss and frustation.Thus, cultural dislocation can affect Chinese professionals both going out and coming back, in each case spawning a form of loneliness linked to identity and belonging (Rajaram & Bordia, 2013; Zhao et al., 2019).

Impact on Loneliness: Culturally rooted loneliness often manifests as a feeling of invisibility or misunderstanding – migrant healthcare workers feel that those around them do not truly "see" who they are or include them as equals. In the U.S., migrants can be surrounded by people yet feel profoundly alone if their colleagues don't make the effort to bridge cultural gaps. One internationally recruited nurse in the UK (reflecting a scenario analogous to the U.S.) described it as giving so much to a system "who barely make the efforts to prove that I do count, to understand the 'me' as a person" (Omiyi et al., 2025). This encapsulates the craving for recognition and understanding that, when unmet, leads to emotional isolation. In China, a foreign clinician might similarly feel that no one truly knows them – colleagues see only the foreign label, not the individual behind it, or avoid deep interaction out of mutual cultural apprehension. These experiences underline that loneliness is not merely the absence of people, but the absence of meaningful connection and mutual understanding.

THEMATIC DISCUSSION

Professional Invisibility and Devaluation

A recurring theme in migrant healthcare workers' narratives is professional invisibility – the sense of being unseen, undervalued, or voiceless in their professional roles. This can take many forms: being passed over for promotions or leadership, having one's skills underestimated, encountering skepticism from patients, or simply not having one's ideas heard in team discussions (Netto, 2024). Migrant professionals often feel they must work twice as hard to receive the same recognition as native peers, yet paradoxically they remain "invisible" when it comes to praise or career advancement. The integrative review of African-born nurses in the U.S. explicitly cited "silencing of voices" and experiences of being treated as outsiders despite their qualifications. One nurse in that review described harrowing periods of feeling like 'an outsider', encapsulating how prolonged invisibility erodes one's sense of belonging and self-worth (Hatton, 2017; Klunk, 1999).

Professional invisibility is often a byproduct of the structural and cultural factors already discussed. Credentialing barriers that force a migrant into a lower position than they are trained for will inherently render their higher-level skills invisible. A foreign-trained surgeon working as a phlebotomist, for example, is literally unseen as a surgeon by those around them; their identity is reduced to a much narrower role. Even once credentialed, subtle biases can keep migrants out of the limelight. Stereotypes (conscious or not) may pigeonhole them into certain roles – e.g., assuming a Filipina nurse is only suited for bedside nursing and not management, or an African doctor being steered towards research rather than patient-facing roles due to accent issues (Sue, 1994). Over time, migrants internalize some of this marginalization. They may stop volunteering ideas or pursuing promotions, believing it's futile because of past dismissals. This self-censorship further perpetuates their invisibility. After experiencing racism, studies found that people often lack the resources to report such experiences. These people are forced to accept these experiences, which can often have a negative effect of their self-confidence and lead to the aformentioned self-censorship.

In the U.S., racism and xenophobia unfortunately contribute to professional invisibility. Numerous studies have found that migrant physicians and nurses report instances of patients refusing their care due to prejudice (e.g., "I want an American doctor" requests), or colleagues making insensitive remarks about their origin. These behaviors send a message that no matter how skilled the migrant is, their personhood is not fully respected; they are seen through the lens of "foreignness" first. That can make someone withdraw and feel they will never be fully accepted – a hallmark of loneliness in the workplace (Klunk, 1999). During the COVID-19 pandemic, for example, Asian healthcare workers in Western countries faced increased discrimination due to racist associations of the virus with China, in effect making some of the very heroes fighting the pandemic feel invisible or even vilified in their communities. Such experiences highlight that professional invisibility is not only about recognition, but about the right to be treated as a full member of the professional community.

China's scenario of professional invisibility might be observed in the limited roles foreigners are allowed. If foreign doctors are largely confined to playing consultative roles or working in special clinics, they are invisible in the mainstream health system – absent from the public eye and from key institutional decision-making. Even highly renowned foreign experts invited to China may be used symbolically (for international image or brief training sessions) without being integrated into the daily fabric of hospital teams. For the individuals, this can feel like being a perpetual guest, never a true colleague (Guo, 2015; Wang et al., 2021). They might not be assigned any leadership in patient management, essentially sidelined to observer status. Such underutilization is demoralizing and lonely; professionals typically derive camaraderie from shared responsibilities and challenges, which these migrants are not fully given.

Impact on Loneliness: Professional invisibility contributes to loneliness by negating one of the fundamental human workplace needs: the need to be seen and validated for one's contributions. When migrant clinicians feel their presence or insights do not matter, they disengage emotionally. Work becomes just a clock-in-clock-out ordeal rather than a meaningful part of life where one has camaraderie and purpose. A lack of recognition can lead to what psychologists call "anomie" – a sense of normlessness and detachment. In healthcare, where teamwork is critical, an invisible member is effectively a detached member, likely not invited into the deeper trust circles that colleagues form. This exclusion, even if polite, is isolation (Wang et al., 2021).

National-Level Policies (U.S. and China)

Immigration and Work Authorization Reforms: National governments have a pivotal role in reducing the structural precarity that fuels loneliness. In the U.S., immigration policy reforms could include increasing and expediting visas/green cards for healthcare workers, and de-linking work visas from single employers. For instance, expanding the Conrad 30 program or creating a federal "National Interest Waiver" fast-track for physicians and nurses (as has been done for some during COVID-19) can provide more permanent stability (Gleeson & Griffith, 2021). Legislative proposals such as the Healthcare Workforce Resilience Act – which sought to recapture unused visas for nurses and doctors – point in the right direction. Moreover, prohibiting or strictly regulating predatory employment contracts, like those with large penalty fees through federal and state labor laws would protect migrant workers from exploitation and give them freedom to change jobs without fear, an essential aspect of well-being (Lim & Paik, 2023).

In China, although the context differs, the government could reconsider its restrictive stance on foreign healthcare professionals in light of globalizing talent flows. Easing the process for foreign experts to obtain longer-term medical licenses, or creating special visa categories for healthcare exchange that allow family accompaniment and multi-year stays, could encourage a more multicultural health workforce (Nakphong et al., 2022). Additionally, China could bolster support for its own citizens who venture abroad and return: for example, establishing re-entry training or credential recognition for Chinese doctors/nurses coming back, to reduce their professional re-adjustment pains (Xu, 2024). On immigration, while China is not traditionally an immigrant destination, pilot programs in regions like Shanghai to hire foreign healthcare talent in certain specialties could be expanded, accompanied by guidelines to promote inclusion of those individuals on language training, cultural liaison officers in hospitals, etc.

Credential Recognition and Bridging Programs: National regulators should streamline credentialing for internationally educated health professionals, without compromising standards. Adopting standardized assessments that quickly identify competence can prevent unnecessary repetition of training. For example, some countries use competency exams or supervised practice periods instead of requiring full re-licensure from scratch. The U.S. might explore allowing experienced foreign physicians to practice in limited settings under supervision while they get licensed – a model similar to apprenticeship that could both utilize their skills and integrate them sooner.

State boards of nursing in the U.S. could harmonize requirements to avoid confusion and ensure that proven international exams or credentials (like the NCLEX-RN, which many foreign nurses do take) are uniformly accepted. Funding should be allocated for bridging programs at universities and teaching hospitals (these are courses or residencies tailored for internationally trained nurses/doctors to upskill in areas like language, cultural competence, and any clinical gaps). Such programs have shown success in Canada and Australia in improving licensure rates and job readiness of IENs. Governments can incentivize institutions to host bridging cohorts through grants or by counting it toward workforce development goals. Ultimately, reducing the time a migrant health worker spends in limbo before practicing not only addresses workforce shortages but also shortens the period of professional isolation that can be so detrimental to their mental health (Alostaz et al., 2024; Nourpanah, 2021; Tsujita et al., 2023; Villamin et al., 2023; Zhong et al., 2023).

Illustrative Reintegration Pathways: Comparative experience suggests targeted bridges can reduce isolation while protecting standards. Canadian and Australian university-hospital "bridging" cohorts for internationally educated nurses combine supervised practice with cultural-linguistic upskilling and show improved licensure and job readiness (Alostaz et al., 2024; Villamin et al., 2023). U.S. limited-practice or supervised-practice pilots for IMGs shorten the interval between arrival and patient-facing roles, rebuilding professional identity and collegial networks (Travis, 2023). For returnee Chinese professionals, structured re-entry supports (clear role definitions, mentorship, and language for team norms) mitigate symbolic recognition without integration and accelerate role congruence (Wang & Liu, 2022; Li et al., 2019; Zhong et al., 2023).

Labor Standards and Enforcement: Both the U.S. and Chinese governments should strengthen labor protections specific to migrant workers. In the U.S., this could mean more rigorous oversight of recruitment agencies – for instance, requiring them to register and adhere to ethical codes. Agencies that violate fair practices through exorbitant fees or misinformation should face penalties. The U.S. Department of Labor can collaborate with professional bodies to issue guidelines for fair contracts for foreign recruits, e.g., limiting the size of any repayment clauses relative to actual costs incurred, as New York's case exemplified (Jones, 2022). On the ground, hospital accrediting organizations, like Joint Commission, could incorporate standards related to equitable treatment of international staff – for example, checking if hospitals provide the same support to a foreign nurse hire as to a local one (Vuohijoki et al., 2025).

In China, labor laws might be extended to explicitly cover foreigners in terms of equal pay and working conditions if they are employed in China, to prevent any covert exploitations. For Chinese nationals being sent abroad via agencies, the government should enforce its own ethical recruitment agreements (Xu et al., 2025). Notably, China did agree to follow the UK Code of Practice for international recruitment; continuing to honor and update such agreements and perhaps striking similar ones with other countries ensures that Chinese migrant nurses and doctors have recourse if they face unfair treatment overseas (Jiang et al., 2022). Additionally, consular support (labor attachés) could be provided for health workers abroad, similar to the Philippines model, which could alleviate the sense of abandonment and loneliness by giving them a link to home that can intervene in issues (Franceschini & Loubere, 2022).

Limitations and Future Research

While this chapter synthesizes extensive interdisciplinary literature, its evidence base remains constrained by uneven data availability, particularly quantitative metrics on loneliness among healthcare migrants and foreign clinician experiences in China. The focus on English-language sources may underrepresent regional or non-published evidence. Furthermore, causal inference is limited: the analysis identifies structural mechanisms but not effect sizes. Future research should integrate administrative and survey datasets to estimate the impact of visa status, credentialing time, and work setting on loneliness; conduct longitudinal studies of re-entry and return migration; and test interventions such as structured onboarding and mentorship through mixed-methods designs. Expanding the comparison beyond the U.S. and China to include other high-migration corridors (e.g., GCC, EU, ASEAN) would also clarify generalizability. These limitations notwithstanding, the chapter establishes a conceptual and empirical foundation for systematically studying loneliness as a structural outcome of global health labor regimes.

CONCLUSION

Loneliness among migrant healthcare workers is a systemic signal, not a personal shortcoming. Across the U.S. and China, different structures, U.S. credentialing and visa dependence; China's hierarchies and cultural barriers, produce the same result: professional isolation. Four mechanisms explain this: bureaucratic precarity (status insecurity and red tape), emotional dislocation (ruptured home and identity), professional invisibility (suppressed voice and undervalued skills), and commodification of care (market logics that reduce people to labor inputs). The costs are practical (retention, performance, inequitable skill distribution) and moral (erosion of dignity and solidarity).

Feasible remedies exist. At the institutional level: structured onboarding and mentoring, anti-bias accountability, mental-health supports, and clear advancement pathways. Nationally: streamlined credential recognition, fair-contract enforcement, and visa reforms that de-link status from a single employer. Cross-border: ethical recruitment under the WHO Code, bilateral supports, and shared investment in training to avoid zero-sum drain. Evidence shows inclusion pays off—lower turnover and better patient outcomes.

"Isolation in White Coats" is a policy choice, not fate. Replacing extraction with reciprocity and community turns migration from a lonely transaction into mutual flourishing. The imperative is simple and universal: those who heal must be seen, heard, and connected, by institutions, by policy, and by each other.

REFERENCES

Adler, P. S., & Kwon, S. W. (2013). The mutation of professionalism as a contested diffusion process: Clinical guidelines as carriers of institutional change in medicine. *Journal of Management Studies, 50*(5), 930–962. DOI: 10.1111/joms.12003

Ahmed, A. A., Hwang, W. T., Thomas, C. R.Jr, & Deville, C.Jr. (2018). International Medical Graduates in the US Physician Workforce and Graduate Medical Education: Current and Historical Trends. *Journal of Graduate Medical Education, 10*(2), 214–218. DOI: 10.4300/JGME-D-17-00580.1

Aktas, E., Bergbom, B., Godderis, L., Kreshpaj, B., Marinov, M., Mates, D., McElvenny, D. M., Mehlum, I. S., Milenkova, V., Nena, E., & Glass, D. C. (2022). Migrant workers occupational health research: An OMEGA-NET working group position paper. *International Archives of Occupational and Environmental Health, 95*(4), 765–777. DOI: 10.1007/s00420-021-01803-x

Al-Btoush, A., & El-Bcheraoui, C. (2024). Challenges affecting migrant healthcare workers while adjusting to new healthcare environments: A scoping review. *Human Resources for Health, 22*(1), 56. DOI: 10.1186/s12960-024-00941-w

Allen, J. A., Diefendorff, J. M., & Ma, Y. (2014). Differences in emotional labor across cultures: A comparison of Chinese and US service workers. *Journal of Business and Psychology, 29*(1), 21–35. DOI: 10.1007/s10869-013-9288-7

Alostaz, N., Walton-Roberts, M., Chen, R., Pratt, M., & Wahoush, O. (2024). Integration trends of internationally educated nurses in Canada and Australia: A scoping review. *International Health Trends and Perspectives, 4*(1), 88–113. DOI: 10.32920/ihtp.v4i1.1958

Angel, Y., & Fire, G. (2023). Healthcare policy changes in an era of health workforce shortage. *Israel Journal of Health Policy Research, 12*(1), 28. Advance online publication. DOI: 10.1186/s13584-023-00576-7

Austin, Z., & Gregory, P. A. (2024). Enhancing integration of internationally educated health professionals in the healthcare workforce: Implications for regulators. *Journal of Nursing Regulation, 15*(1), 24–32. DOI: 10.1016/S2155-8256(24)00026-7

Beaunoyer, E., Dupéré, S., & Guitton, M. J. (2020). COVID-19 and digital inequalities: Reciprocal impacts and mitigation strategies. *Computers in Human Behavior, 111*, 106424. DOI: 10.1016/j.chb.2020.106424

Bhugra, D. (2004). Migration, distress and cultural identity. *British Medical Bulletin, 69*(1), 129–141. DOI: 10.1093/bmb/ldh007

Bludau, H. (2021). Global healthcare worker migration. In *Oxford research encyclopedia of anthropology*. DOI: 10.1093/acrefore/9780190854584.013.231

Boniol, M., Kunjumen, T., Nair, T. S., Siyam, A., Campbell, J., & Diallo, K. (2022). The global health workforce stock and distribution in 2020 and 2030: A threat to equity and 'universal'health coverage? *BMJ Global Health*, *7*(6), e009316. DOI: 10.1136/bmjgh-2022-009316

Brush, B. L., Sochalski, J., & Berger, A. M. (2004). Imported Care: Recruiting Foreign Nurses To U.S. Health Care Facilities. *Health Affairs (Project Hope)*, *23*(3), 78–87. DOI: 10.1377/hlthaff.23.3.78

Cacioppo, J. T., & Cacioppo, S. (2018). The growing problem of loneliness. *Lancet*, *391*(10119), 426. DOI: 10.1016/S0140-6736(18)30142-9

Cai, F., Park, A., & Zhao, Y. (2008). The Chinese labor market in the reform era.

Caliendo, L., Dvorkin, M., & Parro, F. (2015). *The impact of trade on labor market dynamics*.

Caliendo, L., Dvorkin, M., & Parro, F. (2019). Trade and labor market dynamics: General equilibrium analysis of the china trade shock. *Econometrica*, *87*(3), 741–835. DOI: 10.3982/ECTA13758

Carillon, S., Fedyuk, O., Gerbier-Aublanc, M., Gosselin, A., Guidi, C. F., Leite Borges, D. d. C., Malakasis, C., Perna, R., Petel-Rochette, N., Pérez, M., Rodríguez-Newey, I., Rohde-Abuba, C., Sahraoui, N., Sahraoui, N., Santilli, C., & European Commission Horizon (2020). - ERC Project EU Border Care (starting Grant 638259). *Borders across Healthcare: Moral Economies of Healthcare and Migration in Europe*

Chen, C., & Liu, M. (2023). Achievements and challenges of the healthcare system in China. *Cureus*, *15*(5). Advance online publication. DOI: 10.7759/cureus.39030

Cho, H.-J., Kang, K., & Park, K.-Y. (2023). Health-related quality of life of migrant workers: A systematic literature review. *BMC Public Health*, *23*(1), 1004. DOI: 10.1186/s12889-023-15981-5

Clemens, M. A., & Pettersson, G. (2008). New data on African health professionals abroad. *Human Resources for Health*, *6*(1), 1. Advance online publication. DOI: 10.1186/1478-4491-6-1

Collins, F. L. (2021). 'Give me my pathway!': Multinational migration, transnational skills regimes and migrant subjectification. *Global Networks*, *21*(1), 18–39. DOI: 10.1111/glob.12294

Connell, J. (2010). *Migration and the Globalisation of Health Care*. Edward Elgar Publishing., DOI: 10.4337/9781849805186

Cunha, Y. R. (2013). Standing, guy. The precariat. *Revista Aurora*, *7*(1), 203–208. DOI: 10.36311/1982-8004.2013.v7n1.3403

Currie, G., Finn, R., & Martin, G. (2008). Accounting for thedark side'of new organizational forms: The case of healthcare professionals. *Human Relations*, *61*(4), 539–564. DOI: 10.1177/0018726708091018

Dao, M., Furceri, D., & Loungani, P. (2017). Regional labor market adjustment in the United States: Trend and cycle. *The Review of Economics and Statistics*, *99*(2), 243–257. DOI: 10.1162/REST_a_00642

Debesay, J., Kartzow, A. H., & Fougner, M. (2022). Healthcare professionals' encounters with ethnic minority patients: The critical incident approach. *Nursing Inquiry*, *29*(1), e12421. DOI: 10.1111/nin.12421

Dotsey, S. (2023). Foreign healthcare workers and COVID-19 in Europe: The paradox of unemployed skilled labour. *Social Sciences (Basel, Switzerland)*, *12*(4), 211. DOI: 10.3390/socsci12040211

Feng, S., & Guo, N. (2021). Labor market dynamics in urban China and the role of the state sector. *Journal of Comparative Economics*, *49*(4), 918–932. DOI: 10.1016/j.jce.2021.04.002

Feng, S., Hu, Y., & Moffitt, R. (2015). *Long run trends in unemployment and labor force participation in China*.

Franceschini, I., & Loubere, N. (2022). *Global China as method*. Cambridge University Press. DOI: 10.1017/9781108999472

Gauthier, C.-A. (2009). Globalizing Care Economies and Migrant Workers: Explorations in Global Care Chains By Nicola Yeates, New York: Palgrave Macmillan, 2009, 258 pp., ISBN 978-0-23000-534-1. *Relations Industrielles*, *64*(4), 707. DOI: 10.7202/038882ar

General, U. S. (2023). Our epidemic of loneliness and isolation. *The US Surgeon General's Advisory on the Healing Effects of Social Connection and Community, 2023*.

Giroud, A. (2024). World Investment Report 2023: Investing in sustainable energy for all: United Nations Conference on Trade and Development, Geneva and New York, 2023, 205 pp. In: Springer. DOI: 10.1057/s42214-023-00178-9

Gleeson, S., & Griffith, K. L. (2021). Employers as subjects of the immigration state: How the state foments employment insecurity for temporary immigrant workers. *Law & Social Inquiry*, *46*(1), 92–115. DOI: 10.1017/lsi.2020.17

Guay, E., & Drago, A. (2021). Palaces for the People: How Social Infrastructure Can Help Fight Inequality, Polarization, and the Decline of Civic Life, d'Eric Klinenberg, New York, Crown, 2018, 277 p. *Politique et Sociétés*, *40*(2), 224. DOI: 10.7202/1077879ar

Guo, X. (2015). Deskilling and Devaluation of Chinese Immigrant Women in Ottawa.

Hasan, S. I., Yee, A., Rinaldi, A., Azham, A. A., Mohd Hairi, F., & Amer Nordin, A. S. (2021). Prevalence of common mental health issues among migrant workers: A systematic review and meta-analysis. *PLoS One*, *16*(12), e0260221. DOI: 10.1371/journal.pone.0260221

Hatton, E. (2017). Mechanisms of invisibility: Rethinking the concept of invisible work. *Work, Employment and Society*, *31*(2), 336–351. DOI: 10.1177/0950017016674894

Hertz, N. (2021). *The lonely century: how to restore human connection in a world that's pulling apart*. Crown Currency.

Hou, J., Michaud, C., Li, Z., Dong, Z., Sun, B., Zhang, J., Cao, D., Wan, X., Zeng, C., Wei, B., Tao, L., Li, X., Wang, W., Lu, Y., Xia, X., Guo, G., Zhang, Z., Cao, Y., Guan, Y., & Chen, L. (2014). Transformation of the education of health professionals in China: Progress and challenges. *Lancet*, *384*(9945), 819–827. DOI: 10.1016/S0140-6736(14)61307-6

Hu, L., Glavin, Y.-F. W., Yan, R., Pei, C., Yan, M., Zhang, Y., & Liu, Y. (2021). Integrating health and care in China: Lessons learned and future outlook. *International Journal of Integrated Care*, *21*(4), 18. DOI: 10.5334/ijic.5681

Illouz, E. (2007). Cold intimacies: The making of emotional capitalism. *Polity*.

Jakovljevic, M., Chang, H., Pan, J., Guo, C., Hui, J., Hu, H., Grujic, D., Li, Z., & Shi, L. (2023). Successes and challenges of China's health care reform: A four-decade perspective spanning 1985-2023. *Cost Effectiveness and Resource Allocation : C/E*, *21*(1), 59. DOI: 10.1186/s12962-023-00461-9

Jenkins, T. M. (2023). Making the cut: Status, credentials, and hiring in medicine. *Social Problems*, *70*(2), 435–455. DOI: 10.1093/socpro/spab046

Jiang, Q., Horta, H., & Yuen, M. (2022). International medical students' perspectives on factors affecting their academic success in China: A qualitative study. *BMC Medical Education*, *22*(1), 574. DOI: 10.1186/s12909-022-03597-z

Jones, K. (2022). A 'north star'in governing global labour migration? The ILO and the Fair Recruitment Initiative. *Global Social Policy*, *22*(2), 303–322. DOI: 10.1177/14680181221084792

Jossen, M. (2018). *Undocumented migrants and healthcare: eight stories from Switzerland.* Open Book Publishers. DOI: 10.11647/OBP.0139

Kim, J. H., & Silverstein, M. (2021). Are filial piety and ethnic community engagement associated with psychological wellbeing among older Chinese American immigrants? A cultural resource perspective. *Research on Aging*, *43*(2), 63–73. DOI: 10.1177/0164027520937477

Kim, Y. Y. (2017). Cross-cultural adaptation. *Oxford research encyclopedia of communication.*

Kirkpatrick, I., Zardini, A., & Veronesi, G. (2023). Management reforms, re-stratification and the adaptation of professional status hierarchies: The case of medicine in publicly owned hospitals. *Public Management Review*, *25*(11), 2231–2254. DOI: 10.1080/14719037.2023.2222124

Klunk, C. D. (1999). Professionals' Workplace Devaluation: Implications for the Workplace. Midwest Research-to-Practice Conference.

Kuhlmann, , EBrînzac, , M. GCzabanowska, , KFalkenbach, , MUngureanu, , M.-IValiotis, , GZapata, , TMartin-Moreno, , J. M. (2023). Violence against healthcare workers is a political problem and a public health issue: a call to action. *European Journal of Public Health*, *33*(1), 4–5.

Lee, M. A., & Mather, M. (2008). US labor force trends. *Population Bulletin*, *63*(2).

Lee, S. (1998). Estranged bodies, simulated harmony, and misplaced cultures: Neurasthenia in contemporary Chinese society. *Biopsychosocial Science and Medicine*, *60*(4), 448–457.

Leitão, C. A., de Oliveira Salvador, G. L., Idowu, B. M., & Dako, F. (2024). Drivers of global health care worker migration. *Journal of the American College of Radiology*, *21*(8), 1188–1193. DOI: 10.1016/j.jacr.2024.03.005

Li, D., Zhu, L., Zhang, J., & Yang, J. (2021). Decomposing differences of health service utilization among Chinese rural migrant workers with new cooperative medical scheme: A comparative study. *International Journal of Environmental Research and Public Health*, *18*(17), 9291. DOI: 10.3390/ijerph18179291

Li, F., Ding, J., & Shen, W. (2019). Back on track: Factors influencing Chinese returnee scholar performance in the reintegration process. *Science & Public Policy*, *46*(2), 184–197. DOI: 10.1093/scipol/scy047

Li, J., Lowres, N., Koo, F. K., & Gallagher, R. (2021). A systematic review of quantitative and qualitative literature on health professionals' experiences communicating with Chinese immigrants. *International Journal of Nursing Practice*, *27*(6), e12960. DOI: 10.1111/ijn.12960

Li, X., Lu, J., Hu, S., Cheng, K., De Maeseneer, J., Meng, Q., Mossialos, E., Xu, D. R., Yip, W., Zhang, H., Krumholz, H. M., Jiang, L., & Hu, S. (2017). The primary health-care system in China. *Lancet*, *390*(10112), 2584–2594. DOI: 10.1016/S0140-6736(17)33109-4

Lim, S., & Paik, S. (2023). The impact of immigration enforcement on agricultural employment: Evidence from the US E-Verify policy. *Applied Economics*, *55*(19), 2223–2259. DOI: 10.1080/00036846.2022.2102135

Ling, R. E., Liu, F., Lu, X. Q., & Wang, W. (2011). Emerging issues in public health: A perspective on China's healthcare system. *Public Health*, *125*(1), 9–14. DOI: 10.1016/j.puhe.2010.10.009

Lopez-Abuin, J. M. (2010). Review of: 'Increasing access to health workers in remote and rural areas through improved retention: global policy recommendations: Global policy recommendations'. *Rural and Remote Health*. Advance online publication. DOI: 10.22605/RRH1647

Ma, L. (2020). Rethinking democratizing potential of digital technology. *Journal of Information. Communication and Ethics in Society*, *18*(1), 140–156. DOI: 10.1108/JICES-02-2019-0022

Meisters, R., Westra, D., Putrik, P., Bosma, H., Ruwaard, D., & Jansen, M. (2021). Does loneliness have a cost? A population-wide study of the association between loneliness and healthcare expenditure. *International Journal of Public Health*, *66*, 581286. DOI: 10.3389/ijph.2021.581286

Mullan, F. (1995). Medical Migration and the Physician Workforce. *Journal of the American Medical Association*, *273*(19), 1521. DOI: 10.1001/jama.1995.03520430057039

Nakphong, M. K., Young, M.-E. D. T., Morales, B., Guzman-Ruiz, I. Y., Chen, L., & Kietzman, K. G. (2022). Social exclusion at the intersections of immigration, employment, and healthcare policy: A qualitative study of Mexican and Chinese immigrants in California. *Social Science & Medicine*, *298*, 114833. DOI: 10.1016/j.socscimed.2022.114833

Netto, J. J. M. (2024). Invisibility and devaluation of nursing work: Related factors and coping strategies. *Investigacion y Educacion en Enfermeria*, *42*(1), e01.

New China (Xinhua) News Agency. (2009). *Encyclopedia of Journalism*. SAGE Publications, Inc., DOI: 10.4135/9781412972048.n255

Ng, E. (2009). Heartache of the state, enemy of the self: Bipolar disorder and cultural change in urban China. *Culture, Medicine and Psychiatry*, *33*(3), 421–450. DOI: 10.1007/s11013-009-9144-4

Nishio, K., & Bilmes, M. (1987). Psychotherapy with Southeast Asian American clients. *Professional Psychology, Research and Practice*, *18*(4), 342–346. DOI: 10.1037/0735-7028.18.4.342

Nourpanah, S. (2021). Moving, waiting, racing: The emotional and temporal experience of policy for nurses on temporary work permits in Canada. *Anthropologica*, *63*(1), 1–26. DOI: 10.18357/anthropologica6312021186

Oliva-Arocas, A., Benavente, P., Ronda, E., & Diaz, E. (2022). Health of international migrant workers during the COVID-19 pandemic: A scoping review. *Frontiers in Public Health*, *10*, 816597. DOI: 10.3389/fpubh.2022.816597

Olofsson, J., Rämgård, M., Sjögren-Forss, K., & Bramhagen, A.-C. (2021). Older migrants' experience of existential loneliness. *Nursing Ethics*, *28*(7-8), 1183–1193. DOI: 10.1177/0969733021994167

Omiyi, D., Wilkinson, E., & Snaith, B. (2025). Exploring the motivations, challenges, and integration of internationally educated healthcare workers in the UK: A scoping review. *Policy, Politics & Nursing Practice*, *26*(2), 117–135. DOI: 10.1177/15271544241289605

Organization, W. H. (2022). *World report on the health of refugees and migrants: summary*. World Health Organization.

Poon, Y.-S. R., Lin, Y. P., Griffiths, P., Yong, K. K., Seah, B., & Liaw, S. Y. (2022). A global overview of healthcare workers' turnover intention amid COVID-19 pandemic: A systematic review with future directions. *Human Resources for Health*, *20*(1), 70. DOI: 10.1186/s12960-022-00764-7

Qi, Y., Liang, T., & Ye, H. (2020). Occupational status, working conditions, and health: Evidence from the 2012 China Labor Force Dynamics Survey. *The Journal of Chinese Sociology*, *7*(1), 14. DOI: 10.1186/s40711-020-00128-5

Qiu, F., Liu, J., & Zhan, H. J. (2021). Migration and health—Freedom of movement and social benefits for Chinese migrant workers. *Sustainability (Basel)*, *13*(22), 12371. DOI: 10.3390/su132212371

Rajaram, K., & Bordia, S. (2013). East versus West: Effectiveness of Knowledge Acquisition and Impact of Cultural Dislocation Issues for Mainland Chinese Students across Ten Commonly Used Instructional Techniques. *International Journal for the Scholarship of Teaching and Learning*, *7*(1), n1. DOI: 10.20429/ijsotl.2013.070111

Ramji, Z., & Etowa, J. (2018). Workplace integration: Key considerations for internationally educated nurses and employers. *Administrative Sciences*, *8*(1), 2. DOI: 10.3390/admsci8010002

Sanner-Stiehr, E., Stevanin, S., Mikkonen, S., & Kvist, T. (2021). Job satisfaction and generational nursing characteristics among registered nurses in the United States, Italy and Finland: Results of a survey study. *Journal of Nursing Management*, *29*(8), 2364–2373. DOI: 10.1111/jonm.13397

Scott, W. R. (2000). *Institutional change and healthcare organizations: From professional dominance to managed care*. University of Chicago press.

Singh, S., & Steeves, V. (2020). The contested meanings of race and ethnicity in medical research: A case study of the DynaMed Point of Care tool. *Social Science &amp. Social Science & Medicine*, *265*, 113112. DOI: 10.1016/j.socscimed.2020.113112

Siyam, A., Zurn, P., Rø, O. C., Gedik, G., & Ronquillo, K. Joan Co, C., Vaillancourt-Laflamme, C., dela Rosa, J., Perfilieva, G., & Dal Poz, M. R. (2013). Monitoring the implementation of the WHO Global Code of Practice on the International Recruitment of Health Personnel. Bulletin of the World Health Organization, *91*(11), 816-823. DOI: 10.2471/BLT.13.118778

Sue, D. W. (1994). Asian-American mental health and help-seeking behavior: Comment on Solberg et al.(1994), Tata and Leong (1994), and Lin (1994).

Sun, K. C. (2012). Fashioning the reciprocal norms of elder care: A case of immigrants in the United States and their parents in Taiwan. *Journal of Family Issues*, *33*(9), 1240–1271. DOI: 10.1177/0192513X12445564

The State and the Grassroots. (2015). Berghahn Books. DOI: 10.2307/j.ctt9qd9c9

Toyin-Thomas, P., Ikhurionan, P., Omoyibo, E. E., Iwegim, C., Ukueku, A. O., Okpere, J., Nnawuihe, U. C., Atat, J., Otakhoigbogie, U., Orikpete, E. V., Erhiawarie, F., Gbejewoh, E. O., Odogu, U., Akhirevbulu, I. C. G., Kwarshak, Y. K., & Wariri, O. (2023). Drivers of health workers' migration, intention to migrate and non-migration from low/middle-income countries, 1970–2022: A systematic review. *BMJ Global Health*, *8*(5), e012338. DOI: 10.1136/bmjgh-2023-012338

Travis, S. (2023). Bridging the Healthcare Gap: The Critical Importance of International Medical Graduates in the US. *Journal For International Medical Graduates*, *2*(1). Advance online publication. DOI: 10.56570/jimgs.v2i1.73

Tsujita, Y., Oda, H., & Rajan, S. I. (2023). Obtaining a nursing job in Australia and New Zealand: A case study of migrant nurses trained in India. *ERIA Research Project Report FY*, *2023*(07), 47.

Villamin, P., Lopez, V., Thapa, D. K., & Cleary, M. (2023). Nurse migration to Australia: Past, present, and future. *Collegian (Royal College of Nursing, Australia)*, *30*(6), 753–761. DOI: 10.1016/j.colegn.2023.05.001

Vuohijoki, A., Ristolainen, L., Leppilahti, J., Kivivuori, S.-M., & Hurri, H. (2025). Impact of joint commission international accreditation on occupational health and patient safety: A systematic review. *PLoS One*, *20*(6), e0325894. DOI: 10.1371/journal.pone.0325894

Walton-Roberts, M., Runnels, V., Rajan, S. I., Sood, A., Nair, S., Thomas, P., Packer, C., MacKenzie, A., Tomblin Murphy, G., Labonté, R., & Bourgeault, I. L. (2017). Causes, consequences, and policy responses to the migration of health workers: Key findings from India. *Human Resources for Health*, *15*(1), 28. Advance online publication. DOI: 10.1186/s12960-017-0199-y

Wang, M., & Liu, Z. (2022). How Do Green Innovation Strategies Contribute to Firm Performance Under Supply Chain Risk? Evidence From China's Manufacturing Sector. *Frontiers in Psychology*, *13*, 894766. Advance online publication. DOI: 10.3389/fpsyg.2022.894766

Wang, M. S., Raynard, M., & Greenwood, R. (2021). From grace to violence: Stigmatizing the medical profession in China. *Academy of Management Journal*, *64*(6), 1842–1872. DOI: 10.5465/amj.2018.0715

Xie, Y., Guo, Q., & Meng, Y. (2021). The health service use of aged rural-to-urban migrant workers in different types of cities in China. *BMC Health Services Research*, *21*(1), 606. DOI: 10.1186/s12913-021-06638-3

Xu, L. (2024). The regional integration transition of China's immigration policy: The case of Yiwu. *Chinese Public Administration Review, 15*(2), 105–117. DOI: 10.1177/15396754241242851

Xu, X., Ren, P., Shi, W., Deng, F., Wang, Q., Shi, S., Shen, J., Dong, G., & Han, J. (2025). Occupational health and safety regulations in China: Development process, enforcement challenges, and solutions. *Frontiers in Public Health, 13*, 1522040. DOI: 10.3389/fpubh.2025.1522040

Xu, Y., Gutierrez, A., & Kim, S. H. (2008). Adaptation and Transformation Through (Un)Learning. *Advances in Nursing Science, 31*(2), E33–E47. DOI: 10.1097/01.ANS.0000319570.99254.e5

Yang, Y., Chen, B., Huang, P., Wang, Y., Zhang, L., & Cai, F. (2022). Prevalence and influencing factors of depressive symptoms among rural-to-urban migrant workers in China: A systematic review and meta-analysis. *Journal of Affective Disorders, 307*, 11–19. DOI: 10.1016/j.jad.2022.03.061

Yeates, N., & Pillinger, J. (2020). Building resilience across borders: a policy brief on health worker migration.

Zhao, I. Y., Holroyd, E., Garrett, N., Wright-St Clair, V. A., & Neville, S. (2023). Chinese late-life immigrants' loneliness and social isolation in host countries: An integrative review. *Journal of Clinical Nursing, 32*(9-10), 1615–1624. DOI: 10.1111/jocn.16134

Zhao, R., Zhang, H., Zhao, J. S., & Wang, X. (2019). When the west meets the east: Cultural clash and its impacts on anomie in a sample of Chinese adolescents. *Deviant Behavior, 40*(10), 1187–1205. DOI: 10.1080/01639625.2018.1472934

Zhong, S., & Su, B. (2021). Assessing the effects of labor market dynamics on CO2 emissions in global value chains. *The Science of the Total Environment, 768*, 144486. DOI: 10.1016/j.scitotenv.2020.144486

Zhong, Y., McKenna, L., Copnell, B., Zhao, W., & Moss, C. (2023). Professional adaptation experiences of Chinese migrant nurses in Australia: A qualitative study. *Western Journal of Nursing Research, 45*(7), 626–633. DOI: 10.1177/01939459231167711

Chapter 7
Economic, Political, and Demographic Drivers of Social Isolation:
Exploring the Role of Digital Literacy and Migration in Shaping Social Isolation – A Qualitative Study

Spurthi N. Channappaji
Christ University, India

Bindhya Billavara Shivappa
Christ University, India

Akhil Prakash
https://orcid.org/0009-0004-2999-574X
Christ University, India

ABSTRACT

This chapter examines the impact of migration and digital literacy on social isolation amongst workers. Migration can disrupt established social networks, making it challenging for an individual to establish and build new connections. The research employed a qualitative approach, and data were collected through semi-structured interviews with migrant workers residing in Bengaluru. The findings provide contextual information on the causes of social isolation and help acquire more knowledge on how migration and digital literacy relate and influence social isolation. It prioritises individual experience over statistical data, with an increased understanding of the

DOI: 10.4018/979-8-3373-5811-6.ch007

drivers of social isolation. Advanced digital literacy, on the other hand, can reduce social isolation by enabling migrants to maintain connections with their immediate family, access information, and develop innovative social networks. The research study's findings had a significant impact on policies and employers, highlighting the importance of social integration and mental health.

1. INTRODUCTION

Human beings are social animals influenced by individual purposes and interpersonal ties in life. Acceptance sentiments and strong social relationships are beneficial to emotional well-being and predict overall health protection. Social relationships are crucial in fulfilling the human need for attachment and a sense of belonging. Individuals with strong social relationships tend to have more positive life experiences, better psychological well-being, and greater emotional support (Amati et al., 2018). Social isolation is characterised as the deprivation of social association and relationships (Gierveld et al., 2018) and the deprivation of both the quality and quantity of social relationships (Zavaleta et al., 2017). Social isolation also implies physical distance from others and weakened social attachments (Ranjan & Yadav, 2019; Tomaka et al., 2006). Physical distance from others is an emotional matter, but it also causes serious health problems and an escalation of danger. Thus, maintaining social relationships is crucial for safeguarding life (Hodgson et al., 2020). Social isolation refers to the poor quality and limited number of social relationships individuals have with others, both within their own group and in the broader social environment, where human communication occurs (Zavaleta et al., 2014).

Migration is a strong force which helps in building social networking and is a process where peoples from one place moves to another place due to changes in the social, Economic, environmental and political conditions in the initial place, such as state, city, village, or a country and even a continent (Pieter, 1999). Migration takes various forms, including immigration, where people move to a new place in search of better opportunities and settle there, often leaving or abandoning their native place (Tsegay, 2023). From an economic perspective, migration enables individuals and their families to access more labour opportunities and a higher standard of living, while also contributing to individual income growth and promoting economic development, particularly by providing labour as a key element of competitiveness (Gruber & Sand, 2020). However, migration also comes with numerous limitations, including communication barriers and gaps, cultural differences, and feelings of inferiority.

Digital literacy refers to an individual's ability to search, find, evaluate, and create information using digital technologies and the internet (Lopez, 2023). Enhanced digital literacy will contribute to the economic development of individuals in economically weaker sections and also provide a path to improve their lifestyles (Liu & Liao, 2024). Digital literacy is a reference to the consciousness, temperament and ability of people to effectively use digital tools and facilities to recognise, gain access to, handle, incorporate, assess, analyse, and utilise digital content material, construct new knowledge, create media expression and communicate practically in daily contexts, empowering active social involvement and reflective consideration (Ng, 2012). Digital literacy is one of the fundamental elements that enables immigrants to overcome communication barriers and navigate online communities.

Understanding the connections between migration, digital literacy, and social isolation is crucial for developing and implementing policies that support migrants within the community or society. Digital literacy has the potential to reduce social isolation among migrants and improve their social lives and overall well-being. Bengaluru, also known as the Silicon Valley of India, is the capital city of Karnataka, which has a rapidly increasing population due to internal migration, as it is an information technology hub and an educational centre. It attracts a diverse range of talents from across the country and the globe, comprising various socio-economic groups, languages, and cultures. Bengaluru is a place with a high level of migration, linguistic diversity, and a digital environment, making it a key context to examine how social isolation is caused by migration among people working in urban or city areas.

Therefore, the present study aims to determine how migration and digital literacy impact social isolation, and also evaluates how migration and digital literacy levels affect an individual's ability to interact socially with others.

2. REVIEW OF LITERATURE

2.1 Digital Literacy

Older individuals are highly susceptible to social isolation due to a variety of barriers in accessing and benefiting from digital technologies, including poor digital literacy with individuals who do not possess suitable skills, limited technologies accessibility due to lack of funds or paucity of belongings and technologies and fear of error or breaking gear leading to technology anxiety, which significantly eradicates potential for older individuals to stay in touch with loved ones, friends and communities and these issues were worsened through the influence of the COVID-19 pandemic, which saw several older persons more solitary with increased risk of loneliness and unhealthy consequences (Stockwell et al., 2021; Wang et al., 2025). Older persons who derive benefit from internet use on a weekly or monthly basis are significantly less likely to experience social isolation in comparison with daily internet users, frequent and moderate internet use may prove beneficial for older persons, allowing them to stay in touch with friends and loved ones, information provision, and engage in meaningful internet activities with face-to-face relationships accompanying internet interactions, daily internet use comes with heightened risk of isolation, and individual who rarely utilise the net also tend reveal in social isolation and lonely feelings (Batra et al., 2024). In non-linear behaviour, seldom-used internet users are more likely to experience social isolation and loneliness. In contrast, older internet and email users who communicate with their relatives and friends, gain information, and engage with internet communities are generally much less socially isolated and stronger in their social attachments (Jang & Je, 2022). The exposure of older persons to social isolation increased exponentially due to inadequate infrastructural provision and suboptimal digital competence, particularly during the COVID-19 pandemic, as they struggled to afford or access reliable internet. They possessed outdated equipment capable of managing the current era's communication instruments, such as video conferencing or social networking; even when there was provision, it was impractical due to poor digital competence (David et al., 2020).

Older Indian individuals' digital competence during the years 2014-2024 was subject to deliberation, concluding inadequate skill level, socio-economic issues, infrastructural provision restrictions and enormous rural-urban divide are significant determinants of their modest ICT adoption, emphasising the imperative of inclusive policies, social provision targeted towards them and specialist professional training programmes capable of efficiently shrinking the age-related digital divide and realising digital inclusion among older Indian individuals (Jena & Paltasingh, 2025).

Digital competence has been considered crucial to India's socio-economic growth, fostering innovation, entrepreneurship, and access to essential services. However, issues such as poor awareness, inadequate professional training, and enormous infrastructural gaps persist, hindering development. Consequently, community-based projects, policy assistance, and capacity-building programs must be implemented to bolster digital inclusion and reduce the prevalent digital divide (Di & Wang, 2025). Digital divide is not just about internet access but differences in users' online skills, and shows how factors like age, education and experience influence people's ability to use the internet effectively (Hargittai, 2001)

Digitally literate citizens are empowered through enhanced access to fundamental government services, quality education and improved employment options, raising quality of life and general socio-economic well-being, and inclusive development in India is highly reliant on effective awareness and training programs with sensitivity to the differential needs of the population (David et al., 2020). Promotions of digital development in India are deliberated, with reference to vast development accrued through governmental missions like the Digital India, with a focus on critical implementation strategies with increased sense of urgency, skill-based and customised pronged training courses, and special awareness missions to realise equitable and just digital empowerment of diverse communities, socio-economic strata, and geographic locations (Nedeljko et al., 2021).

Digital literacy is mentioned as a critical enabler of social inclusion, emphasising its primary function in increasing employment opportunities, educational achievements, and good governance. Addressing India's digital divide entails expanding training programs, narrowing regional disparities, and promoting equitable access to digital capital (Tinmaz et al., 2022). Luminously ranked as critical to India's sustainable development, achieving digital empowerment entails social inclusiveness plans, skill development, and policy support (Buchan et al., 2024). Gaps in digital literacy exacerbate social and economic disparities in India. Nevertheless, problems such as inadequate access, knowledge, and competence still prevail, and inclusive digital development requires a joint effort through community initiatives, education, and government programs (Sen et al., 2022). Digital literacy has been shown to increase the life satisfaction of South Korean elderly individuals by enhancing their ability to access basic facilities, communicate with acquaintances and loved ones, and utilise lifelong learning facilities. Although notable achievements have been registered, fewer than half of older people are digitally competent, and a high priority now needs to be given to more comprehensive and targeted digital education plans, accessibility plans, and supportive services tailored to their specific needs (Lee, 2024). Recent research stresses the rising significance of information and communication technologies to India's elderly population, allowing them to have greater social interaction, utilise critical services, and handle daily tasks more efficiently and with India's elderly population expected to hit more than 20% of the entire population with the aid of 2050, it is more essential to understand how the demographic employs technology, and the research stresses the importance of age-friendly digital literacy education, cross-generational learning, user-friendly and usable interfaces, and government-supported information and communication technologies to decrease the digital divide and empower India's elderly population thereby increasing their standard well-being and independence (Njonge, 2023).

2.2 Social Isolation

Social isolation has been the focus of considerable study in present-day scholarship, with expanding literature zeroing in on causes, processes, effects, and broader ramifications in diverse populations and venues, thereby becoming a multi-dimensional construct wherein structure, society, biology, and psychological forces, with a multi-level logistic model moderated with individual and regional factors, the research presents robust evidence that social isolation's hazard is considerably increased through some organisations of life, mainly residency in capital cities, limited accesses to conventional markets, and the increasing common domestic structure of independent residency, illustrating general trends across East Asia towards smaller and graying family size (Nguyen et al., 2024). The results of the study, aside from confirming the importance of contextual forces such as endogenous resource availability and community conditions, also unveil how urbanisation and present-day lifestyles have the effect of attenuating social ties unintentionally, reducing social participatory opportunities and yielding places in which social isolation increases, on the biological level, loneliness or isolation has been shown to play effects on the human organism innumerable diverse manner with the research context in which isolation changes gene expression profiles, depresses immune processes, induces hypertrophic stress responses, and disrupts sleep physiology, all of which individually but cumulatively correspond to morbidity and mortality odds, most particularly in older individuals who are already vulnerable to such morbidity and mortality due to the loss of health as an aging correlate. Thus, social connectedness is a social-psychological phenomenon and an underlying determinant of health with an evolutionary biological correlate (Cudjoe & Colburn, 2019). Social isolation and loneliness were independently associated with modestly higher risk of CVD among postmenopausal women in the U.S., and women with both social isolation and loneliness had greater CVD risk than did those with either exposure alone. The findings suggest that these prevalent psychosocial processes merit increased attention for the prevention of CVD in older women, particularly in the era of COVID-19 (Golaszewski et al., 2022).

Migration status influences the association of social isolation with loneliness in Germany so that refugees experience the highest level of loneliness and isolation, while migrants prove to have a surprisingly weaker association of the two, hinting that while migrants may be exposed to isolation in the aspect of fewer social connections, they may be less impacted on an emotional level compared to refugees, possibly due to factors of resilience, coping mechanisms from their culture, or self-selection processes with more resourceful individuals embarking on migration (Löbel et al., 2022). Migration can be a highly stress-inducing phenomenon, yet not all migrants undergo the same process. The clinician needs to be aware of coping strategies and resilience among migrants (Bhugra, 2004). Focusing on non-migrants, migrants, and refugees, this study looks at the effect of social isolation and socio-economic status (SES) on mental health during the period of the COVID-19 pandemic in Germany, while the strength and direction of such association vary across subpopulations, it is found that low SES has a positive correlation with high psychological distress, which is in part channeled through increased social isolation (Touzel et al., 2025). Discrimination and social exclusion have been known to activate the individual's stress response and interfere with neurotransmitter systems with consequent long-term psychologic and physiologic effects, these mechanisms enormously escalate the individual's predisposition to a host of psychiatric illness, including psychosis, depression, substance dependency, and anxiety, such dangers are multiplied in groups already marginalised in society, including the elderly, immigrants, and youth, who are likely deprived of effective social networks and face structural barriers to healthcare utilisation, to reverse these unfortunate trends, scientists reveal the potential of specially developed interventions respectful of culture but sensitive to the unique needs of such groups, in the modern setting, computerised platforms and tech-based support networks have been known to prove promising tools in the correction of social isolation, as they ease the delivery of peer-support networks, culturally sensitive aid, and mental health care to vulnerable groups (Brandt et al., 2022). The study primarily explains how the digital platform helps immigrants feel more included and improves their well-being in a new place. The key concept is that when immigrants use these digital apps, they experience a greater sense of social inclusion (Frounfelker et al., 2019).

Immigrant mental health is significantly affected by stress during all stages of migration since immigrants encounter a host of social, economic, and cultural problems inducing persistent mental strain, the barrier to communication, healthcare, and integration with receiving societies becomes language, causing feelings of exclusion and isolation, unemployment or underemployment contributes to these problems, with a significant number of immigrants unable to achieve stable employment commensurate with their educational level, inducing financial insecurity and loss of self-esteem, discrimination in housing, healthcare, and employment exacerbates feelings of marginalisation, increasing immigrants' susceptibility to mental illness such as anxiety, depression, and psychiatric illness. In addition, social network loss and unfamiliarity with their native culture tend to induce greater social isolation, eroding their ability to cope. Measures to counter such threats include policies and healthcare practitioners developing culturally sensitive, inclusive, and supportive interventions that enhance social integration and promote well-being (Motillon-Toudic et al., 2022). Such effects of social isolation and loneliness on physical and mental health reinforce such perils as depression, strain, and premature death, encapsulating such perils as public health emergencies in so doing highlights the imperativeness of such interventions as going beyond coping mechanisms individual and instead involving broader-based systemic and policy-based responses, in particular advocating designing and implementing targeted interventions and supportive policies capable of enhancing social networks, interpersonal relationships, and provision of necessary supplies to vulnerable groups, such actions are required for strengthening psychological ability to cope and physical health consequently reduced social isolation burden generally on society (Torres & Casey, 2017).

2.3 Migration

Nepalese migration is more than an economic imperative. However, as a socially entrenched standard imposed by social pressure, FOMO, and status-based perceptions, it shows how social comparison and transgenerational transmission maintain a self-sustaining culture of migration (Koirala, 2025). As per the research, more than 70% of the students of medicine proclaimed their desire to emigrate from the country, due mainly to personal needs such as better quality of life and work-life balance, but attachments to the family and emotional disincentives were significant disincentives, privileged educational background, English-speaking ability, and information on migration were substantial predictors (Parvizi et al., 2025). Migration is a crucial livelihood strategy for the poor, and in shaping human development in India, migrants contribute approximately 10% to the national GDP (Deshingkar, P., & Akter, 2009). Germany has attempted to encourage immigrants to become citizens of the country to promote diversity. However, critics argue that immigrants are still treated as outsiders and are mainly viewed as workers. Migration is a complex social process, and researchers have introduced the concept of the post-migrant to understand how migration changes society (Altay et al., 2025). When migrants face challenges such as drought or rising costs, they utilise social media and personal contacts to share information and support one another. These networks depict how communication organises itself, shares resources, and raises awareness (Ou-Salah & Van Praag, 2025). After migration and refugee children and teenagers face mental health issues like anxiety, depression and post-traumatic stress disorder. The article highlights challenges in providing mental health care and support (Frounfelker et al., 2019). Cross-border migrants were prohibited from getting health services like HIV treatment, because of these strict health policies, medical professionals faced Ethical dilemmas to go against their professional duties and values (Balekang et al., 2025). Local people migrate primarily due to water shortages, deforestation, and ongoing climate change. To overcome these environmental challenges, they migrate in search of a better place to live (Rusere et al., 2025). During the COVID-19 pandemic, high-income individuals in the United States were more likely to migrate due to climate-related disasters, such as floods and hurricanes, that affected these areas. This suggests that climate disasters can exacerbate inequality between richer and poorer families, as wealthier families are more likely to have the means to relocate (Clark et al., 2025). For migration and refugee research, the concept of liminality, which involves being in a state of transition between places or identities, is explored. Researchers suggest using a broader framework to better understand how migrants' identities and experiences change over time and in different locations (Marotta, 2025).

The significant impact of social isolation and loneliness on health and well-being of people ties them with greater likelihoods of psychological distress, disease, and premature death, and it becomes apparent how social determinants such as migration, socio-economic status, discrimination, and vulnerable social networks worsen isolation, particularly among high-risk populations such as the elderly, migrants, and refugees, while isolation worsens both mental and physical health, social support networks function as protective mechanisms, and multi-level intervention from community programs and internet-based platforms to health policies and socio-economic changes are required to reduce isolation, foster inclusion, and reinforce resilience (Li, 2016). Loneliness and social isolation are major public health problems with strong correlations to adverse effects on mental and physical health such as depression, pressure, depressed immunity, and premature death, and high-risk populations such as migrants, refugees, the elderly, and low socio-economic status groups are most vulnerable due to determinants such as discrimination, differences in culture, unemployment, and lack of supportive networks. In contrast, social support exerts a protective effect to help people cope with pressure and boost general well-being, and effective intervention must reduce determinants both structurally and individually through health policies, community programs, and internet-based platforms to foster inclusion, reinforce resilience, and reduce harmful effects due to social isolation (Shishehgar et al., 2015).

Construction migrant workers have also pointed out the massive psychological and social issues of migrant group, found from a study of 75 workers, which indicated the vast majority of workers never had formal schooling, the great majority migrated in the past few years, a considerable portion migrated with kinship groups, the average age of respondent workers was 32 years, and 64% were found to have psychosocial care needs, with women workers more revealing psychological distress than their counterparts, on average the quality of community life (QoCL) of workers was sub-moderate, with poor social and living conditions, the results indicate pre-migrant and post-migrant factors such as meager wages, insecurity of work, poor social security, and squalid working and residence environment are responsible for enduring pressure, which contributes to increased psychological pressure and poor QoCL, and thus highlights the need for intersectoral actions and community-oriented psychiatric care in all grades of primary, secondary, and tertiary to reduce pressure and to enrich the quality of life among migratory workers in the construction sector (Sriramalu et al., 2023).

Examining the existing literature, the current study aims to investigate the dynamics with the following research questions, arrived at based on prior discussions on migration, digital literacy, and social isolation in urban settings the literature points to significant disruptions in social networks during migration and highlights the potential role of digital tools in shaping experiences of connectedness while also noting barriers such as limited skills and uneven access these insights guide the formulation of research questions that focus on how migration influences patterns of social interaction in urban spaces how digital literacy mediates the ability of migrants to engage with technology for sustaining and building relationships and how digital platforms intersect with existing challenges of belonging and participation in diverse urban communities these research questions are framed to capture the complexities identified in earlier works while opening space for an in depth examination of the migrant experience in technologically mediated urban settings.

RQ1. How does migration influence social isolation among employees?

RQ 2. How do migrants' backgrounds shape their levels of social isolation?

RQ 3. What challenges do migrants face because of migration?

RQ 4. How does digital literacy affect migrants' ability to cope with or reduce social isolation?

3. METHODOLOGY

3.1 Research Design

This study employs a qualitative research methodology to explore the effects of migration and digital literacy on the daily experience of social isolation among migrant workers in a metropolitan setting. Migration often involves separation from established social networks; therefore, migrants must manage a new, unfamiliar social and cultural environment. While migration offers fresh economic and professional opportunities, it can also trigger feelings of loneliness, isolation, and exclusion when migrants are unable to recreate meaningful social interactions. These processes also escalate in high-speed urban cities, characterised by transient interpersonal relationships and inadequate protection networks. Correspondingly, digital literacy significantly determines how migrant workers adapt to social isolation. As conceptualised here, digital literacy is more than merely a technical competency to operate devices or utilise internet platforms; it is a socially and culturally inscribed competence forged and negotiated through daily life. For migrant workers, efficiently using digital tools can maintain communication lines with their hometowns and similarly connect them with new networks in their destination city. Using internet platforms would reduce feelings of isolation via communication, services, and social interaction avenues.

The quality and scope of social relationships determine how individuals feel integrated or excluded. This study defines social isolation as a condition characterised by narrowed or weakened social connections, resulting in interactions that lack depth, emotional support, or persistence. In exploring the interactions between migration, digital literacy, and social isolation, the study offers a thorough insight into the challenges faced by migrant workers in urban contexts. The study aims to reveal the potential of digital literacy as a tool to fight isolation and realise social well-being.

3.2 Data Collection

This study examines the impact of migration and digital technology competencies on social isolation in urban areas. Digital literacy is more than technical expertise with digital tools; it is socially and culturally constructed during social interactions and everyday use. For this study, social isolation suggests the existence of weak and meagre social connections. Social connections are robbed of their emotional richness and active participation in the community. Migrant workers lose their social protection and become isolated in an urban centre. Other urban residents are insensitive to the emotional needs of workers. Digital worlds tend to favour tech-savvy workers while isolating socially those with low digital competence.

The study used qualitative methods and collected data through semi–structured interviews. A purposive sampling method was employed to select 27 migrant workers residing and working in Bengaluru. Participants were selected through community networks, as well as through friends and family. They included both interstate and intrastate migrants who had been in the city for at least six months.

Interviews were conducted virtually via phone. Each interview lasted about 10 to 15 minutes. The conversations were held in Kannada, Hindi and English, depending on the participant's comfort. In a similar study, 19 interviews were conducted to understand how migrants and their families stay connected by discussing everyday topics, such as memories, weather, and environmental concerns (Ou-Salah & Van Praag, 2025). In our study, a sample size of 27 was selected based on the principle of data saturation, which means that interviews were continued until no new themes or insights emerged from the data. Responses began to repeat after the 25th interview, and by the 27th, no new information emerged, indicating that sufficient data had been collected for a meaningful analysis.

The interviews focused on the experiences of migrants moving to urban areas, their use of digital tools, and the impact these had on their social lives. Some of the main questions asked were:

1. Since moving here, how easy or difficult has it been for you to form new friendships or social networks?
2. What challenges have you faced in connecting with people in Bengaluru?

3. What are the digital tools to stay in touch with family and friends?
4. Do you feel more socially isolated now compared to before you migrated?

All interviews were recorded on audio (with permission) and later prepared for analysis.

3.3 Ethical Consideration

The study adhered to ethical guidelines, prioritising the protection of research participants and maintaining the integrity of data collection. We ensured that all research participants provided informed consent during the interview. This was achieved through a summary of the research, including research questions, methods, and their importance. Participants were allowed to ask any questions and clarify their queries. To protect the participants' identities and personal information, pseudonyms and all identifying details were removed. Audio recordings were stored securely and used solely for research purposes, and were subsequently deleted to prevent any potential risks. By following all these ethical guidelines, we ensured that the participants' privacy was protected, ensured the reliability of our findings, and maintained the integrity of our study. Following ethical research practices fosters trust, safeguards participants, and provides valid results that can be applied to the broader population.

3.4 Participant Profile

The study involved 27 participants, comprising nine males and 18 females, all of whom were working and residing in Bengaluru. Participants were selected to capture a range of migration experiences, including those of interstate and intrastate migrants. Their age, socio-economic status, and stay duration in the urban location varied to provide an inclusive picture of what migration and digital literacy achieve in terms of perceptions of social isolation among urban migrant workers. Informed consent and confidentiality were ensured for all participants throughout the research process.

Table 1. Demographics of the participants

Characteristics	Frequency
Gender	
Male	9
Female	18
Total	**27**
Duration of stay	

continued on following page

Table 1. Continued

Characteristics	Frequency
Less than 2years	14
2 - 4 years	5
Above 4 years	8
Total	**27**
Income	
Less than 50,000	16
50,000 – 1,00,000	8
Above 1,00,00	3
Total	**27**
Qualification	
Undergraduate	21
Postgraduate	6
Total	**27**

4. QUALITATIVE ANALYSIS

The rapid pace of global urbanisation has produced a complex social context, particularly for migrant workers who move to new cities with the aspiration of economic improvement. Although such movement tends to lead to professional development, migrant workers also have the potential to develop an intense sense of social isolation because migrants transfer to new cities without their established networks of social support (Srivastava et al., 2021). For the study's exploratory perspective, a qualitative research framework was chosen to identify the multi-dimensional determinants of social isolation among migrants in Bengaluru and investigate their coping mechanisms to combat these sentiments. Qualitative research best suits this study because it offers depth to investigate individuals' lived experiences and decision-making, and captures nuanced, practice-based knowledge that is impossible to summarise in numerical indicators. The analytical work in this study was inductive and iterative, utilising thematic analysis in NVivo software to allow results to derive from the data, as evidenced by the methodology itself (Nowell et al., 2017).

4.1 Data Coding and Thematic Analysis

Figure 1. Codes and references

Name	File	Reference
(RQ1) Influence of Migration	*25*	*37*
Economic factor	2	2
• Cost of living	2	2
Language gap	8	8
Social factor	21	24
• Diversity	5	5
• Initial difficulty	18	18
• Less talkative	1	1
(RQ 2) Levels of social isolation	*3*	*3*
Decrease in social isolation	2	2
Increase in social isolation	21	22
Separation from networks	8	8
(RQ 3) Challenges of Migration	*3*	*3*
Cultural differences	13	13
Language barrier	20	20
Lifestyle	10	10
(RQ 4) Impact of digital literacy	*1*	*3*
Confident in using digital platform	21	21
Outcome	28	28
• Less social isolation	21	21
• Convenient	7	7
Platform	26	85
• WhatsApp	24	27
• Instagram	24	27
• Facebook	8	10
• LinkedIn	8	9
• Telegram	4	4
• Zoom	4	4
• Snapchat	3	3
• Netflix	1	1

The transcription and interview data were carefully coded and analysed through thematic analysis, breaking down vast amounts of qualitative data into manageable groups and identifying shared patterns. This step-wise approach helped to combine, analyse, and structure participants' responses into meaningful themes and apparent research findings.

A systematic and flexible research methodology was employed in the study, enabling recurring themes and emerging concepts to be identified directly from the data. The process began with the creation of a new NVivo project, into which transcripts and the related papers were imported for detailed analysis.

Within NVivo, data were securely stored and processed on a single platform. From here onwards, preliminary codes (nodes) were generated, each of which was interlinked to key research questions: RQ1 - The Influence of Migration, RQ2 – The Impact of Social Isolation, RQ3 - The Challenges of Migrants, and RQ4 - The Impact of Digital Literacy. And transcripts were coded line by line to ensure that relevant passages were accurately associated with the appropriate codes. While some codes, such as Language Barrier and Cultural Differences, were predetermined, other codes, for example, references to personal digital platforms that reduced social isolation (e.g., Instagram, WhatsApp, Facebook), emerged from the data itself. This movement between data and coding was supported by frequent cross-checks, which strengthened the reliability and robustness of the analysis.

Significant findings were identified across the research questions. The themes related to RQ1, 'Influence of Migration,' and RQ3, 'Challenges of Migrants,' including 20 references to language barriers, were among the most frequently observed, highlighting the significant impact of migration-related factors on social isolation. The high number of reference counts related to RQ2: Impact of Social Isolation, which included 22 references, further highlights the importance of this phenomenon. The finding also demonstrated that RQ4: Impact of Digital Literacy was a significant mitigating factor, and participants who were confident in using digital platforms reported reduced social isolation through active engagement with tools such as Instagram, Facebook, and Netflix. Overall, the findings suggest that social isolation frequently results from migration-related issues and disconnection from existing social networks, while digital tools have considerable potential to mitigate these effects and foster connections.

Figure 2. Qualitative analysis process

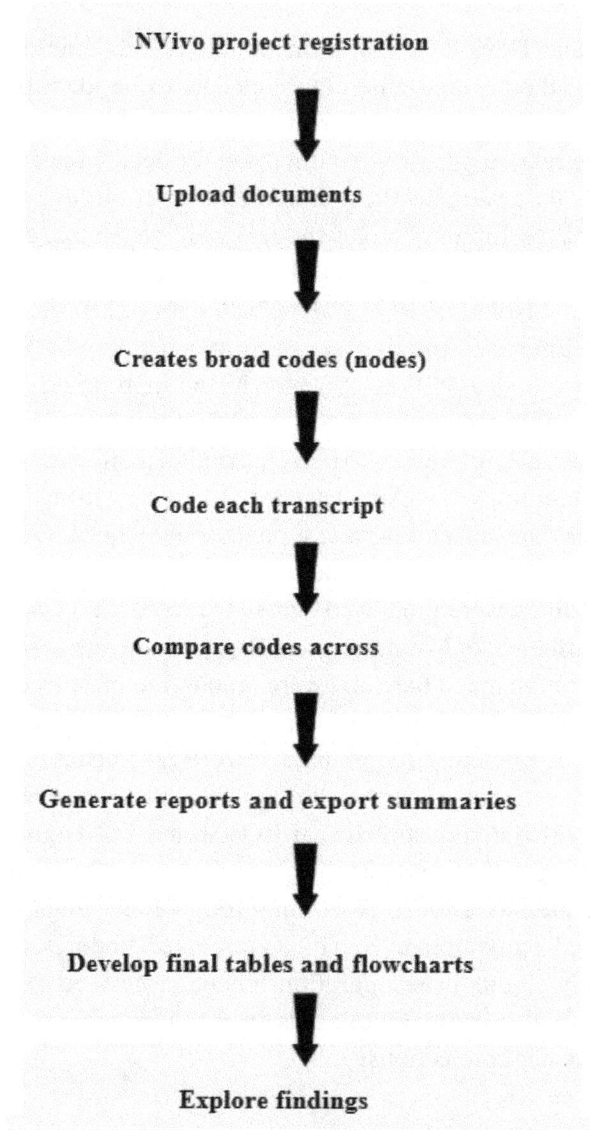

The flowcharts in Fig. 2 describe the systematic process followed to analyse qualitative interview data using NVivo, a computer-assisted qualitative data analysis software. The process ensures that the data is organised, coded, compared, and interpreted in a structured manner.

The first step is to create a new project in NVivo and register it by giving it a name. This creates a workspace where all transcripts and coding activities are stored. Next, all interview transcripts saved in a Word document are uploaded into the project to keep all qualitative material centralised and ready for coding. Later develops initial broad themes, also known as nodes in NVivo. Broad nodes include the influence of migration, levels of social isolation, the impact of digital literacy, and the challenges faced by migrants. For every parent, code children's codes are developed. Once all interviews are coded, NVivo is used to compare patterns across participants. Code frequency reports, Word frequency charts, and Visual models help in understanding which themes are most dominant and how categories relate. Finally, the researcher critically interprets patterns and relationships between themes.

Figure 2 explains the systematic rigour and methodological transparency of the research's data analysis, which is necessary given that the research is founded on rich, qualitative data from semi-structured interviews. From the diagram, we can see the step-wise, structured approach taken, demonstrating the laboriously thorough process of moving from raw interview transcripts all the way to usable information. Specifically, the diagram reflects the workflow of analytics through the NVivo software, from the creation of a project and importing documents through to the chief analytical actions: developing an initial framework through the creation of broad codes (nodes), followed by the time-consuming exercise of individually coding each transcript to mark and categorise textual items. It describes the code comparison stage during interviews to identify general trends and correlations across migrants' orientations. Finally, it demonstrates the reporting and exploration of results—processes that transform the coded data into the contextualised information the study claims to reveal. By diagramming the entire systematic process in this way, the figure ensures that, in the reader's mind, conclusions drawn from the study on how social isolation is impacted through migration and digital literacy are empirically tested and worthy of informing policy.

4.2 Identified Themes

Figure 3. Word Cloud

Figure 3 illustrates the significant themes and oft-cited concepts emerging from the experiences of Bengaluru migrant workers, with isolation, digital technologies, and social media at the core of the findings. The dominance of isolation underscores the emotional and social aspects of migration, where leaving one's hometown is more likely to result in fractured networks of support and strained personal ties. Migrants frequently reported that life in Bengaluru, with its numerous opportunities, presented both challenges and possibilities, but also often compounded loneliness due to unfamiliarity with the culture, linguistic differences, and the absence of robust social ties. Migration is more than just geographic or economic exchange; it also involves social disruption, which enhances the likelihood of loneliness and isolation. The terms migration, reduction, and formation reinforce the evolving nature: while migration intensifies the isolation experiences, it is more likely to be countered by new attachments. These terms highlight migrant agency, illustrating that people are not merely passive recipients of urban stresses or pressures but actively seek out their new environments via companion-seeking, building new networks, and making do with materialised means to confront loneliness directly. Through this struggle, social media and digital technologies appear as significant coping mechanisms. Migrants frequently described platforms like WhatsApp, Instagram, and LinkedIn as lifelines or essential tools for sustaining long-distance relationships, sharing updates, and seeking emotional support. The platforms also played a key role in allowing them to build new social and professional networks in Bengaluru through internet-based groups, workplace communities, or professional mentorship networks. The importance of digital technologies in the picture records the manner in which digital literacy extends beyond technical competence to a socially and culturally embedded skill, allowing migrants to negotiate relationships and build a sense of belonging in an unfamiliar urban landscape.

Nevertheless, migrants also mentioned the limitations of such digital dependence: whilst social networks delivered fleeting relief and options for communication, they couldn't possibly take the place of the emotional depth of face-to-face connections. The regular incidence of terms like confidence, difficulty, challenges, networks, and language also highlights the manner in which migrant challenges are multi-dimensional, emotional, linguistic, and social. Some mentioned struggling with communicating in Kannada, which restricts integration and fosters exclusionary sentiments. Some people shared their experiences of diminished confidence in social interactions and the emotional challenges involved in making new friends in a fast-paced, competitive environment. As a result, even though social networks helped mitigate feelings of isolation, they couldn't completely remove the underlying structural and cultural boundaries that organise migrant life.

Bengaluru, also known as the IT capital of India, has been an attractive destination for migrants from all over who move with hopes of better returns, careers, and professional opportunities. Bengaluru provides economic and social mobility, attracting individuals from diverse social and cultural backgrounds. Despite the optimistic scenario, a different reality altogether exists. Life in Bengaluru is fast, competitive, and individualistic, making it very challenging for new migrants to build strong and deep social networks. This is unlike smaller towns or villages, where neighbours and communities are active advocates of support. Bengaluru's urban location has poor neighbourhoods and a lack of social attachment. This has a high chance of making the migrants feel invisible and lonely, even when they are in crowds. Bengaluru then has multiple selves; there are opportunities for new openings, but also a sense of loneliness. Migrants then struggle to balance the promise of professional growth on one side with the emotional challenge of loneliness on the other. This balancing routine becomes an integral part of their life, determining their way of coping, their approach to doing things, and their attempt to find a sense of belonging in the city.

To overcome these issues, migrants utilise both online and offline strategies to avoid isolation and maintain social relationships. In their offline lives, they try to connect with colleagues, neighbours, or other fellow migrants within urban settings. However, their communication is limited by cultural differences, language barriers, and the fast pace of urban life. Online, migrants first connect with digital tools such as WhatsApp, Facebook, and Instagram to maintain relationships with their loved ones in their place of origin. These platforms offer warmth, emotional reassurance, and a sense of continuity with their pre-migration life, thereby reducing feelings of loneliness in their new environment. At the same time, digital platforms provide some opportunities to form new connections within the host city, although they lack the stability and depth of old connections. Therefore, this dependence on digital tools gives both strengths and limitations.

On the other hand, these digital tools help to overcome distance and reduce feelings of isolation, but they cannot wholly replace the warmth and face-to-face interaction. Figure 3 reflects this reality by illustrating how migration brings both losses and gains together—migration to Bengaluru offers professional success. However, it obliterates social ease and comfort, while digital platforms open new possibilities of connecting, but cannot adequately compensate for the warmth of embodied presence. This way, migrants' daily lives in Bengaluru present an ongoing compromise amidst isolation, adaptation, and tech dependence, with technology serving as a connecting link but never an absolute solution to the problems of belonging in urban life.

Figure 4. Cluster Analysis

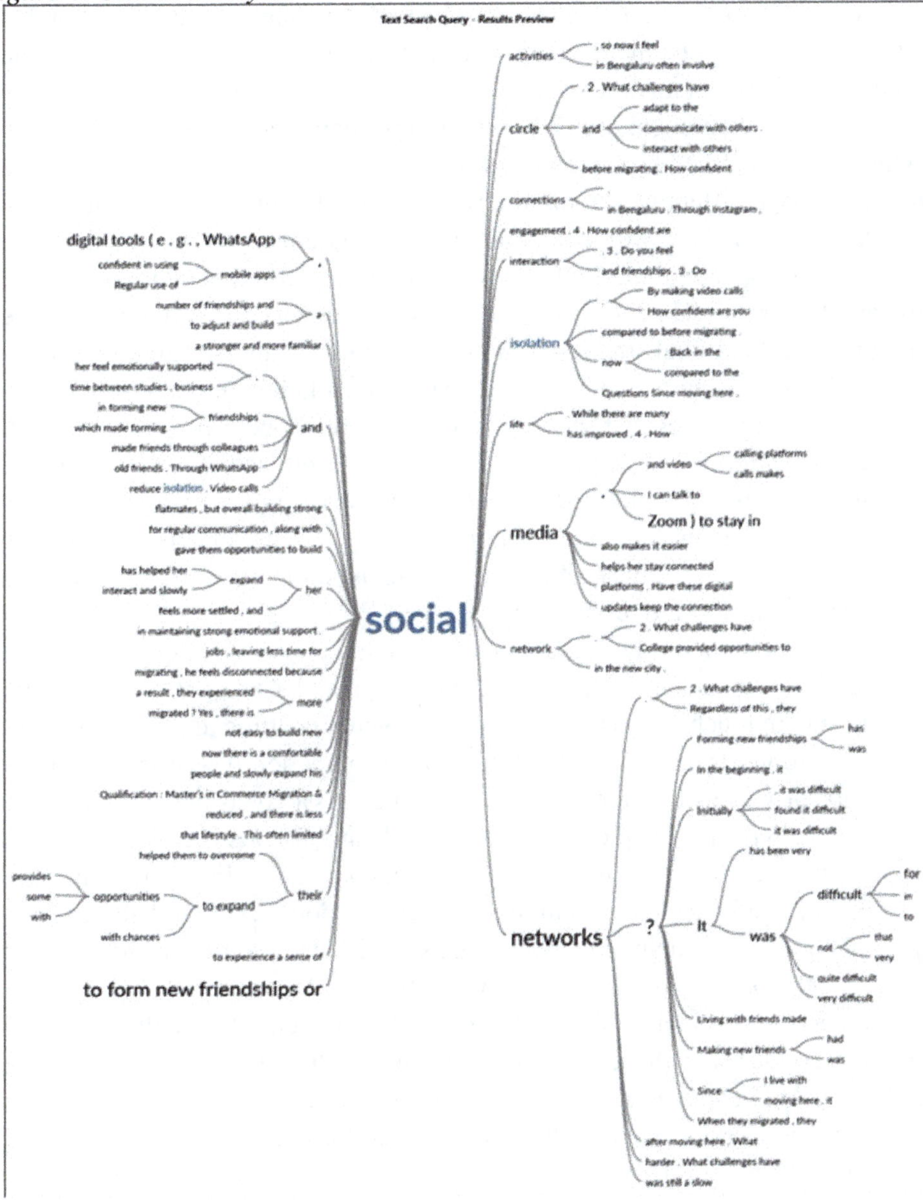

Figure 4 presents a straightforward diagrammatic representation of the significant causes and challenges of feelings of isolation among Bengaluru migrants, framing the problem in a step-wise and systematic manner. The figure highlights that the ultimate cause of isolation is the breakdown of strong and close social networks, which is automatically achieved when people migrate from their hometowns to an unfamiliar city. This deprivation is more than just leaving behind friends and loved ones—leaving behind also means leaving behind the support structures, comfort, and feelings of belonging that come from established networks. Migrants explained in their own voices that making friends in the city was "very difficult," which shows it is more than a theoretical problem but an experiential fact. The first phase after moving is often marked by issues that hinder the formation of new networks, including language differences, unfamiliarity with local culture, and the city's rapid pace, which does not allow time to build intimate relationships. This stage, marked by lost networks and struggles to form new ones, easily lays the foundation for isolation and loneliness. The hierarchical organisation in which Figure 6 is presented highlights that this initial stage—losing old attachments and struggling with new ones—is the most general and immediate cause of isolation among migrant workers. The figure illustrates that physical isolation is only one aspect of the broader concept of isolation for migrants. It has more to do with social isolation, even in the presence of other people. It is challenging for many migrants to connect with others due to both internal and external barriers. The figure clearly illustrates the extent and persistence of this problem. It can persist for a long time after someone has relocated to a city; it doesn't simply go away.

The next part of the analysis examines how digital tools help migrants cope with this isolation. It finds that platforms like WhatsApp and Zoom are key in assisting people to stay in touch. WhatsApp is used for regular chatting and casual updates, while Zoom supports more formal or face-to-face interaction. These aren't just tools people happen to use—they are essential ways migrants actively manage their social lives. They help people keep in touch with family and friends back home and also help build new relationships in work or community settings. In this way, migrants utilise digital platforms to maintain existing connections and establish new ones. Things like video calls help reduce the effects of distance and time zones, allowing people to feel closer to each other even when they are far apart.

However, the figure also shows that not everyone benefits equally from these tools. Success in using them depends on factors such as income, education, and social networks. People with more resources often have better internet, more time, and stronger networks to begin with. They are therefore better positioned to benefit from digital technology. However, it can be challenging for individuals with limited financial resources to access the same advantages.

This section of the analysis is crucial because it demonstrates that although technology can be helpful, not everyone finds that it resolves their problems. Social disparities are still significant. Technology can support connection, but it doesn't remove the barriers many migrants face. Ultimately, the figure presents a clear journey—from the experience of isolation to the use of digital tools for connection, to the uneven results shaped by social and economic factors. It offers a thoughtful and realistic portrayal of how migrants attempt to adapt and build new lives, and how their success depends on much more than just access to the internet.

Table 2. Research questions and Corresponding Themes

Research Questions(RQ)	Identified Themes
RQ1: How does migration influence the experience of social isolation among employees?	Migrants who relocated to Bengaluru often faced the irony of being in physical proximity to large groups of others while feeling emotionally isolated. The new language and varying cultural norms posed challenges in daily interactions. Complex interactions, such as seeking direction or casual chatter, became stressful and sometimes intimidating. Pre-existing social networks from their places of origin were also severed, resulting in the loss of known support structures. This set of circumstances resulted in feelings of loneliness, despite being in continuous proximity with others.
RQ2: How do migrants' backgrounds shape their levels of social isolation?	Adapters relied heavily on their ability to utilise digital communication tools. Micro-migrants with greater digital competence can better maintain contact with kinship and friendship ties online. Familiarity with surroundings, such as navigating urban areas or accessing services, also influenced adaptability—derived background factors included past urban experience and length of stay. Overall, migrants with information technology expertise and a comfort level in environmental settings are better adapted than those without these skills.
RQ3: What challenges do migrants face because of migration?	Migrants found it challenging to make friends due to variations in communication and social behaviour. Members who are more uncomfortable in new social situations avoid social events or interactions. Online interactions then became a critical substitute for face-to-face interactions with others. Affection and ease with the use of online technologies varied from individual to individual. Social engagement then became uneven based on social adaptability or technical expertise.
RQ4: How does digital literacy affect migrant's ability to cope with or reduce social isolation?	Social media sites like Facebook, Instagram, and WhatsApp keep migrants in touch with distant friends. They were able to speak with family and friends, and stay informed about what was happening in the community. However, low-digital-literacy migrants were unable to take full advantage of the platforms. This led to a digital divide, with some who were integrated and others more excluded. Technology hence, bridged and divided, depending on the individual's digital skills.

5. DISCUSSION

The findings of the current qualitative study reveal a multi-layered and rich description of social isolation experienced by migrant workers in Bengaluru. Data, systematically queried using NVivo, verify the principal hypothesis that migration is a significant reason for social isolation, as existing social networks are disrupted. This dimension manifests prominently in the vast number of references concerning the struggles of migrants and the consequences of social isolation, bearing testament to the reality that many participants faced a strong sense of loneliness while being relocated to an urban capital with a vibrant life. This finding verifies existing knowledge about the subject matter, referencing an all-pervasive but oft-neglected aspect of the migrant lifestyle. Feeling "alone in crowds" and being unable to build meaningful, trust-based relationships is consistent with issues concerning migration stress and post-migration social dislocation; that is, the very separation from these well-known social structures creates emotional and practical disadvantages for migrants (Li, 2016; Löbel et al., 2022).

One of the significant inferences is that the experience of social isolation is heterogeneous. The NVivo models capture how individual background predictors—socio-economic background, stay length, and digital literacy—strongly impact a migrant's coping mechanism. Migrants with greater digital competence and more experience using internet-based tools were found to have a more efficient coping mechanism during isolation. The role of digital literacy in buffering against isolation is echoed in research on the second-level digital divide, which examines not only whether migrants have internet access but also the differences in skills and uses that determine who can benefit from digital platforms (Hargittai, 2001; Tinmaz et al., 2022). A direct association between the use of diversified digital platforms, such as WhatsApp, Instagram, and LinkedIn, and a reduced sense of isolation. These tools had a twofold functionality: they connected migrants with their family and friends in their home country. They helped establish new social and professional connections in their destination metropolitan area.

However, the research also revealed that a significant digital divide persists. While digital technologies can serve as effective mitigants, those with lower levels of digital literacy or limited access to devices and the internet are more subject to extended periods of isolation. This finding emphasises that technical solutions are ineffective in unwinding the complexities of urban social integration. Second, the findings unequivocally affirm what is also hinted at in most existing literature: disparities in language and culture are deep-rooted barriers to social integration. The figures show an inability to speak the native language skillfully. An unfamiliarity with domestic norms often led to taciturnity during actual interactions, which validated the sentiments of disconnection. The isolation from a support group of the family also proved an overriding emotional determinant, which augmented the psychological pressure of experiencing an unfamiliar milieu in solitude.

Overall, the findings highlight that a combination of weakened social ties, cultural and language barriers, and gaps in digital resources shapes social isolation among migrants. While digital literacy indeed emerges as an important tool, it only partially resolves the emotional and relational gaps that migrants experience in an unfamiliar urban environment. These insights suggest that the migration experience, rather than being purely economic, is profoundly social and psychological, requiring both interpersonal adaptation and structural support. With these key patterns in mind, the following conclusion synthesises the broader implications of the study.

6. CONCLUSION

This study provides insightful and contextually nuanced information about the daily life of migrant workers in Bengaluru, observing that isolation among them is in no way uncomplicated or single-variable. Instead, it is a multi-dimensional, stratification-based phenomenon subject to linked variables. Migration, a phenomenon commonly driven by the impulse to pursue professional and material success, creates a risky social environment. Migrants are compelled to migrate to unfamiliar urban locations while confronting the absence of established protection networks, such as extended kinship networks, cohesive and tight friendships, and familiarity-based ways of doing things, including culture-based norms. As a result, disconnection from past attachments obliges migrants to consciously reconstruct their feelings of attachment in an unknown, culture-based urban milieu. Reconstruction of social attachments is never an easier feat; it is somewhat overwhelmed by attitudinal problems of adjustment, linguistic dislocation, and negotiating novel social norms. The research findings indicate that migration encompasses both economic and career opportunities, as well as serious personal and social issues. Immigrants are likely to encounter feelings of limited and disconnected social networks within their new communities. Even when they have friends and peers nearby, developing meaningful connections that foster a sense of belonging takes considerable time. Cultural and linguistic diversity can contribute to a feeling of detachment; it may be difficult for individuals to participate in social activities, thereby increasing their sense of isolation. Moreover, the nature of urban life, defined by its fast pace and a lack of personal connections, can compound these challenges. For most immigrants, urban living may evoke a sense of unfamiliarity rather than comfort, especially during the initial phases of settling in.

The study also emphasises the critical role of digital literacy in influencing how migrants adapt and manage these challenges. Social networking sites, messaging apps, and internet bulletin boards were major platforms that enabled migrants to stay connected with friends and family members from their hometowns while helping them build new social connections in their new urban environment. Digital media creates a feeling of sustained social relationships and enables individuals to overcome the physical separation caused by migration. However, while digital literacy mitigates the sense of social isolation, research strongly suggests that it is not a perfect or complete solution. Although online communication is commendable, it lacks the emotional warmth that is often experienced in personal and face-to-face interactions. Leaning too much on online connections can sometimes lead to superficial encounters that are inadequate to address significant feelings of social disconnection. Technology is a vital coping resource, but cannot wholly substitute for the emotional and social payoff of corporeal presence and human-to-human communication. The findings of this study offer strong prospects for informing both policies and employer practices. Employers who interact directly with migrant workers need to recognise that the challenges faced by this group cannot be solely addressed through a focus on the technical aspects of adaptation or work productivity. The success and productivity of workers depend equally on social connection, emotional well-being, and a sense of belonging, alongside their technical abilities. Therefore, data-driven and theory-based interventions should go beyond simple orientation programs designed to educate employees about the organisational policies or urban logistics. Instead, efforts should focus on creating an inclusive work environment that appreciates cultural diversity and fosters interaction, while empowering workers to express their identities. Initiatives such as buddy support groups, mentorship programs, and cultural awareness workshops can help bridge the social gap between migrant and native workers. Policymakers also have a crucial part in addressing the broader social dimensions of migration.

Community and government initiatives could aim to create inclusive urban environments where migrants engage with locals, exchange cultures and develop broad social networks. Personalised strategies to enhance digital skills among migrant workers may also ensure they acquire the necessary expertise for utilising digital platforms for both vocational and personal purposes.

However, these measures must be supplemented by initiatives that cater directly to emotional and cultural requirements, such as counselling services, foreign language learning programs, and community-building activities. By integrating digital access with tangible social support, policymakers can enhance integration and mitigate the risks of long-term social isolation that migrant workers face.

7. RECOMMENDATION

The study's findings indicate that while digital platforms help migrants maintain emotional connections and reduce feelings of isolation, they cannot fully replace in-person social relationships. Digital connectivity offers continuity, but meaningful belonging still depends on supportive social environments, including workplaces and community-level support.

Short-Term Recommendations

Employers: Implement structured onboarding and peer-support or buddy systems to help new migrant workers adjust. Informal social gatherings, such as team lunches, can help reduce early feelings of disconnection.

Local Government: Establish community support kiosks or help desks in areas with high migrant populations that can assist with accessing public services, transportation, healthcare, and legal procedures.

Technology Companies: Simplify user guides and provide them in multiple languages to direct those with limited digital literacy, making these platforms more accessible and less complicated.

Medium-Term Recommendations

Employers: Implement continuous workplace inclusion practices, such as cultural events, peer support groups, or employee well-being groups. These programs can help migrants form deeper social bonds within their work environment.

Local Government: Community centres with language training centres, counselling services, and programs of networking in helping migrants integrate into community life.

Technology Companies: Conduct low-cost digital literacy workshops tailored to migrants to enhance their ability to utilise platforms effectively for both communication and service access.

Long-Term Recommendations

Employers: Include practices that enhance diversity and inclusion in the culture of the organisations. Migrant perspectives should be reflected in training, decision-making, and leadership development to create strong, long-term connections.

Local Government: Develop an integration policy for urban areas that includes safe, affordable housing, community parks, and shared cultural spaces that encourage interaction across diverse groups.

Technology Companies: Innovate digital platforms that facilitate hybrid social engagement—linking online groups to real, in-person community meetups or support networks—to foster meaningful social connections, not just digital presence.

7. SCOPE FOR RESEARCH

The study, as perceptive as it is, offers qualitative data on the migrant workers' experience, but it does pose some limitations to keep in mind while interpreting results. One of the most significant limitations is the nature of qualitative research itself. As the study was conducted with a relatively small number of participants, the results are non-generalisable to the total population of migrant workers in Bengaluru or, more broadly, to migrant workers in urban locations elsewhere. Results drawn from in-depth interviews are richly textured and descriptive but belong to the subjective realm of those who participated. Hence, although the findings provide valuable insights into the matter, they may not capture the complete experiences present within the larger migrant population. The individual experiences presented here reveal personal issues, overcoming strategies, and perspectives; however, they should not be assumed to represent the collective experiences of all migrants.

One of the key limitations of this study is its reliance on self-reported data, which serves as the primary source of data. The interview-based data are naturally prone to various biases, which may affect the accuracy or completeness of the accounts. For example, recall bias can arise when participants struggle to recall past instances, which may unintentionally omit details in ways that reflect their current conditions. Similarly, social desirability bias may also influence participants to present themselves as more favourable, ignoring negative experiences to meet social expectations. These biases may downplay the daily experience of migrant workers. This study aimed to create a safe and nonjudgmental space, as biases of this nature are a significant challenge in qualitative research.

Another significant limitation of the study is its geographic scope. The research was conducted only in Bengaluru, a city with different cultural, economic, and social characteristics. Where Bengaluru is known as "Silicon Valley of India", it has a unique job market with plenty of IT companies and a large number of domestic migrants. Bengaluru has one of the highest levels of exposure to digital infrastructures, with the prevalence of smartphones, reliable internet connectivity, and a digital-first communication work culture. A potential exists for digital literacy to combat isolation, as migration-related isolation is eased by navigational, networking, job-searching, and translocal relationship-keeping apps. For those who lack digital skills, double displacement hits harder, as they deal with the expectation of a technological city along with the usual linguistic and cultural challenges. This digital concentration in Bengaluru facilitates social integration for the digitally competent, while worsening isolation for the digitally disadvantaged. Hence, the findings from this study are directly applicable to Bengaluru city and may not be generalisable to other urban settings. The migrant experience in Bengaluru may differ from that in Delhi, Hyderabad, Mumbai, or any other smaller urban setting, where employment opportunities, social attitudes towards migrants, and access to digital tools vary significantly. As a result, these findings may not be easily generalised beyond this context.

Later research would also need to look beyond the limitations in the following ways: A large-scale, quantitative survey would enable researchers to test the relevance of themes identified in this study and identify trends across a larger population of migrant workers. Using quantitative methods with a larger sample size would enhance the generalizability of the findings and provide stronger insights for researchers to conclude patterns among migrant labour contexts, such as differences in economic development, housing availability, digital connectivity, and civil society support that shape the experience of migrant workers. This approach would help determine whether the challenges faced by migrants in urban India are more common across cities or in particular contexts. By combining both qualitative research and quantitative analysis, future studies could produce a more comprehensive and deeper understanding of the complex issue of social isolation among migrant workers.

REFERENCES

Altay, T., Yurdakul, G., & Foroutan, N. (2025). Undoing one-dimensionality: Reforming German citizenship through the postmigrant framework. *Comparative Migration Studies*, *13*(1), 1–16. DOI: 10.1186/s40878-025-00444-0

Amati, V., Meggiolaro, S., Rivellini, G., & Zaccarin, S. (2018). Social relations and life satisfaction: The role of friends. *Genus*, *74*(1), 1–18. DOI: 10.1186/s41118-018-0032-z

Balekang, G. B., Galvin, T., & Rakgoasi, D. S. (2025). "No, it is not a breach of my oath because it is beyond my control; I use the policies that are in place." Ethical challenges faced by healthcare workers in the provision of healthcare to cross-border migrants in Botswana. *BMC Medical Ethics*, *26*(1), 1–12. DOI: 10.1186/s12910-025-01195-4

Batra, R., Flatt, J. D., Pharr, J. R., Sharma, M., Khubchandani, J., Kanekar, A., Chirico, F., & Batra, K. (2024). Exploring Social Support Strategies and Socio-Cultural Factors Influencing Social Isolation and Loneliness: The Role of Digital Literacy. *Healthcare (Basel)*, *12*(21), 1–10. DOI: 10.3390/healthcare12212149

Bhugra, D. (2004). Review article Migration and mental health. *Acta Psychiatrica Scandinavica*, *109*(4), 243–258. http://doi.wiley.com/10.1046/j.0001-690X.2003.00246.x. DOI: 10.1046/j.0001-690X.2003.00246.x

Brandt, L., Liu, S., Heim, C., & Heinz, A. (2022). The effects of social isolation stress and discrimination on mental health. *Translational Psychiatry*, *12*(1), 1–11. DOI: 10.1038/s41398-022-02178-4

Buchan, M. C., Bhawra, J., & Katapally, T. R. (2024). Navigating the digital world: Development of an evidence-based digital literacy program and assessment tool for youth. *Smart Learning Environments*, *11*(1), 1–24. DOI: 10.1186/s40561-024-00293-x

Clark, M. B., Nkonya, E., & Galford, G. L. (2025). Exodus of the affluent? examining climate hazards, migration, and household income in the U.S. *Population and Environment*, *47*(3), 1–30. DOI: 10.1007/s11111-025-00496-5

Cudjoe, T. K. M., & Colburn, J. L. (2019). Social Isolation. *Home-Based Medical Care for Older Adults: A Clinical Case Book, 1231*(1), 85–90. DOI: 10.1007/978-3-030-23483-6_13

David, D., Toplak, B., & Toplak, B. (2020, January). Digital literacy during the coronavirus pandemic in older adults: Literature Review and Research Agenda. *IFAC-PapersOnLine*, *55*(39), 153–158. DOI: 10.1016/j.ifacol.2022.12.027

Deshingkar, P., & Akter, S. (2009). Migration and Human Development in India. *Human Development Research Paper (HDRP) Series, 13*(19193), 1–85. https://mpra.ub.uni-muenchen.de/19193/

Di, X., & Wang, L. (2025). Impact of digital literacy on aging attitudes of the elderly from the perspective of social cognitive theory. *BMC Public Health*, *25*(1), 1–11. DOI: 10.1186/s12889-025-23377-w

Frounfelker, R. L., Miconi, D., Farrar, J., Brooks, M. A., Rousseau, C., & Betancourt, T. S. (2019). Mental health of refugee children and youth: Epidemiology, interventions, and future directions. *Annual Review of Public Health*, *41*(1), 159–176. DOI: 10.1146/annurev-publhealth-040119-094230

Golaszewski, N. M., Lacroix, A. Z., Godino, J. G., Allison, M. A., Manson, J. E., King, J. J., Weitlauf, J. C., Bea, J. W., Garcia, L., Kroenke, C. H., Saquib, N., Cannell, B., Nguyen, S., & Bellettiere, J. (2022). Evaluation of Social Isolation, Loneliness, and Cardiovascular Disease among Older Women in the U.S. *JAMA Network Open*, *5*(2), 1–12. DOI: 10.1001/jamanetworkopen.2021.46461

Gruber, S., & Sand, G. (2020). Does Migration Pay Off in Later Life? Income and Subjective Well-being of Older Migrants in Europe. *Social Indicators Research*, *160*(2–3), 969–988. DOI: 10.1007/s11205-020-02502-9

Hargittai, E. (2001). Second-Level Digital Divide : Mapping Differences in. *Tprc*, *7*(4), 1–19. DOI: 10.1080/01972240600991514

Hodgson, S., Watts, I., Fraser, S., Roderick, P., & Dambha-Miller, H. (2020). Loneliness, social isolation, cardiovascular disease and mortality: A synthesis of the literature and conceptual framework. *Journal of the Royal Society of Medicine*, *113*(5), 185–192. DOI: 10.1177/0141076820918236

Jang, S. H., & Je, N. J. (2022). International Journal of Advanced and Applied Sciences. *International Journal of Advanced and Applied Sciences*, *9*(4), 71–79. DOI: 10.21833/ijaas.2022.04.009

Jena, B., & Paltasingh, T. (2025). Digital literacy among older adults: A systematic review in Indian context. *Educational Gerontology*, *51*(4), 371–386. DOI: 10.1080/03601277.2024.2397428

Koirala, S. (2025). "Everyone is leaving, so am I": The role of culture in shaping Migration Behaviour in Nepal. *Comparative Migration Studies, 13*(1), 1–18. DOI: 10.1186/s40878-025-00427-1

Lee, H. (2024). Analysis of the impact of digital literacy on life satisfaction (2019–2022) for older adults in South Korea: A national community-based panel study. *Scientific Reports, 14*(1), 1–8. DOI: 10.1038/s41598-024-71397-0

Li, M. (2016). Pre-migration Trauma and Post-migration Stressors for Asian and Latino American Immigrants: Transnational Stress Proliferation. *Social Indicators Research, 129*(1), 47–59. DOI: 10.1007/s11205-015-1090-7

Liu, T., & Liao, L. (2024). Can farmers' digital literacy improve income? Empirical evidence from China. *PLoS One, 19*(12), 1–14. DOI: 10.1371/journal.pone.0314804

Löbel, L. M., Kröger, H., & Tibubos, A. N. (2022). How Migration Status Shapes Susceptibility of Individuals' Loneliness to Social Isolation. *International Journal of Public Health, 67*(December), 1–8. DOI: 10.3389/ijph.2022.1604576

Lopez, M. del P. A. (2023). Digital literacy as a new determinant of health: A scoping review. *PLOS Digital Health, 2*(10), 1–21. DOI: 10.1371/journal.pdig.0000279

Marotta, V. (2025). Rethinking liminality in refugee and migration studies. *Ethnicities, 25*(3), 339–357. DOI: 10.1177/14687968251328675

Motillon-Toudic, C., Walter, M., Séguin, M., Carrier, J.-D., Berrouiguet, S., & Lemey, C. (2022). Social isolation and suicide risk: Literature review and perspectives. *European Psychiatry : the Journal of the Association of European Psychiatrists, 65*(1), 1–22. DOI: 10.1192/j.eurpsy.2022.2320

Nedeljko, M., Bogataj, D., & Kaucic, B. M. (2021). The use of ICT in older adults strengthens their social network and reduces social isolation: Literature review and research agenda. *IFAC-PapersOnLine, 54*(13), 645–650. DOI: 10.1016/j.ifacol.2021.10.524

Ng, W. (2012). Can we teach digital natives digital literacy? *Computers & Education, 59*(3), 1065–1078. DOI: 10.1016/j.compedu.2012.04.016

Nguyen, T. P., Al Asaad, M., Sena, M., & Slewa-Younan, S. (2024). Loneliness and social isolation amongst refugees resettled in high-income countries: A systematic review. *Social Science & Medicine, 360*(August), 117340. DOI: 10.1016/j.socscimed.2024.117340

Njonge, T. (2023). *Influence of Psychological Well-being and School Factors on Delinquency, During the Covid-19 Period Among Secondary School Students in Selected Schools in Nakuru County : Kenya. VII*(2454), 1175–1189. https://doi.org/ DOI: 10.47772/IJRISS

Nowell, L. S., Norris, J. M., White, D. E., & Moules, N. J. (2017). Thematic Analysis: Striving to Meet the Trustworthiness Criteria. *International Journal of Qualitative Methods*, *16*(1), 1–13. DOI: 10.1177/1609406917733847

Ou-Salah, L., & Van Praag, L. (2025). "We always ask about the weather": Using visual mapping to understand how transnational migrant networks share beliefs and values on environmental change. *Digital Geography and Society*, *9*(June), 100126. DOI: 10.1016/j.diggeo.2025.100126

Parvizi, F., Salehi, A., Seghatoleslam, A., Kia, M., & Pope, M. (2025). Factors affecting the migration intention in medical students in Shiraz; south of Iran: A cross sectional study. *BMC Medical Education*, *25*(1), 1–8. DOI: 10.1186/s12909-025-07700-y

Pieter, K. (1999). the Definition of Migration and Its Application: Making Sense of Recent South African Census and Survey Data. *SA Journal of Demography, 7*(1), 19–30. https://journals.co.za/doi/pdf/10.10520/AJA16824482_41

Ranjan, S., & Yadav, R. S. (2019). Social isolation: Development and validation of measures. *Benchmarking*, *26*(6), 1905–1920. DOI: 10.1108/BIJ-11-2018-0371

Rusere, F., Li, Q., Hunter, L., Collinson, M., Ouma, S., Twine, W., & Samimi, C. (2025). Relationships between rural migration and perceptions of environmental change: Insights from Bushbuckridge, South Africa. *Journal of Rural Studies, 119*(April 2024), 103819. DOI: 10.1016/j.jrurstud.2025.103819

Sen, K., Prybutok, G., & Prybutok, V. (2022). The use of digital technology for social well-being reduces social isolation in older adults: A systematic review. *SSM - Population Health, 17*, 101020. DOI: 10.1016/j.ssmph.2021.101020

Shishehgar, S., Gholizadeh, L., DiGiacomo, M., & Davidson, P. M. (2015). The impact of migration on the health status of Iranians: An integrative literature review. *BMC International Health and Human Rights, 15*(1), 1–11. DOI: 10.1186/s12914-015-0058-7

Sriramalu, S. B., Elangovan, A. R., Annapally, S. R., Birudu, R., & Lakshmana, G. (2023). Psychological distress and quality of community life among migratory construction workers in India. *Journal of Neurosciences in Rural Practice*, *14*(3), 533–540. DOI: 10.25259/JNRP_42_2022

Stockwell, S., Stubbs, B., Jackson, S. E., Fisher, A., Yang, L., & Smith, L. (2021). Internet use, social isolation and loneliness in older adults. *Ageing and Society*, *41*(11), 2723–2746. DOI: 10.1017/S0144686X20000550

Tinmaz, H., Lee, Y. T., Fanea-Ivanovici, M., & Baber, H. (2022). A systematic review on digital literacy. *Smart Learning Environments*, *9*(1), 21. Advance online publication. DOI: 10.1186/s40561-022-00204-y

Tomaka, J., Thompson, S., & Palacios, R. (2006). The relation of social isolation, loneliness, and social support to disease outcomes among the elderly. *Journal of Aging and Health*, *18*(3), 359–384. DOI: 10.1177/0898264305280993

Torres, J. M., & Casey, J. A. (2017). The centrality of social ties to climate migration and mental health. *BMC Public Health*, *17*(1), 1–10. DOI: 10.1186/s12889-017-4508-0

Touzel, V., Reifegerste, D., Bozorgmehr, K., & Biddle, L. (2025). Impact of social isolation on mental health changes by socio-economic status: A moderated mediation analysis among non-migrant, migrant, and refugee subpopulations in Germany, 2016–2020. *SSM - Population Health*, *31*(June), 101822. DOI: 10.1016/j.ssmph.2025.101822

Tsegay, S. M. (2023). International Migration: Definition, Causes and Effects. *Genealogy*, *7*(3), 1–10. DOI: 10.3390/genealogy7030061

Wang, K., Feng, Y., Qin, X., & Hu, Y. (2025). Examining the double-edged effects of digital literacy on the social integration of retirement migrants. *Frontiers in Public Health*, *13*(March), 1–15. DOI: 10.3389/fpubh.2025.1470319

Zavaleta, D., Samuel, K., & Mills, C. (2014). Social Isolation: A Conceptual and Measurement Proposal. In *OPHI Working Paper 67*. http://www.ophi.org.uk/social-isolation-a-conceptual-and-measurement-proposal/

Chapter 8
Objectified Bodies: Roots of Disconnection and Isolation

Meenakshi Bose
https://orcid.org/0009-0004-3535-8894
Bandhan, India

ABSTRACT

"Looking glass upon the wall, who is fairest of us all?" The judgment of one's external appearance is prevalent in our society, which, unfortunately, has become normalised in our daily lives instead of being condemned and avoided. Have you ever pondered the extent to which body shaming drives someone into isolation? This chapter attempts to address a serious societal concern addressed through the question above. It further presents the lived experiences of respondents and aims to interpret their perspectives on isolation resulting from body shaming. This chapter proposes a theoretical framework positing that body shaming frequently results in social isolation, highlighting isolation as an adverse outcome of such experiences. Additionally, the chapter critiques the cruelty inherent in body shaming and explores the legal ambiguities that enable these offences. In conclusion, it recommends measures to prevent the objectification of body image and lessen the harmful consequences of body shaming.

1. INTRODUCTION

The sarcasm is that the value of human existence is being relegated to the superficial appearance of an individual, and humiliating others is becoming a deeply ingrained practice in our society. As a consequence, it cannot be denied that body

DOI: 10.4018/979-8-3373-5811-6.ch008

shaming fosters prejudice, diminishes self-worth, induces despair, intensifies social isolation, and heightens the risk of criminal behaviours.

The important and thought-provoking question here is:

"Are we normalizing body shaming to such an extent that it pushes an individual into the dark corners of isolation*?"*

"The honest answer is: *Yes! affirmative—society, in numerous ways, unconsciously normalizes negative criticism and bullying, frequently targeting individuals' appearance, lifestyle, and identity*."

Unfortunately, we have normalised criticising and abusing others based on their external appearance, such as being overweight, having dark skin colour, being bald, or even being differently abled. The purpose of this study is to explore and understand the lived experiences of individuals who have been subjected to body shaming through structural, societal, and digital dynamics (as shown in Figure 1). This research aims to delve into the subjective narratives of respondents to uncover the psychological and emotional distress and behavioural changes resulting to social isolation.

Figure 1. Pathway diagram

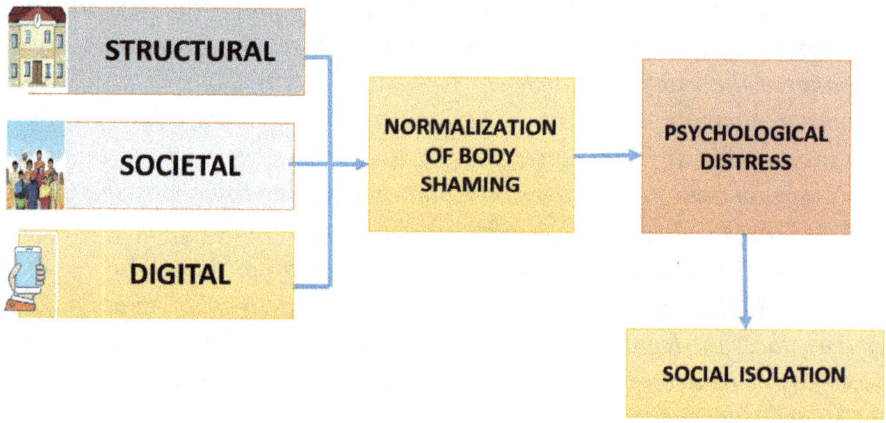

2. RESEARCH QUESTIONS

This section outlines the research questions that underscore the rationale and necessity for undertaking this study.

- How do structural factors such as workplace norms, educational institutions, and media industries contribute to the normalization of body shaming and the emergence of social isolation?
- In what ways do societal attitudes and cultural narratives reinforce body-based prejudice, beauty hierarchies, and experiences of exclusion?
- How is body shaming manifested and sustained within digital spaces through social media interactions and algorithmic visibility, and how does this foster digital isolation?
- How do structural, societal, and digital dynamics intersect to shape individuals' lived experiences of body shaming, particularly in relation to psychological distress, social isolation, and identity negotiation?

3. RESEARCH OBJECTIVE

Main Objective: The main objective of this study is to examine the contribution of structural, societal, and digital factors contribute to the normalization and perpetuation of body shaming, and the influence of these interrelated with individuals' experiences of psychological distress, social isolation, and identity negotiation.

Specific Objectives:

- To analyze structural influences including workplace norms, educational settings, and media industries that normalize body shaming and marginalize non-conforming bodies.
- To investigate societal attitudes and cultural narratives that reinforce body-based prejudice, beauty hierarchies, and social exclusion.
- To explore digital mechanisms such as social media interactions, algorithmic visibility, and online surveillance that perpetuate body shaming and intensify digital isolation.
- To understand the intersectional impact of structural, societal, and digital dimensions on individuals' lived experiences of body shaming, focusing on psychological distress, social isolation, and identity negotiation.

4. CHAPTER PLAN

The thesis is organized into ten interconnected sections that collectively explore how structural, societal, and digital forces normalize body shaming and contribute to social isolation. The introduction familiarizes the study, outlining the background, problem statement, research questions, objectives, rationale, and scope. Following the introduction, the next section unveils the underlying roots of disconnection associated with body shaming through review of relevant literature and theoretical perspectives, identifying research gaps and framing the conceptual foundation. The next explains the mixed-method research design, detailing sampling, data collection, analysis, and ethical considerations. Subsequently, the section on findings examine structural dimensions, analyzing how institutional settings—educational, workplace, and media that reinforce appearance-based discrimination. It discusses societal dimensions, focusing on cultural narratives, familial expectations, and gendered norms that perpetuate prejudice and exclusion. It explores digital dimensions, emphasizing the role of social media, algorithmic bias, and online harassment in shaping digital isolation and body image perceptions. The conclusion section integrates these findings through an intersectional lens, showing how structural, societal, and digital factors converge to intensify psychological distress and identity negotiation. Finally, it concludes the study by summarizing major insights, acknowledging limitations, and suggesting directions for future research, ultimately underscoring the need to foster empathy, inclusivity, and body neutrality as essential elements of social justice and human dignity.

5. THEORETICAL CONNECTIONS

This section elaborates on the theoretical foundations that connect body image, social comparison, and self-perception. Body image refers to the attitudes, beliefs, and evaluations individuals hold about their own physical appearance, while social comparison theory highlights the tendency of individuals to assess themselves in relation to others. Self-perception, in turn, reflects how these evaluations shape one's broader sense of identity, self-concept, and self-esteem. By examining the interplay of these constructs, this section aims to explain how societal standards and interpersonal comparisons contribute to the formation of body image and influence an individual's overall psychological well-being.

According to Festinger's Social Comparison Theory (1954), humans have an inherent tendency to make comparisons in order to evaluate their abilities and opinions. These two dimensions including "ability" and "opinion" that form the primary bases of social comparison and are closely tied to processes such as self-evaluation, self-concept, and self-esteem. In essence, social comparison addresses the fundamental question, *"Who am I in relation to others?"* The principal stimulus behind this process is the pursuit of self-understanding, which often translates into a broader understanding of one's place within society (Bai, 2023). Wood et al. (1994), describe social comparison as the process of evaluating similarities and differences through relevant social information.

Erving Goffman (1963) classically defined stigma as an "attribute that is deeply discrediting." An attribute that may be immediately visible such as skin color or body size or it may remain concealed yet become discreditable if disclosed, as in the case of a criminal record or experiences with mental illness. Further, he contended that most individuals experience the role of being stigmatized "at least in some connections and in some phases of life." His expansive definition of stigma encompasses a wide range of socially discredited attributes, which he classified into three broad categories: *tribal stigmas* (such as race, ethnicity, and religion), *physical deformities* (including conditions like deafness, blindness, and leprosy), and *blemishes of individual character* (for example, homosexuality, addiction, and mental illness).

Mead argued that the most distinctly human and humanizing activity is communication that engages individuals in dialogue with one another. Expanding on Mead's insights, Herbert Blumer of the University of California, Berkeley, introduced the term *symbolic interactionism*. This framework underscores how individuals construct illustrating body-shaming messages become internalized and influence both identity and self-concept. Symbolic interactionism is grounded in three core premises. First, human beings act toward objects, people, and situations based on the meanings these hold for them. Second, such meanings emerge through social interaction with others. Third, these meanings are continually interpreted and modified as individuals engage with their surroundings (Blumer, 2012; Husin et al, 2021).

Urie Bronfenbrenner emphasized that human development unfolds within a complex network of relationships shaped by multiple layers of the surrounding environment. He argued that to truly understand development, one must consider the entire ecological system in which growth takes place. Bronfenbrenner's ecological systems theory proposes that an individual's development is influenced by a series of interconnected environmental systems, ranging from immediate settings such as family and school to broader societal structures, including cultural norms and values (Parris et al, 2010).

Further, research conducted by Fardouly et al. (Fardouly, 2017) indicates that social media plays a substantial role in shaping individuals' body-image perceptions, particularly among young women. This influence stems largely from continuous exposure to appearance-centric content, where unrealistic beauty standards are perpetuated (Anixiadis et.al, 2019) and environments of social comparison are intensified (Perloff, 2014). The visual contents actively shapes self- and other-perceptions by reinforcing narrow, idealized beauty norms. Through repeated exposure, individuals internalize these standards, leading to distorted self-perceptions, increased self-objectification, and a heightened risk of body dissatisfaction (Aparicio-Martinez et al., 2019; Sastre, 2014). Ren et al. (2023) contend that repeated exposure to idealized beauty portrayals on social media intensifies self-objectification and social comparison tendencies. These psychological processes have been consistently associated with elevated body dissatisfaction, heightened body-related anxiety, and a greater risk of disordered eating behaviors.

6. RATIONALE AND SIGNIFICANCE OF THE STUDY

In a society increasingly mediated by appearance-driven norms and digital visibility, body shaming has evolved from a private act of ridicule into a public culture of humiliation. Despite growing global advocacy for body positivity and inclusion, the normalization of shaming continues to thrive in social, institutional, and online spaces, often disguised as humour, discipline, or "constructive criticism." This persistent normalization warrants critical academic attention. The rationale for this study stems from the urgent need to understand body shaming not merely as an individual experience of insult, but as a systemic and structural issue deeply rooted in societal hierarchies, institutional practices, and digital cultures. Much of the existing scholarship treats body shaming as a psychological or behavioural phenomenon; however, limited research explores its intersectional character—how class, gender, digital participation, and institutional norms jointly construct environments that sanction and sustain body-based discrimination.

By examining structural, societal, and digital dimensions together, this study contributes to a comprehensive and intersectional framework for understanding how body shaming operates and persists across multiple layers of social life. It offers insights into how educational systems, workplaces, and media industries reinforce aesthetic standards and influence self-perception, belonging, and professional or academic opportunities. From a social policy and governance perspective, the study holds significant relevance for promoting inclusive institutional cultures and digital ethics. By foregrounding the lived experiences of those subjected to body shaming, the study highlights the emotional and psychological costs of aesthetic conformity in a society that equates worth with appearance. In essence, the significance of this study lies in its potential to transform body shaming from being perceived as an individual vulnerability to being recognized as a collective social concern a reflection of broader inequalities, biases, and exclusions that demand urgent institutional and cultural reform.

7. METHODOLOGY

This study adopts a mixed-method research design integrating both quantitative and qualitative approaches to achieve a comprehensive understanding of body shaming and its multifaceted impacts. The integration of numerical data and narrative accounts allows for triangulation of findings, thereby enhancing the validity and depth of the research.

Research Design

This cross-sectional study adopted a mixed-method design, combining exploratory and explanatory approaches.

Sampling and Participants

Purposive sampling was used to recruit 200 participants from diverse gender, age, geographic, and occupational backgrounds. Respondents from urban, semi-urban, and rural areas were included, representing educational settings, workplaces, and online communities.

Data Collection

Triangulation method was adopted, using a structured questionnaire assessed frequency, contexts, and perceived effects of body shaming across cultural, institutional, and digital domains. In-depth interviews and focus groups captured personal narratives, emotional impacts, and coping mechanisms.

Data Analysis

Quantitative data were analyzed using descriptive and inferential statistics to identify patterns and associations. Qualitative data underwent thematic analysis to generate themes related to structural and institutional bias, cultural beauty norms, and digital harassment.

Ethical Considerations

Informed consent was obtained from all participants. Confidentiality and anonymity were ensured, and participation was voluntary. Sensitive issues were handled with care, and mental-health support information was shared when needed.

Scope and Limitations

Findings are context-specific and may not be universally generalizable.

Table 1. **Methodology — Summary Box**

Aspect	Key Details
Design	Mixed-method, cross-sectional (exploratory + explanatory).
Sample	200 purposively selected participants across gender, age, and geography (urban, semi-urban, rural).
Data Collection	Structured questionnaires, in-depth interviews, and focus groups on experiences, effects, and coping with body shaming.
Analysis	Quantitative: descriptive & inferential stats; Qualitative: thematic analysis (bias, beauty norms, digital abuse).
Ethics	Informed consent, confidentiality, voluntary participation, mental-health support ensured.
Limitations	Context-specific, self-reported data, limited generalizability.

8. FINDINGS AND DISCUSSION

This section presents the key findings derived from quantitative and qualitative analyses, illustrating the prevalence, patterns, and lived experiences of body shaming across structural, societal, and digital domains. The discussion interweaves numerical data with thematic insights to highlight collective normalization and perpetuation of body shaming, fostering experiences of psychological distress and social isolation through institutional cultures, social norms, and digital ecosystems .

Socio-Economic Profile of Respondents

The socio-economic profile of respondents provides an overview of their demographic and structural characteristics, enabling a better understanding of how body shaming operates within diverse social contexts. The study comprised a total of 200 respondents selected from rural, semi-urban, and urban areas. The distribution across gender, age, educational level, occupation, and income status reflects a heterogeneous sample representative of different socio-economic strata (Table 2).

Gender and Age Composition

Out of 200 participants, 55 per cent were female (N = 110), 35.5 per cent male (N = 71), and 9.5 per cent transgender (N = 19). In terms of age, the majority (56 per cent) were within the 18–25 years category, followed by 18 per cent in the 26–35 years range, 13 per cent in the 36–45 group, and the remaining 13 per cent aged 46 and above. This distribution indicates that a substantial portion of respondents belong to the youth demographic, a group often more exposed to social media influences and aesthetic norms (Table 2)..

Educational Qualification

The educational background of respondents was varied: 39.5 per cent were undergraduates, 30 per cent had completed high school, and 30.5 per cent were postgraduates. The inclusion of participants from different educational stages allowed for a nuanced understanding of whether education correlates with awareness or resistance to body shaming practices (Table 2)..

Occupational Status

Regarding occupational engagement, 61.5 per cent of respondents were students, 17 per cent were working professionals, and 21.5 per cent were unemployed. The predominance of students in the sample reflects the study's focus on younger populations and institutional contexts such as schools, colleges, and universities spaces where appearance-based evaluations are often intensified (Table 2)..

Income Level

Socio-economic diversity was also evident in the respondents' income status. Among working individuals, 32 per cent reported a monthly household income below 20,000, 46 per cent earned between 20,001– 50,000, and 22 per cent reported earning above 50,000. This spread suggests that the sample captures both lower- and middle-income groups, allowing for exploration of whether economic background influences vulnerability to or perception of body shaming (Table 2)..

Geographical Distribution

The sample included respondents from rural (30 per cent), semi-urban (17.5 per cent), and urban (52.5 per cent) areas. This geographical diversity was intentional, ensuring representation across spatial and cultural contexts where exposure to digital media and societal expectations of physical appearance differ significantly (Table 2)..

Table 2. Socio-Economic Profile of Respondents **(N = 200)**

Category	Sub-category	Frequency (N)	Percentage (%)
Gender	Female	110	55.0
	Male	71	35.5
	Transgender	19	9.5
Age Group	18–25 years	112	56.0
	26–35 years	36	18.0
	36–45 years	26	13.0
	46 years and above	26	13.0
Education	High School	60	30.0
	Undergraduate	79	39.5
	Postgraduate	61	30.5
Occupation	Student	123	61.5
	Unemployed	43	21.5
	Working Professional	34	17.0
Monthly Income (Household)	Below 20,000	64	32.0
	20,001– 50,000	92	46.0
	Above 50,000	44	22.0
Geographical Location	Rural	60	30.0
	Semi-Urban	35	17.5
	Urban	105	52.5

Source: Author's field survey (2025)

The socio-economic data reflect a demographically diverse sample with variations in geography, education, and occupational background. The concentration of respondents in the youth category and urban areas underscores the growing influence of digital culture and mediated beauty ideals. However, the inclusion of rural and semi-urban participants allows for comparative analysis of traditional and modern forms of body shaming. The data also reveal that economic privilege does not necessarily shield individuals from appearance-based judgment, reaffirming the pervasive nature of body shaming across class boundaries.

Structural Dimension: Institutional Bias and Systemic Exclusion

Interview data indicate that institutional cultures across educational and professional environments frequently reinforce aesthetic norms under the guise of "professionalism," thereby legitimising appearance-based hierarchies. Body shaming within workplaces and academic settings manifests through subtle and explicit exclusion from opportunities, social networks, and leadership roles. Participants recalled being urged to "look fit for the job," "maintain a standard appearance," or "dress according to body type," signalling that academic success and professional mobility are tethered to physical conformity. In educational spaces, respondents reported not only peer mockery but also implicit bias from educators who equated certain body types with laziness, lack of discipline, or diminished capability. Women described being overlooked for client-facing or public-oriented roles, while men narrated pressures to adopt athletic or muscular ideals, highlighting gendered dimensions of aesthetic regulation in institutional settings.

Findings of the empirical study substantiate that students skip school or extra-curricular activities due to bullying or ridicule related to their appearance. During the study, respondents shared that they were bullied and called using offensive nicknames (Kala/Black, Mota/Fat, Haathi/ Elephant, etc) to address them. Narrating her experience, one of the respondents (a student of class 10th) bursted into tears. In the bustling corridors of her school, where laughter often hid unkindness, she had learned early on that silence was her safest armour. Her dark skin had been the constant target of whispered jokes, pointed fingers, and unsolicited advice masked as concern.

"It stole my confidence. I stopped speaking up in class. I doubted my intelligence, my talents, even my right to take up space. Somewhere along the way, I confused my body with my worth."

Sharing her experience on body shaming at the workplace, another respondent asserted that she often faces comments such as:

"Stay out of the sun."

"You'd be prettier if you were brighter."

"You're smart... but so dusky."

These empirical findings confirm that respondents' productivity decreases due to victimisation from body shaming, especially in their workplaces. Furthermore, they eventually withdraw from the labour force and isolate themselves (Morrish & Medina, 2021).

Another respondent claimed:

"Even at the workplace, people are becoming more obsessed with their appearance and physical attractiveness. Such preoccupation with appearance often leads to workplace stress, reduced focus on professional tasks, and diminished productivity. Over time, this can result in disengagement, job dissatisfaction, and even withdrawal from the workforce."

The quantitative findings reaffirm that body shaming is not an incidental interpersonal behaviour but a socially and institutionally embedded phenomenon. Table 3 illustrates that among the 200 respondents surveyed, 136 individuals (68%) reported experiencing body shaming within educational spaces. These responses reveal that both teachers and peers implicitly and explicitly equated physical appearance with discipline, intelligence, and social worth, thereby reproducing dominant bodily norms within educational spaces. Similarly, 108 respondents (54%) identified instances of body-based discrimination in workplace settings, indicating that aesthetic conformity continues to inform professional evaluations, access to opportunities, and career progression. These results highlight the persistence of embodied expectations in formal employment structures, where physical presentation is perceived as a proxy for competence, motivation, or suitability for public-facing roles. In addition, 94 participants (47%) reported avoiding healthcare services due to apprehension about body-related judgement or ridicule. This pattern underscores a troubling dimension of systemic exclusion in which fear of stigma inhibits essential health-seeking behaviour, ultimately contributing to adverse health outcomes and reinforcing socio-medical inequities. Collectively, the data demonstrate that body shaming operates across educational, professional, and healthcare domains, functioning as a mechanism of social stratification that privileges normative bodies while marginalising those who deviate from dominant aesthetic ideals.

Table 3. Institutional Bias and Systemic Exclusion **(N = 200)**

Institutional Context	Number of Respondents	% of Respondents
Educational Institutions	136	68%
Workplace Environments	108	54%
Healthcare Settings	94	47%

Source: Author's field survey (2025)

These findings call for structural interventions, including institutional sensitisation, inclusive policies, and anti-bias mechanisms, to challenge aesthetic hierarchies and promote dignity, well-being, and equitable participation for individuals across diverse body types. The responses of the respondents were gathered through the five statements administered in likert scale *(as shown in Table 4)*. It shows that body shaming significantly affects confidence, social engagement, and mental health. Most respondents reported that body shaming is influenced by others perception about them (88.5 per cent strongly agree) and lowered their participation in discussions (83 per cent strongly agree). Social withdrawal was moderate (35 per cent strongly agree; 60 per cent neutral), and 100 per cent reported negative effects on mental health. Additionally, 39 per cent felt unsupported by faculty or supervisors, indicating gaps in institutional support.This study confirms the pervasive presence of body shaming in academic and work environments and underscores its detrimental effects on confidence, social participation, and mental health.

Table 4. **Body Shaming Affecting Educational/Workplace Isolation (in %)**

Level of Agreement	Feel less confident participating in class/work discussions	Feel my body image affects how seriously others take me	Led me to withdraw socially from classmates or co-workers	Negatively affected my mental health	Feel unsupported by faculty/ supervisors
Strongly Disagree	0	0	0	0	0
Disagree	0	0	0	0	0
Neutral	0	0	60	0	22
Agree	17	11.5	5	100	39
Strongly Agree	83	88.5	35	0	39

Source: Author's field survey (2025)

Societal Dimension: Cultural Beauty Ideals and Body-Based Prejudice

Beyond formal institutions, body shaming was deeply embedded in intimate social spheres such as family and peer groups, serving as early mechanisms of social conditioning. Participants recounted childhood and adolescent experiences where relatives commented on weight, complexion, or body shape in the name of health, marriage prospects, or parental reputation, effectively naturalising body surveillance within domestic environments. Many respondents recalled being criticized during family gatherings, weddings, or community functions events where body commentary was normalized as small talk. Body shaming isn't just about words. It's about looks that includes those lingering glances that scan your external appearance before they meet the eyes. The data illustrate that body shaming is deeply embedded within intimate social environments, particularly families, where early experiences of appearance-based judgement are normalised. Table 5. illustrates that among the 200 respondents, 152 individuals (76%) reported being subjected to body-related comments by immediate family members. These interactions often centred around weight, eating habits, complexion, or height, revealing the way the familial discourses reinforce aesthetic expectations under the guise of concern, discipline, or cultural norms. Such experiences constitute primary sites of socialisation where individuals internalise body ideals and develop body image perceptions from an early age.

Extended family members also played a significant role, with 138 respondents (69%) indicating body shaming from relatives. These interactions were commonly activated during social gatherings or family functions, where comparison with siblings, cousins, or peers becomes a routine practice. The high prevalence suggests that body policing is not merely a private or household-level behaviour but a culturally sanctioned communicative practice within kinship networks. Friends similarly reinforced dominant beauty norms through humour, comparison, and unsolicited advice, normalising "acceptable" body types and marginalising those who deviated from them. These everyday interactions contributed to internalised stigma, emotional distress, and persistent self-monitoring behaviours. It's hearing the friends talk about "needing to lose weight" when they weigh 30 pounds lesser. The individual start to absorb the message that something is wrong with himself/ herself. This fear of being judged results to social isolation pushing the victim in to the silence of loneliness. Tabel 5 illustrates that peers and friends emerged as another key group perpetuating body-related stigma, with 121 respondents (60.5%) citing instances of teasing, derogatory nicknames, and unsolicited advice. Peer-level shaming is particularly salient during adolescent and early adulthood stages, shaping social acceptance, self-esteem, and interpersonal belonging. These experiences reinforce conformity to dominant body ideals, mobility within social groups, and perceived social worth. Michel Foucault's notion of disciplinary power further illuminates how bodies become subject to surveillance, regulation, and corrective narratives within intimate social spaces.

Marriage-related commentary (reported by 49% of respondents) reflects entrenched socio-cultural expectations linking physical appearance—particularly for women—to marital suitability, desirability, and family honour. Such comments often include pressures to lose weight, adjust physical features, or "look presentable" for prospective partners or in-laws, underscoring the intersection of gender norms and aesthetic expectations. Additionally, 87 respondents (43.5%) reported body shaming at social functions, indicating the presence of public surveillance of bodies within extended community spaces. This demonstrates that aesthetic policing is not confined to private spaces but is enacted publicly, often without accountability, reinforcing humiliation and social exclusion. This substantiates Erving Goffman's theory of *stigma* offers a complementary lens, highlighting how deviance from ideal body standards becomes a "spoiled identity."

Collectively, these findings underscore that family and peer networks function as crucial sites where aesthetic norms are reproduced, internalised, and legitimised. Body shaming in such intimate contexts forms the foundation for broader systemic exclusion observed in educational, workplace, and healthcare settings. Thus, interventions aimed at addressing body-based discrimination must account not only for institutional mechanisms but also the micro-social dynamics that shape body image, self-worth, and identity from early life stages.

Table 5. Family and Peer-Level Body Shaming (N = 200)

Context of Body Shaming	Number of Respondents	% of Respondents	Illustrative Behaviours Reported
Immediate Family Members	152	76%	Comments on weight, eating habits, complexion, height
Extended Family/ Relatives	138	69%	Comparison with siblings/cousins, remarks during gatherings
Friends/Peers	121	60.5%	Jokes, nicknames, teasing, unsolicited advice
Marriage-Related Comments	98	49%	Pressure to lose weight/"look good" for marriage
Social Gatherings/ Functions	87	43.5%	Public comments, body evaluation in family events

Source: Author's field survey (2025)

Findings of the study claim that individuals withdraw from gatherings, parties, or group activities due to fear of judgment or ridicule. Victims of body shaming asserted that they lost contact with their friends or were excluded from peer groups because of their appearance or perceived flaws, and thereby, they confined themselves to loneliness. Overweight people are considered visually unattractive, morally and emotionally deficient, estranged from their sexuality, and dissatisfied with themselves. Embarrassment isolates these victims of body shaming from society, which leads to eating problems and drug addiction. Similarly, when body shaming comes from within the family including parents, siblings, or extended relatives- it creates emotional distance, mistrust, and even estrangement. Findings substantiate that if body shamed by family members, individuals may tend to distance themselves from those relatives or feel isolated even within their homes. Families that don't understand the impact of body shaming might fail to provide emotional support. Discussions with the respondents asserted that concerns about being judged by a partner can make individuals avoid romantic relationships or sexual intimacy. Victims were found to avoid meals, outings, or gatherings to escape comments or judgment. In addition, a distorted body image makes the victims feel "unlovable," creating a barrier to dating or forming close bonds. Pieces of evidence from the empirical research reveal that even married women face domestic violence and mental abuse on the grounds of body shaming. It should be noted that such mental and emotional exploitations leave suicidal imprints in the minds of the victims.

Table 6 reveal that 100 per cent avoid social gatherings and no longer participate in activities. In addition, 93 per cent distance themselves from friends and family. These findings signal a severe retreat from both casual and intimate social interactions, indicating a breakdown in community engagement and interpersonal connection. A significant 87 per cent of respondents (strongly agree and agree) worry about being talked about behind their back. This reflects high levels of internalized shame, hypervigilance, and social paranoia, which are known predictors of social anxiety disorders. Interestingly, only 38 per cent reported feeling uncomfortable in group settings, with the majority (62 per cent) selecting a neutral response. This suggests there is a strong prevalence of situational sensitivity (comfort varies by context — family vs strangers) and emotional detachment or numbing, possibly as a coping mechanism (Table 6). Also, the victims reported preferring the companionship of animals as a substitute for human connections. The convergence of behavioural withdrawal and emotional distress aligns with known patterns in individuals facing chronic shame and stigma. Prolonged isolation and avoidance are also risk factors for more severe mental health conditions, including depression, eating disorders, and suicidal ideation.

Table 6. Body Shaming Affecting Social Isolation (in %)

Level of Agreement	Avoid Social Gatherings	Distance Myself From Friends And Family	Feel Uncomfortable In Group Settings	No Longer Participates in Activities	Worry That People Will Talk Behind My Back
Strongly Disagree	0	0	0	0	0
Disagree	0	0	0	0	0
Neutral	0	0	62	0	13
Agree	27	7	19.5	100	49
Strongly Agree	73	93	18.5	0	38

Source: Author's field survey (2025)

Answering the question of body shaming, one of the respondents asserted:

"As soon as I got engaged, the first thing people asked was if I was going to start dieting for the wedding. Even my family members hinted that I should slim down so I'd 'look better in photos.' I felt like my body became a project instead of something to celebrate."

Further, she insisted:

"People kept comparing me to other brides—celebrities, influencers, even friends. I started doubting whether I'd look beautiful on my wedding day because I didn't fit that 'ideal' bridal image."

Another respondent expressed:

"My father often criticized me for my dark complexion. He would make comparisons between my skin tone and that of my lighter-skinned siblings or relatives, often suggesting—directly or indirectly—that lighter skin was more desirable. These comments were not occasional—they were frequent, subtle, and normalized

within our household. Over time, they made me feel ashamed of my appearance. I began associating my self-worth with the acceptance of my appearance to others. Even in social settings, I would feel the urge to hide or change myself, just to avoid being judged. This wasn't just about appearance—it affected my confidence, my ability to speak up, and my relationships."

During the discussions, one of the respondents asserted that:

"Eventually, I internalized it. I became my own critic. The mirror turned into a courtroom, and I was both the judge and the condemned. Every morning, I'd stand in front of it, listing everything I hated. My thighs. My stomach. My arms. It became a ritual of self-punishment. I thought if I hated myself enough, I'd finally be motivated to change and disengage myself from social get-togethers."

Together, these findings reveal that body shaming operates as a systemic form of social exclusion, intersecting across personal, institutional, and digital spheres to shape identity, aspirations, and access to opportunities. Rather than isolated incidents, appearance-based judgements represent a broader socio-cultural apparatus that privileges normative bodies and penalises divergence. This multi-layered exclusion underscores the need for holistic interventions encompassing familial sensitisation, inclusive pedagogical practices, workplace diversity frameworks, and public discourse that challenges aesthetic hierarchies to foster environments that support dignity, mental health, and equitable participation for all body types. The societal acceptance of body shaming reflects Foucault's notion of disciplinary power, where societal norms regulate bodies through subtle surveillance and normalization rather than coercion. The constant reinforcement of aesthetic ideals through everyday discourse perpetuates a culture of conformity that defines worthiness by appearance. This normalization of body shaming as a "corrective" or "well-intentioned" act underscores a dangerous cultural paradox humiliation is moralized as care, and discrimination is rationalized as tradition.

Digital Dimension: Online Surveillance, Algorithmic Visibility, and Digital Isolation

Media fosters the concept of "a perfect body" that can quickly and significantly alter the perception of individuals. The digital landscape functions as a key site where body norms are produced, reproduced, and policed. This section debates that decisive advertisement through media (including social media, print, and television) is mainly to be blamed for many aspects of body shaming. Social media has a significant impact on bridging the gap between individuals and society. Ideologies disseminated by the media, particularly online platforms, news chapters and magazines, have the potential to proliferate throughout society. Evidence from the field asserts that such victims are often addicted to Digital Platforms and Dating

Apps as an escape from criticism and loneliness. This substantiates that technology provides virtual solutions to loneliness. Yet, the findings indicate that individuals subjected to cyber body shaming are disengaged from social media platforms to evade continued harassment. In addition, media and technology play a crucial role in multiplying the impact of body shaming, especially in terms of emotional and mental abuse, particularly among female respondents.

Pieces of evidence claim that persistent exposure often led to digital withdrawal, a self-imposed retreat from online interaction, giving rise to digital isolation which is a modern manifestation of social exclusion in the virtual realm. As shown in Table 7, 71% of respondents reported experiencing body shaming on social media platforms, where visual culture and algorithm-driven content amplify ideals of thinness, muscularity, fairness, and "fitness." Respondents reported encountering derogatory remarks, comparison-triggering posts, and appearance-based trolling, suggesting that social media reinforces aesthetic hierarchies and normalises public scrutiny of bodies.

Messaging platforms also emerged as a significant site of body regulation, with 48% of participants citing experiences of ridicule through memes, unsolicited suggestions on diet or fitness, and privately circulated images. The interpersonal nature of such exchanges indicates that digital shaming often overlaps with existing social relationships. Online dating apps were identified by 37% of respondents as spaces where body judgment is overt, implying that digital intimacy and romantic engagement are influenced by appearance-based gatekeeping. Additionally, 64% acknowledged the indirect effects of influencer and celebrity content, indicating the internalisation of aspirational aesthetics propelled by digital visibility and market-driven beauty standards. Finally, virtual gaming environments and public comment forums, though less frequent (26% and 30.5% respectively), still reflect how anonymity intensifies unregulated body-based harassment. Together, these findings illustrate that the digital ecosystem intensifies body surveillance, fosters insecurity, and reinforces normative beauty ideals, positioning the body as a public object subject to constant evaluation.

Table 7. Digital Dimension of Body Shaming (N = 200)

Digital Platform / Context	Number of Respondents	% of Respondents	Forms of Body Shaming Reported
Social Media Platforms (Instagram, Facebook, TikTok)	142	71%	Negative comments, comparison culture, trolling, filters reinforcing ideal body image
Messaging Apps (WhatsApp, Telegram)	96	48%	Sharing memes, unsolicited weight-loss advice, edited photos of peers
Online Dating Apps	74	37%	Rejection based on appearance, derogatory remarks on body type
Public Forums & Comment Sections	61	30.5%	Anonymous hate comments, fatphobic/ skinny-shaming rhetoric
Influencer/ Celebrity Content Impact	128	64%	Internalised body image pressure, ideal body aspiration, self-comparison
Gaming and Virtual Interaction Spaces	52	26%	Teasing, avatar-based appearance mockery, toxic masculinity norms

The impact of body shaming extends far beyond physical spaces, it deeply influences how individuals navigate and participate in the digital world. The data reveals a striking trend: 81.5 per cent of respondents strongly agreed that body shaming had caused them to reduce their use of social media (Table 8). This indicates a widespread withdrawal from platforms that are typically used to connect, share, and express oneself likely due to fear of judgment, negative comments, or comparison culture. Even more telling, a staggering 99 per cent strongly agreed that body shaming led them to avoid participating in online communities or forums. These are spaces meant for support, conversation, and shared interests, yet for many, they become sources of anxiety or exclusion tied to appearance-based self-consciousness. While 76.5 per cent were neutral on whether they feel isolated or left out in digital spaces, this neutrality may reflect an internal conflict: even if they do not overtly feel excluded by others, they may still voluntarily isolate themselves to avoid discomfort or perceived judgment. Perhaps the most alarming finding is that 100 per cent of respondents agreed that body shaming has caused them to withdraw from online friendships or interactions entirely a unanimous indication that these experiences are not isolated, but systemic and deeply felt. Furthermore, the avoidance of video-sharing platforms with 60 per cent agreeing and 34.5 per cent strongly agreeing suggests a fear of being seen or scrutinized visually, which can be particularly triggering in an image-obsessed digital culture.

Table 8. Body Shaming Affecting Digital Isolation & Withdrawal (in %)

Level of Agreement	Reduced my use of social media	Avoid participating in online communities or forums	Feel isolated or left out in digital spaces	Caused me to withdraw from online friendships or interactions	Avoid video-sharing platforms
Strongly Disagree	0	0	0	0	0
Disagree	0	0	0	0	0
Neutral	0	0	76.5	0	5.5
Agree	18.5	1	17.5	100	60
Strongly Agree	81.5	99	6	0	34.5

Source: Author's field survey (2025)

Objectification of body image is one of the major consequences of advertisements on social and electronic media, which promotes the beauty industry. Advertisements have been condemned for objectifying women's bodies to promote their products. A discussion with a young woman respondent reveals that she uses "Fair and Lovely" cream inspired by the advertisement on television, to transform into a light-skinned beauty. She further reiterated:

"My husband insisted that I should use fairness creams advertised on television so that my skin colour transforms fair. In addition, my mother-in-law often taunts me for being dark-skinned. "

With the exponential rise in social media use, body image discourse has increasingly moved to digital platforms. While these spaces offer support and connection, they are also breeding grounds for negative experiences, including body shaming. It can not be denied that our culture and media fostered the idea of 'the perfect body' and were fundamentally accountable for many components of body shaming (Kalal, 2023). The pieces of evidence substantiate that body shaming nurtured by the socially constructed concept of "the perfect body" influences individuals' online behaviour, particularly focusing on social withdrawal, digital isolation, and reduced participation in online communities. The data reveals a clear pattern that individuals who experience body shaming often withdraw from online platforms. This aligns with the idea that linking negative self-image and online disengagement (Jung et al., 2022; Castellanos Silva & Steins, 2023; and Cohen et al., 2019) .

Simultaneously, digital withdrawal reflects the politics of visibility in online spaces, where algorithmic amplification of "ideal" beauty types reinforces exclusion. Respondents particularly women and transgender individuals reported disengagement from platforms like Instagram and TikTok due to harassment and comparison anxiety, revealing how digital capitalism commodifies beauty and amplifies inequality. Moreover, respondents discussed how algorithmic curation perpetuates aesthetic capitalism, privileging conventionally attractive bodies while marginalizing those who deviate from standardized norms. This reflects what researchers term algorithmic bias, wherein digital systems, though seemingly neutral, replicate social prejudices embedded in data patterns. Thus, the digital dimension of body shaming is not limited to online trolling but extends to the structural logic of platforms themselves, which profit from users' insecurities and continuous engagement with unattainable ideals.

Psychological and Emotional Distress

Evidences from the field substantiate that body shaming often triggers different forms of withdrawal that extend beyond mere avoidance of social interaction. Discussion below elaborates that interaction of an individual with the society is a process of socialisation where behaviour of one affects the other (Cooley, 1902; Marsh, 2002). The processes involved in socialisation influence the social life and an individual's identity as well (Goffman, 1959; Marsh, 2002). The respondents' accounts suggest that isolation is not a uniform experience but rather a set of patterns shaped by the nature and intensity of shaming. These patterns can be understood at multiple levels: Body shaming doesn't motivate; rather, it paralyses individuals both psychologically and emotionally. Findings from the field explain that criticism based on body shaming may lead to victimization of individuals being bullied by lowering their self-confidence, resulting in mental and psychological distress. During the discussions with the respondents, they asserted that due to feelings of embarrassment, they suffer from an inability to express themselves, resulting in the suppression of emotions or avoidance of sharing personal struggles. Also, individuals suffer from the fear of vulnerability and avoid opening up to others due to past ridicule or judgment related to their appearance.

The data suggest that emotional well-being is most directly and universally affected by body shaming. Stress, anxiety, and mental withdrawal were also frequently reported. Interestingly, the relatively low agreement on self-esteem impact (9.5per cent) and the high neutral response (59 per cent) on mental isolation suggest a potential disconnect between experience and recognition (see table 9). Observations reveal that respondents may not fully attribute these emotional or behavioural shifts to body shaming or may lack the language to express these internal changes. This pattern highlights a broader issue: underrecognition of indirect psychological effects. Cultural stigma around discussing mental health or personal appearance may contribute to this gap. However, many values across psychological indicators like self-esteem, emotional well-being, stress, and isolation are consistently rated 4 or 5, showing strong negative effects. Body shaming has a clear negative psychological impact, especially on mental well-being and anxiety levels. Mental withdrawal and social isolation are also affected, though perhaps less consciously acknowledged.

Table 9. Body Shaming Affecting Psychological Isolation (in %)

Level of Agreement	Mentally withdrawn	Negatively affected my self-esteem	Isolate myself mentally from others	Affects my mental well-being	Anxious or stressed
Strongly Disagree	0	0	0	0	0
Disagree	0	0	0	0	0
Neutral	1	0	59	0	12.5
Agree	29.5	9.5	20	100	45.5
Strongly Agree	69.5	90.5	21	0	42

Source: Author's field survey (2025)

Findings of this study authenticate the objectification theory introduced by Fredrickson and Roberts in 1997 as a comprehensive framework to explain socialization among women, and repeated experiences of sexual objectification contribute to the development of mental health concerns—particularly eating disorders, depression, and sexual dysfunction. These conditions are disproportionately prevalent among women compared to men (Muradi & Huang, 2008).

Experiences shared by the respondents claim that psychologically, body shaming breeds anxiety. One of the respondents asserted:

"I couldn't eat in public without feeling like people were judging my plate. Social events made me anxious. Shopping for clothes was a nightmare. I avoided mirrors, photographs, swimming pools anything that forced me to confront my reflection."

She further emphasised:

"I started skipping meals, then entire days of eating. I counted every calorie like it was a sin. I shrank, physically and emotionally. But no matter how much weight I lost, the shame stayed. Because it was never really about the body, rather it was about how I felt inside it."

Analysis of the data reveals a striking consensus on the emotional damage caused by body shaming. Most notably, 98.5 per cent of participants strongly agreed that they struggle to express emotions, and 100 per cent reported feeling emotionally unsupported or fearing judgment. These findings strongly suggest that body shaming leads to internalized shame, suppression of emotional expression, and fear of vulnerability in social contexts. A significant 87per cent of respondents indicated a tendency to withdraw from relationships, and 73.5per cent reported a strong sense of disconnection. This indicates a social ripple effect of body shaming, where victims begin to isolate themselves, potentially as a protective mechanism against further criticism or emotional harm (see table 10). Notably, no participants disagreed with any of the statements, and neutral responses remained low (13–22.5 per cent at most). This near-unanimous agreement reinforces the pervasiveness and severity of body shaming's emotional impact. These are critical factors that indicates that lack of disagreement is a red flag demonstrates that bodyshaming can lead to long-term mental and emotional health challenges such as depression, anxiety, and diminished self-worth.

Table 10. **Body Shaming Affecting Emotional Isolation (in %)**

Level of Agreement	Fear of being judged	Difficult to express my emotions	Feel disconnected	Feel emotionally unsupported	Withdraw from relationships
Strongly Disagree	0	0	0	0	0
Disagree	0	0	0	0	0
Neutral	0	0	73.5	0	13
Agree	24.5	1.5	22.5	100	50.5
Strongly Agree	75.5	98.5	4	0	36.5

Source: Author's field survey (2025)

Statistical Analysis

The quantitative data collected from 200 respondents were analyzed using descriptive and inferential statistical techniques to examine the extent, frequency, and correlational relationships between body shaming experiences and their associated psychosocial outcomes. Statistical analysis was conducted using the Statistical Package for the Social Sciences (SPSS).

Descriptive Statistics

Descriptive statistics were applied to measure the prevalence and frequency distribution of body shaming experiences across demographics and contexts. Percentages, means, and standard deviations were calculated to summarize the data. The mean scores indicate that body shaming experiences are highly prevalent across all three dimensions, with digital exposure emerging as the most pronounced ($M = 4.5$) as shown in Table 11. The high standard deviation in structural and digital contexts suggests varying intensities of experiences depending on institutional settings and individual digital engagement levels.

Table 11. Descriptive Statistics

Variable	Mean (M)	Standard Deviation (SD)	Percentage of Affected Respondents
Structural Exposure	3.9	0.7	68%
Societal Exposure	4.3	0.6	83%
Digital Exposure	4.5	0.6	88%
Psychological Distress	4.1	0.7	72%
Social Isolation	3.9	0.7	66%

Source: Author's field survey (2025)

Comparative Dimensional Analysis

A comparative examination of mean agreement levels across domains reveals variation in the magnitude of isolation effects (as shown in table 12). These values show that emotional and digital isolation are the most pronounced effects of body shaming, whereas institutional and family contexts though still impactful register relatively lower mean intensities. The dominance of emotional and digital isolation underscores that body shaming first damages inner emotional equilibrium and then extends to virtual withdrawal from social spaces.

Table 12. **Comparative Dimensional Analysis**

Dimension	Mean Agreement Score	Relative Severity
Emotional Isolation	4.8	Highest
Digital/Social Media Isolation	4.7	Very High
Psychological Isolation	4.6	High
Social Isolation	4.6	High
Family/Interpersonal Isolation	4.4	Moderate
Educational/Workplace Isolation	4.4	Moderate

Source: Author's field survey (2025)

Correlation Analysis

To identify interrelations among different isolation dimensions, a Pearson correlation test was applied to the aggregated mean scores. Results revealed strong positive correlations across the domains in Table 13. All correlation values ($r > 0.8$) indicate a highly significant relationship, suggesting that body shaming-induced isolation operates in an interconnected manner i.e. distress in one dimension (e.g., emotional) is strongly predictive of withdrawal in others (e.g., social or digital).

Table 13. **Correlation Analysis**

Variables Compared	Correlation Coefficient (r)
Psychological – Emotional Isolation	0.9
Emotional – Digital Isolation	0.9
Social – Family Isolation	0.9
Emotional – Social Isolation	0.8

Source: Author's field survey (2025)

Cross-Dimensional Isolation Index (CDII)

A composite Cross-Dimensional Isolation Index (CDII) was developed by averaging the normalized mean scores from each isolation category. The overall index value stood at 0.87, signifying a high cumulative isolation tendency across the sample. The sub-indices are as follows:

Table 14. **Cross-Dimensional Isolation Index**

Sub-Index	Value
Psychological Isolation Index (PII)	0.8
Emotional Isolation Index (EII)	0.9
Social Isolation Index (SII)	0.9
Institutional Isolation Index (III)	0.8
Family/Interpersonal Isolation Index (FII)	0.9
Digital Isolation Index (DII)	0.9

Source: Author's field survey (2025)

The Emotional and Digital sub-indices record the highest isolation levels, reinforcing that body shaming is internalized both psychologically and through online disengagement, reflecting dual forms of invisibility — emotional suppression and digital withdrawal.

Legal Ambiguities

In a society quick to judge and slow to understand, it becomes imperative to cultivate the ability to listen not only to spoken words but also to silences; to recognize not only visible scars but also the quiet erosion of confidence and joy. Kindness and compassion increasingly prove to be lifelines for those silently enduring psychological distress. While movements promoting body positivity and inclusivity have gained momentum challenging narrow beauty ideals and validating diverse bodies there continue to be unreported and unrecognized cases where body shaming and bullying drive individuals into severe emotional trauma, even to the extent of self-harm or suicide. Despite its profound psychological and social consequences, Indian law does not explicitly criminalize body shaming. This legal vacuum results in limited protection for victims and insufficient mechanisms to hold perpetrators accountable. Current remedies are indirect and largely inadequate. For instance, Section 499 of the Indian Penal Code defines defamation as any spoken, written, or symbolic act harming an individual's reputation. Although punishment may extend to two years of imprisonment, a fine, or both, this provision centers primarily on reputational harm rather than the psychological, emotional, and social injuries arising from body shaming. Importantly, there are no specific statutory provisions addressing body shaming-related crimes or consequences, leaving a significant gap in the legal framework.

Comparing India with a developed nation such as the United States reveals significant legal disparities in addressing body-shaming-related harm. The U.S. also lacks a single federal law specifically prohibiting body shaming, its legal framework imposes stronger institutional accountability through civil-rights statutes in educational and employment contexts. Harassment linked to protected characteristics such as sex, race, disability, or national origin must be addressed under laws like Title VII, Title IX, and the Americans with Disabilities Act, compelling schools and workplaces to act when bullying intersects with discrimination. However, even in the U.S., appearance-based harassment remains challenging to litigate when it does not fall within a protected category. India, by contrast, relies primarily on indirect remedies such as Section 499 of the Indian Penal Code on defamation, which does not adequately capture the emotional, psychological, and social harm caused by body shaming. With increasing instances of online and offline body-shaming abuse and documented links to mental-health distress, isolation, and extreme outcomes such as self-harm, there is a pressing need for India to introduce explicit legal provisions that recognize body shaming as a serious offense and provide robust mechanisms for prevention, protection, and redress. A review of existing literature highlights the urgent need for dedicated legislation or amendments addressing body shaming, given its increasing prevalence and profound mental-health impacts. Strengthening legal safeguards would serve both a preventive and deterrent function, ensuring accountability and reinforcing societal recognition of the seriousness of this issue.

9. CONCLUSIONS

This study demonstrates that body shaming is not merely an interpersonal act but a multifaceted social phenomenon rooted in structural, cultural, and digital hierarchies. The findings reveal how normative body expectations are reproduced across familial spaces, educational systems, workplaces, and online environments, thereby regulating behaviour, shaping identity, and influencing social inclusion. Such normative pressures are internalised by individuals, often resulting in emotional distress, diminished self-worth, and altered self-presentation strategies, particularly among women and young people. Institutional norms around professionalism and appearance further legitimise these biases, translating aesthetic expectations into perceived indicators of competence, discipline, and employability. Concurrently, digital platforms serve as both sites of surveillance and resistance: while they reinforce idealised body standards and perpetuate harassment, they also enable counter-narratives, supportive communities, and emergent body-positivity movements.

Taken together, these findings underscore the systemic nature of body shaming and its implications for mental health, social participation, and equity. Addressing these dynamics requires multi-level interventions, including institutional sensitisation, inclusive policy frameworks, critical media literacy, and community-based programmes that promote body diversity and psychological well-being. Body shaming doesn't stop at emotional harm—it has tangible social and economic consequences. This systemic prejudice proves that body shaming is not merely about appearance—it is a form of social oppression. This chapter advocates the stance that body shaming is vindictiveness against others based on our prejudices and misconceived judgement. Society has normalised the practice of body shaming as a casual part of everyday life, oblivious to the catastrophic effects. In homes, schools, and workplaces, environments meant to nurture and support often become breeding grounds for criticism and judgment, especially when such negativity goes unchecked and normalized. Among the most damaging forms of this is body-shaming, which leaves deep emotional scars, silencing those who experience it. Many who are body-shamed feel overwhelmed by shame and embarrassment, too afraid to speak up or seek help, fearing further ridicule or rejection.

In a nutshell, the concern addressed throughout the entire chapter is how the objectification of the human body leads to a point where they begin to objectify and confine themselves to isolation. This chapter reiterates that individuals are often anxious about their interactions with others, which is influenced by social construction and self-consciousness. An individual tends to avoid social situations and get confined to the walls of isolation due to concerns about their appearance. This highlights that body shaming can trigger feelings of guilt and judgement, underlining the belief that physical appearance defines worth. This can result in mental health issues such as low self-esteem, self-image, and worth, contributing to circumstances like hopelessness and anxiety. Overcoming body shame and regaining confidence can be a challenging journey for individuals.

10. RECOMMENDATIONS

Based on the findings of this study, the following recommendations are proposed to address the pervasive and detrimental issue of body shaming, multi-level interventions are essential.

Institutional Policy Implementation

Since 100 per cent of respondents reported feeling mentally affected hence, peer-support groups and safe spaces should be created within schools, universities, and workplaces. Educational institutions, workplaces, and other formal settings should establish clear anti-body-shaming policies. These policies must outline definitions, consequences, and reporting mechanisms to ensure accountability and a supportive environment.

Integration of Mental Health Services

Given the high prevalence of stress, anxiety, and withdrawal (Tables 5 and 6), institutions must establish dedicated mental health frameworks. This includes trained in-house counselors, confidential helplines, and access to therapy tailored to body image concerns. Mental health services must be made accessible, with specialized counseling and support systems designed for individuals affected by body shaming. These services should prioritize emotional resilience and self-esteem development.

Awareness and Educational Campaigns

The prevalence of derogatory nicknames (*Kala, Mota, Haathi*) and discriminatory remarks at workplaces highlights the urgent need for structured awareness campaigns. Sensitization workshops can shift cultural attitudes, reducing ridicule and increasing empathy among peers and supervisors. Structured awareness programs should be introduced at various levels—particularly in schools and colleges, to educate individuals about the psychological effects of body shaming and to promote body positivity, self-acceptance, and diversity.

Media and Advertising Regulations

The findings highlight a stark impact of body shaming on digital behavior: 81.5 per cent of respondents reduced social media use, 99 per cent avoided online communities, and 100 per cent withdrew from online friendships. Media-driven objectification and unrealistic beauty standards further amplify self-doubt and body dissatisfaction. To counter this, policymakers must enforce stricter regulations on harmful media content, including a rigorous review and active implementation of the Indecent Representation of Women (Prohibition) Act, 1986, to curb the perpetuation of damaging body ideals.

Legal Reform and Recognition

Body shaming should be formally recognized as a punishable offense. It is recommended that existing defamation laws be expanded to include body shaming as a distinct form of reputational and psychological harm.

Parental and Community Engagement

With majority of the participants withdrawing from relationships, community programs and family counseling should strengthen bonds and reduce isolation. Addressing body shaming also requires challenging cultural and familial beauty norms, while encouraging positive communication and support networks to build youth resilience.

Training for Educators and Human Resources Personnel

Respondents' reports of inconsistent or inadequate support (mean $\approx$ 4.0) show the need for capacity-building among educators and supervisors. Training can help them recognize warning signs of withdrawal or distress and respond constructively. Staff in educational and professional settings should receive training to identify signs of psychological and emotional distress related to body shaming and offer appropriate support or referrals.

Future Research Directions

Longitudinal studies are needed to examine the long-term psychological, social, and emotional effects of body shaming. Further research should also assess the effectiveness of intervention programs aimed at reducing its prevalence and impact.

ACKNOWLEDGEMENTS

The author acknowledges the anonymous reviewers for their valuable feedback and the respondents for their participation in the interviews. They declare no conflicts of interest regarding the research, authorship, or publication of this chapter and confirm that no financial support was received.

REFERENCES

Anixiadis, F., Wertheim, E. H., Rodgers, R., & Caruana, B. (2019). Effects of thin-ideal Instagram images: The roles of appearance comparisons, internalization of the thin ideal and critical media processing. *Body Image*, *31*, 181–190. DOI: 10.1016/j.bodyim.2019.10.005

Aparicio-Martínez, P., Perea-Moreno, A.-J., Martínez-Jiménez, M.-P., Redel-Macías, M.-D., Pagliari, C., & Vaquero-Abellán, M. (2019). Social media, thin-ideal, body dissatisfaction and disordered eating attitudes: An exploratory analysis. *International Journal of Environmental Research and Public Health*, *16*(21), 4177. Advance online publication. DOI: 10.3390/ijerph16214177

Bai, J. (2023). Disciplined parenting professionalism: FEPL, changing patterns of power, assumed politics in family education. *International Journal of Learning and Teaching*, *9*(2), 157–162. DOI: 10.18178/ijlt.9.2.157-162

Blumer, H. (2012). Symbolic interactionism [1969]. *Contemporary sociological theory, 62*.

Castellanos Silva, R., & Steins, G. (2023, March 8). Social media and body dissatisfaction in young adults: An experimental investigation of the effects of different image content and influencing constructs. *Frontiers in Psychology*, *14*, 1037932. Advance online publication. DOI: 10.3389/fpsyg.2023.1037932

Cohen, R., Irwin, L., Newton-John, T., & Slater, A. (2019, June). #bodypositivity: A content analysis of body positive accounts on Instagram. *Body Image*, *29*, 47–57. DOI: 10.1016/j.bodyim.2019.02.007

Cooley, C. H. (1902). *Looking-glass self.* Social Media & the Self: An Open Reader https://DOI: 10.32376/3f8575cb.73d69f51

Fardouly, J., Pinkus, R. T., & Vartanian, L. R. (2017). The impact of appearance comparisons made through social media, traditional media, and in-person in women's everyday lives. *Body Image*, *20*, 31–39. DOI: 10.1016/j.bodyim.2016.11.002

Fredrickson, B. L., & Roberts, T. (1997). Objectification theory: Toward understanding women's lived experiences and mental health risks. *Psychology of Women Quarterly*, *21*(2), 173–206. DOI: 10.1111/j.1471-6402.1997.tb00108.x

Goffman, E. (1978). *The presentation of self in everyday life*. Penguin.

Goffman, E. (1979). Gender advertisements. Harper Torchbooks, Harper & Row, Publishers, New York, Cambridge, MA: Harvard University Press. ISBN 0-06-132076-5 (pbk.).

Husin, S. S., Ab Rahman, A. A., & Mukhtar, D. (2021). The symbolic interaction theory: A systematic literature review of current research. *International Journal of Modern Trends in Social Sciences*, *4*(17), 113–126. DOI: 10.35631/IJMTSS.417010

Jung, J., Barron, D., Lee, Y. A., & Swami, V. (2022, October). Social media usage and body image: Examining the mediating roles of internalization of appearance ideals and social comparisons in young women. *Computers in Human Behavior*, *135*, 107357. DOI: 10.1016/j.chb.2022.107357

Marsh, M. (2002). Examining the discourses that shape our teacher identities. *Curriculum Inquiry*, *32*(4), 453–469. DOI: 10.1111/1467-873X.00242

Morrish, N., & Medina-Lara, A. (2021). Does unemployment lead to greater levels of loneliness? A systematic review. *Social Science & Medicine*, *287*, 114339. DOI: 10.1016/j.socscimed.2021.114339

Perloff, R. M. (2014). Social media effects on young women's body image concerns: Theoretical perspectives and an agenda for research. *Sex Roles*, *71*(11–12), 363–377. DOI: 10.1007/s11199-014-0384-6

Sastre, A. (2014). Towards a radical body positive: Reading the online body positive movement. *Feminist Media Studies*, *14*(6), 929–943. DOI: 10.1080/14680777.2014.883420

Wood, J. V., Giordano-Beech, M., Taylor, K. L., Michela, J. L., & Gaus, V. (1994). Strategies of social comparison among people with low self-esteem: Self-protection and self enhancement. *Journal of Personality and Social Psychology*, *67*(4), 713–731. DOI: 10.1037/0022-3514.67.4.713

Chapter 9
From Individualism to Community: Islamic Social Finance as Antidotes to the Loneliness Economy

Khairunnisa Musari
https://orcid.org/0000-0003-0525-9903
Kiai Haji Achmad Siddiq State Islamic University, Jember, Indonesia

ABSTRACT

A paradox exists in contemporary society, characterized by the rise of advanced digital technologies, increasing wealth that supports consumer independence, an increasingly personalized consumer culture, and rising life expectancy, which has given rise to an economy of loneliness, which diminishes the need for human interaction and reduces social dependency. Loneliness has become a product of capitalism and contributed to the creation of an industry that deepens social isolation. Islamic social finance, with its empathy for the socially and economically marginalized, helps build a framework for shifting individualism to community to enhance social cohesion, strengthen social solidarity, and social resilience. This chapter employs an integrative review and netnography techniques through a qualitative research design with thematic analysis to address the economy of loneliness by illustrating the transformative potential of Islamic social finance instruments as antidotes in addressing both material deprivation and social disconnection.

DOI: 10.4018/979-8-3373-5811-6.ch009

INTRODUCTION

Numerous studies have revealed the serious impact of loneliness and social isolation on public health, not only related to mental health issues but also chronic diseases (Adshade et al., 2024; Card et al., 2023), and become a risk factor for premature mortality (Holt-Lunstad, 2021; p. 1). Grounded in evolutionary, social, and developmental theories that view social connection as a fundamental human need, participation in society, or the lack thereof through social isolation, shapes mental health outcomes (Rowe, 2015; p. vii). In addition, rising levels of social disconnection carry significant economic costs, making it crucial for governments, businesses, and society to understand and address these challenges through informed action (Adshade et al., 2024). Policymakers need to acknowledge loneliness and social isolation as pressing public health challenges that carry significant economic consequences (Engel et al., 2025; p. 1048). However, there remains a limited in-depth investigation between loneliness and social isolation, and economic disparities (Kung et al., 2022; p. 1).

A growing body of evidence suggests that loneliness leads to increased healthcare expenditures due to high demand for medical service utilization, as well as lower labor productivity (Engel et al., 2025; p. 1061; Letón, 2025), which in turn leads to lower current and future economic output (Adshade et al., 2024). Individuals, both men and women, of lower economic status are reported to be significantly more likely to experience loneliness, social isolation, and inadequate social support (Kung et al., 2022; p. 1). Therefore, this highlights the need for social finance, policy interventions, and community-based initiatives to break the cycle between isolation and commodified solutions. Strengthening social bonds can help lower healthcare expenditures, enabling public resources to be redirected toward other priority areas, where initiatives that promote social connectedness contribute to the development of human and social capital, laying the foundation for sustainable economic growth (Adshade et al., 2024). However, while some economic evaluations suggest that targeted interventions can be cost-effective, the overall findings remain inconclusive, with few studies considering broader societal costs (Engel et al., 2025; p. 1061).

The World Health Organization (WHO) Commission on Social Connection (2025; pp. 148-149) highlighted that strengthening social infrastructure as the most effective way to expand opportunities for connection. Communities, as the places where people live, work, study, and spend leisure time, are key settings for reducing loneliness. Social infrastructure includes public resources, institutions, and services that foster interaction and build social capital. Strategies such as intentional design, equitable access, investment in community programs, and local participation—alongside measures like adapting the built environment, supporting community groups, and social prescribing—can enhance engagement and the evidences of their benefits are increasing.

Against this background, the paradigm of Islamic social finance offers a compelling counter-narrative. Rooted in principles of mutual care, redistribution, and communal responsibility, instruments such as *zakah, infaq, sadaqah, waqf,* and *hibah* embody a shift from individualism to community. Linking resources of the affluent with the needs of the vulnerable creates not only material support but also social reciprocity and collective identity. Indeed, unlike the loneliness economy that monetizes relationships, Islamic social finance seeks to restore social bonds by embedding financial practice within a moral and communal framework. As stated by Modéer (2018), Islamic social finance can support governments and communities in meeting diverse development needs and holds strong potential to reduce marginalization and vulnerability when allocated to locally driven initiatives that foster social and economic inclusion.

Indeed, as Omar (2022; pp. xx-xxi) highlighted that the establishment of Islamic social finance institutions and instruments is grounded in the pursuit of social justice, equity, and harmony across all segments of society. These mechanisms, namely *zakah, sadaqah* and *infaq, waqf,* microfinance, *takaful* (social insurance), and *qardhul hasan* (interest-free loans), represent powerful yet often underutilized tools with the potential to reduce inequality and bridge the gap between the wealthy and the poor. Historical evidence suggests that when these instruments are fully mobilized within a comprehensive Islamic economic framework, they can play a decisive role in eradicating poverty. This effectiveness stems from their integration into policies designed not only to redistribute wealth but also to empower all societal groups to enhance their economic productivity in a sustainable and self-sufficient manner.

However, although the economic benefits of Islamic social finance are now well recognized, its role in enhancing psychological well-being has not been widely examined (Cahyanti et al., 2024; p. 415). Likewise, evidence regarding interventions designed to enhance social connections or reduce loneliness and isolation remains inconsistent and generally weak, so developing accessible and effective interventions outside clinical environments that can be readily adopted by the broader public is essential Lim et al., 2025; p. 932). For this reason, this chapter explores how Islamic social finance instruments can be reframed not merely as tools for poverty alleviation but as mechanisms to rebuild community bonds and well-being. Then, this chapter uses a literature review approach by employing a qualitative research design with integrative review techniques and netnography, as well as thematic analysis.

Finally, the remaining part of the chapter is organized into three sections. The first section presents the loneliness economy phenomenon globally, including the social isolation issue. As a specific review method that summarizes empirical literature, the exposure of loneliness distribution in several countries worldwide provides a comprehensive understanding of the phenomenon of loneliness, which poses a public health problem in both broad and narrow senses. Through an integrative review, this chapter addresses the issue of loneliness as a mental health crisis that requires attention from all countries. By using this technique, the netnography method serves as a supporting approach to the integrative review, strengthening the argument for shifting from individualism to community to enhance social cohesion, social solidarity, and social resilience.

Then, with a similar technique, in the second section, the concept and practice of Islamic social finance are presented by discussing their roles as a moral and sharing economy, as community-building tools, with selected case studies in several countries. Then, the subsequent section concludes the entire chapter in the conclusion section and policy recommendations. As the book is positioned, this chapter advances the discourse by linking Islamic economic values and Islamic finance instruments to the contemporary global crisis of social isolation, an area largely overlooked in Islamic finance literature. It highlights how faith-driven financial systems can embrace community solidarity, mutual responsibility, and equitable distribution, as well as offering structural and ethical antidotes to the loneliness economy in the age of social disconnection.

THE LONELINESS ECONOMY

The loneliness economy has a variety of meanings and definitions. Among them, the loneliness economy reflects how modern capitalism exploits the need for connection, fostering shallow ties that worsen isolation and highlighting the urgency of prioritizing genuine human relationships. As highlighed by Patel (2023), the loneliness economy represents a troubling side of modern capitalism, where businesses capitalize on people's desire for authentic connection. In this setting, shallow interactions, virtual approval, and superficial ties prevail, often deepening feelings of emptiness and isolation. To counter this growing crisis, society must acknowledge its harmful effects and focus on fostering genuine human relationships.

Indeed, scholars for years have been warning about what many now refer to as the 'age of loneliness', including in the United States (U.S.), where almost half of adults say they feel deeply isolated, a reality that spans generations, income levels, and political views (Thomas, 2025). In 2023, the U.S. Surgeon General declared loneliness a 'public health epidemic' and outlined a strategy to strengthen social ties across schools, workplaces, and digital spaces (Schofield, 2025). Although the U.S. population has steadily increased for decades, the average household size has declined over the same period (Korhonen, 2024). Likewise, in aging societies in Korea, experiences such as divorce or the loss of a spouse often lead individuals to turn to the loneliness economy so unmarried, divorced or widowed individuals have high need for social connections (Whan-woo, 2025).

In the United Kingdom (U.K.), loneliness became a policy priority in 2018 when Prime Minister Theresa May appointed the first Minister for Loneliness, following a survey showing over nine million adults were often lonely; subsequent measures included funding community cafés, promoting social prescribing by general practitioners, and monitoring social wellbeing (Biswas, 2023; Schofield, 2025). In Japan, this country followed in 2021 by creating a similar role to address challenges from an ageing population and high suicide rates, supporting shared housing and local hubs (Schofield, 2025). In China, the lonely economy—emerging in 2015 from the earlier idea of the 'single economy'—now encompasses singles, empty-nesters, couples, dual income no kids (DINK) families, and those choosing to live alone, gaining broad acceptance as shifting social attitudes drive consumers from basic needs toward higher-quality goods that satisfy emotional and lifestyle aspirations (Wang & Liu, 2020; p. 11).

In Spain, as highlighted by Letón (2025), this country leads Europe in life expectancy with an average of 84 years, more than the average of 81.5 years. Other important changes include smaller household sizes, more people living alone, the rise of remote work, urban migration, and increased use of digital platforms. All these factors have led to a reduction in the amount of face-to-face social interaction. In 2021, for every 5,380,853 Spanish residents living with feelings of social isolation, there were associated costs of $1,287. Nationally, the annual direct costs of loneliness reach $16.05 billion. Public health costs generally consist of doctor visits and medication costs, which reached $6.93 billion, and annual costs due to lost productivity (reduced work hours), which increased to approximately $9.08 billion.

In Australia, referring to Proveda at https://proveda.com.au/get-involved/donate, loneliness impacts over 15 percent of Australians and represents more than a passing emotion, where it is a significant concern associated with mental health problems, higher suicide risk, and persistent social isolation. Since 1994, Proveda, formerly Community Care Northern Beaches (CCNB), has helped over 2,500 people each year. Several testimonials from Proveda customers express their gratitude for receiving services that help improve their mental health and thus lead to a better quality of life, for example,

Carolyn, Volunteer, *"I feel fulfilled that I'm helping someone who needs support or feels lonely and just needs company."*

Dot, Belong Club Member, *"The Belong Club can help fill the terrible gap and isolation in their lives."*

In a clear statement, Proveda invites everyone to donate to help this organization connect with individuals who might otherwise remain unnoticed and without support, because government funding often falls short in covering essential services, particularly those related to mental health and suicide prevention. For more than three decades, Proveda has empowered people to contribute to strengthening and expanding meaningful connections within the community through a stronger and better 'village' for all.

No doubt, social isolation, often tied to big cities, also affects small communities facing population decline and loss of services, leaving less-mobile groups—like the elderly, homemakers, and carless households—more reliant on personal networks and vulnerable to isolation (Hortulanus & Machielse, 2006; p. 6). Then, the unsettling is not only the loneliness but how swiftly it has been commodified (Thomas, 2025). As mentioned also, loneliness itself isn't something new, but turning it into a business is in the most digitally connected period of history, with rates of loneliness having never been higher (van de Stadt, 2025). In other words, literally, it is the loneliness economy in the age of socal disconnection (Musari, 2025), where loneliness is becoming more widespread and deeply rooted in a world that is highly digitally connected (Letón, 2025), where the loneliness industry is expanding rapidly, not just be profiting from the social disconnection but also reflecting the deep human need for belonging in a world (Goldstein, 2025).

As Wang and Liu (2020: 15) explained that the lonely economy has emerged from modern economic growth and shifting social values, reflecting the rising share of singles and empty-nesters. Rather than pathological, it represents a market reality where younger generations seek private, undisturbed spaces. This trend, increasingly accepted by society, creates new consumer segments, drives personalized demand, and opens business opportunities for innovative growth. Heim (2023; pp. 20-21) confirmed that self-actualization, linked to thriving, is the drive to realize one's full potential and become one's best self. Often depicted as a pyramid, it illustrates how socio-economic progress enables people to move from meeting basic needs for food, safety, and belonging toward higher goals of esteem and personal fulfillment. As more societies secure fundamental needs, more individuals can pursue self-actualization, showing the connection between economic development and individualism.

A society may reach great heights of material success, yet it cannot sustain them if moral values decline, families break down, younger generations lack proper care and guidance, and social tensions and disintegration increase, including social isolation. Likewise, besides placing a substantial burden on healthcare systems by driving greater use of medical services, social isolation also diminishes both the size and efficiency of the labor force, thereby constraining current productivity and future economic potential (Adshade et al., 2024). The rise of the loneliness economy raises ethical concerns about market-driven approaches to managing human emotions, serving as a troubling example of modern capitalism in which businesses exploit the longing for authentic connection (Biswas, 2023). Social connections have a powerful impact on health as well as longevity, and a lack of them is a risk factor for premature death, but, unfortunately, social factors are often overlooked in medical practice and healthcare services (Holt-Lunstad, 2021: 1)

ISLAMIC SOCIAL FINANCE

A Moral and Sharing Economy

The market for social finance instruments continues to grow rapidly, and investors fund socially beneficial activities so their presence overcome the funding barriers necessary to achieve social goals (Hilbrich, 2021; p. 1). In this regard, social finance refers to investment approaches designed to generate positive social and environmental impacts alongside financial returns, encompassing instruments such as community investment, microfinance, social impact bonds, community loan funds, and philanthropic initiatives (Razak & Dawami, 2013; p. 40). At the same time, Islamic social finance has also recently gained more attention as a distinct model of Islamic financial social responsibility in which Islamic financial institutions and corporations engage in humanitarian initiatives and social development activities (Mohsin & Muneeza, 2025; p. 1).

Islamic social finance has similarities with social finance theories but also has differences due to its foundation in maqasid al-Shari'ah, combining social and faith-based principles, to provide financial support for those in need, alleviate human suffering, including safeguard the environment, particularly in contexts affected by conflict or disaster, through the prudent management and investment of funds to address societal challenges and strengthen communitiess (Razak & Dawami, 2013; p. 40). Islamic social finance serves as a vehicle for socio-economic development and financial empowerment of the poor, and its management is currently being increasingly adapted to current social needs while continuing to uphold the principles of Islamic social finance (Musari & Fathorrazi, 2021; p. 303).

No doubt, Islamic social finance is now remarkably established as the contemporary paradigm that reflects the spirit and intention of Islam, perhaps more effectively than for-profit financial markets and institutions (Al-Suwailem, 2020; p. 2). If, for many, helping those in the developing world, those who are poorer, is a moral issue (Stiglitz, 2006; p. 100), so helping people who are in the loneliness economy or socially isolated is also certainly a moral issue. Loneliness, akin to the deprivation of basic needs such as hunger and thirst, threatens individuals with limited social interaction, who often seek to overcome it by forming new relationships through group activities and community service (Kiliç & Daldal, 2024; p. 148). Indeed, a core principle in Islam is showing care and compassion for others, particularly those who are in need. As stated by Allah SWT in the Qur'an Al-Ma'idah [5]: 2, "…

*Cooperate with one another in goodness and righteousness, and do not cooperate in sin and transgression. And be mindful of Allah..." (*https://quran.com/5*)*

For this reason, among the five essential elements of the *maqasid al-Shari ah*, namely security of: (1) faith/religion (*din*); (2) life (*nafs*); (3) intellect (*aql*); (4) progeny/lineage (*nasl*); and (5) economy as safeguard of property and wealth (*mal*) (Atiq- ur- Rehman, 2019: 35, 38), helping people who are in the loneliness economy or socially isolated is also to security of life (*nafs*) and progeny/lineage (*nasl*). Indeed, Shari'ah seeks to guide both individual transformation and institutional reform, and when centered on the human self, its objectives can be expressed through these five elements that, when accessible to every individual, enable the realization of human development and well-being (Chapra, 2008; p. 6).

During the COVID-19 pandemic, Islamic social finance gained momentum to show how it can mitigate and address social disconnection. As we know, the spread of the COVID-19 led public authorities to introduce several measures, including maintaining physical distance or social distancing from large groups, where these policies were viewed as crucial strategies to slow down the transmission of the deadly virus (AbdulKareem et al., 2021; p. 56). As the result, as explained by Pietrabissa and Simpson (2020: 2-3), prolonged social isolation during and after COVID-19 has deepened loneliness and disconnection, especially among vulnerable groups, leading to fatigue, anxiety, trauma, and potentially severe conditions such as reactive depression. These mental health issues, particularly depression, undermine problem-solving, motivation, daily functioning, and relationships, hindering recovery from crises. Rooted in feelings of hopelessness and withdrawal, depression becomes harder to overcome when isolation limits social contact and support. Sustained disconnection has also been associated with cognitive decline, weakened immunity, greater cardiovascular risk, and even premature mortality.

In Indonesia, in response to the pandemic, a halfway house called "House of Sulaiman" has provided a temporary haven for patients' families. Using netnography, by observing information displayed on its Instagram account at https://www.instagram.com/rumahsinggah.hos, House of Sulaiman, built using *waqf* funds, provides free counseling services to provide psychological support to families of patients experiencing anxiety, helplessness, or despair. Therefore, Islamic social finance can be mentioned as a moral economy, which links wealth circulation to communal well-being by leading to economic justice, social solidarity, and spiritual purpose. Islamic social finance has a mission to reduce marginalization & vulnerability, including facing social isolation and loneliness as a market opportunity. If isolation becomes both a driver of economic costs and a source of new economic markets, as an antidote, Islamic social finance encourages the creation of a sharing economy.

According to Cattelan (2019: 6), the sharing economy, shaped by the digital revolution, redefines market relations by contrasting the notion of 'sharing' in conventional capitalism with that in Islamic economics, where scarcity, division, and competition are replaced by principles of abundance, rooted in *mizan* (balance between resources, human needs, and desires), along with distribution and cooperation among economic actors. A study by Aljarah et al (2025) revealed that social isolation is a significant predictor of the intention to donate virtual gifts, with self-esteem serving as a mediating factor in this relation. In addition, refer to Holt-Lunstad (2021: 7), to improve health outcomes, social connection must be a key component of standard care due to its clear link to morbidity and mortality risks. Addressing this requires coordinated efforts between healthcare systems and community social care providers through team-based care and customized community services. Clinical settings offer valuable opportunities to reduce social isolation and loneliness and promote well-being by fostering social connections.

Instruments as Community-Building Tools

Islamic social finance represents a significant growth area parallel to the development of Islamic finance (Razak & Dawami, 2019; p. 38) and holds substantial potential as a global funding source for empowering underserved communities, provided it is managed prudently and supported by strong national commitment (IRTI IDB, 2020; p. 28). As a critical foundation for an Islamic social finance system, where the objectives of Shariʿah are not limited to the welfare *(falah)* of the Muslim community, *maqasid al-Shari ah* relates also to all human beings and their common prosperity, also in the light of the most recent criteria of sustainable development (Atiq- ur-Rehman, 2019; p. 50). For this reason, Islamic social finance fosters six dimensions of psychological well-being—self-acceptance, positive relationships, autonomy, environmental mastery, life purpose, and self-development—promoting overall well-being and resonating with the Islamic values (Cahyanti et al., 2024; pp. 430-431).

Zakah, infaq, sadaqah, waqf have become the alternate solution of Islamic social finance in mitigating poverty (Musari & Fathorrazi, 2021; p. 303) and income transfer distribution (DEKS-BI & P3EI-FE UII, 2016; p. 49). *Zakah* is one of the most commonly utilized instruments of Islamic social finance to tackle social marginalization and vulnerability (Razak & Dawami, 2019; p. 38). Indeed, *zakah* serves as a socio-humanitarian form of economic support in Islam. It is not only related to fulfilling the basic needs of the poor and the needy, but rather extends further by encompassing spiritual, moral, and educational dimensions, while also promoting social welfare and long-term well-being (Billah, 2019; p. 198). As the third pillar in Islam and the fundamental component of the Islamic social welfare system, *zakah* is the form of the social responsibility of the rich towards the poor and the needy by providing access to a portion of the wealth of the rich, thus working towards social welfare, redistribution of wealth, and poverty alleviation (Ahmad & Habib, 2013; p. 2).

Then, as explained by Atiq-ur-Rehman (2019; p. 37), *infaq* is an altruistic expenditure, especially for social purposes, and for the sake of gaining rewards from the Almighty, not for financial rewards. Here, the main goal is not to earn productive income, but rather to improve the social welfare and well-being of community members, which is why the center of Islamic economic philosophy is the community. As long as social goals can be met, individual private property can be used. Similarly, *infaq* is explained by Rohmah and Harsya (2023; p. 178) as spending or donations from one's funds to meet the needs of another in a way that is acceptable to the Almighty as a form of worship. Rooted in sincerity and faith, *infaq* embodies giving or donating part of one's sustenance to others, regardless of one's level of income, as an expression of devotion to The Almighty.

Regarding *sadaqah*, according to Islamic Relief, literally meaning of 'righteousness', the term has come to signify 'voluntary charity' in contemporary usage. Derived from the root *sidq*, meaning sincerity, *sadaqah* reflects virtuous conduct that demonstrates the genuineness of one's faith to seek the pleasure of God, encompassing acts of generosity, kindness, compassion, and faith that may be material or non-material. Even simple deeds, such as offering a smile or helping someone in need, are considered *sadaqah.* It can be given by anyone in any amount, and while some of the Prophet's companions (peace be upon him) gave away much of their wealth, a balanced approach today may involve dividing one's resources between personal needs, savings, and *sadaqah.*

Further, as explained by International Waqf Fund, *waqf* are perpetual charitable endowments, similar to *sadaqah jariyah,* that have historically played a key role in supporting and developing communities. Typically, *waqf* provides lasting benefits to society by funding services of public value, such as hospitals or universities. The *waqf* endowment is one of the greatest economic practices that Islam offers. It is a long-term investment for the whole community with continuing benefits. In addition, *waqf* provides continuous blessings that endure even after the donor's passing, while supporting the community and allowing the wealthy to fulfill their social responsibility. It also strengthens the bond of trust between donors and society and revives the sunnah of the Prophet (peace be upon him). As Mohsin & Muneeza (2025: 52) mentioned, *waqf* are sustainable service providers for communities.

Then, microfinance and *qardhul hasan* are also the other institutions and instruments of Islamic social finance (Omar, 2021; p. xx). For addressing the Islamic microfinance gap, Islamic nanofinance can be an answer in financing the very poor (Musari, 2020; pp. 265, 267). Nanofinance represents a new paradigm within microfinance and has already been adopted in several Asian countries to support the very poor, which serves as a complement to the shortcomings of conventional and Islamic microfinance, aligning closely with the humanitarian objectives of Islamic economics (Musari, 2019: 4). Nanofinance, distinct from microfinance, addresses extreme poverty by offering very small-scale financial and welfare services to the poorest segments of society, while leveraging subsidized funding, non-governmental organizations (NGOs) support, social security schemes, grants, and interest-free loans in tandem with government investment in health, education, and infrastructure to improve the living standards of the ultra-poor (Ray, 2008; p. 33).

Microfinance is considered a way to alleviate poverty, but this is only partially true, as it continues to leave the poor vulnerable to predatory lenders (Musari, 2020; p. 280). Nanofinance can be an alternative to help vulnerable segments of society escape predatory lenders by employing schemes like *qardhul hasan* for urgent needs such as food, healthcare, education, daily subsistence, funerals, or weddings; and *musharaka/mudharaba* for small trade and ultra-micro enterprises (Musari, 2019; p. 4). Regarding qardhul hasan, the concept has been neglected in scholarly works, even though this is despite the fact that this concept has a higher significance in Islam than most other legitimate contracts because it is specifically approved in the Qur'an and Hadith (Iqbal and Mirakhor, 2011; p. 58; Obaidullah & Khan, 2008; p. 20; Khan, 2008; p. 20).

Of course, as a branch of Islamic finance, Islamic Social Finance is not profit-oriented. It focuses on social justice by providing affordable and accessible funds to those who are economically marginalized and financially excluded from the formal financial system due to various financial and/or locational barriers (Hassan et al. 2022; p. 1). Alongside Islamic microfinance and nanofinance, *takaful* (social insurance) also constitutes a key component of Islamic social finance (Omar, 2021; p. xx). As Islamic insurance, *takaful* is established on Shariah-compliant principles to address the non-compliance of conventional insurance, which is invalid under Islamic law due to excessive uncertainty and the absence of a clearly transferable subject matter in its sale-based contract (Hassan & Muneeza, 2022; pp. 4, 15).

Another voluntary institution in Islam is *hibah* (Nur & Bin-Nashwan, 2022: 224). *Hibah* literally means a gift or donation, while technically it refers to the transfer of a specific property *(mal)* without any form of material compensation. The Prophet encouraged Muslims to give gifts to one another as this practice holds an important place in Muslim society, aiming to nurture love, harmony, and mutual cooperation among people (Khan, 2007; p. 74). Another explanation, *hibah* refers to the unconditional transfer of property or possessions without compensation, serving as a voluntary gift encouraged by the Prophet to foster love, generosity, and cooperation within society (Fauzia & Musari, 2021; p. 44).

Overall, to counter the loneliness economy and social isolation, Table 1 shows how the mechanisms of each Islamic social finance instrument work to overcome them.

Table 1. Islamic Social Finance Instruments

Instruments	Description
Zakah	The true essence of *zakah* lies in fostering social and economic solidarity. *Zakah* has two functions at once, namely the income redistribution function and the functional redistribution function. *Zakah* may be distributed to eligible individuals or groups that fall within the eight categories specified by Allah in the Qur'an, namely: *al-fuqara* (the poor), individuals with no assets and unable to earn a living; *al-masakin* (the needy), those who have earnings but they are not enough to cover their basic needs; *amilun 'ala zakah* (*zakah* administrators/collectors), individuals appointed to collect, store, guard, and distribute *zakah; al-mu'allafate qulubuhum* (recent converts), those whose hearts are to be reconciled, new Muslims or those inclined to Islam who need support to strengthen their faith; *riqab* (to free captives; those in bondage), refers to slaves or captives who are seeking freedom and can use *zakah* to pay for their ransom; *al-gharimin* (those in debt/debtors), people burdened with debt for essential needs, not for sinful activities; *fi sabilillah* (for the way of God; for the cause of Allah), individuals engaged in activities that serve to uphold and promote Islam, such as education, *da'wa* (preaching), or community development; and *ibn al-sabil* (the wayfarer/stranded traveler), travelers who are stranded away from home, out of money, and in need of assistance to reach their destination (Ascarya, 2006; pp. 8-10; Zakat Foundation of America, 2014; Sayah and Musari, 2021; p. 34; Mohsin and Muneeza, 2025; pp. 35). *Zakah* can overcome the loneliness economy by inviting *zakah* givers to interact directly with the recipients of *zakah* so that interactions can occur and directly show how *zakah* funds can help fulfill the basic needs of *zakah* recipients without having to reciprocate with the givers.
Infaq	*Infaq* is a form of voluntary charitable giving in Islam offered solely to seek God's pleasure and promote the welfare of society and family, without expecting any return, without fixed timing or amount, directed toward social causes. *Infaq* does not diminish one's wealth or income, as God promises to replace it with equal or greater rewards. God enjoins all people to practice *infaq,* pious spending in His name, which facilitates wealth redistribution and helps eliminate poverty within communities. When carried out in accordance with its conditions, *infaq* also brings various benefits and protections to the giver (Zakat Foundation of America, 2010; Hassan & Muneeza, 2022; pp. 21-22). *Infaq* can address the loneliness economy by inviting people to fund healthcare programs, counseling, and other community-based activities that can increase interaction and strengthen social bonds in genuine, non-commercial relationships.
Sadaqah	Nowadays, *sadaqah* has come to be defined as voluntary charity or voluntary act of kindness or almsgiving, believed to bring spiritual merit and blessings. *Zakah* should be given within a specific timeframe and in a specific amount, while *sadaqah,* like *infaq,* has no timeframe or limitations. *Zakah* is tied to specific types of wealth, while *sadaqah* can be any act of devotion (Zakat Foundation of America, 2020; Hassan & Muneeza, 2022; pp. 21-22). *Sadaqah* can break the cycle of loneliness and social isolation by spreading the invitation about donations to social causes, including educating people that pleasing others doesn't have to involve money, but can also involve a smile, being a listening ear, or providing motivation and encouragement for life. It is hoped that this, in turn, will encourage genuine, non-transactional acts of kindness, strengthen social bonds, and foster a sense of caring and compassion that doesn't commodify human relationships.

continued on following page

Table 1. Continued

Instruments	Description
Waqf	*Waqf* serve as enduring institutions that provide continuous support and services to communities. Throughout Islamic history, the *waqf* have been central institutions for promoting socio-economic progress, public benefit, and community well-being, guided by values of generosity and sustainability to meet societal needs such as education, healthcare, infrastructure, and environmental protection (DEKS-BI & DES-FEB UNAIR, 2016; p. 44; Mohsin & Muneeza, 2025; p. 52). As perpetual endowments that continuously benefit society, *waqf* combat loneliness and isolation by creating sustainable institutions and spaces that nurture community ties, ensure inclusivity, and embed social solidarity into the very fabric of society, standing as a long-term alternative to market-driven, commodified forms of connection.
Islamic Microfinance; Islamic Nanofinance	Islamic microfinance/nanofinance is a relatively simple financing model that aims to provide between $1-100 within a very short period of time to extremely poor people, without requiring a stable income, collateral, or signed contracts, and without charging interest. One of its goals is to protect the poor from predatory lenders, thereby eliminating their dependence on them, and to promote their independence and dignity, and mobilize both internal and external resources for community empowerment. Access to financing should be minimal, with possible oral applications, same-day disbursement, and flexible repayment terms agreed upon by both parties—ensuring that access to finance becomes a genuine instrument of social justice rather than a source of burden (Musari, 2016; pp. 10-11; Musari & Simanjuntak, 2016; pp. 3-5). When delivered through community-based networks, mosques, or NGOs, the program fosters a culture of empathy, trust, and solidarity, directly addressing loneliness by reminding beneficiaries that they are not abandoned but supported by their community. By empowering microfinance/nanofinance for micro/nano entrepreneurs who typically lack capital, have no collateral, and limited turnover, the program strengthens communal bonds that can reduce social disparities, promote equitable wealth distribution, empower underprivileged communities to start businesses or create jobs, and foster compassionate communities dedicated to eradicating poverty, unemployment, and social inequality.
Qardhul Hasan	*Qardhul hasan* is built on the spirit of benevolence and compassion, interest-free loan granted to those in need for a specific period, often with flexible repayment terms, requiring the borrower to repay only the exact amount borrowed without any profit. Widely used as short-term financial assistance and a tool for social welfare, it reflects Islam's emphasis on brotherhood, mutual care, and sharing among Muslims. *Qardhul hasan* is recommended to be applied as a philanthropic contract of Islamic microfinance/nanofinance and social entrepreneurship (Ismail & Possumah, 2010; p. 6; Musari, 2016; pp. 10-11; Musari, 2019; pp. 19-20; Mohsin & Muneeza, 2025; p. 71). *Qardhul hasan* can reduce the commodification of loneliness and social isolation by providing soft/benevolence loans as sincere financial assistance, without requiring interest, profit sharing, or other commercial benefits, because it does not want to burden those who need loans.

continued on following page

Table 1. Continued

Instruments	Description
Social Takaful	Social *takaful* refers to a system of protection offered to individuals who are financially excluded or socially marginalized. *Takaful* is founded on the principle of mutual protection, where members contribute to a shared pool to support each other in times of hardship (Omar, 2021: xx; Hassan & Muneeza, 2022; p. 23). Beyond financial security, *takaful* nurtures a sense of mutual responsibility and belonging, reducing isolation during crises such as illness, death, or accidents, when people are most vulnerable to loneliness
Hibah & Other Social Donations	*Hibah* and other social donations are symbolic reinforcements of reciprocal, non-commodity relationships, given without any time limit, which refers to the voluntary transfer of legal and beneficial ownership of assets from a donor to a beneficiary (Khan, 2007; p. 74). Other social donations are optional donations and acts of kindness. *Hibah* and other social donations replace transactional, market-based "solutions" to disconnection with hearty, voluntary acts of generosity that strengthen human relationships, rebuild community solidarity, and affirm shared belonging.

Source: Compiled and developed by Author

Thus, Islamic social finance is based on the collaboration between material and spiritual aspects to build a deep and meaningful community through poverty alleviation, community development, and social integration. Its tools not only serve as mechanisms of wealth redistribution but also embody values of solidarity, sincerity, and sustainability that strengthen social cohesion. By funding education, healthcare, infrastructure, and community services, Islamic social finance fosters socio-economic development while simultaneously countering social isolation and marginalization. Ultimately, its integration of ethical, religious, and economic principles ensures that financial practices contribute to inclusive prosperity, empowering underserved groups and reinforcing communal bonds essential for resilient and cohesive societies.

Selected Case Studies

This section presents selected case studies from Islamic social finance in funding the education, healthcare, infrastructure, and community services in order to foster socio-economic development while simultaneously countering social isolation and marginalization. Some case studies as shown Table 2 also show how Islamic social finance provide effects of social disconnection during COVID-19, community breakdown during economic crises, and grassroots solidarity movements.

Table 2. Selected Case Studies in Several Countries

Instruments	Case Studies
Zakah	In Algeria, *zakah* funds have played a significant role in supporting around four million underprivileged families, financing 8,849 micro-enterprises over a 12-year period, and generating employment opportunities for unemployed youth through the use of *qardhul hasan* (Sayah & Musari, 2021; p. 34). In Indonesia, a study by Directorate of Research and Development of Zakah, Infaq, Sadaqah (ZIS) and other Religious Social Funds (DSKL) National Amil Zakah Agency (BAZNAS) found that the higher the income of fishermen, the greater the intensity to make Islamic social institutions as an option, both as a medium to increase business capital and meet daily needs because 60 percent of fishermen borrow money on an interest/profit sharing basis (BAZNAS, 2024; p. 2). In addition, *baitul mal wa tamwil* (BMT) is a community-based microfinance in Indonesia that provides both individual and group financing. It operates through an integrated model combining *zakah* and non-*zakah* funds, such as *waqf* and *sadaqah*, to assist people in need according to specific categories—development, empowerment, or recovery for basic needs. The BMT funding approach blends social and investment financing, with expectations of returns in certain areas. BMT raises capital from its members, similar to cooperatives, while also accepting voluntary deposits and safekeeping funds from non-members. To fill funding gaps, it may source capital from Islamic banks and other institutions (Mahomed & Hydara, 2022; p. 298).
Infaq	In Indonesia, Sinergi Foundation runs the Green Kurban program, which provides Shari'ah-compliant sacrificial animals while empowering breeders, supporting poor communities, and promoting environmental sustainability. In Eid al-Adha 2022, the program distributed 930 sheep and 31 cows across Indonesia, Africa, and Gaza, benefiting an estimated 17,782 people (Musari, 2023; p. 278). In Palestine, *infaq* for humanitarian sector are intitated by several Islamic philanthropy institutions, such as, https://donate.infakpalestin.com/order/form/emergency4gaza https://muslimcaremalaysiasociety.com/ms/kempen/dana-kecemasan-palestin https://www.muslimglobalrelief.org/gaza-emergency-appeal https://kitabisa.com/campaign/baznasuntukpalestina https://www.rumahzakat.org/donasi/palestina https://laznasdewandakwah.or.id/en/infakgandumpalestina/2779 https://donasi.baznas.go.id/bantumuslimdipalestina https://donasi.lazismu.org/bantupalestina https://digital.dompetdhuafa.org/donasi/jagapalestina.
Sadaqah	In Indonesia, Rumah Itqon Zakat and Infak (RIZKI) empowers families by promoting zero-waste practices, teaching housewives to grow crops, raise fish in recycled containers, and develop hydroponic gardens. These initiatives enable underprivileged households to meet nutritional needs, share surplus food through sadaqah, and participate in waste management programs such as a "waste bank" and used cooking oil collection. By integrating green economy, circular economy, and green nano finance principles, RIZKI strengthens family resilience and enhances community well-being (Musari, 2023; pp. 277-278).

continued on following page

Table 2. Continued

Instruments	Case Studies
Waqf	In Malaysia, in the education sector, apart from People's Religious Schools (SAR), State Religious Schools (SAN), and madrasas or Islamic boarding schools which were founded with *waqf* funds, various institutions and universities were also founded with waqf funds, including, Kolej Islam Malaya which is currently known as Universiti Islam Malaysia in Cyberjaya, Albukhary International University (AIU) in Kedah, and the Trengganu Culinary Academy (DEKS BI & DES-FEB UNAIR, 2016; p. 59). In addition, in the healthcare sector, Malaysia also has developed a strong Islamic social finance framework driven by both state and federal governments through Islamic blended finance methods to enhance affordable healthcare development. Through *waqf* funding, such as the An-Nur Waqf Clinic managed by Johor Corporation, a haemodialysis center, medical equipment for healthcare facilities, and the Universiti Sains Islam Malaysia (USIM) Specialist Healthcare Clinic, which began operations in 2015. The main funding instrument is cash waqf to finance a dental chair, a mobile clinic (Klip Mobile), and a haemodialysis clinic (Mahomed, 2022; p. 182). In Pakistan, Hamdard Foundation built Madinat al-Hikmah, a dedicated City of Education, Hamdard Public School, and Hamdard University. It also organizes social and community activities, such as outdoor clinics, free medicine distribution, health education through the media, free eye care, and more (DEKS BI & DES-FEB UNAIR, 2016; pp. 65-67). In Palestine, *waqf* for the humanitarian sector is initiated by several Islamic philanthropy institutions, such as, https://digital.dompetdhuafa.org/wakaf/wakafsumurpalestina https://digital.dompetdhuafa.org/wakaf/wakafambulanspalestina https://digital.dompetdhuafa.org/wakaf/masjidpalestina https://rumahwakaf.org/wakaf/investasi-abadi-untuk-palestina https://donorbox.org/gaza-waqf https://awqafsa.org.za/palestine-waqf-fund/

continued on following page

Table 2. Continued

Instruments	Case Studies
Islamic Microfinance; Islamic Nanofinance	In Pakistan, Akhuwat is an Islamic microfinance organization built upon four core principles: *iman* (faith), *ihsan* (doing good), *ikhlas* (sincerity), and *infaq* (charity). It has since expanded globally, with chapters established in various countries, including the United States. Akhuwat's distinctive approach focuses on fostering solidarity and mutual support between the wealthy and the underprivileged (Hassan & Muneeza, 2022; p. 43). In Malaysia, Amanah Ikhtiar Malaysia (AIM) is an Islamic microfinance institution that provided debt moratoriums during the pandemic to help its members repay their financing facilities without defaulting. As government lockdowns halted most economic activities, many AIM members experienced significant income loss. Some 262,000 members across the country benefited from these moratoriums, which were implemented for five weeks. AIM also initiated the "Love Basket" programme to send necessary items to members who were affected during the lockdown, and it helped 1,500 families until November 9, 2020 (Hassan & Muneeza, 2022; p. 44). Some 262,000 members across the country were helped by these moratoriums, which it made effective for five weeks and featured as many as three deferments with an option to extend one year. AIM also initiated the "Love Basket" (Bakul Kasih) programme to send necessary items to members who had been affected during the lockdown and it helped 1,500 families until November 9, 2020 (Hassan & Muneeza, 2022; p. 44). In Indonesia, BMT offers Islamic microfinance services such as micro takaful, fund transfers, bill payments, and online banking similar to conventional services. The BMT model effectively incorporates Islamic social finance in its financing system to address the needs of poor households (Mahomed & Hydara, 2022: 298). Then, in serving nanofinance, besides Indonesia, several countries have emerged this service through microfinance institutions and rural banks. They provide services to low-income individuals and ultra-micro enterprises. Indeed, nanofinance brings a humanitarian mission consistent with the values of justice, inclusion, and compassion for the poor. However, interest-based nanofinance contradicts Shari'ah principles, so Islamic nanofinance must be operated on an interest-free and collateral-free basis, offering sustainable small loans for emergency needs (Musari, 2016: 10-11; Musari & Simanjuntak, 2016: 3-5). As a community-based Islamic microfinance institution, BMT can provide Islamic nanofinance also.
Qardhul Hasan	In Algeria, *qardhul hasan* becomes a contract *of zakah* funds in supporting underprivileged families, micro-enterprises, and generating employment opportunities for unemployed youth (Sayah & Musari, 2021: 34). In Indonesia, BMT channels financing to both members and non-members for productive ventures using various Islamic equity and debt structures, and may provide *qard* for emergencies (Mahomed & Hydara, 2022: 298).

continued on following page

Table 2. Continued

Instruments	Case Studies
Social *Takaful*	In Brunei Darussalam, Takaful Brunei Keluarga (TBK) offered complimentary COVID-19 special coverage to both new and existing participants of its protection and savings plans (The Scoop, 2021). As part of its efforts to help prevent the spread of COVID-19 and promote the safety of students and teachers, TBK also contributed 233 bottles of 500ml ethanol disinfectant (Takaful Brunei, 2020). In Egypt, Takaful and Karama (TKP) becomes a reform of social protection by providing not just a cash transfer programme targeted to extreme poor households, but also facilitating the integration of some social protection interventions/services in place to help the most vulnerable groups (UNICEF, 2019; p. 8). Its cash transfer initiative was introduced in 2015, where Takaful provides conditional cash assistance to low-income families with children, requiring beneficiaries to ensure school attendance and routine health check-ups, meanwhile Karama offers unconditional cash support to vulnerable groups such as low-income orphans, the elderly, and individuals with disabilities (Hteit, 2023). Across the country, beneficiaries of the conditional (Takaful) and unconditional (Karama) cash transfer programs comprise impoverished women and children, individuals with disabilities, orphans, and widows living in poverty (World Bank, 2020). In Malaysia, the mySalam B40 Takaful Protection Scheme is a government-funded takaful initiative designed to provide free protection for the B40 group—the bottom 40 percent of households earning below RM5,250 per month. This segment includes low-income people who depend significantly on the support of the government through cash transfers, healthcare services, and basic needs subsidies (https://www.mysalam.com.my/mys/info/?url=intro). Moreover, the mySalam Community Protection Takaful is a Shariah-compliant programme held before the pandemic and provides free takaful health coverage for 6.8 million eligible Malaysians at that time (Hassan & Muneeza, 2022; p. 45).
Hibah & Social Donations	In Australia, a disability support provider that collaborates with the National Zakat Foundation (NZF), Hiba Healthcare, is to assist clients, particularly within the Muslim community, in navigating the National Disability Insurance Scheme (NDIS) program and utilizing *zakah* funds for disability care in the form of *hibah* to provide the gift of ability, compassion and inclusion to the participants, their families, and carers by educating and supporting them to be enabled and empowered to achieve confidence and independence (https://hibahealthcare.com.au, https://www.nzf.org.au/partner/hiba-healthcare)

Source: Compiled by Author

Collectively, Table 2 demonstrates that Islamic social finance mobilization serves as a strategic multidimensional tool for socio-economic development, bridging material needs with the spiritual obligation of caring for others, potentially offering a viable framework for addressing the challenges of the economy of loneliness that can be leveraged beyond Muslim communities. Indeed, Islamic social finance instruments are not only mechanisms for wealth redistribution but also platforms for strengthening solidarity, resilience, and social inclusion. By financing micro-enterprises, empowering local communities, promoting a green and circular economy, supporting education and healthcare, and providing disability services, these instruments demonstrate their capacity to alleviate poverty while combating isolation and marginalization.

Thus, it can be stated that the result of the selected case studies are consistent with a study that Islamic social finance has been instrumental in mitigating the effect of the pandemic by attending to economic and social welfare and ameliorate the suffering of communities through various programmes across countries (AbdulKareem et al., 2021; p. 60). However, as Razak and Dawami (2019; pp. 42-43) have noted, the latter's effectiveness and efficiency are hampered by problems including weak governance standards, relatively low human resource capacity, inadequate disclosure and transparency mechanisms, and lack of sound funding structures. Nevertheless, the selected case studies in Algeria, Indonesia, Malaysia, Pakistan, Egypt, Brunei Darussalam, Palestine, and Australia may illustrate the transformative potential of Islamic social finance instruments in addressing both material deprivation and social disconnection from individualism to community.

CONCLUSION

Good prosperity, good income, high technology, and increasing life expectancy have led to greater social disconnection. Capitalism has transformed loneliness into a market commodity, and social isolation is rapidly spreading due to the growing "loneliness" economy and its growing industries. This phenomenon harms the mental well-being of both individuals and society, increasing the cost of economic care and reducing overall productivity. No doubt, the structural and systemic aspects of loneliness, as well as social disintegration and isolation, represent a paradox of contemporary society. People are beginning to recognize the health impacts of loneliness, the economic consequences of social isolation, and social fragmentation as a public health crisis. For this reason, social connections, local community support, counseling, and real-world community engagement activities, aimed at reducing the commodification of loneliness, guide for addressing and mitigating the loneliness economy. To improve the social connection, a shift from individualism to community is essential to foster collective social responsibility.

Islamic social finance holds the potential to develop unique mechanisms in revitalizing the loneliness economy by enabling human compassion and social interconnectedness. It connects core human social needs and the emotion of empathy to build social bonds that can foster strong, cohesive, and prosperous communities. Islamic social finance has mechanisms that seamlessly integrate the spiritual, humanitarian, and socio-economic dimensions of human existence, based on the principles of solidarity, altruism, and brotherhood. This instrument is not merely a redistributive tool, but is designed to stimulate social reciprocity, trust, and cohesion at the community level. As demonstrated in case studies from Australia, Brunei Darussalam, Algeria, Indonesia, Malaysia, Pakistan, and Palestine, and other documented examples, social finance, when mobilized efficiently and effectively, can serve multiple purposes, including poverty alleviation, expanding educational and health opportunities, and promoting active and caring environmental leadership as a mechanism to combat social isolation.

Islamic social finance constructively focuses on human development rather than commodification through its unique social framework within the financial system. Indeed, Islamic social finance primarily aims to address chronic social exclusion and economic poverty. The primary focus is collective participation, shared responsibility, and community-based financial isolation. Islamic social finance addresses poverty and aims to reverse economic decline and chronic social exclusion, not only by redistributing the wealth but also by eliminating social disconnection. Thus, the mission of Islamic social finance is not only to tackle poverty but also to build and facilitate isolated civil and social communities.

POLICY RECOMMENDATIONS

There are several key policy recommendations for policymakers, practitioners, and other stakeholder in managing Islamic social finance to address the loneliness economy. These recommendations can also be replicated by other faith-based and non-faith-based social finance institutions.

First, strengthen the governance of Islamic social finance, including faith-based and other non-faith-based social finance, to increase transparency and accountability to build trust by improving disclosure and reporting standards.

Second, leverage digital platforms for crowdfunding & distribution to reach underserved communities more effectively, and utilize blockchain and/or financial technology solutions to improve traceability, efficiency, and donor confidence.

Third, integrate Islamic social finance, including other faith-based social finances, with public health and social policies, national health and social prescribing initiatives, and then link to programs that reduce loneliness and social isolation, including disability support services.

Fourth, promote multi-sector partnerships by linking Islamic social finance institutions, including other faith-based social finance, with government, NGOs, and private sector actors to co-create community programs or community-oriented solutions. In other words, encourage partnerships that bridge faith-based initiatives with broader social infrastructure investments.

Fifth, embed sustainability and inclusivity by prioritizing green, circular economy, and socially inclusive projects funded by Islamic social finance, then do monitoring, evaluation, and impact assessment by institutionalizing systems for measuring the social and economic impact of Islamic social finance projects, and to refine policies, attract more donors, and ensure alignment with *maqasid al-shari'ah* and Sustainable Development Goals (SDGs).

REFERENCES

AbdulKareem, I. A., Mahmud, M. S., Elaigwu, M., & Abdul Ganiyy, A. F.AbdulKareem. (2021). Mitigating the effect of covid-19 on the society through the Islamic social finance. [JMTP]. *The Journal of Management Theory and Practice*, *2*(1), 56–61. DOI: 10.37231/jmtp.2021.2.1.83

Adshade, M., Khameneh, N. H., & Card, K. (2024, July 31). What are the economic costs of loneliness? *Social Connection Guidelines,* https://www.socialconnection guidelines.org/en/evidence-briefs/what-are-the-economic-costs-of-loneliness

Ahmad, A. U. F., & Habib, F. (2013). *Role of zakah in poverty alleviation through redistributive justice.* World Universities Islamic Philanthropy Conference 2013 'Nurturing Research Culture for Ummah Well Being' held by Institut Kajian Zakah (IKAZ) Malaysia, December 4th-5th.

Al-Suwailem, S. (2020). Foreword. In IRTI IDB, *Islamic Social Finance Report 2020.* Islamic Research and Training Institute, Islamic Development Bank (IRTI IDB).

Aljarah, A., Ibrahim, B., Hazzam, J., & Alam, F. (2025). Isolation marketing: social isolation and virtual gift donation intention. *Management Decision,* ahead-of-print(ahead-of-print). DOI: DOI: 10.1108/MD-07-2024-1685

Ascarya. (2006). Akad dan produk bank syariah: konsep dan praktek di beberapa negara [Islamic banking contracts and products: concepts and practices in several countries]. Bank Indonesia.

Atiq- ur- Rehman. (2019). A critical appraisal of Islamic finance in the light of the maqasid al- Shariʿah. In Cattelan, V. (Ed.), Islamic social finance: Entrepreneurship, cooperation and the sharing (pp. 35-51). Routledge.

BAZNAS. (2024). *Policy Brief: Zakat on fisheries as an alternative solution to poverty alleviation for fishermen and coastal communities.* Center for Strategic Studies - National Amil Zakat Agency (Puskas BAZNAS).

Billah, M. M. (2019). Zakah: its micro- entrepreneurship model and socio- humanitarian impact. In Cattelan, V. (Ed.), *Islamic social finance: Entrepreneurship, cooperation and the sharing* (pp. 199–209). Routledge.

Biswas, A. (2023, December 2). View: There's a growing loneliness economy to tap. *The Economic Times,* https://economictimes.indiatimes.com/opinion/et-commentary/view-theres-a-growing-loneliness-economy-to-tap/articleshow/105683519.cms ?from=mdr

Cahyanti, I. S., Ulfa, U., & Suhendi, E. (2024). How Islamic social finance boosts psychological well-being? *SHARE Jurnal Ekonomi dan Keuangan Islam 13*(2), 415-437. .DOI: 10.22373/share.v13i2.19998

Card, K., Yu, C., Refol, J., Frost, A., & Bombaci, P. (2023, February 9). How does loneliness affect health? *Social Connection Guidelines,* https://www.socialconnectionguidelines.org/en/evidence-briefs/how-does-loneliness-affect-health

Cattelan, V. (2019a). Introduction: Islamic social finance and the importance of roots. In Cattelan, V. (Ed.), *Islamic social finance: Entrepreneurship, cooperation and the sharing* (pp. 1–7). Routledge.

Cattelan, V. (2019b). Experiences in translation: Islamic finance and the sharing economy. In Cattelan, V. (Ed.), *Islamic social finance: Entrepreneurship, cooperation and the sharing* (pp. 71–92). Routledge.

Chapra, M. U. (2008). *The Islamic vision of development in the light of maqasid al-shariah.* The International Institute of Islamic Thought (IIIT).

DEKS-BI & P3EI-FE UII (2016). *Pengelolaan zakat yang efektif: Konsep dan praktik di beberapa negara [Effective zakat management: Concepts and practices in several countries].* Department of Islamic Economics and Finance - Bank Indonesia (DEKS-BI).

DEKS-BI & DES-FEB UNAIR (2016). *Wakaf: Pengaturan dan tata kelola yang efektif [Waqf: Effective regulation and governance].* Department of Islamic Economics and Finance - Bank Indonesia (DEKS-BI).

Engel, L., Rizal, M. F., Clifford, S., Faller, J., Lim, M. H., Le, L. K., Chatterton, M. L., & Mihalopoulos, C. (2025). An updated systematic literature review of the economic costs of loneliness and social isolation and the cost effectiveness of interventions. *PharmacoEconomics, 43*(9), 1047–1063. DOI: 10.1007/s40273-025-01516-w PMID: 40524124

Fauzia, I. Y., & Musari, K. (2021). Waqf crowdfunding for financing the MSMEs: Evidence from ASEAN-3. In de Pablos, P. O., Zhang, X., & Almunawar, M. N. (Eds.), *Handbook of research on disruptive innovation and digital transformation in Asia* (pp. 37-49). IGI Global. DOI: 10.4018/978-1-7998-6477-6.ch003

Goldstein, S. (2025, October 10). Welcome to the loneliness economy. *Psychology Today,* https://www.psychologytoday.com/us/blog/raising-resilient-children/202510/welcome-to-the-loneliness-economy

Hassan, M. K., & Muneeza, A. (2022). *Covid-19 and Islamic Finance*. Cambridge University Press. DOI: 10.1017/9781009189484

Hassan, M. K., Muneeza, A., & Sarea, A. (2022). Introduction. In Hassan, M. K., Muneeza, A., & Sarea, A. (Eds.), *Covid-19 and Islamic Social Finance* (pp. 1–6). Routledge. DOI: 10.1017/9781009189484

Heim, C. (2023). Resilient relationships versus hyper-individualism: Selfish genes, altruism, and attachment. In Heim, C., & Heim, C. (Eds.), *Resilient relationships: Techniques for surviving hyperindividualism, social isolation, and a mental health crisis* (pp. 17–48). Routledge. DOI: 10.4324/9781003263395-3

Hilbrich, S. (2021). What is social finance? Definitions by market participants, the EU taxonomy for sustainable activities, and implications for development policy. Discussion Paper Deutsches Institut für Entwicklungspolitik (DIE)/ German Development Institute 29/2021.

Holt-Lunstad, J. (2021). Loneliness and social isolation as risk factors: The power of social connection in prevention. *American Journal of Lifestyle Medicine, 15*(5), 1–7. DOI: 10.1177/15598276211009454 PMID: 34646109

Hortulanus, R., & Machielse, A. (2006). The issue of social isolation. In Hortulanus, R., Machielse, A., & Meeuwesen, L. (Eds.), *Social isolation in modern society* (pp. 3–12). Routledge. DOI: 10.4324/9780203020142

Hteit, R. (2023, June 4). *Takaful and karama: cash transfer programs for marginalized groups (2015–ongoing).* https://www.sdg16.plus/policies/takaful-and-karama-cash-transfer-programs-for-marginalized-groups

International Waqf Fund. (n.d). *What is Waqf?* https://waqf.org/what-is-waqf/

Iqbal, Z., & Mirakhor, A. (2011). An introduction to Islamic finance: Theory and practice, 2nd Edition. John Wiley & Sons (Asia). DOI: 10.1002/9781118390474

IRTI IDB. (2020). *Islamic Social Finance Report 2020.* Islamic Research and Training Institute, Islamic Development Bank (IRTI IDB).

Islamic Relief. (n.d). *Sadaqah.* https://islamic-relief.org/sadaqah/

Ismail, A. G., & Posummah, B. (2010). *Qardhul hasan principles applied to micro finance facilities*. Working Paper in Islamic Economics and Finance No. 1021, Research Center for Islamic Economics and Finance, Universiti Kebangsaan Malaysia (UKM). https://www.ukm.my/ekonis/wp-content/uploads/2021/02/Qardhul-Hasan-Principles-Applied-to-Micro-Finance-Facilities.pdf

Khan, A. A. (2008). *Islamic microfinance: Theory, policy and practice.* Islamic Relief Worldwide.

Khan, M. A. (2007). *Islamic economics and finance: A glossary*. Routledge International Studies in Money and Banking.

Kiliç, S., & Daldal, K. M. (2024). Economy of loneliness and consumer behavior. *Finans Politik & Ekonomik Yorumlar*, (667), 147–173.

Korhonen, V. (2024, July 5). Average size of households in the U.S. 1960-2023. Statista, https://www.statista.com/statistics/183648/average-size-of-households-in-the-us/

Kung, C. S. J., Pudney, S. E., & Shields, M. A. (2022). Economic gradients in loneliness, social isolation and social support: Evidence from the UK Biobank. *Social Science & Medicine*, *306*(115122), 1–14. DOI: 10.1016/j.socscimed.2022.115122 PMID: 35751988

Letón, S. L. (2025, June 22). Your loneliness is our business: The multi-million-dollar industry of social isolation. *EL PAÍS,* https://english.elpais.com/economy-and-business/2025-06-22/your-loneliness-is-our-business-the-multi-million-dollar-industry-of-social-isolation.html

Lim, M. H., Hennessey, A., Qualter, P., Smith, B. J., Thurston, L., Eres, R., & Holt-Lunstad, J. (2025). The KIND Challenge community intervention to reduce loneliness and social isolation, improve mental health, and neighbourhood relationships: An international randomized controlled trial. *Social Psychiatry and Psychiatric Epidemiology*, *60*(4), 931–942. DOI: 10.1007/s00127-024-02740-z PMID: 39158741

Mahomed, Z. (2022). Assessing financing for healthcare infrastructure in Sub-Saharan Africa: can Islamic finance assist? In Hassan, M. K., Muneeza, A., & Sonko, K. N. M. (Eds.), *Islamic finance in Africa: The prospects for sustainable development* (pp. 167–192). Edward Elgar.

Mahomed, Z., & Hydara, M. (2022). Applying an integrated Islamic social finance model for the empowerment of women farmers in the Gambia. In Hassan, M. K., Muneeza, A., & Sonko, K. N. M. (Eds.), *Islamic finance in Africa: The prospects for sustainable development* (pp. 287–306). Edward Elgar.

Modéer, U. (2018, October 13). Unlocking Islamic social finance to help communities address vulnerability and inequality. *United Nations Development Programme (UNDP),* https://www.undp.org/speeches/unlocking-islamic-social-finance-help-communities-address-vulnerability-and-inequality

Mohsin, M. I. A., & Muneeza, A. (2025). *Inclusive finance: Bridging communities through Islamic social finance*. Edward Elgar. DOI: 10.4337/9781035348770

Musari, K. (2016). *Redefining the Islamic nanofinance and its institutional strengthening: Lesson learned from Asian countries.* A paper was presented at 11th International Conference on Islamic Economics and Finance (ICIEF) "Rethinking Islamic Economics and Finance: Paving The Way Forward for Inclusive and Sustainable Development", Kuala Lumpur, October 11th-13th.

Musari, K. (2019). Promoting qard al-hasan in nanofinance to counter the moneylender in Southeast Asia. *Studia Islamica, 26*(1), 1–16. DOI: 10.15408/sdi.v26i1.5990

Musari, K. (2020). Islamic nanofinance for the very poor by women, hopes for addressing the Islamic microfinance gap. In Azid, T., & Ward-Batts, J. L. (Eds.), *Economic empowerment of women in the Islamic world: Theory and practice* (pp. 265–286). World Scientific Publishing. DOI: 10.1142/9789811212154_0013

Musari, K. (2023). Twinning the green transition and digitalization on the Islamic philanthropy institutions: Evidence in Indonesia. In de Pablos, P. O., Almunawar, M. N., & Anshari, M. (Eds.), *Perspectives on the transition toward green and climate neutral economies in Asia* (pp. 274–285). IGI Global. DOI: 10.4018/978-1-6684-8613-9.ch016

Musari, K. (2025). *From isolation to solidarity: Islamic philanthropy in addressing the loneliness economy in the age of disconnection.* A paper presented at Symposium on Contemporary Muslim Philanthropy held by Management Research Center (MRC) Faculty of Economics and Business Universitas Indonesia (FEB UI) in collaboration with the Muslim Philanthropy Initiative (MPI) Indiana University's Lilly Family School of Philanthropy, Yogyakarta – Indonesia, October 15th-16th.

Musari, K., & Fathorrazi, M. (2021). Islamic helix approach, the Islamic social finance partnership models for MSMEs: Lesson learned from Indonesia. In Azid, T., Mukhlisin, M., Akbar, N., & Tahir, M. (Eds.), *Monetary policy, Islamic finance, and Islamic corporate governance: An international overview* (pp. 303–322). Emerald Publishing Limited. DOI: 10.1108/978-1-80043-786-920211017

Musari, K., & Simanjuntak, R. (2016). Nanofinance, redefinition of microfinance For the very micro society through philanthropy linkage program (case study in Indonesia, Cambodia, Thailand, India). *[AARJSH]. Asian Academic Research Journal of Social Sciences and Humanities*, *3*(4), 455–463.

Nur, A. M., & Bin-Nashwan, S. A. (2022). The potential of cash waqf for poverty alleviation in Somalia. In Hassan, M. K., Muneeza, A., & Sonko, K. N. M. (Eds.), *Islamic finance in Africa: The prospects for sustainable development* (pp. 222–234). Edward Elgar.

Obaidullah, M., & Khan, T. (2008). *Islamic microfinance development: Challenges and initiatives.* Policy Dialogue Paper No. 2. Islamic Research and Training Institute (IRTI) Islamic Development Bank (IDB).

Omar, M. A. (2022). Foreword. In Hassan, M. K., Muneeza, A., & Sarea, A. (Eds.), *Covid-19 and Islamic Social Finance* (pp. xx–xxi). Routledge.

Patel, P. (2023, July 29). The loneliness economy: How capitalism thrives on isolation. *Medium,* https://whatsuppiyush.medium.com/the-loneliness-economy-how-capitalism-thrives-on-isolation-76ccc8c4b93e

Pietrabissa, G., & Simpson, S. G. (2020). Psychological consequences of social isolation during covid-19 outbreak. *Frontiers in Psychology*, *11*, 2201. DOI: 10.3389/fpsyg.2020.02201 PMID: 33013572

Ray, A. K. (2008). Self-help groups, micro finance, and political economy. In Deb, B. J., Sengupta, K., & Ray, B. D. (Eds.), *Globalization and north east India* (pp. 21–36). Concept Publishing Company.

Razak, D. A., & Dawami, Q. (2019). *Achieving Islamic social finance goals through zakah, waqf, and sadaqa in selected countries: Issues and challenges.* In Proceedings of the 7th ASEAN Universities International Conference on Islamic Finance (7th AICIF 2019) - Revival of Islamic Social Finance to Strengthen Economic Development Towards a Global Industrial Revolution, 38-45. DOI: 10.5220/0010114500380045

Rohmah, U. A., & Harsya, R. M. K. (2023). Community economic empowerment through infaq and sadaqah in LAZISMU cirebon regency sharia economic law perspective. *Mu'amalah. Jurnal Hukum Ekonomi Syariah*, *2*(2), 173–187. DOI: 10.32332/muamalah.v2i2.7844

Rowe, K. T. (2015). Preface. In Rowe, K. T. (Ed.), *Social isolation, participation and impact on mental health* (pp. vii-x). Nova Publisher.

Sayah, F., & Musari, K. (2021). Reviving zakah for micro-financing and socio-economic development in Algeria. [IJAZ]. *International Journal of Zakah*, *6*(3), 23–40. DOI: 10.37706/ijaz.v6i3.356

Schofield, P. (2025, July 23). The Viewpoint: The loneliness economy – could emotional connection become a competitive advantage? *Royal London Asset Management,* https://www.rlam.com/uk/institutional-investors/our-views/2025/the-viewpoint-the-loneliness-economy--could-emotional-connection-become-a-competitive-advantage/

Stiglitz, J. E. (2006). *Making globalization work.* W W. Norton & Company.

Takaful Brunei. (2020). *Over 200 bottles of disinfectants donated*, https://takafulbrunei.com.bn/news/over-200-bottles-of-disinfectants-donated

The Scoop. (2021). T*akaful Brunei Keluarga Provides Free COVID-19 Coverage*, https://thescoop.co/2021/09/23/takaful-brunei-keluarga-provides-free-covid-19-coverage

Thomas, E. (2025, July 16). The loneliness economy: How isolation became profitable – And what humanists must do about it. *The Humanist,* https://thehumanist.com/commentary/the-loneliness-economy-how-isolation-became-profitable-and-what-humanists-must-do-about-it/

UNICEF. (2019). *Reform of social protection in Egypt: Takaful and Karama Programme (TKP), A pro-women programme*. https://www.unicef.org/mena/reports/reform-social-protection-egypt

van de Stadt, F. (2025, July 13). The loneliness economy: How capitalism turned our need for connection into a product. *Medium,* https://medium.com/@fvdstadt/the-loneliness-economy-how-capitalism-turned-our-need-for-connection-into-a-product-ae2bf8d6cec2

Wang, L., & Liu, X. (2020). *How loneliness creates economy.* 2020 International Conference on World Economy and Project Management (WEPM 2020), 11-16. https://clausiuspress.com/conferences/LNEMSS/WEPM%202020/20WEPM003.pdf

Whan-woo, Y. (2025, April 18). 'Loneliness economy' emerges as more Koreans live alone. *The Korea Times*, https://www.koreatimes.co.kr/economy/20250418/loneliness-economy-emerges-as-more-koreans-live-alone

WHO Commission on Social Connection. (2025). From loneliness to social connection: charting a path to healthier societies. World Health Organization (WHO).

World Bank. (2020, November 17). *Takaful and Karama: A social safety net project that promotes Egyptian women empowerment and human capital.* https://www.worldbank.org/en/results/2020/11/17/takaful-and-karama-a-social-safety-net-project-that-promotes-egyptian-women-empowerment-and-human-capital

Zakat Foundation of America. (2010, July 23). *The nature of infaq*. https://www.zakat.org/infaq-benefits-nature-infaq

Zakat Foundation of America. (2014, November 19). *The eight kinds of people who receive zakat.* https://www.zakat.org/the-eight-kinds-of-people-who-receive-zakat

Zakat Foundation of America. (2020, June 20). *What is sadaqah?* https://www.zakat.org/what-is-sadaqah

ADDITIONAL READING

Musari, K. (2020). Islamic nanofinance for the very poor by women, hopes for addressing the Islamic microfinance gap. In Azid, T., & Ward-Batts, J. L. (Eds.), *Economic empowerment of women in the Islamic world: Theory and practice* (pp. 265–286). World Scientific Publishing. DOI: 10.1142/9789811212154_0013

Musari, K. (2020). *Cash waqf linked sukuk, a new blended finance of fiscal instrument for sustainable socio-economic development: Lesson learned from Indonesia.* A paper was presented at 12th International Conference on Islamic Economics and Finance (ICIEF) "Sustainable Development for Real Economy", Istanbul, June 14th-20th.

Musari, K. (2025). Between esham and cash waqf linked sukuk to fiscal and development sustainability: Comparative analysis. In Başbay, M. M. (Ed.), *Islamic economics, growth, and development* (pp. 119–140). Routledge. DOI: 10.4324/9781003312864-10

Musari, K., Fajariyah, N. A., & Khotimah, K. (2023). Understanding the behavior of qardhul hassan borrowers in nano-entrepreneurship: A field experiment of Islamic nanofinance. In Rafiki, A., Pananjung, A. G., & Nasution, M. D. T. P. (Eds.), *Strategies and applications of Islamic entrepreneurship* (pp. 21–33). IGI Global. DOI: 10.4018/978-1-6684-7519-5.ch002

Musari, K., & Sayah, F. (2023). Islamic quadruple helix, social finance partnership for developing digital financial inclusion in Maghreb region. In Rafiki, A., Pananjung, A. G., & Nasution, M. D. T. P. (Eds.), *Strategies and applications of Islamic entrepreneurship* (pp. 67–82). IGI Global. DOI: 10.4018/978-1-6684-7519-5.ch005

Chapter 10
Islamic Approaches to Social Inclusion: Addressing the Economic, Political, and Demographic Drivers of Social Isolation

Naseem Akhter
https://orcid.org/0009-0002-7504-1715
Shaheed Benazir Bhutto Women University, Peshawar, Pakistan

ABSTRACT

This chapter analyses the global phenomenon of loneliness and the rise of the "loneliness economy" through Islamic social ethics and an integrative analytical framework. It examines microeconomic, macroeconomic, and political-economic aspects over a decade. At the micro level, Islamic teachings such as Ukhuwwah, Silat al-Rahm, Zakat, Waqf, and Sadaqah are highlighted as means of meeting material needs and strengthening relational capital, countering commodified social bonds. At the macro level, it considers social isolation as a cost to productivity and healthcare, showing how mosques, families, and communal responsibilities reduce alienation. Politically, it critiques neoliberalism and consumerist individualism, proposing Islamic values, Shura, Maslaha, and Adl, to foster inclusive, just, and interdependent communities.

INTRODUCTION

Social isolation has become one of the key socio-historical phenomena of the twenty-first century, and it has a particularly pronounced impact on human health,

DOI: 10.4018/979-8-3373-5811-6.ch010

well-being, community outcomes, and can be taken as an important socio-economic indicator (Holt-Lunstad, 2021). Scholars believe that loneliness and social isolation are not primarily affective states but rather predominantly structural phenomena that emerge out of labour market practices, urbanisation and changing preferences about discrimination (Cacioppo & Cacioppo, 2018; Klinenberg, 2016). Despite the explosion of social isolation literature in recent years, the field of infection control is still influenced by secular constructs with very little room for religious and moral traditions to act (Smith, 2020).

One exception to this discourse is the social inclusion in Islam. Islamic teachings and social ethics in practice give great importance to life in the world as well as in the hereafter. Other care networks (such as *Ukhuwwah* (brotherhood), *Silat al-Rahm* (kinship ties), and charitable institutions such as *zakat, waqf, and sadaqah*) are based on an ideological conception of care, which captures an economic and affective aspect of belonging (Kamali, 2011; Zaman, 2019). These processes are viable alternatives to market-based conceptions of social relations, which commodify social relations through investments in agency or virtual presence (Illouz, 2007).

Economic processes are also internally tied to political and demographic changes, such as urban disaffiliation, migrations, and population ageing, therefore constrained by precarious labour conditions and income inequalities (Putnam, 2000; Victor & Pikhartova, 2020). These structural distortions are systematically counteracted by ethically based mechanisms, namely Islamic *Shura* (consultation), *Maslaha* (public interest), *Adl* (justice), which lead to ensuring equity, accountability and inclusion of villages and communities in decision-making (Esposito, 2018). Such mechanisms make it easier for society to evolve by reducing the effects of social distortions and increasing resilience through the dependence on the members of that community and the practices within the community based on the principles of equality and responsibility.

The chapter questions the way that Islamic thinking engages with social inclusion, imbricated in broader economic, political and demographic dimensions of social marginalisation. Drawing upon theories of theology, economics, and political sociology, the authors maintain that the need for Islamic ethics to evolve, and this need for evolution, should provide a normative model of leadership and pragmatics for the creation of envisaged societies in Pakistan and the contemporary world.

Objectives and Research Structure

The chapter aims to examine the phenomenon of loneliness by considering it in terms of Islamic theology and ethics. These objectives guide the analysis.

1. To view isolation as a spiritual and social state according to Islamic theology.

2. Integrate Islamic ethics with micro- and macroeconomic thinking to establish social isolation as a challenge that has both material and moral implications.
3. To investigate the exploitation of interpersonal connections and market-based alternatives to friendship.
4. For a critical analysis of Islamic teachings in support of care, belonging, and social responsibility that are not market-based.
5. To study the effects of loneliness on macroeconomics, public health, labour productivity and social.
6. To take over Islamic social establishments such as the mosque, *Zakat, Waqf and Sadaq.*, as potential hedges against disconnection costs.
7. To investigate political and economic structures that alienate people and to offer Islamic options based on principles of justice and responsibility for the community.

Research Gap and Significance

Essentially, scholarship on social isolation is founded on secular paradigms and tends to disregard religious or faith-based paradigms, which have historically been the driving force behind community cohesion. The literature on psychological, medical, and economic aspects of loneliness is extensive; however, little attention has been paid to Islamic social ethics as a comprehensive response mechanism.

By highlighting Islamic principles like *Ukhuwwah* (brotherhood), *Silat al-Rahm* (ties of kinship), and institutional frameworks such as *Zakat, Waqf, and Sadaqah*, this chapter seeks to close this gap. Care and solidarity are positioned within religious, ethical, and communal obligations, which distract from changing human relationships. By highlighting the importance of Islamic ethics as a forum for debate on religion, the chapter also offers an effective approach to address the current state of isolation.

LITERATURE REVIEW: THEORETICAL FOUNDATIONS

Secular Perspectives on Social Isolation

The academic literature on social isolation has grown significantly over the past decades and includes cross-disciplinary research papers that are attempting to explain the multidimensionality of the inclination and its adverse implications in terms of the development of the psychological state of an individual, their financial condition, health condition, and societal health outcomes.

It has been recorded that the civic and other types of community involvement in the United States including civic education drastically reduced a conclusive work of

Alexis de Tocqueville at the time of originally documented views followed by subsequent expounding on the works on the subject by Harry, an additional scholar, J. Putnam in a book titled Bowling Alone (2000) which he terms as contraction of trust and compromising the social frameworks that anchor individual existence within community.

Furthering this history, Twenge (2017) flavors the assumption of a cumulative rise in individual existential solitude among modernised people as well as the intercessoristic rate of depression in the demographic, according to which an appreciable segment is debilitated by mental illness and demonstrates a definitive decline in the potential of face-to-face communication.

At the personal level, both studies of Cacioppo and Patrick (2008) assert that loneliness is a biological phenomenon, which reveals that chronic isolation can provoke similar physiological mechanisms alongside autonomy and inflammation as does physical injury.

They thus argue that loneliness is not a social inconvenience but rather a serious and deadly concern in population health.

A meta-analytic study, as described by Holt-Lunstad et al. (2015), supported this viewpoint by determining the risk to mortality linked with loneliness to be identical to that of fifteen cigarettes per day, therefore, necessitating the urgency of prioritising loneliness in the public-health policy dimensions.

The gravity of the problem is further proven by the economic analyses. In the United Kingdom in 2018, the Office for National Statistics estimated the annual economic cost of loneliness, which included absenteeism, decreased productivity, and extra spending on healthcare, among others, to be about 1.5 billion pounds per year.

These kinds of fiscal constituents eventually led to the creation of a ministerial portfolio focusing on the topic of loneliness in the UK government in 2018, and the fact that institutions are urgently trying to address social isolation (Steptoe et al., 2013).

Recent literature suggests that social isolation is increased in various parts of the world including the societies with a majority of Muslim population and that its consequences go beyond the mental health to the economic productivity and stability in the community.

The official global surveys, including those provided by the World Health Organization in 2021 and the Organisation for Economic Co-operation and Development in 2023, demonstrate the increase of loneliness after the COVID-19 pandemic, and this process can be linked to demographic factors, the lack of social trust, and overpopulation in cities.

Similar evidence provided by the Pew Research Center (2020) and the United Nations Development Programme (2022) also records a shrink in community engagement in various Muslim settings. The synthesis of the findings will strengthen the analytical context and help to connect Islamic ethical models with the socio-economic patterns that can be observed.

ISLAMIC SOCIO-SPIRITUAL POLICIES OF PERSONAL IMBIBITION

The Qur'anic Foundations

According to the Quran, social cohesion is a precept on which the well-being of individuals is based. Verse 3:103 exhorts believers to "hold firmly to the rope of Allah all together and do not become divided" (The Qur'an, 3:103). The rope symbol represents how believers are joined. Surah Al-Anam (49:13) reflects on the unity of humanity and confirms that such an activity as social interaction is one of the natural attributes of human nature.

Prophetic Traditions

They are also reinforced by the literature of hadith that lays stress on solidarity, which is obligatory in the theological faith. Prophet Muhammad (PBUH) is quoted saying: he believers in their mutual kindness, compassion, and sympathy are just one body; when a limb suffers, the whole body responds with wakefulness and fever" (Bukhari, n.d.).With this reprimand, we can see an ethical dimension of interdependence at the social plane in the Islamic belief, portraying that one cannot be individually dissatisfied independently of wider existence.

Classical Jurisprudence

These tenets were expounded by the medieval Islamic scholars. Al-Ghazali (1997) assumed that isolation was a contravention of the design by God and the discouragement of innate sociability (*fitrah*). The idea of weakening ties between people triggering social decay was introduced by IbnÌkulthun in Al-Muajam al-Tarahm (1967/2015), who argued that the defence mechanism known as *asabiyyah* exerted a harmful effect on society, as modern sociologists would describe it as the disintegration of agencies.

Research Methodology

The current chapter offers the use of four main methodological dimensions to challenge the modern-day media representations.

Textual Analysis

The most important exegetic works of the Quran, including the commentaries on the Quran, like Tafsir al-Latif, and the classic treatises of jurisprudence, are discussed in order to establish the themes of justice, care, and communal well-being in general.

Comparative Case Studies

Muslim-majority contexts such as Pakistan, Indonesia, and Turkey are juxtaposed with Muslim minority contexts in the United Kingdom and Canada to assess how Islamic social ethics are mobilised to address loneliness and marginalisation.

Interdisciplinary Synthesis

The combination of a critical synthesis of results based on sociological, political-economic, public health, and development studies with methodological approaches that are based on Islamic disciplines would increase analytical rigour.

Critical Engagement

Crossroads between the secular and Islamic paradigms and crossroads among the Islamic paradigms are explained, and they guide the formulation of mechanisms aimed at policy integration.

UNDERSTANDING LONELINESS THROUGH AN ISLAMIC LENS

Under Islamic theology, man is always social in his nature, and he was created to live together and work with each other to help each other. Surah Al-Anam (49: 13) presents the Quranic injunctions which identify the core of diversity and the interaction among people, thus making loneliness a defiance of social stature, which has been ordered by God.

Continuing the ideas of Ibn Kulthun, and his concept of *asabiyyah*, and the ideas of Al-Ghazali in a thesis about the weakening of integration into social fabrics due to bond decay of relatives and friends, the view argues that decaying human relations are an antecedent to societal breakage and the resulting breakdown of community collectivises.

Traditionally, the functions of such institutes as *zakat, waqf, and sadaqah* were used as means of material and non-material solidarity that, being based not on kinship, gave highly stable inter-communal intertwining.

These schools of thought propagated the ideas of economic, psychological, and societal unity and criticised market alienation and market-driven related relationships, advocated the epochally and individually specific forms of relatedness and all-encompassing lifestyle interventions.

MICROECONOMIC DIMENSIONS: INDIVIDUAL AND HOUSEHOLD IMPACTS

The Commodification of Connection

Such intellectualisation of social disconnection between markets, what scholars have called the establishment of loneliness economy, indicates the extent to which markets have sought to embrace the essence of social distance itself. Today, therapeutic services, paid companionship and subscription friendship services focus on curing symptoms but not structural and communal isolation reasons (Illouz, 2007; Hochschild, 2012). Commodification of the human association that is advanced by such services is dangerous since it dehumanises the natural interaction and enables exchange of interaction that can be transactional in nature.

Islamic Thinking When It Comes to Economics

This commodification is opposite to the idea of *barakah* (divine blessing) and *Khidmah* (Serving other people), and Islamic economics foregrounds is challenge to this idea. The Holy Prophet Muhammad (PBUH) instructed that whoever deprives the sister of faith of acute affliction, Allah (SWT) will deprive him/ her of acute affliction, in the Hereafter and the world (Muslim, n.d.). By re-surdicting these kinds of teachings, care is re-branded as the business of the spirit and of civic endeavour rather than a person in the business of it, hence negating the stratification of the social arena in favour of commercial rationality (Kamali, 2011).

The Social Station Islamic Relational Process

***Ukhuwwah* (Brotherhood and Sisterhood)**: the Holy Quran and the Hadith hold that the believers are united in a spiritual fraternity and have a spiritual obligation to offer sympathy, support and help (The Quran, 49:10). One ethic that influences this sort of relational network and is not always dictated by kinship is called *Ukhuwwah*

(Brotherhood and Sisterhood). And is brought forward as a natural solution to the feeling of isolation (Al-Qaradawi, 1999).

Silat al-Rahm **(Kinship Ties):** Kin years maintenance is repeated in a continuum in the teaching of the Islamic religion according to which the nuclear family is pushed further into the extended family and the hierarchy of power as well (The Qur'an, 4:1). Such multigenerational systems and extended families no longer care about solitude particularly in the elderly (Al-Ghazali, 1997).

Communal Worship: Practices such as daily congregational prayers, weekly Jumuʿah gatherings, and Eid celebrations ensure regular opportunities for interaction and community-building. These ritualised encounters not only fulfil spiritual obligations but also integrate individuals into wider networks of solidarity (Esposito, 2018).

Gender: The experiential reality of inclusion among the Muslim communities is conditioned by gender issues; however, the involvement of women in the mosque-related affairs, welfare relationships, and informal care-taking continues to be under-represented. It has been shown that women play an important role, especially in social cohesion by engaging in community-learning groups, charitable activities, and neighbourhood support programs (Bano, 2017). When these views are taken into account, one has a more integral view of the Islamic way of social inclusion.

Social Inclusion Procedure: *Zakat*

The meaning of Zakat goes beyond its monetary aspect, though in most contexts it has been watered down to a limited practice. The Arabic root Z-K-W holds meanings of purification and increase, and therefore implies that Zakat purifies not just material resources but also social relations. According to Al-Qaradawi (1999), Zakat cleanses the individual donor while at the same time promoting collective solidarity and unity among members of society. In this regard, Zakat serves both as a religious practice and a means of fostering social cohesion. The contemporary analysis reveals how the reallocation of finance through the community could be considered under a community programme to enhance the social inclusion aspects, as witnessed in the Selangor *Zakat* Board projects in Malaysia. Here, not only do they support the beneficiaries financially, but also counselling, education, and skills training, and that is why it is easier to successfully reintegrate them into society (Rahman, 2015).

Conventional Uses of Zakat

- Redistribution of wealth
- Poverty alleviation
- Social stability
- Spiritual purification

Contemporary Applications

- Community integration programmes.
- Counselling and mental health services.
- Company development programmes.
- Social networking and frequently changing skills.

Waqf Institutions as Anchors of Community

History *Waqf* (religious endowments) is an institution that recognised and collected funds to be distributed to mosques, schools, hospitals, libraries and similar community advantageous endeavours (Singer, 2008). *Waqf* institutions, in contrast to modern organisations that were compelled to work without charity, were identifiable with a specific location, thereby establishing social stability and solidarity.

Colonialism had disturbed the *waqf* endowments, and it can be seen that an extension of this phenomenon was a decline or even the disappearance or incorporation of this bearer into the creation of states (Hoexter, 1998). In the 21st century, however, it has been some Muslim societies that have rejuvenated *waqf* systems themselves to fit new challenges. On one occasion, the Turkish Directorate of Religious Affairs oversees over 80,000 mosques that are described as the places of worship, learning, counselling and socialising; these are the so-called Third Spaces as introduced by Oldenburg (1999) and the Third Spaces where informal group life is advanced.

Phases of *Waqf* Institutions

Historical Period (7th -13th Century): Liberalisation (9th -16th Century) dad in hospitals, schools, libraries, and the welfare system.

Colonial Period (14th -20th Century): Organised centralisation or fragmentation, weakening of relationships among populations.

Modern Revitalisation (21st century): It is a combination of traditional and innovative services such as mental health, social programmes, and technological services.

Isolation of Society: Macroeconomics Implications

On the one hand, social segregation is inherited at the national level, and on the other, in a family. Not only did Holt-Lunstad et al. (2015) find that persistent loneliness predicts not only these 4 dynamics of death by a factor of 26, but also heightens the prevalence of depression, myocardial disease, cognitive impairment, and anxiety. These impediments to health cost people a fortune. Per the estimates, the US is estimated to spend up to $6.7 billion in Medicare reimbursements annually as a result of the conditions associated with loneliness alone (Flowers et al., 2017). Also, the UK government estimates that the issue of loneliness costs the economy about 32 billion pounds annually, lost productivity, absenteeism and expenditure on health care (Office for National Statistics, 2018).

These statistics demonstrate the uniqueness of loneliness as a macroeconomic problem, which needs to be solved within the system. Linking the society through the establishment of solidarity, redistributive justice and regulatory responsibility, Islamic economic establishments such as that of *Zakat and Waqf* help to mitigate the micro- and macro-cost of disconnection between the societies.

ISLAMIC SOCIAL INFRASTRUCTURE AS ECONOMIC BUFFER

Social institutions that offer Islamic care play a crucial role in countering the economic effects of isolation in society, in that they help in strengthening precautionary communal practices. Ordered groups of support like mosques, extended families, and religious obligations like *Zakat, Waqf, and Sadaqah* form a system of assistance that is classified to support social networks and assist citizens at a tender age who are prone to isolated life (Kahf, 2003; Al-Qaradawi, 1999). According to this integrated model, such institutions are both charged with spiritual and with social responsibility, providing material and emotional support to prevent the expensive health crises or societal crises, i.e., isolation.

Empirical research in highly Muslim settings has indicated a positive correlation between both strong Islamic social infrastructure and the lower incidence of subjective destitution, suicide, and physical illnesses involving the experience of social isolation. The comparative analysis of the empirical data presented by Hassan and Ahmad (2019a) establishes that: higher mosque density and economic activity of religious communities characterise Malaysian states with an exceptionally low utilisation of mental health services and corresponding costs. In parallel research, Al Tamburgholli, Al Khalili, and al-Qaydan (2010) have established that Kuwaiti families that were assimilated into a larger set of kinship enjoyed a resistant loneliness and stress protection, which is a documentary basis of the Islamic institutional structures. As a result, an investment in Islamic social infrastructure can have high social returns: a reduction in health spending and strengthening community resilience (Haque, 2018).

The short-term impact of social isolation on labour market participation and productivity at work is negative. Studies have shown that excluded individuals have higher absenteeism, reduced team building and turnover. The Harvard Business Review (2017) argues that remote employees are less engaged, less ambitious to get promoted, and more likely to resign prematurely, thus derailing individual career tracks and causing organisations and economies, respectively, significant productivity losses.

The workplace Islamic moral constructs tend to focus on and lay stress on collective interests. According to the Barakah concept, an office that is exemplary of a religious dedication and general goodness provides more productivity through the promotion of health and motivational capability of the staff (Beekun & Badawi, 2005). Key values like *Ihsan* (excellence), *Amanah* (trust), *Ta'awun* (cooperation) and Adl (justice) promote equality, collaboration and competence at workplaces. Observational research on Islamic banking and halal-certified commercial practices indicates a higher degree of employee satisfaction and lower employee turnover in the long term than businesses that have not embraced these values (Ali and Al-Owaihan, 2008, and Rice, 1999).

Social isolation should also be placed in the perspective of the transformation of larger political-economic processes. Urbanisation creates economic opportunities and at the same time breaks down old bonds that create anonymity and alienation (Putnam, 2000). Neoliberal systems have undermined the collective institutions, maybe favoring individual responsibility, market solutions and limited state intervention (Harvey, 2005). Spatial privatisation under federal authority, contraction or shrinking of labour and increased geographic mobility further prevent the reestablishment of social relationships and a revitalised community.

These changes serve to break the structures where the Islamic political theory anticipates national interest and national duty. *Maslaha* (public interest) is relevant in guiding policy makers to ensure as much as possible that community welfare is promoted, and *Shura* (consultation) is relevant in encouraging the life of communities, through empowerment (Kamali, 2008). The neoliberalism in such paradigms has alternatives that focus on inclusiveness, equality and making decisions based on communities.

Isolation of consumers caused by consumerism, intimating itself into individualism, is a sufficient cultural determinant that not only brings gratification in the form of material purchasing and commodification of relationships (Bauman, 2000). In this way, promoting emotional bonding covertly on commercial services, this model bolsters alienation. On the other hand, Chinese moral principles support collective contentment through encouraging reciprocal concern, collaboration, and bringing gifts, hence stressing social interdependency.

Tawhid (unity) is not limited to theological aspects but covers the organisation of society, whereby extreme individualism results in the brokenness of spirituality and fragmentation in society. Quranic notion of competition (Quran 5:48) transforms competition as striving to excel in good acts, hence a conflict between an individual and group interest and not individual selfishness. Examples of Islamic micro-financing models in modern usage are the Grameen Bank, microcredit in

Bangladesh, although not necessarily Islamic, which acts as a reflection of the solidarity principle through the concept of financial-social integration (Yunus, 2007). As the example of *Akhuwat* Foundation interest-free loans in Pakistan belongs to a series of Islamic finance, it serves to alleviate material poverty and strengthen social relationships (Mumtaz, 2022).

The recent development of digital technology has produced new isolation patterns, mainly in young people. Although digital religious material is a promising source of educational opportunities and a way to connect with friends, an overuse of digital media has been empirically linked to increased feelings of loneliness and reduced involvement in communal endeavors (Lim, 2020). At the same time, online study circles and virtual *khutbas* are examples of the adaptive practices of Islamic networks to changing social conditions (Campbell, 2021).

THE SOCIAL INCLUSION AND ISLAMIC RULES OF GOVERNANCE

Islamic tradition is rich in creating a governing model in the fore, therefore, performing the interactions among the community and the general welfare, unselfish justice. These do not refer to mere abstract theological concepts alone, but existential work-in-progress policies that define socio-political and economic models of Muslim societies. The three tenets of prayer are *Shura* (consultation), *Maslaha* (public interest), and *Adl* (justice), and that will form one comprehensive schema that will positively influence social inclusion, cushion alienation, and spearhead the inclusive ruling, which recognises everybody in the community. The transfer of these principles into addressing urgent problems in modern societies, such as the alienation of the cities, the presence of socioeconomic inequality, and the decline in civic confidence, is expected of modern Donna Courtioly (Kamali; El-affendi).

The concept of *Shura,* or consultative ruler, is conferred a conspicuous retreat into the mechanism of the Islamic states and necessitates the hearing of opinions of persons affected by policy making directly. After line after line the Holy Quran commands to think collectively: And they when thou (Thou hast ordained) are thought worthy, say unto thy lord and they make the prostration, and whence their dealings are nothing save talk among themselves (Q: 42: 38). It is also the participatory culture that ensures governance is not imposed in a top-down manner but rather it evolves in a form of civic activities that are substantive in nature (Al-Suwaidi, 2011). *Shura* also creates social cohesion by creating a stream through which marginalised groups can have a say in matters that affect them, in order to prevent alienation, which sets in when such groups are left behind during communal discussions. Empirical studies show that Shura-like institutions positively influence the level of confidence in a governance system and improvement in civil order in a society (Sardar, 2014).

The *Maslaha* or interest of the whole is also more than attributable to the consultation approach. Through this idea, follows the guidance that it is the task of policymakers to seek the common good of society rather than individual or corporate interest. Using the *maqashid al-sharify* (objectives of Islamic law) as the basis of its argument, the *Maslaha* gives a significant focus to the key basic human needs, namely faith, life, intellect, family, and property (Chapra, 2000). They come with this principle to an undisputed statement regarding the fact that when integrated within it, relating to social inclusion, policies should be viewed not only within the context of economic performance but should also be seen in how they operate towards the normal satisfaction of the social bond and the communal defence of a vulnerable population. Previously, authorities and lawyers used *Maslaha* when trying to restore peace and stability by using civil works (or non-discriminatory welfare programmes) (Opwis, 2010). The principle can be applied by modern policymakers in such areas as healthcare, housing and social security and, therefore, this feature could be useful in response to contemporary issues (Kamali, 2011).

The third pillar is *Adl* or justice, which requires a fair distribution of resources and equal treatment towards all members of the society. This is always evident in the Quran as God asks someone to do the right things: Indeed, Allah asks you to give people their portion and to judge the people justly. In politics, *Adl* makes them worry about structural inequalities which are founded on the wrong individuals, like the poor, women and minorities (Esposito and Voll, 2001). *Adl* serves as a bulwark for social reorientation, and through the institutionalisation of equity, *Adl* can ecologically heed meaningful participation to all. As presented in the empirical studies of the Muslim-dominant countries, Muslims and non-Muslims think that intense perceptions of equity and justice is connected with heightened civic trust and reduced degrees of social degradation (Hassan & Ahmad, 2019b).

In combination with the *Shura, Maslaha, and Adl* system, Islamic governance offers a model which directly addresses the causes of social isolation. It is an anti-mechanism against the atomising disposition of the neoliberal policy regimes; it ensures participatory representation, has a sense of collective good, and organises fair treatment into institutions. These are joined values to propagate the moral standards of human dignity and community soundness of community folks, major components of a successful society. Consequently, the Islamic rule is not only relevant in preserving an Islamic historical position, but it further provides a sense of how to restructure the existing frameworks of inclusiveness in policymaking (Afsaruddin, 2015).

One of the structures proposed by Islamic governance can be even conducive to social sustainability in the highly globalised and fast urbanised societies, where detachment and alienation are the order of the day. Cohesion of a society would be improved by Muslim societies through the use of consultative governance, investment or development of social cohesion through re-orienting participation, reduction of crisis in isolation and social cohesion. Moreover, the implications of these tenets extend beyond the cultural realms and thereby serve significant lessons to any polity of the necessity to embrace participatory governance as well as policies to provide fair justice, which necessitate the welfare-state. Thus, the Islamic governance does not simply presuppose a spiritually grounded contact but a functional system, also able to produce highly inclusive and strong societies (Mir, 2019).

Empirical Comparisons: The social isolation is different in various societies dominated by Muslims, depending on the urbanization, migration and household rearrangement processes. Comparative studies have shown that Malaysia is reporting a stronger community-based activity in relation to mosque-related activities, and Turkey is facing the loss of trust in relation to blistering urbanization, and Pakistan is facing isolation because of economic insecurity (Hasan and Mahmood, 2021; Yilmaz, 2022). These findings can be incorporated to give empirical evidence to the current chapter.

CASE STUDY: TURKEY'S SOCIAL COHESION INITIATIVES

The practical manifestation of the Islamic teachings can be viewed as an empirical example of the Republic of Turkey, where an Islamic ideal of Islamists is actively integrated into social structures to contribute to cohesiveness and reduce isolation. Religiously-founded Directorate, which manages over 80,000 mosques and community centres nationally, offers community counselling, education, and volunteer services to their community, thus playing a significant role as a communal integrator and counteracting social exclusion (Yilmaz, 2018). Here, the Diyanet becomes an entity of a dynamic, sacred and compensatory society in a stretch whereby the mosques are no longer places of prayer but rather fulfil the functions of ecosystems of stabilising the society.

The mahalle, and the Islamic vision of community life in the context of the contemporary city, is an inalienable part of the Turkish social structure. Traditionally, the mahalle, which is the smallest granular unit of the state of the totaal, was a combination of religious, social, and administrative life and the most basic building block of the Ottoman state. Such a heritage is being continued in modern mahalles, where social and culturally based operations and civic involvement are still to be established. It is assumed that the mahalle system will make the governing process more organised and bring about more trust, solidarity, and civic orientation among families and communities in well-organised neighbourhoods than in their less well-organised ones (Göle, 2013).

These centres provide diversified programmes, which deal with various layers of life in society. These community counselling services are early interventions for people who are stressed, anxious and lonely. Community networks of groups and volunteer pools are being formed through the elder care programmes to reduce the social isolation of patients with age. Young mentorship initiatives are supposed to have high objectives for youth, especially where there is a breakdown in a family setup. The interfaith dialogue platform, as reflected in the Turkish policy, aims to facilitate pluralism and tolerance between religious groups in a pluralist society (Kaya, 2015).

The efficacy of such programmes can be empirically proved. According to the national surveys, the perceived loneliness among the participants of mahalle programmes decreased by 40 per cent, civic engagement by 35 per cent and the indicator of health improved by 25 per cent (Turkish Statistical Institute, 2020). Even additional qualitative research validates the statement that interfaith connectivity is enhanced by community institutions and thus promotes cultural continuity, factored by the cautions of celebration, hospitality, and neighbourhood connections (Çınar, 2019).

Overall, the Turkish experience can be regarded as one of the most common examples of how the harm caused by the isolationist nature can be successfully addressed with the help of implementing Islamic principles of the social order in the modern systems of governance. An Islamic and welfare infrastructure with well-integrated spiritual and social needs has been successfully built in Turkey to serve as a model whereby the spiritual and social needs are met under an integrated institutional framework. This case highlights the ability of faith-based organisations to offer economic and social solutions to the atomising pressures of neoliberal urbanism.

DEMOGRAPHIC VULNERABILITIES AND RESPONSES TO ISLAM

The most notable population issue that is facing modern societies is the rising percentage of the ageing population. The development of demographic transitions is occurring in many countries due to increasing longevity and declining fertility, making social welfare infrastructures atelic and exposing ageing adults to the possibility of social isolation (Harper, 2014). Third-age people are often pressed by a combination of such fragilities as declined physical condition, lack of social support systems through widowhood or loss of more active family members, and inability to use computer technology to support socially distant relationships (Victor

& Scharf, 2005). All of them increase the chances of being lonely and marginalised in late adulthood.

Commodification of elderly services has been the order of the day in contemporary times, where the care institutions have been coming up with fee-based programs. Even though these arrangements do not reflect exceptional needs that are not achieved through alternative systems, they pose a further problem of social fragmentation by isolating the older people to the family, neighbourhood, and cultural spheres they constitute (Estes and Phillipson, 2002). This model is representative of a market logic where efficiency is put over relational well-being and has thereby created a breakdown of intergenerational connections that form the backbone of the community. Thus, the phenomenon of ageing populations is not simply demographic but also moral and cultural in nature regarding the values embraced by the societies as well as by members of the elderly population.

Another paradigm, with many similarities to ideas developed in Islam, is founded on the principle of *Birr al-Walidayn* that extends the idea of filial piety to that of the whole community that has the duty to care about the well-being of elderly individuals. The scripture in Quran says that he or she should be benevolent and humble to parents: and be submissive of them the wing of submission of mercy and say, my Lord, have mercy to them who raised me in infancy, and which nourished me, till I became able to speak, o my Lord, have mercy to them, o my Lord, engage with them playing in caress, and worship him, O my Lord, receive them, o my Lord, with utmost good expectancies, o my Lord, honor them, o my Lord, playing in caress, and worship Combined with this verse along with many prophetic traditions, which equated parental nurturing to worship services, eldercare emerges not only as a religious obligation but also the need of society (Kamali, 2011). Unlike commodified models of eldercare, the Islamic model places the welfare of older adults into the context of families, communities, and faiths; thus, the voice of care is defined as a process of relationship rather than a market relationship.

These moral codes were institutionalised historically in Muslim societies by the long kinship ties and mutual support systems of the community. The ancestors were usually present in the form of large families that followed the old, who were the on-call memory persons regarding exchanging knowledge, settling disputes and preserving cultural practices (Barron, 1997). The elderly population did not avoid participating in the life of society; the infrastructure that was supported through religious endowments *(awqaf)* included hospices, and communities' centres made specifically to socialise with older adults (Singer, 2008). The activities fostered social activities that dignified the old as beings in society, as opposed to dependent ones.

The practices of Islamic eldercare can be seen in Islamic countries like Indonesia today. Research reveals that Islamic boarding schools, which used to focus on the religious education and upbringing of the younger generation, include programs of taking care of elderly adults in their schedule (Rahman, 2019). These projects attract the participation of older people in community education, spirituality and socialisation with students. The resulting dynamic becomes a win-win solution: the youth learn the wisdom and experience of life in old age, and the old receive a chance to retire as well as access to other people and community norms. These are some of the ways in which the Islamic values can be refined to the modern demographic reality needs without compromising on the unity across generations.

Overall, what Islamic strategies are doing to address the vulnerability posed by demographics is the focus on incorporating the spiritual, social, and cultural aspects of policy and practice. The Islamic buildings confront individualism and commodification of most of the current and established strategies by reducing their future consideration within relations, dyadic connections, and age deference. With individual societies around the world struggling to work out the consequences that a continuously ageing population could bring with it, the principles could provide valuable guidance on the creation of inclusive care models that could strengthen instead of weaken social solidarity.

MIGRATION AND DIASPORA INTEGRATION

Acculturation processes in the diaspora migration processes make the migrants vulnerable to a slow disappearance of social connectivity with the indigenous population. Muslim diasporic participants are often faced with limited access to culturally salient social services, institutionalised discrimination and biased views of their cultural identity (Cesari, 2009). These conditions incline the members of communities to feelings of exclusion and warrant the implementation of community-based interventions.

Contemporary policies of integration have been developed by these institutions of Diaspora Islam that ease interaction with the host society while protecting cultural identity. This is the reason why the Islamic Society of North America follows this trend and has been busy creating community centres where religious services are offered along with the teaching of the English language, vocational training, family counselling and interfaith dialogue programmes (Haddad, 2011). Through these activities, newcomers in their host societies are more likely to be integrated into their new communities, and understand each other better between Muslims and non-Muslim.

Mosques regularly become the centre of first-time settlement aid and housing services, job placement and increased access to vital services via networking among new and established members. These spaces are becoming cultural between-ness spaces that maintain Islamic identity but integrate skills and networks to further support integration. Societies thus find openings of civic merit and the interreligious cooperation, and in particular, hovering migrants have the impact of leaving a lasting mark on the religious groups they are involved in and on the community in which these religious organisations are immersed.

Poverty and Inequality in Economies are still present everywhere. Lack of affordable houses, access to social activities and existing economic insecurity contribute to inequity as they bring an escalation of stress within gendered relational processes (Wilkinson and Pickett, 2009). Isolation exacerbates poverty, further forming a self-perpetuating loop that cannot be overturned using traditional policy strategies.

The mechanisms introduced by Islamic economic responses are specifically anti-social (socially cohesive) and anti-material rather than anti-money. The myth of *takful*, mutual guarantee, involves collective liability and sets up economic relations guided by solidarity and not competition (Chapra, 1992). The way such an understanding of the meaning of wealth is viewed as a moral, spiritual duty reflects Islamic perceptions of economic justice and social solidarity.

The harm to social atomism may thereby be reduced, and the economic deprivation diminished with the use of empirical evidence based on Islamic micro-finance institutions. In contrast to the traditional micro-based models of finance, whereby, in most cases, interest is allowed and individual borrowing is encouraged, the Islamic model provides financial services through social networks, thus building upon trust and interdependence.

CASE STUDY: PAKISTAN'S AKHUWAT MODEL

An excellent example is the *Akhuwat* micro-finance network in Pakistan, in which economic interventions have been reoriented to Islamic values. The model encourages inclusion, as opposed to supporting social exclusion. *Akhuwat* is a privately owned credit network whose format is based on interest-free lending clubs, which are arranged in circles of mosques. The rituals of loan are performed on the day of the Friday prayer, and the signatures of the borrowing agreement are traditionally acquired by the community members (Shirazi, Obaidullah, & Haneef, 2015). The practice enables social relationships since those engaged in the practice report increased respect towards their neighbourhoods and religious groups.

The effectiveness of the programme is expressed in the empirical outcomes: over 99 per cent of the beneficiaries show that accountability mechanisms are entrenched in the community, which supports high loan repayment rates (Rafay et al., 2020). When members rethink the idea of borrowing as not a stigmatised behaviour but rather an acceptable one, the participants will feel more relatedness and less isolation. Through empowerment of millions of Pakistani families, *Akhuwat* has inspired other institutions to do the same in majorly-Muslim states like Afghanistan to show that Islamic teachings can be harnessed in modern economies.

POLICY OUTCOMES AND DATA

The most recent studies of the Islamic social finance are pointing out that the regular application of the *Zakat and Waqf* programmes will alleviate the isolation of poverty in the identified regions.

The systematic designation of *Zakat* as the basis of access to basic services, such as housing, health care, and access to community engagement opportunities, is proven by empirical research carried in Malaysia and Indonesia (Johari et al., 2019).

Moreover, community centres which are funded by *Waqf* not only offer practical goods but also reinforce local support systems among communities with low incomes (Sulaiman & Zakariyah, 2020).

EDUCATIONAL APPROACHES AND SOCIAL INTEGRATION

Schools are central to the process of creating social inclusion by creating a climate which gives prominence to interpersonal relationships, civic skills, and cultural education. However, in modern day, the educational systems that focus on standardised tests and personal success do not see through their role in building the community.

In Islamic pedagogy, *Tesbiyah*, which translates into total growth, does not only entail the ABC Cognitivism, but also the social, moral, and spiritual. The traditional *Halaqah* model provides an environment of collaborative learning, maintaining levels of relational attachments and collective responsibility amongst the players.

Modern Islamic secondary and post-secondary schools strongly feature community service and inter-religious dialogue training programs and civic engagement, therefore extending the reach of students to the larger community. According to the empirical evidence offered by Zine (2008), students attending Islamic established schools are found to be more socially connected and civically engaged compared to other students who attend traditional schools.

Spiritual and Mental Health

The interaction between societal isolation and mental health difficulties requires a practitioner to deal with psychological, spiritual, and social aspects of trauma at the same time. Mental-health services may be offered in conformity with the isolation they purport to reduce, as traditional mental-health services commonly tend to focus on individual therapy.

With the interplay between spiritual, social, and mental health, the Islamic mental-health models anticipate this view. Led by the philosophy of *Tazkiyah* (purification), these models assume that mental-health care involves the rehabilitation of every individual and all three facets of proper relations with the Divine, the community and the self.

Spiritual Practice: Hajj, *Khatamiyat* and recitation of the Quran frequently.

Social Support: Peer support groups and community support.

Family Integration: Improving the family relationships efficiently.

Service Engagement: Community and volunteerism.

Professional Care: Competency-based therapeutic intervention.

Community and Technology: Community Digitalising.

The usefulness of digital technology poses some opportunities and some challenges to the Islamic ideas of social inclusion. As much as social media and the World Wide Web can expand geographic distance and connect people to other communities, they also lead to the development of superficial connections that do not stand in support of the knowledge and devotion that is regarded as the key to Islamic social ethics.

Some useful examples of technology application in the Islamic institutions are virtual *Halaqah* study circles, online zakat sites which connect the donor to the recipient, or even mobile applications to manage community services available at the mosques. It is important to note that these technologies are used to complement and not to replace face-to-face interactions.

Islamic Community e-Tools

- Prayer time applications with the involvement of community features.
- Discussion group sites on the study of the Holy Quran.
- The *Zakat* calculators were connected with the local distribution network.
- Applications that give information about Mosques in the community.
- Islamic counselling group support applications.
- Electronic incorporation of Islamic principles into social systems.

Such digital instruments expedited use during the COVID-19 pandemic, showing how effective they might be and how constrained they may be in terms of supporting the connection between the community within the context of physical distancing needs.

RECOMMENDATIONS AND RESULTS

Culturally Responsible Social Policy: Interventions aimed at curing social isolation successfully should respect and integrate various cultural paradigms defining the notions of community, belonging and care. Archetypal strategies are likely to fail where the communities deviate from the predominant secularist orientations.

In the models associated with Islamic solutions, there are views of various policy orientations that can contribute to the improvement of social inclusion as well as protecting religious non-discrimination. Such orientations consist of favouring the work of faith-based community organisations, factoring in spiritual care as a part of communal health care systems, and designing architectural spaces in such a way that could cater to communal gathering sites.

Faith-Based Organisations

Policy frameworks and funding that favour the mosques, Islamic community centres and religious organisations, depending on whether they can provide social services and community-building programmes, ought to be in place.

There is a need to impact culturally competent spiritual care into the system of public health, and to acknowledge the roles played by religious beliefs in mental health and social wellbeing.

Urban Planning: Designing neighbourhoods in such a way that they provide sufficient space to religious institutions, community centres and modest places of assembly so that social interaction can take place.

There is a need to create awareness about cultural competency among nursing personnel and the consumer population.

Make sure that social service providers understand the Islamic values and practices related to family structure, relations, and the community and help-seeking behaviour.

INTERFAITH COORDINATION AND INTERFAITH COHESION

Although the current chapter focuses on the Islamic methods, the ultimate ability to achieve social inclusion requires cooperation that cuts across the line concerning religion and culture. Islamic principles of *Rahmah* (compassion) and *Hikmah* (wisdom) are a conceptual framework of working with other religions that allows Islam to maintain its identity all the time and promotes social integration.

Such cooperation has proved to be possible in practice, as empirical cases such as interfaith community gardens, collaborative community social service efforts, and cooperation in responding to communal disasters all show. The cooperation between the Islamic Society of Orange County and Jewish and Christian communities to alleviate homelessness serves as a perfect demonstration of how religious cooperation may reduce social alienation and develop understanding with each other.

The idea in the Holy Quran that states that there is no compulsion in religion (2: 256) has formed the basis of the various strategies aimed at acknowledging the diversity but finding common ground on which to synergise to address the common challenges facing man, loneliness and the lack of social connection.

FUTURE RESEARCH DIRECTIONS

Longitudinal Impact Studies

The proposed study implies the elaboration of extensive longitudinal studies on the effectiveness of the Islamic interventions in social inclusion through diverse demographic and geographic settings.

Making Cross-Cultural Comparisons

It is advisable to conduct systematic comparative analyses by contrasting the Muslim ways with other community-building and social support models based on other faiths and secular guidelines.

Digital Integration Research

Learners collaborate to explore how the digital world is reshaping the ways tasks are accomplished. Within the framework of human-digital integration, they work together to examine how technology influences daily practices and collective activities.

Research in this area should focus on identifying the most effective strategies for using digital technologies to enhance, rather than replace, social relationships. This is especially important in the context of traditional Islamic community practices, where the aim is to strengthen communal bonds while adapting to modern digital realities.

Policy Studies

Analytical activities should also gauge the effectiveness of the policies that entrench the social principles of Islam in various political and cultural contexts, perhaps both of the majority and minority.

SHORT TREND ANALYSIS

The existing international trends have kept transforming the ideas of inclusion. The latent consequences of the COVID 19 pandemic, the ageing of the population, and the mass migration create new pressures on family and community systems. Results of the United Nations reports (2023) and Euro found studies (2022) prove that such pressures intensify the state of social disintegration, which highlights the specific usefulness of the Islamic ethical model based on solidarity and mutual care to inform the policy of the state and communities.

CONCLUSION: TOWARD INCLUSIVE AND CONNECTED COMMUNITIES

As the chapter shows, the Islamic social ethics provide detailed paradigms that can be used in the context of explaining and dealing with the current crisis of social isolation. By comparing the theological grounds, the mechanisms of institutions, and the stage of application, one notices that the principles of Islam enable other models to receive precedence in valuing the well-being of the community over seeking accumulation by their individual acts and offering personalised attention by the services they provide in markets.

Results indicate that Islamic orientations of social inclusion are applicable at many levels, starting with personal spiritual and social needs, through communal support networks, to the grand design itself of political-economic systems, which foster or hinder human affiliation. Through the method of microeconomics, it induces perspectives that themes like *Ukhuwwah, Zakat, and Waqf* construct caring networks that refuse to capitalise human relationships. The macro-economic analysis will reveal that the Islamic social infrastructure is a buffer of the economy that reduces the expenses felt by society due to seclusion and enhances the resilience of society.

On the level of political economy, the principles of Islamic governance suggest alternatives to the structural forces which foster the disintegration of society, and the principles of consultation, services towards the community, and social justice are treated as the premises of policy-making. The chart of demography shows how Islamic machine reacts to specific weaknesses such as ageing, migration, poverty, and educational inadequacies through an encompassing and dignified nature of intervention.

Most importantly, this discussion highlights the fact that the reduction of the social isolation problem should be methodologically based on measures that recognise the social and spiritual aspects of human nature. The Islamic traditions, which are based on the ideas of divine purpose, community care, and personal responsibility in a community, are the resources to develop societies which follow principles of connection, care, and support for each other.

REFERENCES

Afsaruddin, A. (2015). *Contemporary issues in Islam*. Edinburgh University Press. DOI: 10.1515/9780748632244

Al-Ghazali, A. H. (1997). *The revival of the religious sciences (Ihya' Ulum al-Din)* (Trust, I. B., Trans.). F. Karim. (Original work published 1105)

Al-Qaradawi, Y. (1999). *Fiqh al-zakah: A comparative study*. Dar al-Taqwa.

Al-Suwaidi, J. S. (2011). Shura as a foundation for participatory governance in Islam. *Islamic Studies, 50*(2), 145–162.

Ali, A. J., & Al-Owaihan, A. (2008). Islamic work ethic: A critical review. *Cross Cultural Management, 15*(1), 5–19. DOI: 10.1108/13527600810848791

Bano, M. (2017). *Female Islamic education movements*. Oxford University Press. DOI: 10.1017/9781316986721

Bauman, Z. (2000). *Liquid modernity*. Polity Press.

Beekun, R. I., & Badawi, J. A. (2005). Balancing ethical responsibility among multiple organizational stakeholders: The Islamic perspective. *Journal of Business Ethics, 60*(2), 131–145. DOI: 10.1007/s10551-004-8204-5

Bukhari, M. I. (n.d.). *Sahih al-Bukhari*. Dar al-Marefah.

Cacioppo, J. T., & Cacioppo, S. (2018). *Loneliness: Human nature and the need for social connection*. W. W. Norton.

Cacioppo, J. T., & Patrick, W. (2008). *Loneliness: Human nature and the need for social connection*. W. W. Norton & Company.

Campbell, H. (2021). *Digital religion: Understanding religious practice in new media worlds*. Routledge. DOI: 10.4324/9780429295683

Cesari, J. (2009). Securitization of Islam in Europe. In *Muslims in the West after 9/11* (pp. 19–37). Routledge. DOI: 10.4324/9780203863961

Chapra, M. U. (1992). *Islam and the economic challenge* (No. 17). International Institute of Islamic Thought (IIIT).

Chapra, M. U. (2000). *The future of economics: An Islamic perspective*. The Islamic Foundation.

Çınar, A. (2019). Local governance and community building in contemporary Turkey. *Journal of Social Policy, 48*(3), 411–430. DOI: 10.1017/S0047279418000924

El-Affendi, A. (2010). The elusive reform: Democracy and the rule of law in the Arab world. *Democratization, 17*(3), 492–509. DOI: 10.1080/13510341003700371

Esposito, J. L. (2018). *Islam and the future of tolerance*. Oxford University Press.

Esposito, J. L., & Voll, J. O. (2001). *Islam and democracy*. Oxford University Press.

Estes, C. L., & Phillipson, C. (2002). The globalization of capital, the welfare state, and old age policy. *International Journal of Health Services, 32*(2), 279–297. DOI: 10.2190/5TY7-PD68-QLD1-V4TY

Flowers, L., Houser, A., Noel-Miller, C., Shaw, J., Bhattacharya, J., Schoemaker, L., & Farid, M. (2017). *Medicare spends more on socially isolated older adults*. AARP Foundation. DOI: 10.26419/ppi.00016.001

Göle, N. (2013). The public visibility of Islam and European politics of resentment: The minarets-mosques debate. *Philosophy and Social Criticism, 37*(4), 383–392. DOI: 10.1177/0191453711398773

Haque, A. (2018). Religion and mental health: The Islamic perspective. *Journal of Religion and Health, 57*(1), 5–16. DOI: 10.1007/s10943-017-0489-3

Harper, S. (2014). Economic and social implications of aging societies. *Science, 346*(6209), 587–591. DOI: 10.1126/science.1254405

Harvard Business Review. (2017). *Work and loneliness survey report.*

Harvey, D. (2005). *A brief history of neoliberalism*. Oxford University Press. DOI: 10.1093/oso/9780199283262.001.0001

Hasan, R., & Mahmood, S. (2021). Social isolation indicators in Southeast Asia. *Social Indicators Research, 155*(2), 651–673.

Hassan, M. K., & Ahmad, A. U. (2019a). Social infrastructure and mental health outcomes in Muslim communities. *Journal of Islamic Economics, 45*(2), 234–251.

Hassan, R., & Ahmad, F. (2019b). Mosque density and community mental health: A comparative study of Malaysian states. *The Journal of Muslim Mental Health, 13*(2), 45–62.

Hochschild, A. R. (2012). *The outsourced self: Intimate life in market times*. Metropolitan Books.

Hoexter, M. (1998). *Endowments, rulers, and community: Waqf al-haramayn in Ottoman Algiers*. Brill. DOI: 10.1163/9789004660113

Holt-Lunstad, J. (2021). Social isolation and health. *Annual Review of Public Health, 42*, 101–118. DOI: 10.1146/annurev-publhealth-012420-105148

Holt-Lunstad, J., Smith, T. B., Baker, M., Harris, T., & Stephenson, D. (2015). Loneliness and social isolation as risk factors for mortality. *Perspectives on Psychological Science, 10*(2), 227–237. DOI: 10.1177/1745691614568352

Illouz, E. (2007). *Cold intimacies: The making of emotional capitalism.* Polity Press.

Johari, F., Ali, A., & Aziz, N. A. (2019). The role of zakat in social protection. *Journal of Islamic Accounting and Business Research, 10*(2), 187–203.

Kahf, M. (2003, January). The role of waqf in improving the ummah welfare. In *International Seminar on Waqf as a Private Legal Body* (Vol. 6, No. 1, pp. 1-26).

Kamali, M. H. (2008). *Shari'ah law: An introduction.* Oneworld.

Kamali, M. H. (2011). *The right to life, security, privacy and ownership in Islam.* Islamic Texts Society.

Kamali, M. H. (2011). *Maqasid al-shari'ah made simple.* International Institute of Advanced Islamic Studies.

Kaya, A. (2015). Islam, citizenship, and integration in Turkey and Europe. *Turkish Studies, 16*(4), 537–555. DOI: 10.1080/14683849.2015.1067864

Klinenberg, E. (2016). Social isolation, loneliness, and living alone. *American Journal of Public Health, 106*(5), 786–787. DOI: 10.2105/AJPH.2016.303166

Lim, S. S. (2020). Loneliness in the digital age. *Journal of Communication, 70*(5), 682–703.

Mir, A. (2019). Islamic governance and social inclusion: A critical analysis. *Journal of Islamic Governance, 4*(1), 23–41.

Mumtaz, Z. (2022). Informal Social Protection and Poverty: A Case Study In Pakistan.

Muslim, I. H. (n.d.). *Sahih Muslim.* Dar al-Kutub al-'Ilmiyya.

Office for National Statistics. (2018). *Loneliness: What characteristics and circumstances are associated with feeling lonely?* https://www.ons.gov.uk

Oldenburg, R. (1999). *The great good place.* Marlowe & Company.

Opwis, F. (2010). *Maslaha and the purpose of the law.* Brill.

Pew Research Center. (2020). *Social trust and community life in Muslim-majority countries.*

Putnam, R. D. (2000). *Bowling alone: The collapse and revival of American community*. Simon & Schuster.

Rafay, A., Farid, S., Yasser, F., & Safdar, S. (2020). Social collateral and repayment performance: Evidence from Islamic micro finance. *Iranian Economic Review*, *24*(1), 41–74.

Rahman, A. (2015). Zakat and poverty alleviation: Case of Malaysia. *Asian Social Work and Policy Review*, *9*(2), 118–127. DOI: 10.1111/aswp.12050

Rahman, F. (2019). Islamic education and social welfare: Integrating eldercare in Indonesian pesantren. *Indonesian Journal of Islam and Muslim Societies*, *9*(2), 231–252.

Rice, G. (1999). Islamic ethics and the implications for business. *Journal of Business Ethics*, *18*(4), 345–358. DOI: 10.1023/A:1005711414306

Sardar, Z. (2014). *Reading the Qur'an*. Oxford University Press.

Shirazi, D. N. S., Obaidullah, D. M., & Haneef, M. A. (2015). *Integration of Waqf and Islamic Microfinance for Poverty Reduction* (No. 1436-5).

Singer, A. (2008). *Charity in Islamic societies*. Cambridge University Press.

Smith, J. K. (2020). Faith and community in the age of loneliness. *Journal of Religion and Society*, *22*, 55–72.

Steptoe, A., Shankar, A., Demakakos, P., & Wardle, J. (2013). Social isolation, loneliness, and mortality. *Proceedings of the National Academy of Sciences of the United States of America*, *110*(15), 5797–5801. DOI: 10.1073/pnas.1219686110

Sulaiman, M., & Zakariyah, L. (2020). Waqf governance and community welfare outcomes. *Third World Quarterly*, *41*(8), 1352–1370.

Twenge, J. M. (2017). *iGen*. Atria Books.

UNDP. (2022). *Human development report: Social cohesion and vulnerability.*

United Nations. (2023). *World social report: Demographic change.*

Victor, C. R., & Pikhartova, J. (2020). Lonely places or lonely people? *BMC Public Health*, *20*(1), 778. DOI: 10.1186/s12889-020-08703-8

Victor, C. R., & Scharf, T. (2005). Social isolation and loneliness in old age. *European Journal of Ageing*, *2*(2), 97–104. DOI: 10.1007/s10433-005-0039-7

Wilkinson, R. G., & Pickett, K. (2009). *The spirit level: Why more equal societies almost always do better* (Vol. 6). Allen Lane.

World Health Organization. (2021). *Social isolation and loneliness: A framework for intervention.*

Yilmaz, I. (2018). The role of the Diyanet in contemporary Turkish politics and society. *Journal of Muslim Minority Affairs*, *38*(3), 327–345.

Yilmaz, I. (2022). Urbanization, migration, and social trust in Turkey. *The Middle East Journal*, *76*(4), 563–586.

Yunus, M. (2007). *Creating a world without poverty*. Public Affairs.

Zaman, M. (2019). *Islamic traditions of community welfare: Zakat, Waqf and Sadaqah*. Routledge.

Zine, J. (2008). *Canadian Islamic schools*. University of Toronto Press. DOI: 10.3138/9781442687509

KEY TERMS AND DEFINITIONS

Adl: Foundational Islamic value of justice, requiring fair resource distribution and equal treatment to reduce inequality and exclusion.

Commercialised Companionship: A market sector where services like paid friendship, subscription-based companionship, and therapy monetise human connection to address loneliness.

Maslaha: Principle of public interest in Islamic law, ensuring policies protect collective welfare and vulnerable groups.

Ukhuwwah:: The Islamic principle of brotherhood and sisterhood creates non-market networks of mutual support and solidarity.

Waqf: Religious endowment of property or assets for public benefit, such as mosques, schools, or hospitals, serving as community anchors.

Zakat:: Mandatory charity in Islam that redistributes wealth and purifies social relations, strengthening unity and social responsibility.

Chapter 11

An Assessment of the Commodification of Loneliness

Hüdayi Sayin
https://orcid.org/0000-0002-8994-4088
Istanbul Yeni Yüzyil University, Turkey

ABSTRACT

Humans are a species with a history. Throughout this history, humans have been forced to cooperate and live together. Only through solidarity could they protect themselves from the violence of nature and other species. In addition to the risk of being exposed to violence, his biological characteristics also made this necessary. Unlike other species, humans can only survive for two to three years after birth in a safe shelter, i.e., in their mother's warm arms or a cradle that serves the same purpose. They must be provided with food from outside sources. As soon as the umbilical cord that nourished them in the womb is cut, they need milk from their mother's breasts and food specially prepared for them. This cooperation, which begins within the family, continues and expands within the social networks they join. The development of humans and their species must therefore be studied within the structures in which they live.

INTRODUCTION

We are currently experiencing "interesting times" in which everything is reduced to economics. Eric Hobsbawm, whom we lost at the beginning of the 21st century, described his experiences of the 20th century, which shaped by two world wars, as "interesting times" (Hobsbawm, 2002). In these interesting times, nothing

DOI: 10.4018/979-8-3373-5811-6.ch011

remains that cannot be bought. Anything that cannot find a buyer in the market is doomed to scarcity. Anything that cannot find a buyer in the market is doomed to extinction. The existence of an economic value that creates things or its reduction to an economy that objectifies values. We are living in interesting times. The states responsible for 'high politics' are keen to sell weapons that have been developed for killing. The alienated individual, who has become the object of 'low politics,' watches impassively as their loneliness is marketed amidst the crowds on the neon-lit or dark streets they wander through.

Loneliness is understood as the individual's solitude and is associated with individuality. However, loneliness in the sense of being in solitude is not possible in natural life. Human beings can only attain or be destined for a collective solitude. Therefore, Emile Durkheim demonstrates that even the most extreme act of individual behaviour, such as suicide, occurs within a social context (Durkheim, 2013). The nature into which we are born inherently contains sociality. Friedrich Engels illustrates this with the dialectics of nature and the law of forced motion: "The whole of nature accessible to us forms a system, an interconnected totality of bodies, and by bodies we understand here all material existences extending from stars to atoms, indeed right to ether particles, in so far as one grants the existence of the last named. In the fact that these bodies are interconnected is already included that they react on one another, and it is precisely this mutual reaction that constitutes motion. It already becomes evident here that matter is unthinkable without motion. … When two bodies act on each other so that a change of place of one or both of them results, this change of place can consist only in an approximation or a separation. They either attract each other or they repel each other. … All motion consists in the interplay of attraction and repulsion. Motion, however, is only possible when each individual attraction is compensated by a corresponding repulsion somewhere else" (Engels, 1977, pp. 70-71). Therefore, life is possible within nature as a constant state of motion, interacting with the other parts of the whole in which we exist; when this interaction ceases, life ends.

Attraction and repulsion create a society of coexistence and open the door to other functions of social life. Society takes place through economic activities, and therefore economic relations form the core of society. Therefore, the economy expresses relationships that relate to society or coexistence. Therefore, the economy expresses relationships pertaining to society or coexistence. "Either directly and as a whole, or through the agency of one of its organs, society alone can play this moderating role; for it is the only moral power superior to the individual, the authority of which he accepts. It alone has the power necessary to stipulate law and to set the point beyond which the passions must not go. Finally, it alone can estimate the reward to be prospectively offered to every class of human functionary, in the name of the common interest" (Durkheim, 2005, pp. 209-210). Thus, the economy based on loneliness is not about the individual but about economic relations, and thus it is based on exploitation rather than ensuring the individual's happiness. For this reason, the production relations that encroach upon and usurp the existence of the individual in Karl Marx not only formally contain him, but also transform him (Fuchs, 2019a, pp.59-61). This resulting actual containment is completed by the accumulation of all concrete and abstract assets possessed by the subject and their concentration in the hands of capital (Marx, 1976, pp.100-101).

Mammalian species reproduce sexually and perpetuate their species. This innate characteristic of mammals demonstrates that their existence is only possible through the union of the two sexes of their species. Human beings cannot exist alone, but from the outset he is on a path towards absolute solitude. We can only attain absolute solitude through absence. Where life ends, our solitude becomes absolute with death.

Unlike other mammalian species, humans do not possess the ability to survive alone shortly after birth. "Human babies are helpless, dependent for many years on their elders for sustenance, protection and education" (Harari, 2011, p.11) The evolutionary process adapted the social instincts of Homo sapiens to living in small, intimate groups (Harari, 2011, p.29). From the moment a human being takes its first steps toward life in the womb, it is in a communication environment. We establish our first communication with our mother and her social circle. We feel our mother's reactions to her social environment in our safe haven, and we develop reactions together with her.

Humanity owes its existence as a species to being together. It managed to survive by cooperating and helping each other more than other mammals. As a species, it gained dominance over nature. At this stage, what mattered was cooperation rather than competition. Those who failed to adapt to these forms of cooperation and the resulting new patterns of mental behavior perished. Those who succeeded were able to sustain their existence and ensure the continuation of their species. (Harman, 2002, pp.3-4).

This article offers a critical perspective on the commodification of loneliness experienced at the intermediate stages of humanity's journey towards absolute solitude, which begins within the social environment. Edward Hallett Carr, one of the realist theorists in the discipline of international relations, discusses the political scientist's methodological approach between utopia and reality and, according to him, "The characteristic vice of the utopian is naivety; of the realist, sterility" (Carr, 1946, p.12). Carr states that the utopian focuses on the goal within the desired framework and expresses their wishes, while the realist explains events through the laws of mechanical causality, and he proposes combining the two: "Political science must be based on a recognition of the interdependence of theory and practice, which can be attained only through a combination of utopia and reality" (Carr, 1946, p.13) In this text, within the framework of Carr's proposed method, an effort will be made to combine the critique of the commodification of loneliness instead of utopia with the reality that emerges from the economisation of loneliness. The article assumes that there is a causal relationship between digitalisation and isolation in the ongoing digital revolution.

1. THE SEMANTICS OF LONELINESS

Byung-Chul Han begins his discussion of the meaning of power by posing the following fundamental question regarding the concept of sense: "But what does sense mean? What does it mean to say something has a sense?" (Han, 2019, p.22). He defines meaning as something being in a state of "relational continuum" with something else. Things "become senseless if the form that holds them together completely disintegrates." Therefore, nothing that exists alone has any meaning, or in other words, its existence becomes meaningless. From the moment a human being is conceived, they seek to avoid pain and pursue happiness. When we are happy, serotonin, dopamine, oxytocin and endorphin hormones are released. Individuals need this release in order to be happy. Social approval triggers the release of these hormones and makes us happy. Individuals who fail to gain social approval experience unease, feel uncomfortable and lose their ability to cope with problems. Social approval reveals the need one feels for another person. An individual requires the approval of another. Therefore, loneliness cannot be meaningful as isolation. Loneliness is gaining subjectivity within a unity and occurs within that unity. Solitude means becoming meaningless. The meaning that the human species attributes to the world of objects stems from its biological needs. From the perspective of Marx, human consciousness is formed within the context of its relationship with the material world. History emerges from the continuous transformation of needs; in other words, history is born from the basis of man's physical needs. Thus, nature and history, imbued with meaning, are the two sides of the coin. Civilisation is the conversion of nature into an extension of the human body through human labour. For this reason, human consciousness develops in relation to its own needs in relation to other bodies. "The body can do all this because it has the power to transcend itself—to transform itself and its situation, as well as to enter into complex relationships with other bodies of its kind, in that open-ended process we know as history. Human bodies which cannot do this are known as corpses" (Eagleton, 2011, pp.138-139). The absence of communication with other bodies is the loss of meaning. As human beings, we lose our meaning. Communication breakdown only occurs when life ends. "The Latin word communicare means to do something together, to unite, to give, or to have something in common. Communication is a community-building act. But after a certain point it is no longer communicative, only cumulative"(Han, 2018, pp.105-106). Loneliness in the sense of being solitary is the absence of communication with other members of the species and is impossible. According to the definitions of the United Nations, the World Health Organisation and the International Telecommunication Union, "Loneliness is the distressing feeling that arises when there is a gap between desired and actual social relationships." All three organisations have approached the concept of loneliness with negative connotations. The same institutions have observed a correlation between social isolation and loneliness, but have stated that they are distinct. According to them, social isolation "refers to the objective lack of social ties." Isolation arising from the coercion of a dominant subject reduces the passive subject's search for social support and assistance, leading to loneliness and social withdrawal (Bakırcı, 2022, pp.44-45). Loneliness is seen as "a state characterised by a lack of affection, expressing a search for sincere communication and emotional connection. … Every individual experiences loneliness within their inner world. A person may not feel lonely when alone; however, they may experience the deepest sense of loneliness even in crowds. It can be concluded that loneliness is determined not so much by the number of people around an individual, but rather by the depth of their relationships and communication with those people. Globalisation and rapid developments in information and communication technologies have isolated individuals from society, bringing the issue of alienation to the fore. Spending long periods of time on social media leads to social isolation in individuals. Individuals who become addicted to unlimited and unrestricted social media isolate themselves during this process and become alienated from society" (Karayaman, et al., 2025, p.1628). It is possible to evaluate loneliness positively as well as negatively, as a state of deprivation and detachment leading to alienation. Loneliness can provide a foundation for individuals to establish meaningful and profound relationships with themselves and the beings around them. Loneliness and togetherness do not exclude each other; on the contrary, loneliness gains meaning through interaction with those with whom one is together. Those who establish constructive, meaningful relationships with their surroundings can give meaning to loneliness and, when alone, can utilise the relationships they have established and add value to them. In a state of authenticity, the individual turns inward in solitude, begins to observe themselves, and can initiate the process of understanding themselves (Özdemir & Özaydın, 2025, p.356). Loneliness is man's search for subjectivity as a dated entity within nature. He strives to preserve his subjectivity against being lost in the crowd. Subjectivity is the resistance of the labouring subject to becoming an extension of the factory's machinery, to becoming a mechanical part. Subjectivity gains meaning through the liberation of humans, who are part of nature, from being mere extensions of the factory. While loneliness gains meaning through subjectivity on the path to liberation, it loses its meaning when reduced to an economic commodity, becoming isolated and losing its significance.

2. THE COMMODIFICATION OF LONELINESS

Marx's critique of the capitalist system, which began with an economic-political analysis of the evolution of human societies, is grounded in the reification that lies at the heart of the alienation of humanity throughout history. In Marx, alienation occurs in four stages: the products of human labour, the production processes, the human essence and the severing of the relationship from social environment in which it finds meaning as an entity. Marx's critique concerns the alienation of human beings from themselves through reification within capitalist relations of production. Marx sees alienation from oneself as reaching its highest stage in commodification. Alienation is the separation of humans from their own activities and the products of these activities. The products created by human labour emerge as objects independent of humans, and production is organised not for the use value of objects but for their exchange value. Marx emphasises the inhumanity of reified social relations by comparing the forms of activity appropriate to human nature with their effectiveness in capitalist society (Cornu, 1976, pp.285-291). At this point, the individual ceases to be themselves and becomes a commodity with exchange value. He exchanges his body and labour for money, becoming alienated from himself and his surroundings. According to Marx, liberation from alienation and the establishment of a good model of life are based on the idea of self-realisation. Eagleton interprets Marx as saying that he was more concerned with leisure time than with labour enslaved in material production relations, and that labour would be liberated through leisure time. According to him, Marx "did not make a fetish of material production. On the contrary, he thought it should be done away with as far as possible. His ideal was leisure, not labour. If he paid such unflagging attention to the economic, it was in order to diminish its power over humanity" (Eagleton, 2011, p.239). Leisure time is based on the existence of its opposite, working time. In Marx's view, women and men would become free when they were liberated from work and gained free time. This liberation would free humanity from alienated labour and enable them to realise their full potential. Therefore, reducing objects or situations in which objects are consumed to economics leads to alienation. The commodification of loneliness as a state of leisure also transforms it into a product of capitalist planning. At this stage, loneliness is the absence of cooperation. Capitalist planning shifts the costs of labour cooperation onto the individual, along with the perception of freedom created by isolation. Loneliness is now the alienated subject transforming its own essence into a product from which capital can profit, and becoming isolated and alienated from its social environment. The subject, in their leisure time, distances themselves from their existence, which would otherwise acquire meaning through their surroundings, and becomes a cog in the factory's machinery, a commodity of capital. At work, subjectivity is lost, reduced to a cog in the machine, pushed into isolation within the unity. Here, loneliness becomes solitude. It imprisons the subject in insecurity and unease, deepening the loneliness. Digitalisation is the effective use of information and communication technologies to provide fast and efficient information flow (Lupton, 2013, p.1). Digital transformation has inevitably permeated and transformed everyday social life. However, this transformation has also brought with it the danger of existential and social isolation for humans. In today's world, where the flow of history has accelerated compared to ancient times, digitalisation is leading to human loneliness and commodification, reducing everything to the economy. "In the new forms of being and thought instantiated by digital capitalism, the subject is no longer interpolated as homo oeconomicus a rational reflective subject" (Fuchs & Chandler, 2019, p.13). The insecure and restless subject alone becomes an '"iSlave" in the Big Data universe. Alienated and objectified, the subject opens itself up to slavery. "Digital capitalism revives slavery" (Linchuan Qui, 2019, pp. 114-115; Linchuan Qui, 2016, p.155). The loneliness economy, strengthened by digitalisation, thrives on the commodification and exploitation of individuals' social needs and processes of loneliness. Individuals attempting to fill their loneliness in the digital world become prosumers—a person that both produces and consumes—as they create content and share their data on the platforms where they lose themselves. While using platforms, users' digital labour is combined with their personal data and sold to advertisers. In this way, the user's labour is exploited (Çangüler Kılınç, Avşar, 2023, pp.72-75). The exploitation of digital labour gives rise to the 'human experience,' which is used as raw material for consumption forecasts and sales practices driven by profit expectations. Consumer behaviour is created and directed through the virtual profiling of users. User data is modulated by algorithms, creating advertising sets that influence their desires and needs. When users log into platforms, they consent to the storage of their personal data through terms of service agreements. The personalised information flow generated through the created personal profiles encourages the subject to use the platform while making it mandatory to upload more data, rendering the exploitation of their labour invisible (Sağlam, 2021, pp.52-59). Consequently, individuals require platforms in their daily lives and become dependent on them. This dependency enables individuals to gain control. Digitalisation has distanced people from themselves and the social environment to which they owe their existence. This alienation resulted in being in the midst of crowds but remaining outside of society. Whilst surfing the virtual world on the screens of our smartphones and computers, we have become detached from what is happening in our neighbourhood, on our street and in our community (Harari, 2018, p.88), we have become alienated. This distancing separates the individual from the people as a political subject with whom they coexist and transforms society into "temporary", "fragile" crowds. As gatherings become unplanned and their power to act becomes uncertain, people end up in the crowd of those returning home at the end of the day (Dean, 2019, pp.174-179). We were swept into loneliness amidst the crowds and lost the ability to cooperate that we had possessed at the outset. Crowded loneliness is when an individual, despite being in a community, is unable to communicate with those around them and feels isolated. A causal relationship has been observed between digitalisation and loneliness. It has been determined that as digitalisation increases, loneliness also increases (Süleymanlı, Kalkandeler, 2022, pp.84-88; Karayaman, et al., 2025, p.1628). This isolation, while connecting individuals to digital platforms more, creates a new system of exploitation. The individual's vulnerability to economic exploitation is linked to the nature of the virtual marketplace. First of all, subjects in the virtual world are caught up in a false illusion of sociality. Although it is said that virtual platforms provide an environment that connects subjects with each other, this environment creates an isolating effect due to its lack of substance and superficiality. The subject is unable to communicate with the other user as they would with a real person, unable to establish contact and emotional connection with them, developing only fleeting, transient communication. Secondly, superficial and temporary relationships formed on digital platforms deepen feelings of loneliness. Constant monitoring and reduced privacy in online environments increase superficial relationships and heighten loneliness in crowded spaces. This situation gives birth to a state of "deep loneliness" or "crowded loneliness". Finally, the social bonds that sustain solidarity among the crowds accumulating in urban areas weaken, and the individual finds themselves imprisoned by screens in a deep sense of loneliness (Köktürk, 2022, pp.127-135). In deep loneliness, the subject is cut off from all relationships and connections that give meaning to its existence, becoming isolated. It loses its existential integrity, becoming alienated from the wholeness in which it exists and finds meaning, while remaining isolated within that same wholeness.

3. THE MEANINGLESSNESS OF THE SENSE OF LONELINESS

Our abandonment of living in mutual aid and cooperation, which gives meaning to human life, has caused us to lose our sense of purpose. Commodification has erased the meaning we ascribed to ourselves. Commodification transforms life into a consumer object and domesticates its subject. Chul Han describes this domestication as "bare life". The subject who chooses naked biological life becomes enslaved, clings to a safe life, and relinquishes their freedom (Han, 2017a, pp.18-19). For this reason, everything that becomes commodified loses its meaning. Loneliness becomes meaningless as it becomes commodified, It turns into the reflected image of naked biological life. Chul Han approaches the depletion of humanity's capacity to "Being able to" act together or with others as an isolated commodity, drawing on Canetti's concept of “spiritual nakedness.” According to him, “being able” is only possible through the other and the pain that the other creates. “Being receptive to the other presupposes vulnerability. The painful wound is a primordial opening to the other. ... On account of this state of the soul, I experience restlessness in the face of the other. It makes indifference towards the other impossible ... Our digital bubbles also increasingly shield us from the other. A definite fear for others gives way to a diffuse fear for oneself. Without pain towards the other we do not have access to the pain of the other” (Han, 2021, p.45). Our loneliness, which flourishes where there is no other, thus nakedens our soul. The digitalisation that fosters loneliness results in the loss of meaning in reality. “Digitalisation will ultimately eliminate reality (Wirklichkeit) itself. Or reality will shed its reality and become a window within the digital realm. Soon our field of vision will transform into a three dimensional screen. We are moving further and further away from reality” (Han, 2022, p.120). Industrial capitalism established control mechanisms around three themes: law and order, the state and civil society, and politics of life (Foucault, 2008, p.78). The disciplining of bodies transformed into gears in the factory machine is industrial capitalism's approach to human beings. The liberal concept of freedom is concealed within the disciplined body, legitimising disciplinary techniques. As it becomes a “surveillance regime”, digitalisation is developing into a “protototalitarian trait”. “The individual has been transformed into a data set and exploited for profit. Capitalism has developed into surveillance capitalism. Surveillance generates capital. Digital platforms subject us to constant surveillance and manipulate our behaviour. Our thoughts, feelings and intentions are read and exploited. ... The psychopolitical instrument of Big Data renders human behaviour predictable and controllable. Digital psychopolitics creates a crisis of freedom” (Han, 2021, p.49-50). In the Age of Surveillance Capitalism, “behavioural surplus” was discovered. “Behavioural Value Reinvestment Cycle” processes the user subject's behavioural data as an algorithm and transforms it into a consumption object (Zuboff, 2019, pp. 62–73). Our decoded and processed behavioural data is presented to us as metadata. Surveillance Capitalism sells us back to ourselves. It turns this marketing into a strategy using tools that will make us feel happy, develop behavioural rationality, and stir up heroic emotions. We transform ourselves and our acts of kindness into products of the capitalist market. Initially, we contribute to the transformation of our acts of kindness into elements of capitalist planning; subsequently, we consent to the placement of our compassion, which transforms our loneliness into heroism, as a product consumer in the capitalist market. In the Omnipticon, where surveillance capitalism has imprisoned us, every piece of data we produce-in other words, our own creation-has economic value. Naturally, like anything else with economic value, it has an exchange value and a market where it is sold. The digital prison, into which we voluntarily entered behind bars, isolated by the illusion of freedom and alienated from our surroundings, has transformed into a data pool that we constantly recreate and offer to the market. The "'leisure time'" we spend on digital platforms, which should be our own, has become a "job" owned by capital owners, where we work without realising it. Antonio Negri warns, quoting Marx, that "All the problems begin here": "A use-value, or useful article, therefore, has value only because abstract human labour is objectified or materialized in it. How, then, is the magnitude of this value to be measured? By means of the quantity of the 'value-forming substance', the labour, contained in the article. This quantity is measured by its duration, and the labourtime is itself measured in determinate portions of time such as hours, days, etc." (Negri, 2003, pp.23-30). Negri bases his argument on the quantification of time spent on production, stating that this reification determines the value of labour time within an external social process, which he describes as the "First Displacement: the time of subsumed being". To him (2003, pp.115–119), "displacements" are determined within a dialectical cyclicality in the social organs and constitute "a new Umwelt for the temporal existence of subjects." "The capitalist understanding of command entrusts itself here only to now-time (Jetzt-Zeit), to aesthetics, to enlightenment - more simply, purely to the exogenous mechanisms in force for the reproduction of the system." In this dialectical progression/cycle, time, as the agent of labour, has "reached complete entropy" and time realises itself in "catastrophe". He translates Negri's analysis of 'displacement' into the production of time through the dichotomy of singularity and multiplicity, arriving at the logic of the mechanisms of political control. "In the whole of the history of political thought the one has been pre-eminent and hegemonic over the many." The neoliberal illusion equates being singular with freedom, turning us into the servants of the singular's power. Freedom and singularity are inversely related. "Originally, being free meant being among friends. 'Freedom' and 'friendship' have the same root in Indo-European languages. Fundamentally, freedom signifies a relationship. A real feeling of freedom occurs only in a fruitful relationship - when being with others brings happiness. But today's neoliberal regime leads to utter isolation; as such, it does not really free us at all" (Han, 2017b, pp.2-3). Unlike Han, Negri is optimistic. In the age of communication technologies, the living labour that produces socialised knowledge in political transitions 'will liberate freedom.' According to him, "freedom is a material force" and "today, freedom is a meaningful and essential part of the labour process" (Negri, 2006, pp.202-203). Material production forces singularities into multiplicity and "It is thus for this reason that the singularities endeavour to cooperate and the singular multitudes form constellations, because in that way they may produce more; or better still, they can continuously move beyond the singular measure of productivity and can open themselves increasingly to the immeasurable" (Negri, 2003, p.231). The process referred to as postmodern biopolitics in Negri is defined as digital psychopolitics in Han and exposes the new crisis of freedom. Han persists in the pessimism that underlies his critique of neoliberalism and argues that the mode of production today is characterised by isolation, contrary to what Negri claims. "The cooperative 'Multitude' that Antonio Negri has exalted as the post-Marxist successor to the 'proletariat' does not describe the contemporary mode of production. Rather, conditions are defined by the solitude of an entrepreneur who is isolated and self-combating and practises auto-exploitation voluntarily. He continues his statement, "There is no working class being exploited by those who own the means of production. When production is immaterial, everyone already owns the means of production him- or herself" (Han, 2017b, pp. 5-6) Whether we are optimistic like Negri or pessimistic like Han about the future, singularity eliminates the positive aspects of solitude and drags humanity into a process of objectification, leading to nonexistence. In 'Strange Times', where loneliness is reduced to economics, loneliness is produced as a quantitative value in the first stage of displacement and becomes an object of trade in the market. At this stage, a panoptic control mechanism institutionalises subjugation. Within the dialectic of Negri's analysis, in the second displacement, the subject, mistaking it for its own decision, succumbs to the intoxication of singular power and is swept into complete entropy. It denies that the multitude can only attain power by uniting, arriving at a perverse tautology in which freedom is seen as a freely chosen, solitary state. This omnipticon subjugation leaves the subject alone within the multitude and, by placing it on the brink of a catastrophe that objectifies it, causes the loss of meaning in loneliness. The sense of loneliness becomes meaningless.

4. CAN THE CRISIS OF LIBERALISM OR LONELINESS BECOME A COMMODITY?

Liberalism is a theoretical approach developed by thinkers such as John Locke, Jeremy Bentham, Immanuel Kant, and Adam Smith, drawing its roots from Enlightenment thought. It places fundamental rights and freedoms at the heart of its approach. The 21st century began with the declaration that the real socialist practices of the Marxist economic model, as experienced in the Soviet Union, had failed. Liberal theorists described these events as "The End of History" (Fukuyama, 1992). The recession that emerged at the beginning of the century in 2001 was followed by the 2008 economic crisis, and the world has yet to recover from the effects of this crisis. The latest depression that emerged at the beginning of the 2000s accelerated the pace of technological revolution, transforming daily life on a global scale. As daily life became digitalised, humans found themselves imprisoned within an Omnipticon, a product of their own technological advancement. The Industrial Revolution reshaped the agricultural society and altered the social routine centred around production relations. The traditional structure of the agricultural society has changed, the social core of the family system has shifted, the population concentrated in cities has characterised the social fabric, and power relations have been shaped to suit the new class structure. Society and the city it is confined to are organised like a factory. Everything is integrated into the production processes. As an entity, man has been regarded as a gear in the factory and offered up to serve capital as an object of production. The functioning of the factory's machinery required control over the human body and training according to the job. People were moulded to suit the work. Shelter, nutrition, sleep, socialising with their surroundings and other needs were adapted to fit the job. Michel Foucault conceptualises this transformation as biopolitics, a policy of rationalisation with regard to the body in capitalist society. He defines biopolitics as, "starting from the eighteenth century, to rationalize the problems posed to governmental practice by phenomena characteristic of a set of living beings forming a population: health, hygiene, birthrate, life expectancy, race ... It seemed to me that these problems were inseparable from the framework of political rationality ... This means liberalism," (Foucault, 2008, p.317). Foucault states that in capitalist society, social control is not limited to dominating the individual's consciousness, but also extends to controlling the body. Biopolitics governs life through bodily control, and Foucault explains this through the Panopticon metaphor in relation to state instruments of control (Foucault, 1995, pp.195-231; Foucault, 2003). For this reason, biopolitics consists of systematised policies of oppression in the Panopticon, where the majority of the society is kept under surveillance by the minority. With the transition to a capitalist society, everyday life has become a stage, and social life has evolved into a spectacle (Debord, 1990, pp.11-13). In "society of the spectacle", it is no longer the minority that observes the majority, but rather the majority that watches and follows the minority. The subject observes the lives of others without leaving their position. This surveillance process, known as synopticon, is the construction of a voluntary monitoring system to guide the observer. The major transformation in internet technology, the unrestricted access power and speed of information have compelled a redefinition of surveillance technology. It is considered that surveillance has entered a post-panoptic phase, with digital surveillance technologies creating a digital panopticon. Whilst digitalisation may appear to be moving away from panoptic surveillance through decentralisation, surveillance technologies accumulate Big Data in a centralised location via network connections, and the resulting centralised and panoptic capital is controlled by the state (Fuchs, 2019b, pp.58-59). Law professor Jeffrey Rosen used the concept of Omniptikon in his 2004 book titled 'The Naked Crowd' to indicate the idea that everyone can monitor everyone else, at any time, anywhere (Bitirim Okmeydan, 2017, pp. 60-61). Omnipticon is the entirety of domination practices based on technological surveillance, whereby everyone monitors everyone else through smartphones, social media, and location-based applications. This latest era of transformation we find ourselves in has been referred to by Zuboff as Surveillance Capitalism (Zuboff, 2019, pp. 32-37). According to him, Surveillance Capitalism operates within a mechanism that transforms the individual using technology into a product. The process begins with the subject using technology, the user becomes the product, and the product returns to the user. During this three-stage cycle, the digital capital owner earns high profits. The first stage of the system is "data collection". Social media platforms track members' activities, including their likes, search history, time spent, location, and other information. User actions generate the raw material that will be converted into the system's exchange value, or what Zuboff refers to as "behavioral data". Once the data has been collected, the second phase, in which the raw materials are processed, continues with the production phase of the estimated products. The collected data is converted into algorithm values within artificial intelligence technology. The user's mindset regarding their current and future needs and how they determine these is revealed. Thus, a "digital profile" is created that incorporates the subject's interests, tendencies and weaknesses. After processing the raw materials, the third Marketing-Sales stage is entered. These estimated products are sold to advertising companies, which are the actual customers of the platforms. Companies use processed algorithms to reach potential customers. In the final stage, user behaviour is "predicted, directed and manipulated" for commercial gain. (Zuboff, 2019, s.65-98; Orlowski, 2020). Hereby, the individual, by commodifying themselves within their alienation, becomes an object that is offered to the market of digital capital, only to be repurchased by themselves. Therefore, "Neoliberalism represents a highly efficient, indeed an intelligent, system for exploiting freedom. Everything that belongs to practices and expressive forms of liberty - emotion, play and communication - comes to be exploited. It is inefficient to exploit people against their will. Allo-exploitation yields scant returns. Only when freedom is exploited are returns maximized" (Han, 2017b, p.3). Neoliberal and postmodern culture boosts the economy on the basis of individual happiness and profit growth. The economy created by pushing individuals into isolation is also based on these dynamics. Hedonism and egocentrism, which are dynamics of neoliberal economic culture, have gained greater strength with digitalisation. The hedonistic and self-centred individual pursues pleasure, focuses on their own interests, disregards being beneficial to society, and this approach undermines social bonds (Kaya Deniz, 2019, pp.105-107). Digitalisation has become a useful tool in profit-driven daily life, which glorifies competition, another dynamic of neoliberal culture (Erol, 2021, pp.103-105). The neoliberal order, which has made production a totality through digitalisation, is rendering the need for coming together imperceptible and dissolving society (Kaya, 2024, p.30). The individual who has become disconnected from their social bonds retreats into their digital cave within a virtual universe

(Köktürk, 2021, s.129-133). Like the man in Plato's cave who sees shadows as threats, the alienated and isolated modern human being is also lost within the virtual reality simulation he has created. The individual, confined to solitude within neoliberal daily life, is losing the balance between work and life. The virtualisation of the workplace, the removal of fixed working hours, and the elimination of spatial and temporal constraints have led to an misconception of liberation. Remote working and the ability to access work from anywhere at any time does not allow employees to distance themselves from work and work-related responsibilities outside of working hours. The blurring of the line between work and leisure time leads to persistent work pressure and burnout among employees (Elnur, 2023, pp.293-294; Erol,2021, p.107). The insecurity and unease caused by loneliness in the sense of being alone drives the individual into emptiness and social isolation. Suicide rates among Generation Z youth have shown a significant upward trend since 1996. (Orlowski, 2020). Since the 2000s, young men have shown less interest in the opposite sex, their motivation to live has declined due to concerns about the future, and solitude has become permanent (Farrell, Gray, 2019). On the other hand, in a field study conducted among university students in Turkey on the relationship between Crowded Loneliness and Life Satisfaction, it was observed that women and single individuals exhibited a significantly positive difference in their feelings of crowded loneliness compared to men and married individuals. The same study found that Generation Z (18-25 years old) participants were more exposed to crowded loneliness and negative life satisfaction than other generations Y (26-45 years old) and Z (46-60 years old) (Karayaman, et al., 2025, pp. 1630-1638). In another study conducted on university students in Turkey in 2025 on the theme of the relationship between social media use and loneliness, it was observed that when social media use reached addictive levels, students experienced feelings of loneliness and their communication behaviours deteriorated (Özdemir, Özaydın, 2025, pp. 357–365). According to data from the Turkish Statistical Institute (TurkStat), single-person households showed a steady upward trend from 14.9 per cent in 2016, reaching 20.0 per cent in 2024. The same institution's 2024 Life Satisfaction Survey found that the source of greatest happiness for Turks was their families, at 72.9%. This finding was followed by varying percentages for first-degree relatives, such as parents, spouses and children, at 23.8%. The proportion of those who see themselves as the source of happiness was found to be 4.2% (Turkish Statistical Institute (TurkStat), 2025). According to the Turkish Statistical Institute's 2024 Survey on the Use of Information Technologies Among Children, the internet usage rate among children aged 6-15 is 91.3%. Over 50% of the research sample is aged between 11 and 15, and this age group also spends over two hours a day online. 83.9% of children who use the internet watch videos, 75% participate in their studies, 72.7% download and play games, 72.6% use social media, 68.1% download and listen to music, and 65.2%

use the internet for messaging. According to the report, 76.1 per cent of the children own a mobile phone. Within this ratio, 66.3% of children aged 6–10 own a mobile phone, while 86.2% of children aged 11–15 own a mobile phone. The proportion of children who stated that they regularly use a mobile phone/smartphone was found to be 98.2%. Children use their mobile phones/smartphones 77.9% of the time to browse the internet, 77.3% of the time to make video and voice calls, 75.0% for watching films, series, TV broadcasts and videos, 73.6% for following social media, 72.5% for playing games, 86.8% for school activities, 69.8% for listening to music and 68.2% for messaging. In the study, to determine children's mobile phone/smartphone usage behaviour, the proportion of children who engaged in at least one of the following behaviours—checking their phone at least once every 30 minutes, checking their phone before going to sleep, checking their phone immediately upon waking up, using their mobile phone while watching television, or using their mobile phone while eating with others—was determined to be 68.6%. The percentage of children who play games was found to be 82.8% for boys and 64.8% for girls. In the correlation established with age group, 85.0% of boys and 58.7% of girls aged 11-15 play games. One quarter of children, 25.6%, play games for more than two hours on weekdays, and 40.1% of those who play games regularly have spent more time playing than they had planned (Turkish Statistical Institute, 2024).

According to the Life Satisfaction Survey conducted by TurkStat in Turkey in 2024, Turks see being with family members as a source of happiness, while it was found that one-fifth of them have started living alone. It can be assumed that those living alone consist of relatively young white-collar members of the younger generation. Turkish Vice President Cevdet Yılmaz stated in an exclusive interview with Editor in Chief Mehmet Akif Ersoy and Programmer Dr. Pelin Yantur that 20.0% of Turkey's population lives alone. He added that the social housing project to be implemented nationwide in 2025-2026 will take this percentage into account when planning housing sizes. (Habertürk & Bloomberg HT, 27 August 2025). Loneliness in the sense of being in solitude has reached levels that must be taken into account in high-cost housing projects undertaken nationwide. Another research conducted by TurkStat in 2024 revealed that 90% of Turkish children aged 15 and under, the youngest of whom are starting primary school, use the internet. Around three-quarters of this group use internet technology to communicate with their social circle, engage in leisure activities and study. It is reasonable to predict that these behavioural patterns, which begin in childhood, will increase loneliness in terms of isolation among young people and older age groups. When this situation is reflected in spatial planning, as seen in Vice President Yılmaz's statements, it is evident that generations alienated from themselves and their surroundings will emerge.

5. CALL FOR A RETURN TO FREEDOM

Liberalism constructs its claim to freedom, which it places at the heart of its ideology, through individualisation. The individual will be liberated when freed from control mechanisms. This claim can only come to fruition in an egalitarian social design. In a liberal society dominated by inequality, those who ultimately hold power enslave atomised, dispossessed individuals and purchase their freedom.

The social transformation spanning from the Industrial Revolution to the Digital Revolution we are currently experiencing has fundamentally altered all paradigms of daily life. Whilst digitalisation offers opportunities such as flexibility in time management, it also brings risks such as isolation, social distancing and, as an extension of this, alienation, which undermine human solidarity. Therefore, it is essential to analyse the social costs of digital transformation, manage risks, and plan for the future with a human-centred roadmap.

Globalisation and digitalisation have eliminated the time and place-bound work arrangements in the workplace. For IT workers in particular, the requirement to be present at a specific workplace during specific hours has disappeared, and employees have become global workers. Where the work is physically carried out has become irrelevant. While this creates an illusion of freedom, it also fosters an oppressive atmosphere through the limitless possibilities of digital control. Employers have gained the ability to monitor their employees anytime, anywhere due to technology (Erol, 2021, pp. 98–100). This situation, while virtualising the workplace, eliminates the employee's privacy, anonymises their private life, and isolates them within a crowd. On the other hand, the virtualisation of work and the workplace promotes freelance work, which in turn eliminates employment-related social security. Companies avoid social security responsibilities such as health insurance or severance pay by employing individuals as freelancers. Freelancers are constantly seeking steady employment for a regular fixed income due to short-term, insecure jobs (Kaya Deniz, 2019, pp. 106–110). Pushed into anonymity and deep loneliness, the worker becomes isolated, plagued by insecurity and anxiety about the future. The worker who becomes isolated and experiences alienation grows estranged from their work and what they produce.

Individuals should be legally protected against this system, which causes isolation, abstraction and alienation. Legal protection against isolation must be strengthened. Isolation without legitimate grounds should be regulated as a form of violence and discrimination in future legal texts (Bakırcı, 2022, p.57). Legal regulations should be enacted to enable so-called ‘independent’ workers to join trade unions and benefit from collective bargaining rights, thereby protecting them from the disadvantages that make it difficult to implement occupational health and safety regulations based on the loss of the workplace's fixed and permanent nature (Erol, 2021, pp. 109-110).

In the chaos of daily life, individuals who are pushed into solitude must be brought back into a state of unity where they can find their existential meaning. "The antidote to loneliness is sharing; sharing a space, actions, feelings, the world between individuals" (Köktürk, 2020, p.134). Therefore, social spaces that encourage emotional attachment to the community and genuine sharing with others should be created.

It is neither possible nor right to avoid digitalisation. We must reduce the negative effects of digitalisation and develop our ability to adapt to the new social life that digitalisation brings. We must increase awareness of digital literacy in order to combat digital dependency, which leads to isolation and alienation (Karayaman et al., 2025, p. 1639). We must transform digital platforms into vehicles for developing competencies.

Liberalisation, in its new form as well as in its classical form, caused inequality, enslaved the subject it commodified, and destroyed freedom. Freedom is only possible when the subject is liberated from commodification. The subject attains freedom when it breaks free from the chains that alienate it.

CONCLUSION

Human beings are born to be together and to cooperate. From the very first day, they are with others and embark on a journey towards absolute loneliness. Loneliness is only realised in its absolute form in death. Just as we owe our existence to being together, we become isolated in the absence of others. We must transform our loneliness into a shelter against the forces that shatter our relationships with others.

Digitalisation, in exchange for the virtual socialisation opportunities it offers, creates a platform where shallow and superficial relationships emerge, leading to the individual's isolation and alienation. The loneliness that develops with alienation deepens, evolving into a form of crowded loneliness and becoming a source of capitalist exploitation. The feeling of loneliness within crowds isolates the individual from their social environment, dragging them into a state of solitary solitude amid a lack of communication. A human-centered life and solidarity are being abandoned, and the stripped-down subject is being imprisoned in a digital cave for their social and psychological needs, perceiving the shadows reflected on the screen as reality. Data generated in the pursuit of reality in the world of shadows is exploited by companies seeking to maximise profits. The loneliness economy is a system in which individuals objectify themselves on digital platforms to satisfy needs such as belonging, social approval and entertainment, and in consequence, the data sets and labour produced in this process are commodified by digital capitalists for the purpose of wealth maximisation. As users take refuge in their digital caves, the perception of socialisation that is created leads to their loneliness turning into solitude, their loneliness growing in the shadows.

Human nature finds meaning in unity. Unity protects it from alienation from itself and its surroundings. Neoliberal authority and its techniques of domination seek to prevent singularities, drawing strength from their solidarity, from growing into resilient majorities. Digitalisation provides neoliberal authority with means to atomise individuals, preventing them from merging into a force capable of collective action. Individuals doomed to solitude by these means become estranged from their ontological existence and suffer a loss of meaning.

Throughout this work, a critical perspective has been adopted towards the isolating and alienating effects of the neoliberal order, specifically in relation to digitalisation. Since it is impossible and indeed wrong to turn back the clock on digitalisation, we must seek ways to adapt to this development in a human-centred manner. To this end, it is necessary to increase digital literacy in order to raise awareness of its use, but also to shape its ethical rules. Digital exploitation and the production processes in which the user subject is involved, and the exploitative system in which they essentially transform themselves into data and commodify themselves, must be subject to legal safeguards. It is imperative to bring forth resistance against this typology of human beings who complicate all of this, who accept the exploitation of their existence as entertainment, who have become alienated from themselves and their surroundings, who voluntarily prefer superficial, contactless communication, and who have retreated into a digital cave with their wildness. Balancing the dangers of disorientation and social disintegration within the metaverse will only be possible through ethical and normative regulations, not just technical developments.

REFERENCES

Bakırcı, K. (2022). An essay on the relationship between isolation in business life and poverty, violence, and discrimination from a legal perspective. In Digitalization and Loneliness III: International Loneliness Symposium Book (pp. 41–62). İstanbul: Üsküdar University Press.

Bitirim Okmeydan, S. (2017). Transformation of surveillance society in postmodern culture: From 'Panopticon' to 'Synopticon' and 'Omniopticon'. *Online Academic Journal of Information Technology, Special Issue*, *8*(30), 45–69. DOI: 10.5824/1309-1581.2017.5.003.x

Çalgüner Kılınç, E., & Avşar, Z. (2023). Analysis of Ekşi Sözlük in the context of Fuchs' prosumer commodification and digital labor exploitation concepts. *Yeni Medya Dergisi*, *15*, 69–91.

Carr, E. H. (1946). *The twenty years' crisis: 1919–1939: An introduction to the study of international relations*. Macmillan & Co. Ltd.

Cornu, A. (1976). Manuscripts on economics, politics and philosophy. In Marx, K. (Ed.), *Economic and philosophic manuscripts of 1844* (Somer, K., Trans.). Sol Yayınları.

Dean, J. (2019). Critique or collectivity? Communicative capitalism and the subject of politics. In Chandler, D., & Fuchs, C. (Eds.), *Digital objects, digital subjects: Interdisciplinary perspectives on capitalism, labour and politics in the age of big data*. University of Westminster Press. DOI: 10.16997/book29.n

Debord, G. (1990). *Comments on the society of the spectacle* (Imrie, M., Trans.). Verso Books.

Durkheim, E. (2005). *Suicide: A study in sociology* (Spaulding, J. A., & Simpson, G., Trans.). Routledge. DOI: 10.4324/9780203994320

Durkheim, E. (2013). *The evolution of educational thought: Lectures on the formation and development of secondary education in France*. Routledge. DOI: 10.4324/9781315020594

Eagleton, T. (2011). *Why Marx was right?* Yale University Press.

Elnur, A. (2023). The transformation of the sociology of leisure in the context of digitalization of communication processes. *The Academic Elegance*, *10*(23), 287–311.

Engels, F. (1977). *Dialectics of nature* (Dutt, C., Trans.). Progress Publishers.

Erol, A. (2021). Change of workplace in the age of digitalization: Causes and consequences. İn-san&İnsan, 8(30), 97–113.

Ersoy, M. A., & Yantur, P. (2025, August 27). Special interview – Steel Dome: A new era in Turkey's air defense [Video]. Haberturk & Bloomberg HT. https://tv.haberturk.com/programlar/video/ozel-roportaj-27-agustos-2025-celik-kubbe-turkiyenin-hava-savunmasinda-yeni-donem/888895

Farrell, W., & Gray, J. (2019). *The boy crisis.* BenBella Books.

Foucault, M. (1995). *Discipline and punish: The birth of the prison* (Sheridan, A. M., Trans.). Vintage Books.

Foucault, M. (2003). *The birth of the clinic* (Sheridan, A. M., Trans.). Routledge.

Foucault, M. (2008). *The birth of biopolitics* (Burchell, G., Trans.). Palgrave Macmillan.

Fuchs, C. (2019a). *Rereading Marx in the age of digital capitalism.* Pluto Press.

Fuchs, C. (2019b). Karl Marx in the age of big data capitalism. In Chandler, D., & Fuchs, C. (Eds.), *Digital objects, digital subjects: Interdisciplinary perspectives on capitalism, labour and politics in the age of big data.* University of Westminster Press. DOI: 10.16997/book29.d

Fuchs, C., & Chandler, D. (2019). Big data capitalism – Politics, activism, and theory. In Chandler, D., & Fuchs, C. (Eds.), *Digital objects, digital subjects: Interdisciplinary perspectives on capitalism, labour and politics in the age of big data.* University of Westminster Press. DOI: 10.16997/book29.a

Fukuyama, F. (1992). *The end of history and the last man.* Maxwell Macmillan.

Han, B.-C. (2017a). *The agony of eros* (Butler, E., Trans.). MIT Press. DOI: 10.7551/mitpress/11054.001.0001

Han, B.-C. (2017b). *Psychopolitics: Neoliberalism and new technologies of power* (Butler, E., Trans.). Verso Books.

Han, B.-C. (2018). *Topology of violence* (Demarco, A., Trans.). MIT Press. DOI: 10.7551/mitpress/11056.001.0001

Han, B.-C. (2019). *What is power?* (Steuer, D., Trans.). Polity Press.

Han, B.-C. (2021). *The palliative society: Pain today* (Steuer, D., Trans.). Polity Press.

Han, B.-C. (2022). *In praise of the earth: A journey into the garden* (2nd ed.). (Ermiş, N., Trans.). İnka Kitap.

Harari, Y. N. (2011). *Sapiens: A brief history of humankind.* Vintage Books.

Harari, Y. N. (2018). *21 lessons for the 21st century.* Jonathan Cape.

Harman, C. (2002). *A people's history of the world.* Bookmarks Publications.

Hobsbawm, E. (2002). *Interesting times: A twentieth-century life.* Allen Lane.

Karayaman, S.. (2025). Crowded loneliness scale and field research. *Turkish Studies, 20*(4), 1625–1643. DOI: 10.7827/TurkishStudies.82717

Kaya, İ. (2024). A spatial and temporal critique of the redesign of rituals in the online space: The disappearance of aura. *Folklor Akademi Dergisi, 7*(1), 22–33. DOI: 10.55666/folklor.1384083

Kaya Deniz, A. (2019). Hedonist workers of the digital age: Digital nomads. *IBAD Journal of Social Sciences, 5*, 101–113.

Köktürk, M. (2022). Deep loneliness in the digital world. In Digitalization and Loneliness III: International Loneliness Symposium Book (pp. 123–135). İstanbul: Üsküdar University Press.

Linchuan Qui, J. (2016). *Goodbye iSlave: A manifesto for digital abolition.* University of Illinois Press.

Linchuan Qui, J. (2019). Goodbye iSlave: Making alternative subjects through digital objects. In Chandler, D., & Fuchs, C. (Eds.), *Digital objects, digital subjects: Interdisciplinary perspectives on capitalism, labour and politics in the age of big data.* University of Westminster Press.

Lupton, D. (2013). *Introducing digital sociology.* University of Sydney.

Marx, K. (1976). *Economic and philosophic manuscripts of 1844* (Somer, K., Trans.). Sol Yayınları.

Negri, A. (2003). *Time for revolution* (Mandarini, M., Trans.). Continuum.

Negri, A. (2006). *Movimenti nell'impero: Passaggi e paesaggi* (Atalay, K., Trans.). Otonom Press.

Orlowski, J. (Director). (2020). The social dilemma [Film]. United States: Exposure Labs.

Özdemir, A., & Özaydın, H. (2025). Social media addiction and loneliness: A research on university students. Kent Akademisi, 18 (Special Issue of the International Congress of Social Sciences on Entrepreneurship), 355–371.

Sağlam, Y. (2021). Social media and alienation in the context of surveillance capitalism [Unpublished master's thesis]. Istanbul Gelisim University, Department of Sociology.

Süleymanlı, E., & Kalkandeler, N. (2022). Result of the digitization and loneliness survey in Turkey. In Digitalization and Loneliness III: International Loneliness Symposium Book (pp. 73–91). İstanbul: Üsküdar University Press.

Turkish Statistical Institute. (2024). Research on information technology use in children. https://data.tuik.gov.tr/Bulten/Index?p=Cocuklarda-Bilisim-Teknolojileri-Kullanim-Araştırması-2024-53638

Turkish Statistical Institute. (2025). Family in statistics 2024. https://data.tuik.gov.tr/Bulten/Intex?p=Istatistikler-Aile-2024-53989

Zuboff, S. (2019). *The age of surveillance capitalism*. PublicAffairs.

Compilation of References

AbdulKareem, I. A., Mahmud, M. S., Elaigwu, M., & Abdul Ganiyy, A. F.AbdulKareem. (2021). Mitigating the effect of covid-19 on the society through the Islamic social finance. [JMTP]. *The Journal of Management Theory and Practice*, *2*(1), 56–61. DOI: 10.37231/jmtp.2021.2.1.83

Adenuga, I., Tuncer, B., MacDonald, K. B., & Schermer, J. A. (2025). The relationship between loneliness and school dropout. *Current Research in Behavioral Sciences*, *9*, 100183. DOI: 10.1016/j.crbeha.2025.100183

Adler, P. S., & Kwon, S. W. (2013). The mutation of professionalism as a contested diffusion process: Clinical guidelines as carriers of institutional change in medicine. *Journal of Management Studies*, *50*(5), 930–962. DOI: 10.1111/joms.12003

Adshade, M., Khameneh, N. H., & Card, K. (2024, July 31). What are the economic costs of loneliness? *Social Connection Guidelines,* https://www.socialconnectionguidelines.org/en/evidence-briefs/what-are-the-economic-costs-of-loneliness

Afsaruddin, A. (2015). *Contemporary issues in Islam*. Edinburgh University Press. DOI: 10.1515/9780748632244

Agamben, G. (1998). *Homo sacer: Sovereign power and bare life*. Stanford University Press.

Ahmad, A. U. F., & Habib, F. (2013). *Role of zakah in poverty alleviation through redistributive justice.* World Universities Islamic Philanthropy Conference 2013 'Nurturing Research Culture for Ummah Well Being' held by Institut Kajian Zakah (IKAZ) Malaysia, December 4th-5th.

Ahmed, A. A., Hwang, W. T., Thomas, C. R.Jr, & Deville, C.Jr. (2018). International Medical Graduates in the US Physician Workforce and Graduate Medical Education: Current and Historical Trends. *Journal of Graduate Medical Education*, *10*(2), 214–218. DOI: 10.4300/JGME-D-17-00580.1

Ahuja, M., Miller-Slough, R., Adebayo-Abikoye, E., Williams, C., Haubner, A., Dooley, M. G., Bansal, M., Sathiyaseelan, T., Pons, A., Karki, A., Al Ksir, K., Samuel, B., Tchoua, P., Schuver, T., & Fernandopulle, P. (2024). Loneliness and Alcohol use among College Students During the COVID-19 Pandemic in Rural Appalachia. *Chronic Stress (Thousand Oaks, Calif.)*, *8*, 24705470241264909. DOI: 10.1177/24705470241264909

Akbulut, Ö. F., & Pamuk, K. (2025). Rumination, Loneliness, Task-Oriented Coping and Mental Well-Being Among University Students: A Serial Mediation Model. *Psychological Reports*, *00332941251329788*, 00332941251329788. Advance online publication. DOI: 10.1177/00332941251329788

Aktas, E., Bergbom, B., Godderis, L., Kreshpaj, B., Marinov, M., Mates, D., McElvenny, D. M., Mehlum, I. S., Milenkova, V., Nena, E., & Glass, D. C. (2022). Migrant workers occupational health research: An OMEGA-NET working group position paper. *International Archives of Occupational and Environmental Health*, *95*(4), 765–777. DOI: 10.1007/s00420-021-01803-x

Alabed, A., Javornik, A., Gregory-Smith, D., & Casey, R. (2024). More than just a chat: A taxonomy of consumers' relationships with conversational AI agents and their well-being implications. *European Journal of Marketing*, *58*(2), 373–409. DOI: 10.1108/EJM-01-2023-0037

Al-Btoush, A., & El-Bcheraoui, C. (2024). Challenges affecting migrant healthcare workers while adjusting to new healthcare environments: A scoping review. *Human Resources for Health*, *22*(1), 56. DOI: 10.1186/s12960-024-00941-w

Al-Ghazali, A. H. (1997). *The revival of the religious sciences (Ihya' Ulum al-Din)* (Trust, I. B., Trans.). F. Karim. (Original work published 1105)

Ali, A. J., & Al-Owaihan, A. (2008). Islamic work ethic: A critical review. *Cross Cultural Management*, *15*(1), 5–19. DOI: 10.1108/13527600810848791

Ali, S., George, A., & Ali, S. A. A. (2021, December). Urban isolation-A state of the art report on addressing complexities in urban communities. In. AIP Conference Proceedings: Vol. 2409. *No. 1* (p. 020006). AIP Publishing LLC. DOI: 10.1063/5.0067612

Aljarah, A., Ibrahim, B., Hazzam, J., & Alam, F. (2025). Isolation marketing: social isolation and virtual gift donation intention. *Management Decision*, ahead-of-print(ahead-of-print). DOI: DOI: 10.1108/MD-07-2024-1685

Allen, J. A., Diefendorff, J. M., & Ma, Y. (2014). Differences in emotional labor across cultures: A comparison of Chinese and US service workers. *Journal of Business and Psychology, 29*(1), 21–35. DOI: 10.1007/s10869-013-9288-7

Allen, K.-A., Kern, M. L., Rozek, C. S., McInerney, D. M., & Slavich, G. M. (2021). Belonging: A review of conceptual issues, an integrative framework, and directions for future research. *Australian Journal of Psychology, 73*(1), 87–102. DOI: 10.1080/00049530.2021.1883409

Allison, A. (2013). *Precarious Japan*. Duke University Press. DOI: 10.1215/9780822377245

Alostaz, N., Walton-Roberts, M., Chen, R., Pratt, M., & Wahoush, O. (2024). Integration trends of internationally educated nurses in Canada and Australia: A scoping review. *International Health Trends and Perspectives, 4*(1), 88–113. DOI: 10.32920/ihtp.v4i1.1958

Al-Qaradawi, Y. (1999). *Fiqh al-zakah: A comparative study*. Dar al-Taqwa.

Al-Suwaidi, J. S. (2011). Shura as a foundation for participatory governance in Islam. *Islamic Studies, 50*(2), 145–162.

Al-Suwailem, S. (2020). Foreword. In IRTI IDB, *Islamic Social Finance Report 2020*. Islamic Research and Training Institute, Islamic Development Bank (IRTI IDB).

Altay, T., Yurdakul, G., & Foroutan, N. (2025). Undoing one-dimensionality: Reforming German citizenship through the postmigrant framework. *Comparative Migration Studies, 13*(1), 1–16. DOI: 10.1186/s40878-025-00444-0

Amati, V., Meggiolaro, S., Rivellini, G., & Zaccarin, S. (2018). Social relations and life satisfaction: The role of friends. *Genus, 74*(1), 1–18. DOI: 10.1186/s41118-018-0032-z

Amnesty International. (2023). *"I don't have a future": Stateless Kuwaitis and the right to education* (Report No. MDE 17/6990/2023). Amnesty International.

Anchieta, M. V., Torro-Alves, N., da Fonsêca, É. K. G., & de Lima Osório, F. (2025). Effects of social skills training on social responsiveness of people with Autism spectrum disorder: A systematic review with meta-analysis. *European Child & Adolescent Psychiatry, 34*(7), 2007–2022. DOI: 10.1007/s00787-025-02697-7

Anderson, B. (2013). *Us and them? The dangerous politics of immigration control*. Oxford University Press. DOI: 10.1093/acprof:oso/9780199691593.001.0001

Andersson, M. A., Wilkinson, R., & Maralani, V. (2024). Revisiting Health Disparities Linked to "Some College": Incorporating Gender and High School Experiences. *Social Currents*, *11*(2), 159–180. DOI: 10.1177/23294965231175822

Angel, Y., & Fire, G. (2023). Healthcare policy changes in an era of health workforce shortage. *Israel Journal of Health Policy Research*, *12*(1), 28. Advance online publication. DOI: 10.1186/s13584-023-00576-7

Anixiadis, F., Wertheim, E. H., Rodgers, R., & Caruana, B. (2019). Effects of thin-ideal Instagram images: The roles of appearance comparisons, internalization of the thin ideal and critical media processing. *Body Image*, *31*, 181–190. DOI: 10.1016/j.bodyim.2019.10.005

Ansari, S., Muhammad, T., & Dhar, M. (2023). How does multi-morbidity relate to feeling of loneliness among older adults? Evidence from a population-based survey in India. *Journal of Population Ageing*, *16*(1), 45–66. DOI: 10.1007/s12062-021-09343-5

Aparicio-Martínez, P., Perea-Moreno, A.-J., Martínez-Jiménez, M.-P., Redel-Macías, M.-D., Pagliari, C., & Vaquero-Abellán, M. (2019). Social media, thin-ideal, body dissatisfaction and disordered eating attitudes: An exploratory analysis. *International Journal of Environmental Research and Public Health*, *16*(21), 4177. Advance online publication. DOI: 10.3390/ijerph16214177

Arendt, H. (2004). *The origins of totalitarianism*. Schocken Books.

Ascarya. (2006). Akad dan produk bank syariah: konsep dan praktek di beberapa negara [Islamic banking contracts and products: concepts and practices in several countries]. Bank Indonesia.

Asrani, C. (2022). Spanning the digital divide in India: Barriers to ICT adoption and usage. *Journal of Public Affairs*, *22*(4), e2598. DOI: 10.1002/pa.2598

Atiq- ur- Rehman. (2019). A critical appraisal of Islamic finance in the light of the maqasid al- Shariʿah. In Cattelan, V. (Ed.), Islamic social finance: Entrepreneurship, cooperation and the sharing (pp. 35-51). Routledge.

Audrin, C., & Audrin, B. (2024). Emotional intelligence in digital interactions–A call for renewed assessments. *Personality and Individual Differences*, *223*, 112613. DOI: 10.1016/j.paid.2024.112613

Auerbach, R. P., Mortier, P., Bruffaerts, R., Alonso, J., Benjet, C., Cuijpers, P., Demyttenaere, K., Ebert, D. D., Green, J. G., Hasking, P., Murray, E., Nock, M. K., Pinder-Amaker, S., Sampson, N. A., Stein, D. J., Vilagut, G., Zaslavsky, A. M., & Kessler, R. C.WHO WMH-ICS Collaborators. (2018). WHO World Mental Health Surveys International College Student Project: Prevalence and distribution of mental disorders. *Journal of Abnormal Psychology*, *127*(7), 623–638. DOI: 10.1037/abn0000362

Austin, Z., & Gregory, P. A. (2024). Enhancing integration of internationally educated health professionals in the healthcare workforce: Implications for regulators. *Journal of Nursing Regulation*, *15*(1), 24–32. DOI: 10.1016/S2155-8256(24)00026-7

Aydin, N. (2025). Understanding of a healthy diet in relation to current guidelines: A case study of UK university students. *Health Education Journal*, *84*(2), 125–134. DOI: 10.1177/00178969251316813

Aytaç, I. A., & Rankin, B. H. (2009). Economic crisis and marital problems in Turkey: Testing the family stress model. *Journal of Marriage and Family*, *71*(3), 756–767. DOI: 10.1111/j.1741-3737.2009.00631.x

Babu, K. V., and Prasad, V. N. (2024). Can Replika's Emotional AI Replace Human Companionship?. *IUP Journal of Knowledge Management, 22*(2).

Bai, J. (2023). Disciplined parenting professionalism: FEPL, changing patterns of power, assumed politics in family education. *International Journal of Learning and Teaching*, *9*(2), 157–162. DOI: 10.18178/ijlt.9.2.157-162

Bakırcı, K. (2022). An essay on the relationship between isolation in business life and poverty, violence, and discrimination from a legal perspective. In Digitalization and Loneliness III: International Loneliness Symposium Book (pp. 41–62). İstanbul: Üsküdar University Press.

Bakshi, T., & Bhattacharyya, A. (2021). Socially distanced or socially connected? Well-being through ICT usage among the Indian elderly during COVID-19. *Millennial Asia*, *12*(2), 190–208. DOI: 10.1177/0976399621989910

Balekang, G. B., Galvin, T., & Rakgoasi, D. S. (2025). "No, it is not a breach of my oath because it is beyond my control; I use the policies that are in place." Ethical challenges faced by healthcare workers in the provision of healthcare to cross-border migrants in Botswana. *BMC Medical Ethics*, *26*(1), 1–12. DOI: 10.1186/s12910-025-01195-4

Balibar, É. (2014). *Equaliberty: Political Essays* (J.) Ingram, Ed.). Duke University Press.

Banerjee, A., Duflo, E., Grela, E., McKelway, M., Schilbach, F., Sharma, G., & Vaidyanathan, G. (2023). Depression and loneliness among the elderly in low-and middle-income countries. *The Journal of Economic Perspectives, 37*(2), 179–202. DOI: 10.1257/jep.37.2.179

Banerjee, D. (2021). Loneliness in older people: Spiritual practices as an alternative pathway to action, a treatise from India. *Journal of Geriatric Mental Health, 8*(2), 63–69. DOI: 10.4103/jgmh.jgmh_37_21

Banet-Weiser, S. (2018). *Empowered: Popular feminism and popular misogyny*. Duke University Press.

Bano, M. (2017). *Female Islamic education movements*. Oxford University Press. DOI: 10.1017/9781316986721

Barreto, M., Victor, C., Hammond, C., Eccles, A., Richins, M. T., & Qualter, P. (2021). Loneliness around the world: Age, gender, and cultural differences in loneliness. *Personality and Individual Differences, 169*, 110066. DOI: 10.1016/j.paid.2020.110066

Batra, R., Flatt, J. D., Pharr, J. R., Sharma, M., Khubchandani, J., Kanekar, A., Chirico, F., & Batra, K. (2024). Exploring Social Support Strategies and Socio-Cultural Factors Influencing Social Isolation and Loneliness: The Role of Digital Literacy. *Healthcare (Basel), 12*(21), 1–10. DOI: 10.3390/healthcare12212149

Bauman, Z. (2000). *Liquid modernity*. Polity Press.

Bauman, Z. (2001). *The individualized society*. Polity Press.

Bayraktar, S., & Jiménez, A. (2022). Friend or foe? The effects of harmonious and obsessive passion on entrepreneurs' well-being, strain and social loneliness. *Cross Cultural & Strategic Management, 29*(2), 320–348. DOI: 10.1108/CCSM-03-2021-0056

BAZNAS. (2024). *Policy Brief: Zakat on fisheries as an alternative solution to poverty alleviation for fishermen and coastal communities.* Center for Strategic Studies - National Amil Zakat Agency (Puskas BAZNAS).

Beaunoyer, E., Dupéré, S., & Guitton, M. J. (2020). COVID-19 and digital inequalities: Reciprocal impacts and mitigation strategies. *Computers in Human Behavior, 111*, 106424. DOI: 10.1016/j.chb.2020.106424

Becker, G. S. (1965). A theory of the allocation of time. *Economic Journal (London), 75*(299), 493–517. DOI: 10.2307/2228949

Beck, U. (1992). Risk society: Towards a new modernity. *Sage (Atlanta, Ga.).*

Beekun, R. I., & Badawi, J. A. (2005). Balancing ethical responsibility among multiple organizational stakeholders: The Islamic perspective. *Journal of Business Ethics, 60*(2), 131–145. DOI: 10.1007/s10551-004-8204-5

Belkhir, M., Brouard, M., Brunk, K. H., Dalmoro, M., Ferreira, M. C., Figueiredo, B., Huff, A. D., Scaraboto, D., Sibai, O., & Smith, A. N. (2019). Isolation in Globalizing Academic Fields: A Collaborative Autoethnography of Early Career Researchers. *Academy of Management Learning & Education, 18*(2), 261–285. DOI: 10.5465/amle.2017.0329

Benhabib, S. (2004). *The rights of others: aliens, residents, and citizens.* Cambridge University Press. DOI: 10.1017/CBO9780511790799

Benjamin, R. (2019). *Race after Technology: Abolitionist Tools for the New Jim Code.* Polity Press.

Berlant, L. (2011). *Cruel optimism.* Duke University Press.

Bevens, W., Stoeckl, S. E., Schueller, S. M., Kim, J., Cha, B. S., Chwa, C., Stadnick, N. A., Best, N. C., & Sorkin, D. H. (2024). Loneliness, online learning and student outcomes in college students living with disabilities: Results from the National College Health Assessment Spring 2022. *Frontiers in Psychology, 15*, 1408837. DOI: 10.3389/fpsyg.2024.1408837

Bhugra, D. (2004). Migration, distress and cultural identity. *British Medical Bulletin, 69*(1), 129–141. DOI: 10.1093/bmb/ldh007

Bhugra, D. (2004). Review article Migration and mental health. *Acta Psychiatrica Scandinavica, 109*(4), 243–258. http://doi.wiley.com/10.1046/j.0001-690X.2003.00246.x. DOI: 10.1046/j.0001-690X.2003.00246.x

Billah, M. M. (2019). Zakah: its micro- entrepreneurship model and socio- humanitarian impact. In Cattelan, V. (Ed.), *Islamic social finance: Entrepreneurship, cooperation and the sharing* (pp. 199–209). Routledge.

Biswas, A. (2023, December 2). View: There's a growing loneliness economy to tap. *The Economic Times,* https://economictimes.indiatimes.com/opinion/et-commentary/view-theres-a-growing-loneliness-economy-to-tap/articleshow/105683519.cms?from=mdr

Bitirim Okmeydan, S. (2017). Transformation of surveillance society in postmodern culture: From 'Panopticon' to 'Synopticon' and 'Omniopticon'. *Online Academic Journal of Information Technology, Special Issue, 8*(30), 45–69. DOI: 10.5824/1309-1581.2017.5.003.x

Bjørnskov, C. (2007). Determinants of generalized trust: A cross-country comparison. *Public Choice, 130*(1–2), 1–21. DOI: 10.1007/s11127-006-9069-1

Blitz, B. K., & Lynch, M. (Eds.). (2011). *Statelessness and the benefits of citizenship: A comparative study*. Oxford Brookes University/Kingston University. DOI: 10.4337/9781849808996

Blitz, B. K., & Sawyer, C. (Eds.). (2011). *Statelessness in the European Union: Displaced, undocumented, unwanted*. Cambridge University Press. DOI: 10.1017/CBO9780511921438.001

Bloom, T. (2017). *Noncitizenism: recognizing non-citizen capabilities in the world of citizens*. Routledge. DOI: 10.4324/9781315169736

Bludau, H. (2021). Global healthcare worker migration. In *Oxford research encyclopedia of anthropology*. DOI: 10.1093/acrefore/9780190854584.013.231

Blumer, H. (2012). Symbolic interactionism [1969]. *Contemporary sociological theory, 62*.

Boddy, C. (2020). Lonely, homesick and struggling: Undergraduate students and intention to quit university. (2020). *Quality Assurance in Education, 28*(4), 239–253. DOI: 10.1108/QAE-05-2020-0056

Boniol, M., Kunjumen, T., Nair, T. S., Siyam, A., Campbell, J., & Diallo, K. (2022). The global health workforce stock and distribution in 2020 and 2030: A threat to equity and 'universal'health coverage? *BMJ Global Health*, *7*(6), e009316. DOI: 10.1136/bmjgh-2022-009316

Bose, N. (2021). Citizens' participation in local governance: A study of Residents Welfare Associations in Delhi. In *Decentralisation in Contemporary India* (pp. 240-254). Routledge India.

Bosniak, L. (2006). *The citizen and the alien: Dilemmas of contemporary membership*. Princeton University Press. DOI: 10.1515/9781400827510

Bourdieu, P. (1986). The forms of capital. In J. Richardson (Ed.), *Handbook of theory and research for the sociology of education* (pp. 241–258). Greenwood.

Bourdieu, P. (1986). The forms of capital. In Richardson, J. G. (Ed.), *Handbook of theory and research for the sociology of education* (pp. 241–258).

Bourdieu, P. (1998). *Practical reason: On the theory of action*. Stanford University Press.

Bradburn, N. M. (1969). *The structure of psychological well-being*. Aldine.

Brandt, L., Liu, S., Heim, C., & Heinz, A. (2022). The effects of social isolation stress and discrimination on mental health. *Translational Psychiatry*, *12*(1), 1–11. DOI: 10.1038/s41398-022-02178-4

Brilliant, T. (2022). Loneliness inside of the brain: Evidence from a large dataset of resting-state fMRI in young adult. *Scientific Reports*, *12*(1), 7856. DOI: 10.1038/s41598-022-11724-5 PMID: 35550564

Broadbent, E., Stafford, R., & MacDonald, B. (2009). Acceptance of healthcare robots for the older population: Review and future directions. *International Journal of Social Robotics*, *1*(4), 319–330. DOI: 10.1007/s12369-009-0030-6

Brown, W. (2015). *Undoing the demos: Neoliberalism's stealth revolution*. MIT Press. DOI: 10.2307/j.ctt17kk9p8

Brubaker, R. (1992). *Citizenship and nationhood in France and Germany*. Harvard University Press. DOI: 10.4159/9780674028944

Brush, B. L., Sochalski, J., & Berger, A. M. (2004). Imported Care: Recruiting Foreign Nurses To U.S. Health Care Facilities. *Health Affairs (Project Hope)*, *23*(3), 78–87. DOI: 10.1377/hlthaff.23.3.78

Buchan, M. C., Bhawra, J., & Katapally, T. R. (2024). Navigating the digital world: Development of an evidence-based digital literacy program and assessment tool for youth. *Smart Learning Environments*, *11*(1), 1–24. DOI: 10.1186/s40561-024-00293-x

Buecker, S., Maes, M., Denissen, J. J. A., & Luhmann, M. (2020). Loneliness and the Big Five Personality Traits: A Meta–Analysis. *European Journal of Personality*, *34*(1), 8–28. DOI: 10.1002/per.2229

Bu, F., Steptoe, A., & Fancourt, D. (2020). Who is lonely in lockdown? Cross-cohort analyses of predictors of loneliness before and during the COVID-19 pandemic. *Public Health*, *186*, 31–34. DOI: 10.1016/j.puhe.2020.06.036

Bugallo-Carrera, C., Dosil-Díaz, C., Anido-Rifón, L., Pacheco-Lorenzo, M., Fernández-Iglesias, M. J., & Gandoy-Crego, M. (2023). A systematic review evaluating loneliness assessment instruments in older adults. *Frontiers in Psychology*, *14*, 1101462. DOI: 10.3389/fpsyg.2023.1101462

Bukhari, M. I. (n.d.). *Sahih al-Bukhari*. Dar al-Marefah.

Bull, F. C., Al-Ansari, S. S., Biddle, S., Borodulin, K., Buman, M. P., Cardon, G., Carty, C., Chaput, J.-P., Chastin, S., Chou, R., Dempsey, P. C., DiPietro, L., Ekelund, U., Firth, J., Friedenreich, C. M., Garcia, L., Gichu, M., Jago, R., Katzmarzyk, P. T., & Willumsen, J. F. (2020). World Health Organization 2020 guidelines on physical activity and sedentary behaviour. *British Journal of Sports Medicine, 54*(24), 1451–1462. DOI: 10.1136/bjsports-2020-102955

Cabinet Office of Japan. (2021). *Annual report on the ageing society*. Government of Japan.

Cacioppo, S., Grippo, A. J., London, S., Goossens, L., & Cacioppo, J. T. (2015). Loneliness: clinical import and interventions. *Perspectives on psychological science: a journal of the Association for Psychological Science, 10*(2), 238–249. DOI: 10.1177/1745691615570616

Cacioppo, J. T., & Cacioppo, S. (2018). Chapter Three - Loneliness in the Modern Age: An Evolutionary Theory of Loneliness (ETL). In Olson, J. M. (Ed.), Vol. 58, pp. 127–197). Advances in Experimental Social Psychology. Academic Press., DOI: 10.1016/bs.aesp.2018.03.003

Cacioppo, J. T., & Cacioppo, S. (2018). *Loneliness: Human nature and the need for social connection*. W. W. Norton.

Cacioppo, J. T., & Cacioppo, S. (2018). The growing problem of loneliness. *Lancet, 391*(10119), 426. DOI: 10.1016/S0140-6736(18)30142-9 PMID: 29407030

Cacioppo, J. T., Cacioppo, S., & Boomsma, D. I. (2014). Evolutionary mechanisms for loneliness. *Cognition and Emotion, 28*(1), 3–21. DOI: 10.1080/02699931.2013.837379

Cacioppo, J. T., Hawkley, L. C., & Thisted, R. A. (2010). Perceived social isolation makes me sad: 5-year cross-lagged analyses of loneliness and depressive symptomatology in the Chicago Health, Aging, and Social Relations Study. *Psychology and Aging, 25*(2), 453–463. DOI: 10.1037/a0017216

Cahyanti, I. S., Ulfa, U., & Suhendi, E. (2024). How Islamic social finance boosts psychological well-being? *SHARE Jurnal Ekonomi dan Keuangan Islam 13*(2), 415-437. .DOI: 10.22373/share.v13i2.19998

Cai, F., Park, A., & Zhao, Y. (2008). The Chinese labor market in the reform era.

Çalgüner Kılınç, E., & Avşar, Z. (2023). Analysis of Ekşi Sözlük in the context of Fuchs' prosumer commodification and digital labor exploitation concepts. *Yeni Medya Dergisi, 15*, 69–91.

Caliendo, L., Dvorkin, M., & Parro, F. (2015). *The impact of trade on labor market dynamics*.

Caliendo, L., Dvorkin, M., & Parro, F. (2019). Trade and labor market dynamics: General equilibrium analysis of the china trade shock. *Econometrica, 87*(3), 741–835. DOI: 10.3982/ECTA13758

Campbell, H. (2021). *Digital religion: Understanding religious practice in new media worlds*. Routledge. DOI: 10.4324/9780429295683

Card, K., Yu, C., Refol, J., Frost, A., & Bombaci, P. (2023, February 9). How does loneliness affect health? *Social Connection Guidelines,* https://www.socialconnectionguidelines.org/en/evidence-briefs/how-does-loneliness-affect-health

Carens, J. H. (1987). Aliens and citizens: The case for open borders. *The Review of Politics, 49*(2), 251–273. DOI: 10.1017/S0034670500033817

Carillon, S., Fedyuk, O., Gerbier-Aublanc, M., Gosselin, A., Guidi, C. F., Leite Borges, D. d. C., Malakasis, C., Perna, R., Petel-Rochette, N., Pérez, M., Rodríguez-Newey, I., Rohde-Abuba, C., Sahraoui, N., Sahraoui, N., Santilli, C., & European Commission Horizon (2020). - ERC Project EU Border Care (starting Grant 638259). *Borders across Healthcare: Moral Economies of Healthcare and Migration in Europe*

Carr, E. H. (1946). *The twenty years' crisis: 1919–1939: An introduction to the study of international relations*. Macmillan & Co. Ltd.

Carruthers, S., Pickles, A., Slonims, V., Howlin, P., & Charman, T. (2020). Beyond intervention into daily life: A systematic review of generalisation following social communication interventions for young children with autism. *Autism Research, 13*(4), 506–522. DOI: 10.1002/aur.2264

Casal, B., Rodríguez-Miguez, E., & Rivera, B. (2025). The societal cost of 'unwanted'loneliness in Spain. *The European Journal of Health Economics, 26*(4), 605–617. DOI: 10.1007/s10198-024-01724-9

Castellanos Silva, R., & Steins, G. (2023, March 8). Social media and body dissatisfaction in young adults: An experimental investigation of the effects of different image content and influencing constructs. *Frontiers in Psychology, 14*, 1037932. Advance online publication. DOI: 10.3389/fpsyg.2023.1037932

Cesari, J. (2009). Securitization of Islam in Europe. In *Muslims in the West after 9/11* (pp. 19–37). Routledge. DOI: 10.4324/9780203863961

Çevik Özdemir, H. N., & Ayran, G. (2025). Social isolation in Turkish adolescents: Translation, cross-cultural adaptation, and validation of the social isolation questionnaire. *Children (Basel, Switzerland)*, *12*(9), 1122. DOI: 10.3390/children12091122

Chandra, V. (2024). Changing Landscape of Indian Family. In *Indian Families: Contemporary Family. Structures and Dynamics*, *26*, 65–76. Emerald Publishing Limited.

Chan, L. S. (2018). Online dating apps as a marketing platform. *Journal of Marketing Management*, *34*(15-16), 1373–1392.

Chapra, M. U. (1992). *Islam and the economic challenge* (No. 17). International Institute of Islamic Thought (IIIT).

Chapra, M. U. (2008). *The Islamic vision of development in the light of maqasid al-shariah.* The International Institute of Islamic Thought (IIIT).

Chapra, M. U. (2000). *The future of economics: An Islamic perspective.* The Islamic Foundation.

Charlesworth, H., & Chinkin, C. (2000). *The boundaries of international law: A feminist analysis.* Manchester University Press.

Cheesman, N. (2017). How in Myanmar "national races" came to surpass citizenship and exclude Rohingya. *Journal of Contemporary Asia*, *47*(3), 461–483. DOI: 10.1080/00472336.2017.1297476

Cheetham, L. J. (2024). "Because people don't know what it is, they don't really know it exists": A qualitative study of postgraduate medical educators' perceptions of dyscalculia. *BMC Medical Education*, *24*(1), 896. DOI: 10.1186/s12909-024-05912-2

Chen, C., & Liu, M. (2023). Achievements and challenges of the healthcare system in China. *Cureus*, *15*(5). Advance online publication. DOI: 10.7759/cureus.39030

Chételat, G., Lutz, A., Arenaza-Urquijo, E., Collette, F., Klimecki, O., & Marchant, N. (2018). Why could meditation practice help promote mental health and well-being in aging? *Alzheimer's Research & Therapy*, *10*(1), 57. DOI: 10.1186/s13195-018-0388-5

Cho, H.-J., Kang, K., & Park, K.-Y. (2023). Health-related quality of life of migrant workers: A systematic literature review. *BMC Public Health*, *23*(1), 1004. DOI: 10.1186/s12889-023-15981-5

Chung, A. F., Teasell, M. J., Pergher, V., Thornton, A. E., & Thornton, W. L. (2023). Fear of COVID-19 is associated with trust, subjective numeracy, and differentially with loneliness in older versus younger adults. *Frontiers in Psychology*, *14*, 1080631. Advance online publication. DOI: 10.3389/fpsyg.2023.1080631

Çınar, A. (2019). Local governance and community building in contemporary Turkey. *Journal of Social Policy*, *48*(3), 411–430. DOI: 10.1017/S0047279418000924

Clark, M. B., Nkonya, E., & Galford, G. L. (2025). Exodus of the affluent? examining climate hazards, migration, and household income in the U.S. *Population and Environment*, *47*(3), 1–30. DOI: 10.1007/s11111-025-00496-5

Clemens, M. A., & Pettersson, G. (2008). New data on African health professionals abroad. *Human Resources for Health*, *6*(1), 1. Advance online publication. DOI: 10.1186/1478-4491-6-1

Cohen, R., Irwin, L., Newton-John, T., & Slater, A. (2019, June). #bodypositivity: A content analysis of body positive accounts on Instagram. *Body Image*, *29*, 47–57. DOI: 10.1016/j.bodyim.2019.02.007

Collins, F. L. (2021). 'Give me my pathway!': Multinational migration, transnational skills regimes and migrant subjectification. *Global Networks*, *21*(1), 18–39. DOI: 10.1111/glob.12294

Colquhoun, H. L., Levac, D., O'Brien, K. K., Straus, S., Tricco, A. C., Perrier, L., Kastner, M., & Moher, D. (2014). Scoping reviews: Time for clarity in definition, methods, and reporting. *Journal of Clinical Epidemiology*, *67*(12), 1291–1294. DOI: 10.1016/j.jclinepi.2014.03.013

Connell, J. (2010). *Migration and the Globalisation of Health Care*. Edward Elgar Publishing., DOI: 10.4337/9781849805186

Cooley, C. H. (1902). *Looking-glass self.* Social Media & the Self: An Open Reader https://DOI: 10.32376/3f8575cb.73d69f51

Cornu, A. (1976). Manuscripts on economics, politics and philosophy. In Marx, K. (Ed.), *Economic and philosophic manuscripts of 1844* (Somer, K., Trans.). Sol Yayınları.

Cornwell, E. Y., & Waite, L. J. (2009). Social disconnectedness, perceived isolation, and health among older adults. *Journal of Health and Social Behavior*, *50*(1), 31–48. DOI: 10.1177/002214650905000103

Costello, M. A., Nagel, A. G., Hunt, G. L., Rivens, A. J., Hazelwood, O. A., Pettit, C., & Allen, J. P. (2022). Facilitating connection to enhance college student well-being: Evaluation of an experiential group program. *American Journal of Community Psychology, 70*(3–4), 314–326. DOI: 10.1002/ajcp.12601

Courtin, E., & Knapp, M. (2017). Social isolation, loneliness and health in old age: A scoping review. *Health & Social Care in the Community, 25*(3), 799–812. DOI: 10.1111/hsc.12311

Crary, J. (2013). *24/7: Late capitalism and the ends of sleep*. Verso.

Crenshaw, K. (1989). Demarginalizing the intersection of race and sex: A Black feminist critique of antidiscrimination doctrine, feminist theory and antiracist politics. *University of Chicago Legal Forum, 1989*(1), 139–167.

Cudjoe, T. K. M., & Colburn, J. L. (2019). Social Isolation. *Home-Based Medical Care for Older Adults: A Clinical Case Book, 1231*(1), 85–90. DOI: 10.1007/978-3-030-23483-6_13

Cuijpers, P., Hollon, S. D., van Straten, A., Bockting, C., Berking, M., & Andersson, G. (2013). Does cognitive behaviour therapy have an enduring effect that is superior to keeping patients on continuation pharmacotherapy? A meta-analysis. *BMJ Open, 3*(4), e002542. DOI: 10.1136/bmjopen-2012-002542

Cunha, Y. R. (2013). Standing, guy. The precariat. *Revista Aurora, 7*(1), 203–208. DOI: 10.36311/1982-8004.2013.v7n1.3403

Currie, G., Finn, R., & Martin, G. (2008). Accounting for thedark side'of new organizational forms: The case of healthcare professionals. *Human Relations, 61*(4), 539–564. DOI: 10.1177/0018726708091018

Dabrowski, V., Atas, N., Ramsey, T., & Howarth, N. (2025). 'Money anxiety': Understanding HE students' experiences of the cost-of-living crisis. *Social Policy and Administration, 59*(2), 280–292. DOI: 10.1111/spol.13048

Dagnew, B., & Dagne, H. (2019). Year of study as predictor of loneliness among students of University of Gondar. *BMC Research Notes, 12*(1), 240. DOI: 10.1186/s13104-019-4274-4

Dao, M., Furceri, D., & Loungani, P. (2017). Regional labor market adjustment in the United States: Trend and cycle. *The Review of Economics and Statistics, 99*(2), 243–257. DOI: 10.1162/REST_a_00642

Das, B. (2024). Loneliness of PhD-ing: Migrant bodies of colour and Irish neo-liberal academia. *Irish Journal of Sociology, 32*(1–2), 47–65. DOI: 10.1177/07916035241259254

David, D., Toplak, B., & Toplak, B. (2020, January). Digital literacy during the coronavirus pandemic in older adults: Literature Review and Research Agenda. *IFAC-PapersOnLine, 55*(39), 153–158. DOI: 10.1016/j.ifacol.2022.12.027

Davies, N., Crowe, M., & Whitehead, L. (2016). Establishing routines to cope with the loneliness associated with widowhood: A narrative analysis. *Journal of Psychiatric and Mental Health Nursing, 23*(8), 532–539. DOI: 10.1111/jpm.12339

Davies, W. (2015). *The happiness industry: How the government and big business sold us well-being*. Verso.

De Felice, S., Hamilton, A. F. de C., Ponari, M., & Vigliocco, G. (2023). Learning from others is good, with others is better: The role of social interaction in human acquisition of new knowledge. *Philosophical Transactions of the Royal Society of London. Series B, Biological Sciences, 378*(1870), 20210357. DOI: 10.1098/rstb.2021.0357

De Jong Gierveld, J., & Van Tilburg, T. (2010). The De Jong Gierveld short scales for emotional and social loneliness: Tested on data from 7 countries in the UN Generations and Gender Surveys. *European Journal of Ageing, 7*(2), 121–130. DOI: 10.1007/s10433-010-0144-6

Dean, J. (2019). Critique or collectivity? Communicative capitalism and the subject of politics. In Chandler, D., & Fuchs, C. (Eds.), *Digital objects, digital subjects: Interdisciplinary perspectives on capitalism, labour and politics in the age of big data*. University of Westminster Press. DOI: 10.16997/book29.n

Debesay, J., Kartzow, A. H., & Fougner, M. (2022). Healthcare professionals' encounters with ethnic minority patients: The critical incident approach. *Nursing Inquiry, 29*(1), e12421. DOI: 10.1111/nin.12421

Debord, G. (1990). *Comments on the society of the spectacle* (Imrie, M., Trans.). Verso Books.

DEKS-BI & DES-FEB UNAIR (2016). *Wakaf: Pengaturan dan tata kelola yang efektif [Waqf: Effective regulation and governance]*. Department of Islamic Economics and Finance - Bank Indonesia (DEKS-BI).

DEKS-BI & P3EI-FE UII (2016). *Pengelolaan zakat yang efektif: Konsep dan praktik di beberapa negara [Effective zakat management: Concepts and practices in several countries]*. Department of Islamic Economics and Finance - Bank Indonesia (DEKS-BI).

Dervin, F. (2024). From Language to Listening. *Interculturologies: Moving Forward with Interculturality in Research and Education*, 197-210.

Deshingkar, P., & Akter, S. (2009). Migration and Human Development in India. *Human Development Research Paper (HDRP) Series, 13*(19193), 1–85. https://mpra.ub.uni-muenchen.de/19193/

Dey, D. N. C. (2024). Mental health of adolescents and youth in India: A critical analysis in the era of AI. *Available at SSRN* 5056368. DOI: 10.2139/ssrn.5056368

Dhakal, S. (2018). Citizenship and belonging: Gendered nationality law in Nepal. *Asian Journal of Women's Studies, 24*(2), 137–158.

Diehl, K., Jansen, C., Ishchanova, K., & Hilger-Kolb, J. (2018). Loneliness at Universities: Determinants of Emotional and Social Loneliness among Students. *International Journal of Environmental Research and Public Health, 15*(9), 1865. DOI: 10.3390/ijerph15091865

Di, X., & Wang, L. (2025). Impact of digital literacy on aging attitudes of the elderly from the perspective of social cognitive theory. *BMC Public Health, 25*(1), 1–11. DOI: 10.1186/s12889-025-23377-w

Dotsey, S. (2023). Foreign healthcare workers and COVID-19 in Europe: The paradox of unemployed skilled labour. *Social Sciences (Basel, Switzerland), 12*(4), 211. DOI: 10.3390/socsci12040211

Durkheim, E. (2005). *Suicide: A study in sociology* (Spaulding, J. A., & Simpson, G., Trans.). Routledge. DOI: 10.4324/9780203994320

Durkheim, E. (2013). *The evolution of educational thought: Lectures on the formation and development of secondary education in France*. Routledge. DOI: 10.4324/9781315020594

Dzenovska, D. (2018). *School of Europeanness: Tolerance and other lessons in political liberalism in Latvia*. Cornell University Press.

Eagleton, T. (2011). *Why Marx was right?* Yale University Press.

Egaña-Marcos, E., Collantes, E., Diez-Solinska, A., & Azkona, G. (2025). The Influence of Loneliness, Social Support and Income on Mental Well-Being. *European Journal of Investigation in Health, Psychology and Education, 15*(5), 70. DOI: 10.3390/ejihpe15050070

El-Affendi, A. (2010). The elusive reform: Democracy and the rule of law in the Arab world. *Democratization, 17*(3), 492–509. DOI: 10.1080/13510341003700371

Elder, C., Nidich, S., Moriarty, F., & Nidich, R. (2014). Effect of transcendental meditation on employee stress, depression, and burnout: A randomized controlled study. *The Permanente Journal, 18*(1), 19–23. DOI: 10.7812/TPP/13-102

Ellard, O. B., Dennison, C., & Tuomainen, H. (2023). Review: Interventions addressing loneliness amongst university students: a systematic review. *Child and Adolescent Mental Health, 28*(4), 512–523. DOI: 10.1111/camh.12614

Elnur, A. (2023). The transformation of the sociology of leisure in the context of digitalization of communication processes. *The Academic Elegance, 10*(23), 287–311.

Engel, L., Rizal, M. F., Clifford, S., Faller, J., Lim, M. H., Le, L. K., Chatterton, M. L., & Mihalopoulos, C. (2025). An updated systematic literature review of the economic costs of loneliness and social isolation and the cost effectiveness of interventions. *PharmacoEconomics, 43*(9), 1047–1063. DOI: 10.1007/s40273-025-01516-w PMID: 40524124

Engels, F. (1977). *Dialectics of nature* (Dutt, C., Trans.). Progress Publishers.

Equality Now, & Global Campaign for Equal Nationality Rights. (2025). *Gender-discriminatory nationality laws are fueling poverty and violence against women.* Equality Now.

Eren, F. A., Boz, C., & Sargin, M. (2025). Exploring the relationship between obesity and social isolation: A crosssectional analysis. *Eurasian Journal of Family Medicine = Avrasya Aile Hekimligi Dergisi, 14*(2), 57–67. DOI: 10.33880/ejfm.2025140203

Erol, A. (2021). Change of workplace in the age of digitalization: Causes and consequences. İn-san&İnsan, 8(30), 97–113.

Ersoy, M. A., & Yantur, P. (2025, August 27). Special interview – Steel Dome: A new era in Turkey's air defense [Video]. Haberturk & Bloomberg HT. https://tv.haberturk.com/programlar/video/ozel-roportaj-27-agustos-2025-celik-kubbe-turkiyenin-hava-savunmasinda-yeni-donem/888895

Esposito, J. L. (2018). *Islam and the future of tolerance.* Oxford University Press.

Esposito, J. L., & Voll, J. O. (2001). *Islam and democracy.* Oxford University Press.

Estes, C. L., & Phillipson, C. (2002). The globalization of capital, the welfare state, and old age policy. *International Journal of Health Services, 32*(2), 279–297. DOI: 10.2190/5TY7-PD68-QLD1-V4TY

Eubanks, V. (2018). *Automating inequality: How high-tech tools profile, police, and punish the poor*. St. Martin's Press.

Fakoya, O. A., McCorry, N. K., & Donnelly, M. (2020). Loneliness and social isolation interventions for older adults: A scoping review of reviews. *BMC Public Health, 20*(1), 129. DOI: 10.1186/s12889-020-8251-6

Fardouly, J., Pinkus, R. T., & Vartanian, L. R. (2017). The impact of appearance comparisons made through social media, traditional media, and in-person in women's everyday lives. *Body Image, 20*, 31–39. DOI: 10.1016/j.bodyim.2016.11.002

Farrell, W., & Gray, J. (2019). *The boy crisis*. BenBella Books.

Fassin, D. (2011). *Humanitarian reason: A moral history of the present*. University of California Press.

Fathi-Ashtiani, M., Hosseinchari, M., Ahmadi, F., & Jowkar, B. (2021). Lived Experiences of Dropout University Students: A Qualitative Content Analysis. *International Journal of Behavioral Sciences, 15*(1), 41–47. DOI: 10.30491/ijbs.2021.258913.1440

Fauzia, I. Y., & Musari, K. (2021). Waqf crowdfunding for financing the MSMEs: Evidence from ASEAN-3. In de Pablos, P. O., Zhang, X., & Almunawar, M. N. (Eds.), *Handbook of research on disruptive innovation and digital transformation in Asia* (pp. 37-49). IGI Global. DOI: 10.4018/978-1-7998-6477-6.ch003

Feng, S., Hu, Y., & Moffitt, R. (2015). *Long run trends in unemployment and labor force participation in China*.

Feng, S., & Guo, N. (2021). Labor market dynamics in urban China and the role of the state sector. *Journal of Comparative Economics, 49*(4), 918–932. DOI: 10.1016/j.jce.2021.04.002

Fenn, K., & Byrne, M. (2013). The key principles of cognitive behavioural therapy. *InnovAiT, 6*(9), 579–585. DOI: 10.1177/1755738012471029

Fernández, M. (2020). The politics of denationalization in the Dominican Republic. *Latin American and Caribbean Ethnic Studies, 15*(1), 44–68.

Ferreira, R., Pereira, R., Bianchi, I. S., & da Silva, M. M. (2021). Decision Factors for Remote Work Adoption: Advantages, Disadvantages, Driving Forces and Challenges. *Journal of Open Innovation, 7*(1), 70. DOI: 10.3390/joitmc7010070

Flowers, L., Houser, A., Noel-Miller, C., Shaw, J., Bhattacharya, J., Schoemaker, L., & Farid, M. (2017). *Medicare spends more on socially isolated older adults.* AARP Foundation. DOI: 10.26419/ppi.00016.001

Folbre, N. (2001). *The invisible heart: Economics and family values.* The New Press.

Fortuna, K. L., Solomon, P., & Rivera, J. (2022). An Update of Peer Support/Peer Provided Services Underlying Processes, Benefits, and Critical Ingredients. *The Psychiatric Quarterly, 93*(2), 571–586. DOI: 10.1007/s11126-022-09971-w

Foucault, M. (1995). *Discipline and punish: The birth of the prison* (Sheridan, A. M., Trans.). Vintage Books.

Foucault, M. (2003). *The birth of the clinic* (Sheridan, A. M., Trans.). Routledge.

Foucault, M. (2008). *The birth of biopolitics* (Burchell, G., Trans.). Palgrave Macmillan.

Foucault, M. (2008). *The birth of biopolitics: Lectures at the Collège de France, 1978–1979.* Palgrave Macmillan.

Franceschini, I., & Loubere, N. (2022). *Global China as method.* Cambridge University Press. DOI: 10.1017/9781108999472

Fraser, N. (2013). *Fortunes of feminism.* Verso.

Fraser, N. (2017). Crisis of care? On the social-reproductive contradictions of contemporary capitalism. *Socialist Register, 113*, 21–45. DOI: 10.2307/j.ctt1vz494j.6

Fredman, S. (2011). *Discrimination law* (2nd ed.). Oxford University Press.

Fredrickson, B. L., & Roberts, T. (1997). Objectification theory: Toward understanding women's lived experiences and mental health risks. *Psychology of Women Quarterly, 21*(2), 173–206. DOI: 10.1111/j.1471-6402.1997.tb00108.x

Frounfelker, R. L., Miconi, D., Farrar, J., Brooks, M. A., Rousseau, C., & Betancourt, T. S. (2019). Mental health of refugee children and youth: Epidemiology, interventions, and future directions. *Annual Review of Public Health, 41*(1), 159–176. DOI: 10.1146/annurev-publhealth-040119-094230

Fuchs, C. (2019a). *Rereading Marx in the age of digital capitalism.* Pluto Press.

Fukuyama, F. (1992). *The end of history and the last man.* Maxwell Macmillan.

Fuller-Rowell, T. E., Sultana, S., & Kawachi, I. (2025). Global trends and disparities in social isolation. *JAMA Network Open, 8*(9), e2532008. DOI: 10.1001/jamanetworkopen.2025.32008

Fung, A. (2006). Varieties of participation in complex governance. *Public Administration Review*, *66*(s1), 66–75. DOI: 10.1111/j.1540-6210.2006.00667.x

Furlong, A. (2008). The Japanese hikikomori phenomenon: Acute social withdrawal among young people. *The Sociological Review*, *56*(2), 309–325. DOI: 10.1111/j.1467-954X.2008.00790.x

Galbreath, D. J. (2013). Latvia's non-citizens: Between ethnic discrimination and democratic inclusion. *Ethnopolitics*, *12*(4), 372–391.

Gallie, D., Paugam, S., & Jacobs, S. (2003). Unemployment, poverty and social isolation: Is there a vicious circle of social exclusion? *European Societies*, *5*(1), 1–32. DOI: 10.1080/1461669032000057668

García Peña, L. (2016). *The borders of Dominicanidad: Race, nation, and archives of contradiction*. Duke University Press.

Gaur, P. S., Saha, S., Goel, A., Ovseiko, P., Aggarwal, S., Agarwal, V., Haq, A. U., Danda, D., Hartle, A., Sandhu, N. K., & Gupta, L. (2023). Mental healthcare for young and adolescent LGBTQ+ individuals in the Indian subcontinent. *Frontiers in Psychology*, *14*, 1060543. DOI: 10.3389/fpsyg.2023.1060543 PMID: 36743255

Gauthier, C.-A. (2009). Globalizing Care Economies and Migrant Workers: Explorations in Global Care Chains By Nicola Yeates, New York: Palgrave Macmillan, 2009, 258 pp., ISBN 978-0-23000-534-1. *Relations Industrielles*, *64*(4), 707. DOI: 10.7202/038882ar

Gawande, R. P. (2024). Work-life balance and its impact on employees: Navigating strategies for better work-life balance at workplace. *International Journal of Cultural Studies and Social Science*, *20*(1), 130–136.

Gehl, J. (2010). *Cities for people*. Island Press.

Gelb, A., & Clark, J. (2013). Identification for development: The biometrics revolution. *Center for Global Development Working Paper*, (315).

General, U. S. (2023). Our epidemic of loneliness and isolation. *The US Surgeon General's Advisory on the Healing Effects of Social Connection and Community, 2023*.

Gibney, M. J. (2013). A very transcendental power: Denationalization and the liberalization of citizenship in the United Kingdom. *Political Studies*, *61*(3), 637–655. DOI: 10.1111/j.1467-9248.2012.00980.x

Girmay, M., & Singh, G. K. (2019). Social Isolation, Loneliness, and Mental and Emotional Well-being among International Students in the United States. *International Journal of Translational Medical Research and Public Health, 3*(2), 1–8. DOI: 10.21106/ijtmrph.82

Giroud, A. (2024). World Investment Report 2023: Investing in sustainable energy for all: United Nations Conference on Trade and Development, Geneva and New York, 2023, 205 pp. In: Springer. DOI: 10.1057/s42214-023-00178-9

Gleeson, S., & Griffith, K. L. (2021). Employers as subjects of the immigration state: How the state foments employment insecurity for temporary immigrant workers. *Law & Social Inquiry, 46*(1), 92–115. DOI: 10.1017/lsi.2020.17

Gloria, K. (2022). Loneliness in India: Recognizing the role of history, technology, & culture. Aspen Digital, Aspen Institute.

Goffman, E. (1979). Gender advertisements. Harper Torchbooks, Harper & Row, Publishers, New York, Cambridge, MA: Harvard University Press. ISBN 0-06-132076-5 (pbk.).

Goffman, E. (1978). *The presentation of self in everyday life*. Penguin.

Golaszewski, N. M., Lacroix, A. Z., Godino, J. G., Allison, M. A., Manson, J. E., King, J. J., Weitlauf, J. C., Bea, J. W., Garcia, L., Kroenke, C. H., Saquib, N., Cannell, B., Nguyen, S., & Bellettiere, J. (2022). Evaluation of Social Isolation, Loneliness, and Cardiovascular Disease among Older Women in the U.S. *JAMA Network Open, 5*(2), 1–12. DOI: 10.1001/jamanetworkopen.2021.46461

Gold, J. A., Bentzley, J. P., Franciscus, A. M., Forte, C., & De Golia, S. G. (2019). An Intervention in Social Connection: Medical Student Reflection Groups. *Academic Psychiatry, 43*(4), 375–380. DOI: 10.1007/s40596-019-01058-2

Goldstein, S. (2025, October 10). Welcome to the loneliness economy. *Psychology Today,* https://www.psychologytoday.com/us/blog/raising-resilient-children/202510/welcome-to-the-loneliness-economy

Göle, N. (2013). The public visibility of Islam and European politics of resentment: The minarets-mosques debate. *Philosophy and Social Criticism, 37*(4), 383–392. DOI: 10.1177/0191453711398773

Götz, F. M., Stieger, S., & Reips, U.-D. (2019). The Emergence and Volatility of Homesickness in Exchange Students Abroad: A Smartphone-Based Longitudinal Study. *Environment and Behavior, 51*(6), 689–716. DOI: 10.1177/0013916518754610

Graham, M., Hjorth, I., & Lehdonvirta, V. (2017). Digital labour and development. *Development Studies Research, 4*(1), 13–29. PMID: 28781494

Granieri, A., Franzoi, I. G., & Chung, M. C. (2021). Editorial: Psychological Distress Among University Students. *Frontiers in Psychology, 12*, 647940. DOI: 10.3389/fpsyg.2021.647940

Grant, J. A., Courtemanche, J., Duerden, E. G., Duncan, G. H., & Rainville, P. (2010). Cortical thickness and pain sensitivity in zen meditators. *Emotion (Washington, D.C.), 10*(1), 43–53. DOI: 10.1037/a0018334

Gruber, S., & Sand, G. (2020). Does Migration Pay Off in Later Life? Income and Subjective Well-being of Older Migrants in Europe. *Social Indicators Research, 160*(2–3), 969–988. DOI: 10.1007/s11205-020-02502-9

Guarnera, J., Yuen, E., & Macpherson, H. (2023). The impact of loneliness and social isolation on cognitive aging: A narrative review. *Journal of Alzheimer's Disease Reports, 7*(1), 699–714. DOI: 10.3233/ADR-230011

Guay, E., & Drago, A. (2021). Palaces for the People: How Social Infrastructure Can Help Fight Inequality, Polarization, and the Decline of Civic Life, d'Eric Klinenberg, New York, Crown, 2018, 277 p. *Politique et Sociétés, 40*(2), 224. DOI: 10.7202/1077879ar

Guha, S., and Rajesh Kadam, S. (2024). Review of recent studies on Women in Management. *An Inquiry into Women Representation in Management: A Case Study of Indian Industries*, 23-95.

Gümüş-Demir, Z., & Yılmaz, M. (2024). Loneliness, psychological well-being, depression, and social participation in the older persons: Rural and urban differences. *Current Aging Science, 17*(3), 247–261. DOI: 10.2174/0118746098297063240409070531

Guo, X. (2015). Deskilling and Devaluation of Chinese Immigrant Women in Ottawa.

Hall, S. L., Ryan, D. J., Beatty, J., & Grubbs, L. (2015). Recommendations for peer-to-peer support for NICU parents. *Journal of Perinatology: Official Journal of the California Perinatal Association, 35 Suppl 1*(Suppl 1), S9-13. DOI: 10.1038/jp.2015.143

Han, B.-C. (2017). *Psychopolitics: Neoliberalism and new technologies of power*. Verso.

Han, B.-C. (2017a). *The agony of eros* (Butler, E., Trans.). MIT Press. DOI: 10.7551/mitpress/11054.001.0001

Han, B.-C. (2018). *Topology of violence* (Demarco, A., Trans.). MIT Press. DOI: 10.7551/mitpress/11056.001.0001

Han, B.-C. (2019). *What is power?* (Steuer, D., Trans.). Polity Press.

Han, B.-C. (2021). *The palliative society: Pain today* (Steuer, D., Trans.). Polity Press.

Han, B.-C. (2022). *In praise of the earth: A journey into the garden* (2nd ed.). (Ermiş, N., Trans.). İnka Kitap.

Hansen, T. T., & Budtz Pedersen, D. (2018). The impact of academic events—A literature review. *Research Evaluation, 27*(4), 358–366. DOI: 10.1093/reseval/rvy025

Haque, A. (2018). Religion and mental health: The Islamic perspective. *Journal of Religion and Health, 57*(1), 5–16. DOI: 10.1007/s10943-017-0489-3

Harari, Y. N. (2011). *Sapiens: A brief history of humankind*. Vintage Books.

Harari, Y. N. (2018). *21 lessons for the 21st century*. Jonathan Cape.

Hargittai, E. (2001). Second-Level Digital Divide : Mapping Differences in. *Tprc, 7*(4), 1–19. DOI: 10.1080/01972240600991514

Harman, C. (2002). *A people's history of the world*. Bookmarks Publications.

Harper, S. (2014). Economic and social implications of aging societies. *Science, 346*(6209), 587–591. DOI: 10.1126/science.1254405

Harris, M. A., & Orth, U. (2020). The link between self-esteem and social relationships: A meta-analysis of longitudinal studies. *Journal of Personality and Social Psychology, 119*(6), 1459–1477. DOI: 10.1037/pspp0000265

Harsh, S., Ritik, B., Rushikesh, K., Purvanshu, M., & Suman, S. (2024). AI Being used to Tackle Mental Health Issues Conversify: A Robot Therapist. *International Journal of Trend in Scientific Research and Development, 8*(5), 584–592.

Harvard Business Review. (2017). *Work and loneliness survey report*.

Harvey, D. (2005). *A brief history of neoliberalism*. Oxford University Press. DOI: 10.1093/oso/9780199283262.001.0001

Harvey, D. (2012). *Rebel cities: From the right to the city to the urban revolution*. Verso.

Hasan, R., & Mahmood, S. (2021). Social isolation indicators in Southeast Asia. *Social Indicators Research, 155*(2), 651–673.

Hasan, S. I., Yee, A., Rinaldi, A., Azham, A. A., Mohd Hairi, F., & Amer Nordin, A. S. (2021). Prevalence of common mental health issues among migrant workers: A systematic review and meta-analysis. *PLoS One*, *16*(12), e0260221. DOI: 10.1371/journal.pone.0260221

Haslam, S. A., Haslam, C., Cruwys, T., Jetten, J., Bentley, S. V., Fong, P., & Steffens, N. K. (2022). Social identity makes group-based social connection possible: Implications for loneliness and mental health. *Current Opinion in Psychology*, *43*, 161–165. DOI: 10.1016/j.copsyc.2021.07.013

Hasnain, A., & Hajek, J. (2022). Understanding international student connectedness. *International Journal of Intercultural Relations*, *86*, 26–35. DOI: 10.1016/j.ijintrel.2021.10.008

Hassan Kariri, H. D., & Almubaddel, A. (2024). From theory to practice: Revealing the real-world impact of cognitive behavioral therapy in psychological disorders through a dynamic bibliometric and survey study. *Heliyon*, *10*(18), e37763. DOI: 10.1016/j.heliyon.2024.e37763

Hassan, M. K., & Ahmad, A. U. (2019a). Social infrastructure and mental health outcomes in Muslim communities. *Journal of Islamic Economics*, *45*(2), 234–251.

Hassan, M. K., & Muneeza, A. (2022). *Covid-19 and Islamic Finance*. Cambridge University Press. DOI: 10.1017/9781009189484

Hassan, R., & Ahmad, F. (2019b). Mosque density and community mental health: A comparative study of Malaysian states. *The Journal of Muslim Mental Health*, *13*(2), 45–62.

Hassel, S., & Ridout, N. (2018). An Investigation of First-Year Students' and Lecturers' Expectations of University Education. *Frontiers in Psychology*, *8*, 2218. Advance online publication. DOI: 10.3389/fpsyg.2017.02218

Hatton, E. (2017). Mechanisms of invisibility: Rethinking the concept of invisible work. *Work, Employment and Society*, *31*(2), 336–351. DOI: 10.1177/0950017016674894

Hawkley, L. C., & Cacioppo, J. T. (2010). Loneliness matters: A theoretical and empirical review. *Annals of Behavioral Medicine*, *40*(2), 218–227. DOI: 10.1007/s12160-010-9210-8 PMID: 20652462

Heim, C. (2023). Resilient relationships versus hyper-individualism: Selfish genes, altruism, and attachment. In Heim, C., & Heim, C. (Eds.), *Resilient relationships: Techniques for surviving hyperindividualism, social isolation, and a mental health crisis* (pp. 17–48). Routledge. DOI: 10.4324/9781003263395-3

Heino, R. D., Ellison, N. B., & Gibbs, J. L. (2010). Relationships on the line: Dating and intimacy in the digital age. *New Media & Society*, *12*(3), 477–494.

Helliwell, J. F., & Putnam, R. D. (2004). The social context of well-being. *Philosophical Transactions of the Royal Society of London. Series B, Biological Sciences*, *359*(1449), 1435–1446. DOI: 10.1098/rstb.2004.1522

Hepat, A., Khode, D., Chakole, S., & Chitransha, S. (2024). A narrative review of urbanization and mental health: An Indian perspective. *Cureus*, *16*(3). Advance online publication. DOI: 10.7759/cureus.55381 PMID: 38562368

Hertz, N. (2021). *The lonely century: how to restore human connection in a world that's pulling apart*. Crown Currency.

Herzog, N. J., Celik, D., & Sulaiman, R. B. (2024). Artificial intelligence in healthcare and medical records security. In *Cybersecurity and Artificial Intelligence: Transformational Strategies and Disruptive Innovation* (pp. 35–57). Springer Nature Switzerland. DOI: 10.1007/978-3-031-52272-7_2

Hilbrich, S. (2021). What is social finance? Definitions by market participants, the EU taxonomy for sustainable activities, and implications for development policy. Discussion Paper Deutsches Institut für Entwicklungspolitik (DIE)/ German Development Institute 29/2021.

Hobsbawm, E. (2002). *Interesting times: A twentieth-century life*. Allen Lane.

Hochschild, A. R. (2012). *The outsourced self: Intimate life in market times*. Metropolitan Books.

Hodgson, S., Watts, I., Fraser, S., Roderick, P., & Dambha-Miller, H. (2020). Loneliness, social isolation, cardiovascular disease and mortality: A synthesis of the literature and conceptual framework. *Journal of the Royal Society of Medicine*, *113*(5), 185–192. DOI: 10.1177/0141076820918236

Hoexter, M. (1998). *Endowments, rulers, and community: Waqf al-haramayn in Ottoman Algiers*. Brill. DOI: 10.1163/9789004660113

Holt-Lunstad, J. (2017). The potential public health relevance of social isolation and loneliness: Prevalence, epidemiology, and risk factors. *The Public Policy and Aging Report*, *27*(4), 127–130. DOI: 10.1093/ppar/prx030

Holt-Lunstad, J. (2021). Loneliness and social isolation as risk factors: The power of social connection in prevention. *American Journal of Lifestyle Medicine*, *15*(5), 1–7. DOI: 10.1177/15598276211009454 PMID: 34646109

Holt-Lunstad, J. (2021). Social isolation and health. *Annual Review of Public Health, 42*, 101–118. DOI: 10.1146/annurev-publhealth-012420-105148

Holt-Lunstad, J., Smith, T. B., & Layton, J. B. (2015). Social relationships and mortality risk: A meta-analytic review. *Perspectives on Psychological Science, 10*(2), 227–237. DOI: 10.1177/1745691614568352 PMID: 25910392

Hortulanus, R., & Machielse, A. (2006). The issue of social isolation. In Hortulanus, R., Machielse, A., & Meeuwesen, L. (Eds.), *Social isolation in modern society* (pp. 3–12). Routledge. DOI: 10.4324/9780203020142

Hosein, G., & Nyst, C. (2013). Aiding surveillance: an exploration of how development and humanitarian aid initiatives are enabling surveillance in developing countries.

Hossain, M. M., Purohit, N., Khan, N., McKyer, E. L. J., Ma, P., Bhattacharya, S., & Pawar, P. (2020). Prevalence and correlates of loneliness in India: A systematic review. *Advance.*_https://www.mckinsey.com/~/media/McKinsey/Featured%20Insights/Innovation/Ten%20highlights%20from%20our%202019%20research/MGI-in-2019-A-compendium-of-our-research-this-year-vF.pdf

Hossain, M. M., Purohit, N., Khan, N., McKyer, E. L. J., Ma, P., Bhattacharya, S., & Pawar, P. (2024). Loneliness in India: A systematic review of empirical studies. *Authorea Preprints.*

Hou, J., Michaud, C., Li, Z., Dong, Z., Sun, B., Zhang, J., Cao, D., Wan, X., Zeng, C., Wei, B., Tao, L., Li, X., Wang, W., Lu, Y., Xia, X., Guo, G., Zhang, Z., Cao, Y., Guan, Y., & Chen, L. (2014). Transformation of the education of health professionals in China: Progress and challenges. *Lancet, 384*(9945), 819–827. DOI: 10.1016/S0140-6736(14)61307-6

Howard, M. M. (2020). *The politics of citizenship in Europe* (2nd ed.). Cambridge University Press.

Hteit, R. (2023, June 4). *Takaful and karama: cash transfer programs for marginalized groups (2015–ongoing).* https://www.sdg16.plus/policies/takaful-and-karama-cash-transfer-programs-for-marginalized-groups

Hu, L., Glavin, Y.-F. W., Yan, R., Pei, C., Yan, M., Zhang, Y., & Liu, Y. (2021). Integrating health and care in China: Lessons learned and future outlook. *International Journal of Integrated Care, 21*(4), 18. DOI: 10.5334/ijic.5681

Human Rights Watch. (2011). *Prisoners of the past: Kuwaiti Bidun and the burden of statelessness*. Human Rights Watch.

Husin, S. S., Ab Rahman, A. A., & Mukhtar, D. (2021). The symbolic interaction theory: A systematic literature review of current research. *International Journal of Modern Trends in Social Sciences*, *4*(17), 113–126. DOI: 10.35631/IJMTSS.417010

Husk, K., Lovell, R., Cooper, C., Stahl-Timmins, W., & Garside, R. (2016). Participation in environmental enhancement and conservation activities for health and well-being in adults: A review of quantitative and qualitative evidence. *The Cochrane Library*, *2016*(5), CD010351. Advance online publication. DOI: 10.1002/14651858.CD010351.pub2

Huxhold, O., Miche, M., Schüz, B., & Tesch-Römer, C. (2022a). The role of trust in shaping loneliness trajectories in later life. *The Journals of Gerontology: Series B*, *77*(3), 502–512. DOI: 10.1093/geronb/gbab004

Huxhold, O., Olaru, G., & Windsor, T. D. (2022b). Social expectations and loneliness: Testing the social expectation model of loneliness. *Journal of Personality and Social Psychology*, *123*(5), 1121–1138. DOI: 10.1037/pspp0000414

Hu, Z., Zhu, Y., Li, J., Liu, J., & Fu, M. (2023). The COVID-19 related stress and social network addiction among Chinese college students: A moderated mediation model. *PLoS One*, *18*(8), e0290577. DOI: 10.1371/journal.pone.0290577

Illouz, E. (2007). *Cold intimacies: The making of emotional capitalism*. Polity Press.

Illouz, E. (2007). Cold intimacies: The making of emotional capitalism. *Polity*.

Illouz, E. (2008). *Saving the modern soul: Therapy, emotions, and the culture of self-help*. University of California Press. DOI: 10.1525/9780520941311

Inter-American Commission on Human Rights. (2015). *Report on the situation of human rights in the Dominican Republic*. Organization of American States.

International Waqf Fund. (n.d). *What is Waqf?* https://waqf.org/what-is-waqf/

Iqbal, Z., & Mirakhor, A. (2011). An introduction to Islamic finance: Theory and practice, 2nd Edition. John Wiley & Sons (Asia). DOI: 10.1002/9781118390474

IRTI IDB. (2020). *Islamic Social Finance Report 2020*. Islamic Research and Training Institute, Islamic Development Bank (IRTI IDB).

Isin, E. F. (2009). Citizenship in flux: The figure of the activist citizen. *Subjectivity*, *29*(1), 367–388. DOI: 10.1057/sub.2009.25

Islamic Relief. (n.d). *Sadaqah*. https://islamic-relief.org/sadaqah/

Ismail, A. G., & Posummah, B. (2010). *Qardhul hasan principles applied to micro finance facilities*. Working Paper in Islamic Economics and Finance No. 1021, Research Center for Islamic Economics and Finance, Universiti Kebangsaan Malaysia (UKM). https://www.ukm.my/ekonis/wp-content/uploads/2021/02/Qardhul-Hasan-Principles-Applied-to-Micro-Finance-Facilities.pdf

Jacobs, J. (1961). *The death and life of great American cities*. Random House.

Jahoda, M. (1982). *Employment and unemployment: A social-psychological analysis*. Cambridge University Press.

Jain, S., Singh, R., Agarwal, B., & Singh, A. K. (2025). Understanding the Role of Emerging Technology in Human Resilience in the Digital Age and Artificial Intelligence. In *Exploring Psychology, Social Innovation and Advanced Applications of Machine Learning* (pp. 131-152). IGI Global Scientific Publishing. DOI: 10.4018/979-8-3693-6910-4.ch007

Jakovljevic, M., Chang, H., Pan, J., Guo, C., Hui, J., Hu, H., Grujic, D., Li, Z., & Shi, L. (2023). Successes and challenges of China's health care reform: A four-decade perspective spanning 1985-2023. *Cost Effectiveness and Resource Allocation : C/E*, *21*(1), 59. DOI: 10.1186/s12962-023-00461-9

Jandric, P. (2022). Alone-Time and Loneliness in the Academia. *Postdigital Science and Education*, *4*(3), 633–642. DOI: 10.1007/s42438-022-00294-4

Jang, S. H., & Je, N. J. (2022). International Journal of Advanced and Applied Sciences. *International Journal of Advanced and Applied Sciences*, *9*(4), 71–79. DOI: 10.21833/ijaas.2022.04.009

Järve, P. (2000). *Ethnic and language policy in Estonia*. European Centre for Minority Issues Working Paper No. 6.

Jarvis, H. (2015). Towards a deeper understanding of the social architecture of co-housing. *Urban Research & Practice*, *8*(1), 93–105. DOI: 10.1080/17535069.2015.1011429

Jeffrey, C., & Young, S. (2012). Waiting for change: Youth, caste and politics in India. *Economy and Society*, *41*(4), 507–536. DOI: 10.1080/03085147.2011.635435

Jena, B., & Paltasingh, T. (2025). Digital literacy among older adults: A systematic review in Indian context. *Educational Gerontology*, *51*(4), 371–386. DOI: 10.1080/03601277.2024.2397428

Jenkins, T. M. (2023). Making the cut: Status, credentials, and hiring in medicine. *Social Problems*, *70*(2), 435–455. DOI: 10.1093/socpro/spab046

Jiang, Q., Horta, H., & Yuen, M. (2022). International medical students' perspectives on factors affecting their academic success in China: A qualitative study. *BMC Medical Education, 22*(1), 574. DOI: 10.1186/s12909-022-03597-z

Johari, F., Ali, A., & Aziz, N. A. (2019). The role of zakat in social protection. *Journal of Islamic Accounting and Business Research, 10*(2), 187–203.

Jones, K. (2022). A 'north star'in governing global labour migration? The ILO and the Fair Recruitment Initiative. *Global Social Policy, 22*(2), 303–322. DOI: 10.1177/14680181221084792

Joppke, C. (2019). *Neoliberal nationalism: Immigration and the rise of the populist right.* Cambridge University Press.

Jossen, M. (2018). *Undocumented migrants and healthcare: eight stories from Switzerland.* Open Book Publishers. DOI: 10.11647/OBP.0139

Jung, J., Barron, D., Lee, Y. A., & Swami, V. (2022, October). Social media usage and body image: Examining the mediating roles of internalization of appearance ideals and social comparisons in young women. *Computers in Human Behavior, 135*, 107357. DOI: 10.1016/j.chb.2022.107357

Kahf, M. (2003, January). The role of waqf in improving the ummah welfare. In *International Seminar on Waqf as a Private Legal Body* (Vol. 6, No. 1, pp. 1-26).

Kahneman, D., & Tversky, A. (1979). Prospect theory: An analysis of decision under risk. *Econometrica, 47*(2), 263–291. DOI: 10.2307/1914185

Kamali, M. H. (2008). *Shari'ah law: An introduction.* Oneworld.

Kamali, M. H. (2011). *Maqasid al-shari'ah made simple.* International Institute of Advanced Islamic Studies.

Kamali, M. H. (2011). *The right to life, security, privacy and ownership in Islam.* Islamic Texts Society.

Kang, J. W., Oga-Omenka, C., Tyas, S. L., Dubin, J. A., & Oremus, M. (2025). How social isolation and loneliness leave distinct imprints on memory: A thematic analysis informed by descriptive phenomenology. *Archives of Gerontology and Geriatrics, 139*, 106003. DOI: 10.1016/j.archger.2025.106003

Karayaman, S.. (2025). Crowded loneliness scale and field research. *Turkish Studies, 20*(4), 1625–1643. DOI: 10.7827/TurkishStudies.82717

Kaşak, M., Hacıosmanoğlu, C. D., Tural Hesapcioglu, S., & Ceylan, M. F. (2022). Loneliness in modern world: A case study of Hikikomori from Turkey (eng). *Klinik Psikiyatri Dergisi*, *25*(1), 117–122. DOI: 10.5505/kpd.2022.59265

Katha. (2019, June 19). *Current projects*. https://www.katha.org/current-projects/

Kaufman, A. B. (2021). Pet companionship in the age of urban isolation. *Journal of Urban Studies*, *58*(4), 811–828.

Kaufmann, R., & Vallade, J. I. (2022). Exploring connections in the online learning environment: Student perceptions of rapport, climate, and loneliness. *Interactive Learning Environments*, *30*(10), 1794–1808. DOI: 10.1080/10494820.2020.1749670

Kawachi, I., & Berkman, L. F. (2001). Social ties and mental health. *Journal of Urban Health*, *78*(3), 458–467. DOI: 10.1093/jurban/78.3.458

Kawachi, I., Kennedy, B. P., & Glass, R. (1999). Social capital and self-rated health: A contextual analysis. *American Journal of Public Health*, *89*(8), 1187–1193. DOI: 10.2105/AJPH.89.8.1187

Kaya Deniz, A. (2019). Hedonist workers of the digital age: Digital nomads. *IBAD Journal of Social Sciences*, *5*, 101–113.

Kaya, A. (2015). Islam, citizenship, and integration in Turkey and Europe. *Turkish Studies*, *16*(4), 537–555. DOI: 10.1080/14683849.2015.1067864

Kaya, İ. (2024). A spatial and temporal critique of the redesign of rituals in the online space: The disappearance of aura. *Folklor Akademi Dergisi*, *7*(1), 22–33. DOI: 10.55666/folklor.1384083

Kazantzis, N., Whittington, C., Zelencich, L., Kyrios, M., Norton, P. J., & Hofmann, S. G. (2016). Quantity and Quality of Homework Compliance: A Meta-Analysis of Relations With Outcome in Cognitive Behavior Therapy. *Behavior Therapy*, *47*(5), 755–772. DOI: 10.1016/j.beth.2016.05.002

Kerr, N. A., & Stanley, T. B. (2021). Revisiting the social stigma of loneliness. *Personality and Individual Differences*, *171*, 110482. DOI: 10.1016/j.paid.2020.110482

Keskin, D., & Lajunen, T. (2024). Adaptation of the social and emotional loneliness scale for adults to Turkish culture. *Social Sciences (Basel, Switzerland)*, *13*(3), 174. DOI: 10.3390/socsci13030174

Khalsa, D. S. (2015). Stress, Meditation, and Alzheimer's Disease Prevention: Where The Evidence Stands. *Journal of Alzheimer's Disease*, *48*(1), 1–12. DOI: 10.3233/JAD-142766

Khan, A. A. (2008). *Islamic microfinance: Theory, policy and practice.* Islamic Relief Worldwide.

Khan, M. A. (2007). *Islamic economics and finance: A glossary.* Routledge International Studies in Money and Banking.

Khera, R. (2019). Aadhaar and the invisible exclusion of India's poor. *Economic and Political Weekly, 54*(5), 35–40.

Kiliç, S., and Daldal, K. M. (2024). Economy of loneliness and consumer behavior. *Journal of Financial Politic and Economic Reviews/Finans Politik and Ekonomik Yorumlar, 61*(667).

Kiliç, S., & Daldal, K. M. (2024). Economy of loneliness and consumer behavior. *Finans Politik & Ekonomik Yorumlar*, (667), 147–173.

Kim, Y. Y. (2017). Cross-cultural adaptation. *Oxford research encyclopedia of communication.*

Kim, E. S., Chen, Y., Kawachi, I., & Van der Weele, T. J. (2020). Perceived neighborhood social cohesion and subsequent health and well-being in older adults: An outcome-wide longitudinal approach. *Health & Place, 66*, 102420. DOI: 10.1016/j.healthplace.2020.102420

Kim, J. H., & Silverstein, M. (2021). Are filial piety and ethnic community engagement associated with psychological wellbeing among older Chinese American immigrants? A cultural resource perspective. *Research on Aging, 43*(2), 63–73. DOI: 10.1177/0164027520937477

Kim, Y.-S., O'Sullivan, D. M., & Shin, S.-K. (2019). Can 24 weeks strength training reduce feelings of depression and increase neurotransmitter in elderly females? *Experimental Gerontology, 115*, 62–68. DOI: 10.1016/j.exger.2018.11.009

Kingston, L. N. (2017). *Fully human: Personhood, citizenship, and rights.* Oxford University Press.

Kirkpatrick, I., Zardini, A., & Veronesi, G. (2023). Management reforms, re-stratification and the adaptation of professional status hierarchies: The case of medicine in publicly owned hospitals. *Public Management Review, 25*(11), 2231–2254. DOI: 10.1080/14719037.2023.2222124

Klein, D., Mishra, S., & Müller, L. (2021). Die langfristigen individuellen Konsequenzen des Studienabbruchs. In Neugebauer, M., Daniel, H.-D., & Wolter, A. (Eds.), *Studienerfolg und Studienabbruch* (pp. 279–300). Springer Fachmedien., DOI: 10.1007/978-3-658-32892-4_12

Klinenberg, E. (2012). *Going solo: The extraordinary rise and surprising appeal of living alone*. Penguin.

Klinenberg, E. (2016). Social isolation, loneliness, and living alone. *American Journal of Public Health, 106*(5), 786–787. DOI: 10.2105/AJPH.2016.303166

Klinenberg, E. (2018). *Palaces for the people: How social infrastructure can help fight inequality, polarization, and the decline of civic life*. Crown.

Klunk, C. D. (1999). Professionals' Workplace Devaluation: Implications for the Workplace. Midwest Research-to-Practice Conference.

Koirala, S. (2025). "Everyone is leaving, so am I": The role of culture in shaping Migration Behaviour in Nepal. *Comparative Migration Studies, 13*(1), 1–18. DOI: 10.1186/s40878-025-00427-1

Köktürk, M. (2022). Deep loneliness in the digital world. In Digitalization and Loneliness III: International Loneliness Symposium Book (pp. 123–135). İstanbul: Üsküdar University Press.

Korhonen, V. (2024, July 5). Average size of households in the U.S. 1960-2023. Statista, https://www.statista.com/statistics/183648/average-size-of-households-in-the-us/

Kotozaki, Y. (2025). Editorial: New insights into social isolation and loneliness, volume II. *Frontiers in Psychiatry, 16*, 1675314. DOI: 10.3389/fpsyt.2025.1675314

Kouros, T., & Papa, V. (2024). Digital mirrors: AI companions and the self. *Societies (Basel, Switzerland), 14*(10), 200. DOI: 10.3390/soc14100200

Kross, E., Verduyn, P., Demiralp, E., Park, J., Lee, D. S., Lin, N., Shablack, H., Jonides, J., & Ybarra, O. (2013). Facebook use predicts declines in subjective well-being in young adults. *PLoS One, 8*(8), e69841. DOI: 10.1371/journal.pone.0069841 PMID: 23967061

Kuhlmann, , EBrînzac, , M. GCzabanowska, , KFalkenbach, , MUngureanu, , M.-IValiotis, , GZapata, , TMartin-Moreno, , J. M. (2023). Violence against healthcare workers is a political problem and a public health issue: a call to action. *European Journal of Public Health, 33*(1), 4–5.

Kung, C. S. J., Pudney, S. E., & Shields, M. A. (2022). Economic gradients in loneliness, social isolation and social support: Evidence from the UK Biobank. *Social Science & Medicine, 306*(115122), 1–14. DOI: 10.1016/j.socscimed.2022.115122 PMID: 35751988

Kusurkar, R. A., van der Burgt, S. M. E., Isik, U., Mak-van der Vossen, M., Wilschut, J., Wouters, A., & Koster, A. S. (2021). Burnout and engagement among PhD students in medicine: The BEeP study. *Perspectives on Medical Education*, *10*(2), 110–117. DOI: 10.1007/S40037-020-00637-6

Kuzhabekova, A., & Temerbayeva, A. (2018). The role of conferences in doctoral student socialization. *Studies in Graduate and Postdoctoral Education*, *9*(2), 181–196. DOI: 10.1108/SGPE-D-18-00012

Lancee, B., & Dronkers, J. (2011). Ethnic, religious and economic diversity in Dutch neighborhoods: Explaining quality of contact with neighbors, trust in the neighborhood and inter-ethnic trust. *Journal of Ethnic and Migration Studies*, *37*(4), 597–618. DOI: 10.1080/1369183X.2011.545277

Larkin, B. (2013). The politics and poetics of infrastructure. *Annual Review of Anthropology*, *42*(1), 327–343. DOI: 10.1146/annurev-anthro-092412-155522

Latikka, R., Rubio-Hernández, R., Lohan, E. S., Rantala, J., Nieto Fernández, F., Laitinen, A., & Oksanen, A. (2021). Older adults' loneliness, social isolation, and physical ICT in the era of ambient assisted living: A systematic review. *Journal of Medical Internet Research*, *23*(12), e28022. DOI: 10.2196/28022

Layte, R., & Whelan, C. T. (2002). Cumulative disadvantage or individualisation? A comparative analysis of poverty risk and incidence. *European Societies*, *4*(2), 209–233. DOI: 10.1080/14616690220142790

Le, H. V. (2021). An Investigation into Factors Affecting Concentration of University Students. *Journal of English Language Teaching and Applied Linguistics, 3*(6), 07–12. DOI: 10.32996/jeltal.2021.3.6.2

Lee, H. (2024). Analysis of the impact of digital literacy on life satisfaction (2019–2022) for older adults in South Korea: A national community-based panel study. *Scientific Reports*, *14*(1), 1–8. DOI: 10.1038/s41598-024-71397-0

Lee, M. A., & Mather, M. (2008). US labor force trends. *Population Bulletin*, *63*(2).

Lee, S. (1998). Estranged bodies, simulated harmony, and misplaced cultures: Neurasthenia in contemporary Chinese society. *Biopsychosocial Science and Medicine*, *60*(4), 448–457.

Leider, J. (2018). *Rohingya*. Oxford Research Encyclopedia of Asian History.

Leitão, C. A., de Oliveira Salvador, G. L., Idowu, B. M., & Dako, F. (2024). Drivers of global health care worker migration. *Journal of the American College of Radiology*, *21*(8), 1188–1193. DOI: 10.1016/j.jacr.2024.03.005

Letón, S. L. (2025, June 22). Your loneliness is our business: The multi-million-dollar industry of social isolation. *EL PAÍS,* https://english.elpais.com/economy-and-business/2025-06-22/your-loneliness-is-our-business-the-multi-million-dollar-industry-of-social-isolation.html

Li, D., Zhu, L., Zhang, J., & Yang, J. (2021). Decomposing differences of health service utilization among Chinese rural migrant workers with new cooperative medical scheme: A comparative study. *International Journal of Environmental Research and Public Health, 18*(17), 9291. DOI: 10.3390/ijerph18179291

Li, F., Ding, J., & Shen, W. (2019). Back on track: Factors influencing Chinese returnee scholar performance in the reintegration process. *Science & Public Policy, 46*(2), 184–197. DOI: 10.1093/scipol/scy047

Li, J., Lowres, N., Koo, F. K., & Gallagher, R. (2021). A systematic review of quantitative and qualitative literature on health professionals' experiences communicating with Chinese immigrants. *International Journal of Nursing Practice, 27*(6), e12960. DOI: 10.1111/ijn.12960

Li, M. (2016). Pre-migration Trauma and Post-migration Stressors for Asian and Latino American Immigrants: Transnational Stress Proliferation. *Social Indicators Research, 129*(1), 47–59. DOI: 10.1007/s11205-015-1090-7

Lim, M. H., Eres, R., & Vasan, S. (2020). Understanding loneliness in the twenty-first century: An update on correlates, risk factors, and potential solutions. *Social Psychiatry and Psychiatric Epidemiology, 55*(7), 793–810. DOI: 10.1007/s00127-020-01889-7

Lim, M. H., Hennessey, A., Qualter, P., Smith, B. J., Thurston, L., Eres, R., & Holt-Lunstad, J. (2025). The KIND Challenge community intervention to reduce loneliness and social isolation, improve mental health, and neighbourhood relationships: An international randomized controlled trial. *Social Psychiatry and Psychiatric Epidemiology, 60*(4), 931–942. DOI: 10.1007/s00127-024-02740-z PMID: 39158741

Lim, S. S. (2020). Loneliness in the digital age. *Journal of Communication, 70*(5), 682–703.

Lim, S., & Paik, S. (2023). The impact of immigration enforcement on agricultural employment: Evidence from the US E-Verify policy. *Applied Economics, 55*(19), 2223–2259. DOI: 10.1080/00036846.2022.2102135

Linchuan Qui, J. (2016). *Goodbye iSlave: A manifesto for digital abolition.* University of Illinois Press.

Ling, R. E., Liu, F., Lu, X. Q., & Wang, W. (2011). Emerging issues in public health: A perspective on China's healthcare system. *Public Health*, *125*(1), 9–14. DOI: 10.1016/j.puhe.2010.10.009

Lister, R. (1997). *Citizenship: Feminist perspectives*. Macmillan. DOI: 10.1007/978-1-349-26209-0

Liu, T., & Liao, L. (2024). Can farmers' digital literacy improve income? Empirical evidence from China. *PLoS One*, *19*(12), 1–14. DOI: 10.1371/journal.pone.0314804

Liu, Z., Werneck, A. O., Herold, F., Lowe, C. J., Hallgren, M., Cheval, B., Tari, B., Stubbs, B., Gerber, M., Falck, R. S., Kramer, A. F., Owen, N., & Zou, L. (2025). Bidirectional relationships between television viewing and loneliness in middle-aged and older men and women. *Journal of Affective Disorders*, *388*, 119737. DOI: 10.1016/j.jad.2025.119737

Li, X., Lu, J., Hu, S., Cheng, K., De Maeseneer, J., Meng, Q., Mossialos, E., Xu, D. R., Yip, W., Zhang, H., Krumholz, H. M., Jiang, L., & Hu, S. (2017). The primary health-care system in China. *Lancet*, *390*(10112), 2584–2594. DOI: 10.1016/S0140-6736(17)33109-4

Löbel, L. M., Kröger, H., & Tibubos, A. N. (2022). How Migration Status Shapes Susceptibility of Individuals' Loneliness to Social Isolation. *International Journal of Public Health*, *67*(December), 1–8. DOI: 10.3389/ijph.2022.1604576

Lopez-Abuin, J. M. (2010). Review of: 'Increasing access to health workers in remote and rural areas through improved retention: global policy recommendations: Global policy recommendations'. *Rural and Remote Health*. Advance online publication. DOI: 10.22605/RRH1647

Lopez, M. del P. A. (2023). Digital literacy as a new determinant of health: A scoping review. *PLOS Digital Health*, *2*(10), 1–21. DOI: 10.1371/journal.pdig.0000279

Lorenzetti, D. L., Shipton, L., Nowell, L., Jacobsen, M., Lorenzetti, L., Clancy, T., & Paolucci, E. O. (2019). A systematic review of graduate student peer mentorship in academia. *Mentoring & Tutoring*, *27*(5), 549–576. DOI: 10.1080/13611267.2019.1686694

Lo, T. W., Yeung, J. W. K., & Tam, C. H. L. (2020). Substance Abuse and Public Health: A Multilevel Perspective and Multiple Responses. *International Journal of Environmental Research and Public Health*, *17*(7), 2610. DOI: 10.3390/ijerph17072610

Low, S. (2003). *Behind the gates: Life, security, and the pursuit of happiness in fortress America*. Routledge.

Luhmann, M., & Hawkley, L. C. (2016). Age differences in loneliness from late adolescence to oldest old age. *Developmental Psychology, 52*(6), 943–959. DOI: 10.1037/dev0000117

Luo, W., Zhong, B.-L., & Chiu, H. F.-K. (2021). Prevalence of depressive symptoms among Chinese university students amid the COVID-19 pandemic: A systematic review and meta-analysis. *Epidemiology and Psychiatric Sciences, 30*, e31. DOI: 10.1017/S2045796021000202

Lupton, D. (2013). *Introducing digital sociology*. University of Sydney.

Lyu, C., Siu, K., Xu, I., Osman, I., & Zhong, J. (2024). Social isolation changes and long-term outcomes among older adults. *JAMA Network Open, 7*(7), e2424519. DOI: 10.1001/jamanetworkopen.2024.24519

Macaskill, A. (2013). The mental health of university students in the United Kingdom. *British Journal of Guidance & Counselling, 41*(4), 426–441. DOI: 10.1080/03069885.2012.743110

Mahomed, Z. (2022). Assessing financing for healthcare infrastructure in Sub-Saharan Africa: can Islamic finance assist? In Hassan, M. K., Muneeza, A., & Sonko, K. N. M. (Eds.), *Islamic finance in Africa: The prospects for sustainable development* (pp. 167–192). Edward Elgar.

Ma, L. (2020). Rethinking democratizing potential of digital technology. *Journal of Information. Communication and Ethics in Society, 18*(1), 140–156. DOI: 10.1108/JICES-02-2019-0022

Malani, P. N., Solway, E., Kirch, M., Singer, D. C., Roberts, J. S., & Kullgren, J. T. (2025). Loneliness and social isolation among US older adults. *Journal of the American Medical Association, 333*(3), 254–257. DOI: 10.1001/jama.2024.23213

Mamdani, M. (1996). *Citizen and subject: Contemporary Africa and the legacy of late colonialism*. Princeton University Press.

Mamdani, M. (2001). *When victims become killers: Colonialism, nativism, and the genocide in Rwanda*. Princeton University Press.

Manby, B. (2016). *Citizenship law in Africa: A comparative study* (3rd ed.). African Minds. DOI: 10.47622/9781928331087

Marotta, V. (2025). Rethinking liminality in refugee and migration studies. *Ethnicities, 25*(3), 339–357. DOI: 10.1177/14687968251328675

Marshall, P., Booth, M., Coole, M., Fothergill, L., Glossop, Z., Haines, J., Harding, A., Johnston, R., Jones, S., Lodge, C., Machin, K., Meacock, R., Nielson, K., Puddephatt, J.-A., Rakic, T., Rayson, P., Robinson, H., Rycroft-Malone, J., Shryane, N., & Lobban, F. (2024). Understanding the Impacts of Online Mental Health Peer Support Forums: Realist Synthesis. *JMIR Mental Health*, *11*, e55750. DOI: 10.2196/55750

Marsh, M. (2002). Examining the discourses that shape our teacher identities. *Curriculum Inquiry*, *32*(4), 453–469. DOI: 10.1111/1467-873X.00242

Masiero, S., & Das, S. (2022). The datafied welfare state: Citizenship and social assistance in India. *Information Communication and Society*, *25*(3), 329–346.

McCarthy, J. M., Erdogan, B., Bauer, T. N., Kudret, S., & Campion, E. (2025). All the Lonely People: An Integrated Review and Research Agenda on Work and Loneliness. *Journal of Management*, *01492063241313320*, 01492063241313320. Advance online publication. DOI: 10.1177/01492063241313320

McKinsey Global Institute. (2019). *MGI in 2019: A compendium of our research this year*. McKinsey and Company.

Meisters, R., Westra, D., Putrik, P., Bosma, H., Ruwaard, D., & Jansen, M. (2021). Does loneliness have a cost? A population-wide study of the association between loneliness and healthcare expenditure. *International Journal of Public Health*, *66*, 581286. DOI: 10.3389/ijph.2021.581286

Messenger, J. (2019). *Telework in the 21st century*. Edward Elgar. DOI: 10.4337/9781789903751

Mihalopoulos, C., Le, L. K. D., Chatterton, M. L., Bucholc, J., Holt-Lunstad, J., Lim, M. H., & Engel, L. (2020). The economic costs of loneliness: A review of cost-of-illness and economic evaluation studies. *Social Psychiatry and Psychiatric Epidemiology*, *55*(7), 823–836. DOI: 10.1007/s00127-019-01733-7 PMID: 31119308

Mikolajczak-Degrauwe, K., Slimmen, S. R., Gillissen, D., de Bil, P., Bosmans, V., Keemink, C., Meyvis, I., & Kuipers, Y. J. (2023). Strengths, weaknesses, opportunities and threats of peer support among disadvantaged groups: A rapid scoping review. *International Journal of Nursing Sciences*, *10*(4), 587–601. DOI: 10.1016/j.ijnss.2023.09.002

Mills, C. W. (1997). *The racial contract*. Cornell University Press.

Mir, A. (2019). Islamic governance and social inclusion: A critical analysis. *Journal of Islamic Governance*, *4*(1), 23–41.

Mishra, R. K., Kumari, C. L., Janaki Krishna, P. S., and Dubey, A. (2022). Smart cities for sustainable development: An overview. *Smart cities for sustainable development*, 1-12.

Mishra, P. S., Singh, R., Srivastava, S., & Aditya, A. (2024). Predicting the risk of depression by migration status: A cross-sectional study on older adults in India. *Journal of Population Ageing*, *17*(4), 693–720. DOI: 10.1007/s12062-024-09453-w

Modéer, U. (2018, October 13). Unlocking Islamic social finance to help communities address vulnerability and inequality. *United Nations Development Programme (UNDP),* https://www.undp.org/speeches/unlocking-islamic-social-finance-help-communities-address-vulnerability-and-inequality

Mohsin, M. I. A., & Muneeza, A. (2025). *Inclusive finance: Bridging communities through Islamic social finance*. Edward Elgar. DOI: 10.4337/9781035348770

Morris, A., Mitchell, E., Wilson, S., Ramia, G., & Hastings, C. (2022). Loneliness within the Home among International Students in the Private Rental Sector in Sydney and Melbourne. *Urban Policy and Research*, *40*(1), 67–81. DOI: 10.1080/08111146.2021.2005017

Morrish, N., Choudhury, S., & Medina-Lara, A. (2023). What works in interventions targeting loneliness: A systematic review of intervention characteristics. *BMC Public Health*, *23*(1), 2214. DOI: 10.1186/s12889-023-17097-2

Morrish, N., & Medina-Lara, A. (2021). Does unemployment lead to greater levels of loneliness? A systematic review. *Social Science & Medicine*, *287*, 114339. DOI: 10.1016/j.socscimed.2021.114339

Mosleh, S. M., Kasasbeha, M. A., Aljawarneh, Y. M., Alrimawi, I., & Saifan, A. R. (2022). The impact of online teaching on stress and burnout of academics during the transition to remote teaching from home. *BMC Medical Education*, *22*(1), 475. DOI: 10.1186/s12909-022-03496-3

Motillon-Toudic, C., Walter, M., Séguin, M., Carrier, J.-D., Berrouiguet, S., & Lemey, C. (2022). Social isolation and suicide risk: Literature review and perspectives. *European Psychiatry : the Journal of the Association of European Psychiatrists*, *65*(1), 1–22. DOI: 10.1192/j.eurpsy.2022.2320

Mounk, Y. (2018). *The people vs. democracy*. Harvard University Press. DOI: 10.4159/9780674984776

Mullainathan, S., & Shafir, E. (2013). *Scarcity: Why having too little means so much*. Times Books.

Mullan, F. (1995). Medical Migration and the Physician Workforce. *Journal of the American Medical Association, 273*(19), 1521. DOI: 10.1001/jama.1995.03520430057039

Mumtaz, Z. (2022). Informal Social Protection and Poverty: A Case Study In Pakistan.

Munikrishnappa, D., Majumder, J., Kalita, M., Shivarudraiah, M., Saha, I., & Chakrabarti, A. (2024). Bridging the Mental Health Treatment Gap in India: Opportunities and Challenges: A Narrative Review. *Journal of Mental Health and Human Behaviour, 29*(2), 55–61. DOI: 10.4103/jmhhb.jmhhb_167_24

Munir, T., Shafiq, S., Ahmad, Z., & Khan, S. (2015). Impact of loneliness and academic stress on psychological well being among college students. *Academic Research International, 6*(2), 343.

Murtagh, L. (2012). Enhancing preparation for higher education. *Practitioner Research in Higher Education, 6*(1), 31–39.

Murthy, R. S. (2021). Schizophrenia Research Foundation-Caring for the Mind: A Journey of 35 Years.... and Counting. *Indian Journal of Social Psychiatry, 37*(4), 378–379. DOI: 10.4103/ijsp.ijsp_320_21

Murthy, V. (2020). *Together: The healing power of human connection in a sometimes lonely world*. Harper Wave.

Musari, K. (2016). *Redefining the Islamic nanofinance and its institutional strengthening: Lesson learned from Asian countries*. A paper was presented at 11th International Conference on Islamic Economics and Finance (ICIEF) "Rethinking Islamic Economics and Finance: Paving The Way Forward for Inclusive and Sustainable Development", Kuala Lumpur, October 11th-13th.

Musari, K. (2025). *From isolation to solidarity: Islamic philanthropy in addressing the loneliness economy in the age of disconnection.* A paper presented at Symposium on Contemporary Muslim Philanthropy held by Management Research Center (MRC) Faculty of Economics and Business Universitas Indonesia (FEB UI) in collaboration with the Muslim Philanthropy Initiative (MPI) Indiana University's Lilly Family School of Philanthropy, Yogyakarta – Indonesia, October 15th-16th.

Musari, K. (2019). Promoting qard al-hasan in nanofinance to counter the moneylender in Southeast Asia. *Studia Islamica, 26*(1), 1–16. DOI: 10.15408/sdi.v26i1.5990

Musari, K. (2020). Islamic nanofinance for the very poor by women, hopes for addressing the Islamic microfinance gap. In Azid, T., & Ward-Batts, J. L. (Eds.), *Economic empowerment of women in the Islamic world: Theory and practice* (pp. 265–286). World Scientific Publishing. DOI: 10.1142/9789811212154_0013

Musari, K. (2023). Twinning the green transition and digitalization on the Islamic philanthropy institutions: Evidence in Indonesia. In de Pablos, P. O., Almunawar, M. N., & Anshari, M. (Eds.), *Perspectives on the transition toward green and climate neutral economies in Asia* (pp. 274–285). IGI Global. DOI: 10.4018/978-1-6684-8613-9.ch016

Musari, K., & Fathorrazi, M. (2021). Islamic helix approach, the Islamic social finance partnership models for MSMEs: Lesson learned from Indonesia. In Azid, T., Mukhlisin, M., Akbar, N., & Tahir, M. (Eds.), *Monetary policy, Islamic finance, and Islamic corporate governance: An international overview* (pp. 303–322). Emerald Publishing Limited. DOI: 10.1108/978-1-80043-786-920211017

Musari, K., & Simanjuntak, R. (2016). Nanofinance, redefinition of microfinance For the very micro society through philanthropy linkage program (case study in Indonesia, Cambodia, Thailand, India). *[AARJSH]. Asian Academic Research Journal of Social Sciences and Humanities*, *3*(4), 455–463.

Muslim, I. H. (n.d.). *Sahih Muslim*. Dar al-Kutub al-'Ilmiyya.

Nakphong, M. K., Young, M.-E. D. T., Morales, B., Guzman-Ruiz, I. Y., Chen, L., & Kietzman, K. G. (2022). Social exclusion at the intersections of immigration, employment, and healthcare policy: A qualitative study of Mexican and Chinese immigrants in California. *Social Science & Medicine*, *298*, 114833. DOI: 10.1016/j.socscimed.2022.114833

Nakshine, V. S., Thute, P., Khatib, M. N., & Sarkar, B. (2022). Increased Screen Time as a Cause of Declining Physical, Psychological Health, and Sleep Patterns: A Literary Review. *Cureus*, *14*(10), e30051. DOI: 10.7759/cureus.30051

Namrata Rao, M., Lakshmi Ravikanth, A., Sankaran, L., Bansal, P., & Chowdhury, R. (2024). The Banyan Journey: A Continuum in Community Mental Health Care. In *Mental Health Care Resource Book: Concepts and Praxis for Social Workers and Mental Health Professionals* (pp. 229–250). Springer Nature Singapore. DOI: 10.1007/978-981-97-1203-8_14

Nandamuri, P. P., Rao, K. V. G., & Mishra, M. K. (2020). Sustainable competitive advantage through business model innovation: The Indian perspective. In *Disruptive technology: Concepts, methodologies, tools, and applications* (pp. 191–213). IGI Global Scientific Publishing. DOI: 10.4018/978-1-5225-9273-0.ch010

Nazareth, P., Nikhil, G. B., Chirag, G., Prathik, N. R., & Pratham, P. (2024, June). Exploring the Efficacy of Mental Health Care Chatbots: A Comprehensive Review. In *2024 15th International Conference on Computing Communication and Networking Technologies (ICCCNT)* (pp. 1-6). IEEE. DOI: 10.1109/ICCCNT61001.2024.10725176

Nedeljko, M., Bogataj, D., & Kaucic, B. M. (2021). The use of ICT in older adults strengthens their social network and reduces social isolation: Literature review and research agenda. *IFAC-PapersOnLine*, *54*(13), 645–650. DOI: 10.1016/j.ifacol.2021.10.524

Negri, A. (2003). *Time for revolution* (Mandarini, M., Trans.). Continuum.

Negri, A. (2006). *Movimenti nell'impero: Passaggi e paesaggi* (Atalay, K., Trans.). Otonom Press.

Netto, J. J. M. (2024). Invisibility and devaluation of nursing work: Related factors and coping strategies. *Investigacion y Educacion en Enfermeria*, *42*(1), e01.

New China (Xinhua) News Agency. (2009). *Encyclopedia of Journalism*. SAGE Publications, Inc., DOI: 10.4135/9781412972048.n255

Newall, N. E. G., Chipperfield, J. G., Bailis, D. S., & Stewart, T. L. (2013). Consequences of loneliness on physical activity and mortality in older adults and the power of positive emotions. *Health Psychology: Official Journal of the Division of Health Psychology, American Psychological Association*, *32*(8), 921–924. DOI: 10.1037/a0029413

Ng, E. (2009). Heartache of the state, enemy of the self: Bipolar disorder and cultural change in urban China. *Culture, Medicine and Psychiatry*, *33*(3), 421–450. DOI: 10.1007/s11013-009-9144-4

Nguyen, T. P., Al Asaad, M., Sena, M., & Slewa-Younan, S. (2024). Loneliness and social isolation amongst refugees resettled in high-income countries: A systematic review. *Social Science & Medicine*, *360*(August), 117340. DOI: 10.1016/j.socscimed.2024.117340

Ng, W. (2012). Can we teach digital natives digital literacy? *Computers & Education*, *59*(3), 1065–1078. DOI: 10.1016/j.compedu.2012.04.016

Niedzwiedz, C. L., Richardson, E. A., Tunstall, H., Shortt, N. K., Mitchell, R. J., & Pearce, J. R. (2021). The relationship between community trust and loneliness across the adult life course: Evidence from a national survey. *Social Science & Medicine*, *278*, 113933. DOI: 10.1016/j.socscimed.2021.113933

Nisbett, N. (2009). *Growing up in the knowledge society: Living the IT dream in Bangalore*. Routledge.

Nishio, K., & Bilmes, M. (1987). Psychotherapy with Southeast Asian American clients. *Professional Psychology, Research and Practice, 18*(4), 342–346. DOI: 10.1037/0735-7028.18.4.342

Njonge, T. (2023). *Influence of Psychological Well-being and School Factors on Delinquency, During the Covid-19 Period Among Secondary School Students in Selected Schools in Nakuru County : Kenya. VII*(2454), 1175–1189. https://doi.org/ DOI: 10.47772/IJRISS

Nkrumah, J. (2017). Statelessness and racial exclusion in the Dominican Republic. *Georgetown Journal of International Affairs, 18*(1), 93–103.

Nourpanah, S. (2021). Moving, waiting, racing: The emotional and temporal experience of policy for nurses on temporary work permits in Canada. *Anthropologica, 63*(1), 1–26. DOI: 10.18357/anthropologica6312021186

Noushad Yashan, D. S. R. S., Kohli, N. K., Kalakumari, T., & Mistry, V. (2024). Innovative business models in the digital age: a comparative analysis. *Cahiers Magellanes-NS, 6*(2), 5170–5181.

Nowell, L. S., Norris, J. M., White, D. E., & Moules, N. J. (2017). Thematic Analysis: Striving to Meet the Trustworthiness Criteria. *International Journal of Qualitative Methods, 16*(1), 1–13. DOI: 10.1177/1609406917733847

Nowland, R., Necka, E. A., & Cacioppo, J. T. (2018). Loneliness and social internet use: Pathways to reconnection in a digital world? *Perspectives on Psychological Science, 13*(1), 70–87. DOI: 10.1177/1745691617713052 PMID: 28937910

Nussbaum, M. (2006). *Frontiers of justice*. Harvard University Press.

Nyqvist, F., Victor, C. R., Forsman, A. K., & Cattan, M. (2019). The association between social capital and loneliness in different age groups: A population-based study in Western Finland. *BMC Public Health, 19*, 1337. DOI: 10.1186/s12889-019-7760-y

Obaidullah, M., & Khan, T. (2008). *Islamic microfinance development: Challenges and initiatives.* Policy Dialogue Paper No. 2. Islamic Research and Training Institute (IRTI) Islamic Development Bank (IDB).

Office for National Statistics. (2018). *Loneliness: What characteristics and circumstances are associated with feeling lonely?* https://www.ons.gov.uk

Oldenburg, R. (1999). *The great good place*. Marlowe.

Oliva-Arocas, A., Benavente, P., Ronda, E., & Diaz, E. (2022). Health of international migrant workers during the COVID-19 pandemic: A scoping review. *Frontiers in Public Health, 10*, 816597. DOI: 10.3389/fpubh.2022.816597

Olofsson, J., Rämgård, M., Sjögren-Forss, K., & Bramhagen, A.-C. (2021). Older migrants' experience of existential loneliness. *Nursing Ethics, 28*(7-8), 1183–1193. DOI: 10.1177/0969733021994167

Omar, M. A. (2022). Foreword. In Hassan, M. K., Muneeza, A., & Sarea, A. (Eds.), *Covid-19 and Islamic Social Finance* (pp. xx–xxi). Routledge.

Omiyi, D., Wilkinson, E., & Snaith, B. (2025). Exploring the motivations, challenges, and integration of internationally educated healthcare workers in the UK: A scoping review. *Policy, Politics & Nursing Practice, 26*(2), 117–135. DOI: 10.1177/15271544241289605

Ong, W. J. (2022). Gender-contingent effects of leadership on loneliness. *The Journal of Applied Psychology, 107*(7), 1180–1202. DOI: 10.1037/apl0000907

ONS. (2020). *The cost of loneliness to the UK economy*. Office for National Statistics.

Opwis, F. (2010). *Maslaha and the purpose of the law*. Brill.

Organization, W. H. (2022). *World report on the health of refugees and migrants: summary*. World Health Organization.

Orlowski, J. (Director). (2020). The social dilemma [Film]. United States: Exposure Labs.

Osimo, S. A., Aiello, M., Gentili, C., Ionta, S., & Cecchetto, C. (2021). The Influence of Personality, Resilience, and Alexithymia on Mental Health During COVID-19 Pandemic. *Frontiers in Psychology, 12*, 630751. DOI: 10.3389/fpsyg.2021.630751

Ou-Salah, L., & Van Praag, L. (2025). "We always ask about the weather": Using visual mapping to understand how transnational migrant networks share beliefs and values on environmental change. *Digital Geography and Society, 9*(June), 100126. DOI: 10.1016/j.diggeo.2025.100126

Ousman, Y. I., & Nazir, T. (2023). Loneliness among University students as a growing concerne. *Journal of Family Counseling and Education, 8*(2), 85–99. DOI: 10.32568/jfce.1312556

Özdemir, A., & Özaydın, H. (2025). Social media addiction and loneliness: A research on university students. Kent Akademisi, 18 (Special Issue of the International Congress of Social Sciences on Entrepreneurship), 355–371.

Pandya, S. P. (2021). Meditation program mitigates loneliness and promotes well-being, life satisfaction and contentment among retired older adults: A two-year follow-up study in four South Asian cities. *Aging & Mental Health, 25*(2), 286–298. DOI: 10.1080/13607863.2019.1691143

Park, C., & Shimada, S. (2022). The impact of changing nonimmigrant visa policies on international students' psychological adjustment and well-being in the United States during the COVID-19 pandemic: A qualitative study. *BMC Public Health, 22*(1), 2227. DOI: 10.1186/s12889-022-14698-1

Parvizi, F., Salehi, A., Seghatoleslam, A., Kia, M., & Pope, M. (2025). Factors affecting the migration intention in medical students in Shiraz; south of Iran: A cross sectional study. *BMC Medical Education, 25*(1), 1–8. DOI: 10.1186/s12909-025-07700-y

Pasquale, F. (2015). *The black box society*. Harvard University Press. DOI: 10.4159/harvard.9780674736061

Patel, P. (2023, July 29). The loneliness economy: How capitalism thrives on isolation. *Medium,* https://whatsuppiyush.medium.com/the-loneliness-economy-how-capitalism-thrives-on-isolation-76ccc8c4b93e

Paxton, P. (2007). Association memberships and generalized trust: A multilevel model across 31 countries. *Social Forces, 86*(1), 47–76. DOI: 10.1353/sof.2007.0107

Payne, S. S. C. (2023). Equalization or Reproduction? "Some College" and the Social Function of Higher Education. *Sociology of Education, 96*(2), 104–128. DOI: 10.1177/00380407221134809

Peck, J. (2010). *Constructions of neoliberal reason*. Oxford University Press. DOI: 10.1093/acprof:oso/9780199580576.001.0001

Peck, J., & Tickell, A. (2002). Neoliberalizing space. *Antipode, 34*(3), 380–404. DOI: 10.1111/1467-8330.00247

Pellicano, E., Lawson, W., Hall, G., Mahony, J., Lilley, R., Heyworth, M., Clapham, H., & Yudell, M. (2022). "I Knew She'd Get It, and Get Me": Participants' Perspectives of a Participatory Autism Research Project. *Autism in Adulthood: Challenges and Management, 4*(2), 120–129. DOI: 10.1089/aut.2021.0039

Peplau, L. A., & Perlman, D. (1982). Perspectives on loneliness. In Peplau, L. A., & Perlman, D. (Eds.), *Loneliness: A sourcebook of current theory, research and therapy* (pp. 1–18).

Perlman, D., & Peplau, L. A. (1981). Toward a social psychology of loneliness. In Gilmour, R., & Duck, S. (Eds.), *Personal relationships in disorder* (pp. 31–56). Academic Press.

Perloff, R. M. (2014). Social media effects on young women's body image concerns: Theoretical perspectives and an agenda for research. *Sex Roles, 71*(11–12), 363–377. DOI: 10.1007/s11199-014-0384-6

Pew Research Center. (2020). *Social trust and community life in Muslim-majority countries.*

Pieter, K. (1999). the Definition of Migration and Its Application: Making Sense of Recent South African Census and Survey Data. *SA Journal of Demography, 7*(1), 19–30. https://journals.co.za/doi/pdf/10.10520/AJA16824482_41

Pietrabissa, G., & Simpson, S. G. (2020). Psychological consequences of social isolation during covid-19 outbreak. *Frontiers in Psychology, 11*, 2201. DOI: 10.3389/fpsyg.2020.02201 PMID: 33013572

Płatos, M., Wojaczek, K., & Laugeson, E. A. (2023). Effects of Social Skills Training for Adolescents on the Autism Spectrum: A Randomized Controlled Trial of the Polish Adaptation of the PEERS® Intervention via Hybrid and In-Person Delivery. *Journal of Autism and Developmental Disorders, 53*(11), 4132–4146. DOI: 10.1007/s10803-022-05714-9

Podsakoff, P. M., MacKenzie, S. B., Lee, J. Y., & Podsakoff, N. P. (2003). Common method biases in behavioral research: A critical review of the literature and recommended remedies. *The Journal of Applied Psychology, 88*(5), 879–903. DOI: 10.1037/0021-9010.88.5.879

Pollak, C., Pham, Y., Ehrlich, A., Verghese, J., & Blumen, H. M. (2025). Loneliness and social isolation risk factors in community-dwelling older adults receiving home health services. *BMC Geriatrics, 25*(1), 290. DOI: 10.1186/s12877-025-05947-0

Poon, Y.-S. R., Lin, Y. P., Griffiths, P., Yong, K. K., Seah, B., & Liaw, S. Y. (2022). A global overview of healthcare workers' turnover intention amid COVID-19 pandemic: A systematic review with future directions. *Human Resources for Health, 20*(1), 70. DOI: 10.1186/s12960-022-00764-7

Poortinga, W. (2012). Community resilience and health: The role of bonding, bridging, and linking aspects of social capital. *Health & Place, 18*(2), 286–295. DOI: 10.1016/j.healthplace.2011.09.017

Posel, D. (1991). *The making of apartheid, 1948–1961: Conflict and compromise.* Clarendon Press. DOI: 10.1093/acprof:oso/9780198273349.001.0001

Privacy International. (2021). *Digital identity and human rights: Building inclusive systems*. Privacy International.

Putnam, R. D. (2000). *Bowling alone: The collapse and revival of American community*. Simon & Schuster.

Qiu, F., Liu, J., & Zhan, H. J. (2021). Migration and health—Freedom of movement and social benefits for Chinese migrant workers. *Sustainability (Basel), 13*(22), 12371. DOI: 10.3390/su132212371

Qi, Y., Liang, T., & Ye, H. (2020). Occupational status, working conditions, and health: Evidence from the 2012 China Labor Force Dynamics Survey. *The Journal of Chinese Sociology*, *7*(1), 14. DOI: 10.1186/s40711-020-00128-5

Quadt, L., Williams, G., Mulcahy, J., Larsson, D. E. O., Silva, M., Arnold, A. J., Critchley, H. D., & Garfinkel, S. N. (2024). "I'm Trying to Reach Out, I'm Trying to Find My People": A Mixed-Methods Investigation of the Link Between Sensory Differences, Loneliness, and Mental Health in Autistic and Nonautistic Adults. *Autism in Adulthood: Challenges and Management*, *6*(3), 284–299. DOI: 10.1089/aut.2022.0062

Rafay, A., Farid, S., Yasser, F., & Safdar, S. (2020). Social collateral and repayment performance: Evidence from Islamic micro finance. *Iranian Economic Review*, *24*(1), 41–74.

Rahman, A. (2015). Zakat and poverty alleviation: Case of Malaysia. *Asian Social Work and Policy Review*, *9*(2), 118–127. DOI: 10.1111/aswp.12050

Rahman, E., Webb, W. R., Rao, P., Yu, N., Garcia, P. E., Ioannidis, S., Sayed, K., Philipp-Dormston, W. G., Carruthers, J. D. A., & Mosahebi, A. (2024). A systematic review on the reinforcement loop in aesthetic medicine and surgery: The interplay of social media, self-perception, and repeat procedures. *Aesthetic Plastic Surgery*, *48*(17), 3475–3487. DOI: 10.1007/s00266-024-04016-y PMID: 38724639

Rahman, F. (2019). Islamic education and social welfare: Integrating eldercare in Indonesian pesantren. *Indonesian Journal of Islam and Muslim Societies*, *9*(2), 231–252.

Rajamanikam, S. R. (2024). The Challenges of a Lecturer in a Higher Learning Institution (HLI) in Malaysia. *International Journal of Academic Research in Progressive Education and Development*, *13*(4), 368–382. DOI: 10.6007/IJARPED/v13-i4/23041

Rajaram, K., & Bordia, S. (2013). East versus West: Effectiveness of Knowledge Acquisition and Impact of Cultural Dislocation Issues for Mainland Chinese Students across Ten Commonly Used Instructional Techniques. *International Journal for the Scholarship of Teaching and Learning*, *7*(1), n1. DOI: 10.20429/ijsotl.2013.070111

Ramji, Z., & Etowa, J. (2018). Workplace integration: Key considerations for internationally educated nurses and employers. *Administrative Sciences*, *8*(1), 2. DOI: 10.3390/admsci8010002

Ranjan, S., & Yadav, R. S. (2019). Social isolation: Development and validation of measures. *Benchmarking*, *26*(6), 1905–1920. DOI: 10.1108/BIJ-11-2018-0371

Rawat, S., & Meena, S. (2014). Publish or perish: Where are we heading? *Journal of Research in Medical Sciences : the Official Journal of Isfahan University of Medical Sciences*, *19*(2), 87–89.

Ray, A. K. (2008). Self-help groups, micro finance, and political economy. In Deb, B. J., Sengupta, K., & Ray, B. D. (Eds.), *Globalization and north east India* (pp. 21–36). Concept Publishing Company.

Razak, D. A., & Dawami, Q. (2019). *Achieving Islamic social finance goals through zakah, waqf, and sadaqa in selected countries: Issues and challenges.* In Proceedings of the 7th ASEAN Universities International Conference on Islamic Finance (7th AICIF 2019) - Revival of Islamic Social Finance to Strengthen Economic Development Towards a Global Industrial Revolution, 38-45. DOI: 10.5220/0010114500380045

Rice, G. (1999). Islamic ethics and the implications for business. *Journal of Business Ethics*, *18*(4), 345–358. DOI: 10.1023/A:1005711414306

Richardson, T., Elliott, P., & Roberts, R. (2017). Relationship between loneliness and mental health in students. *Journal of Public Mental Health*, *16*(2), 48–54. DOI: 10.1108/JPMH-03-2016-0013

Rippe, J. (2024). Loneliness and Lifestyle Medicine. *American Journal of Lifestyle Medicine*, *18*(4), 456–458. DOI: 10.1177/15598276231207279

Rodriguez, S. L., & Blaney, J. M. (2021). "We're the unicorns in STEM": Understanding how academic and social experiences influence sense of belonging for Latina undergraduate students. *Journal of Diversity in Higher Education*, *14*(3), 441–455. DOI: 10.1037/dhe0000176

Rohmah, U. A., & Harsya, R. M. K. (2023). Community economic empowerment through infaq and sadaqah in LAZISMU cirebon regency sharia economic law perspective. *Mu'amalah. Jurnal Hukum Ekonomi Syariah*, *2*(2), 173–187. DOI: 10.32332/muamalah.v2i2.7844

Rosa, H. (2013). *Social acceleration.* Columbia University Press. DOI: 10.7312/rosa14834

Rose, N. (2006). *The politics of life itself: Biomedicine, power, and subjectivity in the twenty-first century*. Princeton University Press.

Ross, C. E., & Jang, S. J. (2000). Neighborhood disorder, fear, and mistrust: The buffering role of social ties with neighbors. *American Journal of Community Psychology, 28*(4), 401–420. DOI: 10.1023/A:1005137713332

Ross-Houle, K., & Quigg, Z. (2019). Content, perceptions and impact of alcoholic drink promotions in nightlife venues that are targeted towards students. *Addictive Behaviors Reports, 9*, 100163. DOI: 10.1016/j.abrep.2019.100163

Rowe, K. T. (2015). Preface. In Rowe, K. T. (Ed.), *Social isolation, participation and impact on mental health* (pp. vii-x). Nova Publisher.

Rubenstein, K. (2017). *Gender, citizenship, and the politics of belonging*. Cambridge University Press.

Rusere, F., Li, Q., Hunter, L., Collinson, M., Ouma, S., Twine, W., & Samimi, C. (2025). Relationships between rural migration and perceptions of environmental change: Insights from Bushbuckridge, South Africa. *Journal of Rural Studies, 119*(April 2024), 103819. DOI: 10.1016/j.jrurstud.2025.103819

Ryff, C. D. (1989). Happiness is everything, or is it? Explorations on the meaning of psychological well-being. *Journal of Personality and Social Psychology, 57*(6), 1069–1081. DOI: 10.1037/0022-3514.57.6.1069

Sağlam, Y. (2021). Social media and alienation in the context of surveillance capitalism [Unpublished master's thesis]. Istanbul Gelisim University, Department of Sociology.

Said, E. W. (1978). *Orientalism*. Pantheon Books.

Saini, G. K., Haseeb, S. B., Taghi-Zada, Z., & Ng, J. Y. (2021). The effects of meditation on individuals facing loneliness: A scoping review. *BMC Psychology, 9*(1), 88. DOI: 10.1186/s40359-021-00585-8

Salvi, D., Shah, R., & Tripathi, R. (2025). The Essence of Mindfulness: A Detailed Primer. In Dutta, G., Misra, G., & Gupta, S. (Eds.), *Handbook of Positive Psychology and Indian Thought Systems: Transforming Education for Well-being and Happiness* (pp. 261–280). Springer Nature., DOI: 10.1007/978-981-96-4210-6_17

Samanta, T. (2021). Living solo at midlife: Can the pandemic de-stigmatize living alone in India? *Journal of Aging Studies*, *56*, 100907. DOI: 10.1016/j.jaging.2020.100907 PMID: 33712092

Sampson, R. J. (2012). *Great American city: Chicago and the enduring neighborhood effect*. University of Chicago Press. DOI: 10.7208/chicago/9780226733883.001.0001

Sanghvi, P. B., & Mehrotra, S. (2022). Help-seeking for mental health concerns: Review of Indian research and emergent insights. *Warasan Wichai Witthayasat Kanphaet*, *36*(3), 428–441. DOI: 10.1108/JHR-02-2020-0040

Sanner-Stiehr, E., Stevanin, S., Mikkonen, S., & Kvist, T. (2021). Job satisfaction and generational nursing characteristics among registered nurses in the United States, Italy and Finland: Results of a survey study. *Journal of Nursing Management*, *29*(8), 2364–2373. DOI: 10.1111/jonm.13397

Sardar, Z. (2014). *Reading the Qur'an*. Oxford University Press.

Sastre, A. (2014). Towards a radical body positive: Reading the online body positive movement. *Feminist Media Studies*, *14*(6), 929–943. DOI: 10.1080/14680777.2014.883420

Sayah, F., & Musari, K. (2021). Reviving zakah for micro-financing and socio-economic development in Algeria. [IJAZ]. *International Journal of Zakah*, *6*(3), 23–40. DOI: 10.37706/ijaz.v6i3.356

Schnittker, J., & Bacak, V. (2014). The increasing predictive validity of self-rated health. *PLoS One*, *9*(1), e84933. DOI: 10.1371/journal.pone.0084933

Schofield, P. (2025, July 23). The Viewpoint: The loneliness economy – could emotional connection become a competitive advantage? *Royal London Asset Management,* https://www.rlam.com/uk/institutional-investors/our-views/2025/the-viewpoint-the-loneliness-economy--could-emotional-connection-become-a-competitive-advantage/

Scott, W. R. (2000). *Institutional change and healthcare organizations: From professional dominance to managed care*. University of Chicago press.

Seekings, J., & Nattrass, N. (2005). *Class, race, and inequality in South Africa*. Yale University Press. DOI: 10.12987/yale/9780300108927.001.0001

Sen, A. (1999). *Development as freedom*. Oxford University Press.

Sen, K., Prybutok, G., & Prybutok, V. (2022). The use of digital technology for social well-being reduces social isolation in older adults: A systematic review. *SSM - Population Health*, *17*, 101020. DOI: 10.1016/j.ssmph.2021.101020

Shachar, A. (2009). *The birthright lottery: Citizenship and global inequality*. Harvard University Press.

Shah, A. K., Mullainathan, S., & Shafir, E. (2012). Some consequences of having too little. *Science, 338*(6107), 682–685. DOI: 10.1126/science.1222426

Shahrzad, A., & Kian, A. (2020). Women, nationality, and the politics of belonging in Iran. *International Feminist Journal of Politics*, *22*(3), 369–388.

Shan, C., Hussain, M., & Sargani, G. R. (2020). A mix-method investigation on acculturative stress among Pakistani students in China. *PLoS One*, *15*(10), e0240103. DOI: 10.1371/journal.pone.0240103

Shin, E., Bui, K., & Park, J. (2023). Loneliness Rates among Undergraduates from 2008 to 2022, according to Data from the National College Health Assessment. *Seaver College Research And Scholarly Achievement Symposium*. https://digitalcommons.pepperdine.edu/scursas/2023/posters/29

Shirazi, D. N. S., Obaidullah, D. M., & Haneef, M. A. (2015). *Integration of Waqf and Islamic Microfinance for Poverty Reduction* (No. 1436-5).

Shishehgar, S., Gholizadeh, L., DiGiacomo, M., & Davidson, P. M. (2015). The impact of migration on the health status of Iranians: An integrative literature review. *BMC International Health and Human Rights*, *15*(1), 1–11. DOI: 10.1186/s12914-015-0058-7

Sibai, O., Figueiredo, B. & Ferreira, M.C. (2019, January 30). The Loneliness of the Long-Suffering Researcher. *Social Sciences Space*. The Loneliness of the Long-Suffering Researcher - Social Science Space

Singer, A. (2008). *Charity in Islamic societies*. Cambridge University Press.

Singh, S., & Sirvastva, N. (2024). Loneliness and satisfaction with life among young adults belonging to nuclear and joint families. *International Journal of Indian Psychology*, *12*(2).

Singh, S., & Steeves, V. (2020). The contested meanings of race and ethnicity in medical research: A case study of the DynaMed Point of Care tool. *Social Science &amp. Social Science & Medicine*, *265*, 113112. DOI: 10.1016/j.socscimed.2020.113112

Sinha, C., Meheli, S., & Kadaba, M. (2023). Understanding digital mental health needs and usage with an artificial intelligence–led mental health app (Wysa) during the COVID-19 pandemic: Retrospective analysis. *JMIR Formative Research*, *7*(1), e41913. DOI: 10.2196/41913 PMID: 36540052

Siyam, A., Zurn, P., Rø, O. C., Gedik, G., & Ronquillo, K. Joan Co, C., Vaillancourt-Laflamme, C., dela Rosa, J., Perfilieva, G., & Dal Poz, M. R. (2013). Monitoring the implementation of the WHO Global Code of Practice on the International Recruitment of Health Personnel. Bulletin of the World Health Organization, *91*(11), 816-823. DOI: 10.2471/BLT.13.118778

Slavich, G. M. (2020). Social safety theory: A biologically based evolutionary perspective on life stress, health, and behavior. *Annual Review of Clinical Psychology, 16*(1), 265–295. DOI: 10.1146/annurev-clinpsy-032816-045159

Smith, J. K. (2020). Faith and community in the age of loneliness. *Journal of Religion and Society, 22*, 55–72.

Soni, S. K. & Sharma, S. (2023). *Ayurveda and Social Health: Need for healthy society.*

Southall, R. (2019). *Inequality in South Africa: Nature, causes and responses.* Palgrave Macmillan.

Soysal, Y. N. (1994). *Limits of citizenship: Migrants and postnational membership in Europe*. University of Chicago Press.

Sriramalu, S. B., Elangovan, A. R., Annapally, S. R., Birudu, R., & Lakshmana, G. (2023). Psychological distress and quality of community life among migratory construction workers in India. *Journal of Neurosciences in Rural Practice, 14*(3), 533–540. DOI: 10.25259/JNRP_42_2022

Srnicek, N. (2017). Platform capitalism. *Polity.*

Standing, G. (2011). *The Precariat: The New Dangerous Class.* Bloomsbury Academic.

Stenning, A., & Bertilsdotter-Rosqvist, H. (2021). Neurodiversity studies: Mapping out possibilities of a new critical paradigm. *Disability & Society, 36*(9), 1532–1537. DOI: 10.1080/09687599.2021.1919503

Steptoe, A., Shankar, A., Demakakos, P., & Wardle, J. (2013). Social isolation, loneliness, and mortality. *Proceedings of the National Academy of Sciences of the United States of America, 110*(15), 5797–5801. DOI: 10.1073/pnas.1219686110

Stickley, A., & Koyanagi, A. (2016). Loneliness, common mental disorders and suicidal behavior: Findings from a general population survey. *Journal of Affective Disorders, 197*, 81–87. DOI: 10.1016/j.jad.2016.02.054

Stiglitz, J. E. (2006). *Making globalization work.* W W. Norton & Company.

Stockwell, S., Stubbs, B., Jackson, S. E., Fisher, A., Yang, L., & Smith, L. (2021). Internet use, social isolation and loneliness in older adults. *Ageing and Society, 41*(11), 2723–2746. DOI: 10.1017/S0144686X20000550

Sue, D. W. (1994). Asian-American mental health and help-seeking behavior: Comment on Solberg et al.(1994), Tata and Leong (1994), and Lin (1994).

Sulaimani, M. F., & Gut, D. M. (2019). Hidden Curriculum in a Special Education Context: The Case of Individuals with Autism. *Journal of Educational Research and Practice, 9*(1), 30–39. DOI: 10.5590/JERAP.2019.09.1.03

Sulaiman, M., & Zakariyah, L. (2020). Waqf governance and community welfare outcomes. *Third World Quarterly, 41*(8), 1352–1370.

Süleymanlı, E., & Kalkandeler, N. (2022). Result of the digitization and loneliness survey in Turkey. In Digitalization and Loneliness III: International Loneliness Symposium Book (pp. 73–91). İstanbul: Üsküdar University Press.

Sun, K. C. (2012). Fashioning the reciprocal norms of elder care: A case of immigrants in the United States and their parents in Taiwan. *Journal of Family Issues, 33*(9), 1240–1271. DOI: 10.1177/0192513X12445564

Takaful Brunei. (2020). *Over 200 bottles of disinfectants donated*, https://takafulbrunei.com.bn/news/over-200-bottles-of-disinfectants-donated

Tateno, M., Park, T. W., Kato, T. A., Umene-Nakano, W., & Saito, T. (2012). Hikikomori as a possible clinical term in psychiatry: A questionnaire survey. *BMC Psychiatry, 12*(1), 169. DOI: 10.1186/1471-244X-12-169 PMID: 23061675

Taylor, H. O., Tsuchiya, K., Nguyen, A. W., & Mueller, C. (2023). Sociodemographic factors and neighborhood/environmental conditions associated with social isolation among black older adults. *Journal of Aging and Health, 35*(3-4), 294–306. DOI: 10.1177/08982643221118427

Taylor, Z., Yankouskaya, A., & Panourgia, C. (2024). Social media use, loneliness and psychological distress in emerging adults. *Behaviour & Information Technology, 43*(7), 1312–1325. DOI: 10.1080/0144929X.2023.2209797

Tewari, A., Chhabria, A., Khalsa, A. S., Chaudhary, S., & Kanal, H. (2021, April). A survey of mental health chatbots using NLP. In *Proceedings of the International Conference on Innovative Computing and Communication (ICICC)*. DOI: 10.2139/ssrn.3833914

Thaler, R. H., & Sunstein, C. R. (2008). *Nudge: Improving decisions about health, wealth, and happiness*. Yale University Press.

Thase, M. E., McCrone, P., Barrett, M. S., Eells, T. D., Wisniewski, S. R., Balasubramani, G. K., Brown, G. K., & Wright, J. H. (2020). Improving Cost-effectiveness and Access to Cognitive Behavior Therapy for Depression: Providing Remote-Ready, Computer-Assisted Psychotherapy in Times of Crisis and Beyond. *Psychotherapy and Psychosomatics*, *89*(5), 307–313. DOI: 10.1159/000508143

The Scoop. (2021). T*akaful Brunei Keluarga Provides Free COVID-19 Coverage*, https://thescoop.co/2021/09/23/takaful-brunei-keluarga-provides-free-covid-19-coverage

The State and the Grassroots. (2015). Berghahn Books. DOI: 10.2307/j.ctt9qd9c9

Thomas, E. (2025, July 16). The loneliness economy: How isolation became profitable – And what humanists must do about it. *The Humanist,* https://thehumanist.com/commentary/the-loneliness-economy-how-isolation-became-profitable-and-what-humanists-must-do-about-it/

Thomas, D. N. (2023). The burden of calling out toxic academic practices. *Nature*, *624*(7991), 252–252. DOI: 10.1038/d41586-023-03951-1

Thompson, M., Pawson, C., & Evans, B. (2021). Navigating entry into higher education: The transition to independent learning and living. *Journal of Further and Higher Education*, *45*(10), 1398–1410. DOI: 10.1080/0309877X.2021.1933400

Tinmaz, H., Lee, Y. T., Fanea-Ivanovici, M., & Baber, H. (2022). A systematic review on digital literacy. *Smart Learning Environments*, *9*(1), 21. Advance online publication. DOI: 10.1186/s40561-022-00204-y

Tomaka, J., Thompson, S., & Palacios, R. (2006). The relation of social isolation, loneliness, and social support to disease outcomes among the elderly. *Journal of Aging and Health*, *18*(3), 359–384. DOI: 10.1177/0898264305280993

Torres, J. M., & Casey, J. A. (2017). The centrality of social ties to climate migration and mental health. *BMC Public Health*, *17*(1), 1–10. DOI: 10.1186/s12889-017-4508-0

Touzel, V., Reifegerste, D., Bozorgmehr, K., & Biddle, L. (2025). Impact of social isolation on mental health changes by socio-economic status: A moderated mediation analysis among non-migrant, migrant, and refugee subpopulations in Germany, 2016–2020. *SSM - Population Health*, *31*(June), 101822. DOI: 10.1016/j.ssmph.2025.101822

Toyin-Thomas, P., Ikhurionan, P., Omoyibo, E. E., Iwegim, C., Ukueku, A. O., Okpere, J., Nnawuihe, U. C., Atat, J., Otakhoigbogie, U., Orikpete, E. V., Erhiawarie, F., Gbejewoh, E. O., Odogu, U., Akhirevbulu, I. C. G., Kwarshak, Y. K., & Wariri, O. (2023). Drivers of health workers' migration, intention to migrate and non-migration from low/middle-income countries, 1970–2022: A systematic review. *BMJ Global Health*, *8*(5), e012338. DOI: 10.1136/bmjgh-2023-012338

Train, K. E. (2009). *Discrete choice methods with simulation* (2nd ed.). Cambridge University Press., DOI: 10.1017/CBO9780511805271

Travis, S. (2023). Bridging the Healthcare Gap: The Critical Importance of International Medical Graduates in the US. *Journal For International Medical Graduates*, *2*(1). Advance online publication. DOI: 10.56570/jimgs.v2i1.73

Tricco, A. C., Lillie, E., Zarin, W., O'Brien, K., Colquhoun, H., Kastner, M., Levac, D., Ng, C., Sharpe, J. P., Wilson, K., Kenny, M., Warren, R., Wilson, C., Stelfox, H. T., & Straus, S. E. (2016). A scoping review on the conduct and reporting of scoping reviews. *BMC Medical Research Methodology*, *16*(1), 15. DOI: 10.1186/s12874-016-0116-4

Tsegay, S. M. (2023). International Migration: Definition, Causes and Effects. *Genealogy*, *7*(3), 1–10. DOI: 10.3390/genealogy7030061

Tsujita, Y., Oda, H., & Rajan, S. I. (2023). Obtaining a nursing job in Australia and New Zealand: A case study of migrant nurses trained in India. *ERIA Research Project Report FY*, *2023*(07), 47.

Turkish Statistical Institute. (2024). Research on information technology use in children. https://data.tuik.gov.tr/Bulten/Index?p=Cocuklarda-Bilisim-Teknolojileri-Kullanim-Araştırması-2024-53638

Turkish Statistical Institute. (2025). Family in statistics 2024. https://data.tuik.gov.tr/Bulten/Intex?p=Istatistikler-Aile-2024-53989

Turkle, S. (2011). *Alone together: Why we expect more from technology and less from each other*. Basic Books.

Twenge, J. M. (2017). *iGen*. Atria Books.

Ueno, A., Yu, C., Curtis, L., & Dennis, C. (2024). Job demands-resources theory extended: Stress, loneliness, and care responsibilities impacting UK doctoral students' and academics' mental health. *Studies in Higher Education*, *50*(4), 808–823. DOI: 10.1080/03075079.2024.2357148

UK Government. (2018). *A connected society: A strategy for tackling loneliness.* HM Government.

UNDP. (2021). *Human development report 2021/2022: Uncertain times, unsettled lives.* United Nations Development Programme.

UNDP. (2022). *Human development report: Social cohesion and vulnerability.*

UNICEF. (2019). *Reform of social protection in Egypt: Takaful and Karama Programme (TKP), A pro-women programme.* https://www.unicef.org/mena/reports/reform-social-protection-egypt

United Nations High Commissioner for Refugees. (2014). *IBelong campaign to end statelessness within 10 years.* UNHCR.

United Nations High Commissioner for Refugees. (2023). *Global trends: Forced displacement in 2023.* UNHCR.

United Nations. (1948). *Universal declaration of human rights.* United Nations.

United Nations. (1961). *Convention on the reduction of statelessness.* United Nations.

United Nations. (1979). *Convention on the elimination of all forms of discrimination against women.* United Nations.

United Nations. (1989). *Convention on the rights of the child.* United Nations.

United Nations. (2023). *World social report: Demographic change.*

Uslaner, E. M. (2002). *The moral foundations of trust.* Cambridge University Press.

van de Stadt, F. (2025, July 13). The loneliness economy: How capitalism turned our need for connection into a product. *Medium,* https://medium.com/@fvdstadt/the-loneliness-economy-how-capitalism-turned-our-need-for-connection-into-a-product-ae2bf8d6cec2

van Rooij, E. C. M., Jansen, E. P. W. A., & van de Grift, W. J. C. M. (2018). First-year university students' academic success: The importance of academic adjustment. *European Journal of Psychology of Education, 33*(4), 749–767. DOI: 10.1007/s10212-017-0347-8

van Waas, L. (2008). *Nationality matters: Statelessness under international law.* Intersentia.

Veale, D., Robins, E., Thomson, A. B., & Gilbert, P. (2023). No safety without emotional safety. *The Lancet. Psychiatry, 10*(1), 65–70. DOI: 10.1016/S2215-0366(22)00373-X PMID: 36442491

Venters, S., & Jones, C. J. (2021). The experiences of grandchildren who provide care for a grandparent with dementia: A systematic review. *Dementia (London)*, *20*(6), 2205–2230. DOI: 10.1177/1471301220980243 PMID: 33372548

Verma, S. K., Bhattacharya, S., & Singh, T. (2024). Family Dynamics and Intergenerational Relation in Interdependent Society: An Indian Perspective. In *Indian Families: Contemporary Family. Structures and Dynamics*, *26*, 97–125. Emerald Publishing Limited.

Victor, C. R., & Pikhartova, J. (2020). Lonely places or lonely people? Investigating the relationship between loneliness and place of residence. *BMC Public Health*, *20*(1), 778. DOI: 10.1186/s12889-020-08703-8

Victor, C. R., & Scharf, T. (2005). Social isolation and loneliness in old age. *European Journal of Ageing*, *2*(2), 97–104. DOI: 10.1007/s10433-005-0039-7

Villamin, P., Lopez, V., Thapa, D. K., & Cleary, M. (2023). Nurse migration to Australia: Past, present, and future. *Collegian (Royal College of Nursing, Australia)*, *30*(6), 753–761. DOI: 10.1016/j.colegn.2023.05.001

Vinod, R. (2023). *Modernity in India: Issues, Perspectives and Challenges*. Routledge India. DOI: 10.4324/9781032622880

Vliegenthart, D. (2023). Meaningless spirituality?: The Satsang Network as a Grassroots Response to the Modern Western Crisis of Meaning. In *Combating Crises from Below*

von Soest, T., Luhmann, M., & Gerstorf, D. (2020). The development of loneliness through adolescence and young adulthood: Its nature, correlates, and midlife outcomes. *Developmental Psychology*, *56*(10), 1919–1934. DOI: 10.1037/dev0001102

Vuohijoki, A., Ristolainen, L., Leppilahti, J., Kivivuori, S.-M., & Hurri, H. (2025). Impact of joint commission international accreditation on occupational health and patient safety: A systematic review. *PLoS One*, *20*(6), e0325894. DOI: 10.1371/journal.pone.0325894

Wadhwa, M. (2021). *Digital Mental Health Initiatives in India* (No. 60). ICT India Working Paper.

Walton-Roberts, M., Runnels, V., Rajan, S. I., Sood, A., Nair, S., Thomas, P., Packer, C., MacKenzie, A., Tomblin Murphy, G., Labonté, R., & Bourgeault, I. L. (2017). Causes, consequences, and policy responses to the migration of health workers: Key findings from India. *Human Resources for Health*, *15*(1), 28. Advance online publication. DOI: 10.1186/s12960-017-0199-y

Wang, L., & Liu, X. (2020). *How loneliness creates economy.* 2020 International Conference on World Economy and Project Management (WEPM 2020), 11-16. https://clausiuspress.com/conferences/LNEMSS/WEPM%202020/20WEPM003.pdf

Wang, K., Feng, Y., Qin, X., & Hu, Y. (2025). Examining the double-edged effects of digital literacy on the social integration of retirement migrants. *Frontiers in Public Health, 13*(March), 1–15. DOI: 10.3389/fpubh.2025.1470319

Wang, L., Fagan, C., & Yu, C. L. (2020). Popular mental health apps (MH apps) as a complement to telepsychotherapy: Guidelines for consideration. *Journal of Psychotherapy Integration, 30*(2), 265–273. DOI: 10.1037/int0000204

Wang, M. S., Raynard, M., & Greenwood, R. (2021). From grace to violence: Stigmatizing the medical profession in China. *Academy of Management Journal, 64*(6), 1842–1872. DOI: 10.5465/amj.2018.0715

Wang, M., & Liu, Z. (2022). How Do Green Innovation Strategies Contribute to Firm Performance Under Supply Chain Risk? Evidence From China's Manufacturing Sector. *Frontiers in Psychology, 13*, 894766. Advance online publication. DOI: 10.3389/fpsyg.2022.894766

Wan, L. P., Zhao, Z. Y., Liu, B. P., Zhu, J. H., Jia, C. X., & Wang, X. T. (2025). Association between loneliness, social isolation and incident depression: A prospective study based on UK Biobank. *General Hospital Psychiatry, 96*, 171–177. DOI: 10.1016/j.genhosppsych.2025.07.007

Warner, L. M., Yeung, D. Y.-L., Jiang, D., Choi, N. G., Ho, R. T. H., Kwok, J. Y. Y., & Chou, K.-L. (2024). Effects of volunteering over six months on loneliness, social and mental health outcomes among older adults: The HEAL-HOA Dual Randomized Controlled Trial. *The American Journal of Geriatric Psychiatry, 32*(5), 598–610. DOI: 10.1016/j.jagp.2023.12.022

Warria, A., & Chikadzi, V. (2022). Statelessness, trauma, and mental well-being: Implications for practice, research, and advocacy. *African Human Mobility Review, 8*(3), 41–55. DOI: 10.14426/ahmr.v8i3.1135

Wawera, A. S., & McCamley, A. (2019). Loneliness among international students in the UK. *Journal of Further and Higher Education.*

Webber, M., Reidy, H., Ansari, D., Stevens, M., & Morris, D. (2015). Enhancing social networks: A qualitative study of health and social care practice in UK mental health services. *Health & Social Care in the Community, 23*(2), 180–189. DOI: 10.1111/hsc.12135

Weiss, R. S. (1973). *Loneliness: The experience of emotional and social isolation.* MIT Press World Health Organization (WHO). (2021). *Social isolation and loneliness among older people: Advocacy brief.* https://www.who.int/publications/i/item/9789240030749

Weiss, R. S. (1973). *Loneliness: The experience of emotional and social isolation.* MIT Press.

Whan-woo, Y. (2025, April 18). 'Loneliness economy' emerges as more Koreans live alone. *The Korea Times,* https://www.koreatimes.co.kr/economy/20250418/loneliness-economy-emerges-as-more-koreans-live-alone

WHO Commission on Social Connection. (2025). From loneliness to social connection: charting a path to healthier societies. World Health Organization (WHO).

Whyte, W. H. (1980). *The social life of small urban spaces.* Project for Public Spaces.

Wilkinson, R. G., & Pickett, K. (2009). *The spirit level: Why more equal societies almost always do better* (Vol. 6). Allen Lane.

Wister, A., Kim, B., Levasseur, M., Poulin, V., Qiu, S., Yuwono, E., Meynet, S., Beadle, J., Kadowaki, L., Klasa, K., & Linkov, I. (2025). Resilience applications to social isolation and loneliness in older adults: A scoping review to develop a model and research agenda. *Frontiers in Public Health, 13,* 1589781. DOI: 10.3389/fpubh.2025.1589781

Wood, J. V., Giordano-Beech, M., Taylor, K. L., Michela, J. L., & Gaus, V. (1994). Strategies of social comparison among people with low self-esteem: Self-protection and self enhancement. *Journal of Personality and Social Psychology, 67*(4), 713–731. DOI: 10.1037/0022-3514.67.4.713

World Bank. (2018). *Identification for development (ID4D): The state of identification systems in the world.* World Bank.

World Bank. (2020, November 17). *Takaful and Karama: A social safety net project that promotes Egyptian women empowerment and human capital.* https://www.worldbank.org/en/results/2020/11/17/takaful-and-karama-a-social-safety-net-project-that-promotes-egyptian-women-empowerment-and-human-capital

World Health Organization. (2021). *Social isolation and loneliness: A framework for intervention.*

Worsley, J. D., Harrison, P., & Corcoran, R. (2021). Bridging the Gap: Exploring the Unique Transition From Home, School or College Into University. *Frontiers in Public Health, 9,* 634285. DOI: 10.3389/fpubh.2021.634285

Xie, Y., Guo, Q., & Meng, Y. (2021). The health service use of aged rural-to-urban migrant workers in different types of cities in China. *BMC Health Services Research, 21*(1), 606. DOI: 10.1186/s12913-021-06638-3

Xu, L. (2024). The regional integration transition of China's immigration policy: The case of Yiwu. *Chinese Public Administration Review, 15*(2), 105–117. DOI: 10.1177/15396754241242851

Xu, X., Ren, P., Shi, W., Deng, F., Wang, Q., Shi, S., Shen, J., Dong, G., & Han, J. (2025). Occupational health and safety regulations in China: Development process, enforcement challenges, and solutions. *Frontiers in Public Health, 13*, 1522040. DOI: 10.3389/fpubh.2025.1522040

Xu, Y., Gutierrez, A., & Kim, S. H. (2008). Adaptation and Transformation Through (Un)Learning. *Advances in Nursing Science, 31*(2), E33–E47. DOI: 10.1097/01.ANS.0000319570.99254.e5

Yadav, U., & Prakash, B. (2024). A Socio-Legal Analysis of the Health and Well-Being of the Ageing Population. In *Intersections of Law and Computational Intelligence in Health Governance* (pp. 142–160). IGI Global. DOI: 10.4018/979-8-3693-5976-1.ch007

Yadav, V., Chauhan, S., & Patel, R. (2022). What causes loneliness among household heads: A study based in primary setting in Mumbai, India. *BMC Public Health, 22*(1), 730. DOI: 10.1186/s12889-022-13108-w PMID: 35413809

Yamamoto, M. (2016). Performing family in Japan's rental services industry. *Asian Anthropology, 15*(3), 193–210.

Yan, C. O. (2024). Non-citizens' Continuity of Citizenship in the Baltic States. *The International Journal of Interdisciplinary Social and Community Studies, 20*(1), 1–24. DOI: 10.18848/2324-7576/CGP/v20i01/1-24

Yang, H., Lin, Z., Chen, X., & Peng, J. (2023). Workplace loneliness, ego depletion and cyberloafing: Can leader problem-focused interpersonal emotion management help? *Internet Research, 33*(4), 1473–1494. DOI: 10.1108/INTR-01-2021-0007

Yang, K. (2023). Trust, social engagement, and loneliness among older adults: Evidence from a nationally representative survey. *Aging & Mental Health, 27*(6), 1047–1056. DOI: 10.1080/13607863.2021.2009603

Yang, K., & Victor, C. R. (2011). Age and loneliness in 25 European nations. *Ageing and Society, 31*(8), 1368–1388. DOI: 10.1017/S0144686X1000139X

Yang, Y., Chen, B., Huang, P., Wang, Y., Zhang, L., & Cai, F. (2022). Prevalence and influencing factors of depressive symptoms among rural-to-urban migrant workers in China: A systematic review and meta-analysis. *Journal of Affective Disorders, 307*, 11–19. DOI: 10.1016/j.jad.2022.03.061

Yeates, N., & Pillinger, J. (2020). Building resilience across borders: a policy brief on health worker migration.

Yetim, N., & Yetim, Ü. (2014). Sense of community and individual well-being: A research on fulfillment of needs and social capital in the Turkish Community. *Social Indicators Research, 115*(1), 93–115. DOI: 10.1007/s11205-012-0210-x

Yeung, J. W. K., Zhang, Z., & Kim, T. Y. (2017). Volunteering and health benefits in general adults: Cumulative effects and forms. *BMC Public Health, 18*(1), 8. DOI: 10.1186/s12889-017-4561-8

Yilmaz, I. (2018). The role of the Diyanet in contemporary Turkish politics and society. *Journal of Muslim Minority Affairs, 38*(3), 327–345.

Yilmaz, I. (2022). Urbanization, migration, and social trust in Turkey. *The Middle East Journal, 76*(4), 563–586.

Yin, J., Lassale, C., Steptoe, A., & Cadar, D. (2019). Exploring the bidirectional associations between loneliness and cognitive functioning over 10 years: The English longitudinal study of ageing. *International Journal of Epidemiology, 48*(6), 1937–1948. DOI: 10.1093/ije/dyz085

Young, I. M. (2011). *Responsibility for justice*. Oxford University Press. DOI: 10.1093/acprof:oso/9780195392388.001.0001

Yunus, M. (2007). *Creating a world without poverty*. Public Affairs.

Yuval-Davis, N. (2011). *The politics of belonging: Intersectional contestations*. Sage Publications. DOI: 10.4135/9781446251041

Zakat Foundation of America. (2010, July 23). *The nature of infaq*. https://www.zakat.org/infaq-benefits-nature-infaq

Zakat Foundation of America. (2014, November 19). *The eight kinds of people who receive zakat.* https://www.zakat.org/the-eight-kinds-of-people-who-receive-zakat

Zakat Foundation of America. (2020, June 20). *What is sadaqah?* https://www.zakat.org/what-is-sadaqah

Zaman, M. (2019). *Islamic traditions of community welfare: Zakat, Waqf and Sadaqah*. Routledge.

Zavaleta, D., Samuel, K., & Mills, C. (2014). Social Isolation: A Conceptual and Measurement Proposal. In *OPHI Working Paper 67*. http://www.ophi.org.uk/social-isolation-a-conceptual-and-measurement-proposal/

Zebhauser, A., Hofmann-Xu, L., Baumert, J., Häfner, S., Lacruz, M. E., Emeny, R. T., Döring, A., Grill, E., Huber, D., Peters, A., & Ladwig, K. H. (2014). How much does it hurt to be lonely? Mental and physical differences between older men and women in the KORA-Age Study. *International Journal of Geriatric Psychiatry*, *29*(3), 245–252. DOI: 10.1002/gps.3998

Zhang, N., Fan, F.-M., Huang, S.-Y., & Rodriguez, M. A. (2018). Mindfulness training for loneliness among Chinese college students: A pilot randomized controlled trial. *International Journal of Psychology*, *53*(5), 373–378. DOI: 10.1002/ijop.12394

Zhao, I. Y., Holroyd, E., Garrett, N., Wright-St Clair, V. A., & Neville, S. (2023). Chinese late-life immigrants' loneliness and social isolation in host countries: An integrative review. *Journal of Clinical Nursing*, *32*(9-10), 1615–1624. DOI: 10.1111/jocn.16134

Zhao, R., Zhang, H., Zhao, J. S., & Wang, X. (2019). When the west meets the east: Cultural clash and its impacts on anomie in a sample of Chinese adolescents. *Deviant Behavior*, *40*(10), 1187–1205. DOI: 10.1080/01639625.2018.1472934

Zheng, K., Johnson, S., Jarvis, R., Victor, C., Barreto, M., Qualter, P., & Pitman, A. (2023). The experience of loneliness among international students participating in the BBC Loneliness Experiment: Thematic analysis of qualitative survey data. *Current Research in Behavioral Sciences*, *4*, 100113. DOI: 10.1016/j.crbeha.2023.100113

Zhong, S., & Su, B. (2021). Assessing the effects of labor market dynamics on CO2 emissions in global value chains. *The Science of the Total Environment*, *768*, 144486. DOI: 10.1016/j.scitotenv.2020.144486

Zhong, Y., McKenna, L., Copnell, B., Zhao, W., & Moss, C. (2023). Professional adaptation experiences of Chinese migrant nurses in Australia: A qualitative study. *Western Journal of Nursing Research*, *45*(7), 626–633. DOI: 10.1177/01939459231167711

Zine, J. (2008). *Canadian Islamic schools*. University of Toronto Press. DOI: 10.3138/9781442687509

Zuboff, S. (2019). *The age of surveillance capitalism*. PublicAffairs.

Zuboff, S. (2019). *The age of surveillance capitalism: The fight for a human future at the new frontier of power*. Profile Books.

About the Contributors

Volkan Kaymaz holds a Ph.D. in Economics from Yildiz Technical University (Turkey), where he specialized in applied macroeconomics, environmental economics, and the political economy of crises. Currently, he continues his academic work as a researcher and book editor, having previously held positions as Associate Professor and Assistant Professor at Istanbul Yeni Yüzyıl University. He also recently completed a postdoctoral research position at the University of Coimbra (Portugal), focusing on sustainable energy policy and environmental economics. Dr. Kaymaz has published extensively on topics such as economic crises, financial markets, tourism economics, sectoral structural change, and environmental governance, with research appearing in journals such as Sustainability, Environment, Development and Sustainability, and Tourism: An International Interdisciplinary Journal. He has contributed to multiple international conferences and authored several book chapters, including prior editorial work published with IGI Global. His current research interests include the political economy of loneliness, demographic shifts, public finance, consumption behavior, and structural transformations under contemporary capitalism. His interdisciplinary approach integrates economics, sociology, and public policy, making him well-positioned to serve as editor of this proposed volume.

***

Megha Bakshi holds an MBA, M.Phil., and Ph.D. in Management and brings over a decade of experience across corporate as a certified POSH trainer and academic domains. She currently serves as an Assistant Professor at Sri Balaji University, Pune, and also works as a freelance research consultant. Her academic interests lie in behavior studies, sustainability studies, and human resource studies. As a budding researcher, she has authored peer-reviewed articles in Scopus- and ABDC-listed journals. Her recent publications include the ABDC-listed Journal of Marketing and Social Research and the Scopus-indexed Prabandhan: Indian

Journal of Management. A research paper authored by her has also been accepted for publication in the Scopus listed Journal of Information Systems Engineering and Management and will be published soon. She is a peer reviewer for Web of Science (WoS)-indexed journals and actively engages in faculty development and academic research training initiatives.

Meenakshi Bose is a development professional and academic with over a decade of experience working with nationally and internationally renowned organizations, including UNICEF, the United Nations World Food Programme (WFP), the World Bank, and the KIIT School of Rural Management, KIIT University. She accumulated a decade of research experience conducting baseline studies, endline evaluations, and impact assessments for various development organizations, including the aforementioned UN agencies. She is currently the Manager – Research and Communication at Bandhan-Konnagar (the CSR wing of Bandhan Group), where she has worked extensively on the organization's core thematic areas, including livelihoods, financial literacy, women's empowerment, and community development. At Bandhan, she has played a key role in leading research initiatives, impact assessments, knowledge dissemination, and development communication, contributing to evidence-based programming and stakeholder engagement. Dr. Bose holds a Ph.D. in Management and has qualified the UGC-NET. She possesses dual Master's degrees—an MBA from KIIT University, and an M.A. in Women's Studies from IGNOU underscoring her interdisciplinary strength in development, policy, and gender issues. She has also completed an Executive Education Programme in Data Analytics from IIM Rohtak, enhancing her data-driven decision-making and research capabilities. She is the author of the book "Valuing Women's Unpaid Work: Experiences from Odisha" (Aakar Books, New Delhi), and has published in numerous national and international journals and edited volumes including Scopus indexed. Her research focuses on labour and gender issues, particularly women's workforce participation, unpaid care work, and their role in economic development. A recipient of the Swami Vivekananda Single Girl Child Scholarship for Research in Social Sciences from the UGC, Government of India, Dr. Bose is committed to bridging grassroots realities with strategic policy frameworks. Her work continues to shape inclusive development discourse in India, particularly at the intersection of gender.

Symela Charalampidou is a PhD candidate in Business and Management at Glasgow Caledonian University, where she has recently completed her viva voce examination. With over twenty years of professional experience in banking, finance, and higher education, she combines applied expertise with academic insight. As an Associate Fellow of the Higher Education Academy, she has taught at the university level and supervised student research. Her work explores the intersections of business management, ethics, and society, as well as the challenges of belonging and well-being in higher education.

Santhosh J. is an Assistant Professor in the Department of Public Administration, School of Humanities and Social Sciences, Assam Don Bosco University, Assam, India. His teaching and research interests span governance, public policy, and administrative reforms. He has been actively engaged in academic and institutional development initiatives, contributing to both teaching and research in the field of public administration, dalit studies, caste, and marginality. He can be reached at santhosh.j@dbuniversity.ac.in (ORCID: 0009-0008-2825-1035).

Dylan Lee holds an MD from a leading medical university, a PhD in Strategic Leadership from a U.S. research university, and an MBA from an accredited U.S. program. He currently serves as Chief Medical Officer at a global biopharmaceutical company, overseeing clinical development and multi-region regulatory strategy. His academic attribution rests on formal appointments in molecular medicine and immunology, graduate-level teaching in research design and clinical methodology, supervision of trainees, and contributions to peer-reviewed scholarship with service as a reviewer/editorial contributor. This scholarly base—methods-driven protocol design, transparent reporting standards, and evidence synthesis—directly underpins his industry leadership. In the healthcare and biopharma sector, he has led end-to-end translation from preclinical rationale to first-in-human and late-phase studies, directed IND/CTA authoring across U.S.–EU–Asia jurisdictions, and built cross-functional governance spanning medical, regulatory, pharmacovigilance, and biostatistics. He has run global, multi-site trials with risk-based monitoring and GxP quality systems, executed portfolio and indication-selection decisions tied to payer-relevant endpoints, and managed cross-border partnerships, diligence, and integration. By coupling clinical training and academic rigor with operational execution, he provides the kind of leadership that moves programs from mechanism to marketed value while meeting scientific, regulatory, and commercial thresholds.

Luna Lee, MD, MSN, RN, FNP-C, is a Family Nurse Practitioner with Northeast Ohio Neighborhood Health Services, where they provide primary care (2024–present). Trained first as a physician in China, Luna completed an MD at Sichuan University (2005), and an OB-GYN residency/fellowship at the No. 1 Hospital of Lanzhou University (2005–2011). After moving to the U.S., Luna earned an ADN (2020), RN-BSN (2021), and is completing the Family Nurse Practitioner program (begun 2022) at Kent State University.

Khairunnisa Musari is an Assistant Professor at Faculty of Islamic Economics and Business (FEBI) & Postgraduate Program, Kiai Haji Achmad Siddiq State Islamic University (UIN KHAS), Jember, Indonesia. She is a Secretary of the Indonesian Association of Islamic Economists (IAEI) for the Provincial Board of East Java and a member of the International Association for Islamic Economics (IAIE). Her research interests in sukuk, waqf, esham, fiscal & monetary policies, circular economy, halal logistics, sustainable finance, climate change, and Islamic microfinance & nanofinance. She has several book chapters with international reputable publishers such as IGI Global, Emerald Publishing Limited, World Scientific Publishing, Routledge, Springer, and Palgrave Macmillan. She has experience as a Senior Specialist for Islamic Finance of United Nations Development Programme (UNDP) Indonesia and was listed as one of the Top 300 Most Influential Women in Islamic Business & Finance 2019, 2020, 2021, WOMANi Significancica 2022, and WOMANi Academica 2023, 2024, by Cambridge-IFA.

Ratan Sarkar is an Assistant Professor in the Department of Education, Tezpur University (A Central University), Assam, India. Previously, he served nearly seven years as Assistant Professor in the Department of Teachers' Training (B.Ed.), Prabhat Kumar College, Contai (Vidyasagar University), and as Guest Faculty at National Institute for Empowerment of Persons with Intellectual Disabilities, Regional Centre, Kolkata. He holds a Ph.D. in Education from Pondicherry University, an M.Ed. and M.Phil. in Special Education from Ramakrishna Mission Vivekananda Educational and Research Institute, Belur Math, and an M.A. in Education and Technology from Tata Institute of Social Sciences, Mumbai. He began his academic journey with a B.Ed. in Special Education (Jadavpur University) and a B.A. in English (Hons) from Siliguri College (University of North Bengal), Darjeeling. Dr. Sarkar has published extensively in leading journals (SAGE, Springer, Routledge, Wiley), authored books, chapters, and reviews, and led projects under the Ministry of Education, Govt. of India. He works on inclusive education, educational technology, and policy advocacy to advance equitable learning ecosystems.

Hüdayi Sayin completed his undergraduate studies in 1987, the Department of Forensic Medicine and Criminalistics at the Ankara University Institute of Health Sciences in 1993, the Public Administration Specialization Program at the Public Administration Institute of Turkey and the Middle East in 1995, his master's degree in Political Science and Public Administration at the İnönü University Institute of Social Sciences in 1996, and his doctorate in Political Science and International Relations at the Istanbul University Institute of Social Sciences in 2010. He was honored with the title of Associate Professor in International Relations in 2021. After 41 years of service in public administration, he began his professional academic career at Istanbul Yeni Yüzyıl University in 2015. He has publications on international migration, alienation, international security, and regional studies.

Monica C Singh is a professional with diversified experience of 25 years in Academics (management), Training (Training from the Back of the Room Certified Practitioner), Career & Life Coaching (ICF Credentialed Professional Certified Coach), Mentoring (IMC trained Mentor,)Career Counselling. and Academics (management). She is a doctorate in management who has over 2 decades of teaching experience as a full time and visiting faculty with premier management institutions. including PIMR Indore, NIA, Pune and IFME Pune etc. She has keen interest in research and has published research papers in the areas of behavioural finance and strategy in scopus indexed journals, case studies in the prestigious case centre, and abstracts Dr. Monica as a corporate trainer has conducted more than 300 Management Development programs for prestigious organisations. Currently she is working as Associate Professor at BIIB, Sri Balaji University, Pune, India. She has coaching experience of over 750 hours with executives, senior professionals and students. Her recent publications include a chapter in a scopus indexed book of IGI Global and a research paper in IEEE COnnference published in Grenze International Journal of Engineering and Technology.

Index

A

B

C

D

E

G

H

I

www.ingramcontent.com/pod-product-compliance
Lightning Source LLC
LaVergne TN
LVHW062328300926
849161LV00007B/1618